ENCYCLOPAEDIC HISTORY
OF
THE LIGHT OF CIVILIZATION

How The Vision of God has Inspired all the Great Civilizations

BOOKS PUBLISHED BY NICHOLAS HAGGER

The Fire and the Stones
Selected Poems
The Universe and the Light
A White Radiance
A Mystic Way
Awakening to the Light
A Spade Fresh with Mud
The Warloads
Overlord
A Smell of Leaves and Summer
The Tragedy of Prince Tudor
The One and the Many
Wheeling Bats and a Harvest Moon
The Warm Glow of the Monastery Courtyard
The Syndicate
The Secret History of the West
Classical Odes
Overlord, one-volume edition
Collected Poems 1958–2005
Collected Verse Plays

Encyclopaedic History of The Light of Civilization

How The Vision of God has Inspired all the Great Civilizations

NICHOLAS HAGGER

PENTAGON PRESS

ENCYCLOPAEDIC HISTORY OF THE LIGHT OF CIVILIZATION

ISBN 81-8274-256-0 (HB)

2011

Originally published in UK by John Hunt Publishing Ltd., The Bothy, Deershot Lodge, Park Lane, Ropley, Hants SO24 OBE, UK.
Indian Edition published in 2007 under license from John Hunt Publishing Ltd.

First published in India by
PENTAGON PRESS
206, Peacock Lane, Shahpur Jat,
New Delhi-110049
Phones: 011-64706243, 26491568
Telefax: 011-26490600
email: rajan@pentagonpress.in
website: www.pentagonpress.in

Printed at Chaman Offset Printers, New Delhi.

In our time, the writing and publication of universal histories is an important public service. We are living in an age in which, for the first time in history, the whole human race, over the whole surface of our planet, is growing together into a single world-society.... We have been, first and foremost, adherents of some local nation, civilisation or religion. In future, our paramount loyalty has to be transferred to the whole human race.... If and when the unification of man is achieved... local histories will be seen... as preludes to a universal history of mankind as a whole.

Our time is the first in which it has been possible to take a literally universal view of human history, because this is the first time in which the whole human race all round the globe, has come within sight of coalescing into a single society. In the past, a number of empires, and a smaller number of missionary religions, have aimed at universality. None of them, so far, has ever attained to universality in the literal sense....

These previous attempts at unification on a world-wide scale have inspired some of the great historians of the past to look at our history in universal terms.... These perceptive spirits have been aware that the goal of human and social endeavours is the unification of the human race which we, in our time, may be on the eve of achieving at last.

If these partial unifications of the human race (i.e. under the Persians, Mongols and Timurids) had power to awaken the historical imagination, our present age ought, *a fortiori*, to produce universal historians of even greater stature. It is one of the paradoxes of the present age that the prevalent school of contemporary historians is still working under the

spell of parochial nationalism.... The issue between universalism and nationalism is one of life and death for the human race; and the victory of universalism cannot be taken for granted.

Arnold Toynbee, Foreword to the English edition of the *Larousse Histoire Universelle*, Paul Hamlyn, 1967

• • • • •

***Beatific vision*, in Christianity, the final reward of all those who die in God's grace, namely a direct supernatural knowledge (vision) of God himself.**

Encyclopaedia Britannica, I. 905

***Beatific vision*. The vision of the Divine Being in glory. In Christianity Pope Benedict XII in 1336 formally declared that the Divine Essence would be seen by intuition and face to face. In general Christians have held that this is the ultimate destiny of the redeemed at the last day, but some theologians, including Thomas Aquinas, have held that it was granted to individuals (such as Moses or Paul) for brief periods during their earthly life. Mystics have claimed this or something approaching it....The concept of the Beatific Vision is also found in Islamic mysticism, for example...in Al-Arabi (D.1240): ...'The Vision impregnates the elect with Divine light, each experiencing the Vision according to the knowledge of the Divine Dogma or Dogmas gained by him on earth.'**

John Ferguson, *An Illustrated Encyclopaedia of Mysticism and the Mystery Religions*

O sages standing in God's holy fire.

W. B. Yeats, "Sailing to Byzantium"

History is a pattern
Of timeless moments.

T. S. Eliot, "Little Gidding"

ACKNOWLEDGMENTS

This book's precursor is my work *The Fire and the Stones*, which was published in 1991. At that time I had discussions with many authorities in their fields who are now dead, and I again acknowledge the memories of Ezra Pound (who influenced both Eliot and Yeats), with whom I had a long talk in Rapallo about the culture of different civilizations; of the philosopher E. W. F. Tomlin (an authority on the philosophy of East and West who wrote books on Toynbee and on his long friendship with Eliot); of Sir Laurens van der Post, who recalled a conversation he once heard Jung having about the Light and who told me that my thinking is "of immense importance" as no other living historian holds a Universalist view; and of Kathleen Raine (scholar of Blake and Yeats), who agreed that Toynbee never found the motive force that explains the genesis of civilizations (the vision of the Light) because he looked for it within the subject of history, where it is not to be found, rather than outside history where it can be found. I acknowledge my indebtedness to many living people. I am grateful to Colin Wilson for placing a copy of Husserl's *Ideas* in my hands one evening in Cornwall; to Warren Kenton, alias Z'ev ben Shimon Halevi (probably the world's leading authority on the Kabbalah); and to Carol Andrews, in the early 1990s Assistant Keeper in the Department of Egyptian Antiquities in the British Museum, who helped me interpret some hieroglyphs.

I am grateful to Michael Mann for advice and for his interest in my work. And once again to John Hunt, who immediately grasped the significance of this work and whose wise conceptual powers have benefited its form.

CONTENTS

PART THREE: SUBTRADITION: THE HERETICAL LIGHT IN WESTERN CIVILIZATION

PART FOUR: **THE LIGHT IN CIVILIZATIONS**

APPENDICES

PROLOGUE

Religion is about more than hymns and prayers, the outer forms and rituals you will find in any church, temple or mosque. It is fundamentally about the inner experience of the soul unfolding to God, which the outer forms and rituals are designed to encourage. And how is God characterised? There is a large body of opinion, accumulated over the centuries, that God is Light and is experienced as Light, in inner illumination. Different religions interpret the experience in different ways, but there is much evidence that all who open to God as Light are having essentially the same experience. In fact, for many centuries religion has been based on the experience of the Light, although today the Light is not as well-known as it was in the past.

Religions are very important to history. At school we were taught a history of monarchs and generals, and today many people associate religions with wars: Catholics and Protestants in Northern Ireland, bin Laden's Islam and Judaism/Christendom. In fact, history is about more than *élites* and wars. In certain times civilization flourishes and is expressed in the arts: great painting, sculpture, literature and music. Much of the great art – civilization – has been inspired by a particular religion. A moment's thought about the world's main geographical areas suggests Western art's indebtedness to Christianity and Eastern art's indebtedness to the Buddha and other deities. Religion is the basis for civilization, and is itself based on the experience of the Light. The Light is therefore extremely important to civilization. Is it also important to the history of geographical regions? Can the illumined – the mystics of the great religions – be as important to the sweep of history as kings and wars?

That is the theme of this book – that the (today) little-known experience of the Light, which was once universally known, is fundamental to religion and may be crucial to the history of the world's regions. Recorded history began c.3500-3000 BC. As we recount the tradition of the Light from earliest times and advance towards the present, we find certain local traditions of the Light dominate religions and through them play a part in history.

This book should be read in conjunction with its companion volume, *The Endless Rise and Fall of Civilizations*, which is based on the premiss established at the end of this book. The two books together offer a Grand Unified Theory of Religion and World History.

Looking at all the world's history as one field is called universal history. Universal history regards mankind as a single world-society and is to be contrasted with local national histories. Universalism is a way of looking that embraces all mankind, and is to be contrasted with nation-state nationalism. Universalism incorporates "universal" ("belonging to or done by all persons") and "universe" ("all existing things, the whole creation and the Creator; all mankind"). Religious Universalists have held that all mankind will eventually be saved, and Universalist historians focus on the history of all mankind in relation to the universe and God ("the whole creation and the Creator"). The new Universalism holds that mankind's experience of a universal God perceived or known as the Light is central to all religions and historical traditions, and to civilization and civilizations.

The personal basis for my Universalism can be found in my 45-year-long quest to understand our time, the Age and the pattern underlying world events. This quest through inner experience, cultures and history took me through sceptical Oxford to the Islamic Middle East, where I lived in Baghdad and visited Babylon and the ziggurats, Jerusalem and Qumran. It was in a plane between Baghdad and Basra, high above Ur, that I received and scribbled down the words "life cycle" and first pondered the rise and fall (life cycle) of civilizations. My quest took me to the Far East, where I absorbed the wisdom of the East while spending four years as a Professor in

Japan. There I taught a year's course on Gibbon, Spengler and Toynbee to the postgraduate students, and first glimpsed a fourth way of approaching Western history, which finds its basis in this work. From Japan I visited China (where in March 1966 I was the first to discover the Cultural Revolution) and later the U.S.S.R., India and many Eastern cultural sites, such as Angkor Wat. I absorbed South-East Asian Mahayana Buddhism, having already experienced Japanese Zen in Kitakamakura.

My quest then took me to Libya for two years (during which I was an eye-witness of the 1969 Gaddafi Revolution). From there I visited Egypt and pondered on the Great Pyramid and the Valley of the Kings. Back in London in the autumn of 1971 I experienced the most intense two months of my life. The development is recorded in my poems, and the full story of my personal odyssey belongs elsewhere and reticence is proper here. Suffice it to say that I now knew what was missing from the Christian religion. I grasped from personal experience that there is a void in Western Christendom and I realised that I had been on a quest round the world to find among the typhoons and baking deserts of other cultures what should have been available in my own civilization, what used to be available in it – but what secular Christendom now largely ignores. I could have done with this book at that time, for when I cast around in libraries and bookshops to support my researches into illumination I found bits and pieces in different books, but nothing drawn together. Quite simply this sort of book just did not exist.

The main theme of this book, then, is that religion is based on the experience of the Light, which is interpreted differently in different religions. And that civilization and civilizations are based on religion. Civilization and civilizations decline when the Light is dimmed. The implication therefore is that Western civilization needs a recovery of the Light via its religion if it is to survive and flourish.

Nicholas Hagger
August 2005

Part One

The Origin of The Light

Those who have not seen this Light have not seen God: for God is Light.

St Simeon the New Theologian

1

The Meaning of the Experience of the Light

What is the Light, which is sometimes known as the Fire? The following lines were found sewn in the lining of Pascal's doublet after his death in 1662:

> "The year of grace 1654,
> Monday, 23 November...
> From about half past ten in the evening until about half past twelve
> FIRE."[1]

What was the experience that was so important to Pascal that he *wore* the precise time it happened as a reminder for the last eight years of his life? It clearly amounted to a mystical conversion, for two months later he entered the Jansenist convent of Port-Royal and from a mathematician and physicist became the religious philosopher of the *Pensées,* asserting the Jansenist salvation by divine grace. What happened to him during that "night of Fire"? Judging from the many similar experiences in the Tradition of the Light (or Fire), he probably opened himself to meditative prayer, "looked" into his closed eyelids, and in contemplation "saw" with his inner eye the Light (or Fire) of pure consciousness: first as a dawn-like glimmering out of darkness and then as a watery glow. As he sank deeper into his contemplative trance it may have become the pale watery flaming of a fire-like brightness and eventually a dazzling, blinding sun. (The "fire" and "sun" symbols attempt to describe the indescribable, to approach the raw "thing itself". Christian churches show it as a sun-burst, sometimes out of cloud.) He may have gazed at this Light of the soul in amazement and wonder.

Exactly what had Pascal encountered?

There is a remarkable consistency in the interpretations of the Light or Fire. It is widely seen as having a divine origin, as being "the Divine Light" which originates deep within the cosmos and which created our world. It is identified with Heracleitus' cosmic Fire, the ultimate metaphysical Reality. It is described as a "spiritual sun" which is brighter than our material sun. The vision of the Light (or Fire) has been called "the vision of God"; it has been seen throughout recorded history by people of many religions, and we can call it "the Light (or Fire) of God" as easily as "the Metaphysical Light (or Fire)".

At the same time this divine Light touches the soul (the essence of the mind which can survive death). As a result it is often called "the Inner Light", especially by Quakers; but we will call it "the Light" so as not to narrow its cosmic vastness to an "inner" experience. (The God that created universes is an "outer" as well as an "inner" Light or Fire.) The Light (or Fire) is regarded as grace (as Pascal himself regarded it), the working of a divine and Providential guidance of the human freewill, so that the dancer Nijinsky could justly write in his Diary, "God is fire in the head." (Unfortunately Nijinsky lacked a knowledge of the Tradition of the Light (or Fire) and, unable to interpret it, spent his last thirty years in a mental hospital, from 1919 to 1950.)

The Transforming Power of the Light of God

Here are four "eye-witness" accounts of Western encounters with the Light:

" I entered (within myself). I saw with the eye of my soul, above (or beyond) my mind, the Light Unchangeable. It was not the common light of day that is seen by the eye of every living thing of flesh and blood, nor was it some more spacious light of the same sort, as if the light of day were to shine far, far brighter than it does, and fill all space with a vast brilliance. What I saw was something quite, quite different from any light we know on earth. It shone above my mind, but not in the way oil floats above water or the sky hangs over the earth. It was above me (or higher), because it was itself the Light that made me, and I was below (or lower) because I was made by it. All who know the truth know this Light, and all who know this Light know eternity." (St. Augustine, c.400.)

"These visions which I saw, I beheld neither in sleep, nor in dream, nor in madness, nor with the eyes of the body..., I perceived them in open view and according to the will of God.... From my infancy up to the present time, I now being more than seventy years of age, I have always seen this light, in my spirit (or soul, Jung's translation) and not with external eyes, nor with any thoughts of my heart, nor with the help from my senses.... The light which I see is not located, but yet is more brilliant than the sun, nor can I examine its height, length or breadth, and I name it 'the cloud of the living light'.... But sometimes I behold within this light another light which I name 'the living light itself'. And when I look upon it every sadness and pain vanishes from my memory, so that I am again a simple maid and not as an old woman." (Hildegarde of Bingen, died 1179.)

"All at once the glory of God shone upon and round about in a manner almost marvellous.... A light perfectly ineffable shone in my soul, that almost prostrated me on the ground.... This light seemed like the brightness of the sun in every direction. It was too intense for the eyes.... I think I knew something then, by actual experience, of the light that prostrated Paul on the way to Damascus. It was surely a light such as I could not have endured long."(The Presbyterian evangelist Charles G. Finney, about his conversion of 1821.)

"During prayer on the evening of the third day I entered the interior of my soul, and seemed to descend into the giddy depths of an abyss where I had the impression of being surrounded by limitless space.... The light which has filled my soul has not come from books but from the Holy Ghost.... I felt with delight that he was beautifying my soul.... I longed that the divine gaze, the spiritual Sun, should cause the virtues to flourish in my soul, and was conscious that this longing was granted, and that this profound peace and simple act of love concealed an incomprehensible activity." (Mother Isabel Daurelle, Carmelite nun, died 1914.)[2]

These "eye-witness" accounts indicate how the Light transforms the soul. They claim that it is the truth, that it wipes away sadness and pain and even restores youth. It "converts" or "turns round", as it turned St. Paul round from persecuting the Christians to becoming a Christian. It causes virtues to flourish. Jung, quoting Hildegarde's "I have always seen a light in my soul", claims that it eliminates psychiatric problems: "I know a few individuals who are familiar with this phenomenon from personal experience....Its effect is astonishing in that it almost always brings about a solution of psychic complications, and thereby frees the inner personality from emotional and intellectual entanglements." [3]

We shall see that the Light literally acts as a fire, burning sin from the soul, so that with great abruptness people lose their desire to smoke or drink alcohol, and in some cases cease to be promiscuous. Rational, analytical men find that after experiencing the Light they live from a new centre, a purer and therefore deeper level of consciousness. The Light then enlightens with divine wisdom, giving serenity, "the peace that passeth understanding". The human freewill is fused with the divine Will, and the Light. It brings a sense of the unity of the universe and of man's oneness with all mankind and all creation.

The Light cleanses and energises the soul, and gives abundant energy for action. It gives the soul a zeal to work for the good of others, a zest to create order; thus St Teresa's illumination led her to reform the Carmelite Order and found new religious houses. The Tradition of the Light shows that the illumined often purify their religion to restore conditions in which after a worldly, secularized, Humanistic time the Light can again be seen.

As the illumined apparently receive infused wisdom, divinely revealed knowledge, they become naturally good; for the Light has its own ethic. They become increasingly "divinised" and have a strong sense that a deep meaning and purpose pervade the One. This sense of meaning flows into the soul as divine guidance within the Light. The illumined have a profound conviction that death is not the end, and that illumination is a guarantee of immortality.

In the Western tradition the Light (as it is best known) activates the eternal soul that survives death, while in the Eastern tradition (where it is equally well-known as the Fire) it is the saviour from rebirth. *The Tibetan Book of the Dead* makes it clear that all who experience it will recognise the Clear Light of the Void at death, and that their souls will therefore escape rebirth.

The Light, A Metaphysical Experience

The Light (or Fire) is traditionally seen – directly experienced – in the intellect. This has nothing to do with the reason: *intellectus* in Latin means "perception" (and therefore "understanding", "comprehension") and it is an intuitive faculty which perceives universals and meaning, and therefore understands, while the reason is a logical faculty that analyses particulars, and often sees meaninglessness.[4] The "intellect" is a perceptive faculty that lies outside the five senses. The claim is that when it perceives the Light (which is Shelley's "Intellectual Beauty") it receives wisdom from a source outside the five senses, and this infused, revealed knowledge then influences the reason.

To those who have known and experienced it, the Light has the reality of being known and experienced. To such people, the knowledge or *gnosis* of the Light (or Fire) has the reality of an empirical experience. Strictly, however empiricism sticks to the evidence of the five senses, and as the perceiving intellect is beyond the five senses the Light cannot be perceived by any of the five senses; strictly, therefore, the experience of the Light is not an empirical experience. Intellectual vision or perception of the Light may be regarded as a quasi-visual and therefore a quasi-empirical experience. (It should be pointed out that empiricism is in no position to pronounce judgement upon what is beyond the world of the senses. Empiricism is scarcely a tenable theory regarding the world of the senses since, as Kant argued, our understanding seems to evaluate sense data in terms of categories that are not derived from the world of sense experience.)

In fact, to know the Light is a metaphysical experience. It is "beyond" or "behind" ("meta") the physical world of the five senses. To

Aristotle, metaphysics was literally "what comes after physics". Aristotle distinguished the sensible world, which was the subject of the physics, from "Being as such", "the substance that is free from movement", which was the subject of metaphysics. He followed Plato's distinction between a world of phenomena or appearances, which is unreal, and true Reality. Metaphysics is the study that determines the real nature of things, and as the Light has been widely interpreted as being ultimate Reality – the "ultimate stuff of the universe", the essence within or "behind" the sensible, physical world – a study of it belongs to metaphysics rather than physics. Thus Grosseteste developed a "metaphysics of Light" when he claimed that God, the Eternal Light, created a point of light that spread into the form of matter.[5]

The experience of the Light is the essential mystical experience, for fundamentally mysticism involves a quest for hidden truth or wisdom, and "the treasure" hidden in the centre of the soul is the Light.

Different traditions have different answers regarding the working of the inner Light. The Jewish Kabbalah affirms ten *sefirot* or inner centres, and Kabbalists say that the Inner Light comes down zigzag, like a lightning flash, into the higher centres *Hohmah* (or *Hochma*) and *Binah,* or inner wisdom and understanding (the equivalent of the intellect); it can also come straight down into *Tepheret,* Beauty, the main centre which is in contact with all the four Kabbalistic worlds: the physical, the psychological, the spiritual and the divine. Some traditions, notably the Sufi, see the Inner Light as a reflection of the divine. Others, notably some Christian traditions, see it as a candleflame lit in the soul following a sun-burst; for these, illumination is a consequence in the soul. The Theosophists see the Light as the spiritual sun.

All traditions agree that a seeker only sees the Light by withdrawing from the world of the senses, by moving back from the centre of the wordly rational ego to a purer, deeper, more unconscious centre which Jung called the Self. There, if the consciousness is stilled and the heart calmed in a mystical passive waiting, the Light will break through the mists, the veil, the darkness, the Cloud of Unknowing. Indian devotees of the Tantric Hindu *chakra* system (the centres of the subtle body within the physical body) see this process as the rising of Fire-filled energy and the unfolding of the crown *chakra,* which is the thousand-petalled lotus in the top of the head.

Opinions differ as to when a person is ready for the Light. According to the religious the Light is always near at hand like Jesus in Burne-Jones's painting *The Light of the World*, knocking on the door of the heart (or the soul) which is covered with tangled weeds. Illumination can happen suddenly, as does the Quakers' Inner Light, and the Protestant tradition is full of sudden "repentance" and conversion. Mystics see illumination as crowning a long preparation and ascent; they assert that it only happens when a soul is ready. According to esoteric groups, the Light must be guarded from neophytes until their teachers feel they are ready, and the neophyte moves away from the world of the senses by stages and purifies himself for the world of the spirit. All the initiation ceremonies and mystery religions and schools purge by stages, and the masters in the Far East take their pupils to enlightenment gradually so that the experience occurs when they are ready; after which they swear them to silence. The Tantric Hindu tradition of *Kundalini* Yoga regards the Light as Fire, as a coiled serpent which sleeps at the base of the *chakras*. It seeks to raise the energy gradually for too sudden an awakening in the unready can cause a rush of energy up the *chakras* which can "blow" the mind.

All traditions agree that the Mystic Way regulates the process to create a safe Way of Enlightenment. The Way exists in the religions of all cultures; the starting-point is detachment from the senses, and purification. It is open to all, and in a growing culture, as in the Christian Middle Ages, it has a mass of followers. Neophytes can read the experiences of other mystics on the Way, and can avoid the dangers and make safe progress.

The main exponent of the Christian Mystic Way in the 20th century has been Evelyn Underhill. Her *Mysticism* (1911) sees it as an awakening which leads to detachment, purgation or purification of the senses, and thence to illumination. The soul then seeks quiet and recollection, and may experience voices and visions, raptures and ecstasies until a Dark Night plunges it back into darkness; after which the soul emerges into permanent union with God. William James, in *The Varieties of Religious Experience* (1901/2), adopts a more psychological approach. He distinguishes the "once-born" or "healthy-minded" person from the "twice-born" person who can become a "sick soul" and "divided self" before undergoing a "conversion" experience involving the Light.[6] After this, he has an increasingly saintly outlook in which the carnal appetites of the senses disappear, and he achieves permanent union with God. Both treatments of the Way show that the experience of the Inner Light was the central and most important experience in the mystics' lives.

The individual always derives force from tradition as T. S. Eliot shows in *Tradition and the Individual Talent.* The word "tradition" has two senses: a line of belief handed down from ancestors to posterity, and a doctrine or teaching supposed to have divine authority but not committed to writing (such as the oral teachings of Christ or Mohammed). The individual derives great encouragement and energy from the fact that the Tradition of the Light (both line and teaching) is there, a living reality and not a dead thing. Its evidence is impressive and profound, its 5,000 years of wisdom console him and reassure him when he feels isolated and alone; and his awareness of it nurtures his growth and dynamises his soul. Jesus said, "Except a corn of wheat fall into the ground and die, it abideth alone: but if it die, it bringeth forth much fruit." The individual whose ego dies into the Tradition of the Light finds infused energies that dynamise him and produce fruit in great deeds, many of which have established the stones that have survived the ancient cultures.

Fundamentally, the experience of the Light is an individual one. It is only subsequently ploughed back into the mystics' culture and civilization. The experience need not take place within the context of any sect or religion. It is an existential experience of "Being". Mysticism, metaphysics and the existential philosophy of Heidegger, Jaspers and Marcel all converge and unite in the Tradition of the Light. As all sects and religions turn worldly and secular with time, and lose sight of their metaphysical origins (as does the modern secular doubting Christianity of John Robinson, Don Cupitt and the Bishop of Durham), the individual can do well to retain a degree of independence from all sects and religions so that he can relate to the whole of the 5,000 year old world-wide Tradition – although from time to time, he will inevitably connect himself to the religion that dominates his own culture, which for a Westerner is Christianity.

Our Theme and Method: Phenomenological-Historical-Scientific

The theme of this book is that there is a long tradition of the Light; that civilization is based on religion and that religion is based on experience of the Light, which is interpreted differently in different religions. A civilization rises when the experience of the Light is widely shared. Civilizations decline when the Light is dimmed – not widely shared and forgotten about. This has happened constantly through history. This may now the case with Western civilization, which needs a recovery of the Light if it is to survive and flourish.

We shall have a detailed look at the decline of Western civilization when we follow the stages of different civilizations in the companion volume to this work, *The Endless Rise and Fall of Civilizations*, coming later this year. We shall see that Western civilization is actually a coalition of two civilizations at different stages of their growth, a rising North American one and a declining European one. Here we are narrating the tradition of the experience of the Light broadly chronologically to establish its impact on religions, and therefore (at the end of this book) its role in helping religions/civilizations to rise.

We shall see that for 5,000 years the metaphysical Light (or Fire), which some call God, has inspired the world's cultures and civilizations, and the human response to it has shaped their stones: the megaliths, ziggurats, pyramids, mystery sites, temples, churches and mosques. Of course many different ideas and influences combine to shape a culture. We shall see that the Light has dominated the world's civilizations because from a very early time it was central to their religions. It has manifested in the Christian and Orthodox transfiguration and Hindu Yogic *samadhi*, *Mahayana sunyata* and the Void of *Tao*, Buddhist enlightenment and Zen *satori*.

A Universalist approach (I have already said) holds that the *gnosis* of a universal God perceived or experienced as Light (or Fire) is central to all religions and civilizations, and controls their growth and decay. Our theme states the basis for a Universalist view of world civilizations, and in this book and in its companion volume, *The Endless Rise and Fall of Civilizations* we seek to demonstrate that all civilizations grow and decay in terms of their religions' response to the Light of God.

Although the Light (or Fire) of the religions is the common ground between all the cultures and civilizations, many seekers in our time are simply unaware of the Tradition of the Light which shows 5,000 years of recorded experiences. It has never before been stated in one volume. When assembled, the totality of the recorded experiences seems very weighty in contrast to the anti-metaphysical pronouncements of the Vienna Circle sceptics of the 1920s. Rediscovering this largely lost Tradition is one of the major tasks of our time. The Western tradition has to be reconciled with the very similar tradition to be found in the East, and it has to be made widely available.

In investigating these 5,000 years of recorded specific experiences, we shall be investigating *the reception of the Light (or Fire)* and the illumined's interpretation of their experiences; we cannot investigate the Light (or Fire) itself for according to the Tradition it is divine communication from beyond the senses, and its Absolute nature removes "the thing itself" from human analysis.

Our method will be phenomenological. Phenomenology is a branch of epistemology, which investigates how we know things. As Husserl developed it,[7] it describes concretely experienced phenomena by "bracketing out" (or forgetting about) the object – in our case, the Light (or Fire) itself – and investigating what has been received in the consciousness without theorising about its cause. We can describe 5,000 years of concrete, quasi-empirical experiences of the Light by "bracketing out" the Light perceived and concentrating on the perception of the Light, investigating what is in the perceiving, interpreting consciousness without theorising about the cause of the perception and interpretation. Our descriptive phenomenological approach to the Light in consciousness therefore represents the beginnings of a new objective science of consciousness.

Our method will also be historical. Proceeding historically, telling the story of the unfolding of the Light as chronologically as is possible when developments take place in parallel, will enable us to present the evidence for the universality of the Light as it moves from culture to culture. Starting from scratch, we can see how the knowledge of the Light was slowly accumulated, layer upon layer, and we can relate each recorded perception to the culture in which it took place.

We shall narrate and describe 25 traditions as transmitters of the Light. As we proceed tradition by tradition and pursue the Light of each tradition from start to finish, in some cases from before 3,000 BC to the present, we in no way suggest that each tradition has always been immune from the rest instead of being interconnected and communally influenced by the prevailing *zeitgeist* of each Age. See the chart on pp 534-535. The Light of each tradition was not isolated from the general chronological historical process or flow. In due course we shall propose 25 civilizations as transmitters of the Light. The identification of these civilizations will arise naturally out of our narrative of the Tradition of the Light. We will review the evidence for an unbroken Tradition of the Light over 5,000 years, and leave much historical detail until later. That way we shall proceed from the whole to the individual patterns, and our selection of our patterns will not predetermine the evidence of the whole "carpet".

We therefore aim to present a true and accurate account of the evidence for the appearances of the Light in recorded history in the order in which they happened. In the course of doing this we will establish a Tradition of the Light with many sub-traditions. In *The Endless Rise and Fall of Civilizations* we will relate the appearances of the Light to the growth-and-decay, rise-and-fall movements of their civilizations. In so doing we will provide detailed evidence for a Universalist approach to world civilizations. We shall eventually argue that history is a pattern of events. The question is, which events are significant? It may be that the really significant events have not been emphasised and connected before, but have appeared in isolation as footnotes to particular centuries. Histories of the Crusades, for example, dwell on the outer events and give detailed accounts of all the battles without really probing the inner religious experiences on either side which gave rise to the battles: the Fire Mohammed saw and the Light of St. Bernard, for instance. Our statement of the History of the Light may give some inner events a historical significance they have not had before, and by highlighting events that have largely escaped attention, may come up with some surprising connections which may challenge the conventional wisdom. It is not widely known that the Heavenly Father of the *Bible* emerged from the Light of the Persian Ahura Mazda, and that Christians imported symbols for the Islamic Light during the Crusades. If it is seen that the most significant events in history are inner glimpses of the Light which create religions that dominate cultures, then it may be true that, as Eliot wrote in "Little Gidding", "History is a pattern/Of timeless moments."

Many writings on "timeless" spiritual matters open themselves to "higher worlds", are imprecise about historical causes, and merely have the force of an inspired guess. We reject that way as unacceptable to scholarship, and proceed by a rigorous consideration of the evidence and detailed knowledge of the historical circumstances in each culture. For again and again we see that one idea, or interpretation of the Light, came to govern the thinking of several religious mystics who controlled the direction of their civilization for several decades. Our picture will therefore have the reliability of a carefully observed portrait, not a vague metaphor which says more about the observer than his observation of the thing observed. Only by such exactness can the metaphysical vision again command attention.

Our historical method will enable us to keep both feet firmly on the ground, an essential requirement when dealing with a metaphysical subject and especially one that has not been adequately dealt with before. It will enable us to maintain common sense at all times, to preserve a practical, almost scientific approach, rooting the Light in its historical, cultural context, observing the requirements of scrupulous scholarship, being open and clear about our sources so that the evidence can be impartially weighed by those readers who remain to be convinced. Only by avoiding excessive claims and weird or silly self-deceptions, only by treating the Light objectively and impartially as a cultural phenomenon and only by erring on the side of caution and observing acceptable standards of accuracy (being exact about what is definite and clear about what is only a possibility) can we do justice to our momentous theme and make a painstaking but unassailable case for the universality of the Light at certain times in all cultures. Only then can the conclusions we draw withstand searching scrutiny.

Above all, our method will be scientific. By studying the perception of the Light in consciousness we are laying the foundation for a new objective science of consciousness. Our method will therefore be evidential – never far from the evidence.

Our historical-descriptive-scientific (or -evidential) phenomenology will establish a set of experiences which lie outside the five senses, and this will form the collective experience of the illumined. Individual perceptions of the Light can then be compared or contrasted with this collective standard and its cultural manifestations.

The Tradition of the Light that now follows can be read for the individual's experience of the Light; for how the Light has shaped the world's religions, and through them its societies, cultures and civilizations; and for how the Light provides common ground for a coming world-wide culture (see the chart on pp534-535). It heralds a return to a metaphysical outlook that can restore true values to the lives of Westerners and world citizens.

2

The Central Asian Origin of the Light

The Divine Light is found in all the primitive and ancient cultures and civilizations whose early kings embodied it, whose priests attended it, and whose stones are scattered throughout the Mediterranean, Europe, Africa, the Near East, India, the Far East and the Americas.

All the early cultures were capable of throwing up their own Light as all human beings have a "spark in the soul" which can potentially illumine their culture. Was the experience discovered anew in each separate culture? Or did trading spread it from one culture and civilization to another? Was there one original teaching or system of knowledge that perhaps passed down to Atlantis (if it was not in fact legendary) ten thousand years or more ago, before the cataclysm which ended the Pleisitocene period, and then perhaps on to Lemuria (if it was not in fact legendary), to Central Asia, and the Trans-Himalayan school of Tibet, where Yoga may have originated? And did it eventually pass into Sumerian hieroglyphs, the Egyptian *Book of the Dead*, the Persian *Zend Avesta*, the Indian *Vedas*, Tibetan and Chinese mysticism, the Phoenician cult of Adonis, Greek Pythagoreanism, and the Christian Sermon on the Mount? As we are dealing with the mists of prehistory, the answers are sometimes bound to be inconclusive; but by sticking to the facts, and discounting legends like Atlantis and Lemuria which are not supported by evidence, we can locate a clear pattern.

It may seem incredible that prehistoric nomads should be sensitive to inner knowledge, but we are accustomed to forget that there was a high culture c.8500 BC, long before recorded history began, and that *homo sapiens*, who appeared outside Africa c.70,000 BC, had a larger brain capacity than ours, although his frontal lobes (and therefore his reasoning) were not so well developed.

Cro-Magnon man, who appeared after *homo sapiens*, was tall – he achieved a height of 1.77m – and he had a fine high forehead. He also had a larger brain than we have.[8] He lived in the white cliffs and overhanging rocks and caves of the Dordogne around the modern Les Eyzies, prehistory's Valley of the Kings, from c.30,000 to c.10,000 BC. He made stone lamps and adorned himself with necklaces made of shells. He killed bison, deer, boar, elk and reindeer for their meat and skins, and he fished for salmon, pike and trout. He had a more acute sense of sight and hearing than we have, and he was clearly very intelligent. For his cave paintings he ground pigments on limestone steps and kept his paints in hollow bones: ochre for red and yellow, manganese for black. He painted and engraved from memory, in the gloom of the caves at Lascaux, Font de Gaume and Les Combarelles, and left works of immense aesthetic sensitivity, like the superb frieze of horses at Cap Blanc.

Georges Bataille wrote after visiting the Hall of Bulls at Lascaux: "Nothing supports the contention that we are greater than they were." Henry Miller, a great frequenter of the Dordogne, concluded that as he was capable of such art, Cro-Magnon man had an aesthetic and religious sensibility: "I believe that Cro-Magnon man settled here because he was extremely intelligent and had a highly developed sense of beauty. I believe that in him the religious sense was already highly developed and that it flourished here even if he lived like an animal in the depths of caves." [9]

We have been conditioned to regard Cro-Magnon man as primitive. He had the sensitivity to paint curved bumps in the cave walls into a bison's back or a cow's udder to give a three dimensional perspective in the shadows thrown by his stone lamps. Is it really surprising that he should also have had the sensitivity to close his eyes during the long dark evenings and see the Light – and paint himself as a man with a sun-head?

Southern Africa boasts the oldest men (from perhaps three million years ago). A television study of the cave paintings of Southern Africa ("Images of Another World" by David Drew, shown on London's BBC2 on April 19, 1989) concluded that Palaeolithic paintings interpret trance; that shamans (or medicine men) entered the darkness and silence of the caves (as do the Bushmen of the Kalahari) so that they could enter a trance, experience altered states of consciousness and have visions of "entoptic forms" which are generated by the central nervous system according to American neuro-psychologists, and which appear as squiggles and waves and dotted lines that invisibly bind men to animals in Palaeolithic art throughout the world. If Palaeolithic man used the caves to enter trances, is it not entirely believable that he knew the Light?

The Shamanistic Source of the Light

> **As for the "inner light," which plays a part of the first importance in Indian mysticism and metaphysics as well as in Christian mystical theology, it is...already documented in Eskimo shamanism.**
>
> Mircea Eliade, *Shamanism, Archaic Techniques of Ecstasy*

It seems that the Light was first known in the culture of early shamanistic times. The shamans originated in Siberia and Central Asia in the Altaic area west and south west of Lake Baikal. (Central Asia includes the Mongol and Turkic peoples, and covers the lands of the peoples of Siberia, the Soviet Arctic, Mongolia, Manchuria, Nepal, Bhutan, Sikkim, and of course Tibet.)[10]

Shamanism was the religion of Upper Palaeolithic times, c.50,000 BC,[11] when hunters engaged in rituals involving animals, and their cave paintings have been found in India and China as well as in Central Asia, and in North Africa and Spain as well as in France. The early shamans believed that all animals – indeed, all living creatures including rocks, plants and trees – have personal identities and souls, and that killing animals for food might cause their souls to take revenge on their killers. A modern Eskimo shaman told the Danish explorer Knud Rasmussen: "The greatest peril of life lies in the fact that human food consists entirely of souls. All the creatures we have to kill and eat, all those we have to strike down and destroy to make clothes for ourselves, have souls as we have."[12] Before setting out the early hunters drew a picture of their quarry, and when they returned they put blood and hair from the dead animal on the picture in thanksgiving. They placated and controlled the souls of the animals they killed: hence the many rock-carvings of animals in the Palaeolithic caves in France (c.20,000-12,000 BC).

A shaman means "one who sees" or "one who knows" – it comes from a Tunguso-Manchurian word[13] – and he was essentially a visionary and medicine-man. To the shaman a human being consists of a body, mind and life-giving vital breath which are all extinguished on death; and a soul (the essence of mind) and spirit (the permanent identity which reincarnates) which can be illumined by the divine spark and which do survive death. On death the soul inhabits a spiritual body that preserves the Light, and is simply referred to as a "dead spirit".[14] The shaman was able to contact dead spirits, and he evoked spirits to control his nomadic farming, the sowing and harvesting that were so important in those times.

To become a shaman, the neophyte had to be initiated. This often meant that he had to walk over burning coals to achieve mastery over fire; he was saved from injury if his "command of the spirits" enabled him to give out a mystic or magical heat that left his body immune to extremes of external temperature. He turned away from the secular life either by a ritual self-wounding or through involuntary sickness, and he descended into the Underworld, one of the three shamanistic worlds (sky, earth, underworld) linked by a central axis.[15] His trance, or "temple sleep", was often induced by a drum and lasted three days and symbolized his dying away from the Middle World or Earth. He then ascended to Heaven, the Sky World, either by ascending a notched, ladder-like Tree (which was often a birch tree) or the rainbow or by flying to the Sun Door, his soul a Sun-Bird. He then achieved illumined consciousness, and was shown with a halo round his head. One commentator has written: "The Inner Light has been revealed through the action of a self-achieved submission."[16]

A modern Eskimo shaman has explained this secret ancient knowledge to Knud Rasmussen: "Every real shaman has to feel an illumination in his body, in the inside of his head or in his brain, something that gleams like fire, that gives him power to see with closed eyes into the darkness, into the hidden things or into the future, or into the secrets of another man. I felt that I was in possession of this marvellous ability." Mircea Eliade, in his *Shamanism*, translates the same passage differently when speaking of the "disciple's 'lighting' or 'enlightenment',...a mysterious light which the shaman suddenly feels in his body, inside his head, within the brain, an inexplicable searchlight, a luminous fire, which enables him to see in the dark, both literally and metaphorically speaking, for he can now, even with closed eyes, see through darkness and perceive things and coming events which are hidden from others; thus they look into the future and into the secrets of others." Eliade observes that "the candidate obtains this mystical light after long hours of waiting, sitting on a bench in his hut and invoking the spirits." Elsewhere Eliade reports that "Rasmussen gives several accounts of shamans receiving their illumination, which he took down from their own lips. The shaman Aua felt a celestial light in his body and brain, which, as it were, proceeded from his whole being."[17] The details are instructive: "I had gained my enlightenment, the shaman's light of brain and body, and this in such a manner that it was not I who could see through the darkness of life, but the same bright light also shone out from me, imperceptible to human beings but visible to all the spirits of the earth and sea and sky."[18] The early shamanistic hunters of c.30,000-10,000 BC were sufficiently sensitive to have this Eskimo's illumination.

After his ecstatic illumination, the ancient shaman was ready to return to his people and use his visionary knowledge to heal illnesses, which invariably (shamans assert) have a spiritual cause and involve "loss of soul". The shaman was reborn, and so were his society and in due course the crops, for the shaman's spiritual power made rivers flood and fertilised crops. Pictures often show him wearing stag or reindeer antlers (which symbolise the sacred World Tree) and holding an ear of corn.[19]

The Altaians worshipped a Lord of the Underworld and a Sky-god,[20] and the shaman was found at the centre of the cosmos, where the Underworld with its seven or nine levels,[21] the Middle World or Earth, and

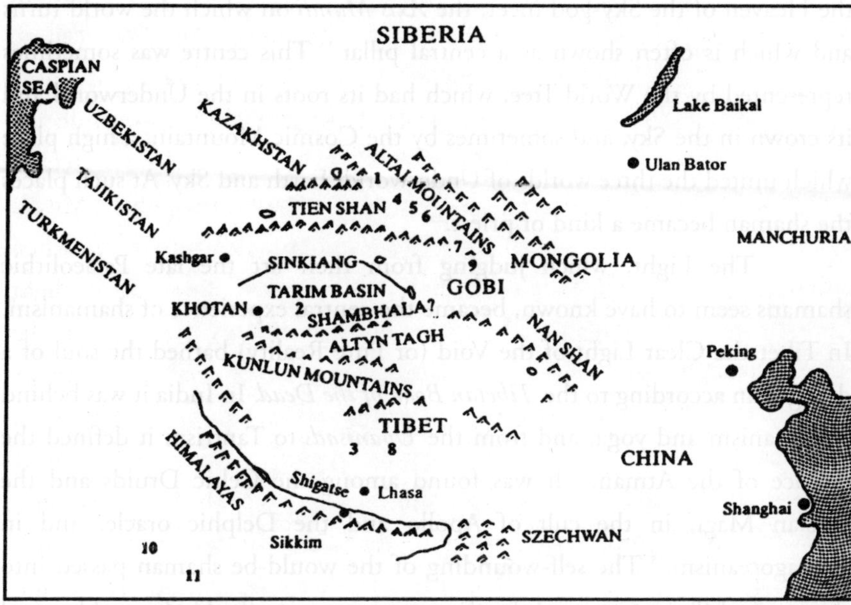

CENTRAL ASIA: THE SPREAD OF SHAMANISM AND BON

1. c.50,000BC Shamanism in Altaic area & Siberia, cave paintings in Central Asia, India & China (& N. Africa, Spain, France)
c.40,000BC *homo sapiens* appears
c.30,000BC Cro-Magnon man appears
2. c.25,000BC? Bon emerges in Shambhala?, which according to tradition is bordered by Siberia in the north, Tibet & India in the south, China in the east & Khotan in the west, & which is therefore in the vicinity of Kunlun Mountains, Altyn Tagh Ridge, the Tarim Basin & the Gobi desert
c.20,000-10,000BC, Bon's Tantrism in Cro-Magnon France
3. c.10,000BC? (or later) Patanjali's Yoga system?
c.8500BC high Neolithic culture, eg in Jericho
4. c.7000BC Kurgans from Altaic region to Russian steppes & Anatolia
5. c.4000-3500BC, Kurgan Sumerians (Anannage?) take Bon from Altaic region to Sumeria
6. c.3903BC? Kurgan Druidism founded in Central Asia?
7. c.2900BC Chinese hexagrams from Bon origins?
8. ?BC Bon-po the indigenous religion of Tibet
9. 2nd C BC Essenes emerge; they originally came from Central Asia
10. 5th C AD Bon enters Hinduism as Tantrism
11. 8th C AD Bon enters Buddhism as Tantrism

the Heaven of the Sky-god meet, the *Axis Mundi* on which the world turns and which is often shown as a central pillar.[22] This centre was sometimes represented by the World Tree, which had its roots in the Underworld and its crown in the Sky, and sometimes by the Cosmic Mountain, a high place which united the three worlds of Underworld, Earth and Sky. At such places the shaman became a kind of priest.[23]

The Light, which judging from their art the late Palaeolithic shamans seem to have known, became the central experience of shamanism. In Tibet the Clear Light of the Void (or Pure Reality) bathed the soul of a dying man according to the *Tibetan Book of the Dead*. In India it was behind Brahmanism and yoga, and from the *Upanisads* to Tantrism it defined the essence of the Atman.[24] It was found among the Celtic Druids and the Persian Magi, in the cult of Apollo and the Delphic oracle, and in Pythagoreanism.[25] The self-wounding of the would-be shaman passed into the myth of Philoctetes, and the shaman's journey to the Underworld passed into the myths of Osiris and Orpheus (both of whom suffered dismemberment) and was reflected in the epic descents of Odysseus and Aeneas. The shaman's World Tree was behind the Kabbalistic Tree of Life, which interiorises it, and the Old Norse Yggdrasil, on which Odin, who was called "the Great Shaman", hanged himself for nine days "as a sacrifice of myself to myself";[26] compare the Buddha's Bo Tree and the Christian cross, both of which united earth and Heaven. The Light is of course found in Christian Mysticism.

Traces of Altaic shamanism run through the architecture of Christianity, Hinduism, Buddhism, and Taoism and the culture of the American Red Indians whose feathers[27] represent the crown of the Light as Fire and suggest the soaring of the Sun-Bird.[28] As the Tradition of the Light widened, the sacred groves of World Trees where it was first known gave way to sacred temples with tree-like pillars, which reproduced groves for the new city-dwellers. (Hence the organic architecture in King's College Chapel, Cambridge, which was built by Freemasons.)[29] The Cosmic Mountain became a Sumerian ziggurat, an Egyptian Pyramid, the Hindu Mount Meru, a representation of which is to be found in the central temple-mountain at Angkor Wat, and many other temples and palaces.

The shaman's Light which could be seen at midnight[30] is the fundamental experience in the cultures of the last 5,000 years. Whether the soul is seen as Horus the hawk or as a Kabbalistic eagle that flies between physical and divine worlds, and whether the shaman survives as the horned figure in Morris dances or as Herne the hunter, wearing antlers, in Shakespeare's *The Merry Wives of Windsor*, shamanism unified the many cultures of recorded history and its experience of eternity has remained constant since Palaeolithic times.

THE BON LIGHT

> **Bon wisdom…includes prophecy, healing and the induction of trances in which the magician can separate soul from body to travel freely, not only in the physical, but also in the spirit, world.**
>
> Ward Rutherford, *Shamanism, The Foundations of Magic*

There is evidence that the first known shamanic religion which transmitted the Light was Bon-po, the indigenous religion of the Central Asian Tibet.[31] Conjecture dates this to c.25,000 BC, though Bon was not known historically until shortly before 1000 BC.[32] In Bon, the gods, ancestral spirits and demons of the three shaman worlds were controlled by priests or shamans. There were a Sky-god who manifested or incarnated in a divine king; an order of oracular priests; and a cult of the gods of the Sky, Earth and Underworld that was linked to such animals as the swan and the bull. (The bull roared in the Underworld and caused earthquakes unless it was appeased like the Minotaur.) There were blood sacrifices over a sacred fire of a horse or bull, which now represented the Sun-god (as did the Egyptian bull of Ra). The shaman ascended to the Sky World of the sun, like the Irish Druid Mag Roth in Celtic myth, by putting on a bull's skin cloak and a bird head-dress and rising up with the smoke.[33]

This early Bon shamanism was the ancient Tibetan wisdom on which Mme Blavatsky claimed to draw. The Bon cult was apparently born in the perhaps legendary land of Shambhala or Shamballa, which seems to have been located near the Kunlun mountains and the more northerly Altyn Tagh Ridge where the River Tarim has its source, and possibly in the Gobi Desert.[34] This lost oasis was first shown on a geographical map in a Bon book about Tibet which can be dated to the 1st century AD, and it has been seen as: the nine-storeyed palace of Hsi Wang Mu, alias Kuan Yin or the Japanese Kannon, goddess of mercy, in the legendary abode of the Immortals; the golden age of the Greeks; the Tebu Land, lost between Tibet and Szechwan, to which Taoists claim Lao-Tze disappeared on the back of a buffalo in the 6th century BC; the kingdom of the Holy Ruler Hiarchas which Apollonius of Tyana visited in the 1st century AD, using the map followed by Pythagoras a few centuries earlier (as described by Philostratus); the legendary kingdom of Presbyter or Prester John, a priest-king who ruled (according to medieval maps) from Turkestan to Tibet and from the Himalayas to the Gobi Desert; and the hidden Bon land in Central Asia inaccessible to all except initiates which is reputed to have an academy of esoteric knowledge and a community of enlightened *arhats* and *bodhisattvas*.[35] This legendary academy in Shambhala is regarded as the origin of the Kalachakra system, a course in astronomy, astrology and Sanskrit whose esoteric knowledge opens the perception to the secret realm of the *bodhisattvas* and which is regarded with such importance in Tibet that the Tibetan calendar dates from its introduction in 1026.[36] The lost spiritual culture of Shambhala has been sought in our own time by the explorer Nicholas Roerich.[37]

The Bon religion proclaimed a secret revelation or esoteric knowledge (the Light) which was available to the elite of shamans and which eventually widened into religion. It seems that the knowledge may have been brought out of the Altaic region north of Tibet by the possibly Mongoloid Sumerians c.3500 BC, who took it with them to the Tigris-Euphrates valley, embodied it in their ziggurats, and passed it on to the Persian Magi.[38] The Magi seem to have had links with Tibet (perhaps with Shambhala), for they passed the worship of Mithras and Ahura Mazda on to the Bon priests, who claimed to have received their faith from Shambhala. From the sacred fire-worshipping Magi, the knowledge passed to the Gnostics and eventually to the Cathars, some of whom fled to Tibet after the fall of Montsegur. It was also brought out from Central Asia by the Indo-Europeans and eventually came to Greece, where the Hyperborean Apollo had a shaman's oracle and was *phoibos*, or "light-bearer"[39] (in the sense that he bore a metaphysical light). It entered Taoism. The knowledge passed into Judaism – the Kabbalistic Tree of Life recalls the shaman's World Tree – and Christianity, Islam, Buddhism and Hinduism, which all have strong Bon shaman elements.

The ancient shamanistic Bon knowledge found its way into all the early cultures, stirring them to religious rites and to civilization. As it became localized over several generations, it differentiated in different regions and formed different religions. Let's explore how this one experience of the Light shaped the early cultures.

Part Two

The Tradition of The Light

The development of culture and the development of religion, in a society uninfluenced from without, cannot be clearly isolated from each other.... What perhaps influences us towards treating religion and culture as two different things is the history of the penetration of the Graeco-Roman culture by the Christian Faith.... The culture (is) essentially, the incarnation (so to speak) of the religion of a people.

T. S. Eliot, *Notes towards the Definition of Culture*

It's not difficult to know where to start as there's general agreement as to which people were the first to show signs of civilization. Back in prehistoric times, the Light of shamanism passed down through the Mesolithic time after 10,000 BC when hunters occupied Jericho (c.8000 BC), Çatalhüyük (c.6700 BC) and Lepenski Vir on the Danube (c.5000 BC).[1] It descended perhaps through Bon to the Indo-Europeans, linguistically connected people who were associated with Central Asia and Tibet and whose homeland by this time was in the Central Russian plain that is bordered by the Urals, the Caucasus and the River Dnieper – to the west of Central Asia and Tibet.[2]

1

The Indo-European Kurgan Light

The End of Old Europe: The Intrusion of Steppe Pasturalists from South Russia and the Transformation of Europe....The Kurgan tradition became manifest in Old European territories during three waves of infiltration: I at c.4400-4300 BC, II at c.3500 BC, and III soon after 3000 BC....Kurgan I people were from the Volga steppe; Kurgan II...developed in the North Pontic area between the lower Dniester and the Caucasus mountains; Kurgan III people were again from the Volga steppe.

Marija Gimbutas, *The Civilization of the Goddess*

The Kurgan people, traditionally the first Indo-Europeans, were in Central Europe from as least c.4500 BC.[1] They buried their dead in long barrows with shafts; hence their name, for *kurgan* is the Russian and Turkic for "burial mound".[2] They were warrior herdsmen of a semi-nomadic pastoralist culture, and they obtained metal weapons (axes and daggers) from the Kuro-Araxes culture which was the first to smelt copper c.4500 BC.[3] Their home was in the copper-bearing Caucasus mountains, and royal Kurgan tombs in the Caucasus date from c.3500 BC[4] and anticipate the royal tombs at Ur (c.2800 BC). The tombs at Ur were chambered palaces, more elaborate versions of the Kurgan model,[5] and both the Caucasian and Ur tombs were filled with a wealth of gold, silver and bronze.

By c.3700 BC the Indo-European Kurgans had spread in force to the Danube,[6] possibly as a result of drought. Their mobility was dramatically enhanced by c.4000 BC when they domesticated the horse. They brought with them a new religion of a Sky Father who ruled over a sun-god.[7]

The old Neolithic Old Europeans worshipped the moon, whose cusp was symbolized in the curve of a bull's horns; hence the origins of the early bull cult.[8] This was an extension of the Palaeolithic cave paintings of bulls as at Lascaux which was already established in Anatolia between c.6700 and c.5650 BC, as can be seen from the fresco of the Great Red Bull at Çatalhüyük, Turkey.[9] The Neolithic religion was a matriarchal one of the moon goddess and Mother Earth (Magna Mater). (Its essence has survived in Robert Graves' *White Goddess*, and in modern witchcraft, which worships the moon goddess Diana and the horned god, now known as Satan.)

By 2000 BC the Europeans had given up the matriarchal religion and adopted the new Indo-European patriarchal system of a Sky Father who ruled over a sun-god.[10] The Indo-European king seems to have embodied the Sky Father. Like the shamans, the Indo-Europeans descended to the Underworld, ascended to the Sky-god in Heaven, and mastered fire.[11] They regarded fire as divine and enshrined it in Fire-temples, and the sun seemed to be the origin of fire while lightning transmitted it.[12] The Sky Father held sway over lightning and fire, including the sun,[13] and fertilised the Neolithic Earth Mother (Magna Mater) and fecundated the soil.[14] He must have resembled the Cerne Abbas giant – Herakles or Hercules, a priapic fertility god with his club, perhaps alias Ogmios or the Sumerian Ogma – which may have been carved by Indo-Europeans if it was not carved by Roman Britons.[15] He was known as Dyaeus or Dyaus Pitar. Dyaeus comes from a root meaning "to shine", and *pitar* is the Sanskrit word for the Greek and Latin *pater*, "father".[16] Bulls, symbolising the old Neolithic moon-religion, and horses, the animal on which Indo-Europeans migrated, were sacrificed by fire in the Fire-temples of the steppes to placate Dyaeus Pitar, the Shining Father, and the Indo-European shamans ascended to the Sky World on the smoke of the sacrifice, which represented a World Tree.[17] The shafts of their burial mounds generally faced eastwards and looked towards the rising Sun.[18]

The Kurgan Light in Europe and Megalithic Sun Cult

Many of the megaliths – gigantic blocks of stone – were probably of Indo-European origin[19] and associated with the Light (or Fire) which was symbolized by the sun. It seems that settlers from Anatolia, who had originated in Central Asia, crossed the Aegean to Thessaly and Crete c.6000 BC, and that descendants moved north and west, cutting through forests and, after 4000 BC, piling boulders into megalithic mortuary shrines.[20] Most of the megaliths belong to the late Neolithic or early Bronze Age (after c.3000 BC), and they are distributed throughout the world, in Europe, the Mediterranean area, Asia and the Pacific Islands (Melanesia).[21] In Europe they are to be found throughout the British Isles, especially in Wales; and in France, especially in Brittany: *menhir* ("isolated megalith") and *dolmen* ("vertical stones" with a horizontal one on top) being Breton words. They are common in Spain and Portugal, Sweden, Denmark and North Germany, but rarer in Holland, Belgium and Switzerland. In the Mediterranean they are to be found on islands (Corsica, Sardinia, Malta, Gozo, Pantellaria, Lampedusa, and Sicily) but not on the mainland (Italy, Greece, and few in the Balkans). They are to be found in North Africa, but significantly perhaps, not in Egypt, where pyramids seem to have taken their place; and there are some in the Sudan. In Asia they are in Transjordania, Syria, Persia, India, Korea, Japan, and even in Alaska.[22] Besides *menhirs* and *dolmens* they comprise trilithons (two vertical stones with a horizontal one on top), alignments (rows of *menhirs*), cromlechs (rows of *menhirs* in a circle with horizontal stones on top), and later megalithic temples.[23] The idea for megalithic temple-pyramids in the Andean, Meso-American and Mexican region probably predated c.1200 BC,[24] but most of those that have survived were built later than 500 BC.

We have seen that Neolithic Old Europe at first worshipped the moon-goddess as a being who was also Mother Earth (Magna Mater) and creative in her own right; the Sun-god was initially worshipped in an earth-orientated fertility cult.[25] Now that a fault in the Libby dating method puts the traditional date of Stonehenge I (c.1800 BC) back to c.2500 BC or even earlier, c.3000 BC,[26] there is evidence that many of the early megaliths in Britain around this date – especially the cromlechs – embodied first a moon-cult, then a sun-cult or sky-cult. The megaliths were eventually places of sun-worship.

Stonehenge I seems to have been a sun-temple or a Fire-temple that looked to the sun.[27] It comprised an outer circular ditch and bank, 56 pits and the Heel (Hele) Stone ("sun stone" as *helios* is the Greek for "sun") or Friar's heel, and Stonehenge II was completed between two and five hundred years later, with bluestones from Pembrokeshire.[28] Stonehenge IIIA was a remodelling with eighty sarsens (and lintels) from the Marlborough Downs.[29] The symmetrical axis of the sarsens is aligned to the solstices in such a way that movements of the sun, moon and major stars could be calculated accurately during the year.[30] Stonehenge was certainly the Greenwich observatory of the time and gematria has been used to show that it was also a solar temple.[31] The fact that the sun rises over the Heel stone on Midsummer's Day has long been an argument for Stonehenge's being a sun-temple.[32] Besides being an observatory, Avebury was also probably a sun-temple, the ancient Westminster Abbey where leaders were buried. An avenue of stones formed the solar serpent, the sanctuary formed its head and its body passed through the Avebury Circle, the sun-symbol.[33]

The giant British hill figures were connected with sun-worship, and may have been signals to the Sun-god. The Long Man of Wilmington, on Windover Hill, Sussex, either opened the doors of Heaven after darkness, or held up two sun discs on poles.[34] It is only this century that we have become aware that chunks of the landscape may have been used pictorially in prehistoric times. The most famous of these is the Temple of the Stars and Zodiacs at Glastonbury, which forms a circle ten miles across, but the Kingston Zodiac near London now rivals this.[35] Mrs Maltwood suggests that the Glastonbury Zodiac was built for the Sun-god, and that it was made c.2700 BC – perhaps c.2500 BC – by the Sumerians, proto-Cimmerians or Cymry,[36] perhaps under the guidance of Hu or Khu Gadarn, the legendary hero with divine solar attributes who has been called the founder of Stonehenge (whether I or II history does not relate).[37] The solar wheel, a wheeled cross, appears in Irish churches (for instance, over the lintel of St

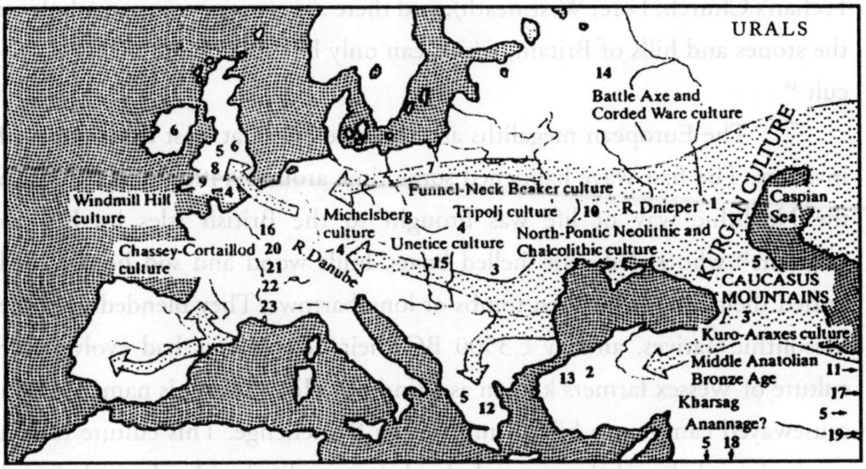

EUROPE: THE SPREAD OF THE INDO-EUROPEAN KURGAN CULTURE AND CIVILIZATION

1. c.7000BC Kurgans from Altaic region to Russian steppes (bordered by Urals, Caucasus & River Dnieper)
2. c.6700-5650BC Kurgans to Çatalhüyük, Anatolia
3. c.4500BC Kurgans in Central Europe & to Kuro-Araxes culture
4. c.3700BC Kurgans at Danube
5. c.4400-3500BC Kurgan Anannage (Tuatha?) to Britain (including Cornwall), Caucasus, Sumeria & Egypt, & Greece
6. c.3500-3000BC Windmill Hill culture (Wessex farmers) including Newgrange, Ireland (c3150BC) & Stonehenge I (c.3000BC)
7. c.23200-2100BC ex-Spanish Funnel-Neck Beaker culture (proto-Indo-Europeans)
8. c.2600BC Funnel-Neck Beaker culture to Britain as Spanish Milesians (?), Anannage Tuatha leave for South America after c.2600BC?
9. c.2700-2500BC British megaliths & Stonehenge II (c.2500BC)
10. c.2400-2300BC Kurgans to land of North Pontians
11. c.2250BC Kurgans to Iran as Iranians
12. c.2200BC Kurgans to Greece as Mycenaeans
13. c.2200-2000BC Kurgans to Anatolia as Hittites
14. c.2200-1500BC Battle-Axe or Corded-Ware culture (& Stonehenge III)
15. c.2300-2000BC Unetice culture
16. c.1850-1200BC Bell-Beaker Celto-Ligurian Bronze-Age Tumulus culture
17. c.1750BC Kurgans to Babylonia as Kassites
18. c.1674-1567BC Kurgans to Egypt as Hyksos
19. c.1500BC Kurgans to Harappa, India as Hindus, with *Vedas*
20. c.1800-1100BC Urnfield culture
21. c.1200BC Kurgans emerge as Celts
22. c.1100-600BC Hallstatt Celts
23. c.600-100BC La Tène Celts

Fechan's Church, Fore, Westmeath), and there are numerous sun-symbols on the stones and hills of Britain, which can only be relics of a prehistoric sun-cult.[38]

The European megaliths are associated with at least three waves of invaders. The first wave happened some time around 4400-4300 BC when the Neolithic way of life was brought to the British Isles by Kurgan migrants[39] who sailed skin-shelled boats, built wood and sod houses, and buried their dead in earthen tombs or long barrows. They blended with the Mesolithic natives, and by c.3500 BC their descendants had evolved the culture of Wessex farmers known as Windmill Hill,[40] which is named after a causewayed camp on a hill 18 miles from Stonehenge. This culture took a precise knowledge of the sun to Ireland. It is credited with what is believed to be the oldest astronomically aligned building in the world: the Newgrange tombs near Dublin c.3150 BC where, four and a half minutes after sunrise on midwinter's day (and only then), the sun shines down a long passage and illuminates a spiral, indicating that the days will now get longer.[41] The Wessex farmers buried their dead communally and attached importance to the sacrificial axe; and they built Stonehenge I c.3000 BC.[42] This new culture may have been the result of the natives dominating the invaders.

Meanwhile, early Bronze Age proto-Indo-Europeans[43] had left Spain and came to the Low Countries and the Middle Rhine in search of metals. They are known as the Funnel-Neck Beaker culture because they buried their dead in megalithic or single graves with drinking cups or beakers.[44] Some came into collision with the main body of Kurgans who were firmly established in Central Europe, and they moved to the British Isles soon after 2600 BC, and arrived at Stonehenge I. They are credited with adding the bluestone pillars of Stonehenge II,[45] which could have been the work of descendants of the builders of Stonehenge I, and some went on to Ireland where they may have added the sun-swirls at Newgrange (2600-2100 BC), and perhaps, as the Spanish Milesians, drove out the Tuatha (who, if they were not legendary, may have set sail for South America).[46] They had shaman-priests and clearly looked to the sun, like Indo-Europeans.[47]

While this was happening, the main body of Kurgans moved on from the Danube.[48] Some invaded the land of the North Pontians and Trans-

Caucasians between 2400 and 2300 BC, in search of metals, and absorbed the ideas of Sumer and Akkad, including Utu and Shamash. Some of these Kurgans were displaced when the Semitic Sargon I conquered Akkad c.2350 BC.[49] With their domesticated horses pulling war chariots they had modelled on the Sumerian wheeled chariot, some entered Anatolia and became the ancestors of the Hittites,[50] and some arrived in Greece c.2200 BC[51] – earlier Kurgans had entered Greece c.3500 BC[52] – and called it Achaea.[53] They displaced some of the descendants of the original Pelasgians (some of whom seem to have gone to Anatolia), and they became the ancestors of the Mycenaeans who built shaft graves in the Kurgan fashion.[54]

The Battle-Axe Light

These Kurgans are known as the Battle-Axe or Corded Ware culture because they were buried in single shaft graves with bronze axes and cord-decorated pottery.[55] Around 2000 BC some reached Scandinavia. Some arrived in France, which repelled them as it was still dominated by the Bell Beaker people, and they settled in Britain.[56]

They built Stonehenge III, probably as an Indo-European Fire-temple, during their occupation of the megaliths (c.2000-1500 BC)[57] – compare the lintels with those of the Lion Gate at Mycenae – and they may have carved the Cerne Abbas Ogma (or Herakles). (Battle-Axe Kurgans acquired Ogma from Britain, but they also found him c.2400-2300 BC when they absorbed Sumer-Akkad.)[58] Meanwhile some conquered Babylonia as the Kassites who also introduced the horse (mid 18th century BC),[59] some briefly overran Egypt as the Hyksos (c.1674-1567 BC)[60] – who worshipped the storm-god Seth and who first introduced the horse and chariot to Egypt – and some went into India and wrecked Harappa (c.1500 BC).[61] All these Indo-Europeans had shaman-priests, and they established the main features of the Kurgan culture: single barrow burials with supine skeletons; bronze axes and daggers; cord-decorated pottery; horse burials; and human sacrifices, including the burial of wives with their husbands in a practice like the Indian suttee, which may be descended from it.[62]

In Britain the Battle-Axe culture intermingled with the Beaker folk who now produced bell-shaped beakers and are known as the Bell Beaker culture,[63] and their extraction of British metals eventually led to the opening of the Cornish tin-mines.[64] These Kurgans came to be known as Wessex chieftans,[65] and their knowledge of Utu and Shamash strengthened the sun-cult that had begun in Britain just before their arrival, and led to the Sumerian Ogma's becoming a god for the Celts. Europeans now buried their dead in kurgans,[66] and they in turn influenced the Kurgan invaders, who absorbed the characteristics of their new regions. As a result individual peoples began to appear: the proto-Germans, Balts, Slavs, Cimmerians and Scythians.[67] The Indo-European *deiuos* or Dyaeus Pitar, the "Shining Father", was worshipped throughout Europe under a variety of names derived from the root "to shine".[68] The Balts worshipped Dieus and his bride, the sun-goddess Saule; the Finno-Ugric peoples (Hungarians, Finns and Estonians) worshipped a Sky-god, Skaj, who visited them at spring ploughing; and the Slavic peoples worshipped Perun, a lightning god, and Svarog, a fire-god who resembles the Iranian-Indian fire-god, Agni.[69]

Since (as we shall see) the Kurgans had absorbed Sumerian and Akkadian ideas (Utu-Shamash), and since (as we shall see) the Indo-European Mithras and Agni, and of course Varuna/Ahura Mazda, had an esoteric significance in Indo-European Iran and India, it is highly likely that like the Iranians and Indians the Kurgans used the megaliths to make fire-sacrifices to their Sky-god, who sent down the power of the sun-like Fire.

A Common Kurgan Light

Before the first Semitic invasions which eventually created Akkad it seems likely that Indo-Europeans associated with the "Great Shining Ones", the "Great Sons of Anu" who, as we shall see, arrived at Kharsag and perhaps founded the Sumerian city-states in a land they called Achaia (later corrupted to Akkad),[70] briefly colonised Greece (which they also called Achaia) and became the Pelasgians (the pre-Hellenic Greeks who preceded the last wave of Indo-European invaders). Later some of the Indo-Europeans seem to have moved on to Denmark, Scotland and Ireland, and finally to Wales and West Britain;[71] to Somerset (or Sumer-set, the land of the Sumerians),[72] Cornwall and Salisbury Plain where they may have built Stonehenge II (using stones from the Welsh hills), Avebury Ring, Glastonbury Tor and the megaliths on Bodmin Moor.[73]

It seems that the Indo-European Kurgans who perhaps brought their shamanism out of Central Asia across the Russian steppes to the Caucasian mountains and to the Sumerian city-states, may have passed their Altaic-Tibetan knowledge into first Sumerian, then Egyptian, and finally British culture, with the result that Sumer, Egypt and Britain all have a common heritage.[74] The knowledge that built such megaliths as the Egyptian stepped pyramid (c.2850 BC) and the Great Pyramid (c.2550 BC); the Sumerian ziggurats and the British observatories at Avebury, Silbury Hill, Stonehenge II (c.2500 BC) and Bodmin Moor; the ziggurat-like World Mountain and spiral maze of Glastonbury Tor and the Cornish cairns, all within 200 years of each other, may have come from the Indo-European Kurgans.[75] The best megaliths seem to have been built from c.2850 BC.

The builders of the best megaliths then seem to have moved to Mexico, where they are remembered through the god Quetzlcoatl, the feathered serpent or snake-bird who recalls the Egyptian vulture and cobra goddesses who appeared side by side on royal documents and often on the Pharaoh's forehead. Among the late Mayans Quetzlcoatl was known as the Sun-god Kukulcan, who is reminiscent of the pre-Celtic Irish Cuchulainn.[76] In Ireland the Mesopotamian Anu (a patriarchal god) became in that still matriarchal Neolithic culture the Celtic goddess Anu, Danu, or Dana, and the Anannage seem to have become known as the Tuatha De Danann or "People of Anu".[77]

The Anu who as we shall see when we consider "The Mesopotamian Light" was worshipped by the pre-Sumerian Anannage and the Tuatha De Danann was a Sun-god as well as at times a Sky-god and a mother goddess. Anu means "brightness" or "radiance", and has associations with the Middle Eastern *el* or *ilu*, the "Shining One" – in Old Cornish, *el* means "Angel" – and among the most important of the Tuatha De Danann was Ogma, who we shall see appeared in the pre-Sumerian Kharsag epic as

Lord Ugmash. Ogma became the Sun-god to the Continental Celts and is known as "Ogma of the Sun-Countenance" (*Ogma grian-aineach*) and "Ogma of Sun-Learning" (*Ogma grian-eiges*), and as "the Sun-Sage". He was the Shamash of the Tuatha De Danann. This Irish sun-sage and early Sumerian solar expert was associated with the Wandlebury observatory in the Gog-Magog Hills, *Gog-Magog* being a corruption of "Ogma".[78]

According to the Irish *Book of Invasions*, in which monastic scholars compiled the Irish tradition between the 6th and 12th centuries AD, the Tuatha were druids skilled in magic who inhabited Ireland until they were pushed out by the Milesians, the sons of Mil who may have been Beaker folk and whose descendants were the Gaels, the dominant Irish people. Irish historians treated the Tuatha as actual people until the 17th century, when they were regarded as gods who were banished from heaven because of their great magical knowledge, and it is as gods that Georges Dumézil regarded them when he related Indo-European gods to the administrative priests, warlike nobles, and agricultural producers of Indian and Celtic society.[79]

Later the Indo-European Kurgan Anannage were perhaps remembered in Greece as the gods of Olympus, and in Scandinavia as the gods of Valhalla. (The hill between Silbury Hill and Avebury is called Waden Hill, after the Teutonic Woden.) Denmark is called Danmark by the Danes, "the land of the Dan people", the people of Anu, the Tuatha De Danann; while Cornwall was known as "*Dan (dun)-monia*", "land of the children of Dan", and many Cornish places seem to have links with the Anannage.[80]

It is likely that Central Asian shamanism was behind the emergence of the Sumerian culture – and of the Egyptian culture, for Egypt was raided by the Kuro-Araxes metallurgists from c.4500 BC,[81] and the Kurgan warriors could have accompanied them on their horses. The Indo-European Kurgans seem to have transmitted Central Asian shamanism to the first civilizations of the near East.

2

The Mesopotamian Light

The First Sumerians: the Anannage or Shining Ones?

The next to reach civilization was the Sumerian culture. It is likely that the founders of the Sumerian city-states came into Mesopotamia from shamanistic Central Asia and Siberia.[1] They were of unknown racial origin, but from linguistic clues it seems they were of Mongoloid stock, and that they came from the Bon-worshipping Altaic Zone, the far north where the fir trees that appear in their art can be found.[2] It has also been thought that they were originally either Hattite Caucasians or Indo-Europeans who spread eastwards, and it is likely that they were a mixture of Altaic and Indo-European influence.[3] It is quite likely that the early Sumerian kings (including Gilgamesh, the epic hero) were descendants from a Kurgan dynasty.[4] Interestingly, the Sumerians first appeared c.3500 BC,[5] long after the Kurgans were in the Caucasus. The Sumerians brought with them the shamans' vision of the Underworld (for example, the poem called "Inanna's Descent to the Netherworld")[6] and the shamans' Light, which they eventually handed on to their conquerors, the Akkadians and Assyrians, and later to the Babylonians, whose contacts with the Persian Medes passed their ideas on to Magianism.

The founders of the Sumerian city-states and Light can perhaps be immediately traced by cuneiform inscriptions to Kharsag in the highlands of the present Lebanese-Syrian border, where "the Great Shining Ones" had brought with them a high culture and were known in Sumer as "the Anannage" or "Anunnaki", "the Great Sons of Anu".[7] Anu was the chief Mesopotamian Sky-god who became the Sumerian An. His name meant "Sky" or "Shining", and he was head of the Sumerian pantheon by c.3000 BC.[8] If the Sons of Anu were sages in pre-Sumerian times – real people not gods – they may have become the Sumerians.[9] Clay tablets discovered in Nippur, where Enlil built the "mountain house" ziggurat of *e-kur*, according to tradition, include one (c.2500 BC) which bears the Sumerian "Creation Myth" that is more properly a Kharsag epic.[10] There are in fact nine Kharsag epics which can be dated to different times throughout the third millennium BC on tablets discovered in Nippur at the beginning of the 20th century and taken to the University of Philadelphia. The "Creation Myth" epic describes how Enlil and his wife Ninlil set up an agricultural farm called Kharsag to benefit the local primitive tribes.[11] Some of epic 2 is so revealing about the flesh and blood actuality of "the great Shining Ones", "the Great Sons of Anu", that it should be quoted in full:[12]

"At Kharsag, where Heaven and Earth met, the Heavenly Assembly,
the Great Sons of Anu, descended – the many Wise Ones.
The Lord of the Granary had not arrived;
there, the grass had not yet become green.
The Lord of the Plough had not yet prepared
the land and the water;
for the Lord of the Plough, the implement had not
turned over the hard earth.

The cattle-shed had not been given running water;
had not been watered from the overflow;
the ass had not been watered;
the seed had not been watered.
Then, the well and the irrigation channels had not been dug;

then, had not been dug for the ass and the cattle.
Because of the sunny enclosure, and the Lord of the Granary,
 the harvest would be heavy.

The Anannage, the Great Lords, had not yet arrived,
the *shesh*-grain* of thirty days did not exist;
the *shesh*-grain of fifty days did not exist;
the small grain, the mountain grain, the animal fodder
 did not exist.
Hand utensils and clothes did not exist.

The Lord of the Plough had not sown the grain;
then, the enclosure had not been erected.
Together with the Great Lords, the Great Lady had not arrived.
The faithful Lord Ugmash had not taken observations of
 the movements of the Sun.

Mankind learned from the Great Shining Ones;
 they set things in order.
Man had not yet learned how to eat and how to sleep;
had not yet learned how to make clothes, or permanent dwellings;
People crawled into their dwellings on all fours;
they ate grass with their mouths like sheep;
they drank storm-water from the streams.

At that time, where the Lords planted greenery,
its fruit covered the extensive enclosure;
the Lord of the Granary made it beautiful.
The Lords rejoiced in the enclosed place –
In its food enclosures – in its shady orchards

Where the Lord of the Granary had planned abundant vegetation,
the Anannage, in their bright dwellings in the spacious enclosure,
ate abundantly, but were not content.
Of the excellent milk from the spacious sheepfold

the Anannage, in their bright dwellings in the spacious enclosure,
drank abundantly, but were not content.

Because of the surplus food from the spacious enclosure,
they made a favourable decision that mankind should be raised to an equal place."
*(The term *shesh* is not yet understood.)

This myth, which has been translated in full by Christian O'Brien, described a very primitive life in a mountainous region ("where Heaven and Earth met") which can be identified as Mount Hermon, above Kharsag.[13] "The Great Shining Ones", who seem very human, arrive and set things in order. The Anannage may well have been Indo-European Kurgans who had made contact with the Kuro-Araxes metallurgists and brought their superior shamanistic and technological skills from the Caucasian mountains to Kharsag. Such a Kurgan migration south of the Caucasus did take place c.3500 BC.[14] Their arrival took place before the birth of the Sumerian sun-cult, before Lord Ogma (Ugmash) had taken observations of the movement of the sun.

The Anannage feature as the Anunnaki in the late *Epic of Creation* about Babylon and Marduk. In that work (on tablets believed to date from the 1st millennium BC) they built the ziggurat at Babylon.[15] This recalls the *e-kur*, the ziggurat-tower or "mountain house" built by Enlil at Nippur and later destroyed by Naram-sin shortly before 2000 BC.[16] Once again, they are very flesh-and-blood, shovelling for a year to make bricks for the ziggurat.

It seems that these probably illumined "Shining Ones" from Central Asia may have been linked with the Biblical Eden, for in another tablet about the founding of Kharsag (epic 1), Ninkharsag, the "lady of Kharsag" and wife of the leader Enlil addresses the Council of Seven and urges a reservoir which will create an "Eden":[17]

"They all turned around as she stood up to answer.
She spoke rebelliously – she spoke strongly:
'With this Settlement will come prosperity;
an enclosed Reservoir – a water trap –

should be established.
The good land is full of water;
because of the water, food will be plentiful.
This perfect Eden is full of water;
it should be irrigated from a cascading water-course.'"

The Sumerian word *edin* means a "plain", but its archaic sign shows water courses and irrigation from a single source: .[18] This reservoir seems to have irrigated and created a Paradisal Garden of Eden, until Kharsag was destroyed when the reservoir burst after a violent thunderstorm, as we learn from Epic 9:

"As the howling storm approached,
the cattle were brought into the long stable building....
The fenced House was destroyed by burning; that place
where the brightness of learning was ravished....The heavens destroyed it....
Learning perished at the House of Life....
The overflowing rain destroyed....
from the reservoir, its water gushed out –
it was a disaster....
The angrily-overflowing Reservoir collapsed....
The House...was destroyed by the thunderstorm....
the Building of Knowledge was destroyed;....the Settlement of Learning – the whole
Settlement with
its food-storage building, and its plantations, became marshland!
The Building of Learning...was crushed by the thunderstorm; it was cut off and
overthrown."[19]

If the *edin* at Kharsag was the Biblical Garden of Eden which had fruit trees and a river that "went out of Eden to water the garden" (*Genesis* 2.10), then Enlil's House of Knowledge anticipates the Tree of Knowledge, and it is possible that the two hundred Angels "who descended in the days of Jared on the summit of Mount Hermon" (*Book of Enoch* I.VI) and taught mankind agriculture and metallurgy were the Central Asian Anannage, just as the seven archangels may echo Enlil's Council of Seven.[20] The words for Angels and Anannage are connected – the *el* means "shining" – and it is possible that the story of Kharsag and the Anannage was deliberately suppressed during the Babylonian times and became the Biblical Garden of Eden and Angels, just as the Flood at Kharsag may have become Noah's Flood which ended in the building of a "tower whose top may reach into heaven"(*Genesis* 11.4): the Tower of Babel which was the ziggurat at Babylon.[21]

It seems that after the flood the Anannage (if they were flesh-and-blood people and not legendary, as O'Brien demonstrates) may have moved from Kharsag to Mesopotamia and founded city-states in what was to become Sumeria. If so, they led the proto-Sumerians, the pre-Sumerian Ubaidian culture,[22] from a primitive race into a great literate nation, and it seems that each Anannage Lord had his own city: Enlil was at Nippur, Enki at Eridu, Shamash at Sippar, and Nanna at Ur.[23] Having left an Achaiyah north of Mount Hermon, near Kharsag, it seems they called their new land Achaia, which was later corrupted to Akkad.[24] There is evidence that an Anannage language was spoken in Sumer, for a tablet overlooked by scholars states that *eme-an* was the language in which Enlil gave some commands that cedars should be felled, not the Sumerian *eme-ku*: *eme-an-ud* ("at that time in the language of heaven (or An)".[25] In due course, in later Babylonian times the sages who were the Anannage may have come to be worshipped as gods; their houses became temples, and Enlil, who is described in Sumerian (c.2500 BC) as "Shining Lord of Cultivation" (*engeli*) – he founded the agricultural project at Kharsag – eventually came to be described in Babylonian (c.1000 BC) as "God of the Wind" (*enlilli*).[26]

The Light seems to have been first recorded by these Sumerians who knew cuneiform writing and produced the oldest known literature c.3500 BC. Because of the scantiness of historical records, there are few personal eye-witness accounts of the Light during the 3rd, 2nd and lst millenia BC, and the knowledge of the Sumerians was symbolized in their gods and vegetation myths, and later in the ceremonies connected with their ziggurats (the word means "towers into the sky"), where the power and wisdom of the Divine Light flowed into the King. Individuals could relate their experience to these public symbols of a metaphysical eternity which permeated Sumerian art and could not have dominated Sumerian life without a widespread knowledge of the Light on the part of the masses.

UTU, SHAMASH AND THE LIGHT

The Light was symbolized in texts about Tammuz, which date back to c.2600 BC. Dumuzi (the Sumerian form of Tammuz),[27] a shepherd-god and vegetation-god, died, was imprisoned in the Underworld, and in one version of the legend rose again with the vegetation in the spring after Inanna, the queen of Heaven and either his wife or his sister, descended to reclaim him.[28] Inanna was the Sumerian form of the Neolithic Earth Mother or Magna Mater.[29] Utu, the sun-god of the Sky World, features in the various versions of this myth, and according to one fragment, Dumuzi appeals to Utu to deliver him.[30] Utu was by now in charge of the universe: Enki (the god who watched over the universe, filled the Tigris with life-giving water and travelled from city to city in a boat) states in the best preserved Sumerian narrative poem, *Enki and the World Order*, "Utu, the son born of Ningal, Enki placed in charge of the entire universe."[31] The brother of the first King of Ur III (Ur-Nammu) was called "Utu-Khegal".[32]

About 2400 BC (or perhaps earlier) Sumer was dominated by the Northern Akkad, and the Sumerian Utu became the Akkadian Shamash[33] (a name that suggests "shaman"), the sun-god whose sign was a disc rising from mountains.[34] He was conqueror of darkness and giver of light, and he was shown on Babylonian seals with tongues of flame or rays from his shoulders.[35] Later the "shining" Shamash figure was shown as a "shining" angel, and the aura of tongues of flame from his shoulders was corrupted to angel's wings. Being all-seeing, he was responsible for justice. He is shown on the pillar which bears the code of Hammurabi, giving laws to the King.[36] In Assyria to the far north he was eventually symbolized by a winged disc, which was the symbol of royalty.[37]

The Utu-Shamash figure was never as important to the Sumerian-Akkadian mythology and pantheon as was Ra to the Egyptian mythology and pantheon. In the early Sumerian pantheon Nanna the moon-god (Akkadian Sin) was the chief astral deity in keeping with the Neolithic worship of the moon, and Utu (like Inanna) was merely Nanna's offspring.[38] Nevertheless, he was definitely worshipped; for example, one of the Flood myths has King Ziusudra worshipping him: "The hero Utu brought his rays into the giant boat. Ziusudra, the King, prostrated himself before Utu, the King kills an ox, slaughters a sheep."[39]

The partial and growing use of the ziggurats (tower-temples made of burnt bricks set in bitumen) as sun-temples (probably Fire-temples, the sun being the source of fire) from c.2200 BC[40] reflected the extent to which sun-worship had grown in Mesopotamia as the Akkadians turned from the moon-god Nanna to the sun-god Shamash, and so changed from the Neolithic to the Indo-European religion. The best preserved ziggurat at Ur (22nd-21st centuries BC), had a shrine to the moon-god Nanna (Sin) on top, because Nanna was the patron deity and divine King of Ur, but it was also used for sun-worship – for the worship of Nanna's son, Utu – when Tammuz returned to the light in the spring.[41]

King Hammurabi of Babylon (18th century BC) identified himself with Shamash, and sun-worship soon replaced moon-worship.[42] As a rule, however, the King himself was not the Sun-god, as was the Egyptian Pharaoh; the King, like Hammurabi, was the High Priest[43] and the head of the priesthood, and it had been an exception for the third dynasty at Ur (22nd-21st centuries BC) to declare itself divine.[44] There was a woman called "Hammurabi-Shamshi" or "Hammurabi is my Sun", but to her the King was not a god; he was the "son of a goddess", and it was rare to find a King claiming identity with Shamash as Hammurabi did, just as it was rare for the King of Assyria to be addressed as the sun like the Hittite King ("Sun Majesty, my Sun"), even though the winged disc was the badge of Assyrian royalty.[45] However the Assyrian King identified himself with Shamash; thus Shamashi-Adad I ruled Assyria c.1813-1781 BC.[46] The sun disc was widely worshipped a few centuries later, and a 9th century BC cuneiform tablet shows a rayed disc and records the foundation of a temple of the sun by the Babylonian ruler Nabu-apla-iddina.[47] The winged Assyrian sun was associated with a winged bull, and a winged bull with a human head guarded the gate of the Assyrian Sargon II's palace at Khorsabad, near Nineveh (c.717-707 BC).[48] Many centuries later the Jews in exile in Babylon, absorbed the Semitic Akkadian Shamash, which, as *shmsh*, is the current Hebrew word for "sun".[49]

Royal Sacred Marriage and Light Cults on Ziggurats

In one myth Tammuz wanted to marry Inanna, and had to seek the consent of her brother and guardian, Utu, and the ceremony of a Sacred Marriage emerged. At the end of the 3rd millennium BC Tammuz's marriage with Inanna-Ishtar was celebrated each year at the Spring Festival at Isin, just south of Babylon in southern Mesopotamia, with the King and the Queen or one of the priestesses playing the roles of Tammuz and Inanna-Ishtar. The Queen or priestess played the dominant partner in rescuing the dead young boy from the nether regions or the Underworld, as befitted a Mother Goddess. After lamentations for the abdicated King, there was joy at his resurrection, and there was a Royal Sacred Marriage as a result of which the earth renewed its vitality under the sun.[50]

In another version of this myth, Tammuz was taken to the Underworld by force to take his wife Inanna's place, and was prevented from returning to earth. He was not resurrected.[51]

When Babylon became the capital in the 18th century BC, Marduk took over the role of Tammuz, and the royal divine union, the marriage, was celebrated each year at the top of the ziggurats. When Tammuz-Marduk died, his body lay in the shrine at the top of the ziggurat, which must have symbolized an inverted nether world or Underworld for the winter. It was guarded by a priestess who acted the part of Inanna.[52] The shrine was initially dedicated to Nanna, the moon-god, because Nanna was nearly born in the dark nether world that claimed Tammuz, and, like Tammuz, was allowed to ascend to the light by journeying across the dark night sky in a *quffah* (a circular boat used on the Euphrates).[53] At the Spring Festival the netherworld of the ziggurat was transformed into Heaven (the Sky World) and Earth, and the Sky Father united with the Earth Mother as the risen Tammuz married his goddess in the topmost shrine.[54]

There was clearly more to this Sacred Marriage than a vegetation cult, although the vegetation cult was certainly present within it. The power of the gods came down into the King through the help of the Goddess, and although the King was separate from, and not identified with, the gods, he was able to use their power for the coming year, partly to make the crops grow, and partly to increase his wisdom and skill in divination. The Sacred Marriage was thus between Heaven and Earth, between the Sky Father and the Earth Mother.[55]

There are grounds for thinking that mystery cults existed in Sumerian-Akkadian times.[56] In *The Righteous Sufferer* there is a descent into the grave and a return to Babylon, each gate of which gives the hero bliss, and he is then admitted to the god Marduk. The doors of the temple of Marduk were known by the names of the gates, and the text may recall a ceremony of initiation. The myth of Tammuz moved further towards spiritual mysteries when Enlil, the Sumerian high god and Nanna's father, was banished to the Underworld for raping Ninlil, for in the later Akkadian Tammuz liturgies Enlil is a title for Tammuz, and Ninlil for Ishtar (formerly Inanna). There is now a motive for Tammuz's descent into the Underworld as Tammuz the rapist died away from his ego, and was reborn sufficiently selfless to marry Inanna-Ishtar.[57]

The sun-worship of the Sumerians may have begun as an exoteric vegetation cult, but, like all vegetation cults, it developed esoteric mysteries that concerned spiritual truths. The exoteric sun of the vegetation cult was also the esoteric Light: the disc rising from mountains was also an inner disc rising deep in the unconscious mind. Shamash conquered the inner as well as the outer darkness as the *Great Hymn to Shamash* bears witness. This Hymn is perhaps the best of the Mesopotamian religious writings in cuneiform, and in it Shamash is clearly the sun. However, as the god of divination who knew the future, he also grants inner revelation: "You grant revelations, Shamash, to the families of men, your harsh face and fierce light you give to them....Which are the regions not warmed by the brightness of your light? Brightener of gloom, illuminator of darkness, dispeller of darkness, illuminator of the broad earth."[58] As a giver of revelations, Shamash was an inspirer of oracles, and thus a god of mental light, and those who opened to his divine influx became "Shining Ones", like the hero in this old Sumerian text:

> "He, whose body is shining splendour,
> Who in the forest of fragrant cedars is cheered with joy,
> Standing in the oracle-lace Apsu,
> Purified with the sparkling lustration."[59]

The ambiguity of outer and inner meanings concerning Shamash was applied to ziggurats, which symbolized the inner as well as the outer world.[60] The ziggurats were shamanistic Sacred Mountains which were built on seven levels, each of which was made of a different metal, and these represented the seven Heavens and the seven gates to the nether world or Underworld as well as the seven planets, and they united the Heavens and Earth (compare Jacob's ladder).[61] They linked Heaven or the Sky World, Earth, and the Underworld, probably embodying each at different times of the year, and the ziggurat that stood near the temple of Marduk in Babylon was called the *Etemenanki* ("the temple foundation of Heaven and Earth"). The sloping sides and terraces often had trees and shrubs on them: hence the *Etemenanki* was called the Hanging Gardens of Babylon, one of the wonders of the ancient world.[62]

The ziggurats were outer observatories for observing the celestial phenomena but they had an inner, religious function as the dead body of Tammuz-Marduk lay in the shrine on the top (probably a Fire-temple) until he emerged at the New Year Festival. The name "Babylon", or *bab-ili*, "the gate of God", emphasises that the city was merely the gateway to the very important religious ziggurat,[63] which the Yahweh worshipping Hebrews (who regarded the Babylonians as idolaters) called "Tower of Babel" (the Hebrew *bll* meaning "confusion").[64] The ziggurats also symbolized the soul's journey up seven hidden levels to the Light or Sun, at the sight of which the power and wisdom of the gods flooded in, and there was an esoteric significance in the Sacred Marriage.[65]

As the sun replaced the moon as the chief god, it seems that the ascent of a ziggurat to worship Shamash became a symbol for this inner opening of the soul to the Light.[66]

3

The Egyptian Light

Like the Sumerians, the Egyptians symbolized the Central Asian shamanistic Light in their gods and State ceremonies, and numerous texts written on papyri and coffins invoke the Light and announce that their writers have become "Shining Ones".[1] As in Sumer and Akkad, the King – the Pharaoh – embodied the power and wisdom of the Light which was symbolized by the sun,[2] and the masses strove to become "Shining Ones" through a ritual that seems to have taken place in the Great Pyramid. This guaranteed survival after death, for the Egyptians interpreted the seeing of the Light as the gift of eternity, a guarantee of immortality in the Elysian Fields.[3]

Mesopotamian Origin and Cult of the Sun-god/Light

The Egyptian Light along with other aspects of the Egyptian civilization may have originated in the Mesopotamian "Shining Ones".[4] Hieroglyphics may have developed from cuneiform, and Thor Heyerdahl's journeys show that the ziggurat could have been exported to Egypt and thence with the pyramid to South America. Some Egyptian religious cults may have originated in Sumeria.[5] The early African Egyptian society worshipped the

African Ra (or Re) and (according to Frankfort's hypothesis) seems to have been influenced by Sumer.[6] Osiris, Isis and Horus may well have been Aryan-Sumerian gods, and there is an obvious parallel between Tammuz and Osiris, both of whom were associated with the Underworld.[7] About the time of the union between the Upper and Lower Kingdoms under Aha (or Menes) c.3100 or c.3032/2982 BC,[8] Osiris became identified with Ra as we see from *The Book of the Dead*: "Osiris...goes into Tattu (i.e. Busiris) and finds there the soul of Ra; there the one god embraces the other, and become as one soul in two souls."[9] As Ra, the god ruled the Sky World and the visible world in his solar bark; as Osiris he ruled the Underworld or the Kingdom of the Dead, and those who died with sanctity; and his son Horus (originally a falcon Sky-god) was the divine Spirit in every man on Earth.[10] To put it another way, Ra was the Infinite aspect of the Godhead, while Horus and Osiris represented God-in-man, first incarnate and then reunited with the Godhead after death. Egyptian religion was thus essentially monotheistic, the various gods being no more than forms, manifestations, phases, or attributes of the Sun-god Ra.[11]

This blending of gods with Ra led to a cult of the Sun-god. The belief that the King or Pharaoh was divine and that his soul blended with the Sun-god began c.2750 BC, when the name Ra was taken by the second-dynasty Pharaohs Nebra and Neferkara. (The second dynasty began c.2853 or, on other datings, 2780 or 2770 BC.)[12] It was well established by the fourth dynasty and intensified when the fifth dynasty associated with Heliopolis took possession of the Egyptian throne. It is referred to in *The Book of the Dead*: "I am Ra...when he began to rule that which he had made.... This means that Ra began to appear as a King."[13] From the early dynasties on, in his life, the Pharaoh was Ra and also Horus, on his death he was Osiris. He crossed the Lily lake to the East and once in the Underworld or Other World accompanied the Sun-god on his voyage out of the darkness and across the skies.[14] The morning sun was Khepri, the scarab beetle which pushed the sun across the sky; the midday sun was Ra; the evening sun was Atum.[15] Ra-Atum, the sun in its midday and evening manifestations, was pushed like a ball of dung by a scarab beetle (or dung beetle), or carried across the sky in a boat or on a falcon's wing, and according to the priests of

Heliopolis could manifest as one of his offspring, Shu, the god of the air, which, in sunshine, meant sunny air.[16] When the moon-cult of the bull was taken over by the cult of the Sun-god, it was asserted that the sacred bull, Apis, was begotten by a ray of Ra's light.[17]

The fourth-dynasty Pharaohs who immediately followed Snefru and his son Khufu, who regarded himself as a god whom all should worship,[18] took the name Ra and identified themselves with the Sun-god. By the 6th dynasty (c.2347 or 2321 BC), the Pharaoh was completely merged with the Sun-god;[19] he was actually the deity, and as the sun which made the crops grow was vital to the well-being of the nation, great care was taken with funeral rites to ensure that a dead Pharaoh actually became the god.[20] (It is now clear that the 3rd dynasty of Ur declared itself divine in the 22nd century BC as a result of Egyptian influence.)[21] At the beginning, only the Pharaoh-King was deified, only he derived magical powers from the sun, the "liquid of Ra" which entered his veins and enabled the Nile floods to appear on time and fertilise the soil.[22] The Pharaoh-King was the Sun-god, and when he died, his son was the Sun-god. Therefore the Pharaoh was reincarnated in his son, and some sort of transmigration from the father's soul into his son's soul must have taken place, via the sun.[23]

The Pharaoh's body, his *ka* (or life force), his *ba* (his renown or impression made on others) interacted after his death, and he became an *akh* (or spiritual soul or spirit state, a glorified being of Light in the afterlife) which ascended to the stars (according to the Pyramid Texts), leaving a "Horus" or new living king behind him, and dwelt with the sun.[24] The *ba* is represented by the hieroglyph of the ibis; the *akh* is represented as a crested ibis.[25] It derives from the term for "radiant light", and the crest transforms the ibis bird of the *ba* into a "Shining One", an *akh*.[26] On death, the *ka* became a kind of double in which the life force could reside, and which required feeding.[27] At the beginning, only the Pharaoh had a *ka* or double and was reincarnated, but later, deification was extended to the royal family and a chosen few, and eventually it became a right to be claimed by all.[28] At first a dead physical body (*khat*) had to be mummified into a cocoon (like the pupa of a scarab) so that it would germinate or sprout a *sakhu* (*s'hw*) or "spiritual body" into which the *akh* ("glorious" or "shining one" or "spiritual soul") could pass.[29] Sir Wallis Budge in his 1899 edition of the *Book of the Dead* wrongly transcribed the *akh* as *khu*, but the hieroglyph for "spirit" or "spiritual soul" is clearly "3h" ("a-kh"), and Budge himself recanted in the 1920s and transcribed the Pharaoh "Akhenaton" correctly rather than as "Khu-enaton".[30] The *akh* in a *sakhu* dwelt in the Elysian Fields or Field of Reeds or Rushes which was the Egyptian Heaven after c.2000 BC.[31] Later, mummification ensured that the *ka* would be born again in a counterpart of Egypt, in whose superior civilization it would have the best chance of ultimately reaching eternity.[32]

AKHS OR "SHINING ONES" AND THE BOOK OF THE DEAD

The widespread cult of the Sun-god did not merely pay honour to the exoteric sun; it also celebrated the esoteric Light. An experience of the Light in this life developed the *akh* and enabled the soul to survive in the Judgement Hall. This can be seen most clearly in the Egyptian *Book of the Dead*, which covers some 200 religious texts, spells and prayers in the form of revised texts (recensions) which were written on papyri or coffins between 1600 and 900 BC, though many began as Pyramid texts and go back to 2400 BC or before.[33]

Traditionally these texts have been understood in terms of the after-life, the references to Ra, Osiris and the sun applying to the Judgement of the Dead; and the title *Book of the Dead* – a mis-translation by the 19th century Lepsius which should really be translated "Chapters of Coming Forth by Day" or "The Book of the Great Awakening" (i.e. the manifestation of the Light)[34] – has been understood in terms of the coming forth into immortality after the first night in the Underworld.[35] It was a well-known Egyptian belief that a deceased spent the first night after his death journeying to the Underworld, and that he did not emerge into the realms of the blessed in Heaven until sunrise (*akhu*) the following morning,[36] when his hymn to Ra celebrated the survival of his soul, his "coming forth by day", which the texts, spells and prayers were designed to secure.[37]

However, the texts are at the same time to be understood in terms of this life, for the gods, who are all manifestations of one god, are all *akhs*,[38] which also means "glorious", "splendid" ones, "Shining Ones"; and the "Shining One", Amon-Ra (or Amun-Re), is the Light which brings eternity *now*. The hymns to Ra which open *The Book of the Dead* should therefore be interpreted spiritually as well as eschatologically. The illustrations in *The Book of the Dead* are of the rituals of living people, in which the high priest and priests put on masks of the various gods to act out roles in the story of Osiris.[39]

The Book of the Dead is thus a primer to help the *ka*, which was attached to terrestrial life and called the being to be born again, develop a *ba*, a supreme heart-soul or ghost that animated the body. This flew to its future abode as a human-headed hawk, as a stork with a flame, or as a "bennu bird" (or phoenix), the "eagle" of Herodotus which was probably a grey heron.[40] The *ba* could then become an *akh* or "Shining One" who was illumined. The *akh* was pure spirit, and was diametrically opposed to the mortal *khat*. *Akh* was the Pharaonic word for "light" in the sense of "glory" or "splendour" – the root meant "shine" or "irradiate", "radiant light"[41] – and as the Egyptians did not distinguish the eternal and temporal worlds in their hieroglyphics,[42] it could mean both physical and transcendental light, the Light of transfiguration and the uraeus (*akhet*) or cobra, the third eye.[43] The crested ibis which represented the *akh* was a migratory bird which lived on the Arabian side of the Red Sea and migrated to Abyssinia in the winter (a geographical equivalent for the spirit migrating to and from Heaven).[44] The glittering specks on the crested ibis's dark green plumage suggested its associations with the Light which was symbolized by the sun.[45] The *akh* preceded creation, and it was the aim of everyone to release it, shining, into the after-life by activating it in this life;[46] for the Egyptians believed that the after-life could be prepared for, and that a virtuous life on earth would increase the chances of the deceased when he stood before Osiris-Ra in the Judgement Hall.

Again and again, *The Book of the Dead* makes it clear that a virtuous life meant becoming an *akh*, seeing the Light. One of the oldest texts is Chapter 64, which occurs in two versions on an eleventh dynasty coffin. The shorter version is called "Chapter of knowing the Chapters of Coming Forth by Day in a single Chapter" – in other words, it contained the whole of *The Book of the Dead* in essence – and its rubric attributes its discovery to the time of "Menthu-hetep" (clearly a mistake for "Men-kau-Ra", Mycerinus, of the fourth dynasty, the man who built the smallest of the three pyramids at Giza c.2539-2511 or 2490-2472 BC) or even to the time of Semti or Den (or Dewen), c.2939-2892 or c.2875 BC, although it may be much later. (See p63.) The text proclaims: "I am Yesterday and Today; and I have the power to be born a second time. (I am) the divine hidden Soul...,the Possessor of two Divine Faces wherein his beams are seen. I am the Lord of those who are raised up from the dead, the Lord who comes forth out of darkness....To the Mighty One has his Eye been given, and his face emits light when he illumines the earth. I shall not become corrupt, but I shall come into being in the form of the Lion-god; the blossoms of Shu shall be in me."

The blossoms of Shu are "the beams of the Sun-god" (Budge's note) – Shu (sunny air) being a child and manifestation of Ra-Atum – and they shall be "in me" (*im-i*), not "upon me" (*hr-i*). The rubric adds "If this chapter is known (by the deceased) he shall be victorious both upon earth and in the Underworld", that is, in this life as well as after his death. The Light shining "in" the writer brings success in this world and protection from evil in the Judgement Hall, and this passage contains what is perhaps the oldest recorded illumination from over 4,500 years ago.

The Book of the Dead charts an awakening – an initiation – from the world of the senses into the world of "the Shining Ones", in which the universe is filled with the "light of Ra". It is a body of advice to initiates whose illumination would stand them in good stead in the Judgement of the Dead. On their illumination they were received into "the sacred Heart of Ra".[47] According to the Hermetic literature of the 4th century BC, a man was released from earthly matter if a ray of Ra (or Amon) penetrated his soul,[48] a fact which resulted in many Egyptian names having something to do with the Light: Tut-ankh-Amon, for instance, meaning "Tut, the living image of Amon (i.e. the Light)" or "Tut who has life in Amon-Ra", the illumined Tut who will receive a favourable Judgement from Osiris. The "Chapter of Making the Transformation into the God who giveth Light in the Darkness" (80) is accompanied by a vignette (picture) of a god with the disc of the sun on his head, and the text is to be understood in terms of the living; indeed, the Egyptian idea of what happened to the dead was founded on their experience of the illumination that could be known by the living: "I am the girdle of the robe of the god Nu, which shines and sheds light upon that which belongs to his breast, which sends forth light into the darkness.... I have come to give light in (or lighten) the darkness, which is made light and bright (by me).... (I) have opened (the way), I am Hem-Nu (the Woman), I have made light the darkness, I have come, having made an end of the darkness, which has become light indeed."

The illumined soul is like a lotus which grows from the neck and unfolds to the sun, like a flower opening to light, as the vignette for the first version of the "Chapter of Making the Transformation into a Lotus" (81A) makes clear. The second version of 81A from the papyrus of Ani, shows a blue lotus in full bloom – the lotus being the symbol of the south (Upper Egypt), the papyrus being the symbol of the north (Lower Egypt) – and it can be translated in three different ways. First, "I am the pure lotus coming forth from the god of light (*akhu*), the guardian of the nostril of Ra, the guardian of the nose of Hathor. I make my journey, I run after him who is Horus. I am the pure one coming forth from the field." Or, "I am the pure lily coming forth from the Lily of Light. I am the source of illumination and the channel of the breath of immortal beauty. I bring the message, Horus accomplishes it." A more accurate translation interprets the hieroglyph *akhu* as "sunshine", in the sense of "Underworldly sunshine" (i.e. the Light): "I am this pure lotus which went forth from the sunshine, which is at the nose of Ra; I have descended that I may seek it (i.e. the sunshine) for Horus, for I am the pure one who issued from the fen."[49]

In the "Chapter of the Four Blazing Flames which are made for the *Akh*" (137A) the text states: "The flame comes to your *Ka*, o Osiris.... I cause it to come to (or, even) the Eye of Horus. It is set in order upon your brow.... The Eye of Horus...sends forth rays like Ra in the horizon." The Eye of Horus is the Light which is *like* the sun on the horizon, and the rubric says, "This shall confer power and might upon the *Akh*" and "these fires shall make the *Akh* as vigorous as Osiris".

The illumination is even more specific in the "Chapter of Kindling a Flame by Nebseni" (137B): "The white or shining Eye of Horus comes. The brilliant Eye of Horus comes. It comes in peace, it sends (or welcome, you who send) forth rays of light to (or like) Ra in the horizon." The movement from within to without recalls Coleridge's "I may not hope from outward forms to win/The passion and the life, whose fountains are within", and the tone becomes ecstatic and Zen-like: "The Eye of Horus lives, yes lives within the great hall; the Eye of Horus lives, yes lives." The joyfully illumined "Chapter of Making the Transformation into a Living Soul" announces: "I am the divine Soul of Ra proceeding from the god Nu; that divine Soul which is God.... I am the lord of light."

Almost every page of *The Book of the Dead* is filled with the vision of the illumined "Shining Ones" (*akhs*), a vision which is reinforced by one of the hieroglyphs for *akhu*, or "Underworldly sunshine",[50] of a meditating god sitting and facing a bird, a crested ibis (his *akh* soul in his spiritual body or *sakhu*), which in turn faces a sun with three pyramid-shaped rays streaming down (the Light symbolized as the sun): "Behold, I have come forth on this day, and I have become an *Akh* (or a shining being)" (65B); "I am...the Great Illuminer who comes forth out of flame (or heat), the bestower (or harnesser) of years, the far extending One, the double Lion-god, and there has been given to me the journey of the god of splendour (*Akh*)" or "of a Shining One" (53); "I am Shu and I draw air from the presence of the god of Light (*Akh*)" (55); "I come forth to heaven and I sit myself down by the God of Light (*Akh*)" (74); and "I am one of those *Akhs* who dwell with the divine *Akh*, and I have made my form like his divine Form, when he comes forth.... I am a spiritual body (*sakhu*) and possess my soul...I, even I, am the *Akh* who dwells with the divine *Akh*" (78). "I, even I...." The ecstatic disbelief at a spiritual good fortune is caught with an amazing simplicity and directness that speaks straight to our hearts from the early Egyptian days.

THE *AKH* AS THE GREAT PYRAMID, OBELISKS, TEMPLE-DANCERS

This obsession with becoming an *akh* or "Shining One" was at the heart of Egyptian life. The early phase of the cult of the Sun-god was behind the building of the pyramids, for although the tomb-pyramid began as a more elaborate version of the Kurgan long barrow with a deep shaft, first a *mastaba,* then a stepped, artificial mountain in a flat desert,[51] the pyramid form came to represent the rays of the sun bursting through cloud and shining down on the earth,[52] up which the king could mount to Heaven as an *akh* as the Pyramid texts indicate: "I have trodden your rays as a ramp under my feet, on which I mount to...the brow of Ra."[53] There is thus a similarity between pyramids and ziggurats.

Khufu (more accurately Khnum Khofoy or Khnum-khuefi, "Khnum protects me"), the name of the Pharaoh who built the Great Pyramid (c.2604-2581 or c.2551-2528 BC), was written *hwfw.*[54] The hieroglyph *hw* (*Khu*) can mean "Protector" but in this combination it is unknown and untranslatable – even such an authority as Faulkner omits it from his dictionary – and it is of a different root from *akh* (*3hw*) meaning "glorious", "splendid" or "shining". Nevertheless Khufu or Cheops (the Greek name known to Herodotus and used at the time of Alexander the Great) is associated with the noun *akhet,* the "horizon".[55] His Great Pyramid was called *akhet,* the horizon of Khufu.[56] *Akhet* also meant "radiant place". Khufu was described as being *akhty* (*3hty*) meaning "horizon-dweller"[57] (literally "belonging to the horizon" as "y" means "belonging to"), the hieroglyph for which includes two suns rising over horizons (one in this world and one in the Other World) and indicates that after death he would be a Shining being in the sunrise of the Light. Khufu, like his father Snefru, did not take the name Ra and is thought to have encouraged his people to believe in him as a Shining god. In consequence, a local divine cult of Khufu was established.[58] The Great Pyramid itself was called *akhty* ("horizon-dweller"),[59] i.e. "belonging to the horizon" – its full title was *Khufu akhty* ("Khufu, the one who belongs in the horizon") or *Akhet Khufu* ("the Horizon of *Khufu*") – and it literally shone like a Shining One for the polished limestone casing stones acted as mirrors and reflected great beams of light from one or other of the pyramid faces between sunrise and sunset.[60] The sides consequently shone gold in the sunlight – the Greek "pyramis" significantly comes in one of its derivations[61] from *pur*, "fire" – and it seems that the Greeks were reflecting the idea of "fire" in their word "pyramid". It seems that the Great Pyramid was built to embody the Light as Fire: its stones shone with divine Light (or Fire).

The Great Pyramid was the only one of the eighty pyramids built between the 27th and 18th centuries to have two chambers above ground, and there are four "air channels" from these chambers which could not have been intended for the *ka* (or double which lived on in the tomb and required food) for the *ka*'s life did not depend on physical air.[62] *Old Kingdom Pyramid Texts* (c.2345-2150 BC) suggest that the *akh* flew (like a crested ibis) to the circumpolar stars, and a north-south section of the Great Pyramid shows that two of the "air channels" are inclined within an accuracy of one degree to the northern Alpha Draconis, the star round which turned the circumpolar stars that were "imperishable" (*Pyramid Texts* 1120-23) as they never dropped below the horizon c.2550 BC and therefore symbolized immortality;[63] and the other two to the southern stars of Orion.[64] It is possible that during the time of the Neolithic moon-cult the *akh* flew to the dark lunar Underworld, in which it survived like an immortal circumpolar star, but as the star-cult of the *Pyramid Texts* predates the sun-cult of the Pyramid-builders, which superseded it, it is certain that in the time of the Pyramid-builders the *akh* emerged into the pre-existent sunshine[65] (*3hw, akhu*) of the Heavenly horizon to "come forth by day" as "one who belongs to the horizon", i.e. a "horizon-dweller". Sun-worship of Ra took place during the second dynasty as we have seen, when Nebra and Neferkara took the name Ra. Nebra's reign was a good 200 years before Khufu's reign.

There is now a school of thought – most notably recently expressed by the authors of *The Orion Mystery* – that alignment with the stars was the predominant factor in Egyptian religious life and governed the building of the three Pyramids of Giza, which (to the Egyptians) represented the three stars in Orion's belt. However, so much is made of the *akh* in the time of the sun-cult and its rebirth to the sunrise, that the night sky could at that time only have been a symbol for the Underworld crossed by the *akh* before it was born in the sunrise of eternity. In short, certainly in the time of the sun-cult and possibly before, it was the sun, not the stars, that governed religious life and the building of the Pyramids. And the Great Pyramid may well have been sun-orientated rather than aligned with specific stars.[66]

In one of the many references to the *akh* in the *Pyramid Texts*, (*Pyramid Texts* 267-8) a Pharaoh is addressed in the Other World, "You are more *akh* than *akhu*", meaning, "You are even more pure spirit than the eternal pre-existent sunshine (i.e. the Light)".[67] The Great Pyramid must similarly be seen in relation to the *akh*. Quite simply, it *was* an *akh* – which is to say, it represented an *akh*.

There is a consensus that although the sarcophagi in the King's Chamber and Queen's Chamber of the Great Pyramid are empty, they did contain the mummy of Khufu, Pharaoh of Upper and Lower Egypt, and his Queen; and that the mummies were stolen by tomb-robbers. But the "air shafts" could not have launched the soul into the eternal sunshine as they were bent and could not admit the sun and each was stopped up half way to the outer walls with two 8-cm-long stops. They were not even "air channels" which allowed living people to breathe.[68] Moreover Khufu may have died before the Great Pyramid was completed and may consequently have been buried in a *mastaba* elsewhere.[69] There is consequently a view that there was never any intention to bury Khufu in the Great Pyramid as the empty granite sarcophagus is too wide for the entrance to the King's Chamber, which shows no sign of having been narrowed. It can only have been dragged to its present place during the building, before the walls and roof of the King's Chamber were erected. The Great Pyramid was possibly therefore a cenotaph, an empty tomb, with one subterranean and two upper chambers, like Snefru's pyramid at Dahshur.[70]

It is possible that the above-ground sarcophagus in the King's Chamber was always an empty coffer, that the Queen's Chamber was for a statue of Khufu and that the underground chamber represented the Underworld.[71] Khufu's name appears on an internal wall of the top of five small chambers above the King's Chamber, as being responsible for building the Great Pyramid ("Wonderful is the White Crown of Khufu"),[72] not for being interred there – and it is possible that alone of the 80 pyramids with underground burials the Great Pyramid had an above-ground purpose.

According to a legend told by Diodorus Siculus[73], Khufu was not buried in his pyramid. It is possible that this decision had much to do with the crack in the ceiling slabs of the King's Chamber, which may have appeared before the pyramid was finished and may have been accompanied by a terrifying noise that could be heard by all the workers. As a result the Great Pyramid may have been declared unsafe.[74] If this was the case, where was Khufu buried? Elsewhere in the Great Pyramid, in a hitherto undiscovered sealed room? Or in a hitherto undiscovered location? That is surely unlikely, given the huge amount of planning and effort that went into the Great Pyramid. If he died before the Great Pyramid was completed, he would have been buried in a *mastaba*, for no Pharaoh in his day could be buried in an uncompleted tomb.[75] The indications are that although he may have died before the subterranean tomb was completed – for it seems to have been left unfinished – the rest of the Great Pyramid *was* finished before he died. Scholarly opinion believes that he reigned longer than the 23 years stated in a Turin papyrus compiled 1,400 years later.[76] (The papyrus gives suspiciously similar lengths for the reigns of Huni (24 years), Snefru (24 years) and Khufu (23 years), suggesting estimates of a generation on the throne. A reign of 30-32 years has been proposed.[77] The whole question of where Khufu was buried is a mystery.

It is possible that the Great Pyramid was a gigantic *akh*, a shining Khufuesque Cathedral where for more than two thousand years neophytes were initiated into the Mysteries of the *akh* by acting out the experience of illumination with high priests and priests wearing head-and-shoulder masks of the gods, playing parts in a Freemasonic-style initiation; just as later neophytes were initiated into the Mysteries of Isis. In this case the upper "burial" chambers were places of initiation rather than tombs, for a ritual whose texts are partly contained in *The Book of the Dead*. Marsham Adams was the first to connect the *Book of the Dead* and the Great Pyramid in texts like "This is a composition of exceedingly great mystery....It is an admirable thing for everyone to know it; therefore hide it. Book of the Mistress of the Hidden Temple is its name" (rubric of ch 162); and "You have not gone dying, you have gone living to Osiris" (coffin of Amamu of Abydos). It has been suggested that the ritual involved passages and opening doors, and also (possibly) a rebuilding of the Great Pyramid (just as the Freemasonry ritual involves a rebuilding of the Temple).[78]

The initiate would have approached the Pyramid at sunset when it was a blaze of light from the evening sun (*atum*), and would literally have "entered the Light (or Fire)" (the horizon-Light of *Akhty*). He then underwent a ritual death in the down passage and ascended the first ascending passage to be reborn to Light among the air pockets of the upper chambers. He opened himself to illumination before the empty coffer (now missing but on record) in the Queen's Chamber,[79] and then followed the Path of the Just[80] up the ramp between the corbeled walls of the Grand Gallery to the ante-chamber and King's Chamber, where another empty coffer symbolized the empty tomb of the risen Osiris, the Hidden Light. There he became "a Shining One". The ritual took a whole night until dawn.[81]

The Great Pyramid was guarded outside by the Sphinx, who was called *Khu* (*hw*) or Protector.[82] There has been much speculation about the age of the Sphinx. It has been suggested that the Sphinx is 12,000 years old because of the amount of wind erosion – yet it was buried under sand for hundreds of years. Traditionally it was thought to have been created during Khafra's reign as it is linked to Khafra's pyramid by a causeway, and many books assert this.[83]

However scholarly research suggests that it was in fact created during Khufu's reign as he was the originator in the fourth dynasty and his two sons who succeeded him followed his innovations: Djedefra (who took the name Ra and reigned nine years) and then Khafra (who also took the name Ra and built his own pyramid at Giza). Rainer Stadelmann of the German Archaeological Institute in Cairo, who organised the sending of a robot camera up the air channels and located the stops, holds this view;[84] he argues that wide-open eyes are more typical of Khufu's reign than of Khafra's; that the ears of the Sphinx are broad and folded forward whereas those of Khafra are elongated and closer to his forehead; and that the slanting causeway connecting Khafra's pyramid to the temples was built round the

Sphinx, suggesting that the Sphinx was already in existence. A headstone from Khufu's time says, "Please make a way round (or to) the Sphinx," suggesting that the Sphinx was known in Khufu's time.[85]

If the Sphinx is Khufu looking at Ra in the east and being illumined by Ra's beams, he has an expression of supreme serenity and tranquillity – perhaps calming down the religious unheavals during his reign, when he had moved against the temple priests, declaring his own divinity.[86] The Sphinx may be saying: "Order has been restored by becoming an *akh*." If the Sphinx was built by either Djedefra (as has been suggested by the French Egyptologist Vassil Dobrev) or by Khafra, then the image is of their father Khufu, identifying him with the Sun-god Ra to restore respect for the dynasty after Khufu's religious persecutions.[87] Khufu is looking at Ra in the east and being illumined by Ra's beams, and his expression of serenity and tranquillity perhaps calms down the religious upheavals of his (i.e. Khufu's, their father's) reign, pledging that the Pharaoh now acknowledges the Sun-god and will not suppress the temple priests. In that the case the Sphinx may say, "Order has been restored because we now become an *akh* through uniting with Ra." The Sphinx's riddle was that, looking to the east at the rising sun on the horizon, he was illumined with the peace of the Sun-god, the Light, and had become a Shining One, an *akh*, a "horizon-dweller". The true riddle of the serene and tranquil Sphinx was thus knowledge of the Light.

The Queen's Chamber and King's Chamber, then, may not have been tombs but may have represented successive stages in the mystic life as long ago as c.2550 BC, and the *akh* was well known in the reign of Semti-Hesep-ti of the 1st dynasty (c.2875 BC),[88] in whose reign (according to the rubric) the longer version of chapter 64 of *The Book of the Dead* ("The Chapter of Coming Forth by Day in the Underworld") was found; suggesting that this extract was written at a still earlier date: "My *akh* shall be as an amulet for my body and as one who watches to protect my soul and to defend it."

The Sphinx, the human-headed lion, then, may have represented Khufu, or possibly his son Khafra, as the Sun-god Khepri-Ra (or as Atum's child the "Lion-god" Shu, sunny air – or as Horemakht, "Horus on (or in) the horizon") whom he became after his death. This interpretation is confirmed by an inscription on the granite stela of Thutmose IV found in a royal chapel at the base of the Sphinx's chest. Thutmose called the Sphinx "this very great statue of Khepri", the god of the rising sun; and "Khepri-Ra-Atum", the Sun-god rising in the morning, at its zenith at midday and setting in the evening.[89] The Khufu- or Khafra-Sphinx guarded the necropolis at Giza (lions being regarded as guardians of the gates of the Underworld in Egypt).[90]

The cult of the Sun-god was also behind obelisks: according to Pliny, an obelisk "is a symbolic representation of the sun's rays and this is the meaning of the Egyptian name for it".[91] It combined the shaman's world axis (*Axis Mundi*), pillar or World Tree with a ray of light, as did the spire, minaret and pinnacle of a church, mosque and Buddhist temple. Obelisks date from the 26th century BC, and the earliest surviving one (12th dynasty, 20th-18th centuries BC) stands outside the Temple of Amon-Ra at Karnak. The one undamaged obelisk from Heliopolis (c.1450 BC) now stands beside the Thames as Cleopatra's Needle. The obelisks weighed between 140 and 230 tons, and their erection was a considerable mechanical feat.

Later, paintings in the tombs of old Thebes's west-bank Valley of the Kings (16th-11th century BC), which is across the Nile from Luxor, showed the angelic "Shining Ones" (*akhs* or "spiritual souls" which dwelt in their *sakhus* or "spiritual bodies") dancing. The temple-dancers of Luxor who lived in the annexe of the Temple at Karnak called the House of Life – the tombs in the Valley were called "Houses of Eternity" – represented the Shining Ones in eternal dances, and to do this they had to receive the Shining Ones, who were reflections of the Light of Ra, and raise their souls into the higher dimensions by *sekhem*, the divine power.[92] The temple-dancers in the Temple of Amon-Ra, Karnak (which was enlarged in the 15th century BC) therefore danced through their souls and became *akhs*.

Akhenaton's Heretical Revolution of the Akh

The *akh* was not affected by the sweeping reforms of Amenhotep IV,[93] who became known as Akhenaton or Ikhnaton (1379-1363 BC), and who briefly replaced the pantheon with Aton (or Aten); it was the *akh* from which

Akhenaton took his name ("He who serves the Aton" but also "The *akh* or shining spirit who serves the Aton").

The importance of the sun-cult in later Egypt is demonstrated by the conflict between Amon (or Amun) and Aton. Amon, a local deity, had been adopted by the Pharaohs at Thebes after 1991 BC, and accepted by the Ra-worshipping Heliopolitans as Amon-Ra.[94] When the 14th-century-BC Akhenaton changed his capital to Amarna and replaced him with Aton (the earlier Ra-Hor-akhty who appeared in the fourth dynasty, the falcon "Horus of the horizon" and a possible derivative from the Sumerian Utu, who had been worshipped in the reign of Thutmose IV, c.1411-1397 or 1397-1388 BC)[95] the dogmas of centuries were swept aside, and the power behind the physical orb of the sun ("Aton") was worshipped without any mythology concerning Osiris, Amon or Ra in a language that recalls the "Great Hymn to Shamash" (or Utu), whose sign was also a disc of the sun. The Aton was the energy *inside* the sun, whereas Ra was the sun.

Aton was more than the physical energy of the sun. Aton was not the sun but the monotheistic power within the sun as Aton's rays were shown as hands that offered the hieroglyph of eternal life and long life, and humans reached out for them with their hands and received them as a gift from the only god.[96] (The *ankh* signified both "eternal life" and "long life" for its shape came from the union of the Delta of Lower Egypt with the straight line of the Nile in Upper Egypt, which brought life and eternal life to men.)

Akhenaton overthrew the pantheon of the Sun-god for a monotheism that resembled that of the Israelite Yahweh; indeed, it is possible that Aton both derived from Yahweh as a result of the exile of the Hebrews in Egypt, and influenced the Yahweh of Moses some 150 years later (and eventually the Allah of Mohammed).[97] Akhenaton asserted the centrality of the sun in the universe and the life-giving nature of its rays, an innovation that anticipated Copernicus by nearly three thousand years[98] and made it hardly surprising that Amon was restored after his death.

Aton was "sole god"[99] as the "Hymn to Aton" shows, and only the divine Akhenaton and his family could worship Aton directly: "There is none other that knows you, save your son Akhenaton, for you have made him skilled in your plans and your might. The earth came into being by your hand, just as you made them (i.e. mankind)."[100] The people worshipped the Pharaoh-King Akhenatòn, and received Aton's gifts through him,[101] and it is doubtful whether they understood the intellectual and contemplative doctrine of *ma'at*, the "truth" of a divinely ordained cosmic order.[102] Since the Sun-god before the time of Akhenaton had always embodied an inner as well as an outer sunlight, and given that Aton – on the evidence of the "Hymn to Aton" at least – was more of a creator of the universe[103] with plans than the physical sun, it is likely that the hands of Aton that proffered the hieroglyph of life (the *ankh*) were also rays of light from an inner sun which had to be received gratefully with open hands. As the Egyptians used the same hieroglyph for "life" and for "eternal life", they could not differentiate them,[104] and indeed, had no need to differentiate them, and the outer sun disc could also represent the inner Light.

It seems, then, that Akhenaton was a heretic and revolutionary who changed his name, his religion and his capital (from Thebes to Amarna) not because he worshipped the physical sun (which has no "plans"), but because he claimed sole right to illumination for himself and his family, because he patented illumination and reflected it, priest-like, from his *akh* to the *akhs* of the Egyptian people[105] who had been accustomed to seek illumination directly in prayers to Amon-Ra, and who preferred direct prayer. (Khufu may have had a similar intention, and its interesting that the Aton was first known in the fourth – Khufu's – dynasty.)[106] Statues of Akhenaton represented him as half-man, half-woman with swollen breasts and a pregnant belly as the Aton was one god and therefore male-female, representing both sexes which related to it. True to tradition, in which gods assumed the facial likenesses of Pharaohs, Aton was shown in the form of Akhenaton.[107]

As Aton symbolized the Light, it is not surprising that there is a tradition that the sun-disc of Aton marked the beginning of Rosicrucianism.[108] In this connection, it is interesting that the worship of Aton was possibly continued after Akhenaton's death by his widow Nefertiti, if we accept the evidence of a gold scarab recovered from a wreck off Turkey in 1986 which couples Nefertiti with Nefernefru-aton, the hitherto little-known Pharaoh who succeeded Akhenaton who may have been none other than Nefertiti.[109] (The official lists have Smenkhara succeeding Akhenaton for four years before Tutankhamon came to the throne.)[110] Rosicrucianism may have its origins in the cult of Aton that was suppressed during Nefertiti's reign.

Egyptian Influence on the Megaliths

If Sumer, Egypt and Britain of the Tuatha and the Druids have a common culture through the megalith-builders, as I suggested on pp36-37, then as Egypt was a culture of the *akh* by 3000 BC and there were already "Shining Ones" at the centre of the Sumerian culture, it is reasonable to suppose that the roughly contemporary British culture of c.2500 BC also celebrated the dawning of the "invisible" Light as well as the rising of the visible sun. On this view it seems that the Anannage were "Shining Ones" because they had become *akhs*, and that the shamanistic magic for which they were known can be attributed to the mysteries of the *akh*, to which they raised their British stones.

Some European megaliths seem to show Egyptian influence, and this is not surprising as the Egyptians colonised many parts of the known world of their time,[111] and they may have occupied and added to the megaliths of the Kurgan-Sumerian shamans who originated in the Near East and Anatolia.[112]

The Egyptians were connected with early Britain through the legendary Spanish Milesius, who invaded Ireland perhaps with the Funnel-Neck Beaker folk and drove out the Tuatha; the Milesian queen was the daughter of Pharaoh.[113] Egyptian-style ceramic beads have been found in the earliest British burial mounds. The inside of Glastonbury's Chalice Well is Egyptian in style, and resembles the work of the 12th dynasty (1991-1786 BC)[114] although it may be later as in Jesus's day the spring was above ground in the vicinity. The axes on Stonehenge might represent "Neter", the first Egyptian concept for almighty God, the picture sign for which was a stone axe-head let into a long wooden handle;[115] although these could have been added at a later date. The solar disc and serpent that are found at Avebury were used in Egypt.[116] St. Piran's cross at Perranzabuloe, Cornwall, is shaped like an *ankh*, the Egyptian symbol of life.[117] There is a similarity in name between the huge Temple of Carnak in Brittany, and the Temple of Karnak in Egypt.[118]

The Egyptians moved to Crete and Mycenaean Greece from as early as c.3400 BC in search of precious metals.[119] Part of the Cyclopean Age can be seen as a colonial offshoot of the cult of the Egyptian Sun-god.[120] On the fringes of a great empire, it seems that some Egyptians did their best in difficult conditions and raised huge stones which would have been more minutely finished had they been back at home by the Nile.

It must however be stressed that the great majority of the far-flung Cyclopean blocks of stone were built by native peoples,[121] and there is evidence that they were occupied by succeeding world-powers. The Minoans, for example, left their traces on the polished sarsens of Stonehenge IIIA, on which appear axes and daggers of a kind used at Mycenae c.1600 BC,[122] but, as Stonehenge IIIA can now be dated to c.2000 BC or before, these are likely to be Minoan graffiti – of no more significance than if Dickens had scratched his name on Shakespeare's birthplace. (It is however possible that Mycenaeans/Minoans, making an Argonaut type of voyage, put an end to the British Kurgan civilization c.1500 BC, and the axes and daggers may record this event.)[123]

The evidence of Egyptianisation at a time when *akhs* were well established and the megaliths were used as sun-temples,[124] reinforces the likelihood that the sun-worship associated with the Cyclopean megaliths had an esoteric, as well as an exoteric side. It seems that the megaliths were used, like the Great Pyramid, as places where initiates were awakened to the Light.

Throughout Egyptian history, then, from the first dynasty to the last, there was an unbroken tradition that held that knowledge of the Light (the "eye of Ra" and of Horus) was crucial in determining the survival of the soul, with the result that instructions to the living were hidden in the periphrasis of a language of the dead.

For Egyptian Gnosticism see "The Gnostic Light", pp393ff. The post-Gnostic Light was based in Egypt's Alexandria, which influenced the Roman Empire and the Near East.

4

The Aegean-Greek Light

The Achaean Mycenaeans' Light

We have seen that c.3500 BC Indo-Europeans settled in Greece, and possibly became the Pelasgians (who are thought to have belonged to a Hittite group);[1] and that c.2200 BC a second wave of Indo-European Kurgans entered Greece and became the ancestors of the Mycenaeans. They called themselves Achaioi or Achaeans, and they seem to have been displaced from Akkad, which was originally called Achaia before it was conquered by the Semitic Sargon I c.2350 BC. Some of the displaced Indo-Europeans went east to settle in Iran and India from c.2250 BC. These Achaean Greeks (or Homeric Danaoi or Mycenaeans) displaced some of the descendants of the original Pelasgians who seem to have migrated to Anatolia.[2]

The bearded Mycenaeans had a warlike, aggressive religion in keeping with the patriarchal Battle-Axe Indo-European religion.[3] The Indo-European Dyaeus became Zeus, the Sky-god with his thunderbolt and storm-god who resembled the Altaic Sky-god[4] just as Pluto resembled the Altaic Lord of the Underworld.[5] To him burnt offerings were made in the course of fire-sacrifices: according to Linear B, the Mycenaean king in Pylos, Knossos and Thebes had the title *wanax* and acted as a king of sacred rites,[6] while the Pythia or priestess of the Delphic Oracle sacrificed animals to the

Sky-god as far back as the Mycenaean period[7] and rose to the Sky World on the smoke which resembled a World Tree. Hyperion-Apollo (who prophesied through the Pythia) was the sun-god; he was *phoibos* or "light-bearer".[8] He was the Enlightener, the god of mental light, and he derived from Shamash, whom the first Achaeans brought with them from Akkad,[9] and who had anyway been absorbed by the Kurgans after c.2400-2300 BC.

The Minoans' Light: The Sacred Bull/Minotaur's Rosette

To the south, across the Aegean Sea, the clean-shaven Cretan Minoans who settled in the Mycenaean civilization by the end of the 17th century BC had a matriarchal religion in keeping with the homely Magna Mater they brought from Anatolia.[10] In Minoan times the Sky Father and the Neolithic Earth Mother, the two aspects of the Indo-European religion, were both present in Greece, the emphasis being on the Sky Father in the north, and on the Earth Mother in the south.[11]

In the Cretan mysteries, Zeus, the Sky-god, became the Neolithic sacred bull which they also brought from Anatolia.[12] (We have seen that there was a bull-cult in Anatolia as early as c.6500 BC.)[13] Its horns symbolized the crescent moon which is on its back in the Middle Eastern sky, and resembles horns,[14] and it appears on the Knossos frescoes as Zeus in the form of a bull who abducts Europa from Tyre to Crete.[15] Their offspring was the priest-king whose title was Minos, just as the title of the Egyptian ruler was Pharaoh. Thus the *Parian Chronicle* mentions a Minos in the 15th century BC and another in the 13th century BC. The sacrificial bull rises from the sea, couples with Minos's wife Pasiphae and fathers the Minotaur (*Minotauros,* "Minos's bull"), which is kept in the labyrinth built by Daedalus.[16]

The priest-king held office for eight years and then ascended to a sacred cave on Mount Ida where Zeus could be found with Hera – the shamanistic Sacred Mountain (compare the Sumerian ziggurat) – to commune with the Bull God, his father, Zeus, and to obtain his approval. If the god was satisfied, he returned for a further eight years and a fresh store of power, which he acquired by sacrificing a sacred bull with the famous double axe (*labrys*) and drinking its blood to receive Zeus's warlike strength and procreative vigour.[17]

The axe of the sacred bull was worshipped throughout Crete, just as it was by the Kurgan Battle-Axe culture, and it was housed in the palace-sanctuary at Knossos, which was a "labyrinth" (home of the *labrys*).[18] The priest-king sat on a throne there and as the adopted son on earth of the Great Mother guarded the entrance to the inner shrine of the Mother Goddess.[19]

On the mainland there were royal cults and shrines (to Hera and Athena) in the royal palaces at Mycenae, Athens and probably Tiryns that were almost identical to the Cretan cult.[20] The Cretans exported their art: the Lion Gate was in the style of Crete, and was the work of the Cretans or of Mycenaean pupils of the Cretans,[21] while a bull with a gold "rosette" on its forehead (c.1550-1500 BC) has been found at Mycenae.[22] It came from the fourth shaft-grave there, and Schliemann described the "rosette" as "a splendidly ornamented golden sun, of two and a fifth inches in diameter" The motif is found in Mycenaean and Cretan art between c.1800 and 1400 BC. It reflected a movement away from the Neolithic moon-cult and the introduction of a sun-cult that connected the bull with the sun, as in Egypt.[23] As in Egypt, the sun also surely represented the Light of the godhead, whose powers the "priest-king" of Mycenae could assume.

The Mycenaeans invaded Crete in due course – the discovery of Linear B by Michael Ventris showed that Mycenaean Greek was spoken in Mycenae and Minoan Knossos during the 15th century BC[24] – and they adopted Anat (Baal's Virgin sister who slew his enemies), whom the Cretans (who were probably of the Hittite group like the Pelasgians) had probably brought from Anatolia;[25] and transformed her into Athena, the Virgin.[26] There was also a cult of the Anatolian Virgin in Egypt under Ramesses II, who kept a harem, and just as Horus was a hawk, so the Virgin was an owl.[27] Athena the Parthenos guarded the Mycenaean priest-king (who lived in the Acropolis) with the wisdom of the Light that was known in Ramesses' Egypt.[28] Much later when the Acropolis was eventually sacked by the Persians in 480 BC and rebuilt under Themistocles, a colossal golden statue of Athena Promachos ("the Champion") stood in the centre, her golden spear tip visible from far out to sea,[29] and the guardianship of the Light was also reflected in Pericles' Parthenon,[30] the ruins of which are still standing.

The Mycenaean culture fell to the Dorians c.1100 BC.[31] The Achaean Greek Mystery religions of this time perpetuated the meaning of the sun-rosette and handed it on to the Dorian Greek culture that succeeded the Mycenaeans c.1100 BC. They guarded the secret of the Light from the unready by symbolising it as bull's flesh, an ear of corn, or fire.[32] These Mystery cults preserved the shaman's experience and offered initiates a way of having religious experiences that were not offered by the public religions; they renewed the neophyte's soul and guaranteed its eternity, for one single contact with the deity (the Light) ensured salvation. Initiates were introduced to the experience of the Light through symbols, and were "divinised". Once they were assured of immortality they were silent. The word "mystery" is derived from *muein* ("to close", to close the eyes to see the Light and to close the lips in silence) and in Greek the initiate was called *mustes* (Latin plural *mystae*, compare our "mystic"), "one who closed his eyes and kept silent".[33]

Dionysiac Bull Mysteries and the Light

The Dionysiac Mysteries perpetuated the bull-cult.[34] They originated in the Mycenaean Age, although they were forgotten for a time and reappeared from Thrace or Phrygia, where they were combined with the Thraco-Phrygian cult of Zagreus. Zagreus was also called Dionysus[35] and he was torn to pieces by the Titans; his heart was preserved and eaten by Zeus, as a result of which a second Dionysus was born.

The Dionysiac Mysteries were also combined with a cult from Asia Minor that identified Dionysus with Bacchus, god of wine. According to this cult, Dionysus-Zagreus was brought up by the Maenads, and so he had a following of ecstatic women called Maenads or Bacchants.[36] He was the god of fruitfulness, vegetation and intoxication by wine, and the physical intoxication which was achieved at his Festivals symbolized a spiritual intoxication,[37] a union with the god as Light. The women wore wreaths of ivy, oak or fir and carried a *thyrsis* or staff wreathed in ivy or vine leaves. They wandered through the mountains and worked themselves into a frenzied ecstasy by drinking wine, dancing themselves dizzy and eating ivy berries, which had a hallucogenic effect. They chanted and indulged in wild sexual orgies, and when they found a wild bull or calf they tore it to pieces and devoured it raw as a way of taking the power of the divinity into themselves.[38]

Dionysus-Zagreus was supposed to incarnate in the bull, and so he was called "bull-horned" (*taurokeros*) and "bull-faced" (*tauroprosopos*) by the Bacchants,[39] and their bull-eating (*omophagia*) recalls the Minoans, who sacrificed bulls to take into themselves the power of Zeus.[40] Like the Mycenaean bull with a "rosette" of Light on its brow, Dionysus, as bull and god, had a Light which could be acquired, and the physical intoxication the women achieved stimulated the inner eye into seeing the *theon eidos* of Euripides' *Bacchoi* or *Bacchae,* the "vision of the gods" or Mysteries sent from Heaven, the coming of the Light.

It was this link between the Dionysiac cult and the Light that led to Dionysus partnering Apollo in the Delphic oracle from the 5th century BC,[41] for the Light brought enlightened knowledge of the future. The orgiastic side of the cult was then tamed and the ecstatic side enhanced as the Pythia went into a frenzy, chewing bay or laurel leaves for their hallucogenic effect to achieve an illumined inspirational vision of the future.[42]

Eleusinian Grain Mysteries and the Light

The Eleusinian Mysteries go back to c.1800 BC.[43] They worshipped Demeter (Ceres), the Earth Mother or Grain-Mother, and her daughter Kore (Persephone), who was carried off into the Underworld by Pluto. The Mysteries concerned the sowing, sprouting and reaping of grain, and by the 8th century BC the Lesser Mysteries of the spring were a preliminary initiation and purification for the Greater Mysteries of the autumn. These included a shamanistic journey to the Underworld.[44] There seems to have been an underground vault beneath the *telesterion*, the hall at Eleusis, and neophytes were led down into this reconstruction of Hades, and then up into a reconstructed Elysium in the *telesterion*. Here the reuniting of Demeter and Kore was celebrated with torches, and a papyrus fragment shows Herakles (the Sky-god figure of the priapic Cerne Abbas giant) saying "I have beheld the Fire (or fire)...I have seen the Maid (i.e. Kore)."[45]

The climax of the Mysteries, the *Philosophoumena*, presented a reaped ear of corn of brilliant gold. This was presented in the *telesterion* in a brilliant light, which was achieved by reflectors: "Suddenly a wonderful light appears before one's eyes; one is transported to delightful places and meadows."[46] The later Eleusinian Epoptic Mysteries recalled a Sumerian-style Sacred Marriage between Zeus and Demeter, and presented in a brilliant light Zeus's son Zagreus as a bull who was torn to pieces, and the ear of wheat which climaxed the Mysteries was presented as growing from Zagreus's grave.[47]

The meaning of the Mysteries seems to have been that the cycle of grain parallelled the cycle of man: the grain that was thrown into a field and buried in earth to bring forth new life represented the seed of Light in man.[48] (Compare the Biblical text we have already considered (p10): "Except a corn of wheat fall into the ground and die, it abideth alone; but if it die, it bringeth forth much fruit.") Thus, classical texts assert that "whoever had been taught the Mysteries would, when he died, be deemed worthy of divine glory", and that "thanks to the beautiful Mysteries, which we received from the gods, death is no disaster for mortals, but rather a benefit". Again: "Happy is he who has seen these sacred ceremonies. He who is not initiated and has not taken part in them, will not have the same fate after death in the cold regions of darkness" (Homeric "Hymn to Demeter").[49]

After the 5th century BC Epoptism was included as the highest of the Eleusinian Mysteries, and a classical text asserts, reflecting the Asian influences that had reached Eleusis: "The Phrygians, the Naassene says, assert that God is a fresh ear of cut wheat, and following the Phrygians the Athenians, when they initiate in the Eleusinia, exhibit in silence to the epoptai the mighty and marvellous and most complete epoptic mystery, an ear of cut wheat." Thus "the soul (at the point of death) has the same experience as those who are being initiated into great mysteries.... Then one is struck with a marvellous light, one is received into pure regions."[50]

Orphic Mysteries: Fire and the Light of Phanes

The Orphic Mysteries also aimed to unite with Dionysus-Zagreus but by means that differed from those of the Bacchic troop.[51] They worshipped Orpheus, the musician, author of sacred writings and priest of Dionysus, who was torn to pieces by Maenads. He suffered the same fate of dismemberment as Osiris, but his head continued to sing.[52]

The Orphics believed that man has a divine soul, the Dionysiac part, which could be liberated from the body, the Titanic part,[53] for (according to Orphism) the Titans killed Dionysus and devoured him, and when Zeus killed the Titans in anger, man was formed from their ashes. The Orphics eliminated the Titanic part by abstaining from meat, wine and sex, and emerged as divine souls who were united with Zagreus-Dionysus and the Light.[54] The soul could be reborn after death, but after three pious or anti-Titanic lives, it was released from the cycle of living to live in the eternal sunshine and bliss of the Isles of the Blest.[55]

The way the Orphics took to unite with Dionysus and the Light, then, was in direct opposition to the way the Maenads of the Dionysiac Mysteries took; it was the way of self-control[56] as opposed to the way of frenzied abandon (which resulted in Orpheus himself being torn to pieces), though the illumination at the end was the same.

The Orphic Light was called Phanes, the Creator, who existed before the sun, which he created. Phanes was the light of reason, the light of life and the light of love. According to Orphic belief, the primal god of Love and Light (Eros-Phanes) sprang from an egg laid by Chronos (Time), just as Ra sprang from an egg, and created a world of gods and men. This Cosmic egg of creation appears on bowls amid flames of fire, and the Orphic revelation was of a phoenix-like rebirth from fire, of an esoteric illumination, to receive which one had to strip off the external Titanic coverings.[57] One then became divine.

Pythagoras, Plato's Fire and Shadows

The Orphic Mysteries had a considerable influence on the Light (or Fire) in Greek philosophy, for they influenced both Pythagoras and Plato.[58] Pythagoras's 20-year long travels to Egypt, Persia and Babylon between 538 and 518 BC put him in touch with a priest (called Abaris) from the "land of the Hyperboreans", the "people from beyond the North Wind" who were probably the northerly Altaic shamans of Central Asia and Siberia, and he seems to have had a shaman-like initiation in a cave on Mount Ida in Crete.[59] Pythagoras left Samos to found a school in Croton, Southern Italy around the time when Rome imported Zeus as Jupiter, and Apollo (c.500 BC), and he found Orphism already established there. Like Orphism and the shamans, Pythagoras taught that the soul was a divine being imprisoned in the body, and that it migrated to another body (or animal or plant) at death unless it was delivered by a discipline of purity,[60] and the Pythagorean Brotherhood adopted the Orphic view of the Light. Indeed, according to a 5th century BC source, Pythagoras wrote under the name of Orpheus.[61] The Pythagorean numbers originated in the Light, for out of the Monad (or Light, the One) came the duad, and out of the duad, numbers; and God revealed Himself in the *tetraktys*, four numbers (1+2+3+4) which made 10 and which contained "the perennial fount and root of Nature" (i.e. 1 and 0, or Being and Non-Being), a mystery that could be expressed as a triangle with a central point (a *tetrahedron* making three triangles). This mystery could not be revealed outside the Brotherhood.[62]

Plato visited Italy and Sicily c.388 BC, and from Pythagoreanism he took the idea that the numbers of geometry are more true of the invisible world of the mind than of the visible world of the senses, a concept that gave him his distinction between the invisible world of Ideas and the visible world.[63] Plato was deeply impressed both by the Orphic belief in the divinity of the soul and the Light of Phanes, and by the Eleusinian search for the Truth which turned out to be the Light, and he compared the beholding of his Ideas with the shades that are revealed in the Mysteries.[64]

Plato expressed the Light in his own philosophy. In his famous simile of the shadows thrown on the wall of a cave by a fire (like the fire in the underground vault at Eleusis or the subterranean cavern of a Mithraeum),[65] he contrasts the illusory nature of the visible world with the "controlling source" of Light in the intelligible world. Just as the sun is the source of growth and light which gives visibility to objects of sense and the power of sight to the eye, so the Good (or Absolute Goodness) is the source of Reality and Truth which gives intelligibility to objects of thought, and the power of knowing to the mind.[66] Plato says that at the age of 50, the shaman-like "guardians of the state...must raise the eye of the soul to the universal Light which lightens all things, and behold the Absolute Good."[67] This is "absolute beauty".[68]

The Achaean descendants of the Kurgans transmitted the Indo-European Light (or Fire), and the Platonic Light can therefore be traced back, through the Orphic and Eleusinian Mysteries, to the Indo-European "fountains of the West" where Plato himself said Greek philosophy originated.[69] However, Plato visited Egypt during his travels, and there is a tradition that he was an initiate at the Temple of Isis at On, Heliopolis,[70] and if this is true then the Platonic Light must also be seen as drawing on, and passing into, the Egyptian Royal Mysteries, into which the Eleusinian, Dionysian and Orphic Mysteries all ultimately passed.[71]

5

THE ROMAN LIGHT

The Etruscans probably emigrated to Italy from Anatolia; their kings go back perhaps to c.1200 BC and certainly to c.800 BC, and they lasted until c.500 BC.[1] Soon after that (c.475 BC), the Latin League unified the Italians round Rome, and the Roman culture came to consist of a State religion, the Latin language, coinage, international legions, an urban network, the rule of law, and civic institutions that were inherited (through trade) from Greece, and in particular from the cultural unity of Hellenism imposed by Alexander the Great (334-323 BC) on both West and East (i.e. from Egypt to India). All these features of civilization were applied to diverse parts of the Roman Empire, to the sophisticated Eastern provinces where urban life was long established, and to the less advanced Western provinces.

The Roman State religion was largely imported. The cult of Jupiter the Sky-god and Thunderer, came from the Indo-European Sky-god Dyaeus Pitar[2] (*Ju-pitar*, compare the Celtic Du-w) and the Greek Zeus when the Etruscans accepted Greek influence and the Olympian gods, including Pluto, God of the Underworld, c.500 BC.[3] Apollo came with him: there was a Greek colony at Cumae from which the Romans imported grain; it had a temple of Apollo and Sibylline books, which the last Etruscan kings brought to Rome, and the cult of Apollo was imported to Rome c.431 BC.[4] The king of the sacred rites (*rex sacrorum*) embodied Jupiter, the Sky-god, and officiated after the expulsion of the Etruscan kings.[5] The cults of Astarte,

Cybele and Mithras came from the East during the general anxiety felt during the Punic Wars of the 3rd century BC,[6] when all gods were appealed to. The cult of Isis was introduced in the 1st century BC[7] and spread from Alexandria in the 3rd century AD along with other pagan mystery cults.

The Roman State religion imported the Inner Light (or Fire) with these cults, and so the shrine in the circular Temple of Vesta in the Forum at Rome, for instance, contained the eternal fire that was attended by the Vestal Virgins and which originated in Vedic India, being known to the Indo-European Indians as *garhapatya*.[8] The Sky-god, solar god and 13 other State deities were served by *flamens* – *flamines*, "those who blow (the sacred fire)" or "those who burn offerings" – the chief of whom was the priest of Jupiter, *Flamen Dialis*.[9] Each day the flamens burnt sacrifices of animals and rose to Heaven on the smoke. Eventually, the Sol cult reflected the Light and was preserved in alchemy.[10] Aurelian built a temple to *Sol Invictus* (Unconquered Sun) in Rome in 274,[11] and the sun is shown radiating out of Constantine's head on some of the coins struck during his rule.

The Light shone through the State religion from the Pillars of Hercules to the Black Sea and unified the diverse peoples within the Graeco-Roman civilization, who all felt they had something in common. Local cultures were subordinated to this Roman culture; they nevertheless existed, and there were local ethnic languages, local customs and practices, pagan temples, Essene communities, Jewish synagogues, Druid universities and Christian baptisteries. Local regimes emerged in opposition to Roman culture, but at first the local leaders were still Romanized, just as the leaders of many independent African states are still Westernised in our own time.

The story of the imperial Roman culture from the time of Augustus is of an imported and disintegrating Roman Light suppressing and persecuting a Christian Light influenced by Iran (during the Jewish captivity in Magi-influenced Babylon), which it did not at first understand as it flourished in the anti-Roman seclusion of Qumran and Britain. After the challenges of other religions, most notably of Gnosticism, the Roman Light was eventually taken over by the Christian Light and Christianity became the State religion.

The Christianization of the Romanized Light

Christianity eventually absorbed the challenges from Neoplatonism (see p406) and Manichaeism (see p410) through the genius of St Augustine. A Manichaean until AD 382 and then a Neoplatonist until his conversion in AD 386, he absorbed both Lights just as Clement had absorbed the Gnostic Light. In doing so, Augustine set the pattern for the Middle Ages. In particular, he let into Christianity the Manichaean view that sexual desire, like the body, belonged to Darkness and the Devil, and in making sexual concupiscence the basis for original sin he reflected Manichaeism, as did the Desert Fathers who struggled against the temptations of the flesh. The evil nature of "the world, the flesh and the Devil" is a fundamentally Manichaean concept[12] which passed into Christianity through St Augustine.

While Christianity was absorbing the Gnostic challenge, the Roman Light was Romanising the local gods throughout the Empire. As their Empire spread and the Romans granted citizenship to the inhabitants of new territories, they offered the gods of the Roman State religion to the local cultures. There was no missionary fervour in this; the Romans wanted to assimilate the local cultures, and they were actually very tolerant of local deities whom they approached in a spirit of agnosticism. The locals were keen to adopt the Roman pantheon for political reasons – to declare for Rome in such an obvious way could result in financial benefits – and so Celts, Gauls and Syrians adopted Jupiter in place of Taran or Baal. The Germanic peoples merged their gods with Roman gods, and according to Tacitus Wotan-Odin became Mercury, Donar-Thor became Hercules and Zin-Tyr became Mars.[13] Odin-Mercury then became identified with the Egyptian Hermes[14] as the god of shamanistic ecstasy and occult knowledge for the Germanic peoples from the Black Sea to Greenland, including Iceland and Scandinavia.

The syncretizing process was well under way by the 3rd century AD, and it gathered force from the Christian movement towards monotheism. Just as the Romans had Latinised Mount Olympus, turned Zeus into Jupiter and imported Apollo, so now Jupiter was fused with Sol who had taken over from Mithras in Asia Minor. Originally the Syrian Sun-god and god of Alchemy, he virtually became the chief god of the Roman Empire in the 3rd century AD[15] when two Roman Emperors, Elagabalus (AD 218-222) and Aurelian (AD 270-275) built temples to *Sol Invictus.* Jupiter-Sol was the Roman god of the Light, whose rays streamed from their heads on coins. Attis had now become a solar deity, and a manifestation of Sol.[16] The Eleusinian, Dionysian and Orphic Mysteries had all passed into the Egyptian Royal Mysteries of Isis.[17] While there were still Pharaohs these worshipped the ruling Pharaoh as an incarnation of Horus, the Sun-god; his mother as an incarnation of Isis, who was also the Earth Mother, Cybele; and his dead father as an incarnation of Osiris, the god of the dead and of fertility.[18] Now Horus became equated with Apollo[19] and Helios with Sol.[20] Isis became Demeter,[21] who, reuniting with Kore, the Maid, conveyed the Light in the Eleusinian Mysteries. (Osiris became identified with Serapis and Dionysus.)[22] In the 3rd century AD the Isis Mysteries spread from Alexandria to Rome, and they symbolized the advent of the Light.

In the Isis Mysteries, the initiation ceremony included a light that appeared round the head of a priest. The priest's head was shaved, and a metal receptacle for alcohol was placed on it. The alcohol was set alight in a dark room, and it shone for some seconds. There "came from Isis a Light and other unutterable things conducive to salvation", and "the eye of the body" could not "bear" the brightness of the divine apparitions. Or, in the words of Apuleius's Lucius, who is reporting his (and Apuleius's own) ceremony of initiation into the Isis Mysteries in the 2nd century AD: "I will record as much as I may lawfully record for the uninitiated.... At midnight I saw the sun shining as if it were noon." (Or, "In the middle of the night I have seen the Sun scintillating with a pure light.")[23] In Corinth Apuleius (AD c.124-c.170) was clearly shown a symbol for the Light.

During the 3rd century AD the Roman Light had united the local regional Lights of the Roman civilization, and as Christianity spread it began the process of Christianizing the regional Lights. We shall see (p101) how it absorbed the Druid Light in Britain through Lucius "the Great Light", and therefore made headway among the Celts and Gauls for whom Yesu became

Jesus. Their Germanic Light was Christianized when Odin-Mercury became the Holy Spirit,[24] the "messenger" of the Christian God. In Asia Minor the cults had already drawn together and they were Christianized when the Vegetation Deity became identified with the Christian God.[25] Attis-Adonis became the dying and resurrected Christ[26] – Attis became sufficiently close to Mithras for the Attic and Mithraic cults to be united in the 3rd century AD[27] – and the Meal of grain became identified with the Mass.[28] The same process happened with the Eleusinian Mysteries, for the Philosophoumena, the sacred offering of an ear of corn, became the offering of bread in the Mass.[29] Clement of Alexandria, who blended Greek and Christian culture, was able to refer to this Christianization of the Greek Mysteries: "O eternally sacred Mysteries, I became holy through initiation. The Lord is the high priest; he imprinted his seal on the Mystic when he granted him enlightenment."[30] (In Christian times, the priest was called "the one who brings enlightenment", *phonotikos,* and the neophyte "the Enlightened One", *photistheis.*)[31] The Isis Mysteries were Christianized when the royal son-mother-father became the triad of Jesus, Mary and God, which in due course became the Trinity of the Father, the Son and the Holy Ghost.[32] According to the Grand Master of the Prieuré Notre-Dame de Sion (1981-4), Pierre Plantard, Isis became the Black Virgin,[33] *Notre-Dame de Lumière,* to whom there is a cult of black effigies all over Europe (for example, at Rocamadour).[34]

The slow Christianization of the Roman Light reached a dramatic conclusion when Christianity captured the imperial throne at Rome and Jupiter-Sol was swiftly replaced by the Christian Light.[35] It was a British coup, which fittingly climaxed the work of Joseph of Arimathaea's Culdees during the long Roman persecution. The daughter of Caractacus's grandson King Coel, who ruled in Colchester probably from a castle that is thought to have been sited where earthworks can still be seen at Lexton, was called Helen (born AD 265). She was brought up as a Christian and married Constantius Chlorus, who became Roman Emperor of Britain, Spain and Gaul. She became the Empress Helena, and she succeeded her husband on his death in AD 306, and reigned with her Christian son, Constantine. They had lived through Diocletian's long persecution of the Christians which had begun in AD 290, during which a Palestinian nobleman, George of Lydda, pleaded with Diocletian for the lives of his fellow Christians, and was beheaded. (He is now the patron saint of England, St George, who marks a further link between Culdee Palestinians and Britain – see "The British Druid Light", pp377-392.) Constantine declared himself Roman Emperor, defeated Maximilian and was welcomed in Rome where, AD c.312, he declared Rome Christian.[36]

There was now one Light throughout the Roman Empire, the Christian Light of the World. The Light of the early Palestinian-British Christians had triumphed as they could never have thought possible.

6

The Anatolian Light

The Hittite Light

The Hittites were Indo-Europeans who originated North of the Black Sea.[1] Some may have been the Pelasgians who settled in Greece until they were displaced by the Achaeans. They seem to have arrived in Anatolia c.2000 BC and absorbed the Hatti, a race that occupied Anatolia from c.2500 BC[2] and whose name has come down to us through Hittite sources.

The Hittite Old Kingdom lasted from c.1700 to c.1500 BC, when the capital was moved to Hattusas (the modern Boğazköy). The Hurrians occupied the south of the Hittite kingdom and conquered Cilicia, but the Hittites controlled North Syria and Mursilis I ended the Amorite dynasty in Babylon c.1595 BC.[3] The Middle Kingdom, c.1500-1400 BC, saw some decline. Syria passed from the Hurrians to the Hanigalbat and thence to Egypt, and eventually Syria was taken by the Mitannians. The Hurrians also made inroads during this time.[4]

The New Kingdom restored the empire: Suppiluliumas defeated the Mitannians and conquered Syria, dominating the Near East, but the young Mursilis II then lost part of Syria to Assyria. There were revolts in Anatolia and the Hittites came into conflict with Ramesses II, the battle of Kadesh in 1299 BC was fought against Egypt. There was an invasion from the Phrygians, who probably came from Macedonia and Thrace, just before the time of the Trojan War (early 12th century), and so the pattern of decline was well established before the Sea Peoples menaced. The Hittite Empire fell suddenly c.1225 BC to the Sea Peoples, probably their ancient enemy the Bronze Age Achaean Greeks, or *Ahhiyawa* according to Hittite tablets.[5] The collapse coincided with the destruction by fire c.13th century BC of Troy, the city of King Priam, and with the Dorian settlement of Anatolia. Northern Anatolia now became Aeolia, Southern Anatolia Ionia, while Western and Central Anatolia was occupied by the Phrygians.

From 1180 to the 8th century BC, the Phrygians established a centralised kingdom although Syria and Cilicia remained Hittite. The Hittites were still in Syria, and North Syrian Neo-Hittite states grew up, for example at Carchemish and Milid, and their gods were the Luwian storm-god, Tarhun, Karkuhas, protector of Nature, and Kubabas-Cybele.[6] In the 9th century BC the Assyrians invaded Syria but did not conquer it, and the state of Urartu rose in the 8th century BC. However, the Assyrians returned, and by 700 BC had absorbed the Neo-Hittite states.

The Phrygians fought the Assyrians in 715 and 709. Soon after Assyria's dispersal of the Lost Ten Tribes[7] following the conquest of Israel in 721 BC, the Cimmerians came from beyond the Caucasus (i.e. Israel's side of the Caucasus) and sacked the capital of the Phrygian kingdom of Midas, Gordium, in 696 or 695 BC and put an end to Phrygia as a major political power. The Cimmerians then withdrew into the countryside to be defeated by the Assyrians in 679 and again between 637 and 626 BC. The cult of Cybele was known in the late 7th century BC as an image of Cybele has been found in the Phrygian citadel at Boğazköy-Hattusas.[8]

From now on Anatolia was under foreign control. The Lydians rose near Izmir in the 7th century BC, and in the 6th century came into conflict with the Medes who were under Croesus. From 546 to 330 BC, Anatolia was dominated by the Iranian Achaemenians. Alexander established a brief empire, but following its decline c.300 BC Anatolia was invaded by Celts in 288-5 BC and finally passed into the Roman hegemony in 133 BC.

Very little is known about the Hittite religion. According to cuneiform tablets discovered at Boğazköy, the Hittite ruler was the earthly deputy for the Storm and Weather god, whose sign in picture-writing was the lightning flash; in life he embodied the Storm and Weather god, and on his death he became a god.[9] The Hittite gods were Anatolian, Syrian and Hurrian. The Hurrians occupied eastern Anatolia after c.1700 BC, and the Hurrian Storm-god was Teshub, and his consort Hebat. Their son seems to have been Sharruma or Sharma (compare Shamash), and the sun-goddess of Arinna was the chief god in the Hittite pantheon and patron of the Hittite rulers.[10] There was clearly an affinity between the Hittite Storm and Weather god, the Indo-European Storm and Weather god Dyaeus Pitar, and the Greek Zeus, and it seems that the sun-goddess of Arinna fulfilled a similar function to that of Apollo[11] who represented the Light. Two other sun deities in Asia Minor – the Hattite sun-god Istanu (from 2nd millennium BC), and the sun-goddess Shams[12] (again compare Shamash) in the early pre-Islamic Arabian religion – both also represented the Light.

The Hittite rule in Syria and Phrygia presided over vegetation cults connected with Cybele, the Great Earth Mother,[13] which had an esoteric side that concerned the mysteries of the divine spiritual life, and as in the case of Zagreus eventually influenced Greece.

Phrygian Attis, the Sacred Bull and the Light

Agricultural mysteries were to be found in a cult of the Phrygian Attis (2nd millennium BC).[14] Attis was loved by the Great Mother of the gods, who was Inanna at Sumer, Ishtar in Assyria, Artemis at Ephesus and Aphrodite in Cyprus; though she was generally called Cybele. Attis castrated himself under a pine tree and bled to death – in one version of the myth, he had been unfaithful to Cybele, who had driven him mad – and there were public Festivals of Mourning and of Joy for the autumn death and spring revival of the god. The priests of Cybele castrated themselves on entering her service, either to give their fertility to Cybele or to preserve its source, the seed, and to resurrect Attis in the spring they went into the whirling dances of the Corybantes, like dervishes, and ecstatically shed blood on his altar and sacred pine.[15]

Apart from public Festivals there were Mysteries of Attis, and initiation comprised a baptism in ram's blood or bull's blood, the initiate lying in a pit under a lattice and being drenched in a "smoking river" of hot blood from the speared animal.[16] Depending on whether the animal was a ram or a bull, he received the *criobolium* or the *taurobolium*, and the initiate emerged with the gift of divine or eternal life which he had received from the sacred animal.[17]

The *mustes* or initiate of Attis actually *became* Attis, and when he emerged, all hailed and worshipped him, the epiphany of the god in the Attis cult being marked with the words, "Hail, Bridegroom, Hail, new Light."[18] The initiate took a mystic, sacramental Meal in which the food was served in the tambourines (or *tympanums*) and cymbals that were used in the ritual, to symbolise his eating the Food of Eternal Life, and as at Eleusis grain was included, Attis being called "the reaped yellow ear of grain".[19] Thus Mother Earth's children won an after-life through her, and were united with the Light.

The Phrygians passed the cult of Cybele, the Earth Mother – and their interpretation of the sacred bull – on to the Greeks together with the pointed Phrygian cap, which was later worn by emancipated Roman slaves as a symbol of freedom, and later still by *Liberté*, when it became the symbol of freedom during the French Revolution.[20]

7

The Syrian Light

Adonis, Baal and the Light

There had been much Hittite influence in Syria, which had been a Hittite colony on and off. The cult of Adonis in Syria and Phoenicia followed the cult of Dumuzi-Tammuz from c.2000 BC in celebrating a boy who was loved by the Earth Mother Cybele,[1] who in Greek mythology was Aphrodite. She gave him to Persephone, the queen of the Underworld, who refused to surrender him, and the similarity of the story to the stories of Tammuz and Ishtar – and of Osiris and Isis – resulted in Adonis being identified with both Tammuz and Osiris as a vegetation spirit who revived nature in the spring.[2] Astarte, the goddess of a fertility cult in Palestine (2nd millennium BC), was identified with Ishtar, Isis and Aphrodite,[3] and therefore she, too, loved Adonis.

In Canaan the Syrian and Phoenician kings embodied the Storm god Baal, the Canaanite god of fertility who rode the clouds, king of the gods, Lord of the Earth from c.1500 BC.[4] Tablets unearthed at Ugarit, North Syria, describe how Baal, the son of Dagon, was in combat with Mot, god of sterility and death, drought and famine.[5]

In these fertility cults, just as the spring sun made the corn grow and return after winter and a ritual (which has come down to us in the form of Morris dances) helped this, so there was an inner sun (the Light) which made the inner corn grow and the vegetation spirit promoted inner fertility.[6]

Just as the rites of the Mesopotamian Tammuz and of the Sacred Bull of the Phrygian Attis involved the Light, so did the rites of Adonis and of the golden calf of Baal.

8

The Israelite Light

The Semitic Hebrews were influenced by the Indo-European fire-cults. Abraham, the first Hebrew, lived at Ur (probably 19th or 18th-17th centuries BC, perhaps c.1750 BC) when the worship of the moon-goddess Nanna was giving way to the Indo-European Sky Father and sun-god,[1] and he would have known that the Akkadians, the speakers of the oldest Semitic language, had adopted the Indo-European Shamash in the 22nd century BC. The Semitic Jews wandered into Palestine from the banks of the Euphrates when the family of the early Hebrew patriarchs migrated from Ur via Harran to Canaan under Abraham.[2] They brought with them King Hammurabi's "eye for an eye" legal code from Ur to the Promised Land, and as Hammurabi identified himself with Shamash[3] they must have brought a knowledge of Shamash. Doubts as to whether the founder of the Hebrew people and pioneer of Judaism in fact existed have been largely dispelled by a find of thousands of cuneiform tablets at Mari, a city on the Euphrates.[4] The family then went to Egypt and lived in bondage until their return to Canaan under Moses (end of 13th century BC), whose Ten Commandments founded Judaism as it has come down to us today.

The Light of Yahweh in the Tabernacle

Old Testament Judaism saw YHWH, pronounced Yahweh, or (less correctly by Christians) Jehovah,[5] as the Light (or Fire). Yahweh (whose name was never uttered from the time of the Exile, *Adonai* or *Elohim* being used instead) was a Person as well as the Being who was First Cause.[6] He evolved from a tribal, "jealous" idol-god who "died" and rose for the spring Passover festival and manifested in sunlight and thunderstorm, who grudged the worship of his rivals, false idols, and who seemed almost cruelly powerful. He became a just and merciful God who ruled first the priest-kings of his chosen people in the Kingdom which David established (c.1000 BC), and then the priests who controlled the country after the Exile (6th century BC). His exploits in the *Old Testament* cover the period from the 20th to the 4th centuries BC, and were written by many hands at different times.

Throughout this time Yahweh was seen in terms of light, fire and lightning in a way that recalls the Indo-European Sky-gods and storm-gods and Fire-temples. Abraham sees Yahweh in the form of "a smoking furnace and a burning lamp" (*Genesis* 15.17) and Yahweh's first appearance to Moses was "in a flame of fire, and the bush was not consumed" (*Exodus* 3.2). Moses was leading a flock on Mount Horeb at the time, and Yahweh identified himself as "I am that I am" and "I am". The incident recalls the Indian Agni who brought the gods down to the fire-sacrifice, and Dyaeus Pitar, who came down as lightning to dwell in the Druids' mistletoe (see pp98-100). Before God spoke out of the bush "the angel of the Lord appeared unto him in a flame of fire out of the midst of a bush", and it is possible that Moses had a vision within his soul, and that Yahweh spoke to him out of the Light rather than the fire. It is worth noting that in *Against Apion* 1.26, Josephus records the story that Moses was a Heliopolitan priest, who as an initiate of the Temple at On, where Plato was reputedly an initiate many years later, might be expected to know about visions; although, to be fair, Josephus prefers the story that Moses was made an Egyptian General and led a campaign in Ethiopia.

Yahweh's appearance on Mount Sinai, when Moses was given the Ten Commandments, was after "thunders and lightnings" (*Exodus* 19.16) when "Sinai was altogether on a smoke, because the Lord descended upon it in fire: and the smoke thereof ascended as smoke of a furnace." This was after Yahweh had led the exodus "by night in a pillar of fire, to give them light" (*Exodus* 13.21). According to another story in Josephus, Moses "erected prayer-houses, open to the air" in Heliopolis. These sound like the tent of the Tabernacle in which stood the Ark of the Covenant that contained the tablets of the Ten Commandments, "all facing eastwards", and "in place of obelisks he set up pillars, beneath which was a model of a boat", which may have been a forerunner of the Ark. (The pillar, like the obelisk, symbolized a ray of the Light.)

Yahweh "shined forth from mount Paran" (*Deuteronomy* 33.2), and in the 9th century BC Elijah challenged Baal by invoking Yahweh, who sent down "fire" from heaven (2 *Kings* I). (The "Baalzebub" of this chapter of *Kings*, Hebrew for "fly-lord" or "lord of the flies", became ***Beelzeboub*** in Greek, and our Satanic Beelzebub.)

Mount Horeb, Mount Sinai and perhaps Mount Paran (each of which is mentioned in the three previous paragraphs) may all be the same mountain. Traditionally it is *Jebel Musa* (Mount of Moses) where in the 4th century AD Christian monks founded the mission of St Catherine's Monastery. An alternative that complies more with the geography of *Exodus* is *Serâbît el Khâdim*, which rises to 2,600 feet over the plain of Paran. Both locations are in southern Sinai.[7]

The *Psalms of David* frequently see Yahweh as Light: for example, "Out of Zion, the perfection of beauty, God hath shined" (*Psalm* 50.2); "the voice of thy thunder was in the heaven: the lightnings lightened the world" (*Psalm* 77.18); and "yea, the darkness hideth not from thee; but the night shineth as the day: the darkness and the light are both alike to thee" (*Psalm* 139.12), which is clearly about the Light.

Yahweh's tongue was "as a devouring fire" (*Isaiah* 20.27), and "the Lord will come with fire...to render...his rebuke with flames of fire" (*Isaiah* 66.15). Ezekiel saw "a great cloud and a fire...and a brightness" (1.4), a cloud which opened to reveal a vision of the throne of Yahweh, who was "fire" and "brightness". The sun and moon went "at the light of thine (Yahweh's) arrows and at the shining of the glittering spear" (*Habakkuk* 3.11), and when Yahweh comes "at evening time it shall be light" (*Zechariah* 14.7). Yahweh's glory shone with a brilliant light: "and the court was full of the brightness of the Lord's glory" (*Ezekiel* 10.4). Yahweh was robed with light, covering himself "with light as a garment" (*Psalm* 104), and light was a symbol of God's presence, as in the "lamp of God" in the temple (*Samuel* 3.3) and the "burnt sacrifices" the Levites made every morning and every evening, again recalling the Indo-European Agni (2 *Chronicles* 13.11).

Yahweh was the Light: "The sun shall be no more thy light by day" in the New Jerusalem; "neither for brightness shall the moon give light unto thee: but the Lord shall be unto thee an everlasting light" (*Isaiah* 60.9). "For with thee is the fountain of life: in thy light shall we see light" (*Psalm* 36.9), and "the light of Israel shall be for a fire, and his Holy One for a flame" (*Isaiah* 10.17). When Yahweh showed a favour to human beings, he made "his face shine" upon them and lifted up "his countenance" upon them (*Numbers* 6.25); thus the people that know the joyful sound "shall walk, O Lord, in the light of thy countenance" (*Psalm* 89.15). The Light protected: "And the light shall shine upon thy ways" (*Job* 22.28); "the lord is my light and my salvation; whom shall I fear" (*Psalm* 27.1); "rejoice not against me, O mine enemy...when I sit in darkness, the Lord shall be a light unto me" (*Micah* 7.8), which is obviously about the Light. The Messiah would come as a Light, so that: "the people that walked in darkness have seen a great light" (*Isaiah* 9.2). "Then shall thy light break forth as the morning" (*Isaiah* 58.8). Yahweh's servant was a light: "I the Lord have called thee...and give thee...for a light of the Gentiles; to open the blind eyes" (*Isaiah* 42.6). All who were enlightened or wise "shall shine as the brightness of the firmament" (*Daniel* 12.3).

Yahweh, then, descended as fire, spoke out of fire, and had a countenance which shone as an everlasting Light. Although fire-sacrifices and burnt offerings were made to him at the ritualistic level in the Indo-European manner, he was clearly also experienced mystically as Light, as an inner sun, and there is much reason for the Kabbalistic Freemasons who built King's College Chapel, Cambridge to have put the Christianized Hebrew characters for JHVH (originally the Hebrew YHWH) in a sun above the west end door.[8] In fact, it was because Yahweh could be experienced mystically as Light that the ritual grew up surrounding the tent of the Tabernacle, the mobile sanctuary which God revealed to Moses in a vision on Mount Sinai (*Exodus* 25), and its successors in the first and second Temples.

In the Tabernacle in the Temple of Solomon (10th century BC) and in the second Temple, there was a divine "Holy of Holies" within a Heavenly

"Holy" and an earthly outer court; and the gold Ark of the Covenant stood in the Holy of Holies, containing the "testimony" which Yahweh gave the people of Israel. "And there I will meet with thee," Yahweh told Moses (*Exodus* 25.22), "and I will commune with thee from above the mercy seat, between the two cherubims which are upon the ark, of all things which I will give in commandment unto the children of Israel."

On the first day of the first month in the year following these words of Yahweh's the Tabernacle was erected, and "a cloud covered the tent of the congregation, and the glory of the Lord filled the tabernacle....The cloud of the Lord was upon the tabernacle by day, and fire was in it by night" (*Exodus* 40.34,38). The journey was only continued when "the cloud was taken up from over the tabernacle". In the mystery of the Tabernacle, Yahweh came down and united with the world below and dwelt in the darkness of the Holy of Holies, from which the glorious Light of his indwelling radiated and his shining being (the bright radiance of his *Shekhinah* or Presence) revealed itself.[9]

Yahweh's Light and the Divine Right of Kings

This Yahweh of Light was closely involved in the destiny of Israel, as was the Apollo of the Delphic Oracle in the destiny of Greece. His *Shekhinah* descended down an obelisk-like pillar or *Axis Mundi* into the first Tabernacle and Solomon's Temple. He made a covenant with the Israelites and appeared in a vision to Jacob, the grandson of Abraham (c.18th-17th century BC), to promise that his descendants would rule Israel. Jacob was at Bethel, "and he took of the stones of that place, and put them for his pillows, and lay down in that place to sleep. And he dreamed, and behold a ladder set up on the earth, and the top of it reached to heaven; and behold the angels of God ascending and descending on it. And, behold, the Lord stood above it, and said...the land whereon thou liest, to thee will I give it, and to thy seed....And Jacob rose up early in the morning and took up the stone that he had put for his pillows and set it up for a pillar" (*Genesis* 28.11-13,18). The prophecy was fulfilled when his descendant David united the Israelites into a single nation as the second king of Israel, before he died c.962 BC.

It is interesting to note in passing that Yahweh's covenant and promise are still active on the international scene, as they are vested in the British Coronation Stone, the Stone of Scone, which is reputed to be Jacob's pillow, the "stone of Israel" (*Genesis* 49.24). It reflects the British monarchs' descent from King David (c.1000 BC), and the continuity of the cry "God Save the King" which hailed the coronation of Saul, the first King of Israel. According to legend, the Stone of Scone derives the Divine Right of the British Kings from Yahweh's promise to Jacob as implemented in David, the ancestor of the British Royal Family, and it pledges that all monarchs crowned on it will receive the divine guidance that Jacob received in his dream.[10]

According to tradition, which may be mixed with legend, the reddish sandstone Palestinian block came to London by a tortuous route. It was apparently carried to Egypt by Jacob's sons and was known to Scottish chroniclers as "Pharaoh's stone". When a daughter of Pharaoh, Scota, married King Gathelus of Ireland, the stone went to Spain with them and was taken to Ireland by Simon Brech, who was crowned King of Ireland c.695 BC. It was at Tara until it was returned to Jerusalem to become the capstone of the Temple. It was saved by the followers of Jeremiah (died c.570 BC) when the Temple was destroyed, and it was returned to Ireland by two daughters of the King of Judah, Tamar and Scota, who had fled to Egypt with Jeremiah. In Ireland, Tamar married Eochaidh, the chief man of Ireland who was descended from Judah's son Zarah and grandson Caled, according to Irish bards. (Judah was Jacob's fourth son and the Palestinian-British line was reinforced by this marriage.) The stone became the coronation stone of the kings of Ireland, later of the kings of Scotland, and eventually of the kings of England after it arrived in Westminster Abbey in 1296, under Edward I.[11]

Yahweh's promise to Jacob is also recalled in the lion and the unicorn which adorn the British Royal Family's coat of arms. The lion stood for the southern kingdom of Judah and the unicorn for a corrupted version of the northern kingdom of Israel's white bull in profile (which went back to the Neolithic moon-cult).[12] The unicorn is first portrayed in Assyrian reliefs after the Assyrians had overrun Israel and taken over the white bull. The lion and unicorn emblem also recalls the words of the prophet Balaam who had blessed the Israelites: "He (Yahweh) hath not beheld any iniquity in Jacob....He hath as it were the strength of a unicorn....It shall be said of Jacob and of Israel, What hath God wrought ! Behold, the people shall rise up as a great lion, and lift up himself as a young lion" (*Numbers* 23.21-24). The lion and the unicorn both represent the strength through Yahweh of Jacob and Israel, and therefore of their descendants, the British Royal Family.[13]

For the Gnostic Mandaean Light, see "The Gnostic Light", p393. For the Kabbalist Light, see p447.

Recent Light

The Western alignment of the 18th century spread to Judaism as the Haskala (rational Enlightenment) among the Ashkenazim of Central and Eastern Europe, and this had the effect of completing the Westernisation of the Sefardic Jews in Western Europe and Italy. Spinoza became a Christian – Novalis called him "God-intoxicated" – and Moses Mendelssohn (grandfather of the composer) turned away from the *Talmud* towards the West.

The Haskala dimmed the Jewish Light, and it spread to Berlin and Russia, and resulted in a reform of Judaism in Germany, and (following German-Jewish immigration in the 1840s) in America. There was a reaction, and many Jews reverted to Orthodoxy and the *Talmuds* under Elijah ben Solomon. Israel ben Eliezer, alias Ba'al Shem Tov, "master or possessor of the good name of God" (c.1700-60), began the Polish pietistic Hasidic movement which transformed the Lurianic Kabbalah and kept alive Jewish mysticism. Rabbi Baer of Mezhirich and Rabbi Levi Isaac of Berdichev contributed to this Hasidic movement.

With Zionism, the *Talmud* became important in Israel, the Soviet Union and the USA, but the Kabbalah and Hasidism have produced contemporary Jewish mystics like Abraham Isaac Kook (died 1935) whose posthumous essays are entitled *Lights of Holiness*, Martin Buber (died 1965) and Heschel (died 1972). But no one thinker has stood for the Light.

9

THE CELTIC LIGHT

The Celts were first distinguishable from the mass of Indo-Europeans c.1200 BC, when their origins can be seen in the Bronze Age Tumulus Culture in France, South Germany and South and Central Bohemia,[1] and they subsequently expanded into Ireland, Britain, the Baltic and Anatolia. The Indo-European Celts reached their height in the La Tène culture between the 5th and 1st centuries BC.[2]

In the 5th century BC they were known to the Greeks as Keltoi, and their kurgan-like barrows were found as far apart as Britain and Ireland, the middle Rhine, the Balkans and Anatolia. They had migrated to Britain in the Hallstatt period,[3] which preceded the La Tène culture. They entered Italy – hence the traditions associated with the Golden Bough, i.e. the mistletoe, near Lake Nemi[4] – and in 387 BC they plundered Rome. There were many Celtic tribes, including the Belgae (Belgians), the Helvetii (Swiss) and the Dumnonii (the Cornish in Britain), and in Caesar's day the Celts were known as the Gauls. Caesar described their sacred sites (*loci consecrati*) as woods with sacred trees (i.e. oak-trees), and there were probably no temples until the Gallo-Roman period when Druids seem to have taken over Stonehenge III,[5] which was apparently attacked and put out of action by the anti-Druid Romans.

The archaeological evidence regards the Celtic Druids as descendants of the Kurgans. They are traditionally regarded as Indo-

Europeans who took over the megaliths. They were the successors of the shamans.

The Light of Du-w as Trinity: Oak-Trees, Mistletoe and Trilithons

There is no record of the priestly order of the Celts before the 3rd century BC.[6] The Druids sacrificed to an Indo-European Sky-god and channelled the Light into public ceremonies. The Light was fundamental to the Druids' thought and rites. The Druids made the creation of man simultaneous with the creation of solar light, and a Druidic Triad says: "Three things came into being at the same moment – light, man and moral choice."[7] They saw the universe as the body of its Creator whose essence was pure mental light, and who was called *Du-w* ("the one without any darkness").[8]

This Godhead, the Yahweh-like Du-w ("Doo-weh"), eventually comprised three aspects or persons: Beli, the creator as regards the past (otherwise known as Teutates), Taran or Taranis, the controlling providence of the present, and Yesu or Esus, the renovator of the future.[9] (Beli was later identified with Apollo, and was a sun-god, while Taran was identified with Zeus-Jupiter and was a Sky-god and god of lightning, and shown with a wheel.)[10] The symbol of the Godhead was three golden rays of light (the Cymric cross), which every Druid wore in gold on the back of his robes.[11] (This has survived in the three ostrich feathers in the crest of the Prince of Wales and in the government mark known as the "broad arrow".)[12]

The Druid Trinity was also symbolized in the three white berries of the mistletoe, which grew on a parent oak-tree,[13] and the oak thus became a symbol for Du-w. *Dru-vid* is probably derived from a root which means "knowing the oak-tree" (*drus* is the Greek for "oak-tree"), the Druids' version of the shamans' World Tree; although it could come from *Dru-thin*, "a servant of Truth".[14] Yesu is identified with the oak, he is shown on an altar cutting an oak-tree, or holding a torch near an oak-tree, in the company of a bull with three cranes on its back, the legend saying *Taruos Trigaranus* ("bull with three cranes").[15]

The elder Pliny describes how Druids cut the mistletoe from the oak on the sixth of every month, and Frazer considers that Virgil's account of the Golden Bough refers to mistletoe at Lake Nemi, where La Tène Celts had expelled the Etruscans c.400 BC. The oak is the tree most commonly struck by lightning, which the Celts believed was a spark from the sun, and the Druids believed that Taran/Dyaeus Pitar (Zeus-Jupiter) came down from Heaven in the fire of a lightning flash to dwell among men in their oak-grove, in Indo-European fire-temples and in the mistletoe, which was therefore divine. It afforded a protection against lightning, and was gathered at the midwinter festival, being seen as a symbol for God's incarnation in man.[16] (The symbol of the divine lightning flash is also to be found in the Jewish Kabbalah.) At the same time Beli came down and dwelt in the bonfires that were lit for the three Druid festivals and burned out evil spirits at Samain ("End of Summer"), the Celtic Festival of the Dead on November 1, at midwinter, and at "Beltane" ("the fires of Beli"), the Celtic Festival of Fire (or Light) which took place on the eve of May 1.[17] These Druid Festivals have survived in the fires on Guy Fawkes Night and Hallowe'en, and on May Day, which recalls the time when after dancing round the phallic maypole the May Queen became the bride of the Sun-god and was sacrificed to Beli. No doubt this happened in the Cornish Helston Floral Dance, "Helston" coming from "*Hele* Stone", "stone of the sun".[18]

The Trinity of Light dominated a pantheon of four hundred Bon-type Celtic gods,[19] and the Druids reflected it in their architecture. The ineffable name of the Deity, the *Awen* (compare the Vedic *Aum* or *Om*, a sacred syllable and mantra which contained a number of Trinities) was symbolized in the rays of the sun at the Solstices and Equinoxes, in "the face of the sun and the Eye of Light", and the Druids placed three stones outside their stone circles so that the rays of the sun passed between them to a central stone.[20]

The trilithons of Stonehenge therefore came to symbolise the Trinity of Light for Druids, and the three bars of light which symbolized the Name – compare the three rays of Light in the Egyptian hieroglyph for *akhu* – were also called the Three Columns of Truth, for the Truth could not be known unless the Light of Du-w was shed on it.[21] As the Light was Du-w, the Druids counted earthly time in darkness – as nights, not days – a practice that has survived in our "fortnight" (or "fourteen nights") and the archaic "senight" for a week.[22] The Druids consecrated their temples as symbols of the Divine Name, believing that at the moment of creation God spoke his own Name, at which "germs" became matter and all creation instantly existed.

This process was symbolized in the oak-tree, whose buds became acorns, and it is likely that the acorns formed a sacred food, being ground into a flour that made small edible cakes.[23] There is a parallel with Egyptian Creation myths in which Ausares (Osiris) uttered his name, and the "Eye of Light" recalls the "Eye of Ra" and the "Eye of Horus"; two similarities which may be cited as further evidence for early Egyptian influence in the founding of Druidism.[24]

The Christianization of the British Druid Light

In the 2nd century Christianity strengthened its position by absorbing British Druidism, which meant that to the north of the Roman Empire there was a solid, growing alternative to the Roman State religion.

Christianity triumphed over Druidism in Britain in AD 156 when King Lucius formally established Christianity as Britain's national religion and consecrated a number of Arch-Druids and Druids as Archbishops and Bishops.

Both Druids and Christians now affirmed the Saviour Yesu or Esus, who fulfilled the Druids' expectations.[25] This development had begun in AD 137 when Timotheus, the other son of Claudia and Pudens, travelled from Rome to Britain to baptise his nephew Lucius, whose seat was at Winchester. Lucius was baptised either at Winchester or at Glastonbury's Chalice Well. He was known as "the Great Light" (Celtic "Lleuver Mawr"), and the Romans latinised his name to Lucius from the Latin "Lux". (Lug or Luc was the Celtic god of light who had lent his name to Lyons, Liegnitz and Leyden, and other Celtic cities.)

Lucius's achievement in being the first British king to declare Britain a Christian nation, a momentous event in the history of Western civilization, was recognised by Sabellius (AD 250): "Christianity was privately confessed elsewhere, but the first nation that proclaimed it as their religion, and called itself Christian after the name of Christ, was Britain." Genebrand wrote: "The glory of Britain consists not only in this, that she was the first country which, in a national capacity, publicly professed herself Christian, but that she made this confession when the Roman Empire itself was pagan and a cruel persecutor of Christianity." The story of Lucius is also confirmed by Bede and the *Anglo-Saxon Chronicle*, and by a tablet now in the vestry room of St Peter's Cornhill, which Lucius founded.[26]

Thus the Druid Light merged with the Light of Christianity, and of Lucius "the Great Light". Taran, who had been Romanized to Zeus/Jupiter, god of lightning and therefore of sparks from the sun, became the Holy Spirit of Beli, the Romanized Apollo, who became the Father's Light whose sparks lit the candle of Yesu, Jesus, the Christian Son. The three rays of the Druid Trinity thus became the Infinite Light (Beli), the finite intermediary (Taran), and illumined man (Yesu). The Druids now symbolized this Christian Trinity in a cross-shaped tree, on which they carved Yesu on the right branch, Beli on the left, and Taran in the centre, and the name of God, Thau (Thor), on the top.[27] Later St Patrick used the shamrock to symbolise the Christianized Trinity.[28] Jesus was readily adopted by the Yesu-worshipping Britons.[29] The Druid spring, summer and winter festivals of Beltane, white-sun-tide (summer solstice) and mid-winter became Easter, Whitsuntide and Christmas, and the Druidic law of tithes was Christianized by St Swithin, the first chancellor-bishop. Likewise, the Druid idea of Creation, in which "germs" became matter when the Creator of Light spoke his name, which had already anticipated the *Logos* or Word of St John, now fused with it.[30]

In AD 170 Lucius founded the church at Winchester which is now Winchester Cathedral. (Hence the burial there of so many later Saxon kings.) In 183 he asked Bishop Eleutherius in Rome for the return of British missionaries who had been taught at Glastonbury, and as a result Elfan, Dyfan and Fagan were made Bishops. They visited Glastonbury, where,

Geoffrey of Monmouth writes (c.1135), "they found an old church built, as it was said, by the hands of Christ's disciples...and afterwards pondered the Heavenly message that the Lord has specially chosen this spot before the rest of Britain as the place where his Mother's name might be invoked. They also found the whole story in ancient writings, how the Holy Apostles were scattered throughout the world. St Philip coming into France with a host of disciples sent twelve of them into Britain to preach, and that there, taught by revelation, they constructed the said chapel which the Son of God afterwards dedicated to the honour of his Mother: and that to these same twelve were given portions of land for their sustenance. Moreover, they found a written record of their doings." From this account it seems that Philip's arrival preceded Jesus's, and it may be that Geoffrey of Monmouth was given a garbled version of what happened. Lucius eventually died in 201.[31]

The Marginalizing of the Celtic Light

The "Dark Ages" was an 18th-century term for the early medieval time in Western Europe when there was no emperor in the West: 476-800. It more loosely came to apply to c.500-1000 when urban life disappeared in the face of warfare, and there was an intellectual darkness and barbarism.[32] During this time, Christian civilization was pressed by waves of invaders, particularly in Celtic Britain where first the Saxons, and then the Danes (the Northmen or Norsemen) spread the Germanic-Scandinavian tradition.

The invaders dispersed the Celtic Church. There were Celtic monasteries in South Wales, Cornwall, Devon, Somerset and Brittany, and St Piran arrived in Cornwall from Ireland in the 6th century AD. His oratory – the oldest Christian building in Cornwall – and his stone cross can still be seen at Perranzabuloe.[33]

King Arthur, a Roman Briton if he was in fact historical and not legendary, seems to have led the Celtic resistance to the Germanic invaders[34] – according to some he led the Welsh, according to others he was based in Somerset and was associated with Cornwall where Tristan's stone still stands near Fowey – and he is reputed to have fought twelve battles and to have achieved a famous victory at Badon in 516 before he was defeated and killed at the battle of Camlann in 537. (It is interesting that the battling King Arthur was a contemporary of the battling Beowulf, who has been dated by Gwyn Jones in *A History of the Vikings* to c.521 when Hygelac, King of the Geats, perhaps Jutes, was killed in battle against the Frisians, or Franks, and when Hrothgar lived in Heorot at Lejre, now Gamle Lejre, in Danish Zealand, where in the 10th century a Viking chieftan was buried in a ship-shaped grave.) A Christian who stood for the Celtic Christian Light, King Arthur seems to have made Avalon (Glastonbury) his spiritual centre because of Glastonbury's legendary connection with Jesus (who is reputed to have lived there before his ministry, having first visited Britain by ship with his guardian Joseph of Arimathaea – see "The British Druid Light", pp380-383). He was reputedly buried at Glastonbury; his standard was the cross, he carried the image of the Virgin Mary into battle, and like Germanus, bishop of Gaul who led the Britons against the marauding Picts, Scots and Saxons in 429, he used "Alleluia" as his call.[35]

There were more invaders between 550 and 600, and the Celtic Britons were driven to the west country and Wales. The Germanic tribes now called themselves "the nation of the English" and it was to their overlord of Kent, Aethelberht that Augustine of Canterbury was sent by Gregory in 597 on a mission from Rome which reconverted Kent and South-East Britain. We shall see that Augustine of Canterbury found evidence of an early Celtic Church at Glastonbury (see pp383-384); he also found Roman-Celtic communities who had retained their faith despite being conquered by the barbarian Saxons, and who resented Augustine's presence as an insult to their faith.[36]

Slowly the Germanic-Scandinavian settlers were Christianized – converted to the Roman Light of Gregory, which emerged from the Dark Ages to illumine Europe. Missionaries from Kent converted Northumbria in 627 and East Anglia in 630, and Celtic missionaries arrived in Northumbria from Iona. Canterbury was now the centre of the Roman reconversion of Britain and it rose in importance. According to Bede, in 656, after Pope Vitalian wrote to the British King Oswy – the letter still exists[37] – the remains of St Peter, St John and St Paul were all apparently taken from Rome to Canterbury and buried there.

From 653 the Celtic Church converted the rest of Britain in some 30 years, and by 687 the last heathen stronghold had been Christianized. From c.690, the Germanic settlers began to convert the continental Germans, with whom they felt a racial and cultural affinity. Wilibrord led the way, and by 732 Germany had its own archbishop (Boniface). Ireland (which had escaped the barbarian invasions) advanced British scholarship. The Irish Celtic monasteries grew into centres of learning from the 6th century onwards, the foremost being at Clonmacnoise, and illuminated Irish manuscripts included the *Book of Kells* (8th-9th centuries AD). Northumbrian scholarship produced Bede (c.672-735), who was pro-Roman.

Communications in the Dark Ages were so poor that knowledge of the role of the early Celtic Church was not available to Bede in the early 8th century. The father of English history devotes a mere two pages to the years between 60 BC and AD 156, does not mention Caractacus or his family's links with Rome, Linus, St Patrick or even King Arthur; he does however give 62 pages to the life and miracles of St Cuthbert who lived at Lindisfarne, which Bede visited. After Bede's time, the Celtic Church was driven into the mountains of Wales and Scotland, and to Iona, Cornwall, Devon, Somerset and Brittany; it survived in Ireland which escaped the Saxon raids, but many churches, monasteries and illuminated manuscripts were destroyed.[38]

The Irish Celtic phase of the Celtic civilization seems to have begun with the Culdees. The Irish raided the west coast of Britain, Wales and Scotland during the 4th century AD when Roman power weakened in Britain, and there may have been missions to the Irish in the 4th century, like St Germanus's mission of 431, before St Patrick's 5th-century mission to Ireland. (Patrick had earlier been captured at a Roman villa in Britain by Irish raiders and spent seven years in slavery in Ireland, according to his *Confessio.*) The Irish Celtic phase of the Celtic civilization grew through the monasticism of the 6th and 7th centuries AD, when Irish works (for example, on the lives of the saints) replaced the Latin works of the Christian schools.

The Irish Celtic phase of the Celtic civilization declined during the invasions of the Norsemen from 795 to 920.[39] There was a sense of relief and renewal from 968 to 1014, but the Norman Western European church reform movement, another foreign influence, reorganised Ireland into dioceses After 1066 the Celtic Church was driven underground, where it resentfully awaited a pretext to express its anti-Roman feelings, which eventually championed the Protestant Reformation.

10

The Iranian Light

The Indo-Europeans who settled in Europe, possibly after being displaced from Akkad after c.2350 BC,[1] also settled in Iran c.2250 BC, and Iranian Mithraism probably dates from c.1700 BC, and certainly predates c.1500 BC when Indo-Europeans migrated from Iran to the Indus Valley.[2] The Indo-European Iranians symbolized the Light in fire to which they made sacrifices and in return received the wisdom of the "Wise Lord", Ahura Mazda, who represented the source of the Light.

The Iranian civilization began with the Elamites in Khuzistan. The Old, Middle and Neo-Elamite periods spanned from c.2700 to c.639 BC, in the course of which Elam was first conquered by, and then overthrew, the 3rd dynasty of Ur. Although the Indo-European Iranians arrived c.2250 BC, it was not until the Iron Age – during which, at least from c.1380 BC, their gods were Mitra (Indian, Mithras in Iranian), Varuna and Indra,[3] all of which occur in the Indian *Rig Veda* – that they rose to become the Medes and the Persians.

The Medes rose to power in the 8th-6th centuries BC: the Magi were their traditional priests, Zurvan was their god, and Median fire-altars were known from c.550 BC; the best known being the ancient Gushnasp fire at Siz (the symbol of Median monarchic and religious unity).[4]

The Persians rose at the Medes' expense from the 7th century BC and became great through Cyrus, the conqueror of Babylon, and his

Achaemenid successors who attacked Egypt and Greece. Ahura Mazda was the god of the Achaemenid kings, and Zoroastrianism may have been the religion of Cyrus the Great, was probably the religion of Darius I, and was certainly the religion of Xerxes, the invader of Greece.[5]

ZOROASTER'S LIGHT: THE SACRED FIRE, FIRE-SACRIFICES AND THE MAGI

The Zoroastrian Light has a long tradition that is regarded dualistically, in terms of darkness. There may have been more than one Zoroaster (Zoroaster is the Greek for the Persian Zarathustra), and the dates of the last Zoroaster are subject to conjecture. The oldest classical writers placed his life between 6000 and 1000 BC, and a 4th century BC Babylonian put it c.2000 BC. Today scholars put his life somewhere between 660 and 500 BC.[6]

Zoroaster saw himself as a messenger of Ahura Mazda, the god of the Achaemenian Kings,[7] the Lord of Light and supreme god who had created the twin spirits of light and darkness (Spenta Mainyu and Angra Mainyu), and who was therefore the source of the alternative vision of light and darkness. Zoroaster hoped for a Saviour who would ensure the victory of light, good and truth over darkness and evil, which were designated under one general term, *The Lie*.[8]

It seems that Zoroaster had access to a very ancient tradition, the religion of the Indo-Iranians or -Aryans, which has not survived. It can, however, be reconstructed from common elements in the sacred books of Iran and India, the *Avesta* and the *Vedas*, and one principal element is Mithras (Indian Mitra) and the cult of fire.[9]

The *Avesta* that survives is a fragment of the whole – only the fourth part of the Sasanian Avesta (3rd-7th centuries AD) survived the Arab conquest of Iran in the 7th century AD – and the *Gathas* ("songs" or "odes") are ascribed to Zoroaster himself (c.7th century BC), and are for the most part in the *Yasna*, the prayer book of the Zoroastrians. Zoroaster is strangely silent about Mithras.[10] The later *Yashts* ("sacrificial hymns") are polytheistic and close to the Indo-Aryan *Rig Veda* – Zoroaster rebelled against the polytheism of the *Vedas*, and the *Yashts* return to ideas he repudiated – and the *Vendidad* or *Videvdat* ("law against demons") is a treatise on ritual impurity. The last *Avesta* on which the Pahlavi (Parthian, a dialect of Middle Persian) books are based was completed by the 4th century AD, and much of it was written by the Persian Magi, the Druid-like priestly caste which followed Zoroaster and served several religions. Mithras is mentioned in the late *Avesta*.[11]

The Light appears in the old Indo-Aryan parts of the *Avesta* which are reflected in the *Yashts*. *Yasht* 22 is addressed to Ahura Mazda: "Glory to you, O Mazda! Lo, I turn from dazzling visions of your home of light and find me weary in the strife again.... Yet in the sacred Fire I pray you let my waking thoughts recall sights that can soothe and strengthen....I passed the Heavens Three...and soared to the place of Everlasting Light." And the fourth step of the soul of the faithful man "placed him in the Endless Lights" (also *Yasht* 22).

The *Gathas* are in an obscure language, and so appear in numerous versions. They are addressed to "the Wise One" or "Wise Lord" (Ahura Mazda), and *Yasna* 30, perhaps the most often quoted *Gatha*, starts: "Now will I speak to those who will hear of the things which the initiate should remember; the praises and prayer of the Good Mind to the Lord and the joy which he shall see in the Light who has remembered them well." Again from the *Gathas* (c.7th century BC): "And the wise walk on the side of Light, while the unwise follow the other until they grow wise.... O Mighty Lord of Wisdom, Mazada! Supreme, Infinite, Universal Mind! Ahura! you that give Life to all! Grant me the power to control this mind, this Lower Mind of mine, this egoism, and put an end to all Duality, and gain the reign of One – as is desired." (32.16). *Gatha* 33 speaks of "the man who is the best towards the righteous saint...having light", and it is clear from the above passages that the "Light" was a "vision" of illumination that was "seen" and which could affect the mind.

The Light that could be "seen" was also the power that governed the universe in the Iranian tradition. Ahura Mazda produced the material of man from light, according to the *Dadistan-i-Dinik*, and in the early *Gathas* he is shown as opposing Angra Mainyu (Evil Spirit), the twin-spirit of

Spenta Mainyu (Good Spirit), both of which he created.[12] There was thus a fundamental dualism in the Iranian tradition, with the Light embodying all that was good. In the later Mazdaean literature, The Lie (the world of Angra Mainyu) emerged in Ahriman, the fore-runner of Satan, who existed independently of Ahura Mazda, and the Magi completed the widening split between the Light and Darkness by combining Ahura Mazda and Spenta Mainyu into Ohrmazd or Ormuzd (a corruption from Ahura Mazda), and dividing the universe into two balanced creations, that of Ohrmazd and that of Ahriman.[13]

The Magi (the Persian *magu* and Indian *magha* mean "gifts" or "riches", suggesting that the priestly Magi received the gift or grace of God, or the Light)[14] were originally Light-worshippers, and they appear as such in the *New Testament* to hail Jesus as an embodiment of their "Wise Lord": the "wise men from the east" (*Matthew* 2.1) are *Magoi* in the Greek, (the plural of *magos* which is the Greek for *magu*). They taught the Light in Chaldean mystery schools[15] – the Chaldeans ruled Mesopotamia in the 8th and 7th centuries BC until the Persian Cyrus the Great conquered Chaldean Babylon and brought the Magi there – and only later turned to "magic", the laws of the world of Ahriman.[16]

The universe of Light was made to go round by fire-sacrifices throughout the Zoroastrian tradition, and the Divine Light was the essential symbol of the Iranian religion, as it was for all the Indo-Europeans and the Hindus. The Light as Fire was kept burning in the altars and was never allowed to go out, and later the Fire-altars developed into Fire-temples where a sacred meal or Mass was celebrated, for example the Fire-temple at Naqsh-e-Rostam near Persepolis.[17]

Mithras

Mithra, or Mithras, and the Persian Earth Goddess Anahita were worshipped in Western Iran,[18] especially in Hellenistic times, but were not accepted by Zoroaster.

Mithras took the side of the Sun in helping the Iranian god of light, Ahura Mazda in his battle with the powers of darkness, which were under

Angra Mainyu or Ahriman. In the myth, Ahura Mazda's first creation was a wild bull. Mithras was born from a rock fully grown and carrying a torch and a knife. He wrestled with the bull and carried it to a cave but the bull escaped. The Sun sent the Raven to look for it and Mithras found it and killed it with his knife, reflecting the replacement of the lunar bull cult by the post-Neolithic solar cult. From the flesh and blood of the bull (the Primal Bull) sprang creation, and the Sun acknowledged Mithras's supremacy.[19]

As a result, Mithras, from being a subordinate, became the central deity in a new Fire-centred religion, and in both the Vedic and Iranian versions he is the genius of celestial Light who sees everything, like Shamash, and is therefore the god of truth.

The king embodied Mithras.[20] In later Roman times the emperor was *felix* because he was illumined by Mithras's divine Grace, and an inextinguishable fire constantly burned in a lamp in the Caesars' palace as it did on the hearth of every Mithraeum, a cult of fire that symbolized Mithras's celestial Light:[21] being divine, the Caesars were incarnations of the Mithraic Light,[22] just as the Pharaohs had been incarnations of Ra, and Mithras was *Sol Invictus*, "the invisible sun", having been equated with Shamash and Helios.[23]

Initiation took place in mountain caverns or in subterranean vaults, and after descending to the crypt the neophyte found himself in a brilliantly illuminated sanctuary where there were flashes of light.[24] There was an open pit-like tomb before the altar of the Mithraeum, above which there was a figure of Mithras slaying the bull, and the neophyte was buried in this tomb to symbolise the death of his sinful nature and his rebirth as an Illuminatus.[25] As in the Attis Mysteries a lattice was put across the pit and a bull was slaughtered. Its blood gushed down onto the neophyte below, who drank some of it to obtain the courage and strength of the bull, and the Primal Bull's gift of divine or eternal life.[26]

The central Mystery concerned the battle between light and darkness for the immortal soul of the neophyte, and there were seven degrees of initiation into the Mysteries of Mithras, which has led to Mithraism's being called the Freemasonry of the ancient world.[27] The oldest degrees were those of the Raven and of the Lion, by the last of which the initiate was fully illumined. The initiation ceremony symbolized the process of illumination and enabled individuals to become Mithras and experience the Light that bestows eternity.[28]

In both Zoroastrianism and Mithraism the Light represented the Truth, the Light which would burn up The Lie (later Ahriman).[29] More than this, as fire the Light actually did burn up The Lie. Moreover, as the sun was the source of the undying Fire,[30] the sacrificial lighting of a fire actually helped to make the sunrise and the universe (which was composed of light and of Agni's lightning and fire) go round. Thus, the *Khorshed Yasht* links the sun-god Mithra and Ahura Mazda as the Lord of Truth and records a sacrifice to the sun in the words, "I will sacrifice unto Mithra." The sacrifice would have burned The Lie and lit the universe. *Yasna* I is likewise addressed to "the Fire of Ahura Mazda", and the Pahlavi texts advise, "Go three times a day to the Fire Temple and do homage to the Fire; for he who makes a habit of doing homage to the Fire Temple and of doing homage to the Fire, will be blessed with a greater share of both worldly wealth and of holiness."[31] The homage to the Fire would have burned The Lie or Ahriman and set the homage-doer in the "holy" direction of the Iranian after-life, which was "Endless Light where is all bliss".[32]

The same outlook must have been present among the fire-worshipping Iranian Scythians from North of the Black Sea, who flourished between the 7th century BC and the 2nd century AD.[33] The Scythians worshipped a Great Goddess of Fire and sun god, Tabiti-Hestia, an Earth Mother[34] who was worshipped in South Russia long before the Scythians appeared there from Central Asia. As the Scythian magicians (Magi) were born with high-pitched voices, a feminine characteristic, because Magi had plundered the shrine of the Great Goddess of Fire at Ascalon, and as a false diviner was burned to death by the Fire with his male relatives on a cart loaded with brushwood, it is likely that the Scythian Light as Fire also represented the Truth (*and* the source of occult knowledge), and that it too, burned The Lie.[35] The Iranian Sarmatians, who were South European Russians and flourished between the 4th century BC and the 4th century AD, were also fire-worshippers,[36] and they sacrificed horses to their fire-god, who must also have embodied Truth and the Light as Fire that burned The Lie.

The Achaemenian empire was conquered by Alexander, and for a while Iranian religion was submerged by Hellenism. It re-emerged during the 1st century BC showing syncretistic Greek-Iranian blends: Zeus Oromazda (i.e. Auramazda or Ahura Mazda), Apollo Mithra, and Helios Hermes.[37]

After the rise and fall of Parthia, Iran entered the Sasanian period from AD c.224. Zoroastrianism, purged of its Greek blending, became the official state religion.[38] The Sasanian coins show a crowned king on one side and a fire- altar on the other side, with the legend "Fire of Ardashir" or "Fire of Shapur"; as we shall see, Zoroastrians never revered fire for itself, but only as a symbol of truth. The best known Zoroastrian fire-altar was the Farnbag fire, which was at Khwarezm until the 6th century BC, wherr it was transported to Kabulistan by Zoroaster's protector Veshtaspa; in the 6th century AD Khosrow I took it to the sanctuary of Karigan in Fars.[39]

It was Zoroastrians who condemned and crucified Mani, who challenged their religion. See "The Manichaeist Light", p410.

11

The European Light

During the centuries following the fall of Rome, the Germanic barbarians triumphed throughout the Roman provinces – the Goths and Ostrogoths in Italy, the Franks in Gaul, the Visigoths in Spain, the Vandals in Africa, the Angles and Saxons in Britain – and in the West civilised urban life disappeared as raiding invaders brought insecurity and intellectual darkness.

Amazingly, a transitional period followed in which the Germanic-Scandinavian barbarian tribes turned into the Christian Germans of the Holy Roman Empire and laid the foundation for the European civilization, which can therefore be seen as the flowering in Europe of the culture of the descendants of the "barbarians" who sacked Rome.

The New Testament Jesus: the Transfiguration and Parables of Light

The European Light of the post-Roman "barbarians" was based on the Biblical Jesus and was associated with Christianity. The Light was fundamental to the Jesus of the *New Testament Gospels*.

The Three Synoptic *Gospels*, the three that give a "synopsis" of the events of Jesus's life, all reveal a ministry that took place between the winter of AD 26 and the spring of 29 (assuming that Jesus was born in 4 BC, the year in which Herod died, and that he was in fact thirty in Luke 3.23 which records "And Jesus himself began to be about thirty years of age").[1]

The central event of these three *Gospels* is Jesus's transfiguration by the Light in AD c.28, when (according to Mark) Yahweh spoke out of a "cloud", saying "This is my beloved Son: hear him" (9. 2-8). The three Gospels look back some forty years or more after the event. *Mark* is the earliest, AD c.65, and there is tradition that Mark was Peter's secretary, and that Peter was a source. Matthew (AD c.70-80) and Luke (AD c.80 or possibly AD 83) both draw on *Mark* – Matthew has about 600 of Mark's 661 verses, while Luke has 350 – but they probably also draw on another source known as Q (German *Quelle*, "source") as well as on their own separate sources.

On the evidence of his teachings, Jesus knew the Light before the transfiguring experience which traditionally took place on Mount Tabor. The mystic begins as a flawed human being who is breached by a little Light and he is then slowly "divinised" until the original human personality has been replaced by a divine personality. Such a process of "divinisation" seems to have been completed in Jesus during his transfiguration on Mount Tabor, which was witnessed by Mark's possible source, Peter, and two other disciples. In Mark's version "his raiment became shining, exceeding white as snow" and he communed with Elijah and Moses before God spoke from a cloud. In Matthew, "his face did shine as the sun, and his raiment was white as the light" (17.2), and in *Luke* "the fashion of his countenance was altered, and his raiment was white and glistering" (9.29). "Transfiguration" is a change of form or appearance, as a result of which a person is elevated, glorified or deified, and in modern terminology, Jesus entered into divine union. The Light shone through him and eliminated the last traces of his worldly self, leaving him purely divine or divinised, and giving the effect of a halo, brightening his aura; a phenomenon that can be observed when a *guru* enters divine union today,[2] and which is commemorated in Eastern Christianity's worship of the deified halo.

The idea of transfiguring Light is central to Jesus's message in the *New Testament.* It occurs in the Sermon on the Mount (AD 27): "Ye are the light of the world. A city that is set on a hill cannot be hid. Neither do men light a candle, and put it under a bushel (i.e. stone measuring pot), but on a candlestick; and it giveth light unto all that are in the house. Let your light so shine before men, that they may see your good works" (*Matthew* 5.14-15).

It is the Light to which Jesus refers as the Kingdom of God in *Luke*: "The kingdom of God cometh not with observation: neither shall they say, Lo here! or, lo there! for, behold, the kingdom of God is within you.... And they shall say to you, See here; or, see there; go not after them, nor follow them. For as the lightning, that lighteneth out of the one part under heaven, shineth unto the other part under heaven; so shall the Son of man be in his day" (17.20-4). This is the familiar idea that the Light cannot be seen by external sense perception, and is neither "here" nor "there" in the outer world.

It is the Light to which Jesus refers in: "Come unto me all ye that labour and are heavy laden, and I will give you rest. Take my yoke upon you" (i.e. the Law, for the Rabbis spoke of 'the yoke of the law' of loving one's neighbour).... For my yoke is easy (i.e. it is love) and my burden is light (i.e. unheavy as it is light that dispels darkness)" (*Matthew* 11.28-30). Jesus means that all who find the Law as expounded by the scribes and Pharisees too difficult to keep will find the love of the Kingdom of God, the Light, an easy way to live, a burden as unheavy as light.

The Synoptic *Gospels* are full of images for the Light, and because a great teacher or Master has to address his words to men who are at different levels of development, and speak to both beginners and the advanced at the same time, Jesus presented these images in the form of parables. The beginners would take the outer husk or shell of the parable, and find some truth that applied to them, while the advanced seekers would take the inner kernel or nut and would understand a truth about the secret Light. Or, as Jesus himself puts it (*Mark* 4.11-12): "Unto you (i.e. the advanced) it is given to know the mystery of the kingdom of God: but unto them that are without, all these things are done in parables: that seeing they may see and not perceive; and hearing they may hear, and not understand; lest at any time they should be converted."

Thus the Light is called mustard seed: "The kingdom of heaven is like to a grain of mustard seed, which a man took and sowed in his field", the "least of all seeds" which grows into "the greatest among herbs, and becometh a tree in which the "birds of the air" lodge. (*Matthew* 13.31-2) Or, it requires one grain of the Light to be sown in the soul for the personality to be transformed and put in harmony with all Nature.

The Light is like a "treasure hid in a field", the field being the spiritual, invisible Kingdom of Heaven, and the man who finds it "hideth" it and "selleth all that he hath", renounces the material world, "and buyeth that field", devotes himself to the spiritual life so that he can know the treasure of the Light (*Matthew* 13.44). Similarly, the Light is like "one pearl of great price" for which a "merchant man" sells all that he has, i.e. gives up the material world to possess it (*Matthew* 13.45-6).

The Light is like the penny that each labourer received in the parable of the vineyard (*Matthew* 20). Each labourer receives the same Light from God, the "householder", whether he joined the work at the beginning of the day, or at the third, sixth or ninth hour. Those who see the Light late in their lives are the "chosen", as opposed to those who have been "called" early. Likewise, those who are "chosen" to attend a wedding from the highways and byways (see the Light late) have as much chance of entering Heaven as those guests who were called – so long as they make the effort of wearing a wedding garment (adapting themselves to the Light) (*Matthew* 22).

All have the potentiality to see the Light if they make the effort and double their "talents" or potentiality for the Light, Jesus suggests in the parable of the talents (*Matthew* 25). So, the servant who buries his talent and makes no effort is cast "into outer darkness" (i.e. the darkness of the outer world in contrast to the Light of the inner world), while the servants who "hath" potentiality for the Light are given still more potentialities, and have "abundance": to see the Light once leads to seeing it in abundance. The same message is contained in the parable of the sower (e.g. *Mark* 4) which concludes with the idea that those who receive seed of the Light with a receptive heart will see the Light in abundance, "some thirtyfold (i.e. thirty times), some sixty and some an hundred".

Again and again, the message of the parables is that one should be ready to receive the Light, like the five virgins who were wise enough to fill their lamps with oil and who were ready when the Bridegroom called to take them to the marriage, whereas the five foolish virgins missed the ceremony as they were out buying oil at the last minute (*Matthew* 25). It is also the message that it is never too late to see the Light. Thus the prodigal son is welcomed with rejoicing, for men can see the Light despite a riotous youth and enjoy its benefits just as much as an elder brother who has never "transgressed" (*Luke* 15).

The lost sheep and the lost coin also represent the sinner who sees the Light (*Luke* 15), as does "the unjust steward" who is commended by the rich man, God (*Luke* 16). The Light is the narrow gate in *Luke* (13.24): "Strive to enter in at the strait gate: for many, I say unto you, will seek to enter in, and shall not be able." The same idea occurs after the parable of the rich young ruler: "It is easier for a camel to go through the eye of a needle (i.e. a very narrow gate in Jerusalem), than for a rich man to enter into the kingdom of God", i.e. turn away from the outer world and his riches and see the Light (*Matthew* 19.23).

It was because all the parables are about the Light that Jesus was so exasperated with his disciples in AD 27 for not understanding the parable of the sower: "Know ye not this parable? and how then will ye know all parables?" (*Mark* 4.13). Jesus believed "He that hath ears to hear, let him hear" (*Mark* 4.9), but he also expected his main point to get across to his most intimate followers, who ought to have had the ears to hear.

Jesus's teachings about the Light are summed up in the Sermon on the Mount: "Lay up for yourselves treasures in heaven.... The light of the body is the eye: if therefore thine eye be single, thy whole body shall be full of light. But if thine eye be evil, thy whole body shall be full of darkness. If therefore the light that is in thee be darkness, how great is that darkness!" (*Matthew* 7.20-3). Luke adds at the end of a similar passage: "Take heed therefore that the light which is in thee be not darkness. If thy whole body therefore be full of light, having no part dark, the whole shall be full of light, as when the bright shining of a candle doth give thee light" (11.35-6). The eye which must be single is the inner eye, the third eye of Hinduism which is painted in the middle of the Indian forehead, when the Light is seen. It is possible that it was to the Light that Jesus cried out on the cross, "My God, my God, why hast thou forsaken me?" (*Mark* 15.34); that he looked for the Light but, in his agony, was too painfully aware of his body to see it, and found only darkness.

Jesus as the Gnostic Light of the World, God as Light

St John's Gospel of Light (later than the three Synoptic *Gospels*, AD c.100) presents a very different view of the Jesus of AD 26-29. For one thing, the eschatology which the Synoptic *Gospels* promised is fulfilled, and eternal life is already present; for another thing, the Christology is emphasised through a number of "I am" pronouncements, the most famous being: "I am the light of the world: he that followeth me shall not walk in darkness, but shall have the light of life"; and "As long as I am in the world, I am the light of the world" (8.12 and 9.5).

John was engaged in a defence of Christianity against the early Gnostics, and he associates Jesus with the Light of the *gnosis* to attract Gnostics to Christianity. He therefore moves away from the historical Jesus and sees the fountain of light in the soul as the Light that is Jesus, and makes Jesus say as much. Jesus therefore sees both bread and wine as the Light in texts which have influenced the Christological Mass and Communion service: "I am that bread of life.... If any man eat of this bread he shall live for ever.... Except ye eat the flesh of the Son of man, and drink his blood, ye have no life in you. Who so eateth my flesh, and drinketh my blood, hath eternal life" (6.48-54); and "I am the true vine, and my Father is the husbandman.... I am the vine, ye are the branches" (15.1,5).

The other "I am" pronouncements are all about the Light: Jesus is the good shepherd, the resurrection and life, "the way, the truth and the life" but by whom no man cometh unto the Father (14.6), and he is the door of the sheepfold: "I am the door: by me if any man enter in, he shall be saved, and shall go in and out, and find pasture (10.9)".

The Light is seen as water: "Whosoever drinketh of this water shall thirst again: but whosoever drinketh of the water that I shall give him shall never thirst; but the water (i.e. Light) that I shall give him shall be in him a well of water springing up into everlasting life" (4.13-14); and "If any man thirst, let him come unto me, and drink. He that believeth on me, as the scripture hath said, out of his belly shall flow rivers of living water (i.e. Light)" (7.37).

The Light is also a grain of wheat (though Jesus is also thinking of his impending death) in a passage we have already quoted: "Verily, verily, I say unto you, except a corn of wheat fall into the ground and die, it abideth alone: but if it die, it bringeth forth much fruit. He that loveth his life shall lose it (i.e. the Light); and he that hateth his life in this world shall keep it (i.e. the Light) unto life eternal. If any man serve me, let him follow me.... Yet a little while is the light with you. Walk while ye have the light, lest darkness come upon you: for he that walketh in darkness knoweth not whither he goeth. While ye have light, believe in the light, that ye may be the children of light" (12.24-6,35-6).

Jesus is the Light of the World in *St John's Gospel* because God is Light: "He that believeth on me, believeth not on me, but on him that sent me. And he that seeth me seeth him that sent me (i.e. the Light/God). I am come a light into the world, that whosoever believeth on me should not abide in darkness. And if any man hear my words, and believe not, I judge him not: for I came not to judge the world, but to save the world (i.e. from darkness)" (12.44-8). This vision of God as Light, which would have appealed to the Gnostics, begins *St John's Gospel* of Light: "In him (i.e. God) was life; and the life was the light of men. And the light shineth in darkness; and the darkness comprehendeth it not. There was a man sent from God, whose name was John. The same came for a witness, to bear witness of the Light, that all men through him might believe. He was not that Light (i.e. God) but was sent to bear witness of that Light. That was the true Light, which lighteth every man that cometh into the world" (1.4-10).

A man must be reborn to see the Light of God: "Except a man be born again, he cannot see the Kingdom of God.... The wind bloweth where it listeth (wishes), and thou hearest the sound thereof, but canst not tell whence it cometh nor whither it goeth: so is every one that is born of the Spirit" (3.3,8). The origin of the spiritual life, then, is as mysterious as the origin of the wind, but all too few are reborn to the Light: "And this is the condemnation, that light is come into the world, and men loved darkness rather than the light.... He that doeth truth cometh to the light" (3.19,21).

The transformation of Jesus from a preacher of the Light in the Synoptic *Gospels* to the Light of the World in *John* is accompanied by an identification of Jesus with the Paschal Lamb, the Lamb of God; for in *St John's Gospel* Jesus is crucified on the same day that the Jewish Passover lamb was sacrificed. It is therefore as well to leave *St John's Gospel* to one side in seeking to obtain a historical view of Jesus (while appreciating John's response to the Light), and the view of Jesus in the Synoptic *Gospels* can then be seen to accord with the view of Jesus in the Essene Gospels – so long as we grant that he was born of a "woman", the "Virgin" beginning as a mistranslation into Greek (*parthenos*) for the Hebrew *alma* of *Isaiah* 7.14 ("Behold a young woman shall conceive and bear a son, and shall call his name Immanuel").

St Paul's Blinding Light: the Gentilised Light in the 'Epistles'

St Paul's work took place against this background of Christian-Roman enmity. His name Paulus was a Romanized form of the Jewish Saul; he was a Jew who trained as a Rabbi and had a knowledge of the *Midrash* (Jewish interpretations of the scriptures). He recognised that Jesus was a threat to Pharisaic Judaism and headed a kind of *Gestapo* that persecuted Christians[3] until his conversion AD c.35. It seems that he never met Jesus.[4] He spent two weeks with Peter and James in Jerusalem, and then returned to his native Cilicia. From AD 47 to 55 he was based in Antioch, and the Roman world empire gave him the model for a vision of a Universal Church commonwealth, just as today our vision of a world-wide civilization offers a model for a world-wide religion. His letters ("epistles") pre-date the *Gospels* and form a third of the *New Testament.* After three dramatic missionary journeys, during which his training as a tentmaker would have stood him in good stead, he was arrested in Jerusalem and finally brought to Rome in AD c.60. He was martyred (probably beheaded) some time before the death of Nero, alias Satan ("enemy"), in AD 68.

The account of St Paul's experience of the Light AD c.35 appears in Acts, which can be dated to AD c.85 (after *Luke*, and, some say, by Luke): "And as he journeyed, he came near Damascus:and suddenly there shined round about him a light from heaven: and he fell to the earth, and heard a voice saying to him, Saul, Saul, why persecutest thou me?" (9.3) He was "three days without sight". Paul later described it to Agrippa: "At midday, O king, I saw in the way a light from heaven, above the brightness of the sun, shining round about me" (26.13). At the same time Paul heard Jesus say that he now sent him to the Gentiles "to open their eyes, and to turn them from darkness to light" (26.17-18).

Consequently in due course, in AD c.46, Paul and Barnabas told the Jews at Antioch: "It was necessary that the word of God should first have been spoken to you: but seeing ye put it from you, and judge yourselves unworthy of everlasting life, lo, we turn to the Gentiles. For so hath the Lord commanded us, saying, I have set thee to be a light of the Gentiles" (13.46-7). This accords with Jesus's last words, according to Matthew, "Go ye therefore, and teach all nations" (28.19); and also with Isaiah's prophecy (60.1-3) that the new Jerusalem would shine; for thy light is come.... And the Gentiles shall come to thy light."

Until this decision to "Gentilise" the Light, which came ten years after the expulsion of Joseph of Arimathaea's party on an oarless boat in AD 36, Christianity had been regarded as a movement within Judaism, and the first people to be called "Christians" were Jews at Antioch (*Acts* 11. 19,26). The oldest of the *New Testament* writings are the letters of St Paul, which were written between AD 52 and 65, and the earliest letter, which may even be dated to AD 49 – the first letter to a Gentile church, the *First Epistle to the Thessalonians* – echoes the Essene "Children of Light" (see pp363-364ff): "The day of the lord so cometh as a thief in the night.... But ye, bretheren, are not in darkness, that that day should overtake you as a thief. Ye are all the children of light, and the children of the day: we are not of the night, nor of darkness" (I *Thess* 5.2, 4-5).

Just as the Essene Dead Sea Scroll, *The War of the Sons of Light Against the Sons of Darkness* described the conflict between the Essene "Sons of Light" and the Jews and Gentiles ("Sons of darkness"), a conflict in which the Sons of Light would conquer the world with the aid of the Angels; so the early Christians, both Jews and Gentiles, were people of darkness who could become "children of light". This idea is to be found in the later writings of the *New Testament,* for instance in the *Epistle to the Ephesians* (early 2nd century AD): "Henceforth walk not as other Gentiles walk...having the understanding darkened, being alienated from the life of God through the ignorance that is in them...For ye were sometimes darkness, but now ye are light in the Lord: walk as children of light" (4.17-18; 5.8). Paul seems to have adapted the Essene vision and applied it to Christian Gentiles, and his drive to make Christianity a Gentile religion was helped by the fall of Jerusalem two years after his death, in AD 70, and the dispersal of the Jews.

Again and again, the Light is behind the words of St Paul, and of his successors, to the Gentiles. Paul's early letters see "the mysteries of God" in terms of the Light, notably the *First Epistle to the Corinthians* (AD c.53-54): "Know ye not that ye are the temple of God, and the the Spirit of God (i.e. the Light) dwelleth in you? (3.16).... Therefore judge nothing before the time, until the Lord come, who...will bring to light the hidden things of darkness" (4.1,5). In their lives, human beings see an obscured reflection of reality (God) as in a small mirror, but the time will come, Paul says, when they shall see that reality (God) is the Light: "For now we see through a glass darkly; but then face to face: now I know in part; but then shall I know even as also I am known (i.e. I shall know the whole of God, the Light)" (13.23).

In the *Epistle to the Philippians* (AD c.53-54) Paul says that the Christians of Philippi "shine as lights in the world" (2.15), and in the *Second Epistle to the Corinthians* (AD c.55) "God, who commanded the light to shine out of darkness, hath shined in our hearts, to give the light of the knowledge of the glory of God in the face of Jesus Christ" (4.6); while "Satan himself is transformed into an angel of light" (11.14).

Paul later records a presumably autobiographical mystical experience of the Light in terms of the third heaven: "I will come to visions of the Lord. I knew a man in Christ above fourteen years ago (i.e. AD 41), (whether in the body, I cannot tell; or whether out of the body, I cannot tell: God knoweth;) such an one caught up to the third heaven.... He was caught up into paradise, and heard unspeakable words, which it is not lawful for a man to utter. Of such an one will I glory: yet of myself I will not glory" (12.2-5). In AD c.57, Paul urges the Romans, in an epistle on which Martin Luther based his doctrine of justification by faith, "Let us put on the armour of light" (*Romans* 13.12).

Some of the *New Testament* letters seem to be much later than St Paul's time, but they too convey the Light. The Epistle attributed to James (1.17, probably AD c.100) sees God as "the Father of Lights" who dwells "in the light no man can approach unto" (*First Epistle to Timothy, attributed to Paul*, 6.16, accepted as Pauline by Catholics but according to Protestants probably 2nd century AD). The *First Epistle attributed to John* (1.5, probably beginning of 2nd century AD) says that "God is light, and in him is no darkness at all" and that "the darkness is past, and the true light now shineth" (2.8). Thus the Word, who is incarnated as Jesus, is a Light-bringer who struggles against darkness, and Jesus reveals the glory of God through his transfiguration – the divine shines through his elevated glorified humanity – and therefore becomes the light of the heavenly Jerusalem: "And the city has no need of the sun...for the glory of the Lord did lighten it, and the Lamb is the light thereof" (*Revelation* 21.23, AD c.80-90). The *First Epistle attributed to Peter* (AD c.117) addresses scattered strangers who have been called "out of darkness into his marvellous light" (2.9), while the *Second Epistle attributed to Peter* (probably AD c.150) urges "take heed, as unto a light that shineth in a dark place" (1.19).

It must be remembered that the canon (the Greek *kanon* meant a "reed" or "cane" used as a measuring-rod) at first included, and then (in the 3rd century AD) excluded, such non-apostolic works as *The Shepherd of Hermas*, which reflected the Light.

The Light of the Christian-Gnostic Alexandrian School: Clement's Gnosis of Light, the Logos of Light

In the 3rd century AD the Gnostic Light (see p393) dimmed. Christian theologians defended Christianity and largely obliterated Gnostic writings until a Gnostic library was discovered at Naj-Hammadi in 1945.[5] Irenaeus, bishop of Lugdunum (modern Lyons, France AD c.120/140-c.200/203) was one of the Church Fathers who refuted Gnosticism, and as he always summarised the Gnostic views he attacked, he was a leading source. The Carthaginian Tertullian (AD c.155/60-after 220), another anti-Gnostic Father, wrote (*Against Praxeas* 9,12): "God said 'Let there be light' and light came into being. And the Word himself was straightway the 'true light which lights every man coming into this world', and through him the light of the world came into being." Hippolytus (AD c.230) and Epiphanius (AD c.375) were two more anti-Gnostics.[6]

But the main attack came from the Alexandrian School (see p401). Alexandria boasted the most famous library of the ancient world – it was founded by Alexander the Great c.332 BC, was the royal library of the Ptolemies, and survived under the Romans until the 3rd century AD – and the School grew up in reaction to the Gnosticism of the Alexandrian Basilides and Valentinus.[7] It was centred on the Christian Catechetical School, the first Christian institute of higher learning at Alexandria, and its curriculum catered for Greek-trained students of Christianity who might wish to be baptised, and this brought together Greek culture and Christian faith. The Greek Stoic philosopher Pantaenus was its first recorded head. He was the teacher and converter of Clement of Alexandria (AD c.150-c.211/215), who succeeded him from c.180 until AD c.201/2, when the Libyan Roman Emperor Septimius Severus forced him to flee to his student Alexander, bishop of Jerusalem. Another pupil of his, Origen (AD c.185-254), then took over as head of the School and established a curriculum that became the basis of the medieval liberal arts course.[8] The orthodox Christian Church of Alexandria was under its bishop Demetrius, from AD c.189 – Alexandria was a see along with Rome and Antioch – and it regarded the School with disfavour; for the Church preached salvation by *pistis*, faith, whereas Clement tried to mediate between Christianity and Gnosticism by making faith (*pistis*) the basis of *gnosis*, and advocating Christian Gnosticism as opposed to heretical Gnosticism, which he condemned. Furthermore, the Alexandrian School interpreted the *Bible* allegorically and emphasised Christ's divinity; whereas the more orthodox Christian School of Antioch (AD c.200) interpreted the *Bible* literally and dwelt on Christ's humanity.[9]

Clement's *gnosis* was knowledge of God, a mystical experience of becoming a part of the being of God, which anticipated the experience of immortality and was the main element in Christian perfection. Clement's *gnosis* was the Light: "And so Knowledge easily translates the soul to the divine and holy which is akin to it, and by its own light conveys a man through the stages of mystery until it restores him at last to the supernal place of rest, teaching the man who is pure of heart to gaze on God, face to face, with perfect science and understanding. For in this consists the perfection of the soul of the true Gnostic, that, rising above all purification and service, it should be with God" (*Miscellanies* 7.10.57).[10] (Compare St Paul's "face to face".)

Clement drew together Greek Platonism, the Jewish Mosaic tradition and Christianity by emphasising the *Logos.*[11] In Stoic and Platonic thought, this was the Reason behind the universe and in the soul.[12] In Jewish thought it was the *memra* (the "Word" of God in *Genesis*),[13] the powerful self-expression of God which in the work of the Jewish Philo of Alexandria (c.15/10 BC-AD 50) became a second God like the Gnostic *Ennoia* or Demiurge. In Christian thought the divine *Logos* was incarnated in Jesus:[14] hence St John's "In the beginning was the *Logos*".

There have been parallels between the *Logos* and the *Tao* (see pp332-334). Both are principles behind the universe, and Stoics lived in accord with the *Logos* as Taoists lived in accord with the *Tao*; and just as the *Tao* was the Light, so too was the truth of the *Logos* the Light, the *gnosis* of Clement which was the end of Greek philosophy, of the Mosaic Law and of Christian *pistis.* Christian belief (*pistis*) was thus acceptable to *Logos*-trained Greeks, and Clement saw the flow of one tradition in terms of a river: "One, therefore, is the way of truth, but into it, just as into an everlasting river, flow streams but from another place" (*Stromateis*).[15]

Clement distinguished Christian Gnostics,who lived according to the *Gospels* and the *Logos* of Light, from orthodox Christians who lived according to the Law, and his attack on orthodox wordly Christianity prepared the way for the desert monasticism of the 3rd century.[16] Clement's successor Origen refuted the Valentinian Heracleon's huge commentary on *St John*, and in the course of defending Christianity against pagan attacks affirmed a good God or Father who created rational and spiritual human beings through an inferior *Logos* or Son, or Light, whose bride was therefore the soul. (Origen anticipated the Arian heresy of the 4th century, which held that Father and Son were not of one substance).[17]

The Alexandrian School, then, defeated Gnosticism by taking over the Gnostic Light and re-Christianizing it, and the influence of the Light of the Alexandrian School can be seen in the late and degenerate Valentinian Christian Coptic-gnostic *Pistis Sophia* ("Faith-Wisdom", 3rd century AD). In this text, "one who hath not found the mysteries" will "question about the mysteries of the Light until it finds them, through the decision of the Virgin of the Light, and inherit the Light for ever". One must "find the mysteries of the Light, go on high and inherit the Light-kingdom". The Virgin of Light is the Sophia who is the *pneuma* or spark in the soul – the Barbelo-gnostics probably called the Sophia "Barbelo" or "the Virgin" – but she is also the *Logos*: "O Light of Lights, in which I have had faith from the beginning, hearken now to my repentance. Deliver me, O Light, for evil thoughts have entered into me.... And I looked upwards so that the Light in which I had faith might come to my help.... And I was in that place, mourning and seeking the Light that I had seen on high.... Now, O Light of Lights, I am afflicted in the darkness of chaos."[18] In the *Pistis Sophia* the saved become rays of the divine Light, an idea that reflects Clement's view that immortality meant becoming a part of God's being.

The New Roman Light in the Early Middle Ages

The "Middle Ages" or "medium aevum" was the Humanist term for the time between the collapse of Roman civilization before the Germanic barbarians c.395 and the Humanist revival of learning c.1500.[19]

The Germanic hegemony in Europe began when the Goths and Franks were admitted to the Roman Empire in 379, and an anti-barbarian reaction appeared in Constantinople[20] which Constantine had founded as a "New Rome" on the site of Byzantium in 324. It was dedicated in 330, when he moved the Roman capital to Byzantium and named it "Constantinople" ("the city of Constantine"). The Visigoths (under Alaric), Ostrogoths and Gauls all invaded Italy between 402 and 407, and in 410 Alaric returned to

Ravenna, the seat of the Emperor Honorius, and demanded land and money. Unsatisfied, he pillaged Rome for three days, but being an Arian he spared the churches. The Visigoths then marched against the Gauls, into whose land, at the end of 406, had gone the Vandals, Suevi, Alani, Burgundians and Alamanni, fleeing from the Huns. They pushed back the federated Franks. Eventually the barbarians arrived in Spain and the Suevi settled in Lusitania, the Vandals in Andalusia (i.e. Vandalusia). The Visigoths were federated and were sent to Spain to fight the Vandals. The Franks, Alamanni and Burgundians now occupied North Italy and could not be dislodged.

In 436 the Romans had some success: they made the Visigoths surrender Arles and Narbonne, they settled the Burgundians in Savoy and the Alani in Orleans. But they lost the other provinces: England (which had been abandoned in 407) to the Angles, Saxons and Jutes, and Spain to the pro-Visigothic Suevi. The dislodged Vandals went to North Africa under Gaiseric (or Genseric), where, in the course of besieging Hippo, they killed St Augustine. In 450 Attila's Huns invaded Gaul and then Italy, where they collected tribute from the Pope. The Franks, Alamanni and Visigoths supported Rome against the Huns, and as a result the German chieftans were now supreme. One of them, Odoacer, deposed the last Roman Emperor in 476 and proclaimed himself king, governing Italy under the theoretical protection of the Emperor of the East in Constantinople, so ending the Roman Empire of the West.

Barbarian kingdoms were then set up: the Vandal kingdom in Africa, the Visigothic kingdom in Spain and Gaul, the kingdom of the Salian Franks and Alamanni in the north. The barbarians co-existed with the Romans; their Arianism allowed the Catholic bishops to retain control over the Church. In Gaul, Clovis, king of the Salian Franks (a Merovingian as the dynasty is named after his grandfather Merovich) expelled the last Roman and set up Frankish domination in Gaul. (The modern "France" is the land of the "Franks".) Meanwhile the king of the Ostrogoths proclaimed himself king at Ravenna in 494.

The new Roman Light was strengthened by St Augustine and Pope Gregory the Great, and in spite of the darkness of the times it spread to every household in Europe.

The Christian Neoplatonist Light: St Augustine's Unchangeable Light, Dionysius's Darkness Beyond Light

There were two schools of the Light in early European Christianity. The first was a Christian Neoplatonist one (i.e. a Christian adaptation of pagan Neoplatonism), and the dominant figure of both was the Christian Neoplatonist St Augustine (354-430). He was born in Algeria, probably a Berber, of a Christian mother, and his autobiographical *Confessions* (c.400) record his early fornications as a student in Carthage in North Africa (he prayed, "Give me chastity and continence but not yet" 8.7) and his passage to Manichaeism. He became a freelance teacher of rhetoric and waited nine years to hear the Manichaean Faustus, only to be disillusioned. At the age of 28 he went to Rome and obtained a Professorship of Rhetoric in Milan, where the Western Emperor ruled. The bishop of Milan was Ambrose. Augustine heard him preach, and he progressed to Neoplatonism probably through the influence of Ambrose who used texts from Plotinus in his sermons. He was converted to Christianity in Milan in 386, and he more than anyone else transmitted Neoplatonism in its Christian form to the Middle Ages. He fused the *New Testament* and Platonic philosophy, and was a Middle Platonist in seeing God as containing all Forms within his mind, but a Neoplatonist in his epistemological doctrine of illumination in which God, the One, is known because his Light shines on the mind of men.[21]

For Augustine, God was at first the pre-Christian, pre-Catholic, Plotinan "Light Unchangeable" or "the Light that never changes", as in a famous passage in *Confessions* (7.10) which has already been quoted: "I entered (within myself). I saw with the eye of my soul, above my mind, the Light Unchangeable" (*Vidi oculo animae meae supra mentem meam lucem incommutabilem*). Other translations render this "beyond my mind" or "casting its rays over the same eye of my soul, over my mind", and in what follows it is clear that Augustine saw it as a Light that was not merely a part of himself: "It was not the common light of day that is seen by the eye of every living thing of flesh and blood, nor was it some more spacious light of the same sort, as if the light of day were to shine far, far brighter than it does and fill all space with a vast brilliance. What I saw was something quite, quite different from any light we know on earth. It shone above my mind, but not in the way that oil floats above water or the sky hangs over the earth. It was above me (or higher) because it was itself the Light that made me, and I was below (or lower) because I was made by it. All who know the truth know this Light, and all who know this Light know eternity." There is perhaps a trace of Augustine's Manichaeism in "the Light that made me", and he continues: "Your light shone upon me in its brilliance.....and I heard your voice calling from on high, saying 'I am the food of full-grown men. Grow and you shall feed on me.... You shall be changed into me'.... And far off, I heard your voice saying *I am the God who IS.*"[22]

Later (7.17) he tries to understand the experience: "This power of reason...withdrew my thoughts from their normal course and drew back from the confusion of (sensuous) images which pressed upon it, so that it might discover what light it was that had been shed upon it.... And so, in an instant of awe, my mind attained to the sight (vision) of the God who IS. Then, at last I caught sight of your invisible nature (Thy invisible things), as it is known through your creatures (things that are made). But I had no strength to fix my gaze upon them. In my weakness, I recoiled and fell back into my old ways."

The vision was not sustained, but he remembered the "fragrance", and his conversion was completed shortly afterwards in his Milan garden. Hearing a girl singing "Take it and read" (*tolle, lege*) from a nearby house, he thought of the Desert Father Anthony who had heard a text beginning "Go home" in a church and had been converted. He opened Paul's *Epistles* and read *Romans* 13.14, "Put ye on the Lord Jesus Christ and make not provision for the flesh, to fulfil the lusts thereof", and "It was as though the light of confidence flooded into my heart and all the darkness of doubt was dispelled" (8.12).

Augustine is reticent about subsequent experiences of the Light, but he evidently had them, for he writes mystically about his love for the Light in general, almost habitual terms: "But what do I love when I love my God?.... It is true that I love a light of a certain kind, a voice, a perfume, a food, an embrace; but they are of the kind that I love in my inner self, when my soul is bathed in light that is not bound by space (or, where for my soul, that shines which space does not contain).... This is what I love when I love my God" (10.6). Again: "I have learnt to love you late, Beauty at once so ancient and so new!...You were within me, and I was in the world outside myself. I searched for you outside myself...You shone upon me; your radiance enveloped me; you put my blindness to flight.... You touched me, and I am inflamed with love of your peace" (10.27). And again: "What is that Light whose gentle beams now and again strike through to my heart, causing me to shudder in awe yet firing me with their warmth? I shudder to feel how different I am from it, I am aglow with its Fire. It is the Light of Wisdom" (11.9).

For Augustine, God is "my Sweetness and my Light" (10.40), "Truth, the Light of my heart" (12.10), "Light of my eyes in darkness" (12.18), and "my Light, my Truth" (13.24), while creation emerged from formlessness when God "the Light" shone on it (13.3). Towards the end of the *Confessions* he wrote of God: "By your gift, the Holy Ghost, we are set aflame and borne aloft, and the fire within us carries us upward.... It is your fire, your good fire, that sets us aflame and carries us upward" (13.9).

This vision of God as Light which is "the illuminator of all Truth" (*De Civitate Dei* 8.4), a vision which is partly Neoplatonic and partly Joannine, is reflected in the rest of Augustine's work. In the *Sermons* (52.16, from AD 391) he writes that he "arrived by some kind of spiritual contact at the Light Unchangeable" (*ad illam incommutabilem lucem*), and in his commentary on *Genesis* (AD 401-415) he records that in the intellectual or mental vision the light by which the soul sees is God: "That light itself whereby the soul is so enlightened that it beholds all things truly the object of the intellect...is God Himself" (*De Genesi* 12.31.59). Thus "God is the intelligible Light" (*Deus intelligibilis lux*) in *Soliloquies* (1.3, AD 387).

Augustine seems to suggest that the divine Light is the divine Essence, the Idea as well as the Form of God. In *De Civitate Dei* (AD 415-420) he praises the Platonists for saying that "the light of our minds for learning all things is the same God Himself by Whom all things were made" (8.7), and "the incorporeal soul is thus illumined by the incorporeal light of the simple Wisdom of God, as the body of the air is illumined by corporeal light" (11.10). The Unchangeable Light and Truth is an ontological truth: "The human mind recognises truth only in the Truth and Light of God....His mind is bedewed (*aspergitur*) inwardly with that Light that abides eternal" (*De Pecc. Mer* 1.37, AD 418); and "the Truth unchangeable shines like a sun in the soul, and the soul becomes partaker of the very Truth" (*De Gen c Manich* 1.43). For Augustine Christ was the "inner teacher" (*magister interior*) of this Truth. Neoplatonists had always seen the soul as a sphere that is *augoeides* ("possessed of a form of radiance or brilliance", and therefore "shining"), and according to the 6th century AD Academy philosopher Damascius, commenting on Plato's *Parmenides*, "in Heaven, indeed, our *augoeides* is filled with radiance".[23]

The human mind, then, only knows Ideas (*Intelligibilia*) in the Light of God, by divine illumination, and this epistemological theory of illumination dominated the early Middle Ages until Aquinas's Aristotelianism replaced it. Even then, Aquinas allowed it to be tenable and even probable ("some Catholic doctors with much probability have made God himself the *intellectus agens*", *In Lib 2 Sentent* 17.2.1), and it was perpetuated by the Franciscan school of St. Bonaventura.

Augustine describes the joy of contact with the Light, the ecstasies when one is rapt (*rapitur*), "withdrawn from the bodily senses and carried away unto God and afterwards restored" (*Sermons* 52.16), and then the recoil of the soul back into normal everyday living where it builds up energy for the next flight. Throughout, there is a distinction between the "spiritual" (imaginative) perception and vision of images such as St Peter's sheet let down from heaven or four-footed beasts, and the "intellectual" perception and vision of the ecstasies, the "intellectual" vision of the Light. This distinction can still be observed today in visionary and mystic poets. For Augustine, the goal of mysticism (union with God) was to be touched by the Light, and as the Light was also Wisdom, and philosophy was the "love of wisdom" (*philosophia*), the Light was also the goal of philosophy. Thus for Augustine, mysticism and philosophy were one.[24]

Second only to St Augustine in influence was another Christian Neoplatonist, Dionysius the Areopagite, whose work was not fully known in the West until the 12th century AD. He is called Pseudo-Dionysius because he took the name of St Paul's convert as a pseudonym and addressed his work to St Paul's fellow-worker Timothy; he was probably a Syrian monk who flourished c.500 and knew Proclus's system.

Dionysius saw God in terms of a Darkness behind the divine Light: writing in Greek, he advocated a turning away from the world of the senses and forms for an ecstatic union with the "light from the divine darkness" which is God. To Dionysius, God was the Darkness beyond light. He was "veiled in the dazzling obscurity of the secret Silence, outshining all brilliance with the intensity of their (i.e. the mysteries') Darkness" and by self-renunciation one may "be borne on high...into the superessential Radiance of the Divine Darkness (or the Ray of that divine Darkness) which exceeds existence (or surpasses all being)" (Dionysius's crucial short treatise, *The Mystical Theology*). God was the Divine Dark who is approached negatively by a *via negativa*: "It is not soul or mind...nor can It be described by the reason or perceived by the understanding, since It...is not power or light...nor is It Godhead or Goodness; nor is It a Spirit...; nor does It belong to the category of non-existence or to that of existence;...nor is It darkness, nor is It light," and so on (*Mystical Theology* 5).

In short, God is unknowable – "the Darkness of Unknowing", which influenced the 14th century *Cloud of Unknowing* – and every affirmation about him is false, though angels filter the Divine Light to the world below in an appropriate intensity, for "it is impossible that the beams of the Divine Source can shine upon us unless they are shrouded in the manifold texture of sacred veils". Prayer is like "a luminous chain" suspended from Heaven, which we seem to pull down with our hands, though we are in fact carried up "to the high splendours of the luminous rays". We are borne up "unto this Darkness which is beyond Light", the divine Darkness which "is the unapproachable light in which God is said to dwell" (Letter 5). Then our intellect "is united to the superlucent rays, being illumined thence and therein by the unsearchable depth of wisdom" (*De Div Nom* 7.3).[25]

Dionysius was the first to describe the workings of the mystical consciousness in terms of the Indian and Greek idea of "divine ignorance", and when the Irish Christian Neoplatonist philosopher John Scotus Erigena translated his work into Latin at the court of the Frankish king Charles the

Bald, along with the works of other early mystics such as Maximus Confessor and Gregory of Nyssa c.850, both Neoplatonism and Western European mysticism became a tradition.[26]

The Benedictines: Pope Gregory's Unencompassed Light

The Benedictine school of practical contemplative prayer derived from the desert mystics, and especially Cassian (died 435); the monks who in the 6th century produced icons in the East like the icon of Christ Pantocrator at St Catherine's monastery, Sinai; and St Benedict (c.480-547).

St Benedict, was the father of Western monasticism: his moderate Rule was adopted in Frankish and German monasteries, and he spent some years in a cave above Subiaco near Rome. The Benedictine tradition was established by the Roman Pope, Gregory the Great (c.540-604), whose *Dialogues* are the only authority for St Benedict's life and for St Benedict's great mystical experience at the window of a tower when "a light shed from above dissipated all the darkness of the night" and "the whole world, gathered as it were under one ray of the sun, was brought before his eyes" (*Dialogues* 2.35). Gregory reluctantly became Pope in 590, and in 597 sent the mission to Britain which resulted in the comment that the English were not Angles but angels (*non Angli sed angeli*). Gregory also encouraged a reform of the Mass, from which came the "Gregorian chant".

Gregory was influenced by Augustine's *City of God* and dreamt of a *societas reipublicae Christianae* ("a society of a Christian republic"), and his *lumen incircumscriptum* mirrors Augustine's *lucem incommutabilem.* Gregory writes a lot about the Light, but is more reticent than Augustine about his own mystical experiences, and only one passage is clearly autobiographical. When Pope, he looks back with envy at the time he was free to contemplate and see the Light which he has now lost: "My sad mind, labouring under the soreness of its engagements, remembers how it went with me formerly in the monastery, how all perishable things were beneath it, how it rose above all that was transitory, and, though still in the body,went out in contemplation beyond the bars of the flesh" (*Dialogues 1 Pref*).

For Gregory, contemplation is a gift from God, and "the greatness of contemplation (i.e. the Light) can be given to none but them that love" (*Homilies on Ezekiel*, i.e. HE, 2.5.17). This "greatness" is caught in 2.2.12-14: "There is in contemplation a great effort of the mind, when it raises itself up to heavenly things.... And sometimes indeed it prevails and soars above the resisting darkness of its blindness, so that it attains to somewhat of the unencompassed (or boundless) Light (*lumen incircumscriptum*) by stealth and scantily; but for all that, to itself straightway beaten back it returns, and out of that light into which panting it had passed, into the darkness of its blindness sighing it returns.... The sweetness of contemplation...carries away (or ravishes, *rapit*) the soul above itself....But...no-one so advances in power of contemplation as to fix the mind's eyes as yet on the unencompassed ray itself of Light. For the Almighty God is not yet seen in this brightness, but the soul beholds something beneath it, by which refreshed it may progress, and hereafter attain to the glory of the sight of Him. When the mind has made progress in contemplation it does not yet contemplate that which God is, but that which is under Him.... As soon as the mind begins to raise itself, and to be inundated with the light of interior quiet, the turmoil of thoughts soon comes back, and it is thrown into disorder from itself, and being disordered, it is blinded."

Contemplation, then, is the endeavour "to fix the eye of the heart on the very ray of the unencompassed Light" (*Morals* which were preached for monks, 23.42), and for Gregory, the Light is beneath God as it is for Dionysius. Unlike Augustine, however, Gregory believed that fallen man could never know God: "(The human mind) is not able to see the glory of God as it is. But whatever of it that is which shines in the mind, is a likeness, and not itself" (*HE* 1.8.30); "with whatever force the eye of the mind in the exile of this life strains after the light of eternity, it is not able to penetrate it; and when we raise the gaze of our mind to the ray of supernal Light, we are clouded over by the obscurity of our weakness. While man is yet weighed down by the corruptible flesh, he is by no means able to see the eternal Light as it is.... It does not see God as He is" (*Morals* 4.45). Thus we "in no wise behold the brightness of the divine power as it abides unchangeable in itself" (*Morals* 5.52), and "the Divinity...shows forth His Brightness scantily to the blinking eyes of our mind" (*Morals* 5.66), while "holy men...cannot see God as He is.... For the mist of our corruption darkens us from the incorruptible Light.... And if the mind already saw it perfectly it would not see it as it were through fog (or darkness, *per calignem*)" (*Morals* 31.101).

For Gregory, God is hidden behind a fog of our own making: "Whatever the progress in virtue, the mind does not yet compass any clear insight into eternity, but still looks on it under the fog of some sort of imagining. And so it is called a vision of the night. And therefore, as contemplating the ray of the interior Sun, the cloud of our corruption interposes itself, nor does the unchangeable Light burst forth such as It is to the weak eyes of our mind, we as it were still see God in a vision of the night, since we must surely go darkling (*caligamus*) under an uncertain contemplation" (*Morals* 5.53).

This view accords with later Western theology, and differs from St Augustine's view, but in one passage Gregory contradicts himself and states the Augustinian view that to see the Light is to see the divine Nature and Essence: "God may be seen by certain semblances, but by the actual appearance (species) of His Nature He cannot....(Moses) was athirst to perceive, through the Brightness of His uncircumscribed Nature, Him Whom he had begun to see by certain semblances, that so the supernal Essence might be present to the eyes of his mind, in order that for the vision of Eternity there might not be interposed to him any created semblance.... By growing in incalculable power by a certain piercingness of contemplation, the Eternal Brightness of God is able to be seen" (*Morals* 18.88).

Gregory's writings are full of the Light. In a famous image he sees the Light as coming through a window or "chink": "In slanting or splayed windows that part by which the light enters is narrow, but the inner part which receives the light is wide; because the minds of those that contemplate, although they have but a slight glimpse of the true light, yet are they enlarged within themselves with a great amplitude....It is very little indeed that those who contemplate see of eternity; but from that little the fold of their minds is extended unto an increase of fervour and love. He who keeps his heart within, he it is who receives the light of contemplation. For they that still think immoderately of external things, know not what are the chinks of contemplation from the eternal light" (*HE* 40.16). Gregory is saying that we see the sunbeam, but not the Sun, and so it is with Truth, for "the Light of Truth...is let into the mind as it were through a narrow slit" (*Morals* 30.8).

The Light is only glimpsed momentarily in Gregory, though other mystics can "sunbathe" in it for an hour or more: "The mind of the elect" – note the Manichaean word (see pp410-416) – "...feeds on the taste of the unencompassed Light, and being carried beyond self, disdains to sink back again into self. But forasmuch as the corruptible body weighs down the soul, it is not able to cleave for long to the Light which it sees in a momentary glimpse" (*Morals* 8.50). The soul is "made to recoil by the very immensity of the light, it is called back to itself" (*Moralia in Job*). Nevertheless, "when it tastes that inward sweetness, it is on fire with love". Once a soul has been "breathed on by the glowing spirit...it gains a taste of something to love" and becomes "vile in its own sight" (*Morals* 23.43), and when the mind "is illumined by the bright coruscations of the unencompassed Light flashing upon it" it "is absorbed in a sort of rapturous security, and carried beyond itself" and "remade in a certain newness", besprinkled with the infusion of heavenly dew from an inexhaustible fountain" (*Morals* 24.11).

The Saints in their Beatific Vision "behold God's face and see the unencompassed Light" (*Hom in Evang* 37.1), and Gregory writes of "the Eternal Light of contemplation", "the invisible Light", "the incorporeal Light", "the true Light" (*HE* 2.5.17-18), and of "the inward Light, a sight whereof flashes in the soul with a ray of brightness by the grace of contemplation" (*Morals* 23.41). Contemplation is "to inhere in the Light, to see it hastily and taste it scantily" (*Morals* 8.50), "to gaze on the very Fountain of Light" (*Morals* 30.8). Those in contemplation endeavour "to behold with their mind the brightness of the Creator" (Morals 30.8), which brings "Wisdom" (*Morals* 22.50) and "the Supernal Intelligence" to the mind (*HE* 2.1.17). There is fervour and joy as the mind is "inflamed with the love of that interior brightness" (*HE* 1.5.13), and the flight of the soul brings ecstasy in numerous passages. The abundance of Gregory's references to the Light makes it easy to understand why he was regarded as a master of mysticism in the succeeding five centuries.[27]

Gregory's Light inspired and Christianized the Dark Ages.

THE WEST ROMAN EMPIRE'S CHRISTIAN LIGHT

The Empire had been revived in Byzantium, where Justinian, the Byzantine Emperor, had reasserted the Christian Light (see p239) in a culture based on a legal Code that regulated the holy life, and he had symbolized the vision in Hagia Sophia, the Church of the Holy Wisdom (c.532-7). Justinian had reconquered Italy through Belisarius from 535, finally recapturing Ravenna in 540. In Rome itself, the Church increasingly functioned as a world state, filling the vacuum left by the Roman Emperors.

However, the Popes in Rome were increasingly unable to rely on the protection of the Byzantine Emperor. The Visigoths rose again in Spain, and there had been a Lombard invasion of Italy in 568 which confined Byzantine power in Italy to Ravenna, Venice and the south. Rome and Constantinople were divided by doctrinal disputes, notably the Byzantine attitude to iconoclasm, and Byzantine-protected Ravenna fell to the Lombards in 751. The Pope now sought protection from the Frankish leader Pepin III, and anointed him king of the Franks. Pepin's son Charlemagne rejected the Byzantine view on iconoclasm and as Christian King of the Franks and Lombards (whom he had conquered) rather than an ex-barbarian, he was crowned Emperor of Rome in 800, thus guaranteeing his protection to the Popes and countering the growing Byzantine influence in the East.

The Church's alliance with Charlemagne, the Christian King of the Germanic Franks, paved the way for the Holy Roman Empire, and Europe became a cultural unit in which hereditary households protected themselves from outlaws in the large tracts of European forest, the hereditary lords protecting their serfs in return for crops. The feudal households were economically self-sufficient, but in matters of religion they all looked to Rome, and the Christian Light blazed against the barbarians who had their own Germanic-Scandinavian tradition. Inevitably Christianity and its classical inheritance blended with the Germanic-Scandinavian tradition, and medieval culture reflected this blend.

The coronation of Charlemagne annoyed the Byzantine Emperor, and there were now effectively two Emperors of Rome. Although schism between the churches of Rome and Constantinople did not follow until

1054, there was now a vast distance between West and East, a distance that was to some extent bridged by the spirit of the Crusades, only to be widened by the West's military actions against the East during the Crusades, as when the Latin Venetians and Crusaders took Constantinople in 1204. Meanwhile Otto I, the Saxon King of Germany, had been crowned Emperor of the Romans in 962, thus founding the Holy Roman Empire. (The Latin phrase "*sacrum Romanum imperium*" dates from 1254, from whose unpromising origins our Western civilization has risen to split the atom and walk on the moon.)

The Norman Conquest – the "Normans" were descendants of "Northmen" or Vikings who had settled in "Normandy" or "Northmendy" – consolidated the hold of the Roman Church over Britain. Ironically, the Romanized Normans were assisted by Bretons who were paying back their old enemies the Saxons and the Danes.

The same pattern occurred in Ireland. In 1171 Henry II's invasion subjected Ireland to five centuries of British rule which lasted until c.1600, and Ireland became a Catholic country.

By the 11th century the new Roman Light had absorbed the Germanic-Scandinavian Light, and it was ready to take on and absorb the Light of Islam.

The Cistercian Light: St Bernard's Consuming Fire

The threat the "infidel" Seljuq Turks posed to the Byzantine Holy City of Jerusalem raised Europe to warlike fervour. Islam had threatened Europe since its expansion into Spain in the 8th century. It was a more advanced civilization than Dark Age Europe, which had been weakened by the Viking attacks; Spanish centres of learning had preserved the Hellenistic science and philosophy of Hippocrates, Galen, Euclid and Ptolemy in Arabic translations, and although Europeans looked up to Islamic culture, art, textiles, clothing, silks, carpets, curtains, tents and pottery, they feared Islamic military power, and the threat to Christian Jerusalem was the last straw. The First Crusade was launched in 1095. In 1098 the Egyptian Fatimids captured Jerusalem.

Jerusalem was recaptured and a Kingdom of Jerusalem was established in 1099, but its fall shocked the West. Christianity was evidently under pressure from Islam, and there was a mood for religious reform. The Benedictine Order had laid the foundations for Western monasticism, and it had been revived in the 11th century by the Italian monastic reformers from Ravenna, St Romuald and St Peter Damian, and by St Bruno (the founder of the Grand Chartreuse and Carthusian Order), all of whom tried to create conditions in which mystics could see the Light. The Benedictine St Anselm founded rational Scholasticism in the 11th century, and the Benedictine abbey at Cluny (which had been founded in 910) attempted to observe the Benedictine Rule more strictly. However, the Cluniac interpretation of Benedictine life was not austere, and the more ascetic Cistercians were in reaction against it and sought to reform it.

The Cistercians were founded in 1098, and spread rapidly as a result of the crusading fervour and Light of the French Benedictine St Bernard of Clairvaux, a Cistercian monk (1091-1153) who dominated the 12th century: he was the spiritual leader of Europe, for he established Pope Innocent II, opposed the Scholiast Abelard who turned mysticism from a matter of experience into a rational dialectic – Abelard was the 12th century A. J. Ayer – and promoted the Second Crusade. The Christian attitude towards Islam must be thoroughly understood. Christianity was intolerant towards Islam as it had been towards the early pagans, the Saxons and Northmen. Islam regarded itself as the fulfilment of the *Old* and *New Testament* revelations, whereas to Christians Islam held up a false prophet and was the religion of the Antichrist of the *Revelation*, against whom was set the image in *Revelation* of a New Jerusalem. Christianity's response to Islam was to destroy it and absorb it.

St Bernard's Light and mysticism are to be found in the 86 *Sermons on the Canticle* (i.e. Song) *of Solomon*, (1130-1145) in which the Light is expressed in imagery of human love. The Bridegroom of the *Song of Solomon* is Jesus Christ and the Bride ("the rose of Sharon") is the Church; the Bridegroom is also the Divine Word, the *Logos*, whose "kiss" is a gift that "conveys both the light of knowledge and the unction of piety" (Cant 8.2-6) to the Bride, who is the soul. Thus, in the spiritual marriage between the soul and the Word, the Word (or Love) is the Light.

Bernard distinguishes two kinds of transport (*excessus*, departure, i.e. rapture or ecstasy) in contemplation, "the one in the intellect, the other in the heart (*affectus*); the one in light, the other in fervour" (*Cant* 49.3). The act of contemplation "is like a sleep in the arms of God, but the soul returns fired with a most vehement love of God" (*Cant* 49.4).

In the contemplation of the heart, the act of love is always initiated by God/the Word who, as husband, "rapes" the soul following a "loving descent", and in the mingling (*commixtio*) and union (*conjunctio*) the soul "feels itself consumed" in a "Fire": "My heart was hot within me, and while I was musing the Fire burned forth" (*Cant* 31.4-6). There is a "love which fires" the heart, and the soul is "set aglow with the love of God" (*Cant* 57.7). Bernard himself experienced this many times, as he describes in an autobiographical passage:

"I confess, then,...that the Word has visited me, and even very often. But although he has frequently entered into my soul, I have never at any time been sensible of (or perceived) the precise moment of His coming.... He is living and full of energy, and as soon as He has entered into me He has quickened my sleeping soul, has aroused and softened and goaded my heart.... He has begun...to illuminate the gloomy spots.... After having, then, such an experience of the Word, what wonder that I should adopt for my own the language of the Bride, who recalls Him when He has departed, since I am influenced by a desire, not indeed as powerful, but at least similar to hers" (*Cant* 74.5-7).

In the contemplation of the intellect, "when the Lord comes as a consuming Fire and His Presence is understood in the power by which the soul is changed and in the love by which it is inflamed; when stain of sin and rust of vices have been consumed in that Fire, and the conscience has been purified and calmed, there ensues a certain sudden and unwonted enlargement of mind and an inpouring of light illuminating the intellect, either for knowledge of Scripture or comprehension of mysteries. But not through open doors, but through narrow apertures does that ray of so great brightness penetrate" (*Cant* 57.7-8).

The "light illuminating the intellect" coming through "narrow apertures" recalls Gregory's "chinks". It brings a revealed wisdom so that intellectual conceptions suddenly become understandable: "For when something from God (*divinitus*) has momentarily and, as it were, with the swiftness of a flash of light, shed its ray upon the mind in ecstasy of spirit...forthwith there present themselves...certain imaginary likenesses of lower things, suited to the meanings which have been infused from above" (Cant 41.3). As in Gregory, contemplation is transient – it has the "swiftness of a flash of light" – but its effects on the soul are permanent. In heaven, "to be thus affected is to be deified (*deificari est*)" – an Eastern idea – for the soul will pass into the will of God "as a kindled and glowing iron becomes most like the fire, having put off its former and natural form; and as the air, when flooded with the light of the sun, is transformed into the same clarity of light so that it seems to be not merely illumined, but the light itself" (*De diligendo Deo* 28).[28]

St Bernard's vision of the Light is embodied in stone at Sarlat in the Dordogne. Near the Cathedral where St Bernard cured the sick in August 1147 by blessing bread and handing it out, there is a puzzling round building called "the Lantern of the Dead". This was built shortly after Bernard's canonisation in 1174, but despite its name no-one is completely certain what its purpose was. It is a round chapel and conical tower that tapers to a point, round whose side winds a "path" up to Heaven, and there is no access to the first floor; and if one goes up the outside by ladder, the narrow slit windows ("narrow apertures" or chinks) are too narrow to squeeze inside. It seems that a light was placed inside the top when a corpse lay in state below, to mark the position of the dead at night in a ritual that may have been Celtic in origin rather than Christian, or which may recall the pre-Islamic ziggurat. The building is peculiar to Western and Central France, and other examples of Lanterns of the Dead can be found at Cellefrouin and Ciron (12th century), and at Antigny (13th century). The Sarlat building has a Templar simplicity, and may have been a place where Bernard himself came down for the dead and "walked" crusading souls up the path round Mount Purgatory (Purgatory is shown as a mountain in Dante) to Heaven. In the *Bible* (*Matthew* 25, 1-13) the wise virgins took oil for their Lights and the Bridegroom came. The Lantern of the Dead may have raised Bernard into the role of Bridegroom, who came for the Bride, the soul; the lantern being a signal to Bernard that there was an illumined soul who needed his services.[29]

The Living Light and Flowing Fire

The Benedictine Light turned prophetic in the 12th century, and in Germany and Italy mystics attempted to influence secular events. The German Benedictine nun Hildegarde of Bingen (1098-1179), the "Sybil of the Rhine", called the Light the *lux vivens* ("living light"), and prefaced her prophecies and denunciations *Lux vivens dicit*, "thus saith the living light", for she lived under the direction of its power. She describes it: "From my infancy up to the present time, I now being more than seventy years of age, I have always seen this light, in my spirit and not with external eyes, nor with any thoughts of my heart, nor with help from my senses....The light which I see is not located, but yet is more brilliant than the sun, nor can I examine its height, length or breadth, and I name it 'the cloud of the living light'.... But sometimes I behold within this light another light which I name 'the living light itself'. And when I look upon it, every sadness and pain vanishes from my memory, so that I am again as a simple maid and not as an old woman."[30]

Hildegarde (sometimes spelt Hildegard) was the first of a line of German Benedictine women mystics: the young St Elizabeth of Schönau (died 1165), Nun Gertrude (died 1291), her sister St Mechthild of Hackborn (died 1310), St Gertrude the Great (died 1301) and the poet Mechthild of Magdeburg (1217-82). Mechthild of Magdeburg wrote her visions in *The Book of the Flowing Light of the Godhead* (compare the *lux vivens*) in which the soul tells the senses that it can bear the "Fire" of God's presence: "Gold in the fire cannot decay but shines more brilliant every way.... Do you think that his Fire will consume my soul? He knows how to burn, and then to gently cool."

For Mechthild, God was a flame or river of "Fire" (or Light) that filled the universe, and the souls of the saints were ablaze with that Fire:

"God showed him in his senses and the eyes of his soul, a Fire which burned ceaselessly in the heights above all things.... This Fire is the everlasting God Who has retained in Himself Eternal Life from which all things proceed. The sparks which have blown away from the Fire are the holy angels. The beams of the Fire are the saints of God.... The comfort of the Fire is the joy our souls receive inwardly from God, with such holy warmth from the Divine Fire, that we too burn with it.... The radiance of the Fire is the glowing aspect of the Divine countenance of the Holy Trinity, which shall so illumine our souls and bodies that we may then see and recognise the marvellous blessedness we cannot even name here (i.e. the Light). These things have come out of the Fire and flow into it again.... Would you know my meaning? Lie down in the Fire, see and taste the Flowing Godhead through your being; feel the Holy Spirit moving and compelling you within the Flowing Fire and Light of God."

Hildegarde's contemporary, the prophetic Italian Benedictine Joachim of Fiore (or Flora) (c.1130-1202) had three so-called "illuminations" which were probably visions. The third certainly was: a triangular psaltry with ten strings, which clarified the meaning of the Trinity for him, and made it the basis for a prophetic historical theory of three ages.[31]

The Scottish Augustinian Platonist and Benedictine Richard of Saint-Victor (c.1123-1173) – he combined both the traditions – spent his life at the Abbey of St-Victor in Paris. He wrote of the "Father of Lights" (Benjamin Minor) and emphasised the practical contemplative life. In *The Four Degrees of Passionate Love* (1173) he crowned the mysticism of the 12th century:

"The Lord...reveals His presence but without showing His face. He infuses His sweetness.... The clouds and darkness are round about Him.... He does not yet appear in the light, and though He be seen in the fire, the fire is a burning rather than an illumination. For he kindles the affection but does not yet illuminate the intellect. He inflames the desire but does not yet enlighten the intelligence. In this state the soul can feel her beloved but she cannot see Him. And if she does see Him it is as one sees by night.... When the mind goes forward to the grace of contemplation with great effort and ardent desire, it moves as it were into the second degree of love.... The shewing of the Divine Light in this state and the wonder of the revelation arising from it, together with the perennial memory thereof bind the soul indissolubly so that she is not able to forget the happiness of her experience.... The brightness she has looked upon binds the thoughts that she may neither forget it nor think about anything else. The third degree of love is when the mind of men is ravished (rapt) into the abyss of Divine Light so that the soul, having forgotten all outward things, is altogether unaware of itself and passes out completely into its God.... And any suffering that is left is absorbed in glory. In this state..., ravished (rapt) into that secret place of divine refuge, when it is surrounded on every side by the divine fire of love, pierced to the core, set alight all about, then it sheds its very self altogether, and puts on that divine life....And soon as she is admitted to that inner secret of the divine mystery...she is wholly dissolved in herself."

Deification is like iron being heated in a fire: "When the soul is plunged in the Fire of divine love, like iron, it first loses its blackness, and then growing to white heat, it becomes like the fire itself. And lastly, it grows liquid, and losing its nature, is transmuted into an utterly different quality of being....As the difference between the iron that is cold and iron that is hot, so is the difference between...the tepid soul and the soul made incandescent by divine love."[32]

The Late Medieval Brightness

In 1187 Christendom had suffered a shattering blow when Jerusalem fell to Saladin, who had made himself master of Egypt. Reform was now considered desperate, and new monastic orders came into being. New ideas were in favour. The Carmelites took up residence at Elijah's Mount Carmel in Palestine (1206-14), and the Franciscans (1209) and the Dominicans (1215) were founded. There was a new focus on Jerusalem, as we shall see from the legends of the Grail (c.1190-1225). (See "The Grail Light", pp428-446.) The Papacy had turned on the Albigensian heretics, the Cathars, in

1209 so that Christendom could remain united internally while resisting the external challenge from Islam, and the Dominicans' mission was to convert the Albigensians. The Augustinians were founded in 1256.

In this determined atmosphere, the Western spirit shone and the 13th and 14th centuries were great periods for the Light. However, the crusader states were lost, and in 1291 Acre, the last city of the Kingdom of Jerusalem, and since 1187 its capital, fell to the Mamluks. Soon afterwards the Hundred Years War broke out between Britain and France, the West was divided within itself, and the crusading spirit declined. The Western soul retired within itself, and the Light shone until the Renaissance.

The Italian Franciscans' Light Supreme, Energising Fire, Infinitesimal Point of Light and Light of Glory

The Radiance of the Kabbalah found its way into the late medieval Brightness of the European mystics. For a full treatment of the Kabbalah, which spread from Palestine, see the Kabbalist Light, pp447-458.

The Kabbalah of the Ashkenazic tradition had been brought to Italy before it reached France through merchants. The "Light Supreme" (God) sent out a spark or ray of the "Light of Glory", by which the intellect saw God, according to the descendants of the Mendicant friars who began a spiritual revival in the 13th century, following the appearance of the first medieval heretics in the 12th century (the Manichaean-Gnostic Cathari or Cathars, the Waldenses or Vaudois and the Lombard *Humiliati*). The main figure was St Francis of Assisi (1182-1226), the founder of the Franciscan Order and of the Franciscan tradition of Italian mysticism which dominated the 13th and early 14th centuries.

St Francis himself had visions, like his Italian forerunner Joachim of Fiore, whose visions Francis must have known. When St Francis was 22 the crucifix in the ruined church of S. Damiano moved and cried out, "Go, Francis, and repair my house, which, as you see, is well-nigh in ruins." Two years before his death, he prayed and in an ecstasy saw a six-winged Seraph-

Christ fixed to a cross in a great light. This vision lasted an hour, and at the end he had the stigmata or wounds of Christ on his hands, feet and side.

St Francis had an Essene-like feeling for Nature, and praised "Brother Sun", "Sister Moon", "Sister Water" and "Sister Earth our Mother" in his *Canticle of the Sun.* He especially praised "Brother Fire", and told a monk not to "harm the fire" when his tunic was burning, and towards the end of his life he asked "Brother Fire" to be good to him when a surgeon tried to cure him of an eye ailment by opening the veins between his eyes and ears. St Francis also had illuminations, and in *The Little Flowers of St Francis* he described the Beatific Vision as "a rapture and uplifting of the mind intoxicated in the contemplation of the unspeakable savour of the Divine sweetness...and a burning sense within of that celestial glory unspeakable", i.e. the Light.

St Francis's Italian disciples included the friars John of Parma (died 1288) who according to the *Fioretti* "gazed into the abyss of the infinite Light divine", and John of la Verna, and the Light is to be found in his disciple, the mystic poet Jacopone da Todi (c.1230-1306), a lawyer who became a lay brother in the Franciscan Order following the death of his wife: "Ineffable Love Divine, sweetness informed, yet bright, measureless, endless Light (*lume fuor di mesura*), flame in this heart of mine." According to Jacopone, the soul progressed through three heavens. The first was the heaven of multiplicity in which the darkness contains "stars" of Light, the second was the heaven of contemplation where the soul has a dim apprehension of God (compare Dionysius), and the third the "hidden heaven" of "measureless Light", where God is to be found.[33]

Jacopone's contemporary Angela of Foligno (1249-1309) lived an immoral life until her conversion. She became a Franciscan tertiary hermit after the death of her husband and children, and expressed the Light in her *Book of Visions*: "The eyes of my soul were opened and I discerned the fullness of God.... I beheld a Thing, as fixed and stable as it was indescribable.... And though my soul did not behold love, yet when it saw that ineffable Thing it was itself filled with unutterable joy." Elsewhere she suddenly exclaimed, "I saw God"; and when her scribe or secretary asked her what she saw, she said, with understandable reticence which her scribe records: "I beheld a Fullness and a Clearness.... What I beheld was not bodily, but as though I were in heaven.... I saw the Supreme Beauty, which contains in itself all goodness."

Angela's language hints, it does not state, but the hints are there: a fullness like a full moon, a clearness like the Clear Light of the Void, a thing that was Supreme Beauty – Angela was describing the Light. "At times", she wrote of her "formless vision", "God comes into the soul without being called; and he instils into her Fire, love and sometimes sweetness." And, "Of these most excellent and divine workings of the soul, when God doth manifest Himself, we can in no wise speak, or even stammer." She put it more strongly: "During last Lent I found myself altogether in God.... And I see and understand that these divine operations...no angel...could comprehend; and all I say now of it seemeth to me so ill said that it is blasphemy."

On another occasion Angela said, "My soul has just been rapt to a state in which I tasted unspeakable joy, I saw all Good." Her scribe recalled that she "told me that her mind had been uplifted three times to this most high and ineffable mode of beholding God in great darkness (i.e. against the background of great darkness), and in a vision so marvellous and complete. Certainly she had seen the Sovereign Good countless times and always darkly; yet never in such a high manner and through such great dark." Angela's Light was such that she could write of her early life: "By God's will there died my mother, who was a great hindrance to me in following the way of God: soon after my husband died likewise, and also all my children. And because I had commenced to follow the aforesaid Way, and prayed God that He would rid me of them, I had great consolation of their deaths." Her Dark Night was "a privation worse than hell".[34]

St Bonaventura (c.1217-1274), the Franciscan intellectual and teacher who was influenced by Dionysius, held in *The Journey of the Mind to God* that the Divine Light of the Creator could not be known by any creature. The Light was the "seventh illumination", the seventh stage in the ascent of the soul, which would only be known after death: the *lumen gloriae* or light of glory. The six illuminations that man is given in this life are the lights of mechanical art, sensitive knowledge, natural, rational and moral philosophy, and revelation of the Holy Writ. Therefore, "if you would truly know how these things come to pass, ask it of grace, not of doctrine;...of that Fire which enflames all and wraps us in God with great sweetness and most ardent love. The which Fire most truly is God" (ch 7). Man may not know the Light of Glory until after death, but he could know the "Energising Fire" of God, which is the Light that can be seen in this life, and the goal of the mystic was "the shaft of light that flashes out from the divine, mysterious darkness", a phrase he took from Dionysius.[35]

The Italian Franciscan Light culminated with Dante (1265-1321), whose Light reflects Mechthild's "Flowing Light" (of which he had read). St Bernard is significantly his guide towards the end of *Paradiso* (c.1318-21), at the climax of which Dante has a vision of the Divine Light. Dante has numerous visions of lights (souls), and he sees Heaven heightened by an increased radiance – the lights of Christ, the Virgin, the Apostles and the saints – and is temporarily blinded by the brilliance of St John's soul. Then, gazing into Beatrice's eyes, he sees a light reflected in them which is the Infinitesimal Point of the Kabbalah: "One point I saw, so radiantly bright, so searing to the eyes it strikes upon, they needs must close before such piercing light." There are nine radiant rings round the Point, which is God; the nine orders of angels. As they fade Beatrice tells him that they have entered the Empyrean ("that heaven which is pure light alone: pure intellectual light", i.e. the highest heaven, the sphere of fire), and "now a living light encompassed me; in veil so luminous I was enwrapt that naught, swathed in such glory, could I see....Light I beheld which as a river flowed." He bathes his eyes, in this river of light (*lume in forma di riviera*, compare Mechthild's "Flowing Light"). He immediately sees the saints of Heaven seated on thrones that rise in tiers and form the petals of a snow-white rose. (Compare a rose window in a Gothic Cathedral.)

The circle of yellow light at the centre of the Celestial or Sempiternal Rose is the light of God's glory, the *lumen gloriae*. This became a dogma a few years before *Paradiso* in 1312, when the Council of Vienna defined the Light of Glory as the necessary help the intellect needs before it can see God face to face: "If in its inmost petals can reside so vast a light, in such a rose as this what width immense must in the rim abide?" The souls of the redeemed Angels are seen as a swarm of bees in the rose, and "their glowing faces were as fire that gives forth flame". St Bernard appears to lead him to the vision of God, and Dante sees Beatrice enthroned in Light: "So I amid the living Light mine eyes directed...and there I saw her in her glory crowned, reflecting from herself the eternal rays." Dante looks higher and sees the Virgin, "a radiance surpassing all the rest", and "is enabled to penetrate with his vision to the True Light of which all other is the radiance" (cf the "Radiance" of the *Zohar*) "or reflection" (summary to canto 33).

This is the Beatific Vision of the Divine Being in glory, the Empyrean. The Virgin raises her eyes "unto the eternal light" (*la luce eterna*). "Now my sight pierced through the ray of that exalted light" (*dell'alta luce*). The "Light Supreme" (*somma luce*) sends "one single spark" of its "glory's light", "the piercing brightness of the living ray" which takes him to "the Infinite Good", "the eternal light", "one simple light" (*un semplice lume*). "The living Light" – "that light supreme", "Eternal light, that in Yourself alone dwelling, alone does know Yourself" – "transforms" Dante, for there are three "spheres" within it. These are the three Persons of the Godhead, and the third of "flame" emanates from the first two.

The universe is therefore *in* God, "the sphering thus begot, perceptible in you like mirrored light". Thus, the universe is permeated by the Divine Light. We do not know anything about Dante's own experience of the Light except what he tells us in the *Divine Comedy*, but only someone who had experienced it could have written the end of *Paradiso*; someone who, to use Dante's words (*Letter to Can Grande, Epist.* X, s28), had "navigated the great Sea of Being".[36]

The German Dominican Light of Wisdom and Spark of the Soul

The Ashkenazic Kabbalah had also reached Germany by 1150, and influenced the Dominican Light after 1215. The Dominican Light now found expression in Dante's sublime vision of the Absolute, and Dante had absorbed the Italian-born St Thomas Aquinas (c.1225-1274), who was the first Dominican of stature following the founding of the Order in 1215. Aquinas was an Aristotelian who accepted the Neoplatonist and Augustinian tradition. He was taught by Albertus Magnus (who in *De Adhaerendo Deo* wrote that through darkness of mind we reach the uncreated Light), and though not himself a mystic he wrote (*De Veritate* 18) that God can be seen by a spiritual light which flows into man's mind from the Divinity, and is an express likeness of the Uncreated Light.

This spiritual light is the Light of Wisdom which uplifts the soul so that it can perceive the Divine, though it falls short of perceiving the divine Essence as it is seen in Heaven. "If the mind be so far uplifted by a supernatural Light that it is introduced to the perception of spiritual things themselves, this is above human measure; and it is caused by the gift of Understanding" (*Comm in Sent* 3.35.2.1.1) which is always a "supernatural light" (*Summa Theol* 22.8.1). Two years before he died Aquinas had a mystical experience during Mass and as a result he left his *Summa* unfinished. He wrote "I have seen that which makes all I have written and thought look small to me" (i.e. the Light).[37]

The German Dominican Meister Eckhart or Eckehart (1270-1327), founder of the Rhineland mystics, saw the Light as the "spark of the soul" (*seelenfünklein* or *scintilla animi*) and anticipated German Protestantism and Existentialism. He, too, was probably taught by Albertus Magnus, and he combined the scholasticism of Aquinas with the work of Plotinus, Augustine and Dionysius; he followed Dionysius in distinguishing between the Godhead, the origin of things which does not act, and God, who does. Thus he wrote of "the desert of the Godhead where no-one is at home". "God is within, we are without, God is at home, we are in the far country", and "God is nearer to me than I am to myself" (*Pred* 69).

Union with God takes place within the soul, which is entered by "Jesus" (the "spark of the soul", the Light). In the spark of the soul or "light of the soul" "God glows and burns unceasingly and in all His glory, with all His sweetness and with all His joy". Here is the "citadel in the soul" where is to be found "that which eternally is, which is neither this nor that" (i.e. the Light). The soul's light is therefore uncreated, and "the eye by which I see God is the same as the eye by which God sees me" (*Sermon* 23). When a person turns from temporal things inwards, into himself, he becomes "aware of a heavenly light" (*Sermon* 21), and "God in the Trinity is the living light in its radiant splendour.... God in human nature is a lamp of living light". "What God is in himself," Eckhart says elsewhere, "no man can tell except he be ravished (rapt) into the light that God is himself", and God "makes the enraptured soul to flee out of herself" (*On the Steps of the Soul*). Thus God is the "Father of Lights".[38]

The German John Tauler (c.1300-61), "the Illuminated Doctor", was a pupil of Eckhart, and, a practical mystic, he often wrote of God "shining" in the soul: "God illumines his true Friends, and shines within them with power, purity and truth, so that such men become divine and supernatural persons." The inner Light brings Truth and shines through to others, but the self must be surrendered or it will see the Light as "dark from its surpassing brightness...as the shining of the sun on his course is as darkness to weak eyes" (*3rd Instruction*). The meeting-place, and emptiness to the intellect but a fullness to the heart, is "the Quiet Desert of the Godhead", but "think not that God will be always caressing His children, or shine upon their head, or kindle their hearts as He does at the first" (*Sermon for the 4th Sunday in Lent*), for there will be a Dark Night. Tauler says that the "Divine illumination" comes not "from our outward life of the human senses" but "from within us and direct from God", and it has an effect like gazing at the sun: "When (a man) turns to look at other objects he sees the sun's disc shining in them." [39]

Tauler played an important part in the Friends of God (*Gottes freunde*), a society of mystics within the Church in Strasbourg who looked back to St Hildegarde, Elizabeth of Schönau and Mechthild of Magdeburg, and who saw themselves as being directly guided by the Holy Spirit, the Light which destroyed selfhood. Another pupil of Eckhart's was connected with this group, the German Dominican Henry Suso (c.1295-1366).

Suso's conversion took place when he was 18, alone in a church: "Of a sudden his soul was rapt in his body, or out of his body.... That which the Servitor saw had no form neither any manner of being; yet he had of it a joy.... And the Friar could do nothing but contemplate this Shining Brightness.... It was, as it were, a manifestation of the sweetness of Eternal

Life.... Then he said, 'If that which I see and feel be not the Kingdom of Heaven, I know not what it can be'" (*Leben und Schriften*, his autobiography, ch 1). Suso refers to himself in the third person as the *Servitor* (Servant) of Eternal Wisdom, and he observes: "It was God Who, by a hidden Light, had caused this return to Himself." This return was the glory of being "illuminated and made shining in the Inaccessible Light" (*Little Book of Truth* ch 4).[40]

Suso's *Little Book of Eternal Wisdom* was widely read throughout the later Middle Ages, whereas his fellow Friend of God, Rulman Merswin of Strasbourg (c.1307-82) was less influential, though in many ways just as interesting. He became a wealthy banker before renouncing business for the spiritual life. His conversion took place in a garden when a radiant Light enfolded him and he felt he was carried round the garden with his feet off the ground. Merswin was probably the author of sixteen tracts that include *The Spark in the Soul*, the spark being smothered in the ashes of worldliness unless the Holy Spirit blows it into flame. In the fifth stage, the divine Light surrounds it until it glows into a white heat. Merswin was probably also the author of the *Book of the Nine Rocks*, in which men are called back to their origin like fish struggling up from pool to pool. The Friends of God included Margaret and Christine Ebner, Henry of Nordlingen and Nicolas of Basel, but one of the most extraordinary was Ellina von Crevelsheim, who was struck dumb for seven years, and then fell into an ecstasy for five days, during which she was "enveloped in light".[41]

The anonymous *Theologia Germanica* (*Book of the Perfect Life* c.1350) was probably written by one of the Friends of God. It says that man has an eye within him which has "the power of seeing into eternity" (ch 7): "The two eyes of the soul of man cannot both perform their work at once: but if the soul shall see with the right eye into eternity, then the left eye must close itself and refrain from working, and be as though it were dead. For if the left eye be fulfilling its office towards outer things...then must the right eye be hindered in its working; that is, in its contemplation." Therefore: "Let no one suppose that we may attain to this true light and perfect knowledge...by hearsay, or by reading and study" (ch 19). "Enlightening" belongs "to such as are growing" (ch 14), while "He who is made a partaker of the Divine Nature neither willeth, desireth nor seeketh anything save Goodness.... Where this Light is, the man's end and aim is...only the One."[42]

The Flemish Eternal Brightness or Light

The Brightness or Light of Flanders was linked to the German Light and to the Ashkenazic Kabbalistic Radiance. Thus, after the anonymous *The Mirror of Simple Souls* (probably written by the Flemish Marguerite Porete c.1300) – which says that in "bright contemplation" the soul is "full gladsome and jolly" – the dominant figure was Jan van Ruysbroeck (1293-1381), who influenced Tauler and Suso. Ruysbroeck was a priest in Brussels, and he spent the last 38 years of his life in the forest of Soignies. There he wrote of the Light as a spring of Living Water which leads the mind to Nudity when it is emptied of sense images. The pure soul can then unite with God, the "Unplumbed Abyss", in a "superessential life" in which enlightened men are "drenched through by the Eternal Brightness" (*Book of Supreme Truth* ch 11) of the "Incomprehensible Light".

In *The Adornment of the Spiritual Marriage*, Ruysbroeck says that God will lift the inward lover "into a superessential contemplation, in the Divine Light":

"Only he with whom it pleases God to be united in His Spirit, and whom it pleases Him to enlighten (illuminate) by Himself, can see God, and no-one else.... Few men can attain to this Divine seeing, because of their own incapacity and the mysteriousness of the light in which one sees.... But he who is united with God, and is enlightened in this truth, he is able to understand the truth by itself....And therefore, whosoever wishes to understand this must have died to himself, and must live in God, and must turn his gaze to the Eternal Light in the ground of his spirit, where the Hidden Truth reveals itself without means. For our Heavenly Father wills that we should see: for He is the Father of Light.... And this is the coming forth and the birth of the Son of Eternal Light. Now if the spirit would see God with God in this Divine Light...he must inwardly cleave to God...even as a burning and glowing fire which can never more be quenched.... He must have lost himself in a Waylessness and in a Darkness, in which all contemplative men wander in fruition...in which the loving spirit has died to itself.... For in this darkness there shines and is born an incomprehensible Light, which is the Son of God, in Whom we behold eternal life. And in this Light one becomes seeing; and this Divine Light is given to the simple sight of the spirit, where the spirit receives the brightness which is God himself.... The loving contemplative...sees and feels nothing but an Incomprehensible Light; and through that Simple Nudity which enfolds all things, he finds himself, and feels himself, to be that same Light by which he sees, and nothing else."

The coming of the Bridegroom is "new enlightenment". For "the ground from which the Light shines forth, and which is the Light itself, is life-giving and fruitful, and therefore the manifestation of the Eternal Light is renewed without ceasing in the hiddenness of the spirit.... And here there is nothing but an eternal seeing and staring at that Light, by that Light, and in that Light." Then a man is enlightened by Divine truth, and he receives anew, every moment, the Eternal Birth, and he goes forth according to the way of light, in a Divine contemplation."

Ruysbroeck is quick to point out the implications of the Light: "All those men who are raised above their created being into a God-seeing life are one with this Divine brightness. And they are that brightness itself,...they are that same onefold ground from which the brightness without limit shines forth the Divine way....And thus the God-seeing men...behold God and all things, without distinction, in a simple seeing, in the Divine brightness." The Light, in fact, is proof of the brotherhood of man which transcends all racial barriers and power politics.

Ruysbroeck also saw God as Fire: "Our own spirit and the Spirit of God sparkle and shine one into the other.... Thereby the spirit is burned up in the Fire of Love" (*Adornment of the Spiritual Marriage* 2.54) and "swallowed up... in the deep Quiet of the Godhead" (*The Sparkling Stone* 9). "The pure soul feels a constant fire of love, which desires above all things to be one with God". And "as the air is penetrated by the brightness and heat of the sun, and iron is penetrated by fire...so likewise is God in the being of the soul" (*Book of Supreme Truth* ch 8). The Light therefore burns the spirit into awareness of the brotherhood of man. "Christ the Eternal Son rises in our hearts and sends His Light and Fire into our wills, and draws the heart from the multitude of 'things', and creates unity and close fellowship, and makes the heart grow and become green through inward love" (*The Adornment of the Spiritual Marriage*).[43]

Ruysbroeck's disciple Gerhard or Geert Groote (c.1340-1384) believed that "the Holy Spirit inwardly visits, illumines and changes the heart of a man". He founded the Brotherhood of the Common Life, which produced the New Devotion of the Low Countries, and practised the imitation of Christ.His notebooks formed the basis of *The Imitation of Christ* by Thomas à Kempis (c.1380-1471), who entered the Windesheim community of the Brethren of the Common Life in the Netherlands and spent 70 years there. The *Imitation* appeared in Latin c.1470 long after the work of Groote's follower, Hendrik Mande (died 1431), the "Ruysbroeck of the North", and of his friend Gerlac Petersen (died 1411), who wrote *The Fiery Soliloquy with God*, but it is the best presentation of the *devotio moderna*.

The *Imitation* begins: " 'He that follows Me, walks not in darkness,' saith the Lord. These are the words of Christ, by which we are admonished how we ought to imitate His life and manners, if we will be truly enlightened." Grace, the working of "intellectual Light from above", is fundamental to Kempis, "for when the grace of God comes unto a man, then he is made able for all things", and is among those "who, being illuminated in their understandings, and purged in their affection, do always breathe after things eternal". Thus, the famous "prayer for mental illumination" can be translated: "O merciful Jesus, enlighten me with a clear shining inward Light, and remove away all darkness from the habitation of my heart.... Send out Your Light and Your truth, that they may shine upon the earth; for until You enlighten me, I am but as earth without form and void."

Kempis distinguishes "the sweetness of the Creator and the creature,...of Light uncreated and of light enlightened (or light illuminate)", and he asks the "Everlasting Light" to "enlighten" his spirit. Grace is "a supernatural light", "the proper mark of the Elect" and only "him that is spiritually and inwardly enlightened" can distinguish "the motions of Nature and of Grace". There is therefore "an incomparable distance between the things which the imperfect imagine in their conceits, and those which the illuminated are enabled to behold, through revelation from above." Jesus is addressed as "You Light of everlasting Light" and is asked "to inflame my coldness with the fire of Your love, enlighten my blindness with the brightness of Your presence" for "You are Fire always burning...and enlightening the understanding".[44]

The *Imitation*, being based on Groote's notebooks, handed on Ruysbroeck's influence to the 15th century, when Henry de Herp, Nicholas of Cusa (who wrote in *The Vision of God* XIII, "it behoveth the intellect to become ignorant and to abide in darkness if it would fain see You") and Denis the Carthusian passed it on to the Renaissance.

The English and Late Italian Fire of Love

English mysticism, which was then open to Continental Kabbalistic influence, can be traced back to the 12th century (*Ancrene Wisse* or *Ancren Riwle* and St Aldred) but its father in the great "flowering time" of the 14th century was really Richard Rolle (c.1300-49). Rolle studied at Oxford, left without taking a degree because of the "disputatiousness" of the academic world and became a hermit. Later he became spiritual adviser to the nuns of Hampole in South Yorkshire.

Rolle describes his conversion in terms of the Light in *The Fire of Love* (ch 15): "From the time my conversion of life (or life-changing) and mind began until the day the door of Heaven (or heavenly door) swung back and his Face was revealed, so that my inner eye could contemplate the things that are above and see by what way it might find the Beloved and cling to him, three years passed, all but three or four months. But the door remained open for nearly a year longer before I could really feel in my heart the warmth (or heat) of eternal love. I was sitting in a certain chapel, delighting in the sweetness of prayer or meditation, when suddenly I felt within myself an unusually pleasant heat. At first I wondered where it came from, but it was not long before I realised that it was from none of his creatures but from the Creator himself. It was, I found, more fervent (or hotter) and pleasant than I had ever known. But it was just over nine months before a conscious and incredibly sweet warmth kindled me."

Rolle expands upon this "Heat" in the "Prologue": "I cannot tell you how surprised I was the first time I felt my heart begin to warm. It was a real warmth too, not imaginary, and it felt as if I were actually on fire. I was astonished at the way the heat surged up.... I realised that...this fire of love...was the gift of my Maker." Thus (ch 14): "To love Christ...will involve three things: warmth (or heat) and song and sweetness.... I call it fervour (or heat) when the mind is truly ablaze with eternal love, and the heart feels itself burning with a love that is not imaginary but real. For a heart set on fire produces a feeling of fiery love."

In the "Prologue" Rolle speaks of "this flame (which metaphorically I call 'fire', because it burns and enlightens)", and later on (ch 19) he makes it clear that the "fire of Love" is the Light: "The mind...blazes up within itself by the fervour of its love....Gradually it grows and glows in spiritual good,...is lifted with heavenly fire to the life of contemplation.... He is held tight in the embrace of eternal love,...and with his whole heart he is attempting to reach up and see that indescribable light." The Light cleanses a man for the next world: "In this way a man is made perfect, and does not need to be purged by fire after this life: the fire of the Holy Spirit burns in him while he is yet in the body. Yet this perfect love does not make a man incapable of sinning, but no sin can persist in him because it is at once purged by the fire of love.... His mind is...rapt...He is taken out of himself into indescribable delight.... Not only does he face death unafraid, but he is even delighted to die" (ch 22).[45]

The anonymous 14th century *Cloud of Unknowing* is an English work influenced by Dionysius. The cloud, or darkness, both separates the soul from and unites the soul with God. It unites by coming between the soul and the material world: "And if ever thou shalt come to this cloud...as this cloud of unknowing is above thee, betwixt thee and thy God, right so put a cloud of forgetting beneath thee; betwixt thee and all the creatures that ever be made. Thee thinketh...that thou art far from God because that this cloud of unknowing is betwixt thee and thy God: but...thou art well further from Him when thou hast no cloud of forgetting betwixt thee and all the creatures that ever be made" (ch 5). One must wait patiently in the Cloud of Unknowing: "This darkness and this cloud is, howsoever thou dost, betwixt thee and thy God, and letteth thee that thou mayest neither see Him clearly by light of understanding in thy reason, nor feel Him in sweetness of love in thine affection. And therefore shape thee to bide in this darkness as long as thou mayest" (ch 3). Patience is rewarded by the fire of love, the Light: "Then will He sometimes peradventure send out a beam of ghostly light (goostly light, i.e. spiritual light), piercing this cloud of unknowing that is betwixt thee and Him; and shew thee some of His privity (i.e. mystery), the which man may not, nor cannot speak. Then shalt thou feel thine affection inflamed with the Fire of His Love, far more than I can tell thee" (ch 26).[46]

There have been attempts to connect the author of *The Cloud of Unknowing* with Walter Hilton (died 1396), who, like Rolle, studied (at Cambridge) and then became a hermit. His masterpiece, *The Ladder* (*or Scale*) *of Perfection*, also derives from Dionysius and the Dominicans. "Whoever loves God dwells in light," Hilton writes. However, a man "cannot pass suddenly from one light to the other, that is, from the love of this world to the perfect love of God." He must "remain awhile in the night" which is "pregnant with good, a glowing darkness." The soul "is not in complete darkness" for "although it (the darkness) conceals it (the soul) from the false light (of the world) it does not entirely conceal it from the true light." Jesus "who is both love and light" is "at work in the soul". This state "is called night and darkness, because the soul is hidden from the false light of the world, and has not yet fully enjoyed the true light."

Therefore "how much better and more blessed must it be to experience His love, to be bathed in His glorious and invisible light, and to see all truth." The Sun of Righteousness, Jesus, will "illumine" the minds of humble souls "to know truth, and will kindle their affections with burning love, so that they burn and shine. Under the influence of this heavenly Sun they will burn with perfect love and shine with the knowledge of God" (2.24-6). When love openeth the inner eyes of the soul for to see this truth," Hilton says of the Uncreated Light, "...then by the sight of God it feeleth and seeth itself as it is" (2.37). "What this opening of the ghostly eye is," Hilton says elsewhere, "the greatest clerk on earth could not imagine by his wit... This opening of the ghostly eye is that lighty murkiness and rich nought that I spake of before, and it may be called...burning in love and shining in light" (2.40). In the third degree of contemplation, a man "is as it were ravished out of his bodily senses, and then by the grace of the Holy Spirit he is illumined, to see through understanding that truth which is God, and also to see spiritual things." The love of Jesus is "to be bathed in His glorious and invisible light, and to see all truth."[47]

The Benedictine nun Julian of Norwich (c.1342-after 1416) had sixteen visions between 4am and 9am on May 8, 1373 and the following night. She was then thirty and very ill, and soon afterwards she was cured. She became a "recluse" at St Julian's Church, Norwich, and wrote two accounts of her "shewings" (revelations), *Revelations of Divine Love.* The second account appeared some twenty or thirty years after the first, and it describes Julian as "a simple creature unlettyrde". However the third "shewing" presents "the whole Godhead concentrated as it were in a single point", Dante's Infinitesimal Point, the *Zohar*'s "hidden, supernal point".

Julian sees the Light as a means of showing us our sin: the Lord "shows us our sin by the gentle light of mercy and grace" and "by that light, lovely and gracious, which shines from himself". The revelations were followed by enlightenment: "I have told you of fifteen revelations...which have been renewed by the subsequent enlightenment and touch of the same Spirit (I hope) that showed me them all." This Light is both faith and God: "Our faith is a light.... By this light Christ, our Mother and Holy Spirit, our good Lord, lead us through these passing years. The light is measured to our individual needs as we face our night. Because of the light we live: because of the night we suffer and grieve.... When we are done with grief our eyes will be suddenly enlightened, and in the shining brightness of the light we shall see perfectly. For our light is none other than God our Maker, and the Holy Spirit, in our Saviour, Christ Jesus. So did I see and understand that faith is our light in darkness, and our light is God, the everlasting Day" (ch 83). "This light is charity, and by the wisdom of God it is measured so as to give us full benefit" (ch 84).

Her visions (including one of a hazel nut, which was "all that is made") gave her a profound conviction that "sin is behovable" (i.e. necessary or inevitable). For it is sin that distinguishes man from God, "but all shall be well and all shall be well, and all manner of thing shall be well" (ch 27), an affirmation which Eliot echoed at the end of "Little Gidding" and which expresses the profound well-being that is the great gift of the Light.[48]

Other, lesser figures contributed to the English mysticism of the fourteenth century. Margery Kempe (c.1373-1440), for instance, also came from Norfolk, but unlike Julian she had fourteen children before turning to a life of devotion and "boisterous" crying, which somewhat devalues her *Book of Margery Kempe*. And William Langland (c.1330-c.1400) was not a mystic, but his *Piers Plowman* (B text 1377-9) was a Benedictine religious allegory that included the Light at the climax, the *lumen Christi*. In Langland's dream, a great Light appears before the gates of Hell, and demands entry as "the King of Glory" so that "Christ, the Son of the King of Heaven, may enter." Immediately the gates burst open, and "Lucifer could not look to see, for the Light had blinded his eyes. And then our Lord caught up into His Light all those that loved him."[49]

The Italian Light shone again before the Renaissance put it out. It was interpreted as God's "Fire" or "furnace" which consumed sin like rust.

St Catherine of Siena (1347-80) tried to reform the Church: "I desire to see you seek God in truth, without anything in between." She carried on the work of St Bridget or Birgitta who was the chief lady-in-waiting to the Queen of Sweden, and who died in Rome in 1373 having founded the *Ordo Sanctissimi Salvatoris*. St Catherine of Siena was a Dominican nun who advised the Pope and was regarded as the greatest of the 14th century mystics, for she had a vision of Christ crucified in a blaze of light. Five blood-red rays streamed from his wounds and turned into pure light as they pierced her body and stigmatised her. "I saw the crucified Lord coming down to see me in a great light," she wrote. "...Then from the marks of His most sacred wounds I saw five blood-red rays coming down upon me, which were directed towards the hands and feet and heart of my body.... They changed their blood-red colour to splendour, and in the semblance of pure light they came to the five places of my body." The pain of the stigmata she received in ecstasy probably contributed to her early death from exhaustion: "So great is the pain that I endure sensible in all those five places, but especially within my heart, that unless the Lord works a new miracle, it does not seem possible to me that the life of my body can endure such agony."

St Catherine of Siena wrote her *Dialogo* at the end of her life, and the Voice of God says to her (ch 63): "In order to raise the soul from imperfection, I withdraw Myself from her sentiment, depriving her of former consolations...which I do in order to humiliate her, and cause her to seek Me in truth, and to prove her in the light of faith....She...awaits the coming of the Holy Spirit, that is of Me, who am the Fire of Love...digging up the root of self-love with the knife of self-hatred." Later Catherine heard the words (ch 85): "I, Fire, the Acceptor of sacrifices, ravishing away from them their darkness, give the Light."

In a letter to an imperfect hermit, Brother William of England, St Catherine wrote about the Light which "I, Fire" gives: "Dearest son...I...write to you...with desire to see you in true light. For without light we shall not be able to walk in the way of truth.... Two lights are necessary. First we must be illumined to know the transitory things of the world.... This is the common light, that everybody in general ought to have.... The soul...ought to go on with all zeal to the perfect light. For since men are at first imperfect rather than perfect, they should advance in light to perfection.... All things ought to be received with reverence by the second class of people, who abide in this sweet and glorious light.... These have known and tasted in the light the eternal will of God.... I wish you and the other ignorant sons to reach this light, for I see that this perfection is lacking to you and to others."[50]

After Catherine of Siena, the Renaissance began to affect the Italian and European spirit, and the French Jean Gerson (died 1429) who saw illumination as part of cognition, the French Franciscan St Colette of Corbie (died 1447), her Italian disciple St Bernardino of Siena (died 1444), and St Catherine of Bologna were all very much end-of-period mystics. So, too, were St Jeanne D'Arc, who heard the voices of saints (Michael, Catherine and Margaret) in a blaze of light, and the Flemish St Lydwine of Schiedam.

However, there was a revival of the Italian Light with St Catherine of Genoa (1447-1510), a would-be nun who was forced into an unhappy marriage. She was twenty-six when, in 1473, her mystical conversion took place. She was visiting her sister's Convent and was persuaded to confess to the confessor of the Convent, "and as she knelt before him, she received in her heart the wound of the unmeasured love of God, with so clear a vision of her own misery and her faults...that she almost fell upon the ground.... She cried inwardly with ardent love, 'No more world! no more sin!'...If she had possessed a thousand worlds, she would have thrown all of them away.... And she returned home kindled (or all on fire)" (*Vita e Dottrina*, a record probably deriving from Catherine herself after 1495, ch 2).

She progressed: "Sometimes, I do not see or feel myself to have either soul, body, heart,...anything except Pure Love" (*Vita* ch 5). And: "When she heard sermons or Mass...she neither heard nor saw...without. But within, in the sweet divine light, she saw and heard other things, being wholly absorbed by that interior light" (ch 6). The soul "is made to know in an instant, by means of a new light above itself, all that God desires it to know". This light "is not sought by man, but God gives it unto man when He chooses", though "he who gazes too much upon the sun's orb, makes himself blind".

The Light purges: "As she, plunged in the divine furnace of purifying love, was united to the Object of her love...so she understood it to be with the souls in Purgatory" (*Tratto di Purgatorio* ch 1). St Catherine of Genoa writes of union with the Light in terms of the purging of an "object" which "cannot respond to the rays of the sun which beat upon it (*reverberazione del sole*), not because the sun ceases to shine – for it shines without intermission – but because the covering intervenes (*opposizione*). Let the covering be destroyed, and again the object...will answer to the rays which beat against it in proportion as the work of destruction advances. Thus the souls are covered by a rust – that is, by sin – which is gradually consumed away by the fire of Purgatory. The more it is consumed, the more they respond to God their true Sun. Their happiness increases as the rust falls off and lays them open to the divine ray...and goes on increasing through the Fire of Love" (*Trattato di Purgatorio* chs 2, 3).

St Catherine of Genoa herself was purged. After four years of being haunted by a sense of sin, all thought of mortifications was "in an instant taken from her mind" (*Vita* ch 5), and underneath was a new centre of consciousness. For her the fire was at first painful and Purgatorial, when "souls have an impediment between God and themselves" and the "extreme fire" is "similar to that of Hell"; but it was finally pleasant and peaceful and Paradisal.[51]

Catherine had served the sick in a Genoa hospital, and she moved into the hospital in 1479 and remained there until her death, being Matron from 1490 to 1496. For twenty of these years she fasted seventy days a year, and her visions were all about "God...as Light and food of the soul".[52] Her goddaughter Battista Vernazza (1497-1587) carried her vision on in such works as *The Union of the Soul with God and On Heavenly Joys,* which reveal her own experience of illumination, but apart from visionaries like Osanna Andreasi of Mantu (died 1505), Columbia Rieti (died 1501) and her follower Lucia of Narni, the Italian Light of Catherine of Siena was gone.

The Renaissance Dimming

The Middle Ages ended with the Kabbalistic and Christian Light in decline in both the West and the East. In the West, the authority of the Catholic Church declined when the Papacy withdrew from Rome to Avignon in the 14th century and eventually split in the Great Schism, when for several decades there were two Popes, one Italian and one French. When the Schism was healed, the Pope became a kind of Renaissance prince with large estates and money to commission works of art, and as the German princes became nauseated at the worldliness of the Church of Rome, the seeds of the Reformation were already sown.

In the East, the fall of Constantinople to the Ottoman Turks in 1453 brought the Byzantine Empire to an abrupt end. The libraries of Constantinople hoarded Greek and Latin texts from the ancient world, and when these libraries were ransacked, the texts found their way to Italy. Italian scholars renewed contact with the ancient world, and the outward-looking Renaissance had begun.

As the early Renaissance scholars studied the classical texts that had been preserved from Roman times in the libraries of Constantinople and searched the monasteries for more works of classical learning, they found their own ideas challenged. From the perspective of the descendants of the Teutonic barbarians who had sacked Rome, they looked back to the origins of Western civilization in Roman culture in the 5th century AD and were fascinated by Graeco-Roman man. A new spirit of intellectual inquiry transformed art, music, literature and science – and religion. Exploring the outside world with a renewed interest in geography – the Spanish discovered America in 1492 – Renaissance man slowly began to lose contact with his inner world, and with the Inner Light. During the High Renaissance, Western culture was enhanced by the rich naturalism of Leonardo and Michelangelo. The body returned to art in classical form; the halo disappeared.

The Reformation Light

Disillusion with the Church led to the Reformation. In the West the Tradition of the Light from the *New Testament* to early Spanish Carmelite mysticism is one undivided flow, but this was broken by the Reformation. With the growth of scientific materialism, rationalism and secularism, individual mystics reacted to specific cultural conditions, and new traditions arose (for example the Quakers, the Quietists, the Pietists). The Protestant experience of the Light co-existed with the Counter-Reformation which the Catholics mounted to deal with the Reformation, and the Light shone.

The roots of the Reformation went back to the end of the Crusades. The reforming Franciscans and Dominicans had opposed the Church, and they paved the way for John Wycliffe's "Lollards" English reform movement in the 1370s. This influenced Jan Hus, a Bohemian who was burned as a heretic in 1415 after the Holy Roman Emperor had abrogated a safe conduct. There was a huge outcry, but the Church silenced the Hussites (who eventually formed the Bohemian or Moravian Brethren). Later there were sermons calling for reforms and, after the overthrow of the Medicis in 1494, there was the puritanical rule of the Dominican Savonarola in

Florence until he was put to death with Papal approval in 1498. According to the most reliable report he told his Papal torturers on May 20, "I have denied my Divine light from fear of torment.... All that I have declared has come to me from God."[53]

There had long been opposition to the Church's practice of raising money by selling indulgences or pardons for sins; those who bought them were guaranteed a place in heaven no matter how wicked a life they had led. Chaucer had criticised this practice in the 1380s in his *Prologue to the Canterbury Tales*, and the Church was clearly abusing its position as intermediary between men and God. Pope Julius II increased the sale of indulgences to pay for the tomb Michelangelo was to sculpt for him, and for the new basilica of St Peter's (on which Michelangelo worked from 1546 to his death in 1564). When a seller of indulgences came to Wittenberg in 1517 Martin Luther (who had promised to enter a monastery during a thunderstorm on July 2, 1505) nailed 95 theses to the church door. In these he sought to make the *Bible*, not the Church, the sole authority over men, and said, "Indulgences confer absolutely no good on souls as regards salvation or holiness." Men could be saved by the mercy of God, and therefore by faith. Salvation was a personal matter between man and God, and "every man his own priest".

Martin Luther began the Protestant Reformation in Germany with his "justification by faith". He wrote: "At last I began to understand the justice of God as that by which the just man lives by the gift of God, that is to say by faith.... 'The just man shall live by faith.' At this I felt myself to have been born again."[54] Luther's discovery that faith alone was necessary for salvation, and that the Catholic Church could be dispensed with, prepared the way for the rise of the Protestant mind in which man made direct contact with God.

Protestantism began as a protest at the Holy Roman Emperor's opposition to the new reformed religion. When the Emperor, Charles V, summoned Luther to a diet, the German princes turned against the Emperor to free themselves from Papal rights. They set up their own churches. The Emperor (who was also King of Spain) opposed the reformed religion in 1521 and again at a diet at Speyer in 1529, and the protest of the German princes at this ruling led to their being called Protestants.

Meanwhile in England Henry VIII, who had in 1521 rebutted Luther and earned the title from the Pope of "Defender of the Faith" (which the English monarch still curiously retains), eventually sided with Luther. He wanted to annul his marriage to Catherine of Aragon, the aunt of Charles V (King of Spain and Holy Roman Emperor), who put pressure on the Pope to refuse permission. Henry broke with the Pope, divorced Catherine, married Anne Boleyn in 1533, and dissolved the monasteries, sequestrating their wealth. The Catholics were appalled. When Henry died he left a Protestant regency council to advise his son Edward VI, and when Edward died in 1553, Mary, Henry's daughter by Catherine of Aragon became Queen. In 1554 she married Philip II of Spain, a devout Catholic.

About the time of Henry's break with the Pope, John Calvin (1509-1564) underwent a sudden conversion to Protestantism in Paris. He said little about it: "When I was too firmly addicted to the papal superstitions to be drawn easily out of such a deep mire, by a sudden conversion He brought my mind (already more rigid than suited my age) to submission [to Him]. I was so inspired by a taste of true religion, and I burned with such a desire to carry my study further, that although I did not drop other subjects, I had no zeal for them. In less than a year, all who were looking for a purer doctrine began to come to learn from me, although I was a novice and a beginner."[55] The "burned" may give a clue that Calvin had suddenly experienced the Light.

In 1534 Calvin left Paris and settled in Switzerland where he wrote *Institutes of the Christian Religion* (1536). He led the Reformed Protestantism movement in Geneva, which spread to France as the Huguenots and eventually to Scotland as Presbyterianism. Calvin's successor, Theodore Beza, made Calvin's philosophy of predestination more deterministic by relating it to God and Providence rather than Christ, and John Knox (died 1572) brought his ideas to Scotland and made Presbyterianism the established Church of Scotland when the Catholic Mary Queen of Scots eloped with the murderer of her former husband.

The Light of the Jesuit and Carmelite Counter-Reformation: St John of the Cross's Supernatural, Burning Light

The Catholic policy of Counter-Reformation was shaped at the Council of Trent (1545-1563). This headed off criticism by desecularizing the Church, a reform which checked the spread of Protestantism in Europe. The movement was called "the Counter-Reformation" by Protestants when the Jesuits – the Society of Jesus which had been founded by a former Spanish soldier, St Ignatius of Loyola – were given the mission of recovering the territories that had been lost to the Church: South Germany, England, and the Low Countries. Charles V attacked the German princes in 1546 and there was war until the Religious Peace of Augsburg in 1555 allowed the German princes to retain the Protestant religion. In England, when the Catholic Mary died in 1558, her husband Philip of Spain sought to impose the Counter-Reformation all through the reign of Elizabeth I, culminating in the defeat of the Spanish Armada in 1588. No concessions were made to Calvinism – the first Puritanism – and the Catholic Habsburgs fought the Thirty Years War to win back Bohemia and Poland for the Counter-Reformation, and eventually admitted defeat under the Peace of Westphalia of 1648.

The roots of the Light of the Counter-Reformation are to be found in the Italian painter and sculptor Michelangelo (1475-1564) who wrote a number of sonnets, letters and fragments. These reveal an aspiring mystic who loved Dante ("Would that I were he!") and who was in search of the Light in the 1530s: "I know not if from uncreated spheres/Some longed-for ray it be that warms my breast..."; "Rend thou the veil, O Lord, break down this wall,/Which by its hardness keeps retarding so/Thy holy sunshine.... Oh send the light.../that so my soul may glow."

It is not often realised that Michelangelo was opposed to the pride of the Renaissance and of the Reformation. He had worked for several Popes after Julius II, and his loyalty was to the Pope who had commissioned him to work on his tomb, not to Luther who opposed Julius's fund-raising for the project; he had supported the Papacy against Savonarola and the Medicis in his time. He worked on the "Last Judgement" fresco of the Vatican's Sistine Chapel from 1533 to 1541 – this was inspired by the medieval hymn *Dies Irae* and by his reading of Dante – and in 1534 (possibly with Henry VIII in mind) he was clearly obsessed by the spiritual pride of the Renaissance and Reformation giants who defied God: "Giants they are of such a height/that each it seems doth take delight/in mounting to the sun, to be blinded by its light"; "A giant there is of such a height/that here below his eyes do see us not..../He yearns for the sun and plants his feet/on lofty towers in order heaven to attain." This last giant is an overreacher who begot the seven deadly sins, but elsewhere Michelangelo writes of attaining heaven: "The pow'r of one fair face spurs me to heaven.../And I rise, living, and with angels go." This Platonist poem speaks of "the light/Which shows the way to God" and completes Michelangelo's "metaphysics of light".[56]

The Light of the Counter-Reformation also appeared in Flanders with the Benedictine Abbot Blosius (1506-1566). He began as a page at the court of Charles V who later wished to make him Archbishop of Cambrai. In the *Book of Spiritual Instruction* Blosius (or Louis de Blois) wrote of being "joined to God in the Divine Light by a mystical and denuded union...through the brilliancy of the Divine Light shining on the mind". The soul is "liquefied by love" and "melts away into God...as iron placed in the fire is changed into fire, without ceasing to be iron". The soul "perceives the surpassing illumination of the Sun of Justice, and learns divine truth (c.11). Its "essence is bathed in the Essence of God" (c.12). In the depth of the soul "we are deiform" and "the heaven of the spirit" is to be found. "The depth, which the uncreated light ever irradiates, when it is laid open to a man and begins to shine on him, powerfully affects and attracts him" (the end of the *Book of Spiritual Instruction*).[57]

The Light of the Counter-Reformation was really centred in Spain, where Charles V became King in 1516. Almost immediately after Charles V came to the throne, the Spanish Light conquered the Andean, Meso-American and Aztec cultures and Christianized the Light of their sun-gods. Cortez destroyed the Meso-American Mayan culture between 1517 and 1523 (with Montejedo), and the Aztec empire in Mexico between 1519 and 1521. Pizarro destroyed the Andean culture of the Incas between 1532 and

1535. When the Andean, Meso-American and Aztec cultures were absorbed into Catholic Christianity, the Inca, Mayan and Aztec sun-gods were absorbed into the Christian God whose enlightenment remained that of an inner sun.

At home, the Spanish Light shone in the Franciscans Francisco de Osuna and her friend St Peter of Alcantara, and in the Dominican Luis de Granada and the Augustinian Luis de Leon. But the Light of the Counter-Reformation really goes back to the Spaniard St Ignatius Loyola (1491-1556), who founded the Society of Jesus to reform the Church within.

A soldier, Ignatius turned to Christianity while recovering from being hit by a cannonball, and in 1522 he experienced the Light while sitting by the River Cardoner at Manresa: "The eyes of his mind were opened, not so as to see any kind of vision, but so as to understand and comprehend spiritual things...and this with such clearness that for him all these things were made new" (*Testament* ch 3). This experience led him to write the first draft of *Spiritual Exercises*, which connect the soul with the Divine will. Ignatius was able to contrast the Light with visions because he "saw the most Holy Trinity as it were under the likeness of a triple plectrum of three spinet keys", and "the Blessed Virgin without distinction of members".[58] In 1529, Ignatius studied in Paris and roomed with St Francis Xavier (1506-52) who became a priest shortly after the founding of the Jesuits in 1534 and took the Jesuit Light to India, Malaya, and Japan.

The Counter-Reformation received new Light from the Carmelite nun St Teresa of Avila (1515-82), who spent eighteen years torn between the world and God. During this time she was ill, but in 1555 she was "addressed by interior voices" and saw "certain visions" and experienced "revelations", and her health improved. She had already had a vision of Christ in 1539, and now she saw Him more frequently, and Satan too, who apparently sat on her breviary until she dislodged him with holy water. Now she experienced "raptures" or trances in which her soul went into a kind of ecstatic swoon: "when I have felt that the Lord was going to enrapture me (once it happened during a sermon...when some great ladies were present), I have lain on the ground and the sisters have come and held me down, but none the less the rapture has been observed."

Such extremes have led to accusations that Teresa was a hysteric who suffered from catalepsy – an illness that brings about a trance-like, paralysed state of consciousness – but this creeping paralysis is often felt by those who know the Light, and is a sign that the Light has come into the soul and should be seen. "The exceeding abundance of the favours granted to the soul clearly indicates how bright has been the sun that has shone upon it and has thus caused the soul to melt away." "This utter transformation of the soul in God," Teresa says elsewhere, "continues only for an instant.... I know it by experience."

In *The Interior Castle* Teresa describes the second degree (or stage) of prayer as "a little spark of true love...which the Lord begins to kindle in the soul....And if we do not quench it through our own fault it begins to light the great Fire which...throws out flames of that mighty love of God.... This little spark is a sign or pledge that God gives to this soul to show that He is already choosing it for great things, if it will prepare itself to receive them. It is a great gift" (ch 15). Divine union is "as if the ends of two wax candles were joined so that the light they give is one: the wicks and the wax and the light are all one; yet afterwards the one candle can be perfectly well separated from the other". Or it is as if "in a room there were two large windows through which the light streamed in: it enters in different places but it all becomes one". In the "union of the Spiritual Marriage", then, "the Lord appears in the centre of the soul, not through an imaginary, but through an intellectual vision". (Again we come across the distinction between imaginary visions and the intellectual perception of the mystic Light.)

Teresa gives glimpses such as these as to what she saw during her mystic union, but otherwise she dwells on the externals – the effect of union on the body for example – and being untaught, lacks the rational power to interpret her experiences. Rather, she concentrates on what the soul *feels* during union and in the Dark Night, when "the light of reason...remains, but it is not clear; it seems to me as if its eyes were covered with a veil".[59] In fact, her emphasis on feeling at the expense of reason is probably a gain, for it gives her a practical down-to-earth side.

St Teresa began to consider reforming the Carmelite order in 1558. She wanted to restore it to its old austerity and enforce withdrawal so that the nuns would contemplate the Light, and in 1562, with the great energy and appetite for work which the Light gives, she opened the first convent of the Carmelite Reform with the Pope's blessing. The Carmelite prior general approved her reform and in 1568 she met a Carmelite priest twenty-seven years her junior, Juan de Yepes, later St John of the Cross (1542-1591), who became her confessor. St John of the Cross initiated the Carmelite Reform for men by opening a discalced ("shoeless", "barefoot") monastery the next year. St Teresa founded another sixteen convents and then the Carmelite general ordered her to stop and (in 1576 and 1577) St John was twice thrown into prison. There he wrote some of his finest poetry. St John's second spell of imprisonment was in Toledo, and he escaped by making a rope of blankets and lowering himself from a window, and after receiving support from Philip II the two lived to see their work accepted.

The Catholic mystic's direct experience of God must have seemed suspiciously Protestant ("every man his own priest") to the Catholic establishment of the 1570s, and St John cannot have reduced the suspicion by taking over and Catholicising the Protestant "burning heart" just as his namesake St John the Evangelist had taken over and Christianized the Gnostic Light of the World in his Gospel of Light. St John's two mystical treatises, *The Spiritual Canticle* – the first 30 stanzas of the poem were written in prison – and *The Living Flame of Love*, reveal the Light he inherited from St Teresa, who overshadowed him until modern times. God touches the soul and rouses it to fire: "There occurs that most delicate touch of the Beloved, which the soul feels at times, even when least expecting it, and which sets the heart on fire with love, as if a spark had fallen upon it and made it burn" (*Cant* 25.5). "As the fire of love is infinite, so when God touches the soul somewhat sharply the burning heat within it becomes so extreme as to surpass all the fires of the world. This is why this touch of God is said to be a 'burn'.... The soul is...entirely burnt up in this vehement fire.... The soul beholds itself as one immense sea of fire" (*Living Flame* 2.3,4,11).

The "light of glory which, in the soul's embrace, God sometimes produces within it" (*Cant* 20.16) is not the divine Essence, however, as it was for St Augustine: "We are not to imagine that the soul sees God essentially...: for this is only a strong and abundant communication from Him, a glimmering light of what He is in Himself" (*Cant* 14.6). The Light, then, appears "as if God drew back some of the many veils and coverings that are before" the soul and "the divine Face, full of grace, bursts through and shines" (*Living Flame* 4.7), causing the poetic cry "O burn that burns to heal!" (*Flama de Amor Viva*). Now there "is a new knowledge of God, wherein the spirit is most gently tranquil, being raised to the Divine Light" (*Cant* 14).

St John wrote two ascetic treatises of renunciation and detachment, *The Ascent of Mount Carmel* and his famous *Dark Night of the Soul*. The Dark Night was an ambivalent concept he borrowed from the Castilian soldier-poet Garcilaso de la Vega, and it was influenced by his youthful admiration for Dionysius the Areopagite. In St John's work there are two Dark Nights: a Night of the Senses, which is really a purgation that transforms the senses into spirit, purifying and detaching the soul from the senses and subjecting it to the spirit; and a later Night of the Spirit, the true Dark Night of the soul, which transforms and divinises the soul by further purging the sensual and new spiritual parts of the soul.

The first Dark Night is a purifying of the lower part of the soul (the physical senses, imagination and emotions), and this is "active", for the individual can contribute by preparing the senses and the spirit. The second Dark Night is a purifying of the higher part of the soul (the intellect and the divine will as opposed to the egoistic will), and this is "passive", for the soul is unable to do anything to unite with God until God has accomplished a stripping away and removal of impurities, working in a Dionysian, "Divine Dark" or Void of fruitful love: "What is meant by 'passive understanding' is this reception of a light that is infused supernaturally."

But that is not the end of the ambivalence for St John uses the image of "darkness" in the Dark Night of the Spirit, the true Dark Night of the Soul, in two different ways. First it describes this stripping away of sensations, images and concepts which impede the soul's unity with God, a state in which the light of perception and love has produced a "night of thought", a darkening of the intellect and its understanding. Secondly, it describes a period of emotional despair in which the Light is no longer seen: for the Dark Night of the Spirit always succeeds Illumination, and in the return to darkness in which the Light is hidden, the mystic feels an emotional desolation and depression which can last months or even years.

St John himself felt this during his time in prison, and he wrote that the "anguished soul" has "the conviction that God has abandoned it, of which it has no doubt" (*Dark Night of the Soul* 1.2.6). The depression is a reaction to the intensity of the illuminative experience, a time of rest for the soul while it is prepared for the unitive life, and all the mystics record a loss of direction at this time, an increase in temptations and an accumulation of disasters and irritations in the outer world, all of which test the patience of the emerging unitive soul.

The last part of St John of the Cross's *Dark Night of the Soul* is a commentary on the first three stanzas of a poem of his, and three quarters of the commentary is devoted to the first two lines: "In a dark night,/With anxious love inflamed...." The Night of Sense burns away the seven Deadly Sins which make men imperfect and brings Illumination: " 'Thy light shall rise up in darkness.' God enlightens the soul." The soul must then spend "some time, perhaps years, after quitting the state of beginners, in exercising itself in the state of proficients". Its joys are now more "abundant and interior than before, and they do not depend on the fatigue of meditation; they come spontaneously.

The Night of the Spirit plunges the soul back into "troubles, aridities, darkness and trials", but God causes "the sun to shine upon them" and then hides "its face" (2.1). There is "an inflowing of God into the soul which cleanses it of its ignorance and imperfections", an "infused contemplation", in which the soul is taught "without efforts on its own part" and enlightened. The enlightenment is "pain and torment" to the soul because "the divine Light" is so high that it "transcends the capacity of the soul": hence St John added "with anxious love" to the lines in *Psalm* 72: "My heart is inflamed."

"The divine light of contemplation," St John writes, "when it beats on the soul not yet perfectly enlightened, causes spiritual darkness, because it not only surpasses its strength, but because it blinds it and deprives it of its natural perceptions. It is for this reason that St Dionysius and other mystic theologians call infused contemplation a ray of darkness, that is, for the unenlightened and unpurified soul, because this great supernatural light masters the natural power of the reason and takes away its natural way of understanding." The "rays of this pure light strike upon the soul" to "renew it and ripen it", and "the more pure and simple the divine light when it beats upon the soul, the more does it darken it, empty it, annihilate it" and "the less pure and simple the light, the less is the soul darkened and annihilated". The natural light of the understanding must be purified and annihilated so that the understanding can be united with the "divine light of the highest nature", and "we learn that the soul, the more it is purified and cleansed in the fire of love, the more it glows with it".

Passing on to the rest of the poem, St John describes how the soul leaves the house of sensuality (his bodily prison) and climbs the ten rungs of the mystic or secret ladder. On the ninth and tenth rungs he encounters the sweet fire of divine love – "the soul is on fire sweetly" – and "the beatific vision", in which "love is like fire, which ever ascends, hastening to be absorbed in the centre of its sphere".

In the last degree of love when the soul is united with God in the spiritual marriage, "the soul is like the crystal that is clear and pure; the more degrees of light it recei.es, the greater concentration of light there is in it, and this enlightenment continues to such a degree that at last it attains a point at which the light is centred in it with such copiousness that it comes to appear to be wholly light, and cannot be distinguished from the light, for it is enlightened to the greatest possible extent and thus appears to be light itself" (*The Living Flame of Love* I).[60]

St John of the Cross's poems are filled with the Light. "Oh flame of love so living,/How tenderly you force/To my soul's inmost core your fiery probe," begins "Song of the Soul in Intimate Communication and Union with the Love of God". Later it appeals to "lamps of fiery blaze" that make "the deepest caverns of my soul grow bright" so that they give "to the belov'd both heat and light". In "Verses Written after an Ecstasy of High Exaltation", a cloud "illuminates the night" – a Dionysian idea – and in "Song of the Soul that is Glad to Know God by Faith" St John describes a fountain out of which "comes the light by which we see/Though it be night" (i.e. the Light). The "Romances" include "You are brilliance of My light.../In whom I am well pleased to shine"(2) and show Simeon "taking fire/With inward love" and being promised he would not die until he saw "The Light descending on its quest"(6). "With a Divine Intention" ends: "And wholly I am burned away."[61]

The Protestant Lutheran Light of Boehme

During the Counter-Reformation Protestant mysticism emphasised the spark of the soul, the Inner Light or "Christ Within", and there were a number of early Protestant mystics who turned away from the Church and justified themselves by faith in their experience of the Light. Sebastian Franck (died 1542), for example, left Catholicism to become a Lutheran, and then left Lutheranism for mysticism after meeting Kaspar Schwenckfeld in 1529. Schwenckfeld (died 1561) had experienced a spiritual awakening (the Light) in 1518, and after disagreements with Luther and the other religious leaders, he founded his own church to focus attention on the experience of Christ (the Light) and to avoid distracting congregations with outer symbols.

Like Franck, the "inspired shoemaker" Jakob Boehme (1575-1624), dissented from Lutheranism but was nevertheless touched by it, and indeed saw his mysticism as being consistent with it, and had direct contact with God as the Light.

Boehme, the greatest Protestant mystic, had his first illumination when he was very young: he "was surrounded by a divine Light for seven days". His second illumination happened in 1600 when he gazed at a polished "pewter dish which reflected the sunshine with great brilliance", fell into an inward ecstasy, and "looked into the deepest foundations of things". Later he went to a green before Neys Gate at Gorlitz, sat down, and, "viewing the herbs and grass of the field in his inward light", he "saw into their essences": "The Gate was opened to me, that in one Quarter of an Hour I saw and knew more than if I had been many years together at an University.... For I saw and knew the Being of all Beings, the Byss and the Abyss, and the Eternal Generation of the Holy Trinity, the Descent and Original of the World and of all creatures through the Divine Wisdom: knew and saw in myself all the three Worlds, namely, The Divine, angelical and paradisical; and the dark World, the Original of Nature to the Fire; and then, thirdly, the external and visible World, being a Procreation or external Birth from both the internal and spiritual Worlds."

The dark world is "the Original of Nature *to the Fire*", which means that the Divine World is a World of Fire; a "Womb of Eternity" from which people can "come to know the hidden unity in the Eternal Being", for "in Yes and No all things exist" (a Taoist viewpoint). Boehme records: "The same was with me for the space of twelve years...as it were breeding...before I could bring it forth into external Form of Writing."

In 1610 he had a similar but more enhanced illumination during his purging: "I began to fight a hard battle against my corrupted nature, and with the aid of God I made up my mind to overcome the inherited evil will, to break it.... Now while I was wrestling and battling, being aided by God, a wonderful light arose within my soul. It was a light entirely foreign to my unruly nature, but in it I recognised the true nature of God and man." It was this illumination that led him to write the *Aurora or Morning Redness* (1612), which is an example of inspired, automatic writing. The *Aurora* was condemned by the local Lutherans and Boehme was forbidden to write any more, an order he obeyed for seven years. (Gerard Manley Hopkins also gave up writing for seven years when he became a Jesuit novice in 1868.)

The *Aurora* is the first of three books, and it states a theosophical system that united "Philosophy, Astrology and Theology". Man is created by the same laws as the planets, microcosm is an image of the macrocosm, and the Trinity is presented in terms of the Light, for God the Father enables his Son to light the soul through the Holy Ghost: "Behold your inward man, and then you will see it most plainly and clearly; if you are not a fool and an irrational beast; therefore observe." (The inward man has been taken as the subtle or astral body.)"...All the powers which move in your heart, in your veins and in your brain, wherein your life consists, signify God the Father. From that power springs up your light....The whole body moves in the power and knowledge of the light, which signifies God the Son.... For as the Father generates the Son out of his power, and as the Son shines back in the whole Father; so in like manner the power of your heart, of your veins, and of your brain generates a light which shines in all your powers in your whole body. Open the eyes of your mind, consider it, and you will find it so.... And the Holy Ghost from God rules in this spirit in you, if you are a child of light.... Thus you find in man three fountain-springs. First, the power in your whole mind, which signifies God the Father. Then secondly, the light in your whole mind, enlightening the whole mind, which signifies God the Son. Then thirdly, there goes forth out of all your powers, and out of your light also, a spirit which has understanding."

It is important to grasp that at one level the *Aurora* of the title is a new age which will change the soul of mankind. Thus the introductory note – "since the time of the writing of this book...the lovely bright day has appeared unto the author" – is not saying that Boehme was illumined *after* the *Aurora*, a claim which makes nonsense of his earlier illuminations of 1600 and 1610. It is saying that he has now seen a new age of Light more fully than the glimpse he had of it in the *Aurora*.

At another level the *Aurora* clearly is a symbol for the Light, the "secret Mystery" or "hidden secret" which, Boehme promises, will become "a manifest knowledge" for all who read his book in singleness of heart. The "secret Mystery of the Deity" cannot be known "if the Dawning or Morning-Redness does not break forth in the centre in the soul."

In the spirit there is hidden "a spark of the light and power of God" and when the soul "is kindled or enlightened by the Holy Ghost, then it triumphs in the body, like a huge fire" which contains "the knowledge of God". The Light of God contains heat "which burns, consumes" in nature, as well as light, "the heart of the heat". The Light in the soul is produced by seven qualities of God acting together in an alchemical way, and the fifth quality, love, produces an azure light, for example, which is seen in the soul. (Compare the seven qualities with the seven *chakras*.) Boehme writes, "From this light now it is that I have my knowledge", and he says: "The light in man, which the Heart of God had breathed in, signifies or resembles the sun."

The kindling of the soul in man is the Dawning of the title and it will lead to the dawn of a new era of Eternity and Light: "The soul...unites with the Heart of God, out of which a new body might come to be.... And therefore in these our present times some beams of the day will more and more break through in the hearts of some men, and make known the day.

But when the Dawning or Morning Redness shall shine from the east to the west, or from the rising to the setting, then assuredly, time will be no more; but the SUN of the Heart of God rises or springs forth." To experience "the ray of the breaking through of the light of God with a fiery impulse", which will bring in a new age, "lay hold on the Heart of God (i.e. the Light), then you have ground enough."

There are dozens of passages about the Light in the *Aurora*, and the Light features in Boehme's *Epistles*: "The divine glimpse and beam of joy arises in the soul, being a new eye, in which the dark fiery soul conceives the Ens and Essence of the divine light." The Light appears in *The Threefold Life of Man*: "The Son of Man, the Eternal Word in the Father, who is the glance, or brightness, and the power of the light (of) eternity, must become man in you, if you will know God: otherwise you are in the dark stable and go about groping." Again: "Behold a bright flaming piece of iron, which of itself is dark and black, and the fire so penetrates and shines through the iron that it gives light.... In such a manner is the soul set in the Deity." The Light appears in his *Dialogue of the Supersensual Life*: "How am I to seek in the Centre this Fountain of Light which may enlighten me..., this true Light, which is the Light of Minds? Master. Cease but from thine own activity, steadfastly fixing your Eye upon one Point.... Be silent before the Lord, sitting alone with him.... So shall your Light break forth as the morning, and after the redness shall arise.... Behold, this is the true Supersensual Ground of Life."

Boehme describes the short cut to the Light, which is an emptying of oneself, a return to the Void: "Behold, if you desire to see God's Light in your Soul, and be divinely illuminated and conducted, this is the short way (i.e. short cut) that you are to take; not to let the Eye of your Spirit enter into Matter or fill itself with any Thing whatever, either in Heaven or Earth, but to let it enter by a naked faith into the Light of the Majesty." Love's duty, then, is to rejoice "therein with its fire-flaming more than the Sun of the world", "ceaselessly to kindle fire in the something, and glow within itself". In short: "Never shall you arrive at the Unity of Vision or Uniformity of Will, but by entering fully into the Will of our Saviour Christ, and therein bringing the Eye of Time into the Eye of Eternity; and then descending by

Means of this united through the Light of God into the Light of Nature" (*The Supersensual Life, Dialogue* 2).[62]

After Boehme's death in 1624 his influence spread all over Europe, his works were translated into many languages and his home town put up a statue of him.

The Church of England Light of the Metaphysical Poets

The Church of England was first established in the 2nd century by Lucius (see pp100-102), and the English Reformation under Henry VIII amounted to a break with the Pope but not with the Catholic Faith, which is preserved in the creeds. *The Book of Common Prayer*, the liturgical book used in churches of the Anglican Communion, was introduced by Cranmer in 1549 and there were revisions in 1552 (a Protestantising reform), 1559, 1604 and 1662. It is still in use, the experimental liturgy of our time being only an alternative.

The Light is present in Morning Prayer: "O Lord, let thy mercy lighten upon us," the *Te Deum* beseeches, while the *Benedictus* asks God "to give light to them that sit in darkness and in the shadow of death". Evening Prayers include the *Nunc Dimittis*, and the words, "To be a light to lighten the Gentiles", while the *Third Collect* begins: "Lighten our darkness, we beseech thee, O Lord." The *Litany* requests "that it may please thee to illuminate all Bishops, Priests and Deacons, with true knowledge and understanding of thy Word" The *Communion Creed* speaks of "God of God, Light of Light", and the priest can say immediately after the Creed, "Let your light so shine before men, that they may see your good works." The Light, then, is not exactly over-present in the Church of England liturgy, but it is there, in hints.

The Church of England Light is reflected in the writings of its literary priests, vicars and thinkers. John Donne (1572-1631) is the earliest. The leading poet of the Metaphysicals with his early love-poems, Donne became a priest in 1615 and Dean of St Paul's in 1621, where he preached his *Sermons* to huge congregations.

There is little about the Light in the poems, though "The Dreame" is clearly about it: "As lightning, or a Taper's light,/Thine (i.e. God's) eyes, and not thy noise wak'd mee..../Perchance as torches which must ready bee,/Men light and put out, so thou deal'st with mee./ Thou cam'st to kindle." In the poem, the God who "cam'st to kindle" was at first mistaken for "an Angell". The "shapeless flame" and "lovely glorious nothing" at the beginning of "Aire and Angels" refer to the Light: "Twice or thrice had I loved thee (i.e. the Light),/Before I knew thy face or name,/So in a voice, so in a shapeless flame,/Angells affect us oft, and worship'd bee;/Still when, to where thou wert, I came,/ Some lovely glorious nothing (i.e. the Light) I did see." The feeling is very Taoist, the Light-*Tao* being experienced before it can be named.

(Donne's contemporary, the Protestant Shakespeare's plays are not known for overt references to the Light. On the usual reading sonnet 33, also written in the 1590s, is a metaphorical statement of human love, in which Shakespeare's aristocratic friend withdraws his love/"heaven's sun", but the poem can also be read in terms of the Light, in which case it is entirely devoted to an experience Shakespeare had. The octet begins "Full many a glorious morning have I seen", and the sestet continues "Even so my sun one early morn did shine/With all triumphant splendour on my brow;/But, out, alack! He was but one hour mine,/The region cloud hath mask'd him from me now." The refrain constrasts the suns of the world of the octet with heaven's sun of the sestet: "Yet him for this my love no whit disdaineth;/Suns of the world may stain when heaven's sun staineth"; "stain" having a double meaning of "being corrupt" and "being obscured".)

Donne's *Sermons*, however, are full of the Light, which is expressed in a wealth of image. "They had a precious composition for lamps, amongst the ancients," Donne says, "reserved especially for Tombes, which kept light for many hundreds of yeares; we have had in our age experience, in some casuall openings of ancient vaults, of finding such lights, as were kindled, (as appeared by their inscriptions) fifteen or sixteen hundred years before; but, as soon as that light comes to our light, it vanished. So this eternall, and this supernaturall light, Christ and faith, enlightens, warmes, purges, and does all the profitable offices of fire, and light, if we keep it...in the proper place,...but when wee bring this light to the common light of reason...it may...vanish." Nowhere has the reason's destructive impact on the Light been more clearly stated. The last thing God "hath reserved to doe" is "the manifestation of the light of his Essence in our Glorification", and the soul, "as a flowre at Sun-rising, conceives a sense of God in every beame of his", and "as a flowre at the Suns declining, contracts and gathers in, and shuts up her selfe, as though she had received a blow".

God comes to us "as the Sun at noon", and a sinner lies as "the slime and mud of the River Nilus...before the Sun-beames strike upon it", the "first beame of grace"; he "cannot so much as wish, that that Sunne would shine upon him, he doth not so much as know that there is such a Sunne.... But if this first beame of Grace enlighten him to himselfe, reflect him upon himselfe." At death, "behold then a new light, thy Saviours hand shall open thine eyes, and in his light thou shalt see light". At death Donne will "never misse the Sunne, which shall then be put out, for I shall see the Sonne of God, the Sunne of glory, and shine myself, as that sunne shines". To the "light of glory, the light of honour is but a glow-worm", and the "beams of glorie which shall issue from my God, and fall upon me, shall make me...an angel of light..., a something I cannot name now, not imagine now". (The "some lovely glorious nothing" was an "angel of light", a beam of the Light; and therefore the Light.) To Donne, the Light or Fire dwells in us like a coal: "a miserable condition of man! which was not imprinted by God, who, as he is immortal himself, had put a coal, a beam of immortality into us, which we might have blown into a flame, but blew it out by our first sin" (*Devotions upon Emergent Occasions, Meditation* 1).[63]

Only Lancelot Andrewes (1555-1626) rivalled Donne as a sermoniser within the Church of England, but in the next generation there were a number of Anglicans (mostly vicars) who were also mystics and poets. They were all Royalists, of course, for the Church of England was of the King's party in the struggle against the Puritans and Cromwell.

The Welsh-born George Herbert (1593-1633) dominated and influenced them. Herbert became an academic and then turned parish priest at Bemerton, near Salisbury. He saw God as the Light in his poem "The Flower": "O my onely light,/It cannot be/That I am he/On whom thy tempest fell all night." In "Sighs and Grones" he writes that "My lust/Hath sow'd fig-leaves to exclude thy light", and in "Heaven" the echo of "delight" is "Light". George Herbert was probably influenced by his elder brother, Edward, Lord Herbert of Cherbury (1583-1648), the father of English Deism (the main philosophy of the rational Enlightenment), who wrote "Elegy over a Tomb" in 1617 about a divine light which gave knowledge and love, and which, perhaps, renews the sun: "Doth the Sun now his light with yours renew?" George Herbert's friend Nicholas Ferrar (1592-1637), the founder of the Christian community at Little Gidding, published Herbert's poems on his death, and gave them the title of *The Temple.* (Herbert had written a prose treatise on the duties of a country parson, *A Priest to the Temple.*) A contemporary of both, Robert Herrick (1591-1674) was ordained in 1623, lost the living of Dean Prior, near Totnes in Devon during the Civil War and lived in London until he was restored in 1662. Herrick wrote in "A Thanksgiving to God, for his House" (one of the poems he published in 1647/8: "Some brittle sticks of thorn or briar/Make me a fire,/Close by whose living coale I sit,/And glow like it."

George Herbert's admirer, the Welsh Henry Vaughan (c.1621-1695) – called "The Silurist" because his family came from Brecknockshire, where the Silures once lived – carried his influence into the 1650s with *Silex Scintillans* ("*The Glittering Flint*"), two volumes of religious poetry (1650-1655) which contain many Herbertisms. The "scintillans" probably came from *Religio Medici* (1635) by Sir Thomas Browne, who, although he seems to have had no mystical experience of his own, wrote of "a common spirit that plays within us yet makes no part of us; and that is the spirit of God, the fire and *scintillation*...which is the life and radical heat of spirits" (1.32). The title suggests a flint that makes sparks, and points to Vaughan's conversion, for "certain Divine Raies breake out of the Soul in adversity, like sparks of fire out of the afflicted flint". In Vaughan's case, the adversity was the death of a brother, the defeat of the Royalists and the destruction of the Church of England by Cromwell.

Vaughan wrote from "th' Inlightned spirit" ("The Retreate"). "The Morning-watch" is all about the Light, and recalls Boehme's *Aurora* (see pp175-179) and St John of the Cross: "O let me climbe/When I lye down!"

The soul "is like a clouded starre whose beames though said/To shed their light/Under some Cloud/Yet are above,/And Shine". The Light has gone, and Vaughan retreats "twelve hundred hours" "unto that hour/Which shew'd thee last, but did defeat/Thy Light", and searches and racks his soul "to see/Those beams again". The "morning" begins as the break of day on the outer world, and becomes the breaking of the Light on the inner world. Similarly, "The Dawning" anticipates the coming of the Light. The "Bridegroome" will come "in the Evening" or "wil thy all-surprizing light/break at midnight?" In "The Men of War" the Light makes the prospect of eternity bearable: "Were not thy word (dear Lord!) my light/How would I run to endless night."

But "The World" is perhaps Vaughan's best-known mystical poem. It also uses the Bridegroom image, only the Light is a ring: "I saw Eternity the other night/Like a great Ring of pure and endless light/All calm, as it was bright." Fools "prefer dark night/Before true light" (the Light), but the Bridegroom provides the Ring only "for his bride", and the soul must therefore aim to be a bride of the Light. The dead "are all gone into the world of light" and death is a Jewel "shining nowhere, but in the dark", while in "Cock-crowing" God is "Father of lights" and "immortall light and heat", and the poet asks: "Brush me with thy light, that I/May shine upon a perfect day,/And warme me at thy glorious Eye!" (i.e. the Light). "The Night" is about the divine darkness. Nicodemus "saw such light/As made him know his God by night", but "there is in God (some say)/A deep, but dazling (sic) darkness". It is not surprising that this writer about the light of Eternity, whose brother was Thomas Vaughan the Hermetical philosopher, should have translated a medical book under the title of *Hermetical Physick* (1655).

Three more Metaphysical poets carried forward the Herbert tradition. Richard Crashaw (c.1613-49) was at first High Church and he probably took Orders. He frequently visited the community at Little Gidding in the early 1640s and wrote an account of it, *Description of a Religious House.* In 1644 he became a Catholic and in 1646 he published *Steps to the Temple,* a title that recalls George Herbert's *Temple.* "Hymn to Sainte Teresa", which was in it, is a Catholic poem about St Teresa's girdle, "sparkling with the sacred flames/Of thousand soules" who were led "to kisse the light/That kindled them" by her "bright/Life". As a result St Teresa walks with God "those waies of light", and in 'The Flaming Heart' (1652) St Teresa is invoked as "O sweet incendiary".

Francis Quarles (1592-1644), an Anglican who came from Essex and had eighteen children, wrote about the absence of the Light in "Wherefore hidest thou thy face, and holdest me for thy enemie?" God denies "the Sun-shine of thy soule-enliv'ning eye" and "without that Light, what light remaines in me?" Quarles tells God: "Thou art my Life, my Way, my Light.... And who's that Light but Thee?" He begs to be enlightened: "O what's thy Light the lesse for lighting mine?"

Thomas Traherne (1637-1674) was ordained in 1660, and was nearly the last of the mystical poets who were also Church of England vicars. He was little known until the manuscripts of his poems and meditations were accidentally discovered in a London bookstall at the beginning of the 20th century. "On News" presents the Light as "the Gem,/The Diadem,/The Ring Enclosing all", "the Heavenly Eye,/Much Wider than the Skie" which was made to appear in the experience of illuminations as "a small and little thing". Traherne's *Centuries of Meditation*, which were written for a small religious society run by a Mrs Hopton of Kington, states a mysticism of joy or "happiness", the beatific vision which helps us see God and his creatures "in a Divine and Eternal Light" (3.60). The world is "a region of Light and Peace, did not men disquiet it" (1.31). Elsewhere Traherne writes: "Those pure and virgin apprehensions I had from the womb, and that Divine Light wherewith I was born are the best unto this day, wherein I can see the Universe."[64]

Sir Christopher Wren lived at the same time as many of the Metaphysicals. Wren's father was Dean of Windsor, and Wren moved in Charles I's court. He was at Oxford during Cromwell's rule – his first architectural commission was in Oxford's Sheldonian Theatre – and he was greatly influenced by the rebuilding of Paris, which he visited in 1665 when the Louvre was nearly finished and Versailles was being improved. The Great Fire of 1666 gave him his chance to rebuild London: he erected 52 parish churches there. He knew about the Light from his father, and (as anyone standing underneath and looking up can see) he put it on the inside vault of the dome of his masterpiece, St Paul's, which took 35 years to rebuild and the idea for which came from the new St Peter's, Rome. The sun-burst (Donne's "Sunne of Glory") – in this instance with a ring of clouds recalling the Cloud of Unknowing – stands above the altar of St Martin in the Fields, the work of Wren's disciple James Gibbs (ceiling by the Italian craftsmen Artari and Bagutti).

Looking back at the Metaphysical poets, one cannot help reflecting that their references to the Light are so numerous that one cannot understand Metaphysical poetry without grasping the Light. Indeed, the Metaphysical Light was principally a phenomenon of the Church of England tradition rather than of the poetry which expressed it. Looking back at these illumined Church of England Royalists who expressed themselves in Metaphysical poetry, one can understand why the illumined American expatriate T. S. Eliot, the one 20th century poet to have written about the Light, pronounced himself Church of England and Royalist.

The post-Metaphysical Church of England mystics grew out of the Cambridge Platonists. At Cambridge, a group of ex-Puritan divines who were opposed to both Calvin and Laud tried to reconcile Christianity and Renaissance Humanism. Benjamin Whichcote (died 1687) probably founded the group, and was its leader, and his main disciples were Ralph Cudworth (died 1688), John Smith (died 1652), Henry More (died 1687) and Peter Sterry (died 1672). The Cambridge Platonists reconciled Christianity and Platonism so that God indwelt in the mind as the Light. "The spirit of man is the candle of the Lord" was their favourite text.

A number of other thinkers were influenced by the Cambridge Platonists without accepting all their ideals, and one of these was John Norris (1657-1711), who became Rector of Bemerton, George Herbert's parish, in the 1690s and adopted Malebranche's theory of divine illumination. (Malebranche, 1638-1715, was a French Catholic who combined Cartesianism, St Augustine and Neoplatonism, so that "we see all things in God", and recalls Bishop Grosseteste who blended Aristotelianism and Neoplatonism at Lincoln in the 13th century.) Norris wrote *Two Treatises Concerning the Divine Light* (1692) against the Quakers, and argued that divine reason differs from human reason in degree, not kind, and that the Quakers were wrong to emphasise faith against reason. Norris wrote "Hymn to Darkness" in which darkness "like the light of God" is inaccessible: "Tho Light and Glory be th' Almighty's Throne/Darkness is his Pavilion."[65]

William Law (1686-1761), who was ordained at Cambridge and was later tutor to the father of Gibbon the historian, was also influenced by Malebranche, and (like the Germans John Gichtel, died 1710, and Dionysius Andreas Freher, flourished 1700-1720) later by Boehme. Law's main theme is the union between the Creator and his creatures, and this is seen in terms of the Light ("the Divine Indwelling") in *The Spirit of Prayer* (1749). Christ was "that eternal Word by which all things were created, which was the life and light of all things.... Thou seest, hearest and feelest nothing of God, because thou seekest for Him abroad with thy outward eyes, thou seekest for Him in books, in controversies, in the church.... Seek for Him in thy heart, and thou wilt never seek in vain, for there He dwells, there is the seat of His Light and holy Spirit. For this turning to the light...within thee is thy only true turning unto God (i.e. conversion); there is no other way of finding Him but in that place where He dwelleth in thee....Awake, then, thou that sleepest, and Christ, who from all eternity has been espoused to thy soul, shall give thee light. Begin to search and dig in thine own field for this pearl of eternity that lies hidden in it" (*The Spirit of Prayer*).

Man has "a spark of the light" in his soul which has a "tendency or reaching after that eternal light and Spirit of God from whence it came forth". Similarly, God has a tendency towards the soul of man, and sent Jesus, "the brightness of His glory", "a sun of righteousness", to unite him with man. Thus, when "the first spark of a desire after God arises in thy soul, cherish it" for it is "a touch of the divine loadstone".

In *An Appeal to all Who Doubt* Law writes of the union between the eternal world and Nature in terms of the Light: "Everything in temporal nature is descended out of that which is eternal.... In Eternal Nature, or the Kingdom of Heaven, materiality stands in life and light; it is the light's glorious Body, or that garment wherewith light is clothed, and therefore has all the properties of light in it."[66]

The Puritan or Nonconformist Light, the Quaker Inner Light

Puritanism began as a late 16th century movement to "purify" the Church of England from all that remained of the Catholic "popery" that had been left behind after Elizabeth I's Settlement. According to the Calvinist James I, it originated with the Familists (or Family of God, or Family of Love), a group founded in Holland by Hendrik Niclaes (c.1502-80), and later influential in England. (Niclaes was enfolded by light when he was eight, and he taught that true Light comes from the Being of Eternal Life.) In fact, Puritanism goes back to Chaucer's parson, though he did not try to impose his way of life on the nation, and to William Tyndale (died 1536), who believed that England, like Israel, had a covenant with God. (Edward VI and Elizabeth I were later seen as the Israelites Josiah and Deborah).[67] Puritanism was evident in the 1560s when the Puritan Matthew Parker turned against the "popery" of the clergy's dress, and in the 1570s, when the Puritan Thomas Cartwright turned against the "popery" of the episcopacy and proposed Presbyterianism.

By the 1580s, some Puritans were ready to go their own way in the face of persecution and to reject the Church of England, as Shakespeare's Malvolio rejected Sir Toby Belch. Some of these Separatists from the Church of England eventually fled to Holland, and fled again on the *Mayflower*. In the 1640s, returned Separatist exiles demanded freedom for their congregations or Independency, as opposed to the power of the Presbyterian elders, and became non-Separatist Independents. Some of these became English Baptists.

The Baptists may have been influenced by the various radical Protestant groups of 16th century European Anabaptists. The Anabaptists blasphemously believed in a second, adult Baptism, and were initially followers of Zwingli in Zurich. Some were mystics like Hans Denck (died 1527), who wrote of "a Spark of Truth",[68] and the ecstatic Nicholas Storch (died 1530), and the most interesting was Thomas Muntzer, c.1490-1535, who saw Luther's Reformation as a revolution. Muntzer broke with Luther in 1522 to assert that true authority was in the Inner Light, not the *Bible*[69]

– a view also taught by Storch – and in 1524 he joined the revolutionary Peasants' Revolt, but was defeated in battle and executed.

The General Baptists emerged from the English Separatists c.1608, and believed that Christ died for all men in accordance with the moderate Calvinism of Jacobus Arminius. They soon dwindled. The Particular Baptists emerged c.1638 from the non-Separatist Independents, and took an extreme Calvinist view that Christ died for an elect who experienced the Light.[70] They survived.

Puritanism opposed the Church of England monarch during the Civil War, and in the 1640s the Calvinist Presbyterian Puritans became supreme in Parliament. The Presbyterians forced Charles I to legislate against bishops and were all set to establish a presbyterian system within the Church of England when Parliament lost control to the army, which was strongly Independent (Congregationalist).

During this highly confusing emergence of the Calvinist Presbyterians, the Congregationalists and the Baptists, the anti-episcopal Puritans were charged with antinomianism: following inner grace – the Light – instead of the Mosaic Law of the Church.[71] The original Separatists and Independents, the Familists before them and the mid-17th century Ranters under Joseph Salmon (who taught an inner experience of Christ), were all charged with antinomianism for following the Inner Light, as were the Collegiants who broke away from the Dutch Calvinist Church and waited on God in silence (among whose number was the philosopher Spinoza, who died in 1677).

The antinomian Puritan Inner Light is to be found in the life of the Congregationalist figurehead of the Puritans, Oliver Cromwell. Cromwell's conversion came just before he was 30, in 1628, when he was outwardly Calvinist. In 1638 he told his cousin, Mrs St John, about it: "Oh, I lived in and loved darkness, and hated light; I was a chief, the chief of sinners.... My soul is with the Congregation of the First-born.... He giveth me to see light in His light." Many years later a friend who knew Cromwell at this time wrote: "Religion was thus 'laid into his soul with the hammer and fire'; it did not 'come in only by light into his understanding'."

After his conversion Cromwell felt he was one of God's Chosen – one of the few, the elect, who according to Calvinists would be saved by contact with the Light – and he therefore opened himself to "the sudden providences in things". He felt he was a blind instrument in the hands of a higher power, and since historical events were determined by God's will – "God's revolutions" – it was his task as Protector to discover the hidden purpose behind events, or "what the mind of God is in all that chain of Providence". Consequently he would suspend judgement and allow events to develop "in order to get more light". In short, he opened his conscience to infused knowledge through the Light, and believed in "dispensations" rather than "revelations".[72]

The Independent Cromwell purged Parliament in 1648 and filled it with Independents, and during the Commonwealth of the 1650s he gave Congregationalism special treatment, much to the disgust of the Presbyterians who worked for the Restoration.

When Charles II was restored, English Protestants (including Presbyterians) had to accept the doctrines of the Church of England, and the Puritans who did not were called "Nonconformists" in the penal acts that followed 1660. They were also called "Separatists" – congregations which had separated from the Church of England – and "Dissenters". (It was only in the 19th century that they were called "Free Churchmen".)

The Puritan Light also shone in the poets Andrew Marvell and John Milton, who both worked in Cromwell's Latin or Foreign Secretaryship in the 1650s. (Milton recommended Marvell as his assistant in the Latin Secretaryship in 1653, and Marvell finally became Latin Secretary in 1657.) Marvell (1621-1678) is the more enigmatic of the two, for he was at heart a moderate and his sympathies seemed to be with the Royalists at first. The son of a clergyman of Calvinist views, he became a Jesuit for a short while before going abroad and missing the Civil War. He returned to be tutor to the daughter of Fairfax, who had disagreed with Cromwell, at Nun Appleton, Yorkshire, c.1651/2. Around then his political views seem to have changed, probably as a result of Fairfax's influence, and he came to admire Cromwell very deeply.

Much of his lyric poetry was written during his time with Fairfax, and "On a Drop of Dew" is about the light in the soul, for the soul, "that Drop, that Ray/Of the clear Fountain of Eternal Day", remembers its former height and "recollecting its own Light,/Does, in its pure and circling thoughts, express/The greater Heaven in an Heaven less". In his best known poem, "The Garden", which is set in the garden of Fairfax's Nun Appleton House, the soul glides into the boughs like a bird and "whets, and combs its silver wings" and "waves in its Plumes the various Light"; and it is clear from the previous stanza (in which the Mind withdraws into itself) that the idea of the soul as a bird in the Light has a deep inner meaning rather than a merely decorative outer one.[73]

John Milton (1608-1674) had been brought up as a Calvinist to believe that only a predestined few are saved – the elect who are illumined – and he hinted at his Puritan sympathies when he denounced hireling clergy in "Lycidas" (1638). From 1641 he came out into the open and pamphleteered for the Puritan cause, attacking the Church of England for the "popery" of its episcopal system, its prayer book and its liturgy. Milton joined Cromwell's administration in 1649, but went blind from excessive reading in 1651/2 when he was only 43; although he continued to work as a translator of state letters until 1659.

"Paradise Lost" was composed between 1655 and 1665 – most of it after 1658, for the "Paradise" was also Cromwell's Puritan Paradise – and the epic poet, blind like Homer, who later created an image of his blindness in "Samson Agonistes" finally came to rest (in "Paradise Regained") in Arminianism: a liberal reaction against Calvinist predestination which asserted that *all* believers – and not merely a few – are the elect, and are saved. (Jacobus Arminius, 1560-1609, had influenced the General Baptists.)

Light sometimes has two meanings in Milton. His most famous sonnet begins "When I consider how my light is spent" (i.e. extinguished). Written in 1652 as an early reaction to his blindness, the sonnet is clearly about extinguished outer light, yet an ambiguous line, "'Doth God exact day-labour, light denied?'/I fondly ask", could include the Puritan Inner Light. From early on Milton's poetry shows an awareness of the Inner Light, which is presented in terms of Christ and God. He saw Christ as "that Light unsufferable", "that far-beaming blaze of Majesty", in "On the Morning of Christ's Nativity" (1629, the year in which he left Christ's, Cambridge). In his versions of the Psalms (1648) he wrote: "Cause thou thy face on us to shine", and "God the Lord both Sun and Shield/Gives grace and glory bright".

"Paradise Lost" is full of the Light of God. The rebellious angels are "far remov'd from God and light of Heav'n" and "the happy Realms of Light", "that celestial light". God "blaz'd forth unclouded Deitie" on his Son, and is the "Fountain of Light", "glorious brightness" with the "full blaze" of his beams, and is "dark with excessive bright". Satan is seen in terms of the Light he once had, as a sun shining through mist or from a cloud. Book 3 begins with an invocation to God as Light: "Hail holy light..../God is light,/And never but in unapproached light/Dwelt from Eternitie..../Thee I revisit, safe,/And feel thy sovran vital Lamp; but thou/Revisit'st not these eyes, that rowle in vain..../So much the rather thou Celestial light/Shine inward, and the mind through all her powers/Irradiate." Milton is clearly saying that as he is blind he needs the Light; or, in the words of the Saviour in "Paradise Regained" (1671): "He who receives/Light from above, from the fountain of light,/No other doctrine needs."

"Samson Agonistes" (1671) makes it clear that Samson knew the inner Light. At first he appears to be without it. He is "exiled from light", "shut up from outward light", "for inward light, alas!/Puts forth no visual beam" (lines 162-3). But at the end, the Semichorus makes it clear that Samson recovered his inner vision: "But he, though blind of sight,.../With inward eyes illuminated,/His fiery virtue rous'd/From under ashes into sudden flame,/ And as an ev'ning Dragon came" (lines 1687-92).[74]

The Puritan Light which shone through "Paradise Lost" in the 1660s, shone through *The Pilgrim's Progress* in the 1670s. (*Part One* appeared in 1678.) Bunyan came into contact with Puritan Seekers and Ranters while serving in Cromwell's army between 1644 and 1647, and when he married in 1649, his wife's dowry comprised just two books, one of which was Arthur Dent's *The Plain Man's Path-way to Heaven*, which showed him how readable a religious tract could be made. In 1650 he started going to church, and gave up dancing and bell-ringing and sports on the green to look for the Light.

The next five years saw "storms" of temptation and despair until the Bedford Separatist church of Baptists rescued him, a church that resembled the modern Congregationalists. Bunyan then became a lay preacher and attacked the Quakers, the Baptists' rivals, arguing that God's Light was quite separate from man. After the Restoration Bunyan was imprisoned for twelve years for holding a service not in conformity with the Church of England, and he wrote his autobiography and began *The Pilgrim's Progress* in prison. He was given a further six months for illegal preaching in 1677.

Bunyan's quarrel with the Quakers shows that he was a Puritan churchman rather than a mystic, but the Light is nevertheless present in *The Pilgrim's Progress.* The book begins as a dream in prison (a "den" in "the wilderness of this world"). Christian sets off in uncertain light with his burden of sin. He leaves the City of Destruction, and passes the Slough of Despond, the Valley of the Shadow of Death and Vanity Fair. He passes the Doubting Castle of the Giant Despair and other torments and temptations and progresses towards the Celestial City. This is seen in terms of the Light throughout. The Evangelist points out "yonder shining light" and says: "Keep that light in your eye, and go up directly thereto, so shalt thou see the gate." Drawing near to the City, Christian sees that it "was builded of pearls and precious stones" and the streets "were paved with gold", and seeing "the reflection of the sunbeams upon it, Christian with desire fell sick."

As they went on "there met them two men in raiment that shone like gold, also their faces shone as the light". Later Christian "saw the two Shining Men again, who there waited for them.... A heavenly host came out to meet them; to whom it was said by the other two Shining Ones, these are the men that have loved our Lord." Then Bunyan sees in his dream "that the Shining Men bid them call at the gate; the which, when they did, some looked from above, to wit, Enoch, Moses and Elijah" (Compare the Egyptian *akhs* or Shining Ones.) "These two men went in at the gate; and lo! as they entered, they were transfigured; and they had raiment put on that shone like gold.... And behold the City shone like the sun."

After Christian has reached the City, his wife follows him in *Part Two* (1684), and again there are references to the Light. Fire fastens on the candlewick "to show that unless grace doth kindle upon the heart, there will be no true light of life in us"; and the Holy Ghost saves us "by his illumination". Mr Standfast says of his Lord, "His countenance I have more desired than they that have most desired the light of the sun."[75]

The Quaker movement, or Society of Friends, carried Puritanism to its logical conclusion, and purged all sacraments, ministers and liturgies as remnants of "popery". The Quaker movement resembled the 14th century Friends of God and the contemporary French Quietism, and it arose when groups of English Quietist Seekers despaired of help from the Church of England or the Puritan Presbyterians, Congregationalists and Baptists during the reign of Charles I.

How this help was denied to its founder, George Fox (1624-91), is graphically described in his *Journal*. Fox was probably apprenticed to a Leicestershire cobbler when at the age of 18 he heard the voice of God say: "Thou seest how young people go together in vanity, and old people into the earth; thou must forsake all, young and old, and be as a stranger to all." He therefore left home in search of enlightenment: "After this I went to another ancient priest at Mansetter in Warwickshire, and reasoned with him about the ground of despair and temptations; but he was ignorant of my condition: he bid me take tobacco and sing psalms.... He told my troubles, sorrows, and griefs to his servants, so that it was got among the milk-lasses.... I heard of a priest living about Tamworth, who was accounted an experienced man. I went seven miles to him, but found him like an empty hollow cask. I heard of one called Dr. Cradock, of Coventry, and went to him.... As we were talking together in his garden, the alley being narrow, I chanced in turning to set my foot on the side of a bed; at which he raged as if his house had been on fire. Thus all our discourse was lost, and I went away in sorrow, worse than I was when I came." During these disillusioning experiences he had a number of "openings" or direct revelations from God, and in view of the episode of the trodden-on flower-bed, it is not surprising that in 1646 "as I was walking in a field on a First-day morning, the Lord opened unto me, 'that being bred at Oxford or Cambridge was not enough to fit and qualify men to be ministers of Christ'".

Fox's salvation came in 1647. He tramped through the Midlands: "My troubles continued, and I was often under great temptations. I fasted much, walked abroad in solitary places many days, and often took my *Bible*, and sat in hollow trees and lonesome places till night came on." When all his hopes "in all men were gone" then: "Oh! then I heard a voice which said,

'There is one, even Christ Jesus, that can speak to thy condition.' Then the Lord let me see why there was none upon the earth that could speak to my condition.... For all are concluded under sin, and shut up in belief, as I had been, that Jesus Christ might have pre-eminence, who enlightens.... Thus when God doth work, who shall let it? This I knew experimentally.... Christ, who had enlightened me, gave me his light to believe in."

What happened was that "one day when I had been walking solitarily abroad and was come home, I was wrapped up in the love of God, so that I could not but admire the greatness of his love. While I was in that condition it was opened unto me by the eternal Light and Power, and I saw clearly therein." Thus: "Now the Lord God hath opened to me by His invisible power how that every man was enlightened by the divine Light of Christ; and I saw it shine through all.... This I saw in the pure openings of the Light, without the help of any man."

Fox became aware of his mission in 1649: "On a certain time, as I was walking in the fields, the Lord said unto me: 'Thy name is written in the Lamb's book of life which was before the foundation of the world'; and as the Lord spake it, I believed.... Then some time after, the Lord commanded me to go abroad into the world, which was like a briery, thorny wilderness....I was sent to turn people from darkness to the light, that they might receive Christ Jesus: for, to as many as should receive him in his Light, I saw that he would give power to become the sons of God; which I had obtained by receiving Christ (i.e. the Light).... I saw that Christ...enlightened all men and women with his divine and saving Light.... These things I did not see by the help of man...but I saw them in the Light of the Lord Jesus Christ.... I was glad that I was commanded to turn people to that inward light." The Inward Light was "that of God in every man".

From then on Fox toured the country, having a vision of the Kingdom of God on Pendle Hill in 1652, preaching to individuals and groups, building the Quaker movement by his personal magnetism, and refusing to be daunted by persecution – there was legislation against the Quakers after the Restoration of the monarchy in 1660 – or by eight spells of imprisonment. Meetings were designed to wait on the Inner Light in silence, without priests or a liturgy, and when a Friend received an "opening" he was encouraged to declare it. And slowly Quakerism absorbed such groups as the followers of Boehme, who found Boehme's Light catered for in the Quaker approach to the Inner Light.[76]

Quakers were at first called "Children of the Light". William Penn (1644-1718), who founded a Quaker colony in the United States, wrote: "If thou wouldst be a child of God, and a believer in Christ, thou must be a child of Light. O man, thou must bring thy deeds to it and examine them by that holy lamp in thy soul, which is the candle of the Lord, that shows thee thy pride and arrogancy, and reproves thy delight in the vain fashions of this world."[77] Fox wrote in his *Epistles*: "And so all be diligent, ye believers in the Light as Christ hath taught you, look up and down in the Light.... With the Light you will see."

Fox regarded the Light as pre-existing the Scriptures – "I saw, in that Light and Spirit that was before the Scriptures were given forth" (ch 2) – but both he and the Friends identified the Light with Jesus Christ. For them, it was Christ manifesting in the hearts of men, and according to Penn, Friends preferred to speak not of the "Light within" but of "the Light of Christ within". The Light was present in all men, even potentially in the heathen, who could be saved by seeing it without knowing the Scriptures or having heard of Christ – Fox cited the conscience of the American Indians as an instance of the universality of the Light – but the Light was still the Light of Christ, a personal assurance of truth. Because the Light was so universal, Penn came to believe it was natural in the sense that it was given to all men and was "that of God in every man"; though in its origin it was supernatural.[78]

The Light grew as a Seed, or acorn, in the unfavourable evil of the human heart, so that James Nayler (who had his tongue bored with hot iron for blasphemy) could write in 1655: "With the Light we see that he that is in the way of God is in holiness, and he that is not, is in the way of the devil; and that he that's in God is out of self, and there sin is blotted out and forgotten."[79] So Fox urged people in his *Epistles* to "wait upon God" for even if they knew little and were full of evil, "it is the Light that discovers all this, and the love of God to you".[80] Francis Howgill (1618-1669) wrote of the "Seed of the Kingdom" which works "through Jesus Christ who hath put the

Light in thee",[81] and John Bellers wrote of "God...who is Light", "The most invisible Light", and "this Inward Light" which "discovers the most hidden thoughts".[82] The Light often reveals itself in a concern for the sufferings of others, and Quakers have been opposed to all forms of brutality, from slavery to war and inhuman prison conditions.

The Quakers sought a genuine mysticism in groups. Their history is a fascinating record of individuals' *experience* of the Light, and the report presented to the Yearly Meeting of 1920 puts its finger on the difference between them and other sects: "The main difference between ourselves and most other bodies of Christians arises from the emphasis we place on the Light of God's Holy Spirit in the human soul – potentially in all human souls, and known in actual experience as these are turned towards the Light and are obedient to it. This direct contact between the Spirit of Christ and the human spirit we are prepared to trust to, as the basis of our individual and corporate life. From this source all our special 'testimonies' flow."[83]

The Quakers influenced Gerard Winstanley (c.1609-after 1660), the founder of the Christian-Communist Diggers movement in England, which cultivated common land in Surrey in 1649-50 before being dispersed. He had a strong belief in the Inner Light: "The Kingdom of God is within you, dwelling and ruling in your flesh." At first he looked for God outside himself, but he came to see that God was the Light within: "You shall no longer feed upon the oil that was in other men's lamps, for now it is required that every one have oil in his own lamp, even the pure testimony of truth within himself." Winstanley identified the Light with Christ: "Your body is his body, and now his spirit is your spirit, and so you are become one with him and with the Father."[84]

The Later Counter-Reformation: the Jansenist Fire, the Light of Quietism

Throughout the rise of the Protestant Light the Counter-Reformation continued. The Catholic Light had briefly reappeared in Italy in St Catherine dei Ricci (died 1590), a Dominican nun, and the Carmelite St

Maria Maddelena dei Pazzi (died 1607), and in Peru in St Rose of Lima (died 1617), who sang duets with birds and had an outlook similar to St Francis's. The French renaissance began with an English Capuchin friar Benedict Canfield (died 1611), who settled in Paris at the end of his life and taught Madame Acarie (died 1618) and Pierre de Bérullc (died 1629).

Between them, these two established St Teresa's reformed Carmelites in France. Of Madame Acarie, Bremond wrote in *A Literary History of Religious Thought in France* "Her message consisted of a sentence from the Gospel, the full sense of which only mystics realise, 'The kingdom of God is within you'. 'One must,' she said, 'penetrate to the depths of the soul, and see if God is, or will be there.'" Madame Acarie and her daughters became Carmelite nuns, and a member of Madame Acarie's circle, St Francis (sometimes written François) de Sales (1567-1622) was spiritual father to St Jeanne Françoise de Chantal (died 1641), who learned contemplation from the Dijon Carmelites. Together, they founded the Order of Visitation, a teaching order. St Francis often speaks of the soul's perception of the divine Presence (e.g. in *Treatise of the Love of God* 6.8,9), and of the soul "outflowing" by "holy liquefaction" to God (6.12).[85]

The French Carmelite development influenced the Venerable Augustine Baker (1575-1641). An English Catholic and Benedictine, he directed Gertrude More (1606-1633), a Benedictine nun who practised a mysticism of love and died of smallpox. Father Baker visited France (Douai) before dying of the plague. "By such fiery trials and purifications," he wrote in *Sancta Sophia*, "as also by so near approaches as are made to the fountain of beauty and light..., love is exalted", while "in regard of the understanding, there is a divine light communicated". Again, being "so illustrated with His heavenly light, and inflamed with His love, all creatures are...perfectly odious" to the soul, which approaches God by "affective prayer" (acts of loving desire).[86]

The French mystic tradition was carried on by Marie de l'Incarnation (1599-1672), who as a widow left her twelve year old son to become an Ursuline nun, and sailed to Quebec. The first time she had a vision of the Trinity, "it seemed that the Divine Majesty granted it to me in order to enlighten me".[87] Later, the friar Brother Lawrence (died 1691) talked to God while running the kitchen of the Carmelite community in Paris.

The 17th century saw other movements within French Catholicism. One was Jansenism, which began when Jansen defended St Augustine's idea of grace against the Jesuits in 1640. Jansenism became a cause célèbre when the French philosopher Blaise Pascal (1623-62) took the Jansenist side against the Jesuits and saw the Light as Fire.

Pascal's great experience (which we have already quoted) was his "second conversion", a mystical "night of fire", on November 23, 1654. He made a note of it on a scrap of parchment, drawing a flaming cross round which were the words: "In the year of grace 1654 Monday, 23 November...from about half-past ten in the evening till about half an hour after midnight. FIRE....Joy! joy! Tears of joy." He carried it about with him, and after his death it was found stitched into the lining of his doublet.[88]

This experience of the Light as Fire resulted in Pascal's becoming increasingly associated with the community at the Convent of Port Royal, and *The Pensées* (1657-8) is concerned with the "Misery of man without God" and the "Happiness of man with God". Man has to wager, or bet, and the believer has the Augustinian "grace which can enlighten" (i.e. the Light) to persevere and penetrate a hidden God, a Deus absconditus. Grace comes from the heart, and so "the heart has its reasons (for betting on God) of which the reason knows nothing", and the main reason is the Light.

"There is enough light for those who only desire to see," Pascal writes, and again: "He (God) has willed to blind some, and enlighten others." Thus: "Objection of atheists: 'But we have no light.'" God "grants by grace sufficient light, that they may return to Him, if they desire to seek and follow Him; and also that they may be punished, if they refuse to seek or follow Him." To put it another way: "If there were no obscurity, man would not be sensible of his corruption; if there were no light, man would not hope for a remedy." The scripture says that "Those who seek God find Him. It is not of that light, 'like the noonday sun', that this is said.... The evidence of God must not be of this nature." Pascal is saying again and again that God is revealed by an inner light, not by an outer one like the sun.[89]

Quietism was another development within French Catholicism. Quietism was a technique of passive contemplation that opened the heart to Augustinian grace (the Light) and avoided direct action. As St Francis de Sales put it, "Desire nothing, refuse nothing."[90]

Quietism can be traced back to the 13th century to Hesychasm and to the Free Spirit heresy, which was based on Neoplatonism. This was taught in Paris by Amalric (or Amaury, died c.1206), who proclaimed a new age based on the opening of oneself to God. He saw the universe as an emanation of God, and therefore God was present in all who opened themselves to the Light. These people were made sinless, and did not need the Church. The idea was taken up by the Beghards and their female counterparts, the Beguines, and it appeared in Spain with the 16th century *Alumbrados* (Spanish for "Enlightened") or Illuminati.

The Alumbrados were mostly reformed Franciscan and Jesuit ecstatics who followed the Gnostics in receiving direct communication from God and in acting under illumination received from the Holy Spirit. They believed that once a soul had received "the Light" in ecstatic and wordless prayer it could make no more progress, and could not retrogress,[91] and so there was no point in worshipping through the sacraments of the Church, a fact which led to their being repressed by the Inquisition. The *Illuminés* probably developed out of the Alumbrados. They appeared in Southern France in 1623, and also received the Holy Spirit (the Light). From 1634 they were led by Pierre Guérin, and they too were suppressed. (The Alumbrados and the *Illuminés* are not to be confused with another group which called itself Illuminati: a Bavarian sect founded in 1776 by Adam Weishaupt, a former Jesuit. These Illuminati wanted a new religion of enlightened reason – in which the reason was enlightened by the Divine Reason, i.e. the Light, and not by the Church or State – and since they saw themselves as the creators of a new world-order, they formed themselves into a secret society to destroy the old order and had a republican and Luciferian outlook until they were banned by the Bavarian government in 1785.)

More immediately, Quietism was prepared for by the Flemish mystics, Constantine Barbançon (died 1632) and John Evangelist of Barluke (died 1635), who were both Capuchins, and by the Franco-Flemish Antoinette Bourignan (1616-1680) who identified herself with the woman clothed with the Sun in *Revelation* 12. It was also prepared for by the Cistercian reform movement, the Trappists, which began at the Norman abbey, Notre-Dame de la Trappe, when de Rancé became abbot in 1664. De

Rancé was converted in the late 1650s after a worldly life, and the silence the Trappists observed was to help them see the Light. But Quietism is mainly identified with the Spanish priest who came to Rome, Miguel de Molinos (1640-1697).

In his *Spiritual Guide*, Molinos argued that men should surrender their individual wills and become passive so that God could work through them. Through silent prayer "we sink and lose ourselves in the immeasurable sea of God's infinite goodness" and make personal contact with the Light. "By not speaking nor desiring, and not thinking," Molinos says of the contemplative spirit, "she arrives at the true and perfect mystical silence wherein God speaks with the soul...and in the abyss of its own depth, teaches it the most perfect exalted wisdom. He calls and guides it to this inward solitude and mystical silence when he says that He will speak to it alone in the most secret and hidden part of the heart."[92]

The *Spiritual Guide* caused a sensation in 1675, because it really said that perfection lay in perpetual union with God and therefore in total inactivity, and doing nothing at all was swiftly condemned by the orthodox Church. (The modern transcendental meditational movements go back to Molinos's extremism.) Unfortunately, Molinos found that his quiet "sinking into God" was helped by sex, and in 1685 he was arrested by the papal police, and his sexual misdemeanours were investigated. Molinos argued that the Devil could take over a passive body and make it commit sexual acts, but because the passive Quietist did not will the acts, they were not sinful. He was tried and imprisoned for life, and two years later his doctrine was declared a heresy.

French Quietism centred round Madame Guyon (1648-1717). She was married at 16 to a man twice her age, and when she was 19 she met a Franciscan friar who told her: "Madame, you are seeking without that which you have within. Accustom yourself to seek God in your own heart, and you will find him." These words, Madame Guyon writes, were "as an arrow, which pierced my heart through and through. I felt in this moment a profound wound, which was full of delight and love – a wound so sweet that I desired it might never heal. These words had put into my heart that which I sought for so many years, or, rather, they caused me to find that which was there. O, my Lord, you were within my heart, and you asked of me only that I should return within, in order that I might feel your presence. O, Infinite Goodness, you were so near, and I, running here and there to seek you, found you not!" Madame Guyon saw her soul opening to flow with the Light as a wound opening and flowing with blood, and "from that moment of which I had spoken, my orison was emptied of all form, species and images; nothing of my orison passed through the mind" (*Life* 1.8).

Madame Guyon was an emotional woman, and she lacked the common sense of many mystics and went to extremes: "If I walked, I put stones in my shoes. These things, my God, Thou didst first inspire me to do" (*Life* 1.10). After the death of her husband, in 1677 she left her children and led a travelling life of religious devotion, and was greatly influenced by Molinos in her *Short and Very Easy Method of Prayer* (1685). Her "passive orison" demanded passivity, and the soul should even be indifferent to eternal salvation, she claimed. She was attacked by Bossuet and imprisoned for a short while. She was released at the request of Louis XIV's second wife, and was publicly defended in 1695 by Archbishop Fénelon, who had been tutor to Louis' heir.

Madame Guyon admitted the extremism that led to these attacks: "I made many mistakes through allowing myself to be too much taken up by my interior joys.... I used to sit in a corner and work, but I could hardly do anything, because the strength of this attraction made me let the work fall out of my hands. I spent hours in this way without being able to open my eyes or to know what was happening to me: so simply, so peacefully, so gently that sometimes I said to myself, 'Can Heaven itself be more peaceful than I?'" (Life 1.17). Her message is clear: be sensible about the Light. "Such quietude," the sensible Ruysbroeck wrote, "is nought else but idleness" (*The Adornment of the Spiritual Marriage* 1.2.66).

On the other hand Madame Guyon's Quietism brought gifts. "I was given light to perceive that I had in me treasures of knowledge and understanding which I did not know that I possessed," she wrote, and perhaps her main gift was automatic writing: "I was myself surprised at the letters which You (i.e. God) did cause me to write, and in which I had no part save the actual movement of my hand: and it was at this time that I received that gift of writing according to the interior mind, and not according to my own mind, which I had never known before. Also my manner of writing was altogether changed and everyone was astonished because I wrote with such great facility.... You did make me write with so great a detachment that I was obliged to leave off and begin again as You did choose. You did try me in every way: suddenly You would cause me to write, then at once to cease, and then to begin again. When I wrote during the day I would be suddenly interrupted, and often left words half written, and afterwards You would give me whatever was pleasing to You. Nothing of that which I wrote was in my mind: my mind, in fact, was so wholly at liberty that it seemed a blank, I was so detached from that which I wrote that it seemed foreign to me" (*Life* 2. 2,21).

Her writings were dictated to her by the Light, and her hymn on the "Acquiescence of Pure Love" begins in Cowper's version: "Love! If Thy destined sacrifice am I,/Come, slay Thy victim, and prepare Thy fires." The fires were the fires of the Light. In the life of union with God which follows illumination in due course, "the soul feels a secret vigour" and "receives a new life". The soul "no longer lives or works of herself: but God lives, acts and works in her" (*Les Torrents* 1.9).[93]

Quietism declined at the end of the 17th century, but disciples of Molinos formed the Molinists on his death in 1697 and followed the Inner Light, and there were still such figures as the Jesuit Jean-Pierre de Caussade (1675-1751). De Caussade's main idea, that we should totally accept God's will, is to be found in *Abandonment to Divine Providence.* Malaval and Poiret also carried Quietism into the 18th century, but the Catholic tradition of mysticism declined as the Age of Reason developed.

The Light of the Evangelical Revival

Evangelicalism began with the German Pietists of the 17th century, who like Johann Arndt (died 1621), Philipp Jakob Spener (died 1705) and August Hermann Francke (died 1727), had their roots in German Lutheranism.

The Pietists carried forward the Anabaptist revival and parallelled Catholic Quietism in protesting against the worldliness of their Lutheran Church, which they revitalised. They believed that Christianity involved a personal inner change, and Spener's *Pia Desideria* (1675) was a six-point plan to achieve this. One of its proposals revived Luther's "priesthood of all believers", an anti-episcopal idea that put him firmly in the Puritan tradition. Radical German Pietists saw this inner change in terms of a mystical and emotional experience, and one of the two Radical traditions stressed the Inner Light, which it identified with the reason.[94] So, German Pietists like Arnold (died 1714), Dippel (died 1734) and Tersteegen (died 1769) were drawn towards the Rationalism of the Enlightenment, which they interpreted as "enlightened reason" through the Light.

Spener's godson, Nikolaus Ludwig Count von Zinzendorf (1700-60), was a pupil at a school of Francke's, and in 1722 Zinzendorf formed a sect for Moravian exiles on his German estate at the modern Herrnhut. He saw it as a Pietist Lutheran sect, but in fact it went back to the 15th century Hussite *Unitas Fratrum* ("Unity of Bretheren"). (Jan Hus had had a conversion about which there are no details, "when the Lord gave me knowledge of the Scriptures",[95] and this was probably an experience of the Light, as was Calvin's equally mysterious "sudden" conversion to Protestantism.) Zinzendorf's contact with the Moravian Kristian David (died 1751) had the effect of reviving the Moravian Church, and more and more his sect formed itself into a separate church. Zinzendorf now stood for a "religion of the heart" or "heart religion", based on personal devotion and fellowship with Christ, which later influenced Goethe and therefore the shaping of Romanticism.

More immediately, the Moravians influenced English Methodism, for in 1736 Zinzendorf travelled to England and America, and Moravian followers of his made a profound impact on John Wesley (1703-91). As a Church of England priest and Oxford don, Wesley had begun a religious study group at Oxford together with his brother Charles in 1729, and the methodicalness of the group had led to their being lampooned as "Methodists". In 1735, far from happy, Wesley went on a mission to the American Indians of Georgia. On the boat were twenty-seven Moravian emigrants who fearlessly sang Psalms during a terrifying storm and revealed the peace Wesley was seeking.

Back in London Wesley met a Moravian called Peter Bohler, who taught him that every man "no matter how moral, how pious, or how orthodox he may be, is in a state of damnation, until by a supernatural and instantaneous process wholly unlike that of human reasoning, the conviction flashes upon his mind that the sacrifice of Christ has been applied to him, and has expiated his sins; that this supernatural and personal conviction or illumination is what is meant by Saving Faith, and that it is inseparably accompanied by an absolute assurance of Salvation, and by a complete domination over sin. It cannot exist where there is not a sense of pardon of all past and of freedom from all present sins.... Its fruits are constant peace – not one uneasy thought."[96] This peace is the familiar tranquillity and serenity – the "peace that passeth understanding" – of those who have experienced the Light. Wesley knew he lacked the emotional experiences Bohler had, but he was unhappy when Bohler told him "My brother this philosophy of yours must be purged away", and: "Preach faith until you have it, and then because you have it you will preach faith."

Wesley's conversion followed soon afterwards, nearly ten years after he had been ordained. On May 24, 1738, aged 35, he went very "unwillingly" to a meeting in Aldersgate Street, London that was held by the Church of England for one of the Moravian congregations. Through his brother Charles he had already discovered Luther's commentary on Paul's *Epistle* (Letter) to the Galatians on justification by grace through faith, and a Moravian preacher now read Luther's preface to his commentary on Paul's *Epistle to the Romans.* Wesley recorded the experience in his *Journal*: "About a quarter before nine, while he (i.e. the Moravian preacher) was describing the change which God works in the heart through faith in Christ, I felt my heart strangely warmed. I felt I did trust in Christ, Christ alone, for salvation; and an assurance was given me that he had taken away *my* sins, even *mine*, and saved *me* from the law of sin and death."[97] The heart-warming was what Bohler had been referring to when he put across his "heart religion". It was the burning of the Fire of Love. It was what Rolle had felt, and St John of the Cross, and numerous other mystics we have considered; it was the working of the Light.

Wesley's heart was on fire, and in later years, looking back on the day in 1709 when he was saved from a fire at Epworth Vicarage, he described himself as "a brand plucked from the burning".[98] The conversion filled him with enthusiasm, though as in Bunyan's case the doubts persisted as the Night of Spirit worked itself out. He evangelised, preached the "good news" of salvation by faith, and the Church of England disapproved of his enthusiasm and closed its doors to him. Wesley founded a Church of England Society along Moravian lines in Fetter Lane, London, and visited Zinzendorf's estate, and though he later separated from the Moravians, the Moravians had already shaped the Evangelical movement's concern for personal conversion experiences and personal salvation. They had also put Wesley in touch with Arminianism – the view that Milton came to share which affirmed that all believers are saved, and not an elected few – and Arminianism, too, influenced the development of Methodism, for Wesley edited *The Arminian Magazine* and wrote in it that "God willeth all men to be saved, by speaking the truth in love."

The Dimming Christian Light

Since the Reformation Christian mystics have emphasised the divine "burn", the touch of God which sets the individual's heart on fire with love. The early Protestants, Puritans and Evangelicals all emphasised the heart, which is perhaps why so many Protestant poets have written of the Light. Since the Reformation, Catholics have done likewise, and St John of the Cross is one of the great poets of all time.

The Light of the Reformation and Counter-Reformation had brought new spiritual energy to Western culture, but the Light was ceasing to shine within Christianity and from the 18th century onwards it was increasingly received within the esoteric movement.

All the Lights in the subtradition (see *Part Three*) have lingered on in groups or heretical sects outside the mainstream Christian tradition. By the 19th century some of these were attracting minds – or rather, souls – away from Christianity, which led to a weakening of the Christian Light. For there were fewer Christian mystics, and many of the literary figures turned to the subtradition for inspiration rather than to the mainstream Christian Light.

Secularized Established Church

Throughout the 19th century we can see a slow secularizing of the Church. The proliferation of heretical sects weakened the Christian Light at a time when the Industrial Revolution with its ethos of progress had brought a widespread scientific materialism, and Darwinism, to Christendom (Blake's "dark Satanic Mills"), and from the 1830s on there was a further fading of the Christian Light. New mystics did not come forward, though the Light continued to be reflected for a while by non-mystics who knew of the tradition from their church.

The 19th century saw no new Catholic mystics of note. The Quietist movement had aroused suspicions that the authority of the Catholic Church was being undermined, and mysticism was officially discouraged, so much so that in the 17th and 18th centuries Jesuits actually denied that it was possible to have a mystical experience. The 19th century was dominated by the Pope's assertion in 1854 that the Virgin Mary was immaculate, and by the dogma of the First Vatican Council in 1870 which asserted that the Pope was infallible. There were doctrinal debates. John Henry Newman became a convert in 1845, but although he wrote "Lead, kindly light" when on a boat between Sardinia and Corsica in 1833, on the evidence of *Apologia Pro Vita Sua* he was led into a tractarian form of rationalism, though his example helped to convert the poet Hopkins in 1866. The Modernist movement within the Catholic Church challenged the reactionary Papacy on *Bible* criticism and freedom of conscience, and was condemned in 1907.

Charles de Foucauld, a Trappist monk, probably kept the Catholic Light alive by becoming a desert hermit in Algeria and living among the Tuareg until his murder by the Senussi in 1916. (His return to the conditions of the early desert fathers comes into Eliot's *Family Reunion*.) Ronald Knox (author of a collection of Sermons, *Captive Flames*, 1940) was converted in 1917, and he and Father D'Arcy had a hand in the conversion of the English novelists Graham Greene (1926) and Evelyn Waugh (1930), but neither of these novelists wrote about the Light. (Indeed, their despair is profoundly connected with the absence of the Light in their literary worlds.)

In Protestantism, mysticism also had to contend with doctrinal disputes. The American Revolution had separated Church and State. It had inherited separation from the Congregationalists, and was anyway opposed to the establishment of the Church of its British colonisers. When the French Revolution set up a secular State, there were moves to disestablish elsewhere in Europe. Both in Lutheran Germany, which was still reacting to the union of Lutheran and Reformed churches in Prussia, and in Scotland, it was the liberals who wanted to disestablish the Church, whereas in England it was the Church of England conservatives who wished to disestablish to emphasise their Catholic links with the Apostles through bishops.

The Evangelical movement had ended with the followers of Wesley leaving the Church of England in 1795, but many sympathisers had remained within the Church and they emphasised personal conversion and piety at the expense of bishops, the sacraments and the liturgy. They formed a Low Church which concerned itself with social problems (as did the Clapham Sect of Wilberforce and other opponents of slavery).

The conservative Anglo-Catholic Oxford Movement, launched by Keble, Newman, Froude and Pusey in 1833, wanted disestablishment to take the Church of England away from the Evangelicals and towards Catholicism. The group put their ideas into 90 *Tracts for the Times*, a publication which Newman edited and which led to the group's being called Tractarians. The Oxford Movement suffered a blow when Newman became a Catholic in 1845, and though it survived to achieve many of its aims, from the way the Movement has been interpreted there does not seem to have been much time for the Light in all the "politicking" and "factionalising". However, there was still a sufficient body of inherited knowledge about the Light at Oxford for it to remain widely known.

The Victorian Dimming of the Christian Light in European Literature c.1880

The secularizing trend in 19th century religion is reflected in Victorian literature, which shows that the "dimming-point" in the slow fading of the Christian Light in Europe was c.1880 (the time of Theosophy, see **pp480-487**). Before c.1880, the Light was sufficiently widely known for it to be reflected in the poetry of non-mystics, whereas after c.1880 this was not so.

Before we turn to Victorian non-mystical poets, it is worth looking at two earlier non-mystics for the sake of comparison. In the 17th and 18th centuries, non-mystics like the English Dryden and Pope referred to the Light, which they knew about from attending church. Dryden wrote at the age of 19, in 1650, of "sparks divine" and "Celestial fire", and later of "Reason's glimmering ray" dissolving "in Supernatural Light" ("Religio Laici", 1682). God was a "Source of uncreated Light", "thrice Holy Fire" ("Veni Creator", 1693). Chaucer's parson "shines by his own proper Light" (1700). Pope gave the Light a secular, humorous, almost pejorative treatment in "The Dying Christian to his Soul" (1708): "Vital spark of heav'nly flame/Quit, oh quit this mortal frame." Poets and critics "both must alike from Heav'n derive their light", and Nature is "one clear, unchang'd, and universal light" ("An Essay on Criticism", 1709). In "Eloisa to Abelard", "gleams of glory brighten'd all the day" as Eloisa knew "eternal sunshine of the spotless mind". Pope wrote of "the soul's calm sun-shine" in "An Essay on Man", and he begins book 4 of "The Dunciad": "Yet, yet a moment, one dim Ray of Light/Indulge, dread Chaos, and eternal Night!"

In the 1830s and 1840s, comparable non-mystical English Victorian poets were also aware of a received tradition of the Light. Tennyson was a "non-mystic" in the sense that though he had mystic gifts and was described by Sir Harold Nicolson as "a morbid and unhappy mystic", he was more of a poet than a mystic. He had a Church of England upbringing as the son of clergyman at Somersby Rectory, Lincolnshire and he was aware of the Light in the 1830s. His St Simeon Stylites sees "a flash of light" after a lifetime up pillars "battering the gates of heaven", and he asks God to lead "this foolish people...to thy light". "In Memoriam" (1842) begins with the idea that our little systems "are but broken lights" of God, and in Tennyson's whimpering "Be near me when my light is low", the light is associated with faith (two stanzas on) rather than a nightlight. Like Adonais, Hallam has entered the Light on his death, "remerging in the general Soul" for on death "we lose ourselves in light". Hallam will return in his "after form/And like a finer light in light". The "stillness of the central sea" of Light surrounds Tennyson's world as much as it does Wordsworth's or Shelley's, and like Wordsworth, Tennyson could fall into a waking trance in which "individuality itself seemed to dissolve and fade away into boundless being". (He records in the same letter to Blood that he could induce this trance almost at will, by repeating his name two or three times to himself silently, like a *Mahayana* Buddhist repeating the divine name.) Tennyson also understood the Grail, which Lancelot sees as "a light...in the crannies" that "blinded" him "as from a seventimes-heated furnace".

Browning had a Congregationalist mother, and his Nonconformism prevented him from going to Oxbridge. From his Congregationalist background he was able to write at the age of 23 in "Paracelsus" (1835): "Truth is within ourselves..../To Know/Rather consists in opening out a way/Whence the imprisoned splendour may escape,/Than in effecting entry for a light/Supposed to be without." Truth is a spring and "source within us; where broods radiance vast,/To be elicited ray by ray", but a sage does not know "how those beams are born/As little knows he what unlocks their fount". Browning goes on to contrast men growing old among books "case-hardened in their ignorance", and "autumn loiterers" being illumined by truth. The poem was well-received.

If 23 is young to have such a mature statement about the Light widely accepted, the Church of England Matthew Arnold was only 20 when he won the Oxford Newdigate prize with "Cromwell": "An inward light, that, with its streaming ray,/On the dark current of his changeless day/Bound all his being with a silver chain." Later, Westminster Abbey is informed that its "light once more shall burn" when Arthur/Cromwell returns.Arnold had a Church of England upbringing with his father, the Head of Rugby, and he was at Oxford during the Oxford Movement; and the strength of the Tradition of the Light is evident from the fact that

Arnold's Empedocles of Etna felt he should see more of the Light than he did. Like St Simeon Stylites, Empedocles despairs of bringing the Light to birth in his soul until he sees it just before he plunges into the crater of the volcano Etna (1852): "Oh, that I could glow like this mountain!/...Oh, that my soul were full of light as the stars!" He has lived "far from my own soul, far from warmth and light", but "the numbing cloud/Mounts off my soul; I feel it..../Leap and roar, thou sea of fire!/ My soul glows to meet you." It is to unite the fire of love with the fire of the volcano that he leaps into the burning crater.

The Scholar-Gipsy still awaits illumination, "the spark from heaven", amid "this strange disease of modern life/With its sick hurry, its divided aims" which Arnold knew as an inspector of schools. In "Dover Beach" (1867) the world has "neither joy, nor love, nor light", and it is the absence of the Light that makes the world a "darkling plain". Human love is a substitute for divine love, and the same feeling was in "Absence" (1852), one of the Marguerite poems in which "I struggle towards the light". Arnold's vision of the Light reaches its climax in his most influential essay, *Culture and Anarchy* (1869), in which "the man who tends towards sweetness and light" is contrasted with the Philistine who is "the enemy of the children of light or the servants of the idea". Arnold quotes St Augustine: "Let the children of thy spirit...make their light shine upon the earth, mark the division of night and day."

The Light was still being reflected in the 1870s. In 1879 another Arnold, Sir Edwin Arnold, chief editor of *The Daily Telegraph*, wrote a poem, "The Light of Asia" based on the *Buddhacarita* of the 1st century AD Asvaghosa, in which the Buddha saw "by light which shines beyond our mortal ken" and died with the word: "Rise, Great Sun!/...The Sunrise comes!/The Dewdrop/slips into the shining Sea!" And in 1875, the Jesuit priest who had been received into the Catholic Church by Newman, Gerard Manley Hopkins, addressed Jesus as "heart's light" in "The Wreck of the Deutschland" and in 1877 he wrote that the grandeur of God "will flame out like shining from shook foil". This energy in things, which he called "instress" (recalling Shelley's "the One Spirit's plastic stress") is a "fire" that breaks from the windhover – just as "kingfishers catch fire, dragonflies draw flame" – and "The Windhover" ends with a wonderful image of illumination in which the heart is like embers: "Blue-bleak embers, ah my dear/Fall, gall themselves, and gash gold-vermilion." (A cold heart can suddenly burst alight with the Fire of love.) Later, in one of his "terrible sonnets" (1885), he wakes and feels the fell of dark and knows that his heart must endure more black hours "in yet longer light's delay", and it is clear from a close reading that the light is not advent of dawn, but "dearest him (i.e. God) that lives alas! away".[99]

About this time the prose-poet and nature-mystic Richard Jefferies wrote lovingly of his Wiltshire countryside, and in his spiritual autobiography, *The Story of my Heart* (1883) he reveals himself as an atheist who saw something higher than a god, "the idea of the whole" which includes the soul, immortality and deity. He called this something a "Higher Soul", but never made the breakthrough into identifying it with the Light during his writing life. However he may have done so on his early death bed in 1887, since it is apparently a fact that he came to know God and Jesus Christ for when "he came to die that divine name uttered in fervent prayer was among the last words to pass his lips".[100]

The Light virtually disappeared from English poetry after Hopkins. It was not in Hardy, whose many lyrics about love and death between 1865 and 1926 lack the profound inward gaze. (It was his outward look that endeared him to some of the poets of the 1950s.) There are hints in Yeats, who joined the esoteric stream. As we have seen, he attached himself to the Theosophical Society in 1887, and was a member of the Order of the Golden Dawn, and he symbolized the mystic marriage in the joined rose and cross in "To the Rose Upon the Rood of Time", "The Lover Tells of the Rose in His Heart", and "The Secret Rose". Otherwise, there are the merest glimmers in the two "Byzantium" poems, when Yeats appeals to the "sages standing in God's holy fire/As in the gold mosaic of a wall", and describes the "flames that no faggot feeds" on the Emperor's pavement. In "Vacillation" he describes how after his "fiftieth year" he sat "a solitary man" when "my body of a sudden blazed" for "twenty minutes, more or less". Yeats was a visionary rather than a mystic, and so he saw the rough beast of "The Second Coming" rather than the Light: "A vast image out of *Spiritus Mundi* /Troubles my sight..../The darkness drops again."

The Light is occasionally glimpsed in the minor poems of the 1890s – in Lionel Johnson's "Mystic" and "Cavalier" where "Yours are the victories of light", and in Vincent O'Sullivan's "The Veil of Light" – but it is missing from Georgian and Modernist poetry. In a novel of the time, Lawrence's *Rainbow* "the light of the transfiguration" has a purely sexual connotation.

The established Protestant churches were now under attack from social thinkers like Karl Marx and intellectuals who held that the *Bible* was not true, like the rationalist Hegel who wanted to restate Christianity as an Idealism. Hegel was denounced by Kierkegaard (died 1855), the founder of Existentialism, but although Kierkegaard wrote in his *Concluding Unscientific Postscript* that "Subjectivity is Truth", he does not appear to have grasped that "Subjectivity" is the Light. Kierkegaard's celebrated "inwardness", then, seems to have been a darkness.

In Britain, there was a mixture of evangelism and social welfare which came to be known in 1878 as the Salvation Army. Then there have been the Negro churches of the 20th century. There is no space to examine each in detail, but from the failure of new Protestant mystics to come forward, it does not appear that the Christian mystical tradition of the Light passed from an increasingly secularized Christianity into its American variations. Individuals kept the Light alive, like the probably illumined Lutheran Dr Albert Schweitzer who gave up a career as a theological scholar and interpreter of Bach (whom he regarded as a mystic) to become a doctor and serve the Africans of the Ogowe River from 1913. And the Protestant Light was certainly kept going by the Quakers.

Scholars continued to make progress in studying the *Bible*, and in the 20th century the Swiss theologians Barth and Brunner began a movement of Neo-Orthodoxy to restore the supremacy of the *Bible*. They opposed theologies (like Kierkegaard's) that were based on religious experience. Such an outlook was hardly likely to favour experience of the Light. Most of the well-known 20th century theologians were touched by Neo-Orthodoxy, and the Lutherans Niebuhr and Tillich contributed in America, while Bultmann demythologised the *New Testament*. The Russian Berdyayev (also spelt Berdyaev) also contributed, though he affirmed "a light which breaks through from the transcendent world of the spirit"[101] into the outside world. The Jewish Martin Buber was also Neo-Orthodox.

As in philosophy, two generations of Protestant theologians have concentrated on what the mystic regards as the wrong questions. The conversions to the Church of England of the poets T. S. Eliot (1927) and Auden (1940), parallelled the Catholic conversions of the novelists Greene and Waugh. Of the two, Auden was not illumined.

The Light only gleams for a moment in the 1930s in MacNeice's "Prayer before Birth" ("a white light/In the back of my mind to guide me") and in Auden's "New Year Letter" of 1941 ("O Dove of science and of light"). In the early 1940s, Eliot reflected it in his work, especially in "The Four Quartets": "The fire and the rose are one." Vernon Watkins writes "O dark, interior flame". David Gascoyne's *Journal* (1937-9) speaks of "men, convinced at last of the existence of a true Light", and of the Future of this Century burning "with an extraordinary, unseen and secret radiance". In his poems Gascoyne progressed from surrealism to Hölderlin, whose poetry, Gascoyne declared, "reaches into the future and the light". Like Hölderlin, Gascoyne became an inspired poet-seer whose "*ars poetica* was an offspring of the Platonic doctrine of inspiration". His "Metaphysical Poems" begin with a quotation from the Egyptian *Book of the Dead* about Osiris-Ra, "the Increated Light", and in "*Lachrymae*" he writes "Slow are the years of light and more immense/Than the imagination" (i.e. the Light fills the human imagination as an ocean fills an harbour). Unless he is partly earthed or grounded the poet who commits the "promethean crime" of glimpsing Paradise – of stealing the "Fire" – is sometimes rewarded with madness, as was Hölderlin, and in Gascoyne's case "the strain which no human mind can stand" led him to an amphetamine-dependency which cut off his inspiration so that he was deserted by the Light. Dylan Thomas's poems contain hints. Most are to do with birth, and "light" is probably "daylight" in "one smile of light across the empty face" and "light breaks where no sun shines". But there is one poem from his "Vision and Prayer" sequence (1945) which may be about the inner Light. Typographically arranged as a cross, it begins: "I turn the corner of prayer and burn/In a blessing of the sudden Sun." It ends: "Now I am lost in the blinding/One. The sun roars at the prayer's end." As if to confirm that this is about the Light, "Poem on his Birthday" (1951) refers to God as "Him/Who is the light of old". There has been no direct mention of the Light in English poetry since then, though Kathleen Raine, a Neoplatonist, has come near to it in "The World" ("It burns in the void").[102]

The same pattern is to be found on the European Continent. In Germany, the Light was strong in the 1830s. Hölderlin (1770-1843) knew the Light. He was steeped in Greece and in Plato's view of the poet as a seer, and on the death of Susette Gontard, the love of his life, in 1802, became deranged. Two years before he had written in "*Die Heimat*" ("Home"), "For they who lend us the heavenly fire, the Gods, give us sacred sorrow too." And around 1826, in "*Überzeugung*" ("Conviction") he wrote of the Light, "As day surrounds men with bright radiance, and with that Light which has its origin on high unites all the dim objects of perception, such is knowledge deeply attained by the human intellect." Goethe died in 1832 saying "More light" (which seems to have been a comment on what he could see within rather than a request for the curtains to be drawn further back) and in *Faust, Part One* (1808), Faust had asked "*Bin ich ein Gott? Mir wird so licht!/Ich schau' in diesen reinen Zugen/Die wirkende Natur vor meiner Seele liegen.*" ("Am I a God? I see the light. I see in these pure, clear features the true nature of my soul", i.e. the Light.)[103] The "Fire" can be found in Mendelssohn's oratorio, *Elijah* (1844), on the conflict between Yahweh and Baal, in which the chorus sing "The Fire descends from heaven" and there is an air "Is not His word like a fire?" The closing chorus "And then shall your Light break forth" contains some of the most inspirational music ever written, and the Light was clearly still widely known in Germany then. Yet at the end of the century, though he knew of the Light, Rilke never experienced it, and wrote little about it. In *The Book of Hours* (1899-1905), the meditations of a Russian monk, there is mention of being "cloaked" from "light's rays"(31), of angels seeking "you in the light"(39) and of "light's realm"(50), but these are instances of Rilke *imagining* what a Russian monk might feel. "Of Pilgrimage" (1900) has the lines: "I dig for you, you treasure, in deep night/-never found it." Rilke dug but never found the treasure; and whether he is writing about the Buddha in Rodin's garden or the "terrible" angels of the *Duino Elegies*, which were supposed to be addressed to an Orphic adept, he is writing as an imaginative poet rather than as a mystic. It is Orpheus the poet that interests him, not Orpheus the mystic.[104]

In French poetry of the same period the nearest to come to the Light were Mallarmé, who wrote "after finding Nothingness I have found Beauty", and Paul Valery whose "Pythoness" asks "*Qui m'illumine?*" ("Who illumines me?") "Come," he writes, "the divine light (*La lumiére la divine*) is not the fearful lightning.... It will teach us.... Dark witnesses of so much light, seek no longer."[105]

The Tradition of the Light, then, ceased to be adequately reflected in the work of English non-mystics before the end of the 19th century, and as we have seen that the Victorian non-mystics obtained the Light they reflected from the Church, there are three possible reasons for this. Either the churches at the end of the 19th century were no longer putting the Light across as effectively as they were during the time of the Oxford Movement. Or, the non-mystical poets were no longer going to the churches. Or, material conditions in the environment had caused a change.

The truth is probably in a combination of all three. There was a decline in church-going at the end of the 19th century, and this probably had something to do with a decline in the quality of the early Victorian emphasis on the Light. At the same time, the Industrial Revolution introduced electricity in 1880, and Edison first lit a street in 1882. The impact of electricity should not be underestimated, and over a period of time it probably took people out of the divine inner dark, so that inner illumination ultimately became lost in fluorescent lighting. The other products of the Industrial and Technological Revolutions have had a similar effect; notably television, which has taken people away from the inner screen of the visionary imagination.

Be that as it may, the failure of non-mystical poets to reflect the Light can be taken as evidence of the fact that it was ceasing to be widely known, and was already becoming only a memory. The less it was widely known, the less it was taught, and the more the mystical knowledge became something which people did not understand, which therefore alienated them, and which finally became lost. The public (as opposed to the esoteric) tradition was in decline.

Secularization of English Hymns between 1889 and 1951: the Vanishing Light

The decline of the Tradition of the Light in Europe is also reflected in the choice of English hymns. The secularization of the Protestant English Light can be seen in action by contrasting the Light-based hymns that appeared in the Church of England prayer-book in 1889 with the Light-based hymns that survived in the 1951 edition, which was more worldly and Humanistic.

The decline of the Tradition of the Light in England lasted throughout the first half of the 20th century during which church attendance dropped. It is currently around 7.5%. To try to bring back the congregations, the Church reached out towards the people, and tried to appear more worldly and Humanistic, more on the public wave length. The traditional language of the *Book of Common Prayer* (1549-1552 with revisions until 1662) and *Bible* (King James version 1611) now co-existed with modern translations, and alternative orders of service emphasised ready comprehension at the expense of familiarity. The Lord's Prayer was recited with "yours" instead of "thys", further weakening the established forms of the past. This trend ended with vicars introducing pop music and supporting political causes. They festooned their churches with posters concerning distant guerilla wars that had nothing to do with the spirit or the Light.

An early contribution to this trend involved a revision of *Hymns Ancient and Modern* in 1951, and in an attempt to reach the people a number of the Victorian Light hymns were excluded and replaced by more "with it" hymns that reflected social settings (Christ on the cross, the child etc). (The rational Movement in English poetry was to favour similar social settings five years later in 1956.)

Many of the Light hymns were in the prayer book long before 1889, and they represented a solid part of the Tradition of the Light as it had always been put across in the Church. To be precise *Hymns Ancient and Modern* go back to 1861, when the first edition brought together the hymn books (Anglican and others) that had appeared in the previous hundred years. An appendix was added in 1868, there was a second edition in 1875, and supplemental hymns were added in 1889 and in 1916 (when there was another addition of "war" hymns). No hymns were deleted between 1861 and 1951.

Of course, selection is an enormously difficult task. At the end of the 19th century there were over 400,000 hymns in common use, 600 of which were by Isaac Watts and 6,500 by Charles Wesley. There have been numerous compilers and there are numerous hymnals. Hymn-singing goes back to the singing of psalms in the Hebrew Temple, and the earliest preserved hymn, the Greek *Phos hilarion* "Go gladsome Light", was written as long ago as AD c.200. The Syrian Gnostics and Manichaeans sang hymns based on the psalms, and St Hilary of Poitiers compiled a hymn book AD c.360. Congregations have sung hymns since St Ambrose of Milan, who drew on Christian Latin poems. In the Middle Ages only choirs sang hymns, and congregational singing only returned with Luther (which is why so many English hymns have German tunes). The Church of England only accepted hymn-singing officially in 1820. Out of this confusion of trends and practices, what criteria should a compiler use?

The compilers of the 1861 edition of *Hymns Ancient and Modern* state in their *Preface* that "they have endeavoured to do their work in the spirit of the English Prayer-book, and in dependence on the grace (i.e. Light) of God". The compilers of the 1951 edition say in *their* Preface that they were reducing the cumbrousness of the supplements by cutting out those hymns "which had never really found favour" and those which "were not likely to last much longer" because "prevailing tendencies" would have swept them away before long. They disclaim any attempt to break fresh ground or exploit "novel ideas", and they conservatively speak of consolidating, but by going along with prevailing Humanistic tendencies, they connived in shifting the emphasis away from the Light. The compilers of the 1925 edition of *Songs of Praise* did the same on stylistic grounds. They say in their Preface that they wanted to make a national collection of hymns and replace "weak and poor hymns", and the 1931 edition speaks of "weak verse and music" which has alienated the nation "during the last half century" in both Anglican and Free Churches. The trouble is that the Light can appear a weak decorative idea to someone who has not experienced it, and there is a danger of throwing the baby out with the bathwater.

Of the 638 hymns of the 1889 edition, 78 on the Light were omitted in the 1951 edition, and 91 have been retained. (See *Appendix* for details.)

The Light is in the selection, but hymns primarily about the Light have been omitted, and by and large it is hymns which have a primary Humanistic meaning, in which the Light is secondary or even incidental, that have survived. By dwelling on the blood, the shepherds, the child and all the socially observable facets of Humanistic Crosstianity, the 1951 compilers helped to exteriorise what had been until Victorian times a deeply interior religion, and by leaving out so many hymns about illumination they contributed to the benighting of a generation of children who were to grow up and become the permissive generation.

Moreover, this Humanistic trend, this process of secularization, has extended to the selection of hymns for church services. How many of the above lines are widely known? If a church-goer finds many of the above lines unfamiliar, then this is a sign that many Light hymns are no longer in fact being chosen or sung. In the next edition of *Hymns Ancient and Modern* we can expect many of these 91 "survivors" to disappear on the grounds that they have ceased to find favour, and so the process of Humanistic secularization will continue; unless something is done to reverse the prevailing tendency.

The mystic will believe that for the last hundred years the Church has got it wrong, that church attendances have fallen in response to the secularization and worldliness, that what is needed is a return to the Light and to the tradition of Christianity's greatest mystics whose vision we have been considering. The mystic Christian who has not turned to esotericism awaits a purging of the Church to retrieve what has been lost and prepare for ecumenical reunification on the Light.

The Christian Light Today

So how strong is the Christian Light today from an ecumenical point of view? The Light symbolism is obvious in Church architecture. The stone spire is a world axis or Tree which joins earth and Heaven. It symbolises in stone the vertical descent of the Light (a pyramid-shaped ray widening from top to base) intersecting the horizontal everyday world of the congregation in the nave, bathed in ethereal light from the stained glass, and the spire points the response vertically back up to the sun, which symbolises the Light of God in Heaven. There is thus a movement from vertical descent to horizontal reception and then vertical ascent, a process which is symbolized by the vertical-horizontal cross, although this dynamic symbolism is today largely forgotten. Pictures with haloes, the eternal lamp before the sacrament, the monstrance and candles further represent the Light.

The Light also descends round each whorled and spinning planet-like Eastern Orthodox dome to the congregation below and then returns back up to point to the sun. On the other hand, a ray of Light splits into 16 and enfolds the post-Copernican Western dome of St Peter's, Rome or St Paul's Cathedral, London, as if it were our round world which it holds like fingers round a fist.

The Light is still in the liturgies of the Church for those who have eyes to see. We have already considered *The Book of Common Prayer*, the liturgical book of the Anglican Communion. The Catholic liturgies also symbolise the descent of the Fire or Light. They are the heirs of the pre-Christian fire-cults, the state ceremonies which channelled the wisdom of the Light into the priest-king's soul.

The Light has always been present in the Catholic liturgical tradition, which goes back two thousand years in parts. The daily service for divine office grew up in the 3rd and 4th centuries AD and was fixed by the 7th century in the Western Roman rite. It contains numerous references to the Light, especially in the hymns of the hours which contrast the permanent Christ-Light with the rising and setting light of day. Vespers were named after the evening star Vesper, and they combined the twelfth hour service and the *Lucernarium*, the blessing of the evening lamp which represented the Light. The Latin liturgy of the Roman rite spread all over Europe and took local forms which became fixed liturgies in the 12th and 13th centuries, when the first portable breviaries appeared.

In 1570 (the beginning of a decade in which mystical prayer and contemplation were replaced by petition and intercession) one form was imposed on all, and until recently, the principal liturgy, the Mass, has been unchanged since then. It includes the Light: "*Et lux perpetua luceat eis*" ("And may eternal light shine on them"). In the Roman Latin rite, the Mass celebrates the redeeming body and blood of Christ in the bread and wine, together with the sacrifice Christ made on Calvary. The Mass also symbolises the coming and presence of the Lord, which fulfils his promise, "Lo, I am with you alway, even unto the end of the world" (*Matthew* 28.20). It assures people that there is a divine reality within their earthly being, and the coming of the Lord is the descent of the Spirit or *Logos* upon the eucharistic offerings so that they become the body and blood of Christ. This descent is the descent of the Light.[106]

The Eastern rite liturgies which are now under Rome also have as their centre a prayer for the descent of the Light (the Spirit or *Logos*) upon the eucharistic offerings. The Eastern rites were all formed in the 4th century AD, and their liturgies are all related.

The earliest, the Antiochene rite, evolved the Liturgy of St James, which proclaims: "We have become the brothers and fellow-servants of the angels, and together with them we perform the service of the Fire and the Spirit.... Servants of the Church, tremble, for ye are partakers of the living fire". Before the sanctification of the eucharistic offerings, it says "show us these holy gifts in radiant light, fill the eyes of our spirit with endless light", and one of the Syrian masses says, "Thus art Thou glorified and dwellest among men, not to burn them with fire but to lighten them."

The Antiochene rite produced the Byzantine rite, which uses liturgies of St John Chrysostom, St Basil the Great and St Gregory the Great. It also produced the Alexandrian rite, which took over the Byzantine liturgy in the 12th century. In addition it produced the Chaldean rite which is used by Catholic Nestorians and the Malabar Christians of India, while the Armenian rite of St Gregory the Illuminator, who made the Armenians the first Christian nation after the British early in the 4th century AD, is based on the Liturgy of St James and the Byzantine Liturgy of St John Chrysostom. All these Eastern Liturgies say the same thing, that the reception of the sacrament sanctifies us, or in the words of a prayer of Simeon Metaphrastes (10th century) "Thou a fire consuming the unworthy, consume me not, O my Creator!...Consume the thorns of all my misdeeds!...Teach and enlighten me."

The presence of the Christ-Light in the sacrament is suggested by the eternal light which hangs before the sacrament in Catholic churches. This has been present in English Catholic churches since the beginning of the 13th century, and it looks back to the Jewish Mosaic Law. The Jews kept a seven-branched lampstand of gold in the temple (*Exodus* 25.31-40) and a light that burned perpetually in the sanctuary (*Exodus* 27. 20-1, Leviticus 24. 2-4, 1 *Samuel* 3.3). According to later Talmudists, this was an act of reverence for the *Torah*, which was in the Ark of the Covenant. The Jews also burned lights before the tombs of prophets and at Jewish festivals (for example, the Feast of the Dedication of the Temple, or Feast of Lights), and a lamp was blessed at the *chaburah* in the name of God "who createst the lamps of fire".

The Catholic liturgy still reflects the Christianizing of the lights that were used at Roman pagan ceremonies. Roman pagans lit lamps and candles in sanctuaries and house doorways during religious festivals, and they burned lights before idols and statues of Roman emperors; they used symbolic torches to light funeral pyres, and left lights in tombs so that the dead would have light. The Church began to burn lights and torches to show respect for dead martyrs – though the Council of Elvira (AD 301-3) condemned this practice – and it permitted lights to be carried in funeral cortèges, as a result of which candles are now placed round a coffin during burial rites in a church. The lights recall the sacredness of the body, which has been a tabernacle for the Light of God, the Christ-Light, and they remind people of the immortality of the soul and the Beatific Vision, for which the Church prays: "Let perpetual light shine upon him" (i.e. the deceased).

The Catholic liturgy also reflects the Christianizing of the lights that were used at Roman civil ceremonies. State officials like Roman consuls and, of course, emperors, were preceded by a torch or thick candle, a custom which continued in Byzantium and in the palaces of the medieval Western kings. The Church began to carry candles before bishops and its Popes, and by the 7th century AD seven candles were carried before bishops and the

Pope, and were put on the pavement above the altar, a practice which is repeated today at any Mass taken by the Pope. These candles represent the Christ-Light, the Word, whereas lights like the bugia, the bishop's candle, were purely functional, to give light so that the bishop could read at services taken by the Pope.

The Catholic liturgical year uses the Light theme. The Christmas liturgy is about the coming of the divine light into the world, the Light shining in the darkness. The Word, born in Light from the Father, is born again in the darkness of Mary's womb; and there is a theological significance in the lights on Christmas trees. Candlemas (February 2) involves the blessing and procession of lighted candles in memory of the meeting between the Holy Family and Simeon, who proclaimed Christ to be "a light of revelation to the Gentiles and a glory to the people of Israel" (*Luke* 2.32). Lent shows the struggle of the "light of the world" against the darkness of sin, which seems to triumph on Good Friday. Christ rises from the tomb with greater radiance than before: "His countenance was like lightning and His raiment like snow" (*Matthew* 28.3). The victory of light over darkness is seen in the Easter Vigil, in the lighting of the paschal candle which in turn lights the candles of the participants; and in the shouts of "*Lumen Christi*". The Easter Vigil of Baptism reminds us that the life of a Christian is a life of the Christ-Light.

The liturgy for Baptism reflects an ancient use of lighted candles. In patristic times, catechumens (converts under instruction before baptism) were called *illuminandi* (those to be enlightened) and the newly baptised *illuminati* (the enlightened). The new baptised person is given a candle: "Receive this burning light and keep the grace of your Baptism throughout a blameless life." As the religious life is a kind of second Baptism, a candidate in a service of profession often receives a lighted candle.[107]

The breakdown of certainties around 1910, the turmoil of the First World War and the rise of Fascism led to a deep disenchantment with modern industrial society, science and progress, and in our time mysticism has undergone a Reawakening in a few Christian individuals who have reacted to the secularization and worldliness of the Church by taking the Mystic Way.

20TH-CENTURY MYSTIC REAWAKENING

The Catholic Reawakening was heralded by St Thérèse of Lisieux as long ago as the 1890s – her autobiography *Histoire d'une ame* in which Jesus is "the Eternal Fire which burns without consuming", "the Sun of Love",[108] was published a year after her death in 1898 – and by two converts: the Jewish Carmelite nun, St Edith Stein (Teresa Benedicta of the Cross), who studied under Husserl and died in an Auschwitz gas chamber in 1942; and Jacques Maritain, who studied under Bergson.

The Catholic Reawakening really began at the beginning of the Second World War. Simone Weil (1909-43) put her spiritual autobiography in the form of a letter. When she was around 30, she had found that reciting George Herbert's poem "Love bade me welcome" helped her bad headaches, and during one of these recitations "Christ himself came down and took possession of me". This was clearly the Light, for she writes: "After this I came to feel that Plato was a mystic, that all the *Iliad* is bathed in Christian light, and that Dionysus and Osiris are in a certain sense Christ himself." The Light came to her without her having to pray for it – "until last September I had never once prayed in all my life" – and appropriately, the last words she ever wrote in her papers (which were published as *Waiting on God*) were: "The most important part of education – to teach the meaning of *to know* (in the scientific sense)",[109] by which she meant knowledge of the Light.

Teilhard de Chardin (1881-1955), a Jesuit palaeontologist, saw Christianity as being renewed by a spiritual understanding of evolution, a view which, for some, puts him in the esoteric stream. Teilhard asserted that both man and his world are evolving towards a unity of the cosmic Christ, and his mixture of religion and science brought a Papal warning against his ideas. Teilhard had mystical glimpses first in Hastings (1911) when he felt the universe as a living presence, and again in 1916, when, as a stretcher-bearer in a church near the front, he saw a picture of Christ blend into the universe, which vibrated with light. "Once again," he writes in *Hymn of the Universe*, which recalls the "instress" of his fellow Jesuit Hopkins and which was published after his death, "the Fire has penetrated the earth... The flame has lit up the whole world from within.... Now, Lord, through the consecration of the world and luminosity and fragrance which take on for me the lineaments of a body and face – in you.... I plunge into the all-inclusive One.... I find in it the ultimate perfection of my own individuality."[110] In Teilhard, the Light is the Word.

Thomas Merton (1915-68), an American who had an English father, became a convert in 1938 and a Trappist monk in 1941. His writings about monasticism have begun a monastic revival, and he was very concerned about social matters and American power politics. In *Contemplation in a World of Action*, which was also published after his death (which was ironically by accidental electrocution from his bedside lamp in a Bangkok hotel room during a visit to the Dalai Lama), Merton writes of the need to renounce the ego to discover "an inner centre of motivation and love which makes us see ourselves and everything else in an entirely new light. Call it faith, call it (at a more advanced stage) contemplative illumination, call it the sense of God or even mystical union: all these are different aspects and levels of the same kind of realisation.... In Blake's words, the 'doors of perception' are opened and all life takes on a completely new meaning.... The real purpose of meditation...is the discovery of new dimensions in freedom, illumination and love."[111] Merton was novice master to a Nicaraguan Trappist, Ernest Cardenal (born 1925), who compares reality to a sun which floods the world with light (and who, encouragingly, is Castro's favourite poet).

The Catholic Reawakening has continued in the work of a less well-known Austrian mystic and artist, Margaret Riley. She brought the Austro-Hungarian Light to Britain after Vienna had been darkened by the anti-metaphysical Vienna Circle philosophers (such as Wittgenstein, Carnap and Ayer), and in the early 1970s she had a vision of Christ in St Ives and was guided by the Light. She revived the better aspects of Quietism and expressed it in her paintings, for example her portrait of St Thérèse of Lisieux as a nun which is based on a vision. Mother Teresa of Calcutta (born 1910), the Albanian Catholic who has served the poor of Calcutta since 1948 and founded the Order of the Missionaries of Charity for Catholic women, has often spoken of the Light, and can be presumed to have been inspired by it.

The leader of the Protestant Reawakening, of the Protestant mystic revival, has undoubtedly been the great American T. S. Eliot (1888-1965), who, living and writing in Europe, saved Protestant mysticism. So important was his Dante-esque journey from the Hell of "The Waste Land" to the Purgatory of "The Hollow Men" and (after he became an Anglican) "Ash Wednesday", and finally to the relative serenity of *The Four Quartets* (1935-41), that he cannot be considered more of a poet than a mystic, and in mysticism as well as in literature, the 1930s and 1940s were the Age of Eliot.

It is the "Quartets" that concern us here. Eliot saw the Light as "the still point" (compare Dante's "infinitesimal Point"), "a grace of sense, a white light still and moving" in "Burnt Norton". He tells his soul to "be still" "so the darkness shall be the light" in "East Coker". The Light is "the point of intersection of the timeless/With time", one of the "hints and guesses" in "Dry Salvages". And, of course, "Little Gidding" ends with "the crowned knot of fire/And the fire and the rose (i.e. Rolle's fire, and Dante's rose) are one (i.e. the Light)". In perhaps his most explicit reference to the Light Eliot had written in "Choruses from 'The Rock'", "O Light Invisible, we praise Thee!/Too bright for mortal vision./O Greater Light, we praise Thee for the less,.../O Light Invisible, we worship Thee!"[112]

Contemporary Protestant mystics are few and far between, so much so that any thought remotely mystical and Protestant is immediately (and probably wrongly) dubbed "Eliotian". The Light can however be found in books by Bishop Kirk and F. C. Happold (see *Bibliography*), who reflect the roots of the Anglo-Catholic tradition. One unlikely mystic has turned out to be Auden's friend, Dag Hammarskjöld (1905-1961), the Swedish Lutheran Secretary-General to the UN until he was killed in a plane crash in the Congo. Hammarskjöld wrote a mystical diary, *Markings*, which Auden translated. It reveals a knowledge of the Light: "To step out of all this, and stand naked on the precipice of dawn – acceptable, invulnerable, free: in the Light, with the Light, of the Light. Whole, real in the Whole....You are one in God.... In prayer you descend into yourself to meet the Other, in the steadfastness and light of this union.... The only real thing, love's calm unwavering flame in the half light of an early dawn."[113]

The contemporary mystical Reawakening comes at a time when the Second Vatican Council of 1962-5 began its key document on ecumenism,

"*Lumen gentium*". The beginning can be translated: "Christ is the light of all nations (or humanity). Hence this most sacred Synod, which has been gathered in the Holy Spirit, desires to shed on all men that radiance of His which brightens the countenance of the Church. (Or: it may bring to all men the light of Christ which shines out visibly from the Church. Or: to enlighten all men by that brilliance of His, which shines in the face of the Church.)" The document goes on to refer to Christ as "the light of the world", a phrase which has an obvious ecumenical meaning.

The Light can still be found in the liturgies, but is it understood by the congregations?

There have been dramatic developments in the relationship between Christianity and Communism. An ecumenically-minded Polish Pope, John Paul II, brought hope to Christians behind the now torn-down Iron Curtain, who re-emerged from under Communism through Gorbachev's *glasnost*, and the Russian Baptists have been going from strength to strength. (The Russian Orthodox Cathedrals have preserved the Byzantine Light as a halo on icons and murals.)

In ecumenical Christendom mysticism has already begun to make a come-back, and the prospects look good. The Catholic and Protestant mystics of the past saw sin as a separation from the divine life, and with hindsight it may appear that for the last hundred years under Lutheran and Calvinist influence, religion has concentrated so much on seeing sin as an effect of a corrupt human nature that outwardly religious men have forgotten to unite the heart with the Light. Emphasis is again being placed on the heart, and a Catholic mystic has declared that the Light flows into the heart (compare the heart *chakra*), whence it goes to the soul.

Some Catholic Quietists came to think the Church irrelevant, but contemporary "heart-based" mystics see the Ten Commandments as the best guide for putting people in the right "frame of heart" to turn away from the senses and receive the Light. Priests are therefore ideally like Zen Masters; they give guidance through regular confession, which, like *koans*, keeps seekers on the Way and therefore opens them to the Light. Such a view assumes that the priesthood is itself illumined, and we have seen that, sadly, this can no longer be taken for granted. Nevertheless, the illumined heart promises to be a basis for a new Catholic-Protestant ecumenism.

It seems that in the European civilization the Light dimmed around 1870-1880 (see pp211-215) and that within European Christianity the Light is not promulgated or preached from the pulpit as it used to be. In America, Christianity remains a force and arguably Churches are still able to sway a Presidential re-election, as may have happened in the case of Bush Jr (who was also assisted by the more powerful Syndicate). Western citizens are more likely to encounter the Light in American rather than in European churches. We shall see in the companion volume to this book that a civilization that is short of Light needs a recovery of the Light if it is to survive and flourish. It follows that the European wing of Western civilization is in urgent need of a recovery of the Light now.

12

The North American Light

The Christian North American Light was deeply influenced by the European Light with which it shares the tradition set out in no. 11 above. Many European dissenters were among the first voyagers to the New World, and they took with them the Nonconformist, Puritan Light that was oppressed in Europe. The North American Light is therefore largely Protestant.

They also took with them Freemasonry. The Founding Fathers of what became the United States were mostly Freemasons. Freemasonry was influenced by Deism, and many of them, including George Washington, were Deists. For the Freemasonic Light, see pp460-463.

The American Great Awakening was influenced by Wesley's Methodism. The Methodist movement developed within the Church of England – it did not break away until four years after Wesley's death in 1795 – but Church disapproval prompted George Whitefield (1714-70) to persuade Wesley to turn to the masses who did not go to church. Whitefield was an Anglican clergyman who had also had a "conversion" experience, and he was, at the age of 23 in 1737, the most popular preacher in England, having already triumphantly visited America. The English Evangelical movement therefore began with an open-air meeting at Bristol in 1739. Shortly afterwards in 1739/40, Whitefield made his second visit to America, having learned from Wesley. He preached to huge crowds and became a leading figure in the Great Awakening of American Calvinists.

The American Dutch Reformed, Presbyterians, Congregationalists and Baptists, as well as some Anglicans, were mainly Calvinist, and since the American colonies had been settled by Puritans like those who crossed on the *Mayflower*, the Puritan idea of a covenant between God and his nation was still strong among the Calvinists there who rejected the new 18th century Rationalism. It was to this Calvinist outlook that Whitefield appealed with an evangelical Calvinism, and he broke with Wesley over Calvinist doctrine.

Jonathan Edwards (1703-58), a Congregationalist pastor, also led the Awakening by preaching justification by faith. Edwards' conversion took place in 1721, when he came to a "delightful conviction" of God's glory, which could be directly apprehended, for it was imparted to the soul as "a divine and supernatural light" (the title of a sermon he delivered in 1734). Edwards had experienced that Inner Light, and as a Calvinist he believed that God had decreed conversion, and in his "New Light" revivalism he saw those touched by the Light as an elect. The Great Awakening was over by 1742, but its effects outlasted the century.

Transcendentalism

Romantic Neoplatonism (see pp475-479) was a source of inspiration for Transcendentalism, which grew out of Unitarianism. Unitarianism had developed in America when Congregationalist churches resisted the emotionalism of the Great Awakening of Whitefield and Edwards, and in the 1780s the Congregationalist churches that did not want controversy turned Unitarian. There was a Second Great Awakening in America from c.1795 to 1835, which began in New England, and in 1832 when Unitarianism was developing, a Unitarian Minister, Ralph Waldo Emerson (1803-82), resigned.

Emerson was overcome by grief at the death of his first wife, and he turned to the Quakers and the Swedenborgians. (He had been reading

Swedenborg before 1829.) He went to Europe and met Coleridge and Carlyle, both of whom had interpreted the German Transcendental Idealism of Kant and Fichte, and he returned with a blend of Romantic individualism and Neoplatonism – he too was influenced by Taylor – and his own brand of Transcendentalism, which he brought to the New England Transcendentalists. They had originated c.1830, and were interested in the tradition of India and China and in Boehme and Swedenborg.

The Unitarians saw God as One, and not a Trinity, and they denied the divinity of Christ. The Transcendentalists saw all creation as One, there being a spiritual correspondence between man and Nature which Emerson had found in Swedenborg and Coleridge (e.g. in *The Ancient Mariner*, where the murder of the albatross unleashes spirits against men). Emerson rejected the established churches, and from reading Swedenborg, and reading and meeting Wordsworth, he had come to believe that wisdom flows into the mind from Nature by divine influx, and that Nature was therefore the source of wisdom. In his *Divinity School Address* of 1838, Emerson challenged the churches, and particularly Unitarianism, by asserting the "impersoneity" of the Transcendental or divine indwelling.

Emerson was referring to the Light, which he had discussed in his lecture on Fox (1835). In this lecture Emerson connected the Quaker Inner Light with Zoroaster, Confucius, Orpheus, and many other mystics we have been considering; and not solely with Jesus, as Fox did. He argued that the Light renews religion: "Nature never fails. Instantly the divine Light rekindles in some one or other obscure heart who denounces the deadness of the church and cries aloud for new and more appropriate practices." The Light that he used as a stick with which to beat Unitarianism into renewal can be found in his poems; for instance, through accepting Fate: "Love it, though it hide its light;/By love behold the sun at night."[1]

Thoreau (1817-62), another of the Transcendentalists and a disciple of Emerson's, acted out the Transcendentalist correspondence between man and nature by moving into a cabin by Walden Pond (on land Emerson owned) in 1845 and keeping a Journal about his ecstatic experiences. He wrote, "I perceive that I am dealt with by superior powers"; by which he meant the influx of the Light.

New Thought

The esoteric Light passed from Theosophy (see pp480-487) into the American New Thought movement, where it was treated as a living experience again, and not part of a system. According to some, New Thought was in fact another new form of Protestant Christianity. However, in the United States the Unity group of the Fillimores (1880s), which claimed to be Christian and was in the New Thought Alliance until 1922, taught reincarnation; Robinson's Psychiana group (1929) was hostile to Christianity; and the I Am movement of the Ballards (1930s) looked back to such Ascended Masters as the occultist, and later mystic, Saint-Germain. All three were influenced by Theosophy, as were other sections of New Thought, and New Thought was clearly more esoteric than Christian.

New Thought began in the 19th century with Phineas Quimby (died 1866) and it drew on Platonism (the view that the "Idea" of the Light is more real than matter, and so thought has an active power, for example in healing) and Swedenborgianism (the view that all situations in the material world have spiritual causes). It drew on Hegel, on the Hinduism of the Theosophists, and on Transcendentalism. The aims of New Thought were defined in 1916: "To teach the Infinitude of the Supreme One; the Divinity of Man and his Infinite Possibilities through the creative power of constructive thinking and obedience to the voice of the indwelling Presence which is our source of Inspiration, Power, Health and Prosperity."

It is as if the dimmed Christian Light gathered strength from the "isms" that influenced New Thought, and shone again through New Thought, which taught continuous revelation through the Light. It asserted that God is immanent as well as transcendent through the Light, and as a result man's nature is divine. The universe is spiritual, and sin and disease are the result of incorrect thinking. To live at one with God is to be healthy – and rich, for financial hardship, too, is the result of incorrect thinking. Such principles appear in works written between the 1890s and 1940s by Trine, Marden, Collier, Fox, Clarke and Peale.

New Thought is best reflected in one of the most popular books of the 1890s, Ralph Waldo Trines's *In Tune with the Infinite* (1897): "The soul is divine and in allowing it to become translucent to the Infinite Spirit it reveals all things. As man turns away from the Divine Light do all things become hidden.... We find the highly illumined seer, Emanuel Swedenborg, pointing out the great laws in connection with what he termed the divine influx." Trine affirmed the Swedenborgian (and, let us not forget, Zoroastrian) idea that "everything is first worked out in the unseen before it is manifested in the seen, in the ideal before it is realized in the real, in the spiritual before it shows forth in the material. The realm of the unseen is the realm of cause. The realm of the seen is the realm of effect."

Therefore "All life is from within outwards", and: "In the degree that we open ourselves to the inflowing tide of this immanent and transcendent life, do we make ourselves channels through which the Infinite Intelligence and Power can work...what I call God. I care not what term you may use, be it Kindly Light, Providence, the Over Soul." Therefore, "Don't shut out the divine inflow.... The thought life needs continually to be illumined from within. This illumination can come in just the degree that through the agency of the mind we recognise our oneness with the Divine, of which each soul is an individual form of expression.... The Light is ever shining, and the only thing that it is necessary for us diligently to see is that we permit neither this thing not that to come between us and the light.... Your friend who keeps his windows clean that the Eternal Sun may illumine all within and make visible all without – know that your friend lives in a different world from yours."[2]

In *Character-Building: Thought Power* (1901), Trine writes: "Thought is the force underlying all. Your every act – every conscious act – is preceded by a thought.... Thought is at the bottom of all progression or retrogression, of all success or failure." Thus, to be illumined one must think of the Light. The connection between thought and the Light is perhaps the main motif of New Thought. James Allen's *As a Man Thinketh* (1902/3) begins: "The aphorism, 'As a man thinketh in his heart, so is he,' embraces the whole of a man's being.... A man is literally what he thinks. His character is the sum of all his thoughts."

Rhodes Wallace's *How to Enter the Silence* applies the same principle to "soul-pruning" for "the barriers that cloud spiritual perception are false human tendencies covering the soul with seven dense veils which must be burned away by divine force within". (Compare Alice Bailey.) Prentice Mulford's *Thought Forces* (1913) states: "There is a Supreme Power and Ruling Force which pervades and rules the boundless universe. You are a part of this power. You as a part have the faculty of bringing to you by constant silent desire, prayer or demand more and more of the qualities, belongings and characteristics of this Power. Every thought of yours is a real thing – a force.... Every thought of yours is literally building for you something for the future of good or ill."

Judge Troward's *The Law and the Word* (1917) begins: "Thought is a power in itself, one of the great forces of the Universe, and ultimately the greatest of forces, directing all the others." Florence Scovel Shinn says the same thing in *The Game of Life and How to Play it* (1925), and so does Emmet Fox's *Power through Constructive Thinking* (1940). All agree that how illumined we are depends on how we think, and Annalee Škarin takes up the idea in her books, notably *Ye are Gods* (1952), which is packed with references to "the fountain of light" which enables us to be gods and partake of the divine life.

Protestant Evangelism

A proliferation of Free Churches was taking place on both sides of the Atlantic. America grew into a world power to rival Germany and England by 1860, and the freedom that was allowed to Protestant groups following the First and Second Great Awakenings attracted Catholic and Lutheran immigrants from Europe. Because of frontier conditions, new denominations grew up, like the Disciples of Christ (1832), which was an alliance of Presbyterian and Baptist revivalists, and conversely, Universalism, which bore no relation to our Universalist view of history and denied hell and eternal punishment, made gains in the mid 19th century. (It finally merged with Unitarianism in 1961.)

Protestants devised new ways of evangelising in the new industrial society, and new sects arose in Britain concerned with the Second Coming: these included the Plymouth Brethren (1827), and the Catholic Apostolic

Church (1832). The millenarian idea spread to America, where Transcendentalism's rejection of the established order had contributed to the rise of Free Churches, and there were such variations of Protestantism as the Seventh-Day Adventists, who unsuccessfully predicted the end of the world and the Second Coming in 1844, and the Jehovah's Witnesses (founded 1879). These looked back to the equally millenarian Shakers, an offshoot of some English Quakers who sang in tongues and shook c.1747. (The movement was taken up by "Mother Ann" Lee, who emigrated to America in 1744, had revelations, and was regarded as the female part of God's nature, like the Gnostic Sophia.)

These variations developed into the Fundamentalist and Evangelical churches of the 1920s which have preserved the Light in America and which have renewed America's vitality. The Wesleyan-based Holiness and Pentecostal churches emerged and advocated a post-conversion experience, a Baptism with the Holy Spirit. One late sect was called the Fire-Baptisted Holiness Church, the Fire representing *the* Fire (or Light). Derivations from old Protestant sects made ground: the Mennonites (who rose from the Anabaptists); the Hussite Moravians; and the formerly German Pietist Brethren. There were new forms of Christianity such as the Mormons, or Church of Jesus Christ of the Latter-Day Saints (founded by Joseph Smith in 1830) and the Christian Scientists (founded in 1879).

The Ecumenical Movement was exclusively Protestant in origin and was influenced by the American missionary leader J. R. Mott (who died in 1955). The World Council of Churches was constituted in Amsterdam in 1948 and had its headquarters in Geneva, but its drive and finance were American. There was now a continuing dialogue between Protestants, eastern Orthodox and Roman Catholics, and the inter-faith movement grew stronger.[3]

Today North America's religion is strong, with an estimated church attendance of 38%, against 1.7% in the UK. The President speaks of God, and the Christian "morality" vote is thought to have swung Bush Jr's re-election. The US currency proclaims "In God We Trust". There are appeals to "a shining city on a hill", and atheist Communism was described by Reagan as an "evil empire". There is now talk of an "Axis of Evil". The Freemasonic Light is intermeshed in these strong religious affirmations.

13

The Byzantine-Russian Light

The Byzantine tradition began with the founding of Constantinople by Constantine the Great in AD 330.[1] Constantine held the imperial throne that had spent 250 years persecuting British Christians, and he formally put an end to all persecutions. There was massive Christianization (see pp81-83). Coins of Constantine now showed him as a Christianized Sol, with a halo of rays of Light shining from his head. Christianity now sought to eliminate paganism, and began the process of destroying the pagan temples and tradition.[2] Alchemy was Christianized. Jesus was identified with the Philosopher's Stone, and Christians proclaimed that man's sulphur (his earthly part) and his mercury (the *pneuma* or spark of the soul) must be united with his salt (the fire of love, the Quintessential Ether), and this trinity of Sulphur-Mercury-Salt was seen as the Christian Trinity of Father-Son (or *Logos*)-Holy Spirit.[3] Constantine gave the British Bishop the seat of precedence at the councils of Arles, Nicaea and Constantinople (AD 314, 325, 337) as Britain was the first country to receive Christianity, and the Christian legacy was honoured by Constantine's sons, who founded the Christian Byzantine Empire, and by his grandson Ambrosius Aurelianus, who became Christian King of the Cotswolds and an uncle of the Christian King Arthur.

The Strengthening Light of the Desert Fathers

However, not everyone was pleased at the coming of Christ's Kingdom on earth, and in the 4th century AD contemplatives chose to leave the new Christian State for the deserts of Egypt, Syria and Palestine where they lived the solitary life of the hermit in Spartan conditions. Many were in reaction against the worldly alliance between Church and State following Constantine's founding of Constantinople. Many had been influenced by the asceticism of Manichaeism, and many were heirs to Clement's Christian Gnostics, who followed the *Gospel* (the Word or *Logos*) rather than the Law. They found ascetics who had preceded them, driven into the desert during the Roman persecutions of Decius and living out a very harsh solitude and bodily denial. By their example these Desert Fathers demonstrated the strength of the Christian spirit in adverse physical conditions, strengthened the power of the Christian Light and led to the founding of the Christian monastic tradition.

Their spiritual vigour seems to have invigorated their bodies, and many of the Desert Fathers are reputed to have lived to incredible ages in the clean desert air. The first hermit was Paul of Thebes who withdrew into the Egyptian desert during the Roman persecution of the Christians under Decius (AD 249-51) – in 250, all citizens were ordered to sacrifice to the Roman State gods in the presence of commissioners, and many Christians defied this edict – and he lived in a cave until he was 113. His disciple Anthony the Hermit, now generally regarded as the first voluntary Christian hermit and founder of Christian monasticism, followed him between AD c.285 and 305, and died at the age of 105. Athanasius wrote a *Life of St Anthony*, and some of his sayings are collected in *The Sayings of the Desert Fathers* (*Apophthegmata Patrum*), a literature which first grew up in the desert in oral form, in the 4th century AD. This reflects the ascetic influence of Manichaeism and dwells on feats of physical endurance rather than inner spiritual matters, but it conveys the feeling of what it was like to be in the desert, consolidating the Christianized Light.[4]

The early monks struggled against evil in the form of the Devil, demons and sensual temptresses – they all had a problem with thoughts of "fornication" – and they saw their asceticism as helping to achieve the victory of God's army and the Light. Pachomius (Egyptian for "falcon") went into the desert c.314 and was the first to draw together hermits' huts into a monastic enclosure with a Rule. Gregory of Nyssa probably took up monasticism in the 360s and developed a Christian Platonism in which the visible universe was the Form of the unseen God. Spiritual Beauty could therefore be ascended to, and one had "to become oneself as beautiful as the Beauty which he has touched and entered, and to be made bright and luminous oneself in communion with the real Light" by which man was deified. When man "observes the beauty of the material sunlight, he grasps by analogy the beauty of the real sunlight".[5]

St Ephraem Syrus also took up monasticism in the 360s and was probably the "Ephrem" of *The Sayings of the Desert Fathers.* A poet, he saw God as the One Light, and a soul could learn to look at the Secret Light, the Beauty of God, and be flooded with Divine Radiance. John of Lycopolis (died c.394) described the action of Christ on the soul as fire that burns away the impurities of iron and turns the iron to the colour of fire, and the soul is enveloped by "the effulgence of God's Majesty" (*The Spiritual State of the Soul*). Macarius spent sixty years in the Egyptian desert of Scetis (c.330-390), and his mystical homilies also speak of fire working on metal, and of Light within light. He was "at all times in a state of wonder at some divine Vision, and he used to become like a drunken man because of some hidden vision."[6] In one of his homilies he writes, "The soul that is perfectly illuminated by the ineffable beauty of the glory of the light of the face of Christ, and perfectly partakes of the Holy Spirit, and is adjudged worthy to be made the dwelling place and seat of God, becomes all eyes, all light, all face, all glory, all spirit" (*Homilies* 1,2).

The desert was full of mystic ecstasies. John the Dwarf, one of the most vivid characters in the desert of Scetis after c.357 – he dug himself an underground cave – said, "Here is what one of the old men in ecstasy said: 'Three monks were standing at the edge of the sea, and a voice came to them from the other side saying, "Take wings of fire and come here to me."'" Silvanus, a desert mystic in Scetis and Gaza around the end of the 4th century AD, was observed by his disciple Zacharias to be "in ecstasy with his hands stretched towards heaven", and when pressed to reveal what he had seen, said, "I was taken up to heaven and I saw the glory of God (i.e. the Light) and I stayed there till now and now I have been sent away." Arsenius retired to the desert of Scetis c.394, and died c.455 aged 101, and it is recorded that: "A brother came to the cell of Abba Arsenius at Scetis. Waiting outside the door he saw the old man entirely like a flame."[7] John Cassian of Marseilles (c.360-435) was trained as a hermit in the Egyptian desert, where he spent seven years. He described how the soul is caught up in an ecstasy which he called the "prayer of fire". He systematised Eastern mysticism for the West, and took the monastic ideal to the West and pioneered it there.

Isaac of Nineveh went into the Iranian desert c.670 and wrote some *Mystical Treatises* which speak of finding God in oneself as in a mirror, and of the soul as being ecstatically at one with God. And Maximus Confessor became a monk c.613 and in his later mystical works saw man as being deified by the incarnate word (i.e. the Light), on whose energy man could draw.

These Eastern desert mystics had prepared the way for Eastern Christianity, which emphasised the divine Light of the Transfiguration, and Eastern Christian mystics later identified with Jesus in his glory. In early Eastern mysticism, God had an essence and attributes or energies (the Light) which penetrated the universe, their emanation, and dwelt in all things. By concentrating on the divine presence through Hesychasm ("stillness"), the mystic could have an ecstatic vision of the divine Light, like Silvanus and Arsenius, and be "divinised". Divinisation could also be achieved by praying to the name "Jesus" (which meant "I am powerful" and therefore brought divine energy to the soul).

We have treated the Desert Fathers as part of the Byzantine tradition as they came to be cherished in Orthodox churches. However, they could equally as well be regarded as being part of the European tradition (no. 11) because they have an important place in the growth of the Christian Light.

Partly as a result of this example and intensity of the Desert Fathers the Christian Light came to dominate the experience of the early medieval mystics, and its hardy metaphysical vision was set to strengthen the growth of the coming European civilization.

The Byzantine Light of Transfiguration

We have seen (p137) that the Roman Empire revived in Byzantium, when Justinian, the Byzantine Emperor, regulated the holy life, symbolized the Light in Hagia Sophia (c.532-7) and then reconquered Italy from 535-540, recapturing Ravenna. Byzantium stood for the Light. When the barbarian invasions destroyed the church schools in the West, the East had become the preserver of culture, and the later Desert Fathers took on an added importance. Ravenna fell to the Lombards in 751. For the development of the Byzantine Empire during the next 300 years, see "The European Light" (pp137-138).

The Byzantine civilization, with its Roman and Christian background, grew in spite of the doctrinal controversy regarding the Alexandrian Monophysites in the 5th century AD, and the Light was renewed in the 6th century AD when Justinian conquered Italy and bequeathed a strong empire. After a brief decline Heraclius and his successors were able to save Byzantine civilization from Islam and renew its vigour, recapturing the True Cross from the Persians. A decline followed during the Age of Iconoclasm in the 8th and 9th centuries, when doctrinal controversy again had a weakening effect, but then the Macedonian dynasty gave Orthodoxy a new vitality.

During the Dark Ages the West had drawn apart from the East, but Byzantium was the centre of Christian civilization. For the most part the Western Popes were protected by Constantinople, and the empire and church were interwoven at Hagia Sophia. In the 9th century the split between the Eastern Greeks and the Western Latins widened when Photius, patriarch of Constantinople, accused the West of heretically altering the creed so that the Spirit came from the Father "Filioque" ("and the Son"); he thus challenged Rome's power over all churches. Photius backed down, but in the 11th century Greek-Latin hostility flared up again, and the patriarch of Constantinople closed Latin churches there and brought about the schism of 1054.

Meanwhile, the Byzantine Light had inspired the growth of Russia, which began with the rise of the Scandinavian Viking Varangians who attacked Constantinople in the early 10th century and were responsible for the growth of Rus through the rise of "Golden" Kiev. In 988, the patriarch of Constantinople was invited to establish an episcopal see in Rus, and the Byzantine Light went with him. By 1100 Kiev declined and Rus disintegrated before the Mongol invasions and the Tatars under Genghis Khan's descendants, and Golden Kiev was replaced by the Golden Horde.

Against this background the Light tradition in the East was preserved by St Symeon the New Theologian (died 1022), the greatest of the medieval Orthodox mystics. Symeon, a monk, taught that prayer could bring the gift of a "vision of light", the "divine Light" which he himself experienced as "Fire uncreated and invisible, without beginning and immaterial". To Symeon the Light was God: "The Light already shines in the darkness, in the night and in the day, in our hearts and minds. This light without change, without decline, and never extinguished enlightens us; it speaks, it acts, it lives and gives life, it transforms into light those whom it illumines. God is Light, and those whom He makes worthy to see Him, see Him as Light; those who receive Him, receive Him as Light. For the light of His glory goes before His face, and it is impossible that He should appear otherwise than as light. Those who have not seen this light, have not seen God: for God is Light. Those who have not received this light, have not yet received grace, for in receiving grace, one receives the divine light, and God Himself" (*Homily* LXXIX. 2).[8] Through the Light man could share the divine Essence and be deified – divinisation being the Eastern tradition's ideal which was based on the Transfiguration – and the illumination had a Christian character, for the Inner Light was from Christ, who spoke through the Holy Spirit.

There was another decline as a result of Western influence and Moslem pressure during the Crusades; in 1204 Byzantium was conquered by the Latins, and by 1265 most of the Byzantine Empire had melted away. There was a cultural revival under the Palaeologi, and a new flowering of the Byzantine mystical tradition through Hesychasm; but a further brief decline was followed by the Turkish assault and the end of the Byzantine civilization.

The Eastern Hesychast Light

Meanwhile, the Eastern Light had also absorbed Jewish Kabbalism and had shone again through another monk, St Gregory Palamas (1296-1359). Gregory was attached to Mount Athos, and he was a defender of Hesychasm, the monastic school of mysticism which Symeon anticipated. (In other words, he was a Quietist in prayer methods, *hesychia* meaning "prayer of quiet"). In his *Apology for the Holy Hesychasts* (1338) Gregory saw man's body and soul as a unity which is filled with the Light: "Through his energies God communicates himself to man, and because God is Light, he communicates himself in the form of Light, not physical light, but uncreated light."

This "uncreated light" could be sought through asceticism and it led to the "deification of the entire man" on the lines of the Transfiguration on Mount Tabor, though "man cannot know the invisible, incommunicable Divine Essence" but only God's "energies or activities", for God is "above all beings" and "nothing created can have communion with the supreme nature". Gregory was initiated into contemplative prayer by a spiritual master after spending 25 years studying the writings of the Church Fathers, and he taught that only the "pure of heart" could see the inner Light.[9] Hesychasm continued as a revival until Constantinople fell to the Ottoman Turks in 1453, and Hagia Sophia became a mosque.

The Russian Light

Russia had inherited the Byzantine Light when, following the rise of Muscovy from c.1396 and the fall of Byzantine Constantinople to the Turks in 1453, the grand Duke of Moscow, later Ivan III ("the Great"), called his capital "the Third Rome" and symbolized the continuity from Byzantium by marrying Sofia, the neice of Constantine Palaeologus, the last Byzantine Emperor.[10] Ivan the Great (died 1505) marked the Roman connection by building national churches in an Italianate Roman style; hence Moscow's Italianate Kremlin.

The Russian Tsars now replaced the Byzantine Emperors as protectors of the Orthodox world, and the Russian Light shone through the haloed murals and icons within the Cathedral of the Archangel (1505-8) in the Kremlin. There was a Time of Troubles with foreign invasions by Poland and Sweden until 1689, when Peter the Great's secular westernising policies replaced the old Tsardom by an "Empire of All Russias", effected a breakdown in the Russian Central Idea and expanded the Empire. In the course of isolating the Church he inadvertently produced a monastic revival in the 18th century through St Mitrofan of Voronezh, St Tikhon of Zadonesk, and Velichkovsky. St Tikhon was the greatest of Russian mystics, and his enlightenment followed a Dark Night of the Soul.

A revival of Hesychasm restored the Russian Central Idea in the 19th century through such men as St Seraphim of Sarov (died 1833), who taught that contemplative prayer could lead to a mystical experience of the Holy Spirit (the Light). The elders (*startsy*, "spiritual teachers") in monastic communities were spiritual models, and those of Optino, like Leonid, Makarius, and Ambrose, were visited by Gogol, Tolstoy and Dostoevsky. Dostoevsky modelled Father Zossima of *The Brothers Karamazov* partly on Stariez Amvrosec (a photograph of whom can be seen in the Dostoevsky Museum in Moscow), and mainly on St Tikhon of Zadonesk. In *The Idiot*, Prince Myshkin's "mind and heart were flooded by a dazzling light" the moment before he had an epileptic fit, "an ecstatic and prayerful fusion in the highest synthesis of life".[11]

Tolstoy reflected the Light in *Anna Karenin* or *Anna Karenina* (1877), when Karenin says in the presence of Landau, the clairvoyant and ex-shop assistant, "The essential thing is not to close one's eyes to the light."[12] Tolstoy himself was won over to Karenin's view, for in 1879 he went through a spiritual crisis and rejected his great novels for a form of Christianity. In *The Death of Ivan Ilich*, the hero discovers the Light just before he dies, and at the turn of the century Tolstoy was writing plays entitled *The Fruits of Enlightenment* and *The Light Shines in the Darkness*.

From 1855 to 1917 Russia disintegrated. After her defeat in the Crimean War, after years of internal dissension at the hands of revolutionary terrorism and after her defeat in the Russo-Japanese war of 1905 and her heavy involvement in the First World War, atheistic Communism (the brainchild of a Westerner, Karl Marx) restored the secular, westernising approach of Peter the Great in a proletarian context and suppressed the

Orthodox religion. The Russian revolution of 1917 stunted the development of the Orthodox Light, but it has been kept alive in exile by such descendants of the "*startsy*" as the Metropolitan Anthony.

In the Orthodox Church the darkening has been made more obvious by Communism. The collapse of Communism has given the Orthodox Light a new chance, but has the Byzantine-Russian society become too secularized for its revival?

14

The Germanic-Scandinavian Light

The Indo-European Germanic or Teutonic peoples had surfaced in North Germany, Denmark and South Sweden c.500-400 BC,[1] and many migrations followed. Migrations took the Vandals, Gepidae and Goths to the south Baltic coast, and more migrations pushed the Celtic peoples of West Germany to the south-west, and the Helvetii into Switzerland.[2]

In the 2nd century BC the Cimbri and Teutoni invaded South Gaul and North Italy and were defeated by Marius in 102/1 BC,[3] and Julius Caesar was able to distinguish the Germans from the Celts (or Gauls).[4] He records in *De Bello Gallico* VI 21-4 that the Germans had no druids (*druides*), no zeal for sacrifice, and that their gods were the sun, the moon and the fire god (equivalent to the Roman Vulcanus), and despite his superficial acquaintance with German religion the Indo-European Light comes through.

In Caesar's time the Germans were west of the Rhine and had reached as far south as the Danube. There were many Roman-German wars, and Tacitus' *Germania* (AD 98) seems to have referred to the Tungri, who were called the Germani, as Germans, and the name was then applied to all the other Germanic tribes. By the end of the 3rd century AD, the Franks, Burgundians and Alemanni (compare the French *Alemagne*) were all near the Rhine, and the Goths, Gepidae and Vandals had moved south-east.[5]

Once the Germanic peoples were federated (given the status of *foederati* or allies) within the Roman Empire, with the right and duty to fight within the Roman army, the tribes became kingdoms with kings (the Ostrogoths in Italy, the Visigoths in Gaul, the Vandals in Africa), and their peoples converted to Arian Christianity: the Visigoths (south of the Danube) in AD 382-395, the Vandals in Spain 409-429, the Burgundians in Gaul 412-436, the Ostrogoths c.456-472.[6]

Germanic-Scandinavian tribes settled in Britain from the middle of the 5th century AD. According to Bede, the first settlers were apparently invited in to defend Britain against the Picts and Scots, and were from three North-West German or Scandinavian tribes, the Angles, Saxons and Jutes. (The Angles probably came from Sleswig or Schleswig, the Saxons from the region between Holstein and the Ems; the Jutes came from Jutland, which forms part of Denmark.) More invaders arrived and pushed west from the Thames. For details of the Celtic resistance, see 'The Celtic Light', pp97-105.

By 500, the Angles and Saxons were in England, the Franks in North East Gaul, the Burgundians and Visigoths were in France, the Ostrogoths in Italy, and the Vandals in Africa. In 507 the Franks drove the Visigoths into Spain, where they were absorbed by the Moslems in 711, and they took Lombardy in 774. From the 7th to the 8th centuries, East Germany was occupied by Slavs, and the end of the 8th century saw the first Viking invasions of England.

During their migrations and federations, the battle-loving Germanic tribes and Vikings had not been without their own Light, which can be traced back to the shamanism of early Indo-European settlers (including perhaps the Anannage) who built long barrows with shafts like the one between Lejre and Øm in Denmark. From c.500 BC to 1st century BC the Germanic tribes worshipped an Indo-European sun-god and fire-god (as Caesar mentions in *De Bello Gallico*, VI.21).

There is certainly a strong shamanistic influence in the Germanic-Scandinavian mythology. The gods dwelt at Asgard, at the centre of which stood the World Tree, Yggdrasil, an ash, the shamanistic tree whose roots linked nine worlds like the Sumerian ziggurats, and formed the seat of Wodan-Woden-Odin.[7]

The cult of Wodan-Woden-Odin developed in the centuries following Christ. Wodan of the Germans, Woden of the Anglo-Saxons, who gave his name to our Wednesday, and Odin of the Scandinavians had evolved from a Bronze Age Sky-god, and he was associated with thunder and the sun disc, and carried an axe. He was the god of death and battle and he lived in Valhalla and received battle sacrifices, victims who were ritually hanged on trees and stabbed by a spear.[8] Wodan-Woden-Odin himself underwent the shaman's false death by hanging on the World Tree for nine days and nights in agony, after which he lifted up the magical runes that brought knowledge to men. His gift was inspiration, and he had the shaman's ability to fly as an eagle to other worlds in spirit form, and to fetch the dead to the spirit world.[9] In the Viking age he is pictured on an eight-legged horse, Sleipnir, which is recognised in Siberia as the steed of the shaman which carries his spirit to other worlds, and he is known as "the Great shaman".[10] His name survives in modern place names, as in Denmark's Odense (originally *Odins-vé*, "consecrated to Odin").

In the Viking age as Odin he was worshipped in wooden Fire-temples and he absorbed some of the functions of the Germanic Sky-god Tiwaz, the Tiw of the Anglo-Saxons who gave his name to our Tuesday (compare the Druid Du-w) and Tyr of the Scandinavians who upheld the universe,[11] and he became a Sky Father who looked down from on high and saw the earth as a whirling disc or moving wheel or hooked cross. This was shown as a *swastika*,[12] which the Nazis adopted. The Germanic Frija or Scandinavian Frigg or Friia, who gave her name to our Friday, was Odin's wife.[13]

The Germanic Thuror, the Anglo-Saxon and Scandinavian Thor who gave his name to our Thursday, had power over storm and lightning. He was equated with Jupiter by the Romans, and his symbols were the oaks of Western Europe, and the axe and hammer[14] (which were symbols among the pre-Christian Lappish shamans); the Anglo-Saxons worshipped him and wore the hammer as a protective amulet and in Western Scandinavia he took over from Odin.[15] Thor is associated with the *swastika* which may also have been a sun-wheel and which was certainly associated with fire. A perpetual fire burnt in front of the iron-topped altars in his Fire-temples, and the late

Kjalnesinga Saga says, "This was the place for the Fire which was never allowed to go out. This they called the sacred fire."[16]

Another god who became important later on was Freyr, the phallic god who was reborn, Horus-like, in the person of each king.[17] His twin-sister Freyja, goddess of love, originated a divination ceremony, *seid*, in which a seeress went into a shamanistic trance and invoked the spirits to help the community.

The Germanic-Scandinavian religion was conducted by the chieftan – it seems that there was no vocational priesthood – and worship took place in a small wooden or stone temple, like the Temple at Uppsala, and led to a sacrifice (of animals or men) in a nearby sacred grove of oak-trees. The bodies hung (like Odin) on a tree.[18] A high-seat pillar in Thor's temples symbolized the sacred World Tree.

With such a strong shamanistic element in their mythology, it is inconceivable that the Vikings were unaware of the principal shamanistic experience of the Light; and it seems only natural that the pagan Viking teachings were eventually reconciled with the Christian Light. As a result carved Viking crosses appeared in Britain, and a scene from the tale of Sigmund appeared in the Cathedral at Winchester, the Viking capital.[19] The Christianization of Nordic and Celtic themes can be seen in the Gosforth cross in Cumbria (which combines Yggdrasil and Heimdall, who guards the shamanistic rainbow bridge, with Calvary),[20] and in the early Gothic church images of the Green Man, a vegetation god descended from the Celtic horned god Cernunnos, who features in the 14th century English poem *Sir Gawain and the Green Knight.*

In the 8th and 9th centuries AD during the rise of Wessex and Mercia an Anglo-Saxon religious poetry flourished, including "The Dream of the Rood" (before 750), an Anglo-Saxon Christian poem carved on a stone cross at Ruthwell, Dumfriesshire, in which the huge cross "seemed to be filled with light brighter than any light you have seen". The poem may have been written by Cynewulf, whose other religious poems include "Christ II (the Ascension)". This is based on a homily written by Pope Gregory the Great, who, as the sender of Augustine to Kent, can be regarded as the source of the Anglo-Saxon Light.[21]

Anglo-Saxon England, then, was a Christian country with thriving monasteries when the exclusively Scandinavian invasions began. The first Viking raid took place at Lindisfarne in 793, and the raids of the pagan Norsemen (Danes, Norwegians and Swedes) took place each year from 835 to 851, during which time the Vikings combined with the Celtic Britons and half Ireland was settled. In 851 they first wintered in England and in 865 began to overthrow the Anglo-Saxon kingdoms of Northumbria, Mercia and East Anglia. In 878 Alfred surrendered three-quarters of England, which became known as Danelaw, and there were heavy Norwegian raids in 900-1. During this time the new invaders nearly wiped out the Christian Church in Britain except in the west country around Glastonbury.

Little by little the West Saxons fought back, and Athelstan was crowned King of all Britain in 925, and defeated the Vikings in 937. By now the Roman Church was in a very strong position as the creation of what was to become the Holy Roman Empire in 800 had made Imperial Rome the centre of the world; all Christianized settlers looked to Rome, and the Celtic Church was ignored and forgotten.

The Angles and Saxons of England converted to Christianity in the 7th century, the Old Saxons after 750, the Scandinavians in the 10th and 11th centuries, and Iceland last of all, after c.1000.

Denmark was officially Christianized in 960, when the worship of Odin and Thor ceased. (At Jelling in Jutland, the ancient royal capital of Denmark, a stone records the event. Erected by Harald Bluetooth, father of Svein Forkbeard and grandfather of Knut or Cnut, King Canute, it shows Christ with a halo and the runic inscription translates: "Harald King bade this be ordered for Gorm his father and Thyra his mother, that Harald who won for himself all Denmark and Norway and made the Danes Christians.")[22] However, there was a new wave of Danish attacks between 980 and 1013, and the invaders levied Danegeld. These invasions were initially launched by Svein Forkbeard from round strongholds built c.980 at Aggersborg and Fyrkat in Jutland, and Trelleborg in Zealand, each of which held some 1200 men who were housed in 16 Heorot-type halls arranged in four squares of four, recalling a *stupa* in a *mandala.* All use Roman feet and show great mathematical precision, and all are aligned to Delphi, a siting that probably began with Pytheas's voyage to Scandinavia between 330 and 300 BC.[23] The invasions used long Viking war-ships of the kind that can be seen at Roskilde, and they were bought off with increasingly huge amounts of English silver which paid the Viking armies until the next invasion. The general demoralisation led to Wulfstan's *Address to the English.* The English and Danes now reached an agreement in which neither encroached on the territory of the other, and in 1018 there was Anglo-Danish Christian unity under Cnut. By then the Germanic-Scandinavian Light had been completely absorbed by the Christian Light.

15

THE ANDEAN LIGHT

The Andean culture stretched throughout modern Peru, Bolivia, Ecuador, North Chile, and North Argentina.

It seems that since Mesolithic times shamanistic hunters from Central Russia journeyed to Siberia and crossed the frozen Bering (or Behring) Strait to America, whence they reached South America, bearing the snake-god design[1] which is found on both Chinese Shang and Mayan masks. Asian peoples first arrived in the New World by this route c.35,000-20,000 BC, and their Mongoloid features are preserved in the American Indians they became.[2] The history of the South American peoples can be tracked back to c.2500 BC.

In the Andean culture, the Chavin pyramid-temples of early Peru date from c.900-200 BC, and the Moche Huaca del Sol, Peru, dates from c.200 BC-AD 600.[3]

These pyramids were connected with sun-cults at a very early stage in their history, and these sun-cults echoed the sun-cults (and, indeed, Mesopotamian moon-cults) connected with the ziggurats and Great Pyramid.[4] Not all scholars accept diffusionism – that all cultural phenomena have one source – and some scholars focus on identical situations in cultures which have had no direct connection. Although scholars point to greater similarities with the Mesopotamian ziggurats – which originated in Indo-

European Central Asia – than with the Egyptian tomb-pyramids, and relate them to migrations from Asia, almost all the South American pyramids explored have a tomb hidden within their base and thus seem to have derived in part from Egypt and to have reflected the Egyptian *akh* and Light as well as Mesopotamian Shamash. The Light (or Fire) of the New World sun-gods can be traced back to the broadly terraced temple-pyramids which mostly date from c.500 BC, although the idea probably goes back to c.1500-1200 BC[5] as one site has an earthen mound which must have supported a perishable building.

The Inca Light

The Andean culture culminated with the Incas who inherited the temple-pyramids and took them over, between c.1200 and 1500.[6] The Sun-god of the Incas was Inti and their main sun-temple was at Cuzco, Peru.[7] Inti was imposed on all peoples whom the Incas conquered. He was readily accepted because the pre-Inca religion at Tiahuanaco worshipped the sun,[8] and its Bolivian site by Lake Titicaca had a famous Gateway of the Sun.[9] The Incas took over the Chimu city of Chan Chan in Peru, where there were already ten temple-pyramids within walled citadels, each of which was at once a palace and a temple-tomb for successive Kings who on their deaths went and dwelt with the sun like the Egyptian Pharaohs.[10]

The Inca Inti's warmth grew the crops, and he was represented as a face on a rayed disc and was regarded as the Incas' divine ancestor and called "My father", his wife was the Moon Mother.[11] At the best known Inca temple, the Sun Temple at Cuzco, there were resident priests and there were initiates or Chosen Women who were sworn to chastity as wives of the sun.[12] The sun's spiritual contact was also present in fire, which was used in divination and in sacrifice; the sun lit a fire, and either guinea pigs or llamas or pure children or Chosen Women were sacrificed while the priests chanted: "Eat this Lord Sun so that you will know that we are your children."[13] After death the good went to live in the sun's warmth while the bad remained as invisible ghosts on the cold earth. Inca festivals whipped up ecstasies in which the inner god of the sun could be seen[14] (the Light).

16

THE MESO-AMERICAN LIGHT

The Meso-American culture stretched throughout modern Mexico, Guatemala and Belize and it produced the highly developed Mayan culture which was in climax AD c.600-900. The first stone monument in Mexico was the pyramid of Cuicuilco (after 300 BC).[1]

THE MAYAN LIGHT

The Mayan sun-god was Kinich Ahau or Itzamna, and the largest Mayan city, Tikal in Guatemala, had numerous temple-pyramids.[2] The similarity between the Mayan culture and Mesopotamia/Egypt is worthy of consideration. The Mayan stepped pyramids were built so that the ruling priests could hold their religious rites there; the priests lived in them, and the people assembled at them.[3] The stone pillars computed the calendars of the Great Cycle or Long Count.[4] The ceremonies made the corn grow.[5]

Like the Incas, the Maya sacrificed to the sun, and their hereditary priests received and offered the hearts of sacrificial victims to the sun-god and were called *Ah kin,* "he of the sun".[6] The Maya believed that the dead went to the nine Underworlds which they could avoid by being enlightened and dwelling with the sun.[7]

At the Temple of the Sun at Palenque, Mexico, Kinich Ahau was worshipped by day; when he set and entered the Underworld, he became the night sun and took on the features of a jaguar.[8] (Compare the Egyptian lion.) The architects designed the buildings at Palenque (AD c.600-900) in such a way that as the sun set on the last day of the winter solstice, and died, when viewed from the new Sun-king's palace its last light shone through a notch in the ridge behind the Temple of the Inscriptions, lit up the steps to the dead Sun-king Pacal's tomb, and spotlit the succession scenes in the Temple of the Cross, confirming the succession of Chan Bahlum, the new Sun-king, before it entered the Underworld through Pacal's tomb.[9]

Another god, worshipped by the Maya Itza was Kukulcan or Kukulan, the special god of the aristocracy and priestly knowledge, who was known to the Aztecs as Quetzlcoatl ("quetzl bird-snake"), the "feathered serpent"[10] (D. H. Lawrence's "plumed serpent") which is found on the head-dress of the Egyptian Pharaohs. Nekhbet, the vulture goddess, represented Upper Egypt, and Wadjet, the snake goddess, represented Lower Egypt, and together they combined the Heavenly feathers of Horus the hawk with the earthly striking power of the serpent.

The Aztec Light

The Aztecs left Northern Mexico (or possibly the south western United States), where they had lived for a thousand years, c.1168 and travelled south to the modern Mexico City where they took power in the 15th century.[11] The Aztecs thought of themselves as "People of the Sun", and they sacrificed to Huitzilopochtli, the god of the sun.[12] The Aztecs took over Teotihuacan ("City of the Gods" or "Where Men Become Gods") which had been sacked about AD 650, and the famous Temple or Pyramid of the Sun and Temple or Pyramid of the Moon there (c.1st century AD) are connected by an Avenue of the Dead which is a mile and a half long.[13]

These relatively late Mayan and Aztec sun-cults echoed the much earlier sun-cults connected with the ziggurats and Great Pyramid and no doubt they were preceded by South American sun-cults that shared the

Sumerian-Egyptian-British culture. It seems that all along South American sun-cults were linked to the Light. On death favoured human beings could dwell with the sun, and initiation into the Light prepared for an after-life with the sun, as it did in Egypt.

The Aztecs believed there had been four suns before the present one, and they kept the present sun going by providing it with nourishment (*tlaxcaltiliztli*), without which it would cease to shine. They fed the sun with the blood and hearts of human beings. Warriors who died fighting for the sun and all victims who were sacrificed in the sun went to the Heavens and had eternal life as "companions of the sun",[14] and they returned to earth after four years as humming-birds, while less favoured mortals went to the ninth Hell.[15]

The Mississippian Indian Light

The Light of the ancient South American sun-cults influenced and has been preserved in the early cultures of the United States. The North American Mississippian Indian culture (AD c.800-1500) grew through the introduction of agricultural techniques and religious practices, including the temple mound, from northern Mexico by 1000.[16] It had settlements grouped round a pyramid on an earth mound; and a temple which was the chief's residence, as in the Meso-American sun culture. The religion was shamanistic and, like the North American Plains and Plateau Indians, and the Mexican Aztecs they perhaps gave rise to, the Mississippian Indians worshipped a sun-god[17] who symbolized the Light in the spirit world, and who was contacted by the medicine man or shaman. Monk's Mound, near Cahokia, Illinois, measures 1000' x 700' x 100' and suggests a strong ziggurat-type religious cult which was probably also Light-based as feathered serpents and falcons' eyes have been found.[18]

The gods of the North American Indians such as Wakan Tanka (Supreme Deity of the Dakota Indians), Gicelemu Kaong (Great Spirit of the Lenape Indians betwen Ontario and Oklahoma) and Tirawa (Supreme God of the Pawnee Plains Indians between Nebraska and Oklahoma) are shamanistic.[19] The medieval South West American Indian culture of Arizona and New Mexico contains strong shamanistic traces and also looked to the sun.[20] Indians such as the Pueblo and Apache (baddies in so many westerns) regarded the universe as being pervaded by an animating One, and seem to have believed that the spring sun returned after winter as a result of human assistance through the Light.[21]

Civilization is traditionally supposed to have spread from the east (*ex oriente lux*)[22], and if the West European and South American megaliths were colonial temples-cum-observatories to an originally Central Asian Kurgan-Sumerian or Egyptian Sun-god, there is no escaping the conclusion that just as the ceremonies in the Sumerian and Egyptian temples celebrated the inner Shamash and Ra as well as the outer sun, so the ceremonies in the British and South American megaliths celebrated their own versions of the dawning of the Light.

17

The Arab Light

Arabs, a branch of the Semites, are mentioned as far back as 854 BC,[1] and a kingdom of "Aribi" occurs in an inscription of the Assyrian king Tiglath-pileser III (died 727 BC).[2] There were various pre-Islamic cults among the Arabic-speaking peoples of Arabia. Many were polytheistic, but a monotheistic influence seems to have arrived in Arabia after 721 BC when the Lost Ten Tribes were dispersed by Assyria.[3] The main early North Arabian god was El or Ilah (*ilah* is "god" in Semitic languages) – compare "Allah" – and there was a Dhu-Samawi ("Lord of the Heavens", compare the Druid Du-w).[4]

It seems that monotheism was already established when a mission from Byzantium arrived in South Arabia in the late 4th century AD.[5] In the 5th century, South Arabia expanded into Central Arabia and made the monotheistic "Lord of Heaven and Earth" the god of the state religion.[6] The god resided in an irregular black sacred stone of basalt (compare the Christian altar), and as each block of stone was a *bet'el* ("house of the god"), Byzantine Christian writers of the 5th and 6th centuries call them *baetyls*. The best known is the Black Stone of the Ka'bah at Mecca, and Dhu-Shara lived in a black stone at Petra.[7]

Mohammed and Islam's Light

At one level the rise of Islam is rooted in a family or tribal quarrel. In the 6th century the Quraysh, the tribe controlling Mecca, allowed caravans to move freely, and as lords of the Ka'bah, the temple at Mecca, they were known as the People of Allah. They allowed the cults of other gods to be linked to the Ka'bah.[8] The Islamic Light emerged in the Arabian desert when AD c.610 the angel Gabriel revealed the *Koran* to Mohammed (AD c.570-632), a camel-driver who had contacts with Jews and Judaism, in the cave of Hira near Mecca. Mohammed came from the Quraysh tribal group or house of Abd Manaf. At 25, the son of a merchant, he married a widow and had at least two sons and four daughters. He was 35 when Gabriel told him "You are the Messenger of Allah", and for the rest of his life Mohammed received "revelations" which were collected c.650 as the *Koran*, and he was inspired to preach the oneness of Allah at the expense of the other cults.

In his first vision, Mohammed saw the opening passage of the *Koran* in letters of fire written on cloth.[9] The Quraysh rejected him. Opposed and scorned by the Meccan establishment, he withdrew to Medina in AD 622, the year from which the Moslem era is dated. (The withdrawal is called the Hijrah.) In Medina Mohammed began reciting prayers in the direction of the Ka'bah at Mecca, the shrine (now in the Great Mosque) which contains a Black Stone that was traditionally given to Adam on his expulsion from Paradise,[10] and pilgrimage to which restores the hope of returning to Paradise on death. He campaigned against the Quraysh, attacking one of their caravans, and after various battles with the Meccans he entered Mecca in triumph with 10,000 men in 630 and eventually became lord of the two sacred enclaves at Mecca and Medina. The Quraysh agreed to worship Allah alone.

Mohammed united Arabia on the idea of Islam. He therefore founded the Arab Empire as well as its religion. Mohammed's vision spread rapidly following his death for one of his early converts, the wealthy merchant Abu Bakr, became first Caliph ("successor") and following Mohammed's approval of *Jihad* ("Holy War") he set about conquering the whole world to place it under Allah.

Mohammed's successors (the caliphs), uniting round the two sacred enclaves, attacked Byzantium and Persia, and Islam soon conquered the Hejaz, Yemen, Oman, Iraq, Syria, Palestine, Persia and later, North Africa and Spain. The conquerors poured money into Mecca and Medina, and united Arabia under the culture of the Arabs. By the 8th century there was a Moslem Empire ("Muslim" or "Moslem" is the past participle of the verb *islam*, and means "those who have surrendered or submitted themselves"). It stretched from Spain to India, and was poised to challenge the Christian Light for the Holy Land.

After Mohammed's death, the succession should have gone to his most direct descendant. Abu Bakr, the first caliph, had seized the leadership that should arguably have gone to Mohammed's cousin and son-in-law Ali (the husband of Mohammed's daughter, Fatimah). Othman, the third caliph and Mohammed's other son-in-law, was descended from the house of Abd Manaf, and he was murdered, and eventually Ali was pronounced caliph. Abu Bakr's daughter raised an army against him in what is now Iraq, and Ali went to Iraq to raise his own followers against her. When Ali was murdered in 661 his eldest son Hasan was persuaded to abdicate by Mu'awiyah, who was already named caliph in Jerusalem.

By now the Islamic world had split over the dispute concerning the Caliphate. The Sunnites differed from the Shi'ites, who supported Ali (Mohammed's son-in-law) and his descendants. The differences gradually became doctrinal, with the Sunnites following the *Hadith*, a collection of sayings of the Prophet (9th century AD), a body of tradition which for them supplanted the *Koran*. (Sunnah meant "well-trodden way".)

The Ummayads now ruled the Islamic empire from Damascus from 661 to 750, and Moslem unity was restored. The conquered territories were Islamised and Arabised and Mecca and Medina were merely the spiritual capitals of Islam. The Ummayads were Sunnis; the pro-Ali Shi'ites believed that the Imam (the Shi'ite version of the caliph) must be descended from Ali by Fatimah, Mohammed's daughter. In this expansionist culture, the Imam ("leader" and successor to Mohammed) was a manifestation of Allah and primordial Light, and had supernatural knowledge and power from the Light to interpret the *Koran* infallibly.[11] The Ummayads enlarged the

Prophet's mosque and executed heretics in the 8th century, but collapsed before the pro-Ali Abbasids in 750.

The Abbasids spent huge amounts on Mecca and Medina between 750 and 861, and the wife of the caliph Harun ar-Rashid built a conduit that brought water to Mecca. Islam became more institutionalised, and the capital was moved to Baghdad. The Abbasids were at their height from 786 to 861, after which until 945 they were in difficulties on account of the Zanj slave revolt in South Iraq (869), the rise of the Saffarids, and the opposition of the Isma'ilis whose offshoots the Qarmatians plundered Mecca in 930 and carried off the Black Stone. Provincial dynasties grew in Persia (the Buyids) and in Central Asia (the Samanids). They used Turkish slaves. In the 10th century the Fatimids (who were pro-Ali but anti-Abbasid) assumed the title of caliph in Cairo. There were also claims from a Spanish Ummayad. However the Fatimids too declined and were overthrown in 1171 by the Kurdish general Saladin.

By now the Shi'ites had split: the Isma'ilis recognised the seventh Imam as Isma'il, and not Musa, and the Nizaris became a branch. (The Aga Khan is the present head of the Nizaris.) Other sects arose: the Nusayris; the peacock-worshipping anti-dualistic Yazidis or Yezzidis who believed that God forgave Satan and made him the Peacock Angel, the foremost of the seven angels; and the Druzes who arose in the 11th century and deified the Fatimid caliph al-Hakim, through whom (they believed) the Light of the Creator (*al-bari*) most recently emanated.

The Sufi Light of *Fana*: Blasphemous Ecstasy under the Abbasids

Islam meant "surrender" to the Will of Allah (*Al-Ilah*, "the Strong One" or *ta'hala*, "the most high or Supreme One") and the Will of Allah was made known in the *Koran* in terms of the Light: "Allah is the Light of the heavens and the earth. His light may be compared to a niche that enshrines (or wherein is) a lamp, the lamp within a crystal (or glass) of star-like brilliance (or as a pearly star). It is lit from a blessed olive tree neither eastern nor western (or neither of the East nor of the West). Its very oil would almost shine forth (or were well-nigh luminous), though no fire touched it. Light upon light; Allah guides to His light whom he will.... Indeed, the man from whom Allah withholds His light, shall find no light at all" (ch 24).[12] As an ancient god who had been known to the Arabs a long time before Mohammed, Allah was one of a number of animistic gods for from early on the Arab tribes worshipped spirits in stones, trees, the winds, and the sun. It was Mohammed's achievement to establish an Arab monotheism that was influenced by Judaism, for as we have said Mohammed had contacts with Jews when he was a camel-driver.

Allah, then, (like Yahweh) is the Light, and the lamp is lit from the intelligential spirit, which is like an olive tree that produces olives which provide oil for the lamp. So Allah says in the *Koran* (ch 50), "We created man. We know the promptings of his soul (or what his soul whispers within him), and are closer to him than the vein of his neck (or the jugular vein)"; i.e. the Light is closer to the soul than the artery in the neck.

The Light of Allah therefore expressed itself through many different sects that grew increasingly worldly, and Islamic mysticism or Sufism, the practice of *tasawwuf* (Arabic for "devotion to the mystical life") developed as an ascetic reaction to this worldliness. *Sufi* means "mystic" and the word derived from *suf*, the clothes of wool worn in penitence, or possibly from a word meaning "purity" or the "line" behind the Prophet, or even from the Greek Gnostic *sophia*, wisdom.

Sufism originated with the Zoroastrian Magi and was taught to Islamic esotericists by Salman Pak.[13] It absorbed Neoplatonism and the Hermeticism of *Poimandres* – Plotinus was called "the *Shaykh*" (guide) by Moslems, and Hermes appears in the *Koran* as "Idris" – and it first appeared in the 7th century. It entered an ecstatic phase with Rabi'a al Adawiya of Basra (died 801), a former slave girl who was known as the Moslem St Teresa. She declined an invitation to view a spring sunset, "Come out and behold the works of God", with the words, "Come you inside that you may behold their maker" (i.e. the Light), and she refused marriage for "I exist in God". Her ecstatic otherworldliness aimed to unite the soul with God in accordance with Mohammed's teachings.

From the 9th century onwards Sufism was a quest for the Light, and its terminology concerned illumination. Sufis aimed to see the Light of Allah, to perceive the "Real", and their term for God, *al-Haqq*, included the sense of "real" and "reality". The Real was perceived in the "heart", and the vision of the heart was to see what is hidden in the unseen world (the Light) by the "light of certainty" (*yaqin*), a beam cast in the heart by God Himself. (Hence Allah is a light in a niche, the heart in the body.) Knowledge of Certainty from books led to the Eye of Certainty (*ain-u'l-yagin*), when one saw the Light with one's own eyes. Beyond this was the Truth of Certainty (*haqq-u'l-yaqin*) when one knew the Light from having been consumed by it. This was direct perception of God with the intuition (*kashf*), and it brought a supernatural power of discernment (*firasat*).

This direct perception of Allah was the Sufi *gnosis* or *ma'rifah*, a concept first introduced by the Egyptian Dhu an-Nun (died 861). The Sufi *gnosis* described a mystic knowledge that was different from ordinary knowledge (*ilm*), for it was knowledge of the Light. This knowledge was of the heart (*qalb*), an organ of spiritual perception related to the physical heart which, when illumined, reflected the whole of the divine mind. For the eye of the heart to see, the phenomenal self (the ego) had to be cleared out of the way, for when the individual self is lost, the Universal Self is found. The losing of the individual self was achieved through ecstasy, and the process was *fana*, a term which, like the Buddhist *Nirvana*, is usually translated "annihilation" but which literally means "blown out" or "passing away". (Indeed many scholars believe that Sufism was influenced by Buddhism and Hinduism, and *fana* may be an Arabic version of *nir-fana* or *Nirvana*.)

In *fana*, which was introduced by Abu Yazid al-Bistami or Bayazid (died 874), the passions and desires were extinguished in the moral self, there was a passing away from all objects of perception and thoughts in the percipient, intellectual self, and finally even the consciousness of having attained *fana* disappeared in the "passing-away of passing-away" (*fana al-fana*). Ultimately, there was a complete passing away from self into abiding with Allah (*baqa*), or eternal life, and this was often accompanied by a loss of sensation. Man was separated from God by ignorance, which was overcome in seven steps: a yearning which renounces worldly things; a love for Allah that burns away all worldly desires; a mind afire with the immanence of Allah in all creation (*marfat*, "enlightenment"); a dark night in which *marfat* is withdrawn, a blowing out of the Light (*fana*); a feeling of the timeless unity within multiplicity (*tawhid*); a trance condition of amazement at the divine; and finally the ecstatic loss of the earthly self and body consciousness, the permanent absorption into the divine (*fuqr wa fana*) which was both passing-away, and the passing-away of passing-away (*fana al-fana*).

The Sufi was then one with the Universal Prototype or Universal Man, and he saw that the universe is a reflection (or shadow) of the Light of Allah, which he also reflected. The Sufi had been unveiled so that the Light was reflected in his light, and his ecstasy was achieved by *dhikr*, "remembrance" or recollection, a concentration of thought which purified the heart.

The early Sufi ecstasies of the 9th century are summed up in Ziyad al-Arabi, who wrote that ecstasy is "assurance of the thing desired...when its light has been shed" though the seeker "is veiled by his own light from its light". In Baghdad and Cairo, which outshone any European city, Sufi schools grew up in which mystical poetry was written in the language of physical passion. In Iraq, al-Muhasibi (died 857) wrote of the Beatific Vision, and his pupil Junayd of Baghdad (died 910) wrote of "ecstatic Grace", while in Egypt, Dhu an-Nun wrote: "Did you not light a Beacon for those who found the true Guidance?"[14]

In Iran, the Persian Abu Yazid al-Bistami, or Bayazid, cried out, in an ecstatic trance, "Glory to Me, how great is My Majesty", so much a part of the Light did he feel. Bayazid came to believe that the Light was enough, that he did not need asceticism or meditation, for they were for the unenlightened, and in carrying a banner of light, he claimed to be above the Prophet: "I have known God by means of God, and what is other than God by the Light of God." The idea that direct knowledge of Allah could be obtained without relying on the Prophet's sole interpretations was blasphemous to orthodox Abbasid Moslems, and Bayazid had gone even further and identified himself with Allah; and he was executed. When asked how old he was at the end of his life he replied, "Four years.... I have been veiled from God by this world for seventy years, but I have seen Him during the last four years: the period in which one is veiled does not belong to one's life." Bayazid also said, "He who discourses of eternity must have within him the lamp of eternity", and it was Bayazid who answered a caller before he found the Light, "Whom do you seek? Bayazid? I too have been seeking Bayazid for thirty years and have not yet found him."[15]

Another ecstatic, Al-Husayn ibn Mansur al-Hallaj (857-922) was also executed for blasphemy. He was crucified for identifying himself with Allah in just two words, *Ana l' Haqq*: "I am God" (or "I am the Creative Truth"), i.e. the Light. These blasphemous words were spoken during his last visit to Baghdad and they were preceded by: "If you do not recognise God, at least recognise His signs. I am that sign."

His servant, Ibrahim ibn Fatik, left an eye-witness account of al-Hallaj's crucifixion in declining Abbasid Baghdad: "When al-Hallaj...saw the cross and nails...he prayed.... When he was finished he said some words...: 'Oh my God, who is revealed in every place, and who is not in any place, I beseech you...sustain me in gratitude for this Your grace, that You hid from others what You revealed to me of the glory of Your countenance (i.e. the Light), and forbad them what You permitted me: the sight of things hidden by Your mystery. And these Your servants, who are gathered together to slay me in zeal for Your religion, seeking Your favour, forgive them. For if You had revealed to them what You have revealed to me (i.e. the Light), they would not have done what they have done; if You had withheld from me what You have withheld from them, I should never have been tested by this tribulation. To You be praise in all You do; to You be praise in whatever You will.' Then he was silent. The Herdsman stepped up and dealt him a smashing blow which broke his nose, and the blood ran onto his white robe.... A riot nearly broke out. Then the executioners did their work."[16]

Al-Hallaj's prayer recalls Jesus's "Father forgive them for they know not what they do", and he seemed to identify himself with Jesus as God incarnate. His last words on the cross echoed an earlier prayer, that God should reduce him to nothing so that all of him might be God: "All that matters for the ecstatic is that the Unique should reduce him to Unity." After which he quoted from the *Koran*. Al-Hallaj is justified today on the grounds that he spoke his offending words under the intoxicating effect of ecstasy, when he had so united with the divine (the Light) that it was Allah who spoke through his lips, and not "the wool-carder" (*al-Hallaj*); and in his death he therefore lived out his description of union as a moth being burnt in a candle (the Light) when "brightly blazing forth, Truth's luminary has driven out of sight each flickering, lesser light". He is now regarded as a martyr.

Al-Hallaj's master, Sahl al-Tustari (died c.896) was reputed to remain in ecstasy (i.e. with the Light) for twenty-five days at a time, during which he ate no food but answered questions from doctors of theology, and even in winter his shirt would be damp with sweat. Al-Nuri was also executed for heresy after offering to die in place of the condemned Sufi, Raqqam. He said, "Once I beheld the Light, and I fixed my gaze upon it until I became the Light," and he wrote: "I adore you, Light Divine, lest lesser lights should make me blind."[17]

After the execution of Hallaj, the problem for Sufis was how to express the intoxicating ecstasy the Light brought without incurring the capital charge of blasphemy. At first Sufis emphasised the distinction between the enraptured contemplator and God, and they were more careful in the language they used.

Abd al-Jabbar al-Niffari (flourished c.961) had a revelation of the Light when he imagined God speaking to him at death and saying: "'Where is your knowledge?' And I saw the Fire. 'And he said to me, 'Where is your act?' And I saw the Fire. And he said to me, 'Where is your *gnosis*?' And I saw the Fire. And he unveiled for me His *Gnosis* of Uniqueness, and the Fire died down."[18] Abu Sa'id ibn Abi l'Khayr (967-1049), a pantheist Sufi, wrote, "In my eye You glow."[19] But despite such apparent blendings and mergings with the Light, the Light merely works on the inner eye that perceives it just as a furnace works on iron, as Hujwiri (11th century AD), the author of the oldest Persian treatise on Sufism, the *Kashf al-Mahjub*, makes clear, suggesting that human attributes cannot become divine ones: "The power of fire transforms to its own quality anything that falls into it, and surely the power of God's will is greater than that of fire; yet fire affects only the quality of iron without changing its substance, for iron can never become fire."[20]

The Persian Ibn Sina, or Avicenna (died 1037) described the Sufi *gnosis* and *fana* in *Stages of the Mystical Life*: "The soul then has reached the light of the Sun and is able to receive the Divine Illumination when it wills, free from all worldly distractions.... Now appear to the gnostic flashes of the Divine Light, like fleeting gleams of lightning, which pass away. By those who experience them, these are called 'mystic states' and every state brings joy and becomes more frequent, as the gnostic is more able to receive them.... In the fifth stage he becomes accustomed to God's presence, the brief flashes of lightning become a shining flame, and he attains to direct knowledge of God.... Then the gnostic passes on to the stage of contemplating God in Himself.... His inmost soul becomes a polished mirror reflecting the Face of God. Then he passes away from himself and contemplates only the Divine Glory." It is remarkable that such knowledge should have begun so unpromisingly: the youthful Avicenna read Aristotle's *Metaphysica* and "did not understand its contents and was baffled by the author's intention; I read it over forty times until I had the text by heart. Even then I did not understand it" (from his autobiography). Understanding came when he found a book by al-Farabi at a bookseller's.[21]

Baba Kuhi of Shiraz, the earliest Sufi poet of Persia (died 1050) saw God in the market, in the valley and on the mountain: "I opened my eyes and by the light of His face around me in all that the eye discovered – only God I saw. Like a candle I was melting in His fire." Pir-I Ansar (died 1088), or Abd Allah al-Ansari, wrote that Allah gives "to my eyes of Your Own Luminousness".

From the 10th century there was a strong Mohammed-mysticism: Mohammed was a light from light, a light from which all prophets were and are created, he radiated Light. Mohammed was Allah saying "I am Ahmad" (i.e. Mohammed) or "I am One" (*Ahad*). This development, along with the extremes of the Sufi ecstasies, and a theosophical element in Sufism which identified Allah with the self and the world, increased the suspicions of orthodox Moslems who distinguished Allah from the self and the world. In the 10th and 11th centuries handbooks on Sufism began to appear to allay fears, like al-Qushayri's defence of Sufism as an orthodox way (1046).

Against this background the last classical Sufi, Abu Hamid al-Ghazali (died 1111) avoided blasphemy by synthesising Sunnism and Sufism in the Seljuq Sultanate: he rooted Sunnism in the heart and rejected the extreme Sufi fusion of the ego and the divine. Al-Ghazali, a pillar of orthodoxy, studied Sufism and came to the conclusion that "I had now acquired all the knowledge of Sufism that could possibly be obtained by means of study; as for the rest, there was no way of coming to it except by leading the mystical life" (his autobiography). He therefore resigned as Professor of Divinity in Baghdad (c.1095), renounced his property and went to Syria to purge himself. In his *The Revival of the Religious Sciences* (ch 4) he avoided charges of blasphemy by defining *fana* in such a way that the distinction between the worshipper and God was preserved: he claimed the worshipper's individuality is effaced when contemplating the unity of God, in whom we live, move and have our being. Thus, the third stage of belief in the unity of God "is to perceive by the inward light of the heart", and "he whose heart Allah has opened to Islam walks in his light".[22]

It is by no means certain that al-Ghazali was himself a mystic, in the sense that he actually experienced the Light. His *The Niche for Lights* (*Mishkat Al-Anwar*), is a commentary on the verse in the *Koran* about the niche of lights. Allah is the Light within the physical body/heart (niche) and spiritual organ of the heart (glass). The olive tree is the Moslem equivalent of the true Vine, an inner tree of vision which is "neither of the East nor of the West", and the Light of the lamp works from the oil of the olive tree, the whole being veiled by the Cloud of Unknowing ("darkness upon darkness").[23] Al-Ghazali makes this existential truth very doctrinaire – there are two kinds of eye (internal and external), two kinds of light, the *Koran* is the Sun of the intelligence and Allah the source of all grades of lights – but he does say that "the light is most of all due to this Light Supernal, above Whom there is no light at all, and from Whom light descends upon all other things", which may be evidence of a glimpse he had had.

The Intoxicating Light Unblasphemously Expressed as Tavern

The Seljuq Turks had come from Persia to Anatolia and Iraq and by 1055 they had spread all over the Middle East. They became the temporal rulers (sultans) of the spiritual caliph-imams. They reached their height between 1072 and 1092 under Malik-Shah and his vizier, Omar Khayyam's schoolfriend Nizam al-Mulk – their policies contributed to the start of the First Crusade – and then they weakened, allowing the Abbasids to survive (a process to which al-Ghazali contributed) until the Mongol invasions resulted in the sack of Baghdad, the murder of the caliph, and the extinguishing of the Abbasid line.

Sufis now began to express their ecstasy through symbols – to escape punishment for blasphemy. The first Sufi symbolist seems to have been Omar Khayyam ("tentmaker") (c.1048-1122), the Seljuq Persian poet and philosopher who was born and died in Nishapur. Omar has not been accurately translated by Edward Fitzgerald. The fact that Fitzgerald himself produced a second totally different version of his arrangement in 1868 indicates how free the first version of 1859 was (although it is inspired English poetry). The *Rubaiyat* ("Quatrains") are in fact independent and self-contained 4-line poems, although there is doubt as to how many of them Omar himself actually wrote for they first appeared two centuries after his death.

The traditional view of Omar is that he was an epicurean. The story goes that when he was at school with Nizam-ul-Mulk (which means "Governor of the Kingdom"), he and another schoolfriend made a vow with Nizam that "to whomsoever (good) fortune falls shall share it equally", and when Nizam became vizier to the Sultan son of Toghril Beg, who had wrested Persia from Mahmud the Great and founded the Seljuq dynasty, his schoolfriends claimed their share. One went into the government – the Sultan accepted his vizier's recommendation – while Omar merely asked "to live in a corner under the shadow of your fortune, to spread wide the advantages of science, and pray for your long life and prosperity". Nizam gave him a yearly pension of 1,200 *mithkals* of gold, and Omar busied himself with knowledge of every kind: astronomy, algebra, philosophy, jurisprudence, history, medicine and alchemy, and he reformed the calendar for the Sultan Malik Shah, whose policies contributed to the causes of the First Crusade, using precise mathematical calculations. He belongs with Michelangelo and Leonardo as the complete, many-sided medieval man. He was supposed to be hated by the Sufis because of his epicureanism and because, being protected by Nizam, he did not have to be obviously pro-Islamic, yet the Sufis (notably Hafez) borrowed his material and used it in a mystical context. He made prophecies, and he told a pupil, "My tomb shall be in a spot where the north wind may scatter roses on it", and eventually it was.[24]

In fact, it seems that Omar was a Sufi who used obscure poetic symbols to express the idea of spiritual intoxication, and his example was followed by his Sufi successors for centuries afterwards. Being of independent mind, he no doubt enjoyed mystifing his readers with poems that seem to be about hedonism but which are in fact about the spiritual intoxication of ecstasy which leads to *gnosis* (the Light).

The point (which has often been missed) is that following the execution of Bayazid and Hallaj for blasphemy, *fana*'s spiritual intoxication came to be expressed in the symbols of drinking (*shirb*) and intoxication (*sukr*) – being in divine contemplation was represented as being in wine – and therefore the cup, the cupbearer and the tavern in the *Rubaiyat* are symbols of spiritual ecstasy. Omar thus had a vision of the Truth which is more profound than that accorded to "doctor and saint". He expresses his vision in terms of the negative way: "O ignorant ones – the Road is neither this nor that!" He tells us he "cannot unfold the secrets of the 'station' (the word is *hale*, the Arabic for "ecstasy") where I dwell", but he hints at it: "My cup in hand, its draughts I drain,/And with rapt heart unconsciousness attain." The "Thou" and "Thee" of the *Rubaiyat* refer to Mohammed, and also Allah: "No heart is there but bleeds when torn from Thee,/No sight so clear but craves Thy face (i.e. the Light) to see." Likewise, the "Thou" of Fitzgerald's "a Flask of Wine, a Book of Verse – and Thou/Beside me singing in the wilderness" is the visionary Mohammed of the *Koran.*

Omar's poetry is Sufi poetry, but it has the human, everyday level of a drinking-song or serenade that can co-exist with the divine vision, though compared with divine Love, human love is inferior: "This worldly love of yours is counterfeit/And, like a half-spent blaze, lacks light and heat."[25] Or, to put it the other way round in the words of the Persian Sana'i of Ghazna (died 1131) whose *The Enclosed Garden of the Truth* represents the Light in terms of a garden – especially a rose-garden – with fountains:

"When the clouds fall away from the Sun (i.e. of Truth), the world of love is filled with light."[26]

The Sufi Light developed into a new phase in Persia in the 12th century, and different Sufi orders grew up around the teachings of their founder and leader. A monastic system was founded by Abu Sa'id ibn Abi'l-Kheyr (died 1049), but Abd al-Qadir al-Jilani (died 1166) was the first to found an order, the Qadiriyya. Then came the pantheistic Suhrawardiyya, a theosophical Sufism that was founded by the uncle of the Persian Suhrawardi al-Maqtul ("killed"), who, sharing the fate of Bayazid and Hallaj, was executed in Aleppo in 1191.

Suhrawardi al-Maqtul led the illuminative school with a philosophy of *ishraq* ("illumination"), and his *Hikmat Al-Ishraq* ("The Wisdom of Illumination") developed a "pan-lightism" in which all existence culminated in the Pure Light of God, the Light of Lights. Suhrawardi tried to unite philosophy and mysticism, and he described the journey of the mystic before he reached *ma'rifah* (the *gnosis* of illumination). He blended Neoplatonism, Hermeticism, Hellenism, Gnosticism, Zoroastrianism and the tradition of Baghdad in a theosophical "mix", and the pantheistic streak that led to his execution was taken over by Ibn al-Arabi (died 1240), a Spanish mystic who taught the Unity of Being (the unity of all existence), having learned mysticism from two Spanish female saints.

Al-Arabi saw the phenomenal and eternal as complementary aspects of the One God's "veil, that is phenomenal existence" which "is but the concealment of His existence in his oneness". The mystic is therefore already one with God: "Those who adore God in the sun behold the sun, and those who adore Him in living things see a living thing." The Beatific Vision "impregnates the elect with Divine light" which "pervades the beings of the elect and radiates from them, reflected as if by mirrors on everything around them." Thus he writes of the soul in one of his poems: "Oh her beauty – the tender maid! Its brilliance gives light like lamps to one travelling in the dark."[27] Al-Arabi's pantheism was carried on by the Eyptian Ibn al-Farid (died 1235), who wrote a "Poem of the Journey" (*Ta'iyat al-kubra*) one of the finest mystical poems in Arabic, in which his pantheistic union with God makes him appear as God incarnate: "My spirit is a spirit to all the spirits; and all visible beauty in the universe flows from my nature."

The Light shifted back to Persia with Farid od-Din Attar (died c.1220), who wrote *The Conference (or Parliament) of the Birds*, an allegorical poem in which thousands of birds pass through seven valleys (the seven stages towards divine union) on a quest to Simurgh, the Lord of Creation. Only thirty birds make it to the palace where they see thousands of suns and moons, and at last the curtain is drawn on the light of lights to reveal – themselves. The Simurgh (the Light) says: "The sun of my majesty is a mirror.... Although you are now completely changed you see yourselves as you were before....Annihilate yourselves gloriously and joyfully in me, and in me you shall find yourselves." The birds lose themselves in Simurgh as the shadow loses itself in the sun "and that is all". The birds had realised "that they were the Simurgh and the Simurgh was the thirty birds". "Strive to acquire the mystic *gnosis*, so that you may learn to know God," Attar says elsewhere. "The Eternal Life means passing away from the personal self."[28]

Attar and the Central Asian Najmuddin Kubra helped to spread the Islamic Light in India, Central Asia, Turkey and Africa, and the great Persian poet Jalal ad-Din ar-Rumi (1207-73) made a great impact on the world. Rumi wrote much of his lyrical poetry for a wandering dervish, Shams ad-Din of Tabriz, a man he met in 1244 and saw as a Beatrice-like image of the Divine Beloved he had been seeking. When Shams was killed by an angry mob c.1261, Rumi called his poems the *Diwan-i Shams-i Tabriz* (*Lyrics of Shams of Tabriz*). Rumi's later *Masnavi* or *Mathnawi* (26,000 couplets), was addressed to a disciple, Husam'l-Din, Shams's successor. It has been called "the Persian *Koran*", and includes much about the Light. It speaks of "Stars immanent in the radiance of the Light of God", of the "lamps" (religions) which are different from each other though "the Light is the same: it comes from Beyond. If you keep looking at the lamp, you are lost: for thence arises the appearance of number and plurality. Fix your gaze upon the Light." Again: "Since you can not bear the unveiled Light, drink the Word of Wisdom (i.e. of the Shaykhs), for its light is veiled, to the end that you may become able to receive the Light, and behold without veils that which is hidden."

Rumi is frequently "drunk" with vision: "He comes, a moon whose like the sky ne'er saw, awake or dreaming, crowned with eternal flame no flood can lay" (i.e. the Light). Rumi was a great admirer of al-Hallaj and frequently refers to Hallaj's blasphemous words in terms of the Light: "O prattler, Mansur's 'I am He' was a deep mystic saying, expressing union with the Light, not mere incarnation." The soul's search for God is seen in terms of oceans and of light: "I sought a soul in the sea, and found a coral there: beneath the foam for me an ocean was all laid bare. Into my heart's night along a narrow way I groped; and lo! the Light, an infinite land of day." Lovers are "moths burnt with the torch of the Beloved's face, O heart, hasten thither! for God will shine upon you." The "lightning spark of love" arises in the heart", and "With You, a prison would be a rose garden, O You ravisher of hearts".[29]

Rumi founded the Mevlevi order of whirling dervishes who remembered God (*dhikr*) through ecstatic trances caused by whirling – their whirl can be found in the rotating wheel of some of his verse – and his contemporary Yunus Emre became the first Turkish mystical poet, his verses being transmitted by another Turkish order of dervishes. Meanwhile ash-Shadhiliyi founded the Shadhiliyah order in Egypt.

The Sufi Light now shone almost exclusively in Persia and further East. Iraqui, the Persian poet and mystic (died 1289), wrote: "When at your love a lamp we light our barn of being is ablaze.... Turn you on us your beauty's sun: our day is dark without your face." [30] Musharrif al-Din Ben Muslih Sa'di (c.1215-92), the Persian poet from Shiraz who wrote *The Rose Garden* (*Gulastan*) about dervishes, wrote of "a raindrop dripping from a cloud" who "was ashamed when it saw the sea. 'Who am I where there is a sea?' it said. When it saw itself with the eye of humility a shell nurtured it in its embrace."[31] The passing-away is a return to the Ocean of Being or Light.

The Persian poet Shams al-Din Mohammed Hafez or Hafiz (c.1326-90) writes even more ambigiously than Omar Khayyam, and his mystical hymns can also be read as drinking-songs or serenades: "Love is where the glory falls of Your face – on convent walls or on tavern floors, the same unextinguishable flame." Again: "O cup-bearer, brighten our goblet with the light of wine" and, "I vow the heavenly Sun is not so bright as heart and soul indwelt by His Love-light." That there is a mystical level is quite clear: "If the radiance of the love of God falls on your heart and soul, surely you will become fairer than the sun.... The light of God will shine on you, enveloping you from head to foot.... If the vision you behold is the Face of God, there is no doubt that from this time forward you will see clearly." And: "There is no difference between monastery and tavern, for everywhere shines the light of the Face of the Beloved."[32]

The erotic (and decadent) mysticism of Hafez is continued by Nur od-Din Abd or-Rahman Jami (1414-92), the last great classical Persian poet. To Jami human beauty reflects the Absolute Beauty of the Divine, which expresses itself in Love: "From all eternity the Beloved unveiled His beauty in the solitude of the unseen....Wherever Beauty peeped out, Love appeared beside it; wherever Beauty shone in a rosy cheek, Love lit his torch from that flame." The divine Beauty is more satisfying than human Beauty: "What profit rosy cheeks, forms full of grace,/And ringlets clustering round a lovely face?/When Beauty Absolute beams all around,/Why linger finite beauties to embrace?" In "Flashes of Light" (*Lawa'ih*) Jami prays to God that he will "remove from our eyes the veil of ignorance". We will then see "every beauty" as "a ray of His perfect beauty reflected therein", and Truth "may cast his beams" into the heart. The Light has to be veiled, Jami writes in "The God Behind the Veil" because its "face uncovered would be all too bright.... What eye is strong enough to gaze upon the dazzling splendour of the fount of light?" When the Light is "tempered by a veil of cloud that light is soft and pleasant to the eye." Jami has a beautiful image for illumination: "Mark me like the tulip with Thine own streaks."[33]

Sufi ideas, which may have originated in India, had spread back to India. Abdul'l Karim ibn Ibrahim al-Jili (c.1365-1412), who came from South of the Caspian and travelled in India, saw three stages of mystical illumination, each ascending nearer to God's Essence or pure Being, and Kabir (1440-1518) was brought up as a Moslem in India and influenced by the Sufi aim of glimpsing Allah. Though he was also influenced by Vaisnavism, he carried on the Sufi tradition of the Light in such verses as: "I was floating down the current of the world and its traditions. In the path I met the True Teacher, who showed me the way to Light." Another Indian poet, Sarmad (died 1657), the martyr-poet-saint of Hindustan, wrote Persian *Rubaiyat* on the Light: "I am a flame, burning smokelessly"; "How can the sensuous one hold the fire of God?"; "The cauldron of Love is lighted in my heart"; "The light of Truth I saw in my citadel, when I had renounced all I was bathed in it". According to Sarmad, "Truth's sunshine" sometimes turns "into the light of the lamp" and scatters "effulgence in the grove".[34]

Such was the Islamic Sufi tradition that confronted Christianity during the two hundred years of the Crusades (1095-1291). The challenge began after the execution of Hallaj in 922 had shown the Sufis that it was dangerous to express their ecstasies in terms that were blasphemous. Some Sufis moved to the Samanid kingdom in Iran, where they converted some of the Turkish tribesmen to Sufism, and eventually the Oguz Turks, led by the Seljuq family, invaded Iran and allied with Persian Sunni Islam. The Seljuq Turks took Baghdad and infiltrated Anatolia, and in 1071 they defeated the Byzantine army, captured the emperor and set up a Seljuq state on Byzantine territory. Byzantium appealed to the Pope and Europe for help, and the First Crusade was born.

After the Seljuqs and Saladin, the Arab Light was dominated by the Ottomans. The Mamluks ("slaves") murdered Saladin's descendant in Egypt and set up a dynasty which lasted until 1517. It reached its height during the Crusades, and after 1258 they installed a caliph in Cairo, and built many mosques, monasteries and tombs. From 1382 the dynasty declined, and they were absorbed by the Ottomans. The Mamluks in fact became Viceroys under Ottoman troops, and in 1798 Napoleon fought a Mamluk army and state when he invaded Egypt and his soldiers damaged the Pyramids with gunfire during target practice.

The Ottomans (Arabic for "Osmans") began as fighters for Islam against the shrinking Byzantine state. Their ancestors defeated Byzantium with the Seljuqs in 1071, and when the Mongols defeated the Seljuqs in 1292, Osman I of Bithynia and his successors fought the Byzantines and, despite a reverse at the hands of Timur (Tamerlane) in 1402, by 1453 they had taken Constantinople, which became their capital as Istanbul. By 1481 they had built a large empire in the North and East Mediterranean. The empire reached its height between 1481 and 1566 (notably under Selim I who, in absorbing the Mamluks, doubled the size of the empire) and in 1514 defeated the Safavids (a Shi'ite Sufi political brotherhood).

There have not been many Islamic mystics since 1500; all mystics within Islam have come from new Sufi traditions in India and Iran.

In India the Naqshbandiyah, an order of Islamic Sufis founded in the 14th century AD in India, was joined by Ahmad Sirhindi in 1593/4, and Sirhindi developed the idea that there is only a subjective experience of unity, that Oneness is in the mind of the mystic and not in the universe. Union between man and God was therefore impossible. His "unity of vision" school opposed the traditional "existential unity of being" school, and there were subsequent attempts at compromise. The mystics Ash-Sha'rani appeared in Egypt in the 16th century, and Abd al-Ghani an-Nabulusi in Syria in the 17th and 18th centuries.

The Sufi tradition continued with Bullah Shah (1680-1752), who wrote, "The fire of Love caught me, who can quench it?" The Turkish poet Sufi Fazil (died 1811), wrote "Through the fire of love, iron is transmuted into gold", and Nazir (1735-1846) wrote, "O creator! Why this my heart has joined to a Beloved, who is callous like the candle-light, which never loses steadiness howsoever passionately the moth burns itself in the fire", and "My heart was a-fire with love". Sir Mohammed Iqbal (1876-1938), one of the originators of Pakistan, wrote in "The New Rose Garden of Mystery" that life "brings light to a pinch of dust. It is its Selfhood that it radiates: it is an ocean from which emanates nothing but pearls. This frame of clay is nothing but a curtain to be burst by Selfhood's light, just as at break of day the sun shines forth, a glorious birth. The rising-place of the Self's sun is in our inmost breast.... There is a lamp alight inside your breast, and bright are the reflections cast in your mind's mirror by its light. Do not forget that you are its trustee." Iqbal again writes: "With You, my flame, I burn, without You, die", and: "His brand has kindled in each heart a light."[35]

The Chishtiyah sect, an Islamic Sufi order in India and Pakistan which goes back to the 12th century AD and follows the "existential unity of being", fathered a Sufi Order founded by Hazrat Inayat Khan in 1910, the first Sufi Master to bring Sufism to the West and whose many books handed on the Sufi Light. His son, Pir Vilayat Inayat Khan, a New Age teacher, later headed it and taught illumination. (His sister was "Madeleine" of the French Resistance, Noor Inayat Khan who was shot at Dachau.)

RECENT LIGHT

The Baha'is appeared in Iran in the 19th century. They were a Shi'ite sect that followed Ali Mohammed of Shiraz who was executed in 1850 for declaring himself to be the Gate (*Bab*) to God – Baha'i was one of his disciples – and a modern Baha'i prayer appeals: "O Lord.... Let the light of Your guidance shine. Illumine our eyes.... Let the light of faith shine forth.... May (mankind) obtain illumination from the same source of light and life." The Baha'is have been persecuted and executed by the Khomeini Islamic regime in Iran.

The Ahmadis appeared in India in the 19th century. They were an Islamic sect that followed Mirza Ghulam Ahmad, who are to Islam what the Mormons are to Christianity. Mirza Ghulam Ahmad announced that Jesus died a natural death in Kashmir, and that he himself was a manifestation of Jesus (as well as of Mohammed and Krishna), and today Ahmadis want the "tomb of Jesus" at Srinagar to be investigated so that they can disprove the Resurrection and achieve what Saladin was unable to do during the Crusades. (See pp374-376.) The Ahmadi claim to the Light is dimmed by their connection with the Light of the World.[36]

The Lebanese Khalil Gibran (1883-1931) has had a following because of *The Prophet.* However, Gibran was not illumined; he studied in Paris from 1908-10 and was influenced by the *Bible*, Nietzsche, Blake and Rodin, and *The Prophet* (together with Blakeian/Rodinesque drawings) is therefore an Islamic-Western hybrid rather than a Sufi work. Mikhail Naimy, Gibran's friend and biographer, wrote *The Book of Mirdad* (1948), which is likewise unillumined.

The Arab republics of the second half of the 20th century have followed the *Koran* and some (like Iran) have embodied Islamic Fundamentalism which interprets the *Koran* literally; but perhaps because attention has been focused on outer rather than inner improvements (such as setting up independent states, catching up with the West and fighting Israel or each other), there has been little emphasis on the Light in 20th century Islam.

However, the Light is still symbolized in the architecture of mosques. The Light descends down the minaret (an obelisk-like spire or world axis or Tree that joins earth and Heaven) into the stucco inside of the mosque, which transforms stone into Light as "Allah is the Light of the heavens and the earth". It then ascends back up the minaret to the sun, which symbolises the Light of Allah in Heaven. The Islamic crescent represents the Light of Allah breaking through the inner dark.

18

The African Light

The Egyptian/African Akh

In 656 BC the 25th Egyptian dynasty retired to Meroe in Nubia (modern Sudan) before the Assyrians and began a Nubian culture.[1] This was founded on the later Egyptian Light of the *akh*, which had survived Akhenaton, and lasted a thousand years.[2] During this time it became progressively cut off from Egypt following the sack of Napata, capital of Kush in which Meroe was situated, by Pharaoh Psamtik II in 590 BC and later Roman invasions.[3]

The Nubian influence spread inland to Lake Chad when the royal family of Meroe fled from an Aksumite invasion to Darfur AD c.325 and probably taught the Bantu to work iron.[4] It may eventually have been responsible for the medieval stone ruins of Great Zimbabwe, which were built by indigenous Africans.[5]

African religion is shamanistic like early Egyptian religion, the material world being linked to the spirits of recently dead or long-dead ancestors and to a Supreme Being, like the Nigerian Yoruba Olodumare (or Olorun, owner of heaven).[6] (Lesser Yoruba gods include Obatala and Shango, deity of thunder and lightning). All Africa absorbed the Egyptian Light of the *akh*, which became the African *akh*.

19

The Indian Light

Death! you know what Fire leads to heaven, show it. I am full of faith. I ask that Fire as my second gift.

Nachiketas or Nachiketa to Yama, King of Death in *Katha Upanisad, from The 10 Principal Upanisads* "done into English" by Shree Purohit Swami and W. B. Yeats

The Indian civilization grew out of the urban Indus Valley culture which rose c.2500 BC and declined c.1750 BC.[1] The Indo-European Aryan-speakers arrived in the Ganges Valley c.1500,[2] and their literature was the Light-filled *Rig Veda* which mentions the Iranian gods Mitra, Varuna and Indra. A chief priest made the crops grow for the king, who embodied a god, and there was a religious fire sacrifice that involved a hierarchy of priests.[3]

The early Hindus, who developed out of the early Iranians, knew the Light. The Hindu Light is first recorded around the end of the Indus Valley culture (c.2500-1500 BC) which centred round the sites of Mohenjo-daro and Harappa in Sind, Pakistan. (*Hindu* in Persian described "the people across the River Sindhu", the Sanskrit for Indus.) The Indo-European peoples who settled all Europe and Iran probably appeared there in waves towards c.1500 BC, perhaps as refugees fleeing the long war between Iranian Elam and Babylon which inflicted crushing defeats on Iran at the hands of the 3rd dynasty of Ur (in the 21st century BC) and Hammurabi (in 1764 BC).[4]

These migrants called themselves *aryas*, "Aryans", as did the Iranians, and they intermingled with the indigenous Indians.[5] They brought their own gods, and Indian gods became identified with them: the non-Aryan Siva (who seems to be the horned cross-legged god who was worshipped at Mohenjo-daro and Harappa) became identified with the Aryan Rudra, for instance.[6] They brought the Iranian sacrificial use of fire, and probably the plant drug *soma*,[7] which gave visions after the manner of LSD, and their descendants, the Indo-Aryans, produced the *Vedic* hymns, the *Rig Veda* (the oldest of the four Vedas, the earliest sacred literature in India, c.1500-1200 BC). These were written to Indo-Aryan deities and especially to Agni, the Iranian fire-god who personified Fire in all its forms, including the sun, lightning and the Fire of the sacrificial altar.[8]

In the *Rig Veda*,[9] which suggests the Iranian and Egyptian Lights, a divine creative flame (*tapas*) is released from the darkness of the Absolute as a sacrificial offering (*yajna*) which is mirrored in the sacrificial religious rites. This flame (the Light as Fire) can be perceived in contemplation by *rsis*, or inspired poets. The Creative Deity or demiurge born of this flame is linked with man through the Light of divine contemplation (*tapas*) and in the *Rig Veda* is personified in Agni, Varuna, Visvakarman and Prajapati, manifestations of the god who both causes and is shaped by the vision (or *dhih*). (Compare the "flame of fire" that appeared to Moses in *Exodus* 3.2 and the text in *Deuteronomy* 4.24, "For the Lord thy God is a consuming fire".) The flame is cosmic, its source is in the divine harmony outside nature; it is mirrored in and at one with nature, and is mirrored by the contemplative human heart when the "luminous" vision is expressed through the ritual (*rta*): "The wise seers watch over their inspired intuition refulgent as heavenly light in the seat of *rta*" (*Rig Vedas* X.177.2); and "By the song born of *rta* the sun shone forth" (X.138.2d). The "universal Light" (IX.48.4) shines in the heart of the inspired poet or *rsi*, and is perceived as an "internal light", the light "set within the heart" (VI.9.6), the "deathless flame" inspired by Agni, the "enlightened one" (I.164.21cd), "the Light-finder" (III.26.lab), and by Soma, "Lord of all those who see by Heaven's light" (IX.76.4ab). It is the "hidden light" or *gulham jyotih* (VII.76.4cd) which is received by the poet as the archetypal vision granted to his ancestors who "found the light; (and) expressed it by means of *dhih*" (devotion or vision) (IV.1.14d) or by chanting. The poet grasps this vision anew as a reliable revelation of truth which was known to his ancestors, and he frames it in song as did the Iranians. We shall see that it is the traditional and perennial task of the poet (*rsi*) in all cultures including our own to restate this contemplative vision of truth for his time – a task in which the modern Western poets have woefully failed as they have lost all knowledge of the vision.

The Fire of Agni

Agni was a fire that brought down the Light as Fire. He was the god who consumed the sacrifice and presented it to the gods above, he mediated between the gods and men and then brought the virtue of the gods down to earth, a virtue that included the Light as Fire; he brought "hitherward the gods" to the sacrifice so that their powers could be tapped (*Rig Veda* 1.2).

"Agni", says the *Rig Veda*, "you are a sage, a priest, a king, protector, father of the sacrifice. Commissioned by us men, you ascend a messenger, conveying to the sky our hymns and offerings....You are...giver of life and immortality; one in your essence, but to mortals three; displaying your eternal triple form as fire on earth, as lightning in the air, as sun in heaven. You are the cherished guest in every household.... Purge us from taint of sin, and when we die, deal mercifully with us on the pyre, burning our bodies with their load of guilt, but bearing our eternal part on high to luminous abodes."[10] Agni purged from sin and gave immortality on behalf of the gods, and so, the *Rig Veda* says: "I call for you Agni, shining with beautiful shine.... The gods have established beloved Agni among the human clans.... May he illuminate the nights that are longing for him." In Agni, the Shining One, the human and divine worlds came together, the meeting place being the Fire on the sacrificial altar; and when Agni illuminated the nights, it was at the divine level in the soul, as well as at the physical level, that the illumination took place.[11]

The *soma* drug was the juice of a type of milkweed (Iranian *haoma*, which is mentioned in the *Zend Avesta* and was used by Zoroastrian priests),[12] a kind of honey mead, and *Rig Veda* VIII,[13] makes it clear that it illumined: "We have drunk the *soma*, we have become immortal, we have entered into Light, we have known the gods." (Or, "Gone to the Light have we, the gods discovered.") The *soma* drug "found" the Light: "*Soma*, thou art our strengthener on all sides; Light-finder art thou; enter us, man-beholder." (From the same passage.)

In due course, Agni ceased to be needed as an intermediary, and a sacrificial mysticism grew up that was more inward than the Zoroastrian kind. In the later commentaries on the four *Vedas*, the *Brahmanas* (ritual writings c.900-700 BC), there is an identification between the objects being sacrificed on the fire-altars, and the fiery power of creation and the universe. "By sacrificing with this (fire)," the Gandharvas told the lonely King Pururavas, "you will become one of us" (*Shatapatha Brahmana* XI 5), and the Indo-Aryans began to use fire-sacrifice as an image for, and a means of achieving, the Light of self-realisation.

The Light of Brahman

The period from c.1000 to 500 BC saw ritual texts such as the *Brahmanas*, the *Upanisads*, the *Dharma-sutras* and probably the *Ramayana*.

The fire now became an image for the interiorised Light of the Self when it united with God. By 600 BC Vedism had grown into Brahmanism: the priestly elite or Brahmins worshipped Brahman as Supreme God, and fire described the union between the Atman (the divine within man) and the eternal Brahman, and the *pranic* energy released in the mystic ecstasy: the Light.

This vision is found in the *Upanisads*, which form part of the final portion of the *Vedas* (*Vedanta*, or "end of *Vedas*") and which elaborated on the *Vedas* in prose and verse. The *Upanisads* mean literally "sitting near devotedly" or "secret teachings", "esoteric doctrines". They are reputedly the work of Indian forest seers, and most of them can be dated to the 5th century BC. Again and again, they record the truth that Brahman (God, OM) is a fire, that individual beings are sparks from the fire which created everything, that the Self (Atman) is an illumined part of this self-luminating, effulgent fire, that one must "unite the light within you with the light of Brahman" (*Svetasvatara*):[14]

"As sparks innumerable fly upward from a blazing fire, so from the depths of the Imperishable arise all things.... Self-luminous is that Being, and formless. He dwells within all.... He is the innermost Self of all.... Self-luminous is Brahman, ever present in the hearts of all.... In the effulgent (or shining) lotus of the heart dwells Brahman...the Light of Lights. Him the knowers of the Self attain.... He is the one Light that gives Light to all. He shining, everything shines.... Hail to the illumined souls!" (*Mundaka.*)

"By the Light of the Self man sits, moves about, does his work, and when his work is done, rests.... The self-luminous being who dwells within the lotus of the heart, surrounded by the senses and sense organs, and who is the light of the intellect, is that Self." (*Brihadaranyaka,* the earliest of the *Upanisads,* c.9th century BC.)

"The truth is that you are always united with the Lord. But you must *know* this. Nothing further is there to know.... Fire, though present in the firesticks, is not perceived until one stick is rubbed against another. The Self is like that fire: it is realised in the body by meditation on the sacred syllable OM. Let your body be the stick that is rubbed, the sacred syllable OM the stick that is rubbed against it. Thus shall you realize God, who is hidden within the body as fire is hidden within the wood.... To realize God, first control the outgoing senses and harness the mind. Then meditate upon the light in the heart of the fire.... Thus the Self, the Inner Reality, may be seen behind physical appearance. Control your mind so that the Ultimate Reality, the self-luminous Lord, may be revealed.... With the help of the mind and the intellect, keep the senses from attaching themselves to objects of pleasure. They will then be purified by the Light of the Inner Reality, and that Light will be revealed.... Great is the glory of the self-luminous being, the Inner Reality.... Follow only in the footsteps of the illumined ones, and by continuous meditation merge both mind and intellect in the eternal Brahman. The glorious Lord will be revealed to you.... Set fire to the Self within by the practice of meditation.... Unite the Light within you with the Light of Brahman.... Cross the fearful currents of the ocean of worldliness by means of the raft of Brahman – the sacred syllable OM.... As you practise meditation, you will see in vision forms resembling snow, crystals, smoke, fire, lightning, fireflies, the sun, the moon. These are signs that you are on your way to the revelation of Brahman.... Said the great seer Svetasvatara: I have known, beyond all darkness, that great Person of golden effulgence. Only by knowing him does one conquer death.... He is the great Light, shining forever. This great Being, assuming a form of the size of a thumb, forever dwells in the heart of all creatures as their innermost Self." (*Svetasvatara.*)

According to the *Upanisads*, the Light, the Self, is the fourth of four states of consciousness which are contained in the letters A, U, M and in their totality OM (compare the Fourth and Blake's "fourfold vision"), and this fourth state is the superconscious vision in which Atman and Brahman, the individual and world souls, are one: "Beyond the senses, beyond the understanding, beyond all expression, is the Fourth. It is pure unitary consciousness, wherein awareness of the world and of multiplicity is completely obliterated. It is ineffable peace. It is the supreme good. It is One without a second. It is the Self." (*Mandukya.*)

THE LIGHT OF THE ATMAN

The inwardness of the *Upanisads* marked a considerable development from the sacrificial mysticism of earlier Vedism. *Mundaka Upanisad* actually states that Brahman is "to be attained neither by austerity nor by sacrificial rites", but "in meditation", and the Light as Fire within became the Light of the illumined soul in the other main *Vedanta* work (excluding the *Brahma Sutras*, attributed to Badarayaaa in the 4th century BC), the *Bhagavad-gita*, which has been dated to the 5th or 3rd centuries BC, or the 1st and 2nd centuries AD.

The *Bhagavad-gita* ("Song of the Lord")[15] has a practical devotional approach (*bhakti*, devotion, a term which appears for the first time in the

Svetasvatara Upanisad, comes from the same root as *Bhagavata*). It is a dialogue between Krishna, an incarnation of Visnu, and Arjuna, who has refused to kill his kinsmen in the battle of Kurukshetra and who is taken to an understanding of salvation. Arjuna asks, "How can one identify a man who is firmly established and absorbed in Brahman? In what manner does an illumined soul speak?" Krishna replies: "He knows bliss in the Atman and wants nothing else. Cravings torment the heart: he renounces cravings. I call him illumined.... This is the state of enlightenment in Brahman. A man...is alive in that enlightenment." Arjuna must fight, and he can still be illumined: "The illumined soul must not create confusion in the minds of the ignorant by refraining from work. The ignorant in their delusion...become tied to the senses and the action of the senses.... Fix your mind on the Atman. Be free from the sense of ego. Dedicate all your actions to me. Then go forward and fight.... The reward of all action is to be found in enlightenment.... When you have reached enlightenment, ignorance will delude you no longer. In the light of that knowledge you will see the entire creation within your own Atman and in me."

The 'I' of the Atman of an enlightened person is quite different from the 'I' of the senses (the ego): "The illumined soul whose heart is Brahman's heart thinks always: 'I am doing nothing.'. No matter what he sees, hears, touches, smells, eats.... This he knows always: 'I am not seeing, I am not hearing: it is the senses that see and hear and touch the things of the senses.'... The Atman is the Light: the Light is covered by darkness: the darkness is delusion.... When the Light of the Atman drives out our darkness that Light shines forth from us, a sun in splendour, the revealed Brahman."

Brahman is "the Light-giver", "shining sunlike, self-luminous", in other words, the Light; and "knowledge of God" is "open vision direct and instant... only made plain to the eye of the mystic." People's "thought is illumined and guided towards Krishna, the Godhead of the Universal Self", who is a "brilliant lamp".

The experience of the Light is described when Krishna reveals himself to Arjuna in his divine form as Lord Visnu: "Suppose a thousand suns should rise together into the sky: such is the glory of the Shape of Infinite God." Arjuna's "hair stood erect" and he "bowed low before God in adoration". He describes God as "shining every way – the eyes shrink from your splendour brilliant like the sun; like fire, blazing boundless". Brahman is "Light of all lights", "self-luminous", and: "The Light that is fire: know that Light to be mine." By the end of the *Gita,* Arjuna has learned to separate himself from the results of his actions – for instance, his fighting – and his "non-attachment" from the "fruits of action" is a measure of his illumined knowledge.

This vision of the "Light of Atman" passed into the growing worship of Visnu and his ten incarnations (chiefly Rama and Krishna), which began in the 7th or 6th centuries BC, and into the growing worship of Siva, who originated in a non-Aryan phallic cult and who is first treated as Supreme God in the *Svetasvatara Upanisad.*

YOGA *SAMADHI*

The Light was also central in early Yoga ("*yoking,* union"), the oral teaching of which was very ancient and may have preceded the ecstasies of the Vedic texts. It was thus at the root of Hinduism, and it certainly preceded the mortification practised in the time of the Buddha. This oral teaching was compiled by Patanjali in his great Yoga classic, *The Yoga Sutras,* the first three volumes of which were written c.2nd century BC, and the last volume during the 5th century AD. Patanjali himself has been placed at varying dates betwen 820 and 300 BC, and even at 10,000 BC,[16] and as the first to reduce the oral teaching to writing, he is regarded as the founder of the Raja Yoga (Royal Yoga) School. *The Yoga Sutras* are claimed to have been the basic teaching of the trans-Himalayan School, South Tibet, which had links with early Altaic shamanism.

The Yoga Light comes from *samadhi,* a concept that usually refers to the Light, and which can be translated "bliss" or "ecstasy". To Patanjali, *samadhi* means intense concentration, so that concentrating mind (*citta*) vanishes, leaving the object concentrated upon as the sole reality, with which the yogi has identified. According to Patanjali *citta* is like a placid lake which is illumined when *purusa* (the seer) is reflected in it. The *citta* can be pacified "by the meditation on the Effulgent Light", which is "beyond all sorrow" Patanjali says (1.36).

"By making *samyama* (self-controlled concentration or perfectly concentrated meditation) on the Effulgent Light comes the knowledge of the fine, the obstructed and the remote." (III 26). "By making *samyama* on 'real modifications' of the mind, outside of the body, called great disembodiedness, comes disappearance of the covering to Light." (III 44). By making *samyama* "on the light emanating from the top of the head" comes "sight of the *siddhas*" (or perfected ones) (III 33), and "by the conquest of the current *samana*" (the vital energy which controls the heart and breath) the yogi "is surrounded by a blaze of Light" (III 41).[17]

This Light is present at the moment of death according to the *Brihadaranyaka Upanisad* : "All the organs, detaching themselves from (a dying man's) physical body, unite with his subtle body. Then the point of his heart, where the nerves join, is lighted by the Light of the Self, and by that Light he departs either through the eye, or through the gate of the skull, or through some other aperture of the body." To the yogi, fire is a purifying force which brings him to the Light, which is in fact an ocean of Light: "Then meditating on the *mantra kshoum*, the ocean of Light situated in the heart, he should, with flames going up, down, and in contrary directions, burn out all impurities" (*Agni-purana* XXIII).

The Buddhist Fire of Craving

By 500 BC there were many states in the eastern Ganges Valley and sects questioned the Brahmanical orthodox tradition, including Buddhism (which was founded by the Buddha, who died c.480 BC).

Fire and Light form the essence of Buddhism, as one might expect of a religion which emerged under ritualistic Hinduism (Brahmanism) in India, and shared the Aryan way of life. (The Buddha was born into an area which was occupied by an Aryan tribe called the Sakyas.) The Light is obvious enough: the very title "the Buddha" means "the Enlightened One" (or "awakened one") and Siddhartha Gautama (c.560-480 BC) achieved his *bodhi* or enlightenment at Bodh Gaya under a pipal or peepal tree (later called the Bo or Bodhi Tree) c.525 BC at the age of thirty-five, after six years of solitude as a wandering shaman-like ascetic who had renounced his wife and baby son.

The Buddhist fire, however, comes as something of a shock, for it is the fire of craving and desire, a bad thing, rather than the spark of the illumined Hindu Atman, and it is a measure of the Buddha's revolution against Vedism that he should stand the main Vedic image on its head.

The heart of the Buddha's doctrine (*dharma*) concerns his realisation that the origin of all suffering is craving or desire ("fire"), and that suffering will cease when the craving ceases, and non-attachment begins (the four Noble or "Aryan" Truths). The Noble or "Aryan" Eightfold Path (the last stage of which is "right concentration", *samadhi*) is the way to eliminate the cravings and achieve enlightenment and *Nirvana*.

The Buddha's premise can be found in his revolutionary Fire Sermon (*Maha-Vagga* I.21) in which he declares that everything is on fire with craving: "All things, O priests, are on fire.... The eye, O priests, is on fire; forms are on fire; eye-consciousness is on fire; impressions received by the eye are on fire...with the fire of passion, say I, with the fire of hatred, with the fire of infatuation.... The ear is on fire; sounds are on fire; the nose is on fire; odours are on fire; the tongue is on fire; tastes are on fire; the body is on fire; things tangible are on fire; the mind is on fire; ideas are on fire; mind-consciousness is on fire; impressions received by the mind are on fire...with the fire of passion, say I, with the fire of hatred, with the fire of infatuation.... Perceiving this, O priests, the learned and noble disciple conceives an aversion for the eye, conceives an aversion from forms...." And so on. "And in conceiving this aversion he becomes divested of passion, and by the absence of passion he becomes free."[18]

The Buddha's Enlightenment: Blowing out the Fire of Desire (Nirvana)

Nirvana, the state Gautama attained under the Bo Tree, is literally a "blowing-out" (or "blown out" state), and it is important to grasp that the concept has been totally misunderstood by European travellers and missionaries in the past. The blowing-out does not mean annihilation, but the blowing out of the flames of craving, ill-will and sensuality, leaving a state of bliss, peace and certainty. *Nirvana* can be attained in this life, and was attained by the Buddha in his life, which is proof that it does not mean extinction. The final *Nirvana* that is obtained after death is in fact called *Parinirvana*, a state of positive bliss although one's separate individuality has perished.

Nirvana, then, is another name for the supreme Buddhist enlightenment experience, the one mystical element in Buddhism which all Buddhists have sought intensely, the experience of unity. The Buddhist Scriptures record this experience. In the second watch of the night of his enlightenment, the Buddha "acquired the supreme heavenly eye" and the world appeared "as though reflected in a spotless mirror", the Light.[19]

The Buddha himself says of his Enlightenment (*Mahasaccaka Sutta*): "When this knowledge, this insight had arisen within me, my heart was set free from intoxication of lusts...becomings...ignorance.... Ignorance was beaten down, insight arose, darkness was destroyed, the Light came, inasmuch as I was there, strenuous, aglow, master of myself."[20]

The Buddha's final entry into *Parinirvana*, on his death, takes him through "nine stages of meditational attainment", whereupon he returned to the "first trance" and "ascended step by step to the fourth trance" after which he "came face to face with everlasting Peace". Another account gives the stages above the fourth trance: infinity of space, infinity of consciousness, nothingness, neither perception nor yet non-perception, the cessation of perception and sensation.[21] It can be deduced from these and other texts that "neither perception nor yet non-perception" is a gazing at the Light, which cannot be perceived through the five senses, and that the cessation of perception and sensation is a merging with the Light in the soul in absolute union which is boundless and infinite.

"Be ye lamps into yourselves", the Buddha advised in his last sermon, "hold fast to the truth as a lamp", and in *Nirvana* the ego, like a lighted candle held up to the sun, is extinguished and yet continues to exist as part of the ocean of light. From the point of view of the world it has escaped rebirth when it attains *Parinirvana*, and is "blown out": "The

Blessed One, O king, has attained *Nirvana* by that kind of *Parinirvana* in which nothing remains which could tend to the formation of another individual.... When there is a great body of fire blazing, is it possible to point out any one flame that has gone out, that is here or there?" (*The Questions of King Milinda* III 5.)[22]

In an earlier passage the Buddha explains to Vaccha that "a fire burning" depends on its clinging to grass and sticks, and that when it goes out it is impossible to say "in what direction has the fire gone...to the east, west, north or south", and that a *Tathagata* (Buddha) who is released from form is "like a great ocean".[23] At death, then, a fire is either transferred, like a flame moving from a burnt-down candle to a new candle, or it is "blown out" and the fire has escaped rebirth for *Parinirvana.*

Jainism and Mahavira: the Expanding Light of the Soul

Another sect to question the Brahmanical orthodox tradition was Jainism. Jainism was a religion which was also founded in the form we know in the 6th century BC, by Vardhamana, a contemporary of Buddha, Zoroaster and Lao-Tze who was later called Mahavira ("great hero").

The origins of Jainism are very ancient, even prehistoric – Jainism may even be the original religion of the Hindu Brahmans[24] – and Mahavira was the twenty-fourth and last of a long line of *tirthankaras,* literally "ford-makers", or "crossing-makers", and therefore "those who lead mankind from the world to perfect bliss". Only two of these "perfect saints" are regarded as having been truly historical, but they were all called *Jinas* ("victors" or "conquerors" in the sense that they had conquered all human passions), and were held up as religious examples of enlightened beings. Mahavira, who is generally thought to have been born in India c.599 BC, reformed Jainism (which comes from the word *Jinas*), and so he is regarded as the founder. His early career parallels the Buddha's. At thirty he left his wife and daughter and spent twelve years as a wandering ascetic (*yeti*), not even wearing a loin cloth, and by the age of forty-two he had reached enlightenment and omniscience.

He died thirty years later (probably in 527 BC) and entered into *Nirvana.* (The Jain *Nirvana* was the divine.)

Like the Buddha, Mahavira was protesting against the ritualistic impersonality of Brahmanism, and Jainism aimed to perfect the soul and realise the Light through asceticism. The huge stone replica of the naked conqueror Gommatesvara at Mount Abu, Sravana Belgola, gazes across South India, indifferent to the world and still. The passions had to be subdued so that the soul, which is identical to the self or Atman of Hinduism, could be purified and reach a state of bliss. The soul was then God – there was no deity outside the soul in Jainism – and being liberated from karma, it could be liberated from being reborn; for in Jainism the soul reincarnated if it had been unable to throw off its impure accretions, which affect future lives.

A soul was purified by its own ascetic effort, then, and exalted to the divine *Nirvana,* and this purity was achieved by the three jewels, right belief, right knowledge and right conduct. Right conduct comprised five vows, which included *ahimsa,* non-injury to all living creatures, the basis of the Jain respect for life.

"One should ever make his own self radiant by the light of the three jewels," says the *Sacred Book of the Jainas* (4.30). The three Jewels "should be followed, even partially, every moment of time without cessation by a householder desirous of everlasting liberation" (4.209).[25] The Jain soul could expand to fill the whole body as the light of a lamp fills a large room as well as a small room, and the Jain *Nirvana* was bliss: the experience of Light which the three Jewels brought.

"The liberated...perceives, he knows but there is no analogy whereby to know the nature of the liberated soul: its essence is without form.... There is no sound, no colour, no smell, no taste, no touch."[26] This is the familiar idea that the Light is beyond the five senses, that it is "neither perception nor yet non-perception". "May He abide always within my heart, 'Supreme Self', the One God of all gods...by deepest meditation reachable," says the *Amita-Gait, Samayika-patha.* "They who have passed beyond all arguments and doubts and false attachments of this world, they only can behold in purity 'the Supreme Self', and in It merge themselves."[27] The Jain self or soul, which it was – and still is – possible to "behold", was of course the Atman-like Light.

After Alexander's fleeting visit to India, the first Indian empire arose, the Mauryan Empire, c.325/1 BC. The first Mauryan Empire was pro-Jain, and the empire reached its height under Asoka, who was pro-Buddhist, c.250 BC. Thus, the Mauryans advanced both Jain and Buddhist Lights.

Theravadic/*Hinayana Anatta* (No Self) and Perception

As the fire of desire is blown out on death, the Buddha asserted that there is therefore "no self", and in this teaching, too, the Buddha openly differs from the teachings of orthodox Vedic belief, which affirm the Atman. According to the Buddha, there is no Atman that reincarnates, there is only a group of five attributes or *skandhas*, cravings which are reincarnated if they are not eliminated. The doctrine of *anatta* (non-self) is a Theravadin or *Hinayana* doctrine, for *Mahayanists*, who saw Buddha more as a god than a teacher, regard *anatta* as applying only to the personal ego and they believe in an Atman-like Universal Self with which they can be united during enlightenment.

During his enlightenment the Buddha "could detect no self anywhere. Like the fire, when its fuel is burnt up, he became tranquil...and finally convinced himself of the lack of self in all that is" (*Buddhacarita* 12).[28] The *Mahayanist* would see the "self" as craving, attachment, and would take the Buddha to have reached a point beyond the fire of passion. (Another disagreement between the Theravadins and Mahayanists concerns *arhats*, the enlightened Theravadins who have worked out "their own salvation with diligence" and, *Mahayanists* assert, with a selfishness which is incompatible with the Buddha's compassion. *Mahayanist bodhisattvas*, the equivalent of *arhats*, therefore delay their entry into *Parinirvana* so that they can be reborn and help their fellow human beings.)

Because of such considerations, between the 4th and 1st centuries BC a number of schools detached themselves from Theravadic Buddhism, but they all possessed a Theravadic Pali canon of three "baskets" or collections: disciplinary rules, sermons and dicta attributed to the Buddha (*dhamma* or *dharma, sutta* or *sutra*), and dogma (*abhidhamma* or *abhidharma*), most of which were written some two hundred and forty years after the Buddha's death. The *dhamma* basket is the most important, and it includes the *Dhammapada* (Way of Virtue), a Buddhist poem which (like the work of our Kempis) is a call to the common man to rouse himself from sloth and achieve spiritual joy.

This joy is to see the Light: "And he who lives a hundred years, not seeing the highest law, a life of one day is better if a man sees the highest law.... How is there laughter, how is there joy, as this world is always burning? Do you not seek a light, you who are surrounded by darkness?.... The sun is bright by day, the moon shines by night, the warrior is bright in his armour, the Brahmana is bright in his meditation; but Buddha, the Awakened, is bright with splendour day and night."[29] In the *Mahayana Surangama Sutra* (1st century AD in Sanskrit) the Buddha distinguishes "the perception of our eyes and the intrinsic Perception of Sight by our enlightened Mind that is conscious of the fallible perception of the eyes", and, doctrines of self and non-self aside, it is this second perception, which is accompanied by radiating "beams of Light",[30] that is so crucial to the Buddha's Light; a divesting oneself of the illusions of the world of the senses and a rising to a higher, ideal world.

THE *MAHAYANA* BUDDHIST LIGHT

The Light dominated the Eastern cultures while Europe was still in the Dark Ages. In India, it was central to a new Buddhist metaphysical theology that spread into the rural, feudal, bureaucratic cultures of South East Asia, Tibet, China and Japan, and blended with their traditional shamanistic religions (for example the Bon, which underlies Tibetan Buddhism). It reached the people of Asia through the monasteries of Lhasa (the Tibetan spiritual centre which has been destroyed by the materialistic Chinese Communists) and the Zen monasteries of Japan; seats of learning which preserved the Light.

The South-East Asian *Mahayana* Light must be seen in terms of the Indian background from which it originated.After the Mauryan decline there were many small kingdoms from c.150 BC to AD 300, and there were foreign invasions from Bactria (c.180 BC) and the Scythians (or Sakas, 1st century BC). Jain and Buddhist temples date from this time, but no pre-Gupta Hindu temples have survived, although they are referred to in literature. North India then saw the Gupta Empire from AD c.320 to 540, and there was a Classical Age until the invasion of the Central Asian Huns or *Hunas* who had migrated from the Volga to Persia and Afghanistan.

The *Mahayana* Light began when *Mahayana* Buddhism emerged in the 1st century AD[31] and called itself a Greater Vehicle (*Mahayana*) as opposed to the orthodox Theravadic Buddhism which it called a Lesser Vehicle (*Hinayana*). The image was of a large ferry boat which would carry more people to the distant shore of *Nirvana* than a small ferry boat. *Nirvana*, the enlightened state when the fire of desire is "blown out", meant the same in *Mahayana* as it did in *Hinayana*, but *Mahayana* was more metaphysical, and more selfless, than *Hinayana*; more metaphysical because the Buddha had three bodies, the physical, phenomenal one being an earthly manifestation of a transcendent celestial Buddha, and more selfless because its *bodhisattvas* (who had a tendency to attain enlightenment) nobly postponed their own entry into *Nirvana* until they had helped all other beings to enter it first.

For details of the spreading of the *Mahayana* Light, see "The South-East Asian Light" (pp311-318).

The Hindu Light

The Hindu Light had shone through the cult of Siva. We have seen (p279) that the cross-legged god of Mohenjo-daro and Harappa may have been an early form of Siva. Siva was first treated as the supreme God in the *Svetasvatara Upanisad* and first worshipped by the Hindu Pasupatas (a sect of the 2nd century BC-2nd century AD). Later Saivism (the worship of Siva) developed during the Gupta Empire (which supported Visnu and

Vaisnavism AD c.320) and spread to South East Asia – to Vietnam, Borneo and Bali – between the 2nd and 4th centuries. It reached the Mediterranean, where it may have influenced Plotinus and Clement of Alexandria. (Plotinus in particular seems to have drawn on the Indian tradition, especially on Patanjali, who lived at least a century and probably several centuries earlier than he did if, as is thought, he flourished in the 2nd century BC.)

After the Puranic period (4th-8th centuries AD), there was a rise in devotional Hinduism in Tamil-speaking Southern India between the 8th and 11th centuries AD. The ascetic Siva and his virgin consort Sakti, who is in fact a part of him, represent a world-denying pair, for their senses are under such control that although Siva is shown with an erect *lingam* or phallus, no ejaculation of semen takes place (a practice also adopted in later Taoism). In this respect, Hindu Saivism differs from Tantrism, which affirms the sensuality of the *lingam* in the *yoni*.

"Permanently ithyphallic" (i.e. straight-phallused) "yet perpetually chaste",[32] Siva is in Yogic contemplation on the cremation-ground, wearing an elephant-hide or tiger-skin, skulls round his neck and serpents in his hair, and his illumined third eye ignores all sensual temptation. As "Lord of the Dance" (*nataraja*) he dances creation into being out of joy, and dances it towards destruction in frenzy down the mountain. He is both creator and destroyer, and Sakti mirrors these two aspects, first as the mild Uma or Parvati, and then as the bloodthirsty Durga or Kali who drinks blood from a human skull.[33]

Siva reconciles the opposites, and the theology of the Tamil Saivites was known as *Saiva-siddhanta* (Sanskrit for "The Conclusion of the Followers of Siva"), which included the Kashmir Saivism.[34] The hymns of the Southern Indian Saiva saints embody Siva as the Light and completely surrender to the Lord in adoration (*bhakti*). In the 7th century AD Sambandhar, who converted the local Southern Indian King from Jainism, addresses Siva as "You Light whom Brahma, being's fount, and Visnu could not see", and writes, "Never fades Your light away.... In your heart will dawn true light.... Scatter golden blossoms fair (i.e. the Light)." Tirunavukkarasu Swami (or Apparswami) addresses Siva as "O light, O flame" and "Siva, our flaming king", and in *Garlands for God* writes: "Like the fire in the wood waiting to be lit...so the dear Lord unseen waits for your call." In the 8th or

9th century AD, Sundaramurti (or Sundarar) writes of Siva "O Lord, are you not our Saviour.... Lead us out of darkness you kindly light." Elsewhere he says "He is the flame and light" (hymn 84), and: "He is the light of all the living beings of this world.... He is the flower of my crown (hymn 59)." Mannikkavacakar or Manikkar Vasahar (probably 9th century AD) addresses Siva as "our kindly light", and in *In Praise of God* speaks of Siva as "flooding my soul with inward light".[35]

The Tantric Hindu Light: Siva-Sakti and the *Lingam*, *Kundalini* the Serpent-Fire and *Tummo* or Psychic Heat

Tantrism (the Bon knowledge) also passed into Hinduism from the 5th century AD.[36] The *Mahayana* outlook of Nagarjuna and Asanga influenced the main Indian religion, and its esoteric system, which controlled vital forces to make illuminations possible, was practised in India, Nepal, Bhutan and Tibet.

In Tantric Hinduism,[37] Reality comprises male and female aspects: Siva and Sakti, who represent pure consciousness (the Light) and mental activity. The human body is a reflection of the cosmos. The spinal column is the axis between the two poles and represents Mount Meru, while the nerve connections which run up it represent sacred rivers. The female force, Sakti, who is also called the Goddess "*Kundalini*", lies coiled at the bottom of the spine like a serpent. Meditation awakens and raises her life force from the lowest psychic centre or *chakra* (*cakra*, "wheel"), which is "four fingers" below the navel *chakra*. It rises up past the five higher *chakras* along the *susumna* (the nerve connection up the middle of the spinal cord), to be united with the male force, Siva, in the top *chakra* in the crown of the head. There it spreads out into a fountain-like crest, the thousand-petalled lotus which is the Bliss of the Beyond, and from there the *Kundalini* life-force passes out into the freedom of the cosmos. Snake-charmers symbolise the rising of the *Kundalini* serpent-fire by charming a coiled cobra into an upright position, and pilgrims bathe in the sacred river Ganges to recall the cosmic flow of *Kundalini*-Sakti energy.

The union between *Kundalini*-Sakti and Siva is the ecstatic experience of illumination, and this goal of "*Kundalini* Yoga" is symbolized in Tantric art. Scroll paintings show the central figure (e.g. Vairocana) sitting with a *sakti* in one arm, and *yantras* (diagrams) show the *lingam* (phallus) within the *yoni* (vagina), affirming the sexual act. A *mantra* (syllables), "*Om, mani padme, Hum*", means "Enlightenment, jewel in the lotus (or *lingam* within the *yoni*), power" (also "I", and "semen"), and since Tantric Hinduism was interwoven with Saktism – which was the worship of Sakti rather than Siva, both in her benevolent aspect (as Uma, Parvati and Ambika) and in her destructive aspect (as Kali, Durga and Sitala) – in Tantrism the *yoni* symbolized the world of becoming, both the mother-creator and the destroyer (Kali) whose sexual rites included necrophily in burial-grounds. The serpent *Kundalini* was held to ascend from the inner *lingam* of the subtle body (which is first mentioned in the later Upanisads of the later centuries BC and earlier centuries AD, e.g. the Aitarega, Varaha, and Yogatattva Upanisads).

The Mystic Way to the divine Light can therefore be seen in terms of *Kundalini*. The seminal fluid is transmuted into *ojas* by the *prana* or vital force which flows in from Nature and is stored at the base of the spine. The *ojas* travels up, round and down the nerve currents which form a figure 8 round the spine, and makes the skin of the front and back feel silky. It travels down onto the bone over the *Kundalini*-Sakti which begins to rise up the spinal column in the *susumna* like mercury in a thermometer. Its progress can take weeks, months or even years, and as it passes beyond the three lowest *chakras*, the ego "dies". (Compare the lotus of fire at the navel in Buddhist *Tantra*, which immolates the ego.)

When it reaches the heart *chakra*, the seeker has his first experience of the Light. When it reaches the eyebrow *chakra*, he sees God as a Light with which he cannot quite unite. When it reaches the crown *chakra* (*sahasrara*) and unites with Siva, *samadhi* takes place. He receives "gift-waves" through the crown of his head, is illuminated like an electric bulb, and experiences the Clear Light of the Void which is seen at death when the life-force travels up the spinal cord and leaves the body for good through the crown of the head.

The Divine Light is thus seen as the opening of the "petals" of a *chakra* to the pranic energy. It is to some extent a light lit within oneself by the divine energy or Light, and the journey from purification to illumination and the unitive life is seen in terms of the progress of *Kundalini*-Sakti up the *chakras* on the *susumna*. Once the mystic union between Sakti and Siva is achieved, a bliss-creating nectar drips down like seminal fluid and floods the body and mind with "*rasa*-juice", which is often represented as milk dripping from the udder of the cow Kamadhenu, or as a white flower.[38] It has also been described as a cloudburst over the mind. Once this process has taken place, it can be repeated much more quickly several times a day, and the rising of *Kundalini* to the crown *chakra*, tingling the spine and prickling the scalp, can soon be almost instantaneous, as it came to be for *Gopi* Krishna.[39]

The *Six Teachings* or *Six Doctrines* start with this process for they deal with *Tummo*, the Tibetan word for generating a psycho-physical bodily warmth or heat by yogic means. This involves receiving *prana* from Nature, storing it in the body, then using it to transmute semen into a subtle fiery energy which circulates in the nerve-channels (Sanskrit *nadis*) of the psychic nervous system. The fiery energy produces a heat that allows a hermit *yogin* to sit naked in a cave amid the freezing snows of the Tibetan mountains and not feel cold. It can also be used instead of an overcoat in our modern Western winters, but requires a measure of sexual continence as seminal fluid is involved; and it may be present during healing.

Western mystics, too, have found that *Tummo*, the fire of love, causes the flesh to burn. Maria Magdalena de Pazzi (died 1607) could not wear woollen clothes in winter because the psychic heat ("fire") in her was so warm that she even had to plunge into a well to cool off. Philip Neri (died 1595) could not sleep under bedclothes in winter, and St Catherine of Genoa actually heated cold water by dipping in her psychically hot hands.[40]

In the Yoga of the Psychic Heat which is in the *Six Teachings*, the *yogin* is taught how to visualise, meditate, sit, and breathe in the manner of Hatha Yoga (which also releases the subtle body). He is taught to direct thought, and train the nerve-system so as to obtain the psychic heat, and he is instructed to pray to the first Kargyutpa *guru* Dorje-Chang, alias Vajra-

Dhara: "Vouchsafe your 'gift-waves' that the Clear Light may be recognised as being within me.... Vouchsafe your 'gift-waves' that all phenomenal appearances shall dawn upon me as the Clear Light." The experience of psychic heat is in fact the experience of the Clear Light when "blissfulness is experienced" and "the mind assumes its natural state", while "the forming of thoughts ceases automatically...and something resembling the light of dawn, and something resembling a cloudless sky are seen".

When the nectar has dropped its molten heat from the crown of the head, "the Clear Light of All-Voidness being realised, one becomes immersed in a condition of consciousness unaffected by all worldly (or external) stimuli."[41] This is illustrated by a story about Milarepa who, despite a diet of nettles, was in a cave, "sitting in *samadhi*" when some hunters came and "prodded" his thin body with the ends of their bows to see if he was a man. Eventually Milarepa sang to them of his Five Comforts, which included the body and "the Lucid Mind", and he concluded: "No time have I to waste on useless talk; therefore shall I into the state quiescent of *samadhi* enter now."[42] Once the Clear Light has been seen in *samadhi* and the nectar of heat released, the *yogin* does not feel the cold (or extreme heat). Contact with the divine Light numbs the senses, a condition that is symbolized by the practice of "fire-walking" across red-hot cinders, during which the *yogin* is without apparent pain.

The Vaisnavist Hindu Light's Triumph over the Saivist Light: Visnu and Bhakti

After the Gupta empire there were small successor kingdoms which the Arabs invaded in the 7th-8th centuries AD. In South India, which had seen Tamil kingdoms and literature soon after the Mauryas, there were conflicting kingdoms, and in the 6th century AD the Pallavas rose. They followed Vaisnavism and temple-building increased, and monasteries spread.

The Vaisnavist Light really goes back to Sankara or Sankaracarya (AD c.788-820, though possibly c.700-750). For although Sankara was brought up in a Saivite family and taught to worship Sakti, his works incline towards Vaisnavism, the worship of Visnu, and he was the giant whom all the succeeding Vaisnavists opposed.

To Sankara, Brahman was the ultimate reality, not Siva; and Reality was an impersonal, "self-luminous" being which true perception could see, while the phenomenal world including the individual ego – everything else – was *maya*, a concept he introduced and interpreted as "illusion" or "appearance" in the sense of "unreal".[43]

Sankara started with the experience of the immortality of the Self or soul, the Atman which was identical with the self-luminous, all pervading Brahman. His monist continuation of the spirit of the *Upanisads*, on which he wrote commentaries, led to his founding the *Advaita* ("non-duality" or "monist") *Vedanta* ("End of the Veda") School.

So, he writes of the awakening of the Self in terms of the Light: "The Self alone lights up the mind and powers, as a flame lights up a jar.... A light does not need another light; it shines of itself.... Thus setting the fire-stick of thought in the socket of the Self, let the kindled flame of knowledge burn away the fuel of unwisdom.... The joy of the Self...shines pure within like the flame in a lamp....The Eternal shines forth glowing of red-hot iron.... The Self, the eye of wisdom beholds not, as the blind beholds not the shining sun.... The Self, rising in the firmament of the heart, a sun of wisdom...shines forth and illumines all." Again: "Here, verily, in the substantial Self, in the hidden place of the soul, this steady shining begins to shine like the dawn; then the shining shines forth as the noonday sun, making all this world to shine by its inherent light." And: "When the real Self with its stainless light recedes, a man thinking 'this body is I', calls it the Self.... The Self, wrapped in the five vestures beginning with the vesture formed of food, which are brought into being by its own power, does not shine forth, as the water in the pond, covered by a veil of green scum."[44]

What this scum might be is illustrated in a story about Sankara. Walking in a street in Kasi, he heard a scholar learning a grammatical rule by rote. He rebuked the grammarian for wasting his time over a futile formula, and composed a song: "Adore Govinda (i.e. Brahman), adore Govinda, adore Govinda, O fool ! When your appointed time arrives, the repetition of a grammatical rule will not save you."[45]

Sankara's insistence on adoration (*bhakti*) anticipated the Age of *Bhakti* (11th-19th centuries), which was based on the adoration (*bhakti*) of a personal God, and here was a movement away from the impersonality of Sankara's Brahman. The hymnodists and *Bhakti* saints were Vaisnava rather than Saiva, and their goal was to escape the cycle of birth and death and live in the presence of Visnu.

Visnu was mainly known through his incarnations (*avataras*) and especially as Rama, the hero of the epic *Ramayana*, and as Krishna, the divine cowherd who gazed on naked cowgirls or *gopis* – symbolising God's love for the soul – in the *Bhagavata-Purana*, and the charioteer of the *Bhagavad-gita*. Visnu (or Vishnu, *vis* being Sanskrit for "to pervade") is connected with the sun in the six hymns that are dedicated to him out of the 1,017 in the *Rig Veda*; hence the legend that he took three strides across the universe. He is shown with his consorts Lakshmi (or Sri) and Bhumidevi, or asleep on the cosmic ocean within the coils of a serpent, waiting to wake up and renew the world by descending in the form of a new incarnation.

In Hindu cosmology, according to the *Atharvaveda*, in each world-cycle or *maha yuga* of 12,000 years there were four world ages (*yugas*). In our world-cycle we have had the Krta, which lasted 4,800 years; the Treta, which lasted 3,600; the Dvapara, which lasted 2,400; and the Kali, in which we now live. This will last 1,200 years. Visnu appears at the end of each age to renew it. There is a dawn and dusk, each of 400 years, contained within the length of the above figures, and now at the end of our Kali *yuga*, the shortest and nastiest age, evil has proliferated and *dharma* is submerged in luxury and vice. The Kali *yuga* will end violently with a conflagration and natural disasters, and a new *maha yuga* will begin, a new age, through Visnu's renewal.[46] Visnu is shown holding a conch or a discus (*chakra*), or a lotus, and he rides a Garuda bird to heaven. His thousand names include "Hari". ("Hari Krishna" therefore contain two names for Visnu.)

Visnu, like Siva, was seen as the renewing Light, and the Vaisnava Schools of such Southern Indian *Bhakti* mystics as Ramanuja and Madhva continued the tradition of the Vaisnava saints Nammalvar (7th-9th century AD) and Andal (mid-7th century AD). However, Ramanuja and Madhva differed from Sankara's monism (that Atman and Brahman were one) in the way they interpreted the relationship of the Atman to their personal God. Ramanuja (c.1017-1137), who is reputed to have lived to be 120, qualified Sankara's monism (*visistadvaita*, "qualified monism") following a vision he had of Visnu. As a result he became a temple priest and asserted that the soul is immortal, that the material world must be seen in the light of the soul, but that to know the Atman or Self is not to be united with God, for divine union takes love (*bhakti*). The goal, then, was not to be released from transmigration through Brahman, but to unite with Brahman as identified with the personal God Visnu, and be saved by *bhakti*. Despite his opposition to Sankara, Ramanuja adhered to the *Vedanta* school and argued that the *Upanisads* teach the soul's union with a personal God, whose world of creation was not an unreal *maya* but a *sesa*, a spilling from the plenitude of his being. For Ramanuja, God's "divine form is the depository of all radiance", an "ocean" of compassion and tenderness, and "he came down to...give light to the whole world" (Ramanuja on the *Bhagavad-gita* 6.47).[47]

Madhva (c.1199-c.1278) went further in opposing Sankara. He pronounced a dualism (*dvaita*) between soul and God, Atman and Brahman, which he held to be different in kind. He was probably influenced by some Nestorian Christians in his youth, when he ran away from home and was found arguing with priests of Visnu, and he came to assert a Hell, Purgatory and Heaven where the soul went after death, from a world that was real and not *maya*. The Light in Madhva is more like the Christian Light.

Nimbarka (flourished 12th-13th centuries) taught a dualistic monism (*dvaitadvaita*) in which souls were both different from and united with God, the crucial factor being devotion (*bhakti*) to Krishna and his consort Radha. This liberated from the cycle of rebirth as it brought the Light. (Compare the Tibetan Clear Light, which originated in India and which similarly liberated from rebirth.)

Vallabha (1479-1531) taught pure monism (*suddhadvaita*) or non-dualism (*advaita*), and saw reality as Krishna, who appears as Brahman in the *Upanisads* and who is all creation and every soul. To him, the end of devotion (*bhakti*) was union with Krishna as the Light and liberation from rebirth.

Caitanya (1485-1533) worshipped Krishna and his consort Radha, his favourite among the *gopis* (daughters of the cowherds), and he identified with Radha so as to be near his lord, Krishna. The soul therefore had to be female in approaching the male God – "as an immoral woman constantly thinks of her illicit lover while living in the midst of her family, so do thou silently and ceaselessly meditate on Hari while doing thy earthly work" (*Contem* 523)[48] – and Caitanya used ecstatic songs and dances which led to trances. He preached "inconceivable duality and nonduality" (*acintyabhedabheda*), meaning that the relation between the soul and God could not be grasped by thought and that they were both different and the same. The ecstasy was that of *samadhi*, and Caitanya had a great impact on Vaisnavism in Bengal.

Popular *bhakti* cults continued to flourish through the writings of Ramananda (15th century), a follower of Ramanuja and *guru* of the Sufi-Hindu Kabir, and the poets Narima Mehta (15th century), Mira Bai (16th century), who sang as a *gopi* of her love for Krishna, and Tulsidas and Tukaram (17th century).

In the 11th and 12th centuries, Saivism declined at the expense of Vaisnavism and *Mahayana* Buddhism. One effect was the creation of the *Lingayats* ("*Lingam*-wearers") or *Virasaivas* (heroes of the Saiva faith) by Basaya in the 12th century. The *Lingayats* were influenced by the qualified monism and *bhakti* of the *Vaisnavist* Ramanuja. They wore a small phallus or *lingam* round their necks, and they worshipped the image of the *lingam*, which they took out of a case twice a day before meals and held in their left hands, meditating on it and adoring it. They were extremely puritanical, and saw the *lingam* as a symbol of the ascetic personal God Siva who brought the Light to the world, and whose illumination was detached from sensuality. The *lingam* was thus a symbol of the Light.

The *lingam* also incarnated the Light in the erotic sculptures of India at Sanchi, Mamallapuram, Ajanta, Elura, Orchha, Puri, Bhuvanesvar, Konarak and Khajuraho. These sculptures were more than mere examples of erotic art. They were symbols (carved at different times between the 3rd century BC and the 13th century AD) for the soul's love for Siva, for the Atman's love for Brahman, and for the naked *gopis'* love for Krishna; symbols which draw on a natural everyday eroticism that found expression in Vatsyayana's Kamasutra (4th century AD).[49]

The Sikh Light

The Sikh Light was a development from the Hindu Vaisnava *bhakti* movement, for its founder, *Guru* Nanak (c.1469-1539), was born a Hindu. Reacting to the Moslem pressure on India since the 12th century, which ended in the Moghul rule of the 16th century, Nanak founded Sikhism in the Punjab at the end of the 15th century to combine the Islamic and Hindu outlooks. He even wore a mixture of Moslem and Hindu dress during his wanderings in the Punjab forests at this time, and since he was a follower of Kabir, whom he regarded as a Sikh ("disciple") though he was as much a Sufi and a Hindu, the Hindu influence was the stronger.

Nanak was a strict Monotheist, and his God (*Om Kar*, "Creator God") was close to Kabir's Sufi immanent God who was manifest in creation to the spiritually illuminated eye once *maya* was overcome and the divine teacher (*guru*) admitted to the heart. Nanak taught that Sikhs should open themselves to the divine name (*nama*) by repeating it, and that this would put them in harmony with the divine order (*hukam*) and achieve a mystical union with God as Light. The salvation to which meditation on the *nama* led, the beatific vision of God immanent in the human spirit as Light, would liberate man from rebirth and reabsorb him into the divine life of *Nirvana*: "Love the Lord, o my soul....A shrine in darkness – so are you without him, o my soul." The Light is in all creation: "The sun and moon, O Lord, are Your lamps.... The perfume of the sandal is Your incense, the wind is Your fan, all the forests are Your flowers, O Lord of light.... The light which is in everything is Yours, O Lord of light." Again: "He is pure, endless, and infinite; all light is Yours, O Lord. God is concealed in every heart: His Light is in every heart."[50] The fourth *guru*, Ram Das, wrote in a Hymn: "O refractory Soul, my beloved, think within your body."[51]

Anecdotes about the deeds of Nanak (*janam-sakhis*, "life-stories") began to be collected some fifty to eighty years after his death, and the fifth of the line of ten Sikh *gurus*, Arjun, collected these anecdotes and sayings, and edited and enlarged the collection of Sikh religious poems (including Kabir's) into the one canonical scripture of the Sikhs, the *Adi Granth*. Later Arjun was executed by the Moslem authorities. The Sikhs then opposed the

Moslems, by which time they had already broken with the Islamic – and the Hindu – origins of their religion. Their claim to be an independent religion is based on their scriptures, their observances and way of life, their sacred city by the lake of Amritsar ("the Lake of Nectar") and its Golden Temple (or Harimandir, which was built in 1604 and rebuilt and overlaid with gold foil in the early 19th century), and their prophet and line of *gurus*.

The Moghul Light

From 750 to 1200 North India had been decentralised, and Turkish power arrived in the 10th century. This led to the Turkish Moslem conquest of North India until, during a decline c.1365, the Turkish Timur (Tamerlane or Tamberlaine the Great) invaded and sacked Delhi in 1398. There were Moslem states in South India from c.1350 to 1680, when central control was lost, and the Moghul Empire, which stemmed from Timur, was established from 1526 to 1761, especially through Akbar the Great who ruled for over 50 years (1556-1605) and who allowed all religions to practise alongside Islam.

The builder of the Red Fort (which was begun in 1638) in New Delhi, Shah Jehan, left an inscription on the wall of the Hall of Private Audience (*Dewan-i-Khaf*) from the height of the Moghul time: "If there is Paradise on earth, it is here, it is here." Here in the white marble pavilion Shah Jehan, grandson of Akbar the Great and builder of the Taj Mahal, Moghul Emperor, sat on the Peacock Throne.[52] Was his inscription a geographical statement, or a statement of ecstatic contemplation of the Light?

Recent Light

The Hindu Light made a comeback after the Moghul Empire. The Moghul Empire declined in the 18th century, dwindling to little more than Delhi. The vacuum was filled first by the Hindu Maratha Empire in the west, and then by the British, who, having arrived in India c.1600, competed with the

French from 1740 to 1762, and conquered India by 1818. The rise of Indian nationalism, at first in the late 19th century and then through Ghandhi, saw a renewal of the Hindu Light – Gandhi's movement did not discriminate between religion and politics – and following the anti-imperialist policies of the British Liberals and Labour Party there was a transfer of power, with the result that the Hindu tradition is still very much alive.

The Indian Hindu Light is strong today. This is largely a result of the continuing influence of the *Vedas* and especially the *Upanisads* through Sankara's *Vedanta* school, which, we have seen, has had a great influence on Theosophy and other contemporary esotericists.

The Light is still symbolized in the architecture of Hindu temples. Hindu temples tend to be shaped like pyramid-mountains. Like the Temple of the Sun at Konarak, they widen downwards from the top like a shaft of sunlight. Inside the Light is suggested by a lit image of the god – generally Siva or Visnu on a thousand-petalled lotus – which is invoked often with the aid of Vedic fire until the Light enters the soul. It ascends back up the pyramid-mountain to the sun, which symbolises the Light of transcendent Reality.

From the early 19th century on, Hinduism was in contact with the West and Christianity, and Rammohan Ray founded the pro-Western, monotheistic *Brahmo Samaj* ("Society of God") which became more mystical under Debendranath Tagore and then Keshab Chuder Sen. (Sarasvati founded the Arya Samaj as an anti-Western reaction following the Indian Mutiny.) The Light shone out in Ramakrishna (1836-86) who followed Sankara's *Vedanta* school and whom members of the *Brahmo Samaj* visited. Ramakrishna wrote nothing, but his disciples left written records of his life and sayings, and his continuation of the *bhakti* tradition.

Ramakrishna first experienced the Light as an uneducated young Bengali in the Temple of Kali at Dakshinesvar, just outside Calcutta. He was made assistant priest there at the age of 18, and lived in the nearby woods. He was about to kill himself with a sword when "suddenly I had the wonderful vision of the Mother and fell down unconscious... In my heart of hearts, there was flowing a current of intense bliss, never experienced before, and I had the immediate knowledge of the light, that was Mother." Again,

"The buildings..., the Temple...vanished from my sight, leaving no trace whatsoever, and in their stead was a limitless, infinite, effulgent ocean of consciousness or spirit. As far as the eye could reach, its shining billows were madly rushing towards me.... I was caught up in the billows and fell down senseless." Later, with a trained mountaineer, Totapuri, who had attained *samadhi*, he "tore the veil of name-and form, and beheld his individuality dissolving in a limitless blaze of spiritual light".[53] He continued to have visions of the Divine Mother (Kali) and of Krishna, and later on, he had a vision of Mohammed among Moslem mystics, and a vision of Christ while studying the *New Testament*, after which he taught the unity of all religions.

As a great Master, Ramakrishna was sitting in his room describing divine forms when he "went into an ecstatic state and said, 'I have become! I am here!' Uttering these words he went into *samadhi*. His body was motionless. He remained in that state a long time and then gradually regained partial consciousness of the world. He began to laugh like a boy." On another occasion about 8pm, Ramakrishna asked Mahimacharan to recite a few hymns from the scriptures and when he heard the words "the yogis who have attained samesightedness", "then he stood up and went into *samadhi*.... Speechless, the devotees looked at this yogi who had himself attained the state of samesightedness. After a long time the Master regained consciousness of the outer world and took his seat. He asked Mahima to recite verses describing the love of God.... Master: 'Ah! Ah!' On hearing these verses the Master was about to go again into an ecstatic mood, but he restrained himself with effort."[54]

Ramakrishna also knew *Kundalini*: "(The Serpent) comes to rest in the heart.... A great brilliance is seen.... (The serpent) moves thus through six stages (i.e. *chakras*) and coming to (the highest one) is united with it. Then there is *samadhi*. When (the serpent) rises to the sixth stage, the form of God is seen. But a slight veil remains, it is as if one sees a light within a lantern, and thinks that the light itself can be touched, but the glass intervenes.... In *samadhi*, nothing external remains.... If he remains twenty-one days in this condition, he is dead."

Ramakrishna's disciple, the sophisticated Vivekananda (1862-1902), continued the Hindu Light, but concentrated his energies on improving the social conditions of Indians. In *Six Lessons on Raja-Yoga* he taught: "Give up all ideas of enjoyment.... Man must struggle on...until he sees the light."[55] Meanwhile the 19th century South Indian mystic, Ramalinga, left an account of his vision of the Light: "O Light of lights! O Self-radiance, the dispeller of darkness of ignorance, I am fully illumined now. All my doubts and delusions have vanished. I am one with the Divine. I am Absolute Existence, Absolute Knowledge, Absolute Bliss."

In the 20th century the Hindu Light has continued to shine. Sri Aurobindo (1872-1950) took part in the independence movement and was imprisoned by the British in 1908 before retiring for a while to develop a philosophy of "the gnostic man". The gnostic man is the illumined man, for the gnostic man comes into being when the drive of the spiritual mind or supermind achieves yogic illumination, and unites with enlightenment which descends from the cosmos. A new dialectic is therefore created, the light of Brahman and man's illumined mind – the two opposites – being reconciled in a new spiritual man. A man's evolution makes him divine, and a new spiritual age is approaching in which such divinity will happen.

The Light is therefore very important in Aurobindo's work, and it does not favour the spirit escaping from the body but its coming more perfectly into the body. His own mystical experience may be deduced from a passage in *The Divine Life* (1940): "At the gates of the Transcendent stands that mere and perfect spirit described in the *Upanisads*, luminous, pure, sustaining the world..., the pure Self..., the inactive Brahman, the transcendent Silence. And the mind when it passes those gates suddenly...receives a sense of the unreality of the world and the sole reality of the Silence." The Silence is identified with the "inactive Brahman" which is the Light. So, "the earliest formula of Wisdom promises to be its last – God, Light, Freedom, Immortality." Elsewhere he asks, "By what alchemy shall this lead of mortality be turned into the gold of divine Being?"[56]

In *The Lights and Visions of the Mother*, Aurobindo connects the Light with Kali: "The white light is the Mother's light. Wherever it descends or enters, it brings peace, purity, silence and the openness to the higher forces" (31.7.1934); and, "It is the Mother's diamond light that is the essential Force. The diamond light proceeds from the heart of the Divine

Consciousness" (13.11.1936). Aurobindo identified the divine Mother with Mother India, and so took the Light back into the Indian independence movement, where it was carried on by Mahatma Ghandi, who lived out the teachings of the *Bhagavad-gita.*

Ramana Maharishi (1879-1950), a Tamil mystic, also followed Sankara. He found *samadhi* by asking who he was and answering in terms of what he was not; as a result he reached a state of consciousness beyond the mind which was the Light.

On August 30, 1896 he walked ten miles to the temple of Arayani-nallur on a rock and "sat down in the pillared hall. He had a vision there – a vision of brilliant light enveloping the entire place. It was no physical light." He defined this light as the Light of the Self falling on the ego and being reflected back from it in *Erase the Ego*: "The light of the Self...falls on the ego and is reflected therefrom.... To destroy the ego and BE the Self, is the Supreme method of attainment.... To see the Self, the mind has simply to be turned inwards... The Self is the Heart, self-luminous. Illumination arises from the heart and reaches the brain, which is the seat of mind. The world is seen with the mind; so you see the world with the reflected light of the Self."[57] Ramana Maharishi's disciples saw his body "shining like the morning sun" or "like a column of pure light" during one of his transfigured hours.[58]

The Bengali poet Rabindranath Tagore (1861-1941) saw God as Light in "Gitanjali" ("Song of Offerings"): "Light, my light, the world-filling light, the eye-kissing light, heart-sweetening light!" The essays on art of Ananda Coomaraswamy (1877-1947) made him the major interpreter of India to the West, and his Vedas include a diagram to show the correspondence between the "Light of Heaven" and the "Light of Nature" (which is "the reflection...at the circumference of the 'Light of Heaven' at the centre"), and these lights or suns both appear in the individual's conscience.[59] Swami Sivananda (died 1963), the founder of the Divine Life Society, and Krishnamurti (born 1895), who founded the World Order of Star with the Theosophist Annie Besant and was hailed as the reincarnated Buddha until he retracted in 1928, both carried on the Tradition of the Light.

The anonymous *Vedanta Moola Saram* ("the Essence of the *Upanisads* ") by "a science graduate", a series of articles which appeared in

The Hindu Organ between 1945 and 1950, analyse 21 of the thousand or more *Upanisads.* These articles have been reprinted, and under the front page banner headline "*Triambagan* (Three-Eyed Lord), God's Light is the Source of the World Light", the following appeared on June 12, 1970: "The peerless Eye (of fire) in His Forehead opened and made the darkness flee.... That Three-eyed Lord indeed is our refuge." In other articles the science graduate writes of *samadhi,* enlightenment, and the seed-like nature of the Light, and he invokes Agni as "Enlightener".

We have already seen that the most influential *Vedanta* school, *Advaita* (Sanskrit for "Nondualism", i.e. Monism) was founded by Sankara. In fact it draws on the *Upanisads* and the *Vedanta-sutras,* and is indebted to Gaudapada, the 7th century AD author of the *Mandukya-karika,* a verse commentary on the *Mandukya Upanisad* which draws on the *Mahayana* Buddhist Emptiness (*Sunyavada*). According to Gaudapada the individual belongs to the Atman (all-soul) just as the space in a jar belongs to all space and is indistinguishable from it when the jar is broken; there is no more duality between the self and the All than between the air inside and outside a jar. We have seen that Sankara fused the Atman and Brahman, so that the Self is Brahman, the Light, and there is no duality between the Light of the Self and its Light within all creation. (This is also the message of the *Mahayana* Zen Buddhist Ryoanji stone garden in Kyoto, Japan, in which individual pebbles of Light also belong to a sea of pebbles that is artificially bordered and limited, but which need not be so.)[60] The *Advaita* school, which stresses the scientific economy of creation (just as Freemasons see God as an Architect), has found modern expression in the School of Economic Science's semi-Gurdjieffian philosophy courses which have been advertised in London tube stations since the 1950s and where many an awakening has been encouraged. A leading modern exponent of the *Advaita* school is the New Age teacher Jean Klein, a Czech who experienced the Light of the Atman-Brahman "one evening, on Marine Drive, in Bombay". He writes: "I was aimlessly watching the flight of some birds when I came to feel that all and everything was happening inside myself; and, in so doing, I knew myself consciously. Next morning...I was seized in full consciousness by an all-penetrating light, without inside or outside. This was the awakening in

Reality, in the *I am.*" The Self is the Light: "This mind...can only function harmoniously when illuminated by the Self.... The Self you are is resplendent of its own light."[61]

Add to such "scientific" developments the continuing influence of the neo-Hindu Theosophical Movement of Mme Blavatsky, and the Hari (or Hare) Krishna movement – a ***bhakti*** movement based on Caitanya and called the International Society of Krishna Consciousness, which was founded by Swami Prabhupada and which thrived among Hindu migrants – and add recent illumined figures like Sai Baba, Gururaj, and *Gopi* Krishna (born 1903), who had a profound and disturbing experience of *Kundalini* ("a halo of light") in 1937 on which he based his autobiography as it is "the most wonderful achievement in front of man",[62] and there can be no doubt that the Light is stronger in modern India than it is in the Middle East.

20

The South-East Asian Light

The Mahayana Buddhist Light: Sunyata/the Void, Mind-Essence, the One, Endless Light

Mahayana Buddhism declined in India and spread throughout South-East Asia when an enormous number of Buddhist monasteries was destroyed by the Central Asian Huns (or *Hunas*) under the Saivite King Mihira Kula in the 6th century AD and the Saivite Bengal King Sasanka in the 7th century. Its schools spread eastwards to Central Asia, Korea, Tibet, Java, Sumatra and Sri Lanka (Ceylon), and were especially influential in China – Indian monks travelled to China along the silk route from the 3rd century BC onwards – and in Japan, where *Mahayana* became the state religion in the Nara period (8th century). Thus, the Indian Madyamika School was founded by Nagarjuna in the 2nd or 3rd centuries AD, and it spread to China as San-lun (5th century) and Japan as Sanron (7th century).

A missionary, Kumarajiva, translated the main text *Maha-prajna-paramita-sastra* ("Great Perfection of Wisdom Treatise", which is attributed to Nagarjuna) from Sanskrit into Chinese. This text sees Reality as "the Void" (*sunyata*) or *Nirvana*: "All things having the nature of emptiness (*sunyata*) have no beginning and no ending. They are neither faultless nor not faultless; they are neither perfect nor imperfect." There is a Middle Way between all the pairs of opposites, and this is the Void-*Nirvana*, which is both the denial of extremes and the All, the Light. A part of Nagarjuna's *Diamond Sutra* states that "all things are in *Nirvana* from the beginning", and everything came out of the Void or Light, which is a diamond, or *prajna* ("wisdom").[1] *Sunyata* is therefore the Light.

The Indian Yogacara or Vijnanavada School was founded by Asanga and his brother in the 5th century AD, and it spread to China as Fa-hsiang (6th century) and to Japan as Hosso (7th century), where it centred on the oldest temple in Japan, Horyu-ji (completed 607). The Yogacara School taught that mind (*manas*) was the source of all things, together with its "store-consciousness" (*alaya*). It was an Idealistic doctrine: mind, not *sunyata*, gives the "suchness" or "thusness" (*tathata*) to things, and "at the stage of *Tathagatahood* where the flowers of the *Samadhis*, powers, self-control and psychic faculties are in bloom", the *bodhisattva* "shines like the moon in water with varieties of rays of transformation" (*Lankavatara Sutra*, a scripture already in China in the 1st century AD, on which the School is partly based).[2] The term *Tathagata* means "he who has gone in that manner" (i.e., "he who has trodden the path"). It can also mean "he who has come from the suchness" (i.e., after reaching enlightenment).

The concept of *Tathagata* appears in another Indian scripture of the School, Asvaghosa's 1st century AD *Awakening of Faith* (*Mahayana-sraddhotpada-sastra*), the work which gave *Mahayana* its name. In this work, "the Pure Essence of Mind" or "Mind-Essence" has both "an emptiness aspect" and "a non-emptiness aspect" – it is emptiness because it is reached by emptying the mind of multiplicity, but it has its own reality – and though "we think of Mind-Essence as the Womb of *Tathagata*" in fact "nothing comes forth and nothing returns and there is no Womb of *Tathagata*". The Mind-Essence is in fact *Alaya-vijnana*, the "storage of Universal Mind" which has one aspect "of Enlightenment" and another "of Ignorance". The Mind-Essence then, is the Light, from which all creation comes as from a womb, although there is no birth or death connected with the Light and so it is not a womb.[3]

The main concepts of the two main *Mahayana* schools, *sunyata* and "Mind-Essence", then, describe the Light. So did the main concepts of the remaining *Mahayana* schools.[4] The Indian Avatamsaka (or Avatanshaka) School spread to China as Hua-yen (7th century) and to Japan as Kegon (8th century). Its main text, the *Avatamsaka-sutra* tells the truth of the Buddha Vairocana's Enlightenment. Vairocana is Sanskrit for "the Illuminator", the supreme Buddha who is often called *Mahavairocana*, "the Great Illuminator". (Compare Mani's title.) In Japan he is known as "the Great Sun" (*Dainichi Nyorai*) and in Tibet as "Maker of Brilliant Light" (*Rnam-par-snang-mdzad*); in Mongolia as "Maker of Brilliant Light". (The Japanese Dai-butsu or colossal bronze Buddha at Todaiji, Nara, is a Kegon image of Vairocana, the original body of Sakyamuni or Gautama, which was dedicated in 752.)

According to the Avatamsaka School, all objects and energies are under one law. This is the Law-nature (*dharma-dhatu*, "totality", "universal principle") or One behind each of the many, and there is therefore sameness in difference, and difference (multiplicity) in sameness (unity), a metaphysics that later passed into Zen. An enlightened Buddha experiences the harmonious whole, and the Oneness is the Light which is behind all creation.

This is symbolized as stone in the famous stone garden at the Ryoanji temple in Kyoto, where pebbles and rocks represent sea and rocks, or earth and mountains, or clouds and mountains; in short, the sea of Becoming and the rock of Being that make up the unity of all creation,[5] and which its 15th-century Zen designer, Soami, is supposed to have hidden by describing it as "a tiger fleeing from one island to another with it cubs against the attack of a leopard".[6] Everything is made of the Light-based material, everything is made of "matter" which is in fact Light. To a perfectly enlightened Buddha, all things have Buddha-nature, and the oneness of the stone garden is what the giant Buddha sees.

The Indian Saddharmapundarika School (6th century AD) spread to China as *T'ien-t'ai*, and (through the monk Saicho, later Dengyo Daishi) to Japan as Tendai (9th century AD). Its main text, the *Lotus Sutra* (first translated into Chinese AD c.250, literally "the Lotus of the True Law", i.e. the Light), makes it clear that the aim of all is to be a Buddha, that Buddhahood (Enlightenment by the Light) is the one way for all. The

Buddha himself is represented as an eternal being surrounded by a thousand *arhats* and *bodhisattvas* like the 1,000 Kannons or Deva Kings at the Tendai Sanjusangendo temple in Kyoto – there are 1,000 realms in Tendai, each containing three divisions – and according to the Lotus Sutra truth can be reached by gestures, exclamations and silences, which has led Tendai to be regarded as a form of Zen. The central threefold truth of Tendai regards all things as of the Void and temporary, and therefore at one in their Voidness and temporariness. The Void is the Light, a truth that can be known and directly contacted.

The Indian Pure Land or Sukhavati School (2nd century AD) spread to China as Ching-t'u (3rd century AD) and to Japan as Jodo, *Shin* (which Nō expressed) and Ji. Its main text, the *Pure Land Sutra* (*Sukhavativyuha*, before 2nd century AD), is about a monk called Dharmakara who attained Buddhahood and a Pure Land. In this Pure Land all might obtain *Nirvana* and all could be reborn into it by calling on the name of the Buddha at death. Dharmakara became known as the Buddha of Unlimited Light (Sanskrit *Amitabha*, "endless light", Japanese *Amida*) and one of his assistants was the Japanese Kannon.

The Tendai School brought the sect to Japan, but by the 13th century the Jodo sect separated from Tendai through the work of Honen who advocated a constant calling on *Amida* ("endless light") or saying the *Nembutsu* (a shortened version of the Japanese invocation, *Namu Amida Butsu*). His disciple Shinran founded the True Pure Land sect (*Shin*), and taught that a man had to call on *Amida* only once to obtain salvation – some Nō plays express such an invocation – while Ippen founded the "Ji" sect which invoked *Amida* at set times of the day.

Later the *Lotus Sutra* and pure Land were combined by Nichiren ("Sun Lotus", 1222-82). Nichiren distinguished the original being of the Buddha as taught in the *Lotus Sutra* from his incarnation, and held that all can "climb the precipice of Bodhi" (Enlightenment)[7] and possess Buddha-nature (the Light) by repeating a salutation. The modern Soka-gakkai (Value Creation Society) worships Nichiren as the True Buddha of the *Lotus Sutra*.

Tantric Buddhism

The Light of Tantric Buddhism or Vajrayana ("the Diamond Vehicle") was a form of *Mahayana* Buddhism that began in India and Sri Lanka (Ceylon) in the 2nd or 4th centuries AD. Its founder was either Nagarjuna or Asanga. *Tantras* were "looms" or "works", post-Vedic treatises in Sanskrit, and Tantrism aimed to purify and control the psychological processes: "Just as gold is freed from its dross only be fire and acquires its shining appearance from heat, so the mind of a living being, cleansed from the filth of his actions and desires through his love for me, is transformed into my transcendent likeness. The mind is purified through the hearing and uttering of sacred hymns in my praise" (*Bhagavata-Purana* 11.14.25).[8]

Indian Tantrism sought to recapture the experience that made Gautama the "Enlightened One" (Buddha), and its goal was enlightenment. In the "age of degeneration" ("Kali *yuga*", "age of darkness") enlightenment was gained by bodily exercises, the body containing the cosmos (*Kalacakra Tantra*). The initiate did yogic exercises which corresponded to the stages of spiritual growth, and identified with cosmic forces (gods and goddesses). Eventually he saw that *Nirvana* or the Void (*sunyata*) are a passive wisdom (*prajna*) that has an indestructible or diamond-like (*vajra*) nature, while destroying ignorance like a diamond (or a thunderstorm, for *vajra* has a second meaning), but that the best course of action (*upaya*) is the compassion of the *bodhisattva* (*karuna*).

The diamond was the Light, which is shaped like a diamond and which creates an immortal diamond-body as in Neo-Taoism. Enlightenment meant seeing that the opposites of Void and compassion are in fact One – that the Void is to be identified with compassion – and that (as in Taoism) union of the opposites can be symbolized in the sexual act, which represented the last stage of spiritual growth.

A late Tantric Indian form of *Mahayana* Buddhism called Mantrayana (*Mantra*, "spell", i.e. the "Path of the Sacred Formulas") spread to China as Chen-yen (7th and 8th centuries AD), and to Japan as Shingon (9th century AD). Shingon was introduced by Kukai or Kobo Daishi (the Great Master who propagated the *Dharma*), and it meant "True Word", a translation of the Sanskrit *mantra.* It approached the wisdom of Maha-Vairocana, "the Great Resplendent One" or "the Great Illuminator", the Buddha in his *dharmakaya* (cosmic body) rather than the historical Buddha Sakyamuni. Its main text, the *Dainichi-kyo* (or in Sanskrit, the *Mahavairocana-sutra,* "Great Sun Sutra") saw the universe as being within Maha-Vairocana, or the Light. Maha-Vairocana was both Womb and Diamond (Void and Light), both within all things as their Buddha-nature, and beyond impurity.[9] The initiate could be enlightened within a human body provided he became one with Maha-Vairocana, and he reached unity through symbolic gestures (*mudras*) and syllables (*mantras*), *mandalas* and yoga.

Angkor Wat: The Triumph of Buddhism over Hinduism

The decline of Saivism can be measured at Angkor in Cambodia, which the Khmer kings built between the 9th and 13th centuries to symbolise the Hindu universe. The kings changed first from Siva to Visnu, and then from Visnu to the *Mahayana* Buddhist cult based on the *bodhisattva* Avalokitesvara (of whom the Tibetan Lamas are reputedly incarnations). They built the city of Angkor round a central mountain, which represented Mount Meru (compare the shamans' World Mountain). Lakes represented the cosmic ocean that surrounded the Indian cosmic mountain, and the temples of the central mountain or pyramid observed the cult of a god-king (*devaraja*). The king was identified first with Siva, then with Visnu, and finally with the Buddha, and his temple became his mausoleum when he died.

Beginning with Jayavarman II (9th century), the royal essence or "inner self" resided in a *lingam* in a pyramid in the exact centre of the royal city. This *lingam* was a palladium of the kingdom. It was supposed to have been given by Siva to a Brahmin priest, through whom Siva and the king could commune in the sacred city which was a microcosm for the world. At the end of the 11th century the Baphuon temple was built to house the golden *lingam* of Udayadityavarman II, which also contained the king's inner self. The king was Siva in his life, and the people prostrated themselves before his *lingam* in acknowledgement of this fact, and he was entombed and embodied as Siva on his death.

The change from Siva to Visnu took place in the 12th century, when the famous Angkor Wat identified Suryavarman II with Visnu, both during his life and after his death (c.1150). When *Mayahana* Buddhism was adopted during the second half of the 12th century, the god-king left his *lingam* to enter a statue of the Buddha and become the king-as-Buddha. The *lingam* and the Buddha were both symbols for the Light, and the god-kings of Angkor embodied the enlightenment of Siva and Buddha, and were "enlightened ones". The *lingam* was thus an incarnation for, and symbol of, Siva's Light, as it was for the Lingayats of the 12th century.[10]

The Khmers were later converted to Theravada Buddhism, and when Thai armies sacked Angkor in 1431, the city was abandoned and the jungle closed in until it was rediscovered in the 19th century.

Recent Light

The Light is strong in contemporary Buddhism. The Light is symbolized in the architecture of Buddhist temples or *caityas*. It descends down a pinnacle which is often golden into a hall with a central nave, on either side of which are two rows of pillars, where there is an image of the meditating Buddha (very often with an aura of flames), whose enlightenment is to be imitated, or a *stupa* which contains relics (and is shaped like a pre-Buddhist Kurgan-style burial mound). Buddhism disappeared from India after Moslem invaders sacked the Indian monasteries in the 12th century AD, and it declined in Central Asia after the spread of Islam.

The Tibetans had spread the Buddhist Light to Nepal, Bhutan, and Sikkim, and Buddhism influenced Burma, Thailand, Indo-china and Indonesia. Buddhism supported the anti-colonialists in all the Buddhist countries except for Thailand and Japan, and as a result it entered politics in a number of countries. In Sri Lanka (Ceylon), for example, Gunanda's movement challenged Christian missionaries, and there political Buddhism was helped by the Theosophical Society of Olcott, and the Maha Bodhi Society (1891). In Burma, Buddhism was sufficiently a channel for the Light for the Venerable Ledi Sayadaw to write a manual called *The Requisites of Enlightenment* in which seven "factors of Enlightenment" lead to the Light, as a result of which a man will experience "joy in the knowledge that he can now perceive the light of *Nibbana*". (*Nibbana* is *Nirvana*, the state that is beyond attachment.)

Buddhism spread throughout China and Korea by the 14th century, when it began to be replaced by Neo-Confucianism. In Japan it stayed. From being the state religion in the 8th century, in the 17th century it was still able to throw up a third Zen sect, the Obaku, which was close to Rinzai but invoked *Amida* and embodied the Light – and it became an arm of government between the 17th and 19th centuries. Then the revived Shinto religion was established in the Meiji Era and the Buddhist lands were confiscated. However, Buddhism made a come-back through the new religions Soka Gakkai (which was based on Nichiren) and Rissho-Kosei-kai. The Tibetan Buddhist Dalai Lama fled from the Chinese in 1959.

There has been a Buddhist revival in the West, partly through the late Christmas Humphreys, the retired English judge. As a result, the writings about Japanese Zen Buddhism of such interpreters as Daisetzu Suzuki and the late Dr. Blyth (my sometime colleague in Tokyo) are well-known in the West and to New Age audiences. This revival reflects the strength of the Buddhist Light today, and confirms the spiritual strength of the Far East. A young seeker could do worse than go out to the Far East (as I did) and discover the Light there – it is more likely to be found in the Far East than in the Middle East – and if he goes to a Buddhist country like Japan, he will grasp that even today "the pursuit of enlightenment...is the purpose for which Buddhism exists".[11]

21

The Japanese Light

Bon

Bon (see pp23-25) seems to have pre-dated Shinto in Japan. It has long had a following in Japan, and at the New Year and on July 15 the dead spirits return to their families at Bon festivals. (Compare our All Hallows E'en.) They are welcomed with fires, and thousands of fire-flies are released in public places such as Tokyo's Chinsanzo Gardens. Each fire-fly represents an illumined spirit. Such a spectacle makes one wonder if our "bonfire", which shoots up sparks, is not so much a "bone-fire" (OED) as a "Bon-fire", a fire for Bon which celebrates the close relationship between the living and the dead.

Shinto Kami

Shinto, the indigenous pre-Buddhist shamanistic religion of Japan, derived from China and from the *Mahayana* influence on Taoism.[1] The name is an adaptation of two Chinese words, *Shin* and *To* (compare *Tao*), "the Way of the Spirits" – the native form is *Kami-no-michi* – and under the influence of Chinese Taoism which had spread throughout Japan by the 7th century AD, the *kami* of the Imperial Household and the tutelary *kami* of powerful clans became the *kami* of the whole nation, an equivalent of the *Tao*: the one Light which Shinto channelled.[2]

The *kami* were gods, rather like the Hindu *devas*.[3] (Further Indian influence can be found in the *torii*, the gateway to a Shinto temple which recalls the gateways to Indian temples, the *toranas*). The word can be translated "mystical", "superior", or "divine", for the *kami* were deities or spirits which ruled men or nature, and each Japanese became *kami* after death. Until the end of the war the Emperor and Empress were regarded as *kami* in their lifetime, and the Imperial palaces in Tokyo still have "nesting-boxes" in the trees for the *kami* of their ancestors.[4] (This is a shamanistic idea. According to the Tungus and Yakuts of Eastern and North-Eastern Siberia, the souls of future shamans live in nests in high trees in the Upper World.)

But behind the polytheism and the plurality, there was a single principle. The Divine Being "is at one and the same time the 800 myriads (i.e. ten thousands) of deities. It is the One Great Root of Heaven and Earth and all things in the universe are in this One God."[5] It was this One principle that was behind the original *kamikaze*, the divine wind or typhoon which blew away Genghis Khan's threatening Mongol fleet in 1281, but at the level of the *Tao* it transcended cognition and could only be known by faith.

Shinto mythology is based on the Sun Goddess Amaterasu, the ancestress of the Imperial Household. The mirror, sword and jewels of the Imperial Regalia which are revered in Shinto temples and shrines were originally given by the Sun Goddess to her grandson, the first Emperor. Hence Japan is "the Land of the Rising Sun".[6] Shinto was originally linked with agricultural rites and shamanism. When it became "*Tao*-ised", the One *Kami* of the universe, which contained the spirits of the departed, could be known as an inner sun[7] in accordance with whose will man should live "as *Kami*'s child".

It is because the instinctive Shinto was already open to the influences of the human interior that the first Zen made such an impact in the Japanese unconscious mind. In a sense, Shinto anticipated Zen, and the Imperial golden chrysanthemum, the symbol of the Imperial family, which still appears on some Imperial gifts (the most favoured of which is an urn for one's *kami* after death, for such a gift from a divine *kami* guarantees immortality), represents the Golden Flower,[8] the Light. There were thirteen Shinto sects in the 10th century AD Meiji period, and it is significant that one of them was called Konko-kyo; for "Konko", the religious name of its founder, means "golden light".

ZEN *SATORI*

The Light of Zen originated with the Indian *Dhyana* School (4th century AD), which spread along the silk route to China as *Ch'an*, an amalgamation of *Mahayana* Buddhism and Taoism, through the Indian monk Bodhidharma (6th century). There was already an "Inner Light School" in China in the 4th and 5th centuries based on the teachings of the Buddhist monks Tao-sheng (360-434), Hui-yuan (334-416, the founder of Chinese Pure Land) and Seng-chao, and in particular on Tao-sheng's "thesis of sudden enlightenment for the achieving of Buddhahood" and "thesis of making clear the Buddha-nature in every man".[9]

But it was Bodhidharma's Ch'an School which held that meditation ("*dhyana*", "*ch'an*") was the way to experience enlightenment. *Ch'an* was influenced by the *Tao*, which, like the Buddha-mind or Buddha-nature, was present in all things. Its main text, the *Lankavatara Sutra* which was already in China in the 1st century AD, held that all possess Buddha-nature. This was equated with the Void (*sunya*) in *Ch'an*, and the perception of the Buddha-nature as the Void or the Light was enlightenment (*wu* in Chinese, later *satori* in Japanese).

Ch'an's Northern School held that enlightenment comes gradually, while Ch'an's Southern School held that enlightenment comes suddenly. This was the "School of Sudden Enlightenment" near Canton. It was founded by Hui-neng (638-713), who held that the body is the "lamp" for the Light, which is "the real Buddha...within our minds".[10] (Compare the lamp of Allah c.650.) In his *Sutra of Wei Lang* Hui-neng wrote: "Within the domain of our mind there is a *Tathagata* of Enlightenment who sends forth a powerful light which illumines externally the six gates (of sensation) and purifies them. This light is strong enough to pierce through the six heavens of desire, and when it is turned inwardly to the Essence of Mind it eliminates at once the three poisonous elements, purges away our sins which might lead us to the hells, and enlightens us thoroughly within and without."[11] The Southern school triumphed over the Northern school and spread to Japan as Zen between the 7th and 12th centuries.

The aim of Zen *satori* was an awakening to the experience of enlightenment which Gautama the Buddha had under the Bo tree. The Ch'an Southern School split into Lin-chi and Ts'ao-tung in the 9th century, and these offshoots spread to Japan as Rinzai (12th century) and Soto (13th century), which emphasised different ways to the Light. Eisai, the founder of the Rinzai school, was a Tendai monk who brought *Ch'an* (Zen) back from China and stressed the *kung-an* (Japanese *koan*), a paradoxical question which transcended all thought and prepared the way to Enlightenment. This approach was accompanied by Tendai shouts and exclamations, laughter and beatings with a wooden stick during meditation to shock seekers abruptly out of their reason into enlightenment.

Dogen, the founder of the Soto school, was also a Tendai monk who went to China and he brought back *zazen* ("sitting straight") so that in the words of Hui-neng "with no thought arising in the heart, this is sitting" (*Za*): "inwardly to see one's own nature and not move from it, this is Meditation" (*Zen*), i.e. to see one's own Buddha-nature or self-nature. No effort was made to strive after enlightenment (*wu-wei*, non-action of the mind): but calming the thoughts could bring enlightenment.[12]

Zen gave rise to Nō drama in the 14th century AD. Nō drama was particularly developed by the actor-author Seami (or Zeami) Motokiyo (1363-1443), who wrote a manual for Nō pupils, *Kadensho* (or *Kwadensho*), the "Book of the Flowery Tradition" or "Book on the Handing on of the Flower" (1440-2). This dwells on the difficult and untranslatable *yugen* ("mystery and depth"). *Yugen* suggests "what lies beneath the surface", the subtle rather than the obvious, the hint as opposed to the statement. The essence of *yugen* is "true beauty and gentleness" (Seami), and it is the spiritual core of Nō, the joy that is felt at a perfectly achieved beauty, which the Nō actor should aim to catch through symbolism rather than go for mere realistic representation. Seami writes that the symbol of *yugen* is "a white bird with a flower in its beak", and: "If one aims at the beautiful, 'the flower' is sure to appear.... If the 'flower' is lacking, there will be no beauty in his impersonation."[13]

Yugen, restrained beauty, is a Zen term. It is derived from Zen literature, in which Seami was imbued – the ruler of Japan, Yoshimitsu was devoted to Zen and may have been his master – just as the Nō chorus chants were derived from Buddhist prayer chants. (This same restrained hinting at beauty, the essence of the best of Japan, also rules the tea ceremony, the landscaping of Japanese gardens and the *haiku*, all of which reflect the Zen *yugen*, and Japanese flower-arrangement, which began as a 6th century AD ritual offering of flowers to the Buddha.) Zen, a mixture of *Mahayana* Buddhism and *Taoism*, came from China at a time when *The Secret of the Golden Flower* was being written under the influence of *Ch'an*. We will see (p338) that "Golden Flower" (*Chin Hua*) may have hidden the Chinese character for Light (*kuang*), and the flower of the *yugen* was also the Golden Flower, the Light. The "mystery and depth" which the Nō actor was to hint was the inner beauty of the Light, and when a Nō actor caught the *yugen*, he hinted at his character's contact with the "inner beauty and gentleness" of the Light which lay "beneath the surface". In typical Taoist-Zen style, Seami himself hints at the Light in *Kadensho*, calling it "the Flower".[14]

"Our attainment of enlightenment," says a Zen authority, "is something like the reflection of the moon in water. The moon does not get wet, nor is the water cleft apart. Though the light of the moon is vast and immense, it finds a home in water only a foot long and an inch wide. The whole moon and the whole sky find room enough in a single dewdrop, a single drop of water. And just as the moon does not cleave the water apart, so enlightenment does not tear man apart. Just as a dewdrop or drop of water offers no resistance to the moon in heaven, so man offers no obstacle to the full penetration of enlightenment. Height is always the measure of depth. (The higher the object, the deeper will seem its reflection in the water.)"[15]

Satori is "another name for Enlightenment", the famous Daisetzu Suzuki writes, and "Zen devoid of *satori* is like a sun without its light and heat. Zen may lose all its literature, all its monasteries, and all its paraphernalia; but as long as there is *satori* in it, it will survive to eternity.... The life of Zen begins with the opening of *satori*." Zen is "like a great mass of fire; when you approach it, your face is sure to be scorched", and "another name for *satori* is "*ken-sho* meaning 'to see essence or nature', which apparently proves that there is 'seeing' or 'perceiving' in *satori*.... *Satori* is thus a form of perception, an inner perception, which takes place in the most interior part of consciousness.... Zen is like drinking water, for it is by one's self that one knows whether it is warm or cold. The Zen perception being the last term of experience, it cannot be denied by outsiders who have no such experience." Therefore a Zen master can say, "O monks, lo and behold! A most auspicious light is shining with the utmost brilliancy over the great chiliocosm (i.e. world in a thousand forms, multiplicity).... O monks, do you not see the light?"[16]

The whole of Zen, then, is a way to the Light, or, to quote a famous Zen saying, "the practice is enlightenment". And the collections of sayings of the Zen masters are justly called *The Transmission of the Lamp* (AD 1004), *The Five Lamps meeting at the Source* and *The Finger Pointing at the Moon*. It is this practical approach to the Light that has drawn so many contemporary seekers to Zen.

The Zen Light is still very strong in Japan. In the 1960s, for example, Prime Minister Sato, dismayed at the performance of the Japanese economy, booked into a Zen temple for a weekend's reflection. He presumably contemplated economic matters from within the calm of the Light.

22

The Oceanian Light

Before c.20,000 BC, S.E. Asians entered Australia and became the ancestors of the Aborigines, whose shamanism includes the worship of gods such as Bunjil, Baiame and Daramulun.

The *Hunas* or Huns from Mongolia invaded India from Central Asia (beyond the Volga in Russia) soon after AD c.415, and had earlier reached China; they were superb horsemen in the Central Asian Indo-European Kurgan tradition. They seem to have absorbed Tantric Hinduism. Settlement from S.E. Asia continued into the Christian era. The Polynesian Light can thus be seen as a Central Asian export via India and China.[1]

Polynesian Mana, the High Self of Light

The Polynesian religion is supposed to have reached Polynesia (islands in a triangle bounded by Hawaii, Tahiti, Samoa, New Zealand and Easter Island) from India and China via Melanesia (islands from Fiji to New Guinea).[2] There is a strong Indo-European and Tantric element in the Polynesian Creation Myth: all creation came from the union between a Sky Father and Earth Mother.[3] There is also an interiorisation of the Indo-European outlook that we have found in the energy of Tantric Hinduism's *ojas* and Taoism's *ch'i* in both the Melanesian and Polynesian views: all creation is one and is pervaded by a force or power known as *mana* (compare the *Mahayana* Yogacara *manas*), which is beneficial if it is rightly directed. *Mana* had to be kept intact, and so there were certain social taboos (*tapu*); a chief's *mana* affected the *mana* of his people, as did the Pharaoh's Light, and so he could not be approached on pain of death.[4] To preserve the purity of his, and therefore of his people's *mana*, a Hawaiian chief was encouraged to marry his sister. There was a strong shamanism in Polynesia, and initiates wore masks to ward off the spirits who surrounded them. Headhunting, cannibalism and human sacrifice all served to capture another spirit's *mana* and take it into oneself.

The Polynesians lived at a Neolithic cultural level before they were discovered by the West towards the end of the 18th century and although there seems to have been an invasion from South-East Asia AD c.800 (when displaced Polynesian Maoris arrived in New Zealand and worshipped Io) and another invasion from South America (the Andean civilization) c.1100, the Polynesian language was preserved from outside contamination until the middle of the 19th century. Consequently it has preserved the purity of the lore guarded by the Polynesian *kahunas* ("Keepers of the Secret") of Hawaii from AD c.400, and especially the root meanings of symbol words used by Polynesian initiates which were also found in Jewish, Christian and Gnostic writings. This parallelism has led to suggestions that the lore of the *kahunas* contains the original lost Eastern teaching that found its way into all religions, that it is possibly the source from the East of the Druid Trinity, that it was known in Egypt and ancient India, and that it returned to North Africa about the time of Christ and may have influenced the Essenes. (We shall see – on pp398-400 – that the Mandaeans of the 1st century AD saw people as *manas*, divine spirits who longed to return to the Light.) Champions of such a view[5] go so far as to claim that the lore of the *kahunas*, which they call *Huna* (or "Secret") is a system of coded information which passed into all religions as teaching that became garbled over the years.

The main *Huna* teaching as it is found in Hawaii, which Hun ideas may have reached through Indian trading ships, according to the decoding of Max Freedom Long, was the fact of the High Self, which is an intermediary between the praying individual and God, and which has to be presented with *mana* or vital force by the two low selves. The *mana* travels to the High Self up a "ladder of words" (the Goddess *Kundalini* in Tantric Hindu thought). The High Self sends a return flow of purified *mana* down the ladder to the two low selves. This is in fact a beam of the Light which contains revelation. The High Self in fact consists of mirrored Light for it reflects God's Light, and it is the Kingdom of Heaven. Long equates it with the Egyptian *akh* (which he called by the obsolete mistranslated word, *khu*).[6]

The Polynesian religion interiorises the Indo-European Sky Father and Earth Mother, and follows the Tantric Hindu union of Siva and Sakti-Kali and of the Taoist *Yang* and *Yin*, in seeing the High Self as being a pair of selves, a Father and a Mother; an idea that tallies with the Heavenly Father and Earthly Mother of the Essenes. Champions of *Huna* argue that the idea of a Father and a Mother who were part of a High Self was too much for the early Church Fathers, who worshipped not the "Virgin" Mother of the High Self but the "Virgin" Earthly Mother, Mary the Mother of Jesus, as a Virgin.

The *kahunas* used the word *aumakua* ("I-parents") for this composite High Self, and it is possible that this was corrupted to the sacred syllable "aum" or OM. Similarly, the movement of the vital force from the low to High Self may have been corrupted into the movement of *Kundalini* from the base of the spine to the head, although the experience of *Kundalini is* accompanied by waves of physical shivers up the spine. Champions of *Huna* claim that decoding *Huna* opens new depths in Yoga, Hinduism, Buddhism, and sun-worship. To *Huna*, this was always the worship of the Light of the High Self and of the vital force or *mana* in its symbol of life-giving sunshine. Champions of *Huna* claim that it is particularly revealing when applied to the teachings of Jesus: to *Huna*, the Lord's Prayer calms the hates, fears, desires and hurtful feelings of the low self so that it can present vital force to the High Self, and Jesus showed the ladder or "way" to the High Self.

The Easter Island Giants and the Light

How the idea of *mana* applied to Polynesian culture can be vividly seen on Easter Island, which since 1888 has been owned by Chile (which is 2,100 miles away). In addition to the walls of huge blocks of stone which seem to have been a solar observatory and which date from AD c.380, there are over 600 gigantic stone statues (*moai*) which date from c.1100 to 1680. Some 200 of these are faces hewn on the sides of the volcano, and at least 300 had legless trunks that stood on burial monuments (*ahu*) until they were overturned in a civil war. Most of these are faces between 10 and 20 feet high, with long ears, and weigh about 25 tons, and reconstructions show that they were probably manoeuvred by 12 islanders using two wooden logs as levers. They represent important people who were deified on their death: the Easter Island ancestors or priests in their burial places. They have topknots of red tuff, which came from a special quarry quite separate from the rest of the Easter Island stones, so there was clearly great significance in the red crowns on the heads as they face the sun, overlooking the sea.

In fact, they have all directed their *mana* well so that they have achieved their High Selves – these gigantic stone heads are High Selves – and they are therefore illumined in their crown *chakras*. Easter Island shows over 600 spiritual heroes who have achieved illumination, and who like Mandaean *manas* gaze at the Light to which they long to return, which is symbolized in the sun. They can thus also be seen as enlightened Buddhas, and it may be that Buddhism was the strongest Indian influence on the primitive Easter Islanders.[7]

What happened c.1680 to put an end to the sculpting of these giant statues? A legend suggests that Easter Island contained two races, who are still to be found on the island: a "master race" of foreign invaders who arrived from South America c.1100, had long ears, and carved the statues; and a "slave race" of indigenous short-eared Polynesians who were ordered to clear the land of rocks to make it suitable for farming. According to a legend c.1680 the short ears rose and massacred the long ears.[8]

There are two possible explanations for the statues. The giant statues could be *Mahayana* Buddhas with *manas*. The Central Asian Mongolian Huns or *Hunas* who threatened China in the 3rd century BC and destroyed the Buddhist monasteries in India in the 6th century AD, may have absorbed the giant Buddhas of India and brought a modification of the idea to Easter Island AD c.800 or at the latest c.1100, as symbols of men enlightened by Tantrism; or more simply, Indian traders might have brought the idea on their trading ships. In other words, the sculptors came from South-East Asia and influenced pre-Columbian art in Peru. Alternatively, the "long ears" were perhaps South American descendants of the Andean or Mayan cultures, which collapsed suddenly AD c.800, and they brought the idea of giant men illumined by the New World sun-god to Easter Island perhaps taking between 50 and 300 years on carving each giant statue, and created statues that recall pre-Columbian art. In which case perhaps the solar observatory of AD c.380 was New World in conception. What seems certain is that, whether Buddhist or New World in conception, the statues show illumined men.

23

The Chinese Light

"When the Great *Tao* prevailed the whole world was one community. Men of talent and virtue were chosen to lead the people, their words were sincere and they cultivated harmony.... This was called 'the Age of Universality'."

Confucius, *Li Chi*

The history of the Chinese civilization spans 4,600 years. From its first Lung-shan (or Longshan) Culture city c.2600 BC (which was discovered in Shantung or Shandong province in 1990) and from semi-legendary beginnings in the Yu and Hsia dynasties and the early Huang Ho, China progressed to the first archaeologically secure dynasty, the Shang, c.1766-1122 BC.[1]

With northern China so close to Central Asia it is not surprising that there was a shamanistic influence, and the Shang was an intensely religious dynasty whose kings were not war leaders but shamanistic intermediaries between man and the unseen Heaven (*T'ien*) where the Supreme Ruler (*Shang Ti* or *Ti*) dwelt with the royal ancestors. The Shang kingship was sacral and the Shang king, the intermediary between the spirits and the human world, was thought to be descended from God (*Ti*) who ruled the spirits. *Ti* formed part of the posthumous names of the last two

Shang monarchs, and later *huang-ti* was the term for "emperor" *Ti* guaranteed good harvests and was the Chinese civilization's central idea. It is known that in the 14th century a Shang ruler moved his capital to Yin, and tombs suggest a high civilization at this time.[2]

More is known of the Chou dynasty, which flourished from 1122 to 481 BC and included towards the end Confucius (551-479 BC) and Lao-Tze (born c.570 BC), who (according to his biographer c.100 BC) met Confucius and criticised his pride and ambition. The first Chou leaders, whom Confucius so much admired, had a central court round which feudal states lived in orderly stability. After 722 BC revolts broke out and feudalism declined; in fact Chinese society was becoming less stratified and a new elite was thrown up, a *shih* historian-class that mediated between the kings and the common people, and both Confucius and Lao-Tze belonged to this new class. (Lao-Tze was an archivist at the Chou court.) The social changes should be seen as anticipating the coming Ch'in dynasty rather than representing a futureless decline from classical Chou, and this was therefore a time in which the Light was renewed as the *Tao* rather than a period of unabated decline. The Chou decline set in between 481 and 221 BC, which is known as the period of Warring States, and many movements flourished as the states warred, Confucianism and Taoism being the only two movements that have survived. Mencius and other philosophers belong to this late Chou time as a unified China was slowly being born, partly as a result of the changes called for by Confucius and Lao-Tze.

The Indo-European Iranian Light (or Fire) of Zoroaster seems to have spread through India and reached China – Iranian was the language in Chinese Turkestan in the 1st millenium BC – and there was an Indo-European influence on Taoism. The fire-sacrifice to the Sky Father was internalised so that a subtle fire blended Heaven and Earth; it was a Zoroastrian belief that all Heavenly things have earthly counterparts.

The Light is crucial in Taoism although translations have tended to obscure the fact. Although the doctrine of the *Tao* existed earlier, the founder of Taoism is traditionally Lao-Tze or Lao-Tzu, who lived (like Zoroaster, the Buddha and Mahavira) in the 6th century BC. He was born c.570 BC, but there are doubts as to whether he in fact existed, and it has been suggested that his poems, the *Tao Te Ching* ("Book of the Way and its Power", *te* being the power of *Tao* rather than "virtue") were a compilation made in the 3rd century BC. Lao-Tze means "Old Master" or "Old Boy", his real name being Li-poh-yang, and as the arrangement of his poems is as confused as some of the Chinese characters are obscure, there are differing versions in English.

The Light of Tao

The main point to grasp is that the idea *Tao* (Way) can be understood at different levels. It can be the way of one's life (and especially how a King should govern his country), or the way of the universe, or it can have a mystical meaning. In its mystical sense, the *Tao* is a Void out of which all creation came (poems 4,11) and is similar to the Hindu Brahman; it is the One, the unity under the plurality and multiplicity of the universe (poems 14,42), the source of the impersonal, eternal energy (*ch'i*) behind the universe. The aim of life is to live in harmony with the *Tao*, and one will then know old age, which is a reward for living with gentleness.

Tao, then, is the basis for all things without actually having form itself (poems 14,41), it is First Cause that existed "like a preface to God" or prior to God (poem 4). It is the "mother" and "ancestor" of all things (poems 52,4) that existed before heaven and earth (poem 25). It is the "storehouse" (or possibly "shrine") of all things (poem 62). It is "invisible", "inaudible", "vague and elusive" (poems 14.35), it is "everlasting" and "unchangeable" (poems 7,16,25) and it "flows everywhere" like an ocean (poem 34). It is "the great Form" (poem 35) and it is nameless for it is not a concrete, individual thing and it cannot be described in known terms (poems 1,32,37,41). It is Non-Being or *wu* (poems 1,40), and "all things in the world come from being, and being comes from non-being" (poem 40). (Chuang Tzu takes this idea even further back: "There was being. There was non-being before there was being. There was no-non-being before there was non-being. There was no-no-non-being before there was no-non-being.")[3] It is "Subtle" (formless) (poem 14).

The *Tao* is certainly all these things, but in addition it is the mysterious Light which is neither perception nor yet non-perception: "We look at it and do not see it.... Its name is The Subtle (formless).... Going up high, it is not bright, and coming down low, it is not dark. Infinite and boundless..." (poem 14). (Or: "At rising, it does not illumine; at setting, no darkness ensues; it stretches far back to that nameless estate which existed before creation.") In other words, we do not see the Light with our sense-perception, and it does not obey the laws of the sun, but is eternally there.

The Light of *Tao* gives wisdom: "In order to grasp it is necessary first to give. This is called subtle light" (poem 36). Or, "This indeed is Subtle Light." In other words, there is a subtle understanding from the formless Light of *Tao*.

The Light protects from danger. Poem 52 repays close attention: "Close the mouth. Shut the doors" (of cunning and desires or the senses). "And to the end of life there will be (peace) without toil.... Seeing what is small is called enlightenment.... Use the light. Revert to enlightenment. And thereby avoid danger to one's life – this is called practising the eternal." Arthur Waley's translation of the last part is interesting: "He who having used the outer-light can return to the inner-light (*ming*) is thereby preserved from all harm. This is called resorting to the always-so."

The aim of life is to return to the Light of *Tao*: "All things come into being, and I see thereby their return. All things flourish, but each one returns to its root. This return to its root means tranquillity. It is called returning to its destiny. To return to destiny is called the eternal (*Tao*). To know the eternal (i.e. *Tao*) is called enlightenment.... Being in accord with *Tao*, he is everlasting" (poem 16). Other translations substitute for "eternal": "Eternal Law", the "Unchanging", or "constancy". In other words, we came from the Light of *Tao* and we return to it by seeing the Light as we must when we die.

This message is put unforgettably in poem 56, part of which echoes poem 52: "He who knows does not speak. He who speaks does not know. Close the mouth. Shut the doors. Blunt the sharpness. Untie the tangles. Soften the light. Become one with the dusty world. This is called profound identification." (Or: "Let turmoil be subdued. For this is mystic unity.") Stop talking, this poem is saying, and blunt the sharpness of the reason, untie its problems, and soften the light of day to the inner Light and experience mystic union.

Self-knowledge has to be understood within the meaning of this Light: "He who knows others is wise; he who knows himself is enlightened" (poem 33). In other words, to know oneself is to know that one can achieve union within the Light of *Tao.* Thus the "established saying" of poem 41 refers to those who have not discovered the Light within themselves: "The *Tao* which is bright appears to be dark." (This can be translated: "The way (*Tao*) out into the Light often looks dark.")[4]

The Taoist, then, experiences in ecstasy a Reality which cannot be understood with the reason and which has nothing to do with abstract knowledge. He empties his mind and mirrors Heaven and Earth in its underlying Void (the Light), which inhabits his heart once it is cleansed (*hsin chai*). In the *chiao* ("pure") ritual in a Taoist temple, a priest lights an incense burner to symbolise the burning of the Light inside his own body; which he then mirrors as a mediator to the community.The macrocosm of the universe and the microcosm of man obey the same laws, and how one should live was developed by Chuang Tzu (died 275 BC) and Lieh-Tzu, who made Taoism into a philosophy.

Yin and Yang, and the Light

To the Taoist, everything is in a flux, and the kaleidoscopic permutations of the changes are recorded in the very ancient *I Ching* ("Book of Changes"), one of the five classics that Confucius edited and preserved. (Confucius, or Kung Fu Tzu, 551-479 BC, was a contemporary of Lao-Tze but he was not a religious teacher of the Light, rather a teacher of social ethics whose ideas dominated the Chinese educational system for 2000 years; in troubled times he harked back to the "Former Kings", the legendary King Wen and the emperors Yao and Shun of the 24th/23rd century BC, the founders of the Hsia and Shang dynasties, and to the stability of the first Chou ruler, c.1122 BC, whose regional fiefs were subordinate to the central Chou court and not independent of it, and who therefore respected *T'ien*, the power of Heaven.[5] Confucius's system is religious in so far as it regarded the enlightened man as the mediator between Heaven – *T'ien*, which is endowed with consciousness

– and Earth, as when back in the golden age "the Great *Tao* prevailed", and temples to Confucius like the Confucian temple in Peking are memorials to Confucius rather than functioning "churches" and show the tablet of Confucius as their only image.)

The trigrams of the *I Ching* were reputedly discovered by the legendary Fu Hsi (24th or even 29th century BC) on the back of a tortoise shortly after the Huang Ho or Yellow River culture began (c.3000-2500 BC). The hexagrams were formed and written down by Wen Wang in 1143/2 BC[6] shortly after writing was discovered in China, and the appendices were completed some seven hundred years later. The *I Ching* was primarily a work of divination rather than of mystical instruction, and it became increasingly popular as Taoism degenerated into magic, alchemy and divination.

Nevertheless, Taoists saw in it sixty-four possible permutations of the two opposing forces in the Taoist universe, the force of darkness and inactivity, and the force of light and activity, which proceed from the Supreme Ultimate (*T'ai Chi*).

These two forces (which recall the Zoroastrian dualism) are called *Yin* and *Yang* for the first time in the Third Appendix of the *I Ching* (1.32, 4th century BC): "That which is unfathomable in (the movement of) the inactive and active operations is (the presence of a) spiritual (power)." The footnote in the Legge edition says "The 'Spirit' is that of 'God'", but we have seen that *Tao* existed "prior to God" (poem 4).[7] The unfathomable is, again, the formless Light that cannot be perceived with the senses, and if it is true that the *Tao Te Ching* was not compiled until the 3rd century BC, then this Appendix to the *I Ching* may have had a considerable influence on the growth of the idea of the Light of *Tao*. And *Yin* and *Yang* clearly have an illuminative, mystical significance.

Yin and *Yang* are also represented as Heaven (*Yang*) and Earth (*Yin*), with Man in between, a metaphysical triad of the human condition that recalls Man's position between the Heavenly Father and Earthly Mother in the Essene teachings, and which is today shown by the arrangement of three flowers in the Taoist Japanese *ikebana* (flower-arrangement). Man's position between these two forces is symbolized in Taoist art as the sexual act, the union between *Yang* (male) and *Yin* (female), which recalls the Sky Father's fertilising of the Earth Mother in Indo-European times. There are also correspondences with Tantrism as the subtle fire rises. Taoist gardens unite *Yin* (water, e.g. rivers and lakes that reflect the moon) and *Yang* (mountains and rocks).

The Heavenly ruler was *Shang Ti*, the protector and tribal Lord of the Shang dynasty (c.1766-c.1122 BC) who lived in *T'ien* or Heaven, and later *T'ien Ti* of the Chou dynasty (c.1122-221 BC), the power from Heaven that gave the emperors their divine mandate (*T'ien Ming*) to rule. The power of the Heavenly Ruler was the Light. Heaven gave the emperor a mandate to keep harmony between Heaven, the Earth and Man. The Supreme Ruler (*Shang Ti* or *Ti*) dwelt in Heaven (*T'ien*), and the emperor was his representative on earth and joined him on his death, along with his own royal ancestors who sent down the Light of *Tao* to him during his lifetime.

The emperor was Man's representative and as the "Son of Heaven" he humbled himself before Heaven (*T'ien*) and Earth (*Ti*) in Ming times at the altar of the *T'ien T'an* (Temple of Heaven) in Peking, a circular building approached by a long cobbled walk set in a square, for Heaven was considered to be circular and the Earth square.[8] The Ming emperors were divine in the Light. *Ming* means "brightness", and reflects the Manichaean Light[9] which had been introduced to China in the T'ang dynasty (618-907) along with Zoroastrianism, Islam and Nestorian Christianity, and which combined with Taoism and Buddhism to influence the Ming founder, Chu Yuan-chang.

The Later Taoist Light: Tantric Dragon-Fire, the Golden Flower and the Circulation of the Light

As the silk route brought Buddhist and Hindu monks from India to China from the 3rd century BC onwards, Tantric *Mahayana* Buddhism and Hinduism influenced China, and in particular later Taoism: the Neo-Taoism that began in the 3rd and 4th centuries AD when Ko Hsuan and his great-nephew Ko Hung evolved Tantric alchemical techniques in search of immortality.

The Eastward spread from India to China was helped by upheavals which affected the homegrown Chinese religions. After 221 BC the Ch'in and Han dynasties flourished in China, beginning with the Emperor who was buried with a recently discovered army of terracotta soldiers. In 31 BC cults that honoured the Supreme Unity and Lord of the Soil were replaced by Sacrifices to Heaven and Earth. In AD 184 Taoism was suppressed as being responsible for revolutionary messianism that caused political revolts. In China, Buddhism had always had a larger following than Taoism, and from AD 65 the two had become linked. From AD c.100 there was an unsettled period as Han declined. Now there were six dynasties in swift succession, and until c.580 there were barbarian invasions from the North. Then first the Sui and then the T'ang dynasties rose and established central control and great prosperity until c.753. From 755 to 960 there was a decline. There were rebellions and five dynasties followed in quick succession.

The 3rd and 4th century AD alchemical techniques were based on the Light, and were influenced by Tantrism. The Chinese subtle body has *ching*, semen or sexual energy; *ch'i*, the moving vitality which attunes to the *Tao* (to attain which the Taoist artist saw with the eyes of his spirit so that he caught *ch'i*); and *shen*, the luminous personal spirit behind the eyes, the Light. These forces were circulated (like *Kundalini*) round the subtle body in meditation, so that *ching* was raised from its "crucible" at the base of the spine to the top of the head, and brought back down the front of the chest to the sexual organ. From there it circulated again until the energy became "an inner fire" that was symbolized as a dragon (the Chinese version of the *Kundalini* serpent) in later Taoist art.

The *ching* rose and blended with the *ch'i* – this was represented in later Taoist art as the copulation of the Dragon and the Tiger – and the inner light of the *shen* was stirred into a rotation of its own. The Taoist then saw with his inner sight his "face before he was born" (i.e. the Light). The circulation of the *shen* transformed it into the golden elixir (*chin-tan*) or liquefied gold (*chin-i*). This flowed down and joined the fused *ching* and *ch'i*, where the personal merged into the cosmic *ch'i* and *shen* of the *Tao.* Two liquid radiances were produced: one silver or moon, the other gold or the sun. A special saliva then formed in the mouth which was swallowed into the lowest crucible, where it congealed into the Seed of Immortality. It grew into a "crystal child" and rose to the head as an immortal body.

The root of the whole process was therefore the *ching*, the semen or the sexual energy, and this was acquired by stimulating one's own sexual organ or by taking in massive amounts of the energy of the opposite sex (*yin* in the case of a man, *yang* in the case of a woman); for later Taoism held that women secreted essences in sexual intercourse which were absorbed by men, and vice versa. The Taoist often made love without ejaculating, retaining his semen so that it could circulate as inner fire and repair his brain, giving longevity. (Compare the Indian Siva's *lingam*, which never ejaculated because Siva was detached from sensuality.) The whole point of the inner alchemy was that the fire of the heavenly heart (or heart *chakra*) produced light in the mind which led to immortality, but later the imagery tended to be taken literally – the liquid gold was thought of as an edible solution – and a degeneration set in.[10]

The Light of inner alchemy can be found in the Religion of the Golden Elixir of Life, which was founded by Lu Yen or Yu Tung-pin (born c.796). Lu obtained his esoteric lore and Chinese yoga from Kuan Yin-hsi, the Master Yin-hsi of the Han-ku pass for whom Lao-Tze wrote down the *Tao Te Ching.* Lu appears as Lu-Tsu in the Neo-Taoist *The Secret of the Golden Flower* (*T'ai Chin Hua Tsung Chi*), which was written in the 9th century, and he was influenced by *Ch'an.* His movement was persecuted, and he may have hidden the main idea of *Ch'an*, the Light, in the characters for "Golden Flower" (*Chin Hua*), for they can be written one on top of the other, and touching, so that the middle reveals the character for "Light" (*kuang*), which is formed from the lower half of the top character and the upper half of the bottom one.[11] The Religion of the Golden Elixir of Life was influenced by the Iranian Light religion of Manichaeism – in the T'ang period there were many Persian temples in China – or by Gnostics or Nestorian Christians: the Uigers, allies of the Emperor, were Nestorians, and in AD 781 a well-known Nestorian monument was erected in Sianfu.

The Secret of the Golden Flower [12] is a textbook that describes how to circulate the Light, which is known as "the Golden Flower": "That which exists through itself is called the Way (*Tao*). *Tao* has neither name nor shape. It is the one essence, the one primal spirit...contained in the light of heaven. The light of heaven cannot be seen. It is contained in the two eyes.... The Golden Flower is the light.... One uses the Golden Flower as a symbol. It is the true energy of the transcendent great One.... The Golden Flower is the Elixir of Life" (*Chin-tan*, "golden ball", "golden pill"). We must therefore look inwards to discover the Light, for "the heavenly heart lies between sun and moon" (i.e. between the two eyes) in "the square inch field of the square foot house" (i.e. the face), in "the purple hall of the city of jade" (i.e. the topmost gate or crucible which produces *shen*), where dwells the God of Utmost Emptiness and Life.

We must close our eyes and meditate and breathe rhythmically and we then bring the energies of *Tao* into ourselves: "When the light is made to move in a circle, all the energies of heaven and earth, of the light and the dark are crystallised.... Only after concentrated work of a hundred days will the light be genuine, then only will it become spirit-fire. After a hundred days there develops by itself in the midst of the light a point of the true light-pole (*yang*). Then suddenly there develops the seed pearl.... The light is not in the body alone, nor is it only outside the body. Mountains and rivers and the great earth are lit by sun and moon; all that is light. Therefore it is not only within the body. Understanding and clarity, perception and enlightenment, and all movements (of the spirit) are likewise this light; therefore it is not just something outside the body.... As soon as the light is circulating, heaven and earth, mountains and rivers, are all circulating with it at the same time. To concentrate the seed-flower of the human body above in the eyes, that is the great key of the human body. Children, take heed ! If for a day you do not practise meditation, this light streams out, who knows whither? If you only meditate for a quarter of an hour, by it you can do away with the ten thousand *aeons* and a thousand births."

The Light rises in quietness: "If, when there is quiet, the spirit has continuously and uninterruptedly a sense of great joy...it is a sign that the light principle is harmonious in the whole body; then the Golden Flower begins to bud. When, furthermore, all openings are quiet, and the silver moon stands in the middle of heaven, and one has the feeling that this great earth is a world of light and brightness, that is a sign that the body of the heart opens itself to clarity. It is a sign that the Golden Flower is opening. Furthermore, the whole body feels strong and firm.... Rotten and stinking things on earth that come into contact with one breath of the true energy will immediately live again.... The fragile body of the flesh is sheer gold and diamonds. That is a sign that the Golden Flower is crystallised."

The illumination, the opening of the Golden Flower, recalls the beautiful descriptions of the Egyptian *Book of the Dead*: "At times the following can be experienced: as soon as one is quiet, the light of the eyes begins to blaze up, so that everything before one becomes quite bright as if one were in a cloud. If one opens one's eyes and seeks the body, it is not to be found any more.... Or when one sits in meditation, the fleshly body becomes quite shining like silk or jade." The self is freed from the conflict of opposites and the spirit rises to become part of the one *Tao*. "At the third watch the sun's disc sends out blinding rays.... When the rotating light shines towards what is within...the energy of the dark is fixed, and the Golden Flower shines concentratedly....Related things attract each other. Thus the polarised light-line of the Abysmal presses upward.... It is creative light which meets creative light. As soon as these two substances meet each other, they unite inseparably, and there develops an unceasing life.... One is aware of effulgence and infinity. The whole body feels light.... This is the return of the one light, the time when the child comes to life.... The heavenly heart rises to the summit of the Creative,...it demands the deepest silence.... Not a single thought arises; he who is looking inward suddenly forgets that he is looking.... The crystallised spirit goes into the space of energy. The One is the circulation of the light." The condition of all this is calm: "As long as the heart has not attained absolute tranquillity, it cannot move itself."

The Golden Flower, then, is finally an immortal spirit-body of light (*shen*) which returns to the immortal *Tao*. Light reunites with light, and the hiddenness of the secret Light of the Religion of the Golden Elixir of Life is summed up in a parable by the Sung Su Tung-p'o (1036-1101): "There was a man born blind. He had never seen the sun and asked about it of people who could see. Someone told him, 'The sun's shape is like a brass tray.' The blind man struck the brass tray and heard its sound. Later when he heard the sound of a bell, he thought it was the sun. Again someone told him, 'The sunlight is like that of a candle,' and the blind man felt the candle, and thought that was the sun's shape. Later he felt a (big) key and thought it was a sun. The sun is quite different from a bell or a key, but the blind man cannot tell their difference because he has never seen the sun. The truth (*Tao*) is harder to see than the sun, and when people do not know it they are exactly like the blind man."[13]

The Sung dynasty rose from 960 to 1085 but entered a decline until c.1206 under pressure from the Manchurian Juchen, and the decline deepened from 1211 to 1368 with the Mongol conquest of China under the Yuan dynasty of Genghis Khan and his grandson Kublai Khan (Coleridge's "Kubla Khan"). The Mongols had a shamanistic cult of Heaven and Nature, but during their occupation of China they allowed religious freedom. However, Taoism and Buddhism declined into badly organised popular religions.

From 1368 to 1571 the *Ming* ("Brightness") shone out from a strong central government. Eventually the *Ming* went into decline – the last Ming emperor did not believe in his own divinity – and from soon after 1550 there were raids from Japan and from the Manchurian Manchus (descendants of the Manchurian Juchen) who flourished in the Ch'ing dynasty c.1640 to 1796, in the course of which there was peace for 100 years.

Recent Light

In Taoism there was one notable contribution to the Light in the flourishing Ch'ing of 1794. *The Book of Consciousness and Life (Hui Ming Ching)* by the monk Liu Hua-yang was printed with the first published version of *The Secret of the Golden Flower* in 1921. It has a lot to say about the Light: "If you would complete the diamond body with no outflowing, diligently heat the roots of consciousness and life. Kindle light in the blessed country ever close at hand.... One must diligently fill oneself with light.... The thousand-petalled lotus flower opens, transformed through breath-energy.... A halo of light surrounds the world of the law.... The emptiness is irradiated by the light of the heart and of heaven.... Consciousness reverts to contemplation; the moon-disc rests alone."[14]

The Ch'ing dynasty declined from 1796 to 1911, after which there were internal uprisings and wars with the West (Britain and France). Centralisation was restored under Mao's Communists in 1949, and although religion has been suppressed, and the Christian missionaries expelled, as in the case of Russia the persecution seems to have had the unintended effect of keeping the Light alive.

Today the Taoist Light survives on Taiwan. Taoist temples symbolise the Light when the priest lights an incense burner to symbolise the Light in his own body, which he mirrors to the community.

However Taiwan is now better known for its impressive displays of *ch'i* (life energy) by the Taiwanese magic acrobats than for its *shen* (Light): following a tradition that goes back to 200 BC the Taiwanese acrobats defy gravity (draw up a heavy jar with an outstretched hand or lie in midair, supported only by the blade of a sword between the shoulders) and withstand pain (smash bricks with their hand, endure bricks being smashed over their head, hammer six-inch nails into wood with their forehead, and bend steel rods with their neck). They marshal an energy akin to the Tibetan *Tummo* or "psychic heat" which numbs the senses and makes possible fire-walking across red hot cinders without pain being felt or any blemish being left on the skin.

24

The Tibetan Light

As we have seen (pp23-25), Bon-po was the indigenous religion of Central Asian Tibet. This shamanic religion dominated Tibet before recorded history c.25,000 BC.

The Tantric Buddhist Light: Tibetan Buddhism, One Mind, the Clear Light of the Void

As Tantrism,[1] whose coiled, serpentine symbols adorned caves in Palaeolithic Europe c.20,000 BC, the Bon knowledge taught the existence of seven *chakras* or centres of energy in the spirit or subtle body, up which the female (Sakti) *Kundalini* energy that is coiled at the base of the spine rises to unite with Siva in the crown of the head; and sexual rituals (*maithuna*) which, as in Taoism, symbolise enlightenment. As Tantrism, the Bon knowledge entered Hinduism in the 5th century AD and Buddhism in the 8th century.[2]

Tantrism spread from India to Tibet, and to the temples and monasteries of Lhasa, between the 6th and 11th centuries. Tibetan Buddhism was a synthesis of *Mahayana* (the Madhyamika and Yogacara Schools) and Vajrayana (Tantric Buddhism), the monasticism of early Theravadic Buddhism and the Tibetan Bon religion.[3]

The Indian Buddhist missionaries in Tibet were so impressed by the Bon magicians that they absorbed the Bon religion – hence the Tantric *mandalas* of Tibetan Buddhism, hence the Dalai Lama was a reincarnation of the Sky-god,[4] and hence Tibet's soothsaying oracular priests. In the 8th and 9th centuries there was a struggle in Tibet between the pro-Buddhist rulers and the pro-Bon noble families, and although Bon was persecuted by the 8th century King Khri-srong-Ide-brtsan, it survived and is still practised in North East Tibet.

The Tibetan Light was revealed through eight Tibetan Buddhist sects which grew up between the 11th and 14th centuries.

The *Rning-ma-pa* (or *Ningmapa*, "Old Order") Sect was founded in 749 by the 8th Century Indian *Tantric* Master Padmasambhava who brought Tantric Buddhism from India to Tibet in 747 (just as Bodhidharma took the *Dhyana* School to China in 527). Padmasambhava transmitted the wisdom he had acquired in India, Burma, Afghanistan and Nepal in his work *The Yoga of Knowing the Mind, the Seeing of Reality, called Self-Liberation* in which the Mind is the One Mind or the Light and *Nirvana* is the Light. [5]

"All Hail to the One Mind", Padmasambhava wrote, "that embraces the whole *Sangsara* and *Sangsara* and *Nirvuna*.... that although ever clear and ever *Sangsara* and *Nirvana*... that although ever clear and ever existing, is not visible, that although radiant and unobscured, is not recognised....These teachings... will also be sought after by ordinary individuals, who, not knowing the One Mind, do not know themselves.... Others...having become fettered by desires, cannot perceive the Clear Light."

This One Mind, knowledge of which gives self-liberation, is timeless, "non-created and self-radiant" and "of the Voidness", yet "has in reality been shining forever, like the Sun's essentiality", and one's own mind is "of the Clear Light of the Voidness", "this self-originated Clear Light" which is "Natural Wisdom" and "Total Reality". "This changeless Great Light", which was originally an Indian perception, "is of the unique Clear Wisdom, here set forth, which, illuminating the Three Times (i.e. the past, present, and future), is called 'The Light'." One should "look into the True State, wherein self-cognition, self-knowledge, self-illumination shine resplendently. These, so shining, are called 'The *Bodhisattvic* (i.e.

enlightened) Mind'. To Them who have passed away into *Nirvana*, this Mind is both beginningless and endless.... Unless one sees the Buddha in one's mind, *Nirvana* is obscured. Although the Wisdom of *Nirvana* and the Ignorance of *Sangsara* illusorily appear to be two things, they cannot truly be differentiated.... The whole visible Universe also symbolises the One Mind.... For the sake of future generations who shall be born during the Age of Darkness (*Kali yuga*), these essential aphorisms...were written down in accordance with Tantric teachings." Thus, the True State or One Mind, *Nirvana* or Voidness (or Pure Reality), shines unceasingly like the sun.

The *Bka'-brgyud-pa* ("Transmitted Command") or *Kargyutpa* ("White Line of *Gurus*") sect separated from Padmasambhava's Rning-ma-pa as a result of a 12th century reform movement. It transmitted esoteric Buddhist teachings that go back to the 1st century AD Indian Saraha and his disciple Nagarjuna. These were handed down from the first *Kargyutpa guru*, Dorje-Chang to Tilopa (middle of the 10th century), who passed them on to his disciple Naropa. The *Kargyutpa* sect emphasised the breathing exercises of Hatha Yoga. The *Six Teachings* – techniques for attaining enlightenment both before and after death – are a Yogini or Sakti *Tantra* that goes back to Lawapa of Urgyan (or Odyana, Afghanistan). This was brought to Tibet in the 8th century by Padmasambhava, who came from Urgyan, and compiled by Naropa's disciple Marpa, and his successor, the poet and mystic Mi-la Ras-pa or Milarepa.

The *Six Teachings or Six Doctrines*[6] add to Padmasambhava's treatment of the Clear Light (*Hod-gsal* or *Od-Sal*), the colourless Light of pure *Nirvanic* consciousness which, apparently everyone momentarily experiences at the moment of death – hence Goethe's descriptive "more light" – and which masters can experience in *samadhi* at will. This Clear Light, which is the mystic radiance and which marks the attainment of Buddhahood as well as the Voidness from which creation takes place is hard to know *after* death, in the Bardo state between death and rebirth, and so the purpose of life is to know it during one's present life.

The fourth teaching or doctrine, the *Yoga of the Clear Light*, presents the way to the Clear Light during waking ("the day time") as a negative way: "The identification (or realization of the Clear Light) is to be attained in the interval between the cessation of one thought and the birth of the next thought. The Clear Light is made use of on the Path by practising the Six Rules of Tilopa. They are: 'Imagine not, think not, analyse not, meditate not, reflect not, keep in the Natural State.' "

The Clear Light can be known during the "deep sleep" ("during the night-time") and "after death" when (the *Yoga of the After Death State* says) "the Primal Clear Light dawns", and "the recognising of the Clear Light is to be accomplished in the interval between the cessation of consciousness in this world and the arising of consciousness in the after-death state", when the inner landscape is like "an autumn sky without a cloud".

The art of dying is to die seeing the Clear Light, "free of thought-forming" and merging "into the natural state of quiescence": "By abiding in the state of the Clear Light as long as desired and then rising out of it in the body of the Divine United Clear Lights...and transferring the consciousness through the Aperture of Brahma, on the crown on the head, one who is adept (in the yoga of consciousness-transference) passes into the Buddha State of Complete Enlightenment). One who is weaker in the practice becomes a Holder of the Dorje in some one of the tenth-degree states (of the highest celestial *bodhisattvas*)."

In other words, by seeing the Clear Light during death, one can become a Buddha rather than a *bodhisattva.* However, "inability to recognise the Clear Light" after death is a state of ignorance, when a light inferior to the Clear Light is seen: "The resultant light dawns; the Greatly Void (or vastness of the Voidness) is experienced." After death there is a state of "unconsciousness (or swoon) for a period of three and one-half days", after which "the deceased coming to know that he is dead, feels great sadness (or regret at having died)". He must then unite Compassion and the Voidness and place himself "in the state of the Clear Light".

The Tibetan *Book of the Dead* is a commentary on the part of the earlier *Six Teachings* that deals with the Yoga of the After-Death State and the Clear Light.[7] It was written down in the time of Padmasambhava in the 8th century AD, and rediscovered by a successor of Marpa and Milarepa, Rigzin Karma Ling-pa, who began the Karma-pa sect. It is superficially about the Art of Dying, and in particular the art of dying while looking at the "Clear

Light of the Void" – "clear" because it is "colourless", for the "Formless" is colourless – and the text which was to be read over a dying person or near a dead body by a lama describes the 49 days a deceased spends in an intermediary state (*Bardo*) between death and rebirth. (The figure 49 has an esoteric significance, being a multiple of 7.) Just before death the prayer is: "O nobly born, the time has now come for you to seek the Path (in reality). Your breathing is about to cease. The *guru* has set you face to face before with the Clear Light; and now you are about to experience it in its Reality in the *Bardo* state, wherein all things are like the void and cloudless sky."[8]

On death, the deceased "swoons" for three and a half days, during which empiric consciousness of objects disappears, unveiling Pure Consciousness, and he sees the Clear Light "for up to a meal-time period": "When the expiration has ceased, the vital-force will have sunk into the nerve-centre of wisdom and the Knower will be experiencing the Clear Light of the natural condition (or state)."

If he has already reached enlightenment and has already unveiled the Clear Light so that he is ready for Liberation, then he immediately recognises the Clear Light and becomes *dharmakaya*, or a Buddha in his cosmic body who has Perfect Enlightenment, and is identified with the blue god Samanta-Bhadra.

In the case of a lama the prayer is: "Reverend Sir, now you are experiencing the Fundamental Clear Light, try to abide in that state which now you are experiencing." In the case of anyone else, the prayer is: "O nobly born, listen. Now you are experiencing the Radiance of the Clear Light of Pure Reality. Recognise it.... Your own consciousness, shining, void and inseparable from the Great Body of Radiance, has no birth, nor death, and is the Immutable Light – Buddha *Amitabha*."

The conscious recognition of the Clear Light induces an ecstatic condition of consciousness (*samadhi*) "such as saints and mystics of the West have called Illumination".[9] By recognising the boundless Light of the Void as the true Reality of his self, and surrendering all attachment to his ego, he is liberated from the cycle of rebirth. This experience of the primary Clear Light may follow only a "snap of the fingers" after death.

If the deceased does not recognise the Clear Light – and lamas maintained that "comprehension of the nature of the Clear Light is quite impossible for the unilluminated"[10] – then the secondary Clear Light dawns, karmically obscured, "in somewhat more than a mealtime period" after death, and the dead person will wonder "Am I dead, or am I not dead?" If the deceased does not recognise the secondary Clear Light, he is definitely not ready to be liberated, and he is under the illusion that he still possesses a body, and the karmic illusions begin: "sounds, lights and rays" which "awe, frighten and terrify". On successive days, dazzling lights drive the impure deceased towards dim (white, green, yellow, blue, red and smoke) lights, and if he develops an overwhelming desire to possess a body and becomes fond of any one of these dull lights, and becomes attached to it, he will be drawn into the world it represents (gods, titans, humans, brutes, ghosts or Hell). In that case he is reborn, and there is no Liberation.

On the other hand, if he resists any one of these dim lights, he achieves a degree of Buddhahood in the Realm set aside for each light and acquires a rainbow halo. A Peaceful Deity dawns each day, and there is a succession of Buddhas and *bodhisattvas* in radiant light, the first of which is the dazzling blue of the *Dhyani* ("meditation") Buddha *Vairocana* (Sanskrit for "The Illuminator"), the Thatness of the Void, the Manifester of Phenomena; who is often identified with Samanta-Bhadra. Each Peaceful Deity represents the conquest of a vice (bondage, anger, egoism, lust, envy).

After the fifth day the lights become less and less divine, the deceased sinks deeper and deeper into the lights of the lower nature, and the Peaceful Deities give way to the Wrathful Deities, visions which personify reasonings rather than sublime human feelings. After the fourteenth day the After-Death dream slowly exhausts itself and rebirth will follow, though there is first a Judgement before Dharma-Raja (Tibetan) or Yama-Raja (Theravadists), a figure so like Osiris of the Egyptian *Book of the Dead* that it has been suggested the two works have "a common source, at present unknown".[11]

The Light of the Tibetan *Book of the Dead*, like the Light of the *Six Teachings*, was to be experienced by the living as well as the dying. The Wrathful Deities and the Judgement after death could be avoided if the deceased recognised the Clear Light, and he could only do this, we have seen, if he had already experienced the Light in this life. And so initiates were trained to experience the Clear Light through Yoga and Tantrism, and thereby escape the light-path cycle of rebirth after death. The *Tibetan Book of the Dead*, was itself used as a manual to instruct initiates who sought the Clear Light. It resembles the Egyptian *Book of the Dead* in being a guide-book to illumination that is couched in the language of the after-death state – the "Clear Light" had the same place for Tibetan initiates that Amon-Ra had for the Egyptian "Shining Ones" – and just as the Egyptian *Book of the Dead* is really "the Book of the Great Awakening", so the Tibetan *Bardo Thodol* means "Liberation by Hearing on the After-Death Plane". In other words, the liberation from rebirth followed a *hearing* about the Clear Light from a lama. Death and rebirth can thus be interpreted to mean an awakening and a new consciousness, and the deceased can represent an initiate.

It has been ingeniously suggested[12] that the esotericism of the *Tibetan Book of the Dead* lies in the fact that initiates read it backwards. Reading backwards an initiate passed the terrifying God of Death (the destroyer of the ego); then the goddesses who were thought-forms from himself (28 "power-holding" and sinister goddesses and 58 "blood-drinking" goddesses who are shown in terms of the coloured lights and light-paths); and then the green, red, yellow and white lights of the gods of the Four Wisdoms. He reached the dazzling blue light of the Dharma-Dhatu, the Buddha-body which is also the glorious blue light of the Dhyani-Buddha Vairocana, the Thatness of the Void. Then, the karmic illusions ceased and attachments were forgotten, and the Clear Light of the Void could be experienced.

Thus, illumination comes at the end as a goal, rather than at the beginning, and it follows an ascent from confusion rather than anticipates a descent into confusion. The original intention of the *Bardo Thodol* was that it should be read as a descent after death, everyone is agreed on that. The reversal of the order of the chapters "in no way accords with the original intention, though it was "possibly sanctioned by lamaistic custom",[13] and it is by no means certain that as a primer of Illumination it was read as an ascent. But no matter how initiates used the text, the Clear Light was Reality, and in so far as that was the goal, the way down and the way up were the same.

The Tantric Buddhist Light appeared in other Tibetan Buddhist sects. The Sa-skya-pa sect (based on a monastery of the same name, which was founded in 1073) saw the Light as a characteristic of mind (*sems*, Sanskrit *citta*). The Gcod-pa sect grew out of an Indian sect in the 11th century AD and arrived at the Light of the Void by eliminating the thoughts, which prevented the Light from being seen. These thoughts were symbolized as demons. The Bka'-gdams-pa sect (11th-15th centuries AD) also eliminated thoughts so that the Light of *sunyata* (the Void) could be seen, and this sect was absorbed into the Dge-lugs-pa sect (14th-15th centuries AD), which asserted that the mind is light, that each person is a luminous energy, that light is the nature of mind (*sems*). This is the sect of the Dalai Lama. The Jo-nang-pa sect, based on a monastery which was founded in the 14th century AD, saw Reality as a luminous mind element, the *tathagata-garbha* ("Matrix of the Buddhas").[14]

MANDALAS

It is worth noting that *mandalas* (Sanskrit *mandala*, "circle"), the more pictorial form of *yantra* or sacred diagram in Tantric Buddhism (and Hinduism), represent the Light. The *mandala* originated in the ancient Tibetan Bon-po religion. The Bon-po masters constructed *mdos*, or symbolical representations of the world, and identified themselves with the gods outside the circle. They became Reality, and were able to control the forces in the universe.

When interpreted correctly, *mandalas* take the yogin step by step to Enlightenment. They should be followed clockwise like the sun, and they start from the East. Since they were originally drawn in the dust in front of a meditator, East is the point nearest him and is South on a compass; thus the left side of the *mandala* is South, the right hand side North, and the top West. All *mandalas* are based on the dome-shaped *stupa* at Sanchi, India (2nd-1st century BC), a stone monument that enshrined some relics of the Buddha. It is surrounded by a stone railing and has four open gates which open to the four quarters of the universe. These gates symbolise the openness of Buddhism, and the Vajrayana *mandalas* show a square temple with four open gates round an inner circle. Worship at the *stupa* involved walking round it from East to West, and following the course of the sun. When the *stupa* design developed into the multi-storied pagoda of Peshawar, India (2nd century AD), on which the pagodas of China, Korea and Japan were based, the principle of following the sun was preserved; and the worshipper remembered that "as the sun illuminates the physical world, so does the Enlightened One illuminate the spiritual world".[15]

At another level, the Eastern gate represented the Buddha's birth, the Northern gate his *Parinirvana.* Each gate had a presiding Dhyani-Buddha and colour, and Vairocana, the total of all the Wisdoms, occupied the centre. There are three protective circles outside the gates of a *mandala*: an outer circle of flames, known as a Mountain of Fire (*me ri*), which bars entry to the uninitiated and burns ignorance; a middle one of diamonds (*vajras*), which stands for illumination and the creation of a new spiritual body, the "Diamond Body" (*vajra-kaya*); and an inner one of lotus petals representing spiritual rebirth. The meditator moves inwards from the many to the One, and the five innermost circles within the gates contain at the centre an image of the One Light. For *mandalas* share with *Tantras* the aim of teaching "ways whereby we may set free the divine light which is mysteriously present and shining in each of us, although it is enveloped in an insidious web of psyche's weaving".[16]

25

The Central Asian Light

The Central Asian culture began c.50,000 BC, as we have seen (p18). Recorded history did not begin until c.3500-3000 BC, and although in a sense the Central Asian shamanistic Light is the oldest of them all, Central Asian historical records did not really begin until the *Hsiung-nu* or Huns, c.500 BC onwards.[1]

As we saw on pp18-23, the Central Asians received the Light from Altaic shamanism around 500 BC, and the Mongolians migrated as the *Hsiung-nu* in the 4th century BC.[2] During their many migrations they took with them the Light of *Huna*, evidence for which can be found in Hawaii as we saw when considering the Oceanian Light. We have seen that the Easter Island giants may be Hun-inspired (pp325-329), a restating of the giant Buddhas of India.

The Huns of Attila ravaged Europe in the 5th century AD and sacked the Roman Empire. According to legend, for which there is some historical evidence, soon afterwards the *Hsiung-nu* confederation was overthrown by the Orkhon Turks, who ruled until the rise of the Mongol Khitan. They controlled north China and established a Chinese dynasty (907-1125). However, their homeland was in Manchuria rather than present Mongolia, which was ruled by "All the Mongols". The Juchen, who took the name Chin ("Golden"), succeeded the Khitan in China and supported the Tatars against "All the Mongols". Genghis Khan, ruler of "All the Mongols" challenged both the Juchen-Chin and the Tatars. He sacked Peking in 1215. By 1279 the Mongols controlled the whole Chinese empire, which was ruled by Genghis's successor, Kublai Khan (Coleridge's Kubla Khan). By now contact with China and Tibet had strengthened Buddhism among the Mongols, and a successor, Altan Khan, conferred the Mongolian title "Dalai" on a Tibetan prelate, who became the first Dalai Lama. The Mongolians soon adopted Tibetan Buddhism.[3]

Besides its own tradition of the Light, Central Asia has been deeply influenced by Tibetan Buddhism; see 'The Tibetan Light' (pp343-351). In more recent times Central Asia has shared the Tibetan Buddhist Light of Tibet. In that sense, its Light is one of the more recent.

• • •

THE LIGHT IN ANCIENT CULTURES

The Light of all cultures has a common origin in Central Asia. In our consideration of the Tradition of the Light we must appreciate that it spread simultaneously into several geographical regions and that civilizations have a common culture of the Light although different ancient religions reacted to it in different ways and accorded it different gods.

It has to be said that the simple rural peasant cultures of the East kept the Light alive through religions which transmitted it from one generation and century to another so successfully that today we think of the East as a place of spiritual power, despite the material backwardness of some of the Eastern countries. The shivers of *prana* up the spine felt in *Kundalini* Yoga are realities that are widely taken for granted in the East today, whereas the equivalent shivers of spirit during contemplation before and during Mass, such as (according to contemporary accounts) St Teresa evidently knew, are not the general rule at increasingly secularized European church services.

Enough has been said to establish our theme, that in all these originally primitive and ancient cultures the Light (or Fire) had a central importance as it dominated their ideas, attitudes, values, ideals, traditions, beliefs, customs, rituals, religious ceremonies, technology and works of art. In fact, as we have seen, the Light-based rituals and religious ceremonies were at the heart of the common social life and coloured the cultures' attitudes, values and ideals; or created their traditions, beliefs and customs. The King represented the god of the religion and transmitted the mystic Light in social ceremonies. As all the people shared the rituals and sacred ceremonies, the Light, which shone from the beyond and was known within by all, was fundamental to each primitive and ancient culture.

The cave-paintings of the Palaeolithic shamans, the ceremonies on the *ziggurats*, the initiation ceremonies in the Great Pyramid, the symbolic sun-worship in the Cyclopean megaliths, the Indo-European fire-sacrifices in Greece, Iran and India, the bull rituals of the Cretan priest-kings, the Eleusinian mysteries with their ear of corn, the Bacchic frenzies and Greek Oracle, the Druid rituals in the sacred oak-groves, the ceremonies for Mithras and Attis, the Hindu rituals for Agni and later the Atman, the Buddhist ceremonies that put out the fire of desire, the Jain ceremonies and the Chinese ceremonies that honoured the *Tao* – all had a tremendous influence on the cultures of the Mediterranean, Europe, the Near East, India, the Far East and the Americas in primitive and ancient times. All these sun-cults and fire-cults show that these early cultures and civilizations were *inspired* by the Light, which through symbols and ceremonies gave meaning to the everyday life of all who shared its common, unifying metaphysical vision.

It is clear that once the knowledge was known, it was carried from one culture to another (see the chart on pp534-535), and what was known in one culture at a particular time was probably known in most, if not all of the other cultures at that time. The megalithic sun-worshippers must be seen alongside the worshippers of Ra and *akhs*; the Indo-European Sky Father and Earth Mother must be seen alongside the Sumerian Royal Sacred Marriage; and the Indo-European and Druid fire-cults must be seen alongside Zoroastrian and Hindu fire-sacrifices, Agni, Ahura Mazda and Brahman. When the Light was known in several cultures at a particular time, and there were extensive trade routes, it is inconceivable that it was totally unknown in other cultures which appear to have worshipped the sun and fire at that same time.

We shall see in the companion volume to this book that the first ten Lights' religions, and the religion of no. 14, are defunct. If there rites are still occasionally celebrated then they are kept going as cults and are part of the occult – the hidden, heretical knowledge that is quite separate from the living religions of the remaining fourteen Lights.

But whether their religions are defunct or still living, the gods of the ancient world have to be seen in relation to each other and not in isolation. What is certain is that after 2600 BC, there was a flow of recorded tradition about the Light which preserved the knowledge from the past for each generation to rediscover and experience afresh.

We have established that all the religions are based on the Light, which is interpreted differently in different religions. We shall be seeing in the companion volume to this book that civilizations decline when the Light dims. As there is intense interest in Western civilization, it is important to take a closer look at the Light in a subtradition of the European and North American civilizations – on the margins of European and American Christianity – to consider more fully, and in greater depth, to what extent the Christian Light is dimming because of defections to the subtradition, and whether part of the coalition that is Western civilization is in decline.

We shall see in the companion volume to this book that the first ten Lights' religions, and the religion of no. 14, are defunct. If their rites are still occasionally celebrated then they are kept going as cults and are part of the occult – the hidden, heretical knowledge that is quite separate from the living religions of the remaining fourteen Lights.

But whether their religions are defunct or still living, the gods of the ancient world have to be seen in relation to each other and not in isolation. What is certain is that after 2000 BC there was a flow of recorded tradition about the Light which preserved the knowledge from the past for each generation to rediscover and experience afresh.

We have established that all the religions are based on the Light, which is interpreted differently in different religions. We shall be seeing in the companion volume to this book that civilizations decline when the Light dims. As this is now the situation in Western civilization, it is important to take a closer look at the Light in a subtradition of the European and North American civilizations – on the margins of European and American civilizations – to consider more fully and in greater depth, to what extent the Christian Light is dimming because of defections to the subtradition, and why part of the civilization that is Western civilization is in decline.

Part Three

Subtradition: The Heretical Light In Western Civilization

The aim of the *Tantras* is to teach the ways whereby we may set free the divine light which is mysteriously present and shining in each one of us, although it is enveloped in an insidious web of the psyche's weaving.

Guiseppe Tucci, *The Theory and Practice of the Mandala*

In all the traditions we have been examining there was a mainstream religion and a subtradition of sects that was influenced from outside and was regarded as heretical. Because of the domination of Western civilization, which is a combination of the European and North American traditions (nos. 11 and 12), in this Part we are taking a look at the subtradition that has had such an influence on the European tradition's mainstream but which has always remained separate, opposed by the mainstream and often suppressed as heretical.

In "The European Light" (no. 11) we have stated the pure mystic tradition of the Light within Christianity. Alongside this pure tradition, co-existing with it, feeding it and sometimes merging with it, is a subtradition that is less mainstream, more disputed, apocryphal, even heretical. This subtradition is outside mainstream Christianity and sometimes borders on the occult. The occult was hidden because it was unacceptable to the Church; the Cathars and Templars, for example, had a high regard for Lucifer/Satan. This subtradition is open to foreign influences (Gnosticism, Neoplatonism and Sufism for example), which dilute the Christian Light.

As we are investigating the dimming of the European Light it is important that we should take account of this subtradition for it helps to explain why at certain times in the history of Western civilization, including the present, the Christian Light has not shone as purely as at other times. This subtradition also gives a clear indication of the rival thinking and philosophies that Europe's religion had to contend with as it kept awareness of the Christian Light alive.

The European Light, then, has been stated in no. 11. What follows are the accretions that gathered round it over two thousand years, which enable us to measure the strength, or weakness, of the mainstream Light in each century by taking account of the challenges to it by mystics operating within a subtradition outside the mainstream.

1

THE ESSENE LIGHT

This subtradition begins with the Essenes as there is a tradition that Christ was an Essene. The Essenes were part of the Israelite religion and Light (no. 8) but always remained outside the mainstream as a sect.[1] The Essene sect influenced Christianity, which also began as a sect before influencing the mainstream religion of the European tradition. As this influence is somewhat speculative and may be legendary rather than historical, it is best dealt with under the European subtradition rather than in the mainstream Israelite or European traditions.

Against a Roman background the Jewish Essenes emerged in the 2nd century BC.[2] Jonathan and then Simon Maccabeus usurped the office of high priest in Jerusalem and used their secular authority to persecute their opponents, who included the Essenes. Now deemed heretics, the Essenes fled into the wilderness and, called themselves "the Children of Light", and they lived in natural surroundings, on the edge of Lake Mareotis in Egypt – where they were called *Therapeutae* or healers (from which came our words "therapy" and "therapeutic") – and by the Dead Sea in Palestine, where they established a monastic community in the caves near Qumran, studying the scriptures and storing their Dead Sea Scrolls in clay jars, until the centre was destroyed by Vespasian's Roman legions in AD 68. They knew "the One" through Nature, and their angels (which derived from Babylon) were cosmic energies whose power they harnessed. They lived according to natural therapy, having inherited the Egyptian art of healing along with Chaldean astronomy, and were brilliant agriculturalists who had a vast knowledge of crops and soil conditions. They were very learned, and flourished until the 1st century AD, when the Jews were dispersed by the Romans.

From the portraits of Josephus, Philo of Alexandria, Pliny the Elder and Solanius, we know that they lived in quasi-monastic communities, generally without women, and that they shared all their property; they observed the Sabbath but did not worship at the Temple in Jerusalem, believed in immortality and divine punishment, and awaited a divine Messiah in the desert. There were only about four thousand Essenes in Pliny's day, and Pliny described them as "a race by themselves, more remarkable than any other in the world".[3]

Central Asian Origin of the Essene Teaching

The Essenes were "the oldest of the initiates, receiving their teaching from Central Asia" according to Philo of Alexandria.[4] They preserved this teaching in a pure form and it passed into Christianity, so that Bishop Eusebius, writing in the 3rd century AD, could say, "The ancient Therapeutae were Christians and their ancient writings were our gospels and epistles."[5] The Essenes can be linked to the Central Asian Bon region and Tibet through Esses (Jesus), the "wonder-worker" who according to an ancient Bon book[6] visited north Tibet. We shall see (pp374-376) that he may have been the Esses (or Eshe or Isa) who preached in Persia in the 1st century AD. If the Essene teaching did originate in the Tibetan region it is possible that their Heavenly Father and Earthly Mother were a refinement of the Indo-European Kurgan Sky Father and Earth Mother (or *Magna Mater*).[7]

It is certain that the Essenes had existed for a very long time, perhaps under another name, before they became known as "Essenes" in the 2nd century BC. They were reputedly called Essenes because they claimed descent from Esnoch (or Enoch), "the Founder of Our Brotherhood" and subject of an ancient Essene text called *The Vision of Enoch*, or from Esrael (or Israel), the elect of the people to whom Moses gave the Communions at

Mount Sinai in the 14th-13th century BC (*Exodus* 18.21-6).[8] Moses had a great influence on Essene thought – there is an Essene *Book of Moses* – for he taught "the Law" or *Torah*, deviation from which caused all suffering, and the Essenes were very strict followers of "the Law".

There is also a strong Zoroastrian influence as a result of the exile of the Jews in Babylon from 587/6 to 538 BC. The Judaistic Light went through a great change when it came unto contact with the Iranian Light during the Babylonian exile. Chaldean Babylon had been conquered by the Persian Cyrus the Great, and the Jews of the southern kingdom of Judah, lamenting their exile "by the waters of Babylon", absorbed the Iranian monotheism of Ahura Mazda and a hierarchy of Babylonian angels.[9] (All the angels with proper names derive from Babylon.) The Jews opened themselves to the Iranian dualism of Light and Darkness, to the Iranian Satan (Ahriman), to guardian angels and spirit forms, not to mention the astronomy of the Magi, and brought back home a more deeply monotheistic outlook.[10]

Enoch's God as Fire

The Jewish work that transmitted these ideas was the *First Book of Enoch*,[11] which is a compilation written at different times between the 3rd and 1st centuries BC, though parts may be older than that. The only extant version is an Ethiopic translation of a Greek translation of the original Hebrew or Aramaic, and it concerns the esoteric journeys and visions of Enoch, the seventh patriarch of *Genesis*, who was later thought to have been given secret knowledge by God.

This tradition is partly Babylonian, for Enoch was associated with the Babylonian myth about the seventh antediluvian King, Enmenduranna,[12] who was given divine revelation by the sun-god. It is also partly Biblical, for "Enoch walked with God: and he was not; for God took him" (*Genesis* 5.24). This was the famous "translation" (in the religious sense of the word) during which Enoch was "raised aloft" to join "the Son of Man" and "the Lord of Spirits" or "Head of Days" in Heaven; an episode that derives partly from the "Wise Lord", Ahura Mazda, but mainly from the "Son of Man" in Daniel's vision (7.13), who "came with the clouds of heaven" to "the Ancient of days". (The *Book of Daniel* dates to the 2nd century BC and relates to Antiochus IV's persecution of the Jews, not to the exile in Babylon.)

In an earlier vision of the Head of Days, Enoch says that he saw a "house of fire", and that his "spirit was transfigured". In another vision from the oldest part of the book, Enoch entered Heaven which was a house "built of flames of fire", and saw God as Fire: from underneath the lofty throne of God "came streams of flaming fire so that I could not look thereon. And the Great Glory sat thereon, and His raiment shone more brightly than the sun." Elsewhere, the angels of light were "like flaming fire", and the Lord of Spirits "caused His light to appear" to the righteous.

Teachings of the Essene Children of Light: Enoch's 14 Communions

The literature of the Essenes transmitted the Light. It comprises: *The Gospel of Peace of Jesus Christ by the disciple John* concerning the healing works of Jesus (a fragment of a 1st century AD Aramaic manuscript which seems to contain the pure, original words of Jesus in the language both he and St John spoke, and can therefore claim to be an uncorrupted version of the teachings of Christ before they were garbled into their *New Testament* form towards the end of the 1st century AD); a number of Essene scriptures from *Enoch* and *Moses* to Jesus and the *Essene Revelations*, and some scrolls, most of which were found at the buried Essene library at Qumran.[13]

The esoteric teachings of the Essenes are a collection of texts within these works concerning the Essene Communions with the Angels, the Tree of Life and the Sevenfold Peace, in all of which the Essenes are seen as "Children of Light". The Light was transmitted by the Essene Master – it seems that Jesus was such a Master – and its secret had to be guarded, so that an Essene swore as part of his Sevenfold Vow to "obey with reverence my Master who gives me the Light of the Great Masters of all times", and "to keep secret all the traditions of our Brotherhood which my Master will tell me". And so in the Essene Sermon on the Mount, Jesus says, "And the Children of Light shall guard and preserve their written word" (Essene *Book of Jesus*).

The Essene mission was to perpetuate the Light, and the *Prologue to their Worship* required them to recite: "When God saw that his people would perish because they did not see the Light of Life, he chose the best of Israel, so that they might make the Light of Life to shine before the sons of men, and those chosen were called Essenes." The Essene worship used the terms "Heavenly Father" and "Kingdom of God" which Jesus uses in the *New Testament* (e.g. Brothers: "We will build the Kingdom of God with the Power of the Heavenly Father"). It is important to grasp that the goal of all Essenes was union with the Heavenly Father, who was also the Creator, the Light, and Ahura Mazda of Zoroastrianism (via Babylon). They therefore sought union with the One Law, the cosmic ocean of life and thought in the universe.[14]

The Heavenly Father was the One of the powers and forces of the invisible or unseen realms, and the Friday evening Communion with Him began: "The Heavenly Father and I are One." Conversely, the Earthly Mother, or Mother Earth (*Magna Mater*), was the One of the powers and forces of the visible or seen realm of Nature. As in Zoroastrianism, all Heavenly things have earthly counterparts which are filled with spiritual power.

There were fourteen Essene Communions, seven with the Angels or forces of the Heavenly Father and seven with the Angels or forces of the Earthly Mother, and in *The Communions* man's relationship to these Angels or forces and to his "parents" is seen by Jesus in terms of the Tree of Life. Man is the trunk, the ground is his Earthly Mother, the roots are the Angels or forces of his Earthly Mother; the stars are his Heavenly Father, and the branches are the Angels or forces of the Heavenly Father. The Earthly Mother's six Angels (to be contemplated in the morning) are the Angels or forces of the Sun, Water, Air, Earth, Life and Joy, while the Heavenly Father's six Angels (to be contemplated in the evening) are the Angels or forces of Power, Love, Wisdom, Eternal Life, Work and Peace.

"The morning sun encircled his head with glory" as Jesus said: "My children, know you not that the Earth and all that dwells therein is but a reflection of the Kingdom of the Heavenly Father?" In other words, the seen is a Platonic reflection of the unseen, of "the Sea of Eternity" in which the sacred Tree of Life stands and from which flow the "healing waters" of the Angel or force of Love, by which "we know the Children of Light". The seen is therefore a reflection of the Light which is unseen by the five senses.

Jesus urges the multitude to grasp this now: "Do not wait for death to reveal the great mystery; if you know not your Heavenly Father while your feet tread the dusty soil, there shall be naught but shadows for thee in the life that is to come. Here and now is the mystery revealed. Here and now is the curtain lifted.... Lay hold of the wings of the Angel of Eternal Life, and soar into...the endless Light." The force of Eternal Life of course proceeds from the One, as Jesus makes clear in a very Zoroastrian passage: "Who, O Great Creator! is the fountain of Eternal Life within our souls? Who hath made the Light and the Darkness?"

The fourteen Communions are said to have originated with Esnoch (or Enoch), and to have appeared on the first of the two stone tablets, which, according to the Essene *Book of Moses*, Moses brought down from Mount Sinai and gave to Esrael, the elect of the people. (The Ten Commandments were on the second tablet.) They were thus very much a part of the Mosaic Law to the Essenes, and the Sevenfold Peace (which is in the Essene *Book of Jesus*) is a result of being in harmony with the Law (the One). The seven peaces (to be contemplated at noon) are, Jesus says: peace with the Body, the Mind, the Brotherhood, Mankind, the Wisdom of the Ages, the Kingdom of the Earthly Mother and the Kingdom of the Heavenly Father

In the Essene *Book of Jesus* Jesus goes up "into a mountain" and addresses his disciples and "all those who hungered for his words": "Like the hollow blackness of a window when the wind puts out its candle is the body alone, with no heart and mind to fill it with Light. And the heart alone is a sun with no earth to shine upon, a light in the void." Jesus uses a Platonic image to describe the body as a chariot, the heart as a "fiery steed", and the mind as the driver, and then passes to a succession of beatitudes of Light, for the Essene Sermon on the Mount is a sermon on Light:

"Blessed is the Child of Light who is strong in body, for he shall have oneness with the earth.... Blessed is the Child of Light who is wise in mind, for he shall create Heaven.... As the sheaf of golden wheat lieth hidden within the tiny kernel, so is the Kingdom of Heaven hidden within our thoughts.... Neither can evil thoughts abide in a mind filled with the Light of the Law.... Blessed is the Child of the Light who is pure of heart, for he shall see God.... Blessed is the Child of Light who doth build on earth the Kingdom of Heaven, for he shall dwell in both worlds.... Thou, Child of Light, do ye gather with thy brothers and then go ye forth to teach the ways of the law to those who would hear. He who hath found peace with the brotherhood of man hath made himself the co-worker of God.... Blessed is the Child of Light who doth study the Book of the Law, for he shall be as a candle in the dark of the night.... Beyond the icy peaks of struggle lies the peace and beauty of the Infinite Garden of Knowledge, where the meaning of the Law is made known to the Children of Light.... He who hath found peace with the teachings of the Ancients, through the light of the mind, through the light of nature, and through the study of the Holy Word, hath entered the cloud-filled" (compare the cloud that covered the Tabernacle) "Hall of the Ancients.... Blessed is the Child of Light who knoweth his Earthly Mother, for she is the giver of life.... Blessed is the Child of Light who doth seek his Heavenly Father, for he shall have eternal life.... From the beginning until the ending of time doth the holy flame of love encircle the heads of the Heavenly Father and the Children of Light: how then can it be extinguished? For not as a candle doth it burn, nor yet as a fire raging in the forest. Lo, it burneth with the flame of Eternal Light, and that flame cannot be consumed.... He is covered with Light as with a garment.... If we say the Heavenly Father dwelleth within us, then are the heavens ashamed; if we say he dwelleth without us, it is a falsehood.... Only this do we know: we are his children, and he is our Father. He is our God.... He who hath found peace with his Heavenly Father hath entered the Sanctuary of the Holy Law and hath made a covenant with God which shall endure for ever.... May the Sevenfold Peace of the Heavenly Father be with thee always."

The logic of this Sermon is unmistakable: we are Children of Light because God is a Father of Light, the Peace is a Peace of Light, and the law of the Heavenly Father is a Law of Light. Therefore, in the words of Essene fragments that are identical with a Dead Sea Scroll, "The law was planted in the garden of the Brotherhood to enlighten the heart of man" and "the Law was planted to reward the Children of Light with healing and abundant peace... with eternal joy in immortality of eternal Light" (from the *Manual of Discipline of the Dead Sea Scrolls*).

The Endless Light and the Law

This inner vision of Eternal Light is celebrated in *The Book of Hymns of the Dead Sea Scrolls* and also at the end of *The Essene Book of Revelations* (the texts are identical): "I have reached the inner vision and through Thy spirit in me I have heard Thy wondrous secret. Through Thy mystic insight thou has caused a spring of knowledge to well up within me, a fountain of power, pouring forth living waters, a flood of love and of all-embracing wisdom like the splendour of eternal Light."

Some of the lost scrolls expand on the One Light, which can be experienced by Children of Light: "The people that walked in darkness shall see a great Light, and they that dwell in the land of the shadow of death, upon them shall shine the Light of the Holy Law.... The Law is the best of all good for the Children of Light" (*Angel of Joy*); "What is the Deed well done? It is that done by the Children of Light who regard the Law as before all other things" (*Angel of Power*); "What is the thought well thought? It is that which the Child of Light thinketh, the one who holdeth the Holy Thought to be the most value of all things else" (*Angel of Wisdom*); "He who, to obtain the treasures of the material world, destroyeth in him the world of the Law, such an one shall possess neither force of life, nor the Law, neither Celestial Light. But he who walks with the Angels and who follows the Holy Law, he shall obtain everything good: he shall enter the Eternal Sea...converting the soul from darkness to light" (*The Holy Law*).

"The Law was planted in the Garden of the Brotherhood to illumine the hearts of the Children of Light.... The Children of Light are the servants of the Law, and the Heavenly Father shall not forget them.... He hath lit the candle of Truth within their hearts.... The Heavenly Father hath kindled his flame in the hearts of the Children of Light" and "purifieth the followers of the Light" while "the fourth step that the Child of Light did make, placed him in the Endless Light (*The Brotherhood*). Again, "the Angel of Light" is invoked (*Stars*) and thanks are given "unto the Lord Of Light" (*Psalms of Praise and Thanksgiving*).

The Essene Light demands that we take a fresh look at the *Bible*, and there are some interesting comparisons to be made. In the Essene *Book of Moses*, one of the oldest of the Essene documents, Yahweh "called unto Moses out of the mountain, saying, Come unto me, for I would give thee the Law for thy people, which shall be a covenant for the Children of Light". (Compare *Exodus* 19.) Later Yahweh says "I am the Law" (not Lord) "thy God.... Thou shalt have no other Laws before me." God originally tells Moses, "Honour thy Earthly Mother, that thy days may be long upon the land, and honour thy Heavenly Father, that eternal life be thine in the heavens," but he then recognises that "only the Children of Light can keep the Commandments of the Law" and so he gives "another Law", "a stern law" (the Ten Commandments, which include "Honour thy father and mother") "for they know not yet the Kingdom of Light".

The beginning of the Lord's Prayer echoes the noon peace contemplations, which begin "Our Father who art in heaven (i.e. Heavenly Father, Ahura Mazda), send to all your Angel of Peace". "Thy will be done on earth as it is in Heaven" refers to the Earthly Mother, to whom there was a parallel prayer: "Our Mother which art upon earth, hallowed be thy name, Thy kingdom come, and thy will be done in us, as it is in thee. As thou sendest every day thy angels, send them to us also. Forgive us our sins, as we atone all our sins against thee. And lead us not into sickness, but deliver us from all evil, for thine is the earth, the body and the health."[15]

The Law of the Heavenly Father, the Light, is why "the kingdom of heaven is like unto a merchant man, seeking goodly pearls; who, when he had found one pearl of great price, went and sold all that he had and bought it (*Matthew* 13. 45-6): "My children, only the kingdom of heaven within thee, where the Law of thy Heavenly Father doth dwell, doth belong to thee.... And if this one precious pearl be thine forever, why dost thou barter it for pebbles and stones?" (The Essene *Book of the Teacher of Righteousness*).

The Essene *Gospel of John* begins "In the beginning was the Law" (not Word), "and the Law was with God, and the Law was God," which makes the *Logos* comprehensible. Instead of saying that he was a "man sent from God...to bear witness of the Light, that all men through him might believe" and that he himself "was not that Light" (verses 6-8 of the *New Testament Gospel*), John says: "From the far place in the desert came the Brothers, to bear witness of the Light, that all men through them might walk in the light of the Holy Law. For the true light doth illumine every man that cometh into the world, but the world knoweth it not. But as many as do receive the Law, to them is given the power to become the Sons of God, and to enter the Eternal Sea where standeth the Tree of Light. In the same Essene Gospel Jesus explains the "born again" passage: "Verily, verily, I say unto thee, except a man be born of the Earthly Mother and the Heavenly Father, and walk with the Angels of the Day and the Night, he cannot enter into the Eternal Kingdom." Jesus was clearly irritated (as was God in the presence of Moses) at man's preference for darkness as opposed to Light, and he complains: "Man is born to walk with the Angels, but instead he doth search for jewels in the mud. To him hath the Heavenly Father bestowed his inheritance, that he should build the Kingdom of Heaven on earth, but man hath turned his back on his Father, and doth worship the world and its idols. And this is the condemnation, that Light is come into the world, and men loved darkness rather than Light, because their deeds were evil. For every one that doeth evil hateth the Light, neither cometh to the Light."

In *The Gospel of Peace* John deals with natural healing by the forces of Angels of water, sun and air, and makes it clear that to Jesus, diseases were caused by sin, and that the cure was therefore to stop sinning, for sinlessness meant living in healthy harmony with the One Law. After the cleansing of the body by natural healing, the Light should come, Jesus says, but he again recognises that man is too used to darkness to receive the Light: "I am sent to you by the Father, that I may make the Light of life to shine before you. The Light lightens itself and the darkness, but the darkness knows only itself, and knows not the Light. I have many things to say to you, but you cannot bear (sic) them yet. For your eyes are used to the darkness, and the full Light of the Heavenly Father would make you blind. Therefore you cannot yet understand that which I speak to you concerning the Heavenly Father who sent me to you. Follow, therefore, first only the laws of your Earthly Mother, of which I have told you. And when her angels have cleansed and renewed your bodies and strengthened your eyes, you will be able to bear the Light of our Heavenly Father. When you can gaze on the brightness of the noonday sun with unflinching eyes, you can then look upon the blinding Light of your Heavenly Father, which is a thousand times brighter than the brightness of a thousand suns. But how should you look upon the blinding Light of your Heavenly Father, when you cannot even bear the shining of the blazing sun? Believe me, the sun is as the flame of a candle beside the sun of truth of the Heavenly Father."

The dazzling brightness of the Light is taken up in the Essene *Book of Revelations.* There are thirteen seats round the throne of the Heavenly Father in the "sea of blazing light" and "blinding ocean of radiance" which is Heaven, one for each Angel and one for the Earthly Mother; and the seven seals on the Heavenly Father's book are opened by the Angels of the Earthly Mother, who opens the seventh seal herself.

Enough has been said to suggest that Jesus may have been an Essene Master (which is how he appears in the Essene Gospels), along with Elijah, John the Baptist and John the Beloved. This possibility may account for the tradition that (like Plato) Jesus went to Egypt, where the Essene *Therapeutae* lived by Lake Mareotis, and became an initiate at the Temple of Isis at On, Heliopolis, and danced with his Apostles. Hence the existence of paintings in the Vatican which show Jesus dancing, for the Essene Brotherhood used sacred music and dancing to raise the soul to communion with the Angels, just as the Egyptian temple-dancers used music and dancing to raise their souls to the level of *akhs.* It is therefore possible that Jesus was linked with an Egyptian temple in the course of his training as a potential Essene Master, and it is fascinating to think that Jesus may have studied the Egyptian *Book of the Dead* in the course of becoming an *akh* and opening his soul to the Essene Light.

The Two Essene Messiahs and the Reason for the Crucifixion

Comparing the Essene Light and the Synoptic Light offers a fresh approach to the historical Jesus; it confirms that the Light was central to his teaching and parables, and it brings his message vividly alive for us today. It also solves problems. In particular, it makes clear how a fundamental misunderstanding about the nature of the Messiah led to Jesus's crucifixion.

We have observed that Jesus seems to have taught within the Essene tradition. According to the *Dead Sea Scrolls*, the Essene tradition expected two Messiahs: a priest Messiah (of the House of Moses' brother Aaron) and a King Messiah (of the royal House of David); a spiritual one who would be "the Son of Man" (the Judge of the world from *Daniel* and 1 *Enoch*) and a political one who would be "the Son of God". The two Messiahs would parallel the two Essene Kingdoms of the Heavenly Father and Earthly Mother.[16]

This Essene tradition of a spiritual, as opposed to a political, Messiah was probably anticipated in *1 Enoch*, which seems to contain Essene elements. In this work, sin is traced back to angels who fell when committing sexual misdeeds with the daughters of men (the 200 on Mount Hermon we have linked with the Anannage in the Sumerian tradition), and Enoch intercedes for them and is shown in dreams the archangels, *Sheol* (the ancient Israelite Hell) and Heaven, and the Tree of Life, and the Apocalyptist argues that the cause of sin must be eliminated before righteousness can return. Celibacy and the after-life feature strongly, themes which appear in the works of the Essenes. There are references to the "Son of Man", a phrase which is echoed in the possibly later *Book of Daniel*. They anticipate a mystical and heavenly, apocalyptic Messiah who would descend to save his people, rather than the traditional, political Messiah who was "Son of David" or "Son of God", the title of the anointed sacral King of Israel.

No fragments of the main part of *1 Enoch* have so far been discovered among the *Dead Sea Scrolls*, and it has been suggested that *1 Enoch* was written in the 2nd century AD by a Christian who wrote the "Son of Man" passages after the death of Christ and wanted to give his thoughts the authority of Enoch. However, if *1 Enoch* is in fact a Jewish work dating from the 3rd century BC and if the Messianistic passages were in fact written between 165 and 161 BC, then it clearly provided the context for the Essenes' spiritual Messianism and had an enormous influence on the *New Testament* as it adds an apocalyptic interpretation to the *Daniel* text that is behind Jesus's replies to Caiaphas in the *New Testament*.

Jesus does not appear to have thought of himself as the spiritual Messiah until his meeting with Caiaphas, and the references to the "Son of Man" in the *New Testament* before then are either corrupt texts added by the Church, or eschatological and apocalyptic texts referring to the last Judgement, and Jesus is not explicitly identified with that. How then according to the Essene *Gospels* did an Essene Master come to be crucified as "the Messiah" (the political "anointed one", or *Christos* in Greek, "the Christ")?

First, the Master became an itinerant preacher with twelve disciples, and in the Essene *Gospel of Peace* the phrase he uses, the "Son of Man", appears on nearly every page to mean "man" rather than the Messiah. For example, "when the Son of Man resists the Satan" (Hebrew "enemy") "that dwells in him and docs not his will, in the same hour are found the Mother's angels there.... For no man can serve two masters. For either he serves Beelzebub (i.e. "Baal") and his devils or else he serves our Earthly Mother and her angels."

Secondly, Jesus proclaimed a message which owed much to John the Baptist, that the Kingdom of Heaven (the Light) could be known here and now, and that since God was Heavenly Father (or *Abba*, meaning "Daddy"), then he, Jesus, like all Sons of Men and Children of Light, was a "Son of God" (*Mark* 1.1).

To Jesus, this title "Son of God" expressed an intimate relationship with the Light, but it had a political connotation for the Romans and the Jews as the King of Israel was "the Son of God"; for to the Zealots, the anti-Roman liberation movement of the day, the "Son of God" or royal Messiah would be the King of Free Israel, and therefore an anti-Roman political leader.[17] The Jewish Sadducean establishment collaborated with the Romans to the disgust of the nationalistic rank and file, and when Jesus entered

Jerusalem to challenge the Sadducees and warn Jerusalem of its impending destruction (a prophecy that was fulfilled shortly afterwards) he was seen as a political leader. Jesus regarded himself as the King of a spiritual Kingdom, the Kingdom of Heaven, when Caiaphas asked him if he was the Biblical and political Messiah ("Christ").

It is worth comparing the answers Jesus gives to Caiaphas in the *Gospels*. In *Matthew* 26.63 Jesus is asked if he is "the Christ, the Son of God", and he replies, "Thou has said: nevertheless, I say unto you, hereafter shall ye see the Son of Man sitting in the right hand of power, and coming in the clouds of heaven." In *Mark* 14.62 (written AD c.65, the earliest version) Jesus is asked "Art thou the Christ, the Son of the Blessed?" and he replies "I am; and ye shall see the Son of man sitting on the right hand of power, and coming in the clouds of heaven." In *Luke* 22.67 Jesus is asked "Art thou then the Christ (i.e. the Messiah)?" and he replies, "If I tell you, ye will not believe: and if I also ask you, ye will not answer me, nor let me go. Hereafter shall the Son of man sit on the right hand of the power of God." He is asked "Art thou then the son of God?" He replies, "ye say that I am." There is no conversation with Caiaphas in *John*, but in *John* 18.34 Jesus is asked by Pilate, "Art thou the King of the Jews?" Jesus replies, "Sayest thou this thing of thyself, or did others tell it of thee?.... My kingdom is not of this world.... Thou sayest that I am a king."

Only in *Mark* is he not evasive, and even here some commentators prefer the reading "You say that I am" in place of "I am".[18] Otherwise Jesus is inclined to say "The 'Messiah' is your term, not mine" and nowhere does he actually admit to being the spiritual Messiah, the "Son of Man", although he clearly prophesies the coming of the apolcalyptic Judge of the world from *Daniel* and *1 Enoch*, the spiritual Messiah the Essenes awaited.

In a disputed text in *Mark*, then, Jesus claimed to be the spiritual Messiah, but in the other Gospels he merely supported the Essene tradition, admitting to being neither the spiritual nor the political Messiah. Likewise he had refused to be trapped into criticising Tiberius Caesar when shown the tribute money ("Render therefore unto Caesar the things which are Caesar's; and unto God the things that are God's"). Nevertheless, his replies to Caiaphas led the Sadducees to understand him politically (perhaps to misunderstand him deliberately) and hand him over to the Romans, probably as the leader of an armed band of Jewish rebels; and Jesus was crucified under a notice that mocked him with a political title: King of the Jews.

Neither the Essene nor the Synoptic *Gospels* explain what happened to Jesus between his appearance in the temple at the age of twelve in AD 8 (*Luke* 2.42) and his baptism in AD 26 by the probably Essene John the Baptist ("a burning and shining light", *John* 5.35) at the age of "about thirty" (Luke 3.23); or where he might have studied to obtain the understanding that produced the parables concerning Light. It is possible (as we have already seen) that he spent some of these missing years in the Essene Brotherhood.

Jesus in Kashmir?

An alternative, additional theory, which does not contradict the Essene connection, is that one "Isa", or "Esses" (Jesus), according to a Tibetan manuscript, travelled to Kashmir at the age of thirteen and studied the Vedas under Hindu priests, and then the Buddhist *Sutras*, before returning to Jerusalem via Persia, where, according to some evidence, he attacked the dualism of the Magi. He could then have contacted the Essenes.

An ancient Bon book says: "The wonder worker Esses then came to the land of Shanshun-Mar (north Tibet)". Esses is shown as one of the supreme Bon gods in sacred *thankas.* Did this Esses give his name to the Essenes, who were linked with Central Asia? Another passage describes how a teacher Esses (or Eshe) preached in Persia in the 1st century AD. Was this Esses Jesus, and did he visit Tibet in the course of his visit to India? We have seen (p361) that the Christian historian of the 3rd century AD, Bishop Eusebius, says, "The ancient *Therapeutae* (i.e. Essenes) were Christians and their ancient writings were our gospels and epistles."

This speculative theory has been fascinatingly developed in a book[19] which argues that Jesus was influenced by the example of the Buddha, the "Enlightened One", into calling himself the "Light of the World", and which quotes a little known letter from Pilate to Tiberius (who was presumably at

Capri). In it Pilate sympathises with Jesus, who engagingly preached "leaning against the trunk of a tree". In view of the obvious interest of the letter if it is genuine I quote it in full:

"To Tiberius Caesar.

A young man appeared in Galilee and, in the name of God who sent him, preached a new law, humility. At first I thought that his intention was to stir up a revolt among the people against the Romans. My suspicions were soon dispelled. Jesus of Nazareth spoke more as a friend of the Romans than as a friend of the Jews.

One day I observed a young man among a group of people, leaning against the trunk of a tree and speaking quietly to the crowd that surrounded him.They told me that he was Jesus. This was obvious because of the great difference between him and those around him. His fair hair and beard gave him a divine appearance. He was about thirty years old, and never before had I seen such a pleasant, kind face. What a vast difference there was between him, with his fair complexion, and those, wearing black beards, who were listening to him. As I did not want to disturb him, I went on my way telling my secretary, however, to join the group and listen.

Later my secretary told me that he had never read in the works of the philosophers anything that could be compared with the teachings of Jesus, and that he was neither leading the people astray nor an agitator. That is why we decided to protect him. He was free to act, to talk, and to call a gathering of people. This unlimited liberty provoked the Jews, who were indignant; it did not upset the poor but it irritated the rich and powerful. Later I wrote a letter to Jesus asking for an interview at the Forum. He came. When the Nazarene appeared I was taking my morning stroll, and looking at him, I was transfixed. My feet seemed fettered with iron chains to the marble floor; I was trembling all over as a guilty person would, although he was calm. Without moving, I appraised this exceptional man for some time. There was nothing unpleasant about his appearance or character. In his presence I felt a profound respect for him. I told him that he had an aura around him and his personality had an infectious simplicity that set him above the present-day philosophers and masters. He made a deep impression on all of us, owing to his pleasant manner, simplicity, humility and love. These, worthy sovereign, are the deeds that concern Jesus of Nazareth, and I have taken time to inform you in detail about this affair. My opinion is that a man who is capable to turning water into wine, who heals the sick, who resuscitates the dead and calms rough seas is not guilty of a criminal act. As others have said, we must admit that he is really the son of God.

Your obedient servant,
Pontius Pilate."

The letter, is in the Vatican library in Rome and copies of it can be acquired at the Library of Congress in Washington, but despite the vivid, eye-witness picture of Jesus AD c.28 with fair hair and a beard, it may be an early Christian forgery as Pilate seems to accept the miracles very readily.

The Kashmir claim is that Pilate crucified Jesus to appease the mob, but arranged for him to be taken to the tomb alive, as the bloodstains on the Turin Shroud, it can be argued, confirm.[20] Jesus then fled back to Kashmir where there was a Jewish community and where he lived to a ripe old age. He was buried there, and his tomb is now a shrine of the Ahmadiyya Movement.

There is no space to consider this theory here in full, but while it has obvious attractions in linking the Essenes and their Central Asian source, and Buddhism and Christianity, it must be said that the parables concerning Light contain very few hints of the Fire of Brahman or of the Buddha's fire of craving, and that the Kingdom of Heaven and the ideal of neighbourly love are rather in the Judaistic-Essene tradition than in the tradition of India or Tibet. So far as our picture of Jesus as a preacher is concerned, we do not need Jesus to be Isa; and the Essene Jesus fits the historical view better than a Buddhist Jesus.

2

The British Druid Light

There is another heretical tradition (which can be reconciled with the Essene tradition) that Jesus spent some of his missing years on another fringe of the Roman Empire, Britain, where he absorbed the Druid Light.

Legendary Origins of the Druid Light

The Druid Light is evidently very ancient. It is claimed that Druidism was founded in shamanistic Asia in 3903 BC (a very precise, astronomically calculated date) by the Egyptian Seth who murdered Osiris, and that the Druids were the shamanistic originators of early Mediterranean civilization and the builders of the megaliths; in which case the Druids inspired the Kurgans.[1]

There is a strong Levitical strain in Druidism, and there are claims that it may have been the original Hebrew religion from Canaan, the region of Mount Hermon.[2] It will be helpful at this point to recall the history of Israel. The Shemites (Shem was the son of Noah) became "Hebrews" ("Colonisers") after Abraham's exodus, and Jacob, Abraham's grandson, formed 12 tribes, ten named after each of his own ten sons, and two named after his son Joseph's sons. The 10 northern tribes revolted under the tribe of Ephraim, the descendants of the son of Joseph, and in 922 BC Israel divided into two kingdoms: the northern kingdom of Israel whose capital eventually became Samaria, and the southern kingdom of Judah whose capital was Jerusalem. We have seen that the emblem for Israel was the white bull (later corrupted to a unicorn) and for Judah a lion.

The Assyrians (whose descendants may be the modern Kurds) overran Israel in 721 BC, and the tribe of Ephraim and the other nine northern tribes became the Lost Ten Tribes of Israel. The southern kingdom of Judah was overrun by the Babylonians in 587/6 BC, when the Temple was destroyed and many Jews (as the people of Judah were known) were in exile in Babylon until 538 BC. Then the Persians conquered Babylonia and the Magi found their way to Babylon, and the Jews were allowed to return.

Tradition, which may be mixed with legend, has it that many of the northern Israelites found their way to Britain. The Israelites were known as the Kymri, pronounced K'Omri, the people of King Omri who founded Samaria in 880/879 BC, and these became the Welsh Cymri. There are claims that the word was corrupted into the Greek Kimmerioi or Cimmerians, their land became Crimea, and they came to be known as Keltoi or Celts. The Black Obelisk of Shalmaneser III in the British Museum shows the son of Omri, Jehu, on his knees, paying tribute to the Assyrian ruler. The Cimmerians believed in the One invisible God of the Hebrews and in the coming of a Messiah, as did the Hebrews, and they carried the Ark of the Covenant in their processions as did their forefathers in Israel. When they settled in the Isles of the West (Britain) the Kymri became the "British": in the ancient Hebrew language that co-existed with old Cymric *B'rith* means "covenant" and *ish* "man" or "woman", so "the British" were "the people with whom Yahweh had made a Covenant".

According to tradition the Ephraimites were known as the "sons of Isaac", and there are claims that this was corrupted to *I-Saccasuns, I-Saksuna, Sakasuna, Saksens* and finally Saxons. The Angles, or *Engles*, were called "God-men" by contemporary worshippers of stone idols (*Engles* meaning "God-men" in their language), and they, and the Frisians and Jutes, along with the Saxons, all seem to have originated in the northern kingdom of Israel, where they were first led by Ephraim.

Before the division between north and south, the Levites were in service to the official priestly sect across the whole of Israel, in 48 cities

(*Numbers* 35. 1-8). Moses gave the official priestly functions to his brother Aaron and his descendants, and he gave special priestly functions to Levi, Jacob's third son, and his descendants because they had slaughtered the idolators who worshipped the golden calf (*Exodus* 35. 25-9). The Levites received no land like the other 12 tribes; "the sacrifices of the Lord God of Israel made by fire are their inheritance" (*Joshua* 13.14).

Some of these Levitical servants who served Ephraim in Israel seem to have become Celts. It seems that a branch of this unofficial priesthood of the Levites established "The Truth" ("Druid"), which was brought to Britain along with their patriarchal structure and the white bull of Israel, which became the Druid emblem.[3]

There is a legend that Hu Gadarn Hysicion (or Hu the Mighty, son of Isaac), an Egyptian Hebrew who was nearly a contemporary of Abraham, led the first colony of Cymri (Welsh) into Britain from Defrobane (on the site of Istanbul) and established "The Truth" in Britain, and ever since the Druid battlecry and motto has been "*Y givir erbyn y byd*" ("The Truth against the World").[4] The name Hu (*Khu*) is Egyptian and was used of the Sphinx ("Protector") and as a "son of Isaac" he sounds like an Ephraimite, but Hu's personal role is uncertain as he is also credited with founding Stonehenge. Stonehenge I is now considered to have been founded c.3000-2500 BC rather than c.1800 BC (the time of Abraham); this was closer to the founding of Stonehenge III, which was probably a Light-temple. Was Hu an Ephraimite who joined the Indo-European Kurgans of the Battle-Axe culture who knew of Utu-Shamash, and brought the Levitical religion of the early Hebrew patriarchs to Britain soon after c.2000?

It is possible that Egyptian Hebrews came to Britain after the bondage, when the Levites had been in existence some while (after c.1200 BC), and it is possible that an advance guard left in Jacob's day – Jacob and his sons, including Levi, moved to Egypt – and brought the Egyptian knowledge which is perhaps preserved on the inside of the Chalice Well in Glastonbury, a Druid centre. There are certainly links between the Druids and the ancient Hebrews, and the Druid term for the stone cairns of megalithic times, *si'uns*, recalls the Hebrew "Zion" ("fortress" or "mount of stone").

The prehistoric poets of Greece were certainly shamans, and there have been claims that they were Druids as their names suggest: Musaeus ("knowledge"), Orpheus ("the harp") and Linus ("the white-robed"). Metre was the Druid vehicle of instruction, and if the early Greek poets were Celtic Druids in touch with Britain, then Plato was right in claiming that Greek philosophy originated in the "fountains of the West".

Besides the claims that Hu Gadarn founded the Druid order as we know it, c.1800 BC, there have been claims that an Aed Mawr founded it c.1000 BC, that the Celtic King was a Druid of Truth, that the Order influenced Orphism, and that Pythagoras was a Druid: the Druids taught the Orphic-Pythagorean concept that "souls do not disappear, but wander from one body to another". It is claimed that the Druid Bull celebrates the fact that Druidism was founded in Taurus. (Another story is that Hu Gadarn's standard showed an ox.) Later, it is claimed, the symbol became the thing signified, and the widespread Neolithic bull-worship of the ancient world which was linked with the moon was immediately Druid in origin. The Tauric Chersonese (the Crimea), Mithras in Persia, Baal in Canaan, Brahma in India, Astarte or the Dea in Syria, Apis in Egypt, the two calves in Israel, the Minotaur in Crete, and the bull with three cranes on its back which was worshipped by the British Gomeridae – all were fundamentally Druid, according to these claims.[5]

Archaeological evidence cannot confirm these claims, and as the Druids left no literature on the Continent, and later Irish and Welsh writing has to be used with caution.

Jesus in Britain: Joseph of Arimathaea and the Virgin Mary at Glastonbury?

The British Druid Light was part of the Celtic tradition (no. 9) but its impact on Christian refugees remained separate from its mainstream and may have influenced the European tradition (no. 11). A Druid influence on Jesus also solves many problems regarding Jesus's life, but may be legendary rather than historical. It is therefore best excluded from the traditions we considered in *Part Two*, and dealt with as part of the European subtradition.

There is a tradition[6] that Joseph of Arimathaea was the uncle of the Virgin Mary, being a younger brother of her father, and that as her husband died when Jesus was young, Joseph of Arimathaea became Jesus's guardian in accordance with Jewish law. That was why Pontius Pilate granted him the body of Jesus. Joseph owned a large house in Jerusalem, another one outside Jerusalem, and an estate in Aramathaea, and he was a member of the Sanhedrin and a legislative member of the Roman senate. He also owned a fleet of ships that traded regularly with the Cornish tin mines.

Britain was the source of the world's tin supply in those days; both Herodotus (c.450 BC, Bk 3.115) and Aristotle (c.350 BC) called Britain "the Tin Island", *Cassiterides.* Joseph particularly went to Ding Dong mine at Penwith, and the lead mines at Priddy in the Somerset Mendips in England, and as *Nobilis Decurio* he had the sole right to import tin and lead into Palestine. He sailed to Glastonbury, which was probably the island "Ictis" where Pliny situated the British tin trade, down the river Brue – in those days the sea was further inland than it is now – and he took the boy Jesus with him. There is a tradition in Maronite and Catluci villages in Northern Galilee that Jesus went to Britain as a shipwright in a trading vessel from Tyre, and that he wintered once in Britain, and the same story is told in the Land's End region of Cornwall where it is said that Jesus's foster-father Joseph was a ship's carpenter on boats seeking tin, and that on one occasion he took Jesus to Ding Dong Mine, Penwith.

In those days Glastonbury was an island of three hills – Wearyall Hill, Chalice Hill and the Tor – surrounded by sea which has since receded. It was known as the isle of Avalon. Jesus may have liked the seclusion of Glastonbury, and the Tor would have reminded his Palestinian eye of Mount Tabor (where the transfiguration later took place). At that time Britain was inhabited by the Celts. We have seen that they may have come from Samaria. Their language seems to have derived from the time of King Omri, founder of Samaria, and the Celtic or Cymric (Welsh) language is the oldest living language according to some philologists, and had an affinity with Hebrew, which would have been a further attraction to a Palestinian. We have seen that the Levitical servants to the Ephraimite Israel seem to have become British Druids who carried the Ark of the Covenant in their processions and called themselves "the people of the Covenant" ("B'rith-ish"), and the Celtic Druid "Du-w" clearly echoed Yahweh.

The Druidical religion was highly organised in Jesus's day. It had 40 Druidical seats of learning or universities, one for each of the 40 Druid tribes, and over 60,000 students (Gildas, *Cottonian* MS), and the Druids were significantly advanced to use the Greek script in all commercial transactions (Caesar, *Gallic War* 6.13). The Druid religion had spread to Spain, Gaul, Germany and Scandinavia, all the territories across the northern frontier of Roman civilization, and it appealed to Palestinian exiles as it was an "anti-Roman" religion. Glastonbury was a Druid centre.

It seems that Jesus may have returned to Britain and contacted the Druids and resided at Glastonbury. If so, as a Messiah-conscious Essene he could not fail to have been aware of the Druid belief in a Messiah, which the Celts could have brought out of Samaria, and which the Sadducean descendants of Judah, the southern kingdom, seemed to have lost. An ancient Celtic Triad gives a Druid slant to the Hebrew psalm 24, substituting Yesu for the Lord, and predicts that Yesu will be the Messiah or "King of Glory": "The Lord our God is One. Lift up your heads, O ye gates, and be ye lift up, ye everlasting doors, and the King of Glory shall come in. Who is the King of Glory? The Lord Yesu; He is the King of Glory."[7] This British Celtic tradition of the Messiah was known to every Briton, but it was not known to the Sadducean Judeans.

In Britain Jesus could have studied the old Israelite Levitical Druid religion and the Druid Triad of Beli, Taran and Yesu (or Esus) "the King of Glory" (see pp81, 100-101), and with an Essene knowledge of a spiritual as opposed to a political Messiah he would have seen the Light of the sun-god Beli and the "sparks of the sun" of Taran as the Light of the Heavenly Father and the Light of the spirit. He could not fail to have been impressed by the fact that Yesu or Esus, who bore his own name (Jesus), was the Druid Messiah, the King of Glory, the Essene Son of Man.

Jesus may have resided at Glastonbury until the beginning of his Ministry at the age of 30 (AD 26) and he may therefore have been in Britain immediately before he surfaced in Palestine as the *New Testament Gospels* describe.The first British historian Gildas (516-570) says: "Christ, the True

Son, afforded his Light, the knowledge of his precepts (i.e. the Mosaic law), to this island during the height of, or the last year of the reign of Tiberius Caesar" ("*summo Tiberii Caesaris*"). Tiberius retired from Rome to Capri in AD 27, and he died in AD 37; if "the last year of the reign" means the last active year before his retirement, then Gildas is saying that Jesus was in Britain in AD 26.

There is a heretical tradition that Jesus built a hut of mud and wattles in AD 26, and led a mystic, hermit life near the ancient Chalice Well at Glastonbury, which is known as "The Secret of the Lord". (*Secretum* can also mean "retiring place".) St Augustine wrote to Pope Gregory the Great c.600 (*Epistolae ad Gregorium Papam*): "In the Western confines of Britain there is a certain royal island of large extent, surrounded by water, abounding in all the beauties of nature and necessaries of life. In it the first neophytes of the catholic law, God beforehand acquainting them, found a Church constructed by Christ himself."[8] As Jesus's father was a carpenter it is likely that Jesus would have known how to construct a church. There is a story in William of Malmesbury (early 12th century) that Jesus appeared to St David in Glastonbury in 540 and told him that it was not necessary to rededicate the church "as he himself had long before dedicated the church in honour of his mother". William of Malmesbury reports the charter which King Ina gave to Glastonbury c.700: "To the ancient Church, situate in the place called Glastonbury (which Church the Great High Priest and Chiefest Minister – i.e. Christ – formerly through his own ministry, and that of angels, sanctified by many an unheard-of miracle to Himself and the ever-virgin Mary, as was formerly revealed to St David) do grant....." On the outside south wall of the Norman successor to St Mary's Chapel is a stone with archaic lettering that was greatly venerated; it says "Jesus Maria". The answer to Blake's question, "And did those feet in ancient time/Walk upon England's mountains green?" may have been: Yes.

If it happened, Jesus's stay in Britain until AD 26 is important because it explains how the early Church came to be founded in Celtic Britain, at Glastonbury, some years before it was founded in Rome. This story is generally not well known, although there have been several books on the subject. As it has great implications for the Ecumenical Movement and brings together many of the Light traditions we have considered so far, but in particular the Christian, Druid and Roman Light, it is worth describing the historical events at some length so that the statements on the Light made during the 1st and 2nd centuries AD (and the later Grail traditions) can be seen in better perspective.

After the Crucifixion of AD 29 Joseph of Arimathaea may have been imprisoned for "stealing" Jesus's body and burying it in his own tomb (4th-5th century apocryphal *Gospel of Nicodemus*). In AD 36 it seems that Joseph of Arimathaea and a party of Christians were persecuted and deported in a sailless, oarless boat. They left Palestine and drifted to France. They then returned to Britain, which was still across the frontier from the Roman civilization which had executed Jesus, Julius Caesar's attempt to conquer it having proved abortive. They never went to Rome but came straight to Britain from the mother church in Jerusalem. The *Ecclesiastical Annals* for AD 36 say: "In that year, the party mentioned were exposed to the sea in a vessel without sails or oars. The vessel drifted finally to Marseilles and they were saved. From Marseilles, Joseph and his company passed into Britain, and after preaching the gospel there, died." From Marseilles it seems that Joseph and his company journeyed along the Rhône valley to Rocamadour, where Zachaeus took up residence on the rocky slopes which apparently reminded him of Palestine, and from there they continued to Morlaix in Brittany, whence they sailed for Britain, a voyage that took four days.

They settled in Glastonbury having arrived at Wearyall Hill, and built a wattle church (which was destroyed by fire in 1184) on what is now the site of the Abbey. There is a mass of corroborative evidence that St Philip sent them to Britain, and that among those who accompanied Joseph were St Mary Magdelene (on one view, Jesus's widow), Martha, and Lazarus, the man Jesus raised from the dead who wrote the well-known *Triads of Lazarus* (the triad being a Druid form of thought that later found its way into the Christian Trinity). There are records of visits to Britain by St James (AD 41), St Luke, and St Peter, who was absent in Britain after being banished by Claudius when Paul wrote his *Epistle to the Romans* without mentioning him in the dedication. An extract from ancient church records at Lyons reads:

"Lazarus returned to Gaul from Britain to Marseilles, taking with him Mary Magdalene and Martha. He was first appointed Bishop. He died there seven years later" (AD 44 or 45). Joseph of Arimathaea frequently went to Gaul and returned with more helpers, including Simon Zelotes (AD 44) and Aristobulus (Barnabas's brother, Peter's father-in-law, and one of the original 70 disciples elected by Jesus). He was Paul's representative in Britain.

There is a tradition that the Virgin (i.e. "Woman") Mary accompanied her uncle, Joseph of Arimathaea, to Britain, and that Joseph looked after her for 15 years before she died, and was buried, in Glastonbury. Although there is a rival tradition that Mary spent the rest of her life at Ephesus, this tradition is given support by a Breton tradition that Mary's mother was British.

According to this tradition, which is even told in an edition of Hachette's *Guide Bleu, Bretagne*, the Virgin Mary's mother was Cornish, Anna of *Cornouaille*, which could explain how Jesus had fair hair according to the letter purporting to be from Pilate. Anna was of royal blood but was brutally treated by her jealous first husband (Joseph of Arimathaea's elder brother who must have gone to Britain with Joseph's tin trade). With child, she fled to Jaffa, presumably on one of Joseph of Arimathaea's boats, whence she reached Nazareth and gave birth to Mary. Mary married the carpenter Joseph at 15, and Anna then returned to Cornwall and ended her days beside the "bay of Palue", near the well, where Jesus is reputed to have visited her "several times", both as a boy (with Joseph of Arimathaea) and later on. There is a tradition that during this time the Virgin Mary visited Marazion. Palue seems to have been Looe, where a bridge was dedicated to St. Anna, as was a well in the nearby Isle of Lammana (Looe Island) which belonged to Glastonbury Abbey. Lammana was probably Lan Anna, the Church of Anna, and the nearby rock Essa's Bed was probably Eesa's Bed (Aramaic for "Jesus's" Bed). The church at Hessenford was also dedicated to Anna. St Anna became the patron saint of Brittany when the British overran it in AD 387, and when many west country bishops and clergy fled there after the defeat of Arthur's uncle Aurelius Ambrosius, and during the heathen/Saxon raids, they took Cornish traditions, cults and place-names with them, with the result that there is now a Bay of La Palue in Brittany. This tradition offers additional family reasons for Jesus and Joseph of Arimathaea to visit Britain, the land of Jesus's mother and Joseph's neice.[9]

Several British manuscripts make Joseph of Arimathaea uncle to both St Mary and St Joseph, who were cousins. According to ancient records preserved in Britain[10] Anna or Anne married three times: first Joachim by whom she had the Virgin Mary; secondly Cleophas, by whom she had another Mary who became the mother of St James the Less, St Simon, St Jude and Joseph Barsaba, all of whom were either Jesus's cousins of the half-blood or half-brothers; and thirdly Salome, by whom she had a third Mary who married Zebedee (possibly Aristobulus), and was the mother of St John the Divine and St James the Great (St James of Compostela) – who were also Jesus's cousins of the half-blood.

According to another manuscript Heli, the father of the Virgin Mary, was the brother of Jacob, the father of St Joseph; both the Virgin Mary and Joseph were cousins, and Joseph of Arimathaea was therefore the uncle of both of them. Joseph of Arimathaea had a daughter, Anna, who married King Beli, while Anna's daughter Penardin married Beli's grandson Llyr (King Lear). Thus two members of the Holy Family married into the British Royal Family, whose line continues today. St John of Glastonbury states that King Arthur claimed descent from St Joseph, who was a widower before he married St Mary according to the *Protevangelium* (a very ancient apocryphal gospel claiming to be written by St James the Less, who calls himself "the cousin and the brother of the Lord Jesus", and whose authenticity was believed in by SS Chrysostum and Cyril).

Meanwhile Joseph of Arimathaea converted first King Llyr (Shakespeare's King Lear), and then Arviragus, the ruler of South Britain (and son of Shakespeare's Cymbeline) who shared the rule of the country with Caradoc, or Caractacus as he was known to the Romans, the ruler of Wales (*British Chronicles*). It seems that Arviragus gave the church Joseph founded to proclaim the Saviour Yesu or Esus, whom the Druids expected, the same tax-exempted status at law as the Druid seats, according to the Domesday Book (*Survey Folio,* page 249b): "The *Domus Dei,* in the monastery of Glastonbury, called the Secret of our Lord. This Glastonbury Church possesses its own ville XII hides of land which have never paid tax."

Arviragus may have been related to the royal Anna and this may explain his generosity to Joseph, who was the uncle of Anna's daughter. In any event, the Silurian royal family welcomed the former metal merchant turned missionary and allied with the Christian enemies of Rome at a time when, as a result of Saul of Tarsus's (i.e. Paul's) persecution during the 30s, "the Church of Jerusalem was scattered abroad" (Acts 8.1-4). Joseph's convert King Llyr (Shakespeare's King Lear) later founded the first Christian church in Wales at Llandaff.

This was the origin of the Culdees, originally "*Culdich*" or "*quidam advanae*" (John Colgan, *Trias Thaumaturga*), "certain strangers" or refugees who arrived in Britain in AD 37.[11] They became Christianized Druids, established centres in remote islands out of reach of the persecution of the Romans, such as Enlii (off the coast of Wales) and Lindisfarne, and eventually lived in Iona, where they followed St Columba who said "Christ is my Druid".[12] "Culdees" are also "*Ceile-De*" or "*Gille-De*", "servants of our Lord".

Additional evidence that there was an early mission at Glastonbury comes from William of Malmesbury: "They also found (in AD 183) the whole story in ancient writings how the holy apostles, having been scattered throughout the world, St Philip the Apostle coming to France with a host of disciples, sent twelve of them into Britain to preach, and that – taught by revelation – they constructed the said chapel which the Son of God afterwards dedicated to the honour of his Mother. Their leader, it is said, was Philip's dearest friend, Joseph of Arimathaea, who buried our Lord."

Eventually Joseph died on July 27, 82, and he was buried in Glastonbury in the wattle Church of St Mary on the site of what is now the Abbey; the inscription on the lid of his sarcophagus under his initials read: "*Ad Brittanos veni post Christum sepilivi. Docui. Quievi.*" ("To the Britons I came after I buried the Christ. I taught. I have entered my rest.") In one MS found by the Rev. H. A. Lewis and quoted by L. S. Lewis, Maelgwyn of Avalon wrote c.450, "Joseph of Arimathaea, the noble Decurion, received his everlasting rest with his eleven associates in the isle of Avalon. He lies in a bifurcated line (or linen garment) at the southern angle (or next to the southern corner) of the Oratorium over or above (*super*) the Adorable

Virgin." This indicates that the Virgin Mary was also buried there. (Joseph of Arimathaea is called *paranymphos* or attendant to the Blessed Virgin in *Magna Tabula Glastionae.*) "Avalon" means "Land of the Dead" and the earlier form "Avilion" means "Isle of the Departed Spirits", which may refer to Joseph and the Virgin Mary.

Joseph's body remained buried on the site of his church until 1345, when Edward III gave a licence to John Bloom of London to dig for it, and a Lincolnshire monk states in 1367 that the body was found. The Abbot and monks placed the body in a silver casket let into a stone sarcophagus, at the east end of Joseph's Chapel in Glastonbury Abbey. It was there in 1662 and when the chapel was ruined by Puritan fanatics it was secretly removed by night into the churchyard of the parish church and interred in a tomb which bears the simple initials JA. In 1928 the Vicar of Glastonbury, Rev L. S. Lewis, found it and brought it back into the parish church where the tomb (still marked JA) can be seen today.[13]

The Culdee Light in Rome

The heretical British Light of Jesus and Joseph of Arimathaea, if the story we have been examining is true, influenced Rome through the British Royal Family.[14] Rome was alarmed at the rise of Christianity in Britain and Gaul, and in AD 42, following the examples of Augustus and Tiberius, Claudius proclaimed in the Roman senate that to accept the Druidical or Christian faith would be punishable by death by the sword, torture or the Colisseum lions. The same year Claudius launched an invasion of Britain to exterminate Druidism and Christianity, and on and off until 118 Britain became the Romans' Vietnam or Iraq.

For the next nine years, Caractacus, aided by Arviragus and Guiderius, bravely defied the Roman army whose generals had conquered the rest of the known world, despite huge losses. The British supported Christian Druidism's defiance of the Roman Empire as they later supported Protestantism's defiance of the Popish Spanish Armada.

In AD 45 there was a truce, and Caractacus and Arviragus went to Rome. To clinch the peace, Claudius offered his daughter, Venus Julia, in marriage to Arviragus, and incredibly they were married; while the Roman commander, Aulus Plautius, married the sister of Caractacus, Gladys, who had been converted to Christianity by Joseph of Arimathaea, and who was renamed Pomponia Graecina, the last name reflecting the fact that she was a Greek scholar. She was shortly afterwards put on trial for being a Christian, but was acquitted.

Meanwhile the war resumed, and the British continued to be indifferent to death as a result of their religious beliefs (Lucanus, AD 38). The Romans were victorious in AD 52 when Claudius personally directed the battle of Clune in Shropshire, at which Caractacus was betrayed and captured. Caractacus was paraded in chains through Rome behind the Emperor's chariot, after which he was set free provided he remained in Rome.

Caractacus resided at the *Palatium Britannicum* ("Palace of the British"), where a Christian community was established, and his two sons were allowed to return to Britain. Caractacus's daughter, who was another Gladys, was adopted by Claudius as his own daughter in AD 53. She was renamed Claudia, and she married Aulus Plautius's aide, Pudens, in a Christian ceremony at the Palace of the British, where they lived. For a while the Culdee Light shone in Rome virtually in the presence of the Emperor.

St Peter had arrived in Rome in AD 44 – the house of Pudens was the first to entertain Peter in Rome – and there is evidence that St Paul arrived in AD 56 or 58. In 58 Linus, son of Caractacus, was consecrated by St Paul as the first bishop of the Christian Church in Rome, which was in the grounds of the Palace of the British. It can now be visited as the shrine of St Pudentiana. Linus (and Pudens and Claudia) are mentioned in 2 *Timothy* 4-21, which links the Apostles and the Britons in Rome.

In AD 59, Caractacus returned to Britain and died in Glamorganshire, and his daughter Princess Eurgain founded 12 colleges of Christian Druids for Culdee initiates. Meanwhile Nero (who was referred to as Satan) ordered a huge massacre of the Druids and Christians, and Boadicea, a relative of Claudia, recaptured Colchester from the Romans, defeated Suetonius Paulinus's London garrison of Romans at Ambresbury Banks, near Epping (the Druid "Ambreshiri" or "Holy Anointed One" was a term also applied to Avebury) and was finally defeated near Newmarket

AD c.61. The massacre of Christians and Druids mentioned in Tacitus (*Annals* XIV ch30) spread to Rome, and the daughters of Claudia buried 3,000 martyrs in the church in the grounds of the Palace of the British, and the inscription in the church still reads: "In this sacred, most ancient of churches, known as that of Pastor (Hermas), dedicated by Sanctus Pius Papa (St Paul), formerly the house of Sanctus Pudens, the Senator, and the home of the holy apostles, repose the remains of three thousand blessed martyrs which Pudentiana and Praxedes, virgins of Christ, with their own hands interred." (Compare the Christian "virgins of Christ" with the earlier fire-cult of the Vestal Virgins.) During further persecutions, Pudens was martyred in AD 86, Claudia died in 97, her daughter Pudentiana was executed in 107, Claudia's son Novatus in 137 and Claudia's other daughter in 140.

St Paul in Britain?

There is a heretical tradition that St Paul was in Britain for much of the six years that are not accounted for in the Bible between his liberation from his first imprisonment to his martyrdom (AD c.61-67).[15] According to the *Long Lost Acts of the Apostles* (the Sonnini MS) Paul preached from the summit of Ludgate Hill, on the spot where St Paul's Cathedral was later erected. References to Paul's visit to Britain are made by Irenaeus, Tertullian and Origen, all of whom were born in the 2nd century AD, and by many other Roman writers. St Paul is reputed to have founded the Abbey at Bangor, and references to his stay in Siluria can be found in the exchange of letters between St Paul and the Roman philosopher Seneca, which are contained in the Paulian Manuscript in Merton College, Oxford.

It is said that while at Bangor he wrote his rule for living a Godly Christian life, and this is recorded in *Ancient British Triads* as *The Triads of Paul the Apostle.* Because it is little known, and shows how St Paul may have adopted the Druid triad as a literary form, it is given in full:

"There are three sorts of men: The man of God, who renders good for evil; the man of men, who renders good for good and evil for evil; and the man of the devil, who renders evil for good.

Three kinds of men are the delights of God: The meek; the lovers of peace; the lovers of mercy.

There are three marks of the children of God: Gentle deportment; a pure conscience; patient suffering of injuries.

There are three chief duties demanded by God: Justice to every man; love; humility.

In three places will be found the most of God: Where He is mostly sought; where he is mostly loved; where there is least of self.

There are three things following faith in God: A conscience at peace; union with heaven; what is necessary for life.

Three ways a Christian punishes an enemy: by Forgiving him; by not divulging his wickedness; by doing him all the good in his power.

Three chief considerations of a Christian: Lest he should displease God: lest he should be stumbling-block to man; lest his love to all that is good should wax cold.

The three luxuries of a Christian feast: What God has prepared; what can be obtained with justice to all; what love to all may venture to use.

Three persons have the claims and privileges of brothers and sisters: The widow; the orphan; the stranger."

From his contact with the Druids through the Palace of the British and through Aristobulus, his representative in Britain, St Paul would have known of the Druid triads for some years. As Jesus may have done before him, he would have studied the triad of Infinite Light (Beli), the illumined man (Yesu or Esus) and the finite intermediary (Taran), and connected them with God the (Heavenly) Father, the Son and the Holy Spirit or Holy Ghost; or to use St Paul's own words in the first text to anticipate the Trinity AD c.55, "The grace of the Lord Jesus Christ, and the love of God, and the communion of the Holy Ghost, be with you all" (2 *Corinthians* 13.14). This was developed in *Matthew*, AD c.70-80: "Go ye therefore, and teach all nations, baptising them in the name of the Father, and of the Son, and of the Holy Ghost" (28.19). It was extended in the Nicene Creed with its 6th century addition of "and the Son" in "I believe in the Holy Ghost...who proceedeth from the Father and the Son"; and in the 5th century Athanasian Creed: "We worship one God in Trinity.... But the Godhead of the Father, of the Son, and of the Holy Ghost is all one."

Paul presented Christianity in the idiom of the British, using triads to make Christianity more understandable. At the same time, he may have been influenced by the Druid triad, which advanced the eventual Christianization of Druidism.

We have seen that the spreading of the Christian Light cannot be separated from the spreading of the British Culdee Light. We have touched on a number of traditions concerning the presence in Britain of the Holy Family and the disciples. How true they are we cannot finally know; certainly different parts of the Roman Empire claimed to have housed members of the Holy Family at different times. All that can be said is that the British tradition is the strongest, and that there is some documentary evidence to connect Jesus with both the Essene and Druid teachings.

3

The Gnostic Light

Gnosticism was a syncretistic religion which emerged in first Syria, then Egypt in the 1st and 2nd centuries AD. It superseded classical antiquity and the Orphic and Dionysiac mystery cults of Greece and Italy, it had its own rites and places of assembly, it emphasised salvation, and it blended: Iranian dualism; the thought of Mesopotamia and India; the thought of Greece (Platonism and Hellenism); and Judaism and Christianity.[1] The Church Fathers whose writings against it form one of the main sources regarded it as a Christian heresy because it distorted the Christian message (in the case of Simon Magus), or developed it (in the case of Valentinus), or adapted Christ to alien teaching (in the case of the Naassenes).

In fact Gnosticism must now be seen to include a pre-Christian Jewish Kabbalism (for example the library found at Naj-Hammadi or Chenoboskion in Upper Egypt in 1945); a Hellenistic paganism (Hermeticism, see pp401-409); Mani's Manichaeism (see pp410-416); and Mandaean poetry from Palestine (see pp398-400).

The Syrian-Egyptian Gnostic Light

Syria was the inspiration for Gnosticism, which later spread to Egypt. Although the first Gnostic, the heretic Simon Magus, came from Samaria in

Palestine (now northern Israel), his influence was most felt in Syria. His partner Helena came from Tyre and his followers practised in Antioch.

Gnosticism was the main rival to Christianity before AD 150. Its *gnosis* ("knowledge") was the Light. Gnostics interpreted the Light as a spark which transformed the soul and brought divine revelation as it was the principle that created the universe, and they constructed elaborate doctrinal systems to explain the Light's creative powers.

Gnosticism was dualistic, for God opposes the world of matter, which was created by an anti-God (the Platonic "Demiurge" or Judaistic Yahweh or Babylonian "Archons") and not by the "Heavenly Father" of the *New Testament.* The divine realm of Light is opposed to the cosmos, which is a realm of darkness, and the transcendent God is hidden and unknowable except by supranatural revelation and illumination beyond the five senses.

The *Pneuma* or Spark: the Gnosis as Recovery of Vanished Light

In Gnosticism man's spirit (*pneuma*) was enclosed in his soul (*psyche*). The soul was the product of the cosmic powers of darkness, and when lit by the *pneuma*, which was also called "the spark" – an illumined person was called a *pneumatic* – the inner man achieved *gnosis* or certain knowledge of the realm of light, as opposed to *pistis* or mere faith. "Gnostics" were "the Knowing Ones" who were released from the imprisoning world to return to the divine realm of light after death, and the Gnostic salvation was an experience of the Light. The Archons tried to keep the soul a prisoner in the world of darkness, and a messenger from the realm of light had to outwit the Archons so that the spark could be lit and the spirit liberated. This liberating messenger was the spiritual Christ. He was contrasted with the physical Jesus, who was a part of the world of matter and darkness. The *gnosis* or knowledge was therefore an inner illumination, not a rational theory, in each of the works that can be thought of as Gnostic.[2]

The Gnostic tradition of the Light began with the Jewish Simon Magus ("the Magician", 1st century AD), who according to *Acts* (8.9-24) "bewitched" the people of Samaria into believing he was "the great power of

God", and attempted to buy from the apostles the power to lay on hands and transmit the Holy Spirit. Hence our word "simony". In later sources Simon was the supreme god, a redeemer figure who rivalled Jesus and who appeared variously as Son, Father and Holy Spirit, professing "a Power of the immeasurable and ineffable light, whose magnitude is to be held incomprehensible, which Power even the creator of the world does not know, not the lawgiver Moses, nor your teacher Jesus".[3]

According to Hippolytus, this pre-existent limitless power of Simon's, the Light, turned into Thinking (*Nous*, Mind) from which came Thought (*Epinoia* or *Ennoia*), a lower fallen female creative principle which Simon embodied in a prostitute called Helena (also called Selene, the moon-goddess). He had found Helena in a Tyre brothel and she accompanied him everywhere. Simon himself was Thinking or Mind, the upper male principle which was Son of the Power and Father of Thought. The creative Thought was superior to the world which was created by Babylonian-Iranian angels that emanated from the *Ennoia*, and the *Ennoia* was a divine principle that had sunk by being involved in creation. Simon's disciple, Menander, taught in Antioch that Simon was sent down as a saviour, and that the Light ultimately produced an *Ennoia* that was superior to the world-creating angels. Saturninus of Antioch dropped the *Ennoia* and taught that one unknown Father emerged from the Light and made the angels.

The Light systems of Basilides and Valentinus, and of Marcion and the Barbelo-gnostics, came from Christianity. Basilides (first third of 2nd century AD), a Syrian born in Alexandria, saw the First Cause, or God, as a nameless "Non-Existent" or "Non-Being" who created the Archon Abraxas. From him came *Nous* and *Logos* and 365 generated heavens, the last of which is inhabited by the angels who made our world. The Light, issuing from the Sophia (the transmundane Mother), illumined the Darkness below, which "lusted" for the Light's brightness and tried to retain it. As a result an image was formed and our world was fashioned, and the higher powers tried to recover the "raped" particles of Light (*Hippolytus 7*). Basilides drew on the Indian *maya* and *Nirvana* for his idea that our cosmos is illusory, and in Basilides' system Jesus (*Nous*) became Saviour when he was illumined by Light from above and Simon of Cyrene died in Jesus's place. Basilides' son Isidore kept his sect going and it survived until the 4th century AD.

Valentinus (an Egyptian from Alexandria who lived in Rome AD c.135-60 and later Palestine) taught the *pneuma* or spark from the Light, and culminated Syrian-Egyptian Gnosticism. In his system, darkness originated within the godhead, so that there were two Absolutes: the pre-existent Abyss (also called Fore-Beginning or Fore-Father) and the *Ennoia* (Thought, also called Grace and Silence), who may or may not have come into being after the Abyss. The double Absolute had emanations (*aeons*) in pairs. From Abyss and the *Ennoia* came Mind (*Nous*) and Truth, and from them came Word (*Logos*) and Life, and from them came Man and Church. Altogether there were thirty *aeons* (fifteen pairs) of the Light; they were called the Fullness (*Pleroma*), and the last female *aeon* was Sophia. Only Mind (*Nous*) could know the Abyss.

Not realising this, Sophia longed for him and penetrated into his realm of light, but was driven back, purified and steadied by Limit. Her desire for the impossible, however, gave birth to a lower Sophia outside the *Pleroma* (a sensual and low Sophia as opposed to the spiritual, high one), who was called "*Sophia-Prunikos*", "Wisdom the Whore" (a concept which drew on Simon Magus's Helena and who was likewise identified with the moon-goddess or white goddess), or *Achamoth* (after the Hebrew *chokmah*, the Wisdom *sefira* in the Kabbalah). Because of the ignorance which had appeared within the *Pleroma*, the *aeons* created a new pair of *aeons*, Christos and Holy Spirit. Christos made the *Pleroma* serene again by enlightening all *aeons* about the unknowability of the Abyss, and bringing *gnosis*.

However, the lower Sophia was outside the Light and Fullness, and pined for the vanished light. The *aeons* took pity on her and sent a later emanation, Jesus, to be her consort, and Sophia joyfully received the light that surrounded the illumined Saviour. Their marriage took place in the bridal chamber of the *Pleroma*, and "darkness dissolves at the appearance of the light" (ch 25 of the Valentinian *Gospel of Truth* AD c.150, which was found at Naj-Hammadi, and which may have been written by Valentinus himself). The lower Sophia then shaped the Demiurge who created seven heavens, and who, as the world-creating God of the *Old Testament*, believed he was the highest God until he was enlightened by the Sophia. The Sophia was the *pneuma* or spark inside his soul – "the Sophia is called '*pneuma*', the

Demiurge 'soul'" (*Hippolytus* 6.34.1) – and when Sophia recovered the Light, order was restored within the *Pleroma* of Light. Valentinianism grew through Valentinus's disciples Ptolemaeus, Marcus and Theodotus, and Ptolemaeus's disciple Heracleon interpreted *St John's Gospel* as a Valentinian work.

Marcion of Sinope (died c.160), who taught in Rome, was the most Christian of the Gnostics – he was in the Church until he was excommunicated in AD 144 – and he provided the biggest Gnostic challenge to Christian orthodoxy, because his sect of Marcionites defied the Church in every main city from the 2nd to the 5th centuries. However, he was the one major Gnostic who did not make the Light the centre of his teaching. Marcion was only a Gnostic in so far as, like Valentinus, he affirmed two gods: a supreme but Alien Father, and an inferior, oppressive creator and Demiurge. There was no *pneumatic* experience of illumination of the elect by a *gnosis*, no treatment of the Light; only faith (*pistis*), for Christ saves or redeems ("buys") men from the world and its oppressive god to make them children of a new Alien God, who is alien even to the objects of his salvation. Marcion's Gospel, which is lost but which is reflected in Tertullian, claims that Jesus revealed the Father but that his teachings were corrupted, and that Paul received a new revelation which was similarly corrupted: hence Marcion's *Gospel* restated "the truth" in its original purity.

In the 2nd century AD, Gnostic Gospels were written under pseudonyms, and the most important, the *Apocryphon of John* ("Secret work of John"), the chief work of the *Barbelo-gnosis*, parallelled the Valentinian Light. There was an equivalent to the Abyss, a Spirit-Father who was surrounded by the "pure (or living) water of His light", and whose reflection created an *Ennoia* or "First Man", the female *Barbelo* (or "Virgin"). Further *aeons* were created until the *Pleroma* was complete, and there was a Christos. Sophia conceived a Thought from herself, called Ialdabaoth, the First Archon and the *Old Testament* Yahweh, who produced in the water of light an image of the "First Man" as man. This was the psychical Adam who had *pneuma* breathed into him at the suggestion of Christos and his four "Lights" (*aeons* sent by the Light-God). The "Thought of Light" hid herself in Adam so that the archons could not see her, and Adam shone from the light within him.

The Ophites of the 2nd century AD also saw the *gnosis* as the Light. They also called the First Archon Ialdabaoth, but they made Sophia transmit *gnosis* to Adam and Eve through the serpent, which was the *pneuma* because it had given secret knowledge that came from the unknown God. The Ophites (*ophis* is Greek for "serpent") therefore stood the Biblical view of the serpent on its head, and saw it as the means whereby man was reunited with the primal Light. The serpent was a Serpent of Light. They believed in a spiritual Christ who taught *gnosis*, and cursed the physical Jesus at their initiation ceremony, a practice which did not endear them to the Church Fathers.

The Naassenes were closely linked to the Ophites (*nahash* is Hebrew for "serpent"). The Naassenes claimed that the *Gospel of Thomas* contained Jesus's secret sayings. In this Gospel, which comprises papyri discovered in Egypt between 1896 and 1907, Jesus says, "There is light within a man of light, and it illuminates the whole world; if it does not illuminate it, it is darkness" (saying 24). Again, "If people ask you 'Where have you come from?' say to them, 'We have come from the light, from the place where light is self-originated'" (saying 50). Again: "I am the light which shines upon all. I am the All; All has gone forth from me and All has come back to me. Cleave the wood, and there am I; raise the stone, and there you will find me" (saying 77). And: "Images appear to man, but the light which is in them is hidden in the image of the Father's light" (i.e. Christ). "He will reveal himself; his image is concealed by his light" (i.e. he cannot be adequately perceived by those who are still in their mortal body) (saying 83).

The Mandaean Light

The Gnostic Mandaean Light was outside the Christian or Hellenistic influences. The Mandaeans or Sabaeans probably originated in Syria-Palestine, from where their priestly caste (known as Nasoreans) migrated to Mesopotamia in the 1st century AD. They adopted Babylonian magical texts and the Iranian calendar, revered John the Baptist – their sect may have sprung from him – and regarded Jesus as a false Messiah. Mandaean works date from this early time, although they were mainly written down from the 7th and 8th centuries.[4]

The Mandaean *gnosis*, or *Manda*, was personified in Manda d'Hayye ("Knowledge of Life"), the central divine saviour of Mandaean religion. He was called forth by the Life in the world of Light, and was sent down to the lower world. Mandaean works generally open "In the name of the great first alien Life from the worlds of Light, the sublime that stands above all works", for Life was alien to this world, or *Tibil* (the Mandaean suggests baseness), as was the unknown Father or Neoplatonist One.

The Mandaean *gnosis* involved a return or ascent to the Light. The first alien life was the "King of Light" whose world was "of splendour and of light without darkness", a world which was opposed to the "world of darkness". Human beings were *manas*, divine spirits who longed to return to the Light: "I am a *Mana* of the great Life. Who has made me live in the *Tibil*, who has thrown me into the body-stump?...A *Mana* am I of the great Life. Who has thrown me into the suffering of the worlds, who has transported me to the evil darkness?" They were therefore *akh*-like "beings of light" who were mixed with darkness: "I am I, the son of the mild ones (i.e. the beings of light)"; "they brought shining light and cast it into the dense darkness".

As a result of the mixture, unity became a plurality. The soul, a part of the first Life or Light, *fell* into the body, and "the Light fell into the darkness", "slept" there and was "drunk" with the "din" of the world until Manda d'Hayye called to the elect. "Manda d'Hayye spake unto Anosh... Fear not and be not dismayed, and say not, They have left me alone in this world of the evil ones.... Since terror overcame thee in this world, I came to enlighten thee.... It is the call of Manda d'Hayye.... He stands at the outer rim of the worlds and calls to his elect.... My eyes, which were opened from the abode of light, now belong to the (body-) stump."

The call was uttered by "the Alien Man", the Messenger who was sent into the world for the purpose, who had "gone forth" and prayed from "the place of light", and the call was to awaken the elect to the Light, "to awaken them and shake them up, that they might lift their faces to the place of light", to "our Fathers, the Sons of Light in their city", and "rise up victorious to the place of light".

The call was answered: "If a person has the *gnosis*, he is a being from on high. If he is called, he hears, replies, and turns towards Him who calls him, in order to reascend to Him.... We believed in thee, Good One, we beheld thy light and shall not forget thee.... From the place of light have I gone forth, from thee, bright habitation.... I asked him for smooth paths to ascend and behold the place of light." There was thus an ascent from the Many back to the One, the Light, and the *gnosis* was the Light, the *gnosis* of the soul's divine origin which was known by the mystical experience of illumination. Indeed, in Gnosticism, "the enlightenment by a ray of the divine light which transforms the psychic nature of man may be an article of faith, but it may also be an experience."[5]

4

The Hermetic Light

Christianity was further challenged when the Light of the Alexandrian School (see pp123-126) gave rise to three pagan Alexandrian Lights: the heretical Lights of Hellenistic pagan Hermetic thought (some of which was Gnostic), Alchemy and pagan Neoplatonism. These three Lights were connected, for the *Hermetica* (discourses) and the main Alchemical work are both attributed to a teacher referred to as Hermes Trismegistos, who came from the Alexandrian School where (from AD 232 to 242) Ammonius Saccas (died AD c.245) taught Plotinus and together with him founded pagan Neoplatonism.

The Hermetic Light and the Tarot's Sun Card

Hermes Trismegistos ("Thrice-Greatest") was the Greek name for the Egyptian god Thoth or Tehuti, the god of learning. His books were carried in sacred possession and he was honoured by the small mystic sect which produced the *Corpus Hermeticum*, the 18 scriptures of Hermetic thought (middle of 1st century – end of 3rd century AD).

There are claims that Hermetic thought is far older than its writings, and that it goes back to the mysteries of the Great Pyramid, where (according to one tradition) an initiate spent forty hours sleeping in the sarcophagus of the King's Chamber in total darkness, with the result that the powerful vibrations changed his metabolism and enabled him to see the Light. In that case, the two sceptres and crowns of the Pharaohs symbolized the spiritual and material worlds as well as the two kingdoms of Upper and Lower Egypt. Be that as it may, the *Corpus Hermeticum* is of Greek rather than Egyptian origin – the dialogue form betrays its Platonism – and the most important and the most Gnostic of the 18 discourses is the first, *Poimandres* ("Shepherd of Men"), which records a divine revelation. For *Poimandres* himself is the Light (*Nous*).

Poimandres begins with a vision:[1] "Once, when I engaged in meditation upon the things that are (real things) and my mind was mightily lifted up, while my bodily senses were curbed... I thought I beheld a presence of immeasurable greatness that called my name." This presence is "*Poimandres*, the *Nous* (Mind) of the Absolute Power" and Hermes is shown a vision of reality: "Everything became light, serene and joyful. And after a while there was a Dark-ness...resembling a serpent.... From out of the Light a holy Word (*Logos*) came over the nature (watery substance).... Then *Poimandres* said to me, 'That light is I, *Nous* (Mind), thy God (or the foremost God, the first God), who was before the humid nature (watery substance) that appeared out of the Darkness. And the luminous Word that issued from the *Nous* is the Son of God....Now then, fix your mind on the Light and learn to know it.'...I beheld in my *nous* (mind) the Light consisting in innumerable powers and became a boundless Cosmos." *Poimandres* spoke again: "The divine *Nous*, being androgynous, existing as Life and Light, brought forth by word another *Nous*, the Demiurge.... Now the *Nous*, Father of all, being Life and Light, brought forth Man like to himself."

The Hermetic *nous*, then, replaced the Gnostic *pneuma* as the spark, the capacity to see the divine Light,[2] and *Nous*, the Light, created the Word, then the Demiurge, and finally Man, as *Light*. The Primal Man then descended into the lower world of Nature as he does in Gnosticism: "Man entered the demiurgical sphere...and having broken through the vault showed to lower Nature the beautiful form of God. When she beheld him who had in himself inexhaustible beauty...she smiled in love; for she had seen the reflection." This is the familiar Gnostic idea that there was a mutual attraction between Light and Darkness, that the Light on high appears as a reflection below and is "raped" and detained by Darkness. Man, then, turned "from Life and Light into soul and mind (*Nous*), into soul from Life and into mind from Light", and as he came from a Father who is Life and Light, he must "enter again into Life and Light", return to the Light: "And thereafter, man thrusts up" past seven zones, shedding his bad qualities one by one until he becomes a Power and enters the Godhead again, for "this is the good end of those who have attained *gnosis*: to become God."

Man's ascent through seven zones recalled the seven levels of the Babylonian *ziggurat*, and the seven gates on ascending steps represented the seven planets through which a Mithraic initiate had to pass in the *klimax heptapylos* of the initiation ceremony. There are other references to the Light in the discourses – to "the brilliance of God", to the "clear light" at the "gates of understanding", to the sun which "does not illuminate, as does a vision of the Good", to all things and reality being "full of light" – but the main point of the discourses is in the *Hymn of Praise for him who is reborn* and in the invocation, "And Light, illuminate Mind in us".[3] For like the Gnostic creation myths, the mythological metaphysics of the Hermetic God and Demiurge are only important in so far as they impose a duty on the initiate to be reborn in this life, and *experience* the Light.

The pagan Alexandrine *Hermetica* may have been reflected in the Tarot cards, which are reputed to have been connected with the Serapeum at Alexandria, and therefore with the Hermetic mysteries.[4] Initiates are said to have been led through a gallery containing 22 pictures which had a deep spiritual meaning. Serapis was at first a Sun-god who was associated with the sacred Egyptian bull, Apis, but among the Gnostics he became the universal Godhead, which Man had to enter in the Hermetic mysteries, as we have just seen. There is a legend that when the Serapeum at Alexandria was destroyed in AD 391 by Theophilus, (the anti-pagan patriarch of Alexandria who also destroyed all the temples to Mithras and Dionysus in North Africa), the priests banded together to preserve the rites of Serapis, and the pictures, and their descendants, the Gypsies, carried the Books of Enoch or

Thoth (Tarot) with them on their travels until they arrived in England some time before the reign of Henry VIII. The 22 pictures were preserved in the 22 "major trumps" of the Tarot cards. Another tradition relates the Tarot to the Egyptian *tar* and *ro* ("road", "royal"), indicating that it was the Royal Road to Wisdom, and it seems that the Tarot may contain the temple of Serapis's version of the initiation into the Egyptian mysteries of the Great Pyramid.

The Royal Road to Wisdom meant exploring each card in turn from 1 to 21 (the Fool is not a numbered card), and if read correctly the sequence traces the death of the ego and the advent of the Light (the Sun card is number 18). There is a view that the Tarot is derived from the Sanskrit for North Pole Star (*Tar*), and that by a magic law of inversion the order of the cards should be reversed to begin with the Universe and end with the Magician, to be which was the goal of the quest. However, this advances the Sun card to number 3, which is very early in the sequence for the climactic illumination, and overvalues the concept of the magician: for the word *magus* can be derived from the Sanskrit for "higher", "major", suggesting that the magician controls a "higher" level of Nature than the material level and seeks egoistic control over forces which the mystic serves selflessly. The magician should be at the beginning of the initiatory quest precisely because he symbolises the ego which must die.

THE GOLD LIGHT OF ALCHEMY

Alchemy,[5] whose gold symbolized the Light, originated in Egypt. ("Alchemy" comes from Arabic *al*, "the", and probably *Khem*, Coptic for "Egypt".) Egypt had long had knowledge of pigments for embalming, but Alchemy as we know it began with the discovery of mercury c.300 BC, and the earliest Alchemist was Democritus, who is identified with Bolos of Mende, a Hellenised Egyptian who lived in the Nile Delta c.200 BC and who wrote *Physica and Mystica*, the first major Greek Alchemistic work. The first authenticated Egyptian Alchemist was Zosimos of Panopolis (2nd-3rd century AD).

Egyptian Alchemy was also called Hermeticism, after Hermes Trismegistos, whose *Emerald Tablet* from the *Book of the Secret Creation* (now sometimes attributed to Apollonius of Tyana or Balines, 1st Century AD) called Alchemy the operation of the Sun: "And as all things have been, and come from One...all things have been born from this single thing....The Sun is its father....It is finished, what I have said of the operation of the Sun."

Alchemy was therefore connected with the mysteries of Sol, the Sun-god who protected the Roman Emperors of the 3rd century AD until he was replaced by Christianity. From the beginning Alchemy was far more than a branch of chemistry that sought to transmute base metals into gold by means of the philosopher's stone, the missing and miraculous ingredient of transformation. In fact, Alchemy transmuted consciousness from lead-like everyday perception to a subtle, gold perception which saw every object as being contained within the Absolute; and its cosmic symbolism emphasised the oneness of the world at the level of Eternity, Infinity and Unity. This was known in the Egypt of c.1450 BC when the outwardly earthly Sphinx in her later form of Sekhmet, the lion-headed goddess (and "Eye of Ra" of the uraeus) apparently disgorged the "blood of the green lion", the gold sun of the Light, in a rite which is reputed to have taken place in the sanctuary in the temple of her consort Ptah at Karnak.

The Alchemist used a sealed vessel as a model of the universe and human consciousness, in which the opposing forces (symbolized by Male and Female, Sulphur and Mercury, Earth and Air, Fire and Water) were synthesised into the gold Light. The gold in the vessel therefore represented the Light, the inner Sun of which the outer Sun, Sol, was a Platonic shadow, and the adept (*adeptus*, "he who has attained" the gift of God) was crowned with Enlightenment and Eternal Love. The texts of the Alchemists were therefore deliberately obscure to deter the unworthy, and their later pictures had to be contemplated for inner meanings. Thus a man with a head of the sun climbing out of a pot showed liberation from the material world through illumination, and Sol was shown with a halo that was essentially spiritual.

The Philosopher's Stone, then, transmuted base mind into the Light, and there were three stages in this process, all of which formed the Great Work or *Magnum Opus*. The first stage was Purgation, the formation of *materia prima*: the subject (i.e. the initiate) was distilled and solidified into a perfectly mercurial substance which appeared as a Blackness. The second stage was Illumination: the subject was cooked into an incombustible sulphur which appeared as a Whiteness (the White Rose). The third stage was Union: the subject was fermented to Ultimate Perfection, the Philosopher's Stone, which appeared as a Redness, the colour of Alchemical gold. This could lead to the discovery of the Panacea, the Elixir of Life, which could transmute the human body into an incorporeal "body of Light". The whole process was symbolized in Alchemical paintings, as the "blood of the green lion", the green and black lion suggesting raw matter, mercury and sulphur which have disgorged the Light (the gold sun) and the Elixir of Life (the blood).[6]

In the Fire of Love (the salt or secret fire) the King (Sol) was reunited with his Queen (Luna) – these are figures in the Tarot, too (and in the Royal Sacred Marriage of the Sumerians) – and the opposites were reconciled. To the pagan Hermetic Alchemist, after purgation and illumination the natural man was transmuted into the spiritual man, Sol and Luna were married, divine and human were united, and infinite and finite became one.

The Neoplatonist Light: Plotinus's Flight to the One

Neoplatonism was a syncretistic pagan Alexandrian philosophy that drew on the Hermetic Gnostic Mysteries, which sought to return to the Light of the One. The Hermetic Mysteries were known to Ammonius Saccas, the teacher of its founder Plotinus (AD c.205-c.270).

Neoplatonism also drew on Platonism and Middle Platonism, which came from Plato's *Dialogues*, his absolute Ideas and the Light. Platonism was taught in the Academy by Plato's successors, and it comprised a Reality that was independent of the world perceived by the senses. It described the Ideas and Forms in terms of Pythagorean mathematical numbers and geometrical circles, which Aristotle found useless. Middle

Platonism (1st century AD) proclaimed One Reality with a hierarchy of Forms in the divine mind, to which a human mind as ascetic as Philo of Alexandria's could ascend.

Neoplatonism under Plotinus affirmed One Reality and a descending hierarchical order of spheres of being.[7] The lowest of these is our universe, which can be perceived with the senses. The One Reality created *Nous* (Intellect, Mind or Spirit) from which came Soul; Soul is in contact with *Nous* and with the lower nature, and the Forms are emanations downwards from Soul. Thus, although matter is evil the material world is not, and the ecstatic mystic Plotinus opposed the Gnostics in refusing to disparage the Demiurge and his creation (*Against the Gnostics, or against those who say that the Creator of the World is evil and that the World is bad, Enneads* II.9). The Neoplatonist universe is symbolized in the maze on the floor of Chartres Cathedral: concentric circles widening from a point in the centre (our universe) until they merge into the One.[8]

The Soul must ascend through *Nous* back to the One as in *Poimandres*, and it must therefore awaken to the Light, which is the Light of the One. Plotinus is quite specific about this:[9] "We may believe that we have really seen, when a sudden light illumines the Soul: for this light comes from the One and is the One. And we may think that the One is present, when, like another god, he illumines the house of him who calls upon him; for there would be no light without his presence. Even so the Soul is dark that does not behold him; but when illumined by him, it has what it desired, and this is the true end and aim of the Soul, to apprehend that light, and to behold it by that light itself, which is no other than the light by which it sees. For that which we seek to behold is that which gives us light, even as we can only see the sun by the light of the sun. How then can this come to us? Strip thyself of everything.... In the vision that which sees is not reason but something greater than and prior to reason.... We ought not even to say that he will see, but he will *be* that which he sees, if indeed it is possible any longer to distinguish seer and seen, and not boldly to affirm that the two are one.... (The Soul) ceases to be Being; it is above Being while in communion with the One. If then a man sees himself become one with the One, he has in himself a likeness of the One." Then "it will be possible for the soul to see both God and herself divinely, and she will see herself illumined, full of intelligible light; or rather she will be light itself – pure, unfettered, agile, becoming a God or rather being a God, and wholly aflame" (*Enneads* VI, 9,9).

To see – and be – the One Light, a man must turn away from the body by purifying himself, and he must become *Nous* by contemplating it and uniting with it as a preparation for mystic union with the One. "This light of *Nous* shines in the soul and illumines it: that is, it makes it intelligent: that is, it makes it like itself, the light above." Like the sun's rays, the downward rays of the divine become dimmer and dimmer until light becomes darkness, which is a deprivation of light; and the upward return of the soul recovers the Light. Plotinus himself often made the shamanistic "flight of the alone to the Alone" into ecstatic union with the One, and his disciple, editor and biographer Porphyry records that he saw his master "rapt" on four occasions. (Plotinus was "ever tending towards the divine which he loved with all his heart. He strove strenuously to set free his soul and to ascend above the bitter waves of this sanguinary existence. And thus by a divine illumination and by meditation and the methods described by Plato in the *Symposium*, he would lift himself up to the First and All-transcendent God.")[10]

Plotinus says little about his experiences, as opposed to his metaphysics, but he writes: "Many times it happened. Lifted out of the body into myself; becoming external to all other things and self-centred; beholding a marvellous beauty;...acquiring identity with the divine." It is not enough to have a mere glimpse: "Some there are that for all their effort have not attained the Vision.... They have received the authentic Light, all their soul has gleamed as they have drawn near; but they come with a load on their shoulders which holds them back from the place of Vision."[11]

Plotinus's Neoplatonist successors continued his vision of the One Light. Plotinus's disciple in Rome, Porphyry (c.234-c.305), insisted that the pagan Trinity of One-*Nous*-Soul was all One, while Iamblichus (died c.325), a pupil of Porphyry's, posited a One behind Plotinus's One. Proclus (410-485) believed that the soul possesses an imperishable light by which it perceives the divine.

Largely through the efforts of Iamblichus and Proclus, Neoplatonism became a pagan theology, whose revealed divine truth rivalled Christianity – the soul ascended to the One with the help of pagan gods – and, growing up at a time when paganism was destroyed and Christianity had not conquered the educated world, its pagan ecstasies had an immense impact on the Roman culture. It influenced later contemplatives and mystics like St Augustine and Pseudo-Dionysius, who reasserted Christianity by blending Neoplatonism and the Christian Vision. Christianity absorbed Neoplatonism just as it absorbed Gnosticism, but as a result the mysticism of early Europe was fundamentally Neoplatonist and Alexandrian.

5

The Manichaeist Light

In the 3rd century AD, Manichaeism, a semi-Gnostic Iranian higher religion rather than a heresy, challenged Christian Orthodoxy. It could be treated under "The Iranian Light" in *Part Two*, but is best treated as a form of Gnosticism. Christians regarded it as being as heretical as Gnosticism.

Iranian Gnosticism

In Iranian Gnosticism Darkness attacks and engulfs Light, whereas in Syrian Gnosticism Light approaches Darkness and is darkened by it; and Manichaeism, the system of Mani (AD 216-274/7),[1] marked the maturity of the Iranian form just as Valentinianism marked the maturity of the Syrian form. Mani's Gnosticism contains no esoteric *pneuma* because it was designed as a higher religion, and it had to have a mass appeal. As such it did very well – it was the only Gnosticism to become a higher religion – and its threat to Christianity can be judged from the fact that St Augustine was a Manichaean from 373 to 382.

Mani was influenced by Marcion and by Bardesanes (or Bardaisan), the Syrian Gnostic (154-c.222). The *New Testament Apocrypha*, which comprises numerous Apocryphal Gospels, Acts, Epistles and Apocalypses, contains Gnostic material concerning the Light, and the poem "The Hymn of the Pearl", which is found in the apocryphal *Acts of Thomas* (probably early 3rd century) has been ascribed to Bardesanes, or Bardaisan. It embodies a strong Iranian strand of Gnosticism in which Darkness attacks the Light.[2]

It is in the form of an allegory. A king's son is sent from his Father's home to Egypt (the world of matter) to fetch the Pearl which is guarded by a serpent (probably the Demiurge, the evil ruler, rather than the Ophite agent of *pneumatic* illumination). He puts on Egyptian clothes (a body), and is drugged so that he forgets about the Pearl until his Father awakens him. He seizes the Pearl, after which his parents send his robe (his true self or "garment of light"). The allegory is about man's need to return to God and find his true spiritual self.

Interpreters have always puzzled over the meaning of the Pearl, and have tended to see it as the soul, and the king's son as the Saviour. But the Pearl is the Light, as it is in the *New Testament* parable; and the king's son is the soul of every man which descends at birth from the realm of light to the realm of darkness. The Pearl is, then, the luminous self or power of Light, the *Ennoia* or Sophia, the *pneuma* not just of the Ophites, but of St Paul, who, writing in Greek, always preferred the word *pneuma* to *psyche* for our "spirit", and contrasted the *pneumatic* and *psychic* man.

Mani, the Apostle of Light

Manichaeism was a religion of the Light. At the age of 24, on April 19, AD 240, Mani experienced a spiritual illumination and received his "call" (compare the call of Manda d'Hayye): "The Living Paraclete came down to me and spoke to me.... He revealed to me the mystery of the Light and the Darkness, the mystery of the conflict and the great war which the Darkness stirred up. He revealed to me how the Light (turned back? overcame?) the Darkness by their intermingling and how (in consequence) was set up this world" (*Kephalaia* ch 1, Mani's own book which was among the library of 4th century AD Manichaean papyri discovered in Egypt in 1930). He declared himself the "Apostle of Light" and supreme "Illuminator", and his execution in chains parallelled the fate of the Light of the World: his "crucifixion" followed a passion of twenty-six days at the hands of the Zoroastrian Magi, during which the Illuminator relived the trials of Jesus. Mani was influenced by Christianity, for he was brought up among the Jewish-Christian Gnostic-influenced Baptistai or Elkhasaites, whom his father had joined after hearing a voice in the temple at Ctesiphon (the Iranian Parthian winter capital) ordering him to renounce meat, wine and sex, and Mani was taught about Jesus – and the Gnostics – by them.

Mani's *gnosis* – the "mystery" of his vision – was expressed in the form of a creation myth which could be understood by a mass audience, but it is clear that the myth was intended to interpret the *experience* of the Light. In this myth, which is recorded in Syriac by Theodore bar Konai, the primal principles of Light and Darkness were infinite, had always existed and were their own origins. The good principle lived in the place of Light (the "Father of Greatness") together with his five "beings of light", and the evil principle lived in Darkness (the "King of Darkness") together with his five worlds. To the Persians the King of Darkness was Ahriman, to the Greeks *Hyle* or "matter", which was evil in Manichaeism (as it was not in Zoroastrianism) and which had a spiritual aspect that made it evil.

Desiring better, the Darkness *aggressed* against the Light and battled against it, and being pacifist, the Light was unable to fight. The Deity, the Father of Greatness, was therefore forced to call forth the Mother of Life to create the Primal Man to preserve peace in the worlds of Light. The Primal Man is a figure that occurs throughout the Gnostic writings. He is in *Poimandres* and he is Adam Kadmon of the Kabbalah; in Manichaeism he is an emanation from the godhead, the god Ohrmazd (who is God of Light in Zoroastrianism). Ohrmazd the Primal Man was sacrificed, for he fought against the Devil with the soul as his weapon, and was defeated and eaten by the Sons of Darkness, with the result that the soul was mixed with matter and fettered in corruption. The Deity was forced to call forth the Great Architect. He created the Living Spirit or Demiurge to liberate the Primal Man, whose "resurrection" (like Christ's) was a guarantee for all salvation in the future, a guarantee that Manichaeans symbolized in the daily practice of grasping right hands.

However, the Primal Man was compelled to leave behind the soul, which was lost to matter, and the Living Spirit, or Demiurge, or King of

Light, then created the world out of intermingled Light and Darkness to liberate the soul (the light parts) from the powers of darkness which were imprisoned in the world (the dark parts), so that the devoured light could be extracted from the *Hyle* and purified back to Light. The deity was then forced to make his third creation, of the Messenger (or Third Messenger), the liberator and saviour who created plants and animals. The King of Darkness countered by producing Adam and Eve and pouring in the remaining light – man was thus created in the image not of God but of Darkness – and he therefore imprisoned soul.

The powers of Light sent the luminous Jesus (an emanation from the Messenger) to Adam, and he made Adam eat from the Tree of Knowledge. In fact, Jesus played the role of the serpent in a variation of the Ophite myth, and he personified all Light that is mixed into matter (*Nous*) and the suffering form of the Primal Man, as a Manichaean psalm makes clear: "Come to me, my kinsman, the Light, my guide.... I am in everything, I bear the skies, I am the foundation, I support the earths, I am the Light that shines forth, that gives joy to the souls.... Now go aboard the Ship of Light" (246.54.8-55.13). Jesus warned Adam not to reproduce, but he did, thereby extending the Darkness to all mankind.

Mani therefore appeared as the "Illuminator" who, according to the Pseudo-Clementines (*Homilies* 3.20), was the one "true Messenger", and as the fourth of a line of "apostles of God". "From aeon to aeon the apostles of God did not cease to bring here the Wisdom and the Works. Thus in one age their coming was into the countries of India through the apostle that was the Buddha; in another age, into the land of Persia through Zoroaster; in another, into the land of the West through Jesus. After that, in this last age, this revelation came down and this prophethood arrived through myself, Mani, the apostle of the true God, into the land of Babel."[3] Mani was an "Apostle" ("messenger") of the Light, and he claimed to be superior to Jesus, so when he called himself "the apostle of Jesus Christ" he meant the eternal Light-Jesus, of which Jesus was also an apostle.

Mani's approach to the Light owed much to the Buddha, Zoroaster and Jesus: his ascetic ethics came from the Buddha, his cosmogony from Zoroaster (as we have seen), and his eschatology from Jesus. His asceticism arose from the myth that the body had been created by Darkness, that it imprisoned Light (the soul) and that the animal world contained Light. His followers should not marry or make love lest Darkness was reproduced, and they should eat only vegetables so as to mortify the body and release Light into it, and so as not to hurt the Light in animals. They should not plough, reap, kneed or bake for fear of harming particles of the Light. Hegemonius, the son of Bardesanes, wrote in *Acta Archelai*, "When someone walks on the ground he injures the earth (i.e. the Light mixed with it); he who moves his hand injures the air, for this is the soul of men and beasts." (Compare the compassion of the Buddha.)

Those who kept these ascetic rules were the "Elect", a monastic elite who influenced Christian monasticism, and the masses who kept the Elect were "Hearers" or "Soldiers"; all others were "sinners". The Elect became part of the Kingdom of Light on earth and therefore went to the "Paradise of Light"; the Soldiers returned to the world after death until their Light was freed (a Buddhist idea) and they themselves became Elect; and the sinners went to the Devil and Hell.

Mani's eschatology concerned the Light. The history of man involved freeing of the Light, and the sun helped this process by extracting and purifying Light from the *Hyle* and bringing it to the world of Light and praise, where the souls of the dead resided. On death, souls (i.e. beings of Light) were ferried to the moon by the "Ship of Light" and transferred to the rotating wheel of the zodiac which raised them to the sun like a gigantic fairground wheel, whence they were taken to the world of Light. Thus, the parts of Light ascended and the parts of Darkness descended incessantly until Light and Darkness could be free of each other, when the world would be burned up and Light would end. Then a new emanation of the Messenger would appear, the "Great Thought", or Hunter or Fisher of Light, who would be as powerful as the earlier emanations of Jesus (who appeared to Adam) and the Paraclete (who appeared to Mani).

The power of Darkness (but not Darkness itself) would be destroyed – the ruin of the *Hyle* was decreed – and Light would be safe from Darkness, as a psalm makes clear: "His net is his Living Spirit, for with his Spirit he shall catch the Light.... A new Aeon will be built in the place of the world that shall dissolve, that in it the powers of the Light may reign. This is the Knowledge of Mani, let us worship him and bless him." As in the case of the Egyptian *Book of the Dead*, the after-life could be anticipated in this life, the Paradise of Light could be obtained by becoming one of the Elect, and one could become soul (Light) by turning away from the body (*hyle*) and achieving illumination by ascetic effort.

The mythology, cosmogony and eschatology of Manichaeism all emphasised the need to be illumined in this life, to follow the example of the "Apostle of Light", the "Illuminator"; to experience the Light. This same vision ran through the sects which Manichaeism produced. The first was the optimistic Mazdakism (3rd-5th centuries), which worshipped a god of Light and which released the Light into the world by an ascetic life (though women were in common to reduce greed). The founder was not the 5th century Mazdak but the much earlier Zaradust-e Khuragan, and no books survive, our knowledge being confined to a few mentions in Near Eastern sources.

The later writings of the Magi reflect the influence of Manichaeism. In the Mazdaism of the 3rd-7th centuries and the Pahlavi books, some versions have Ohrmazd creating the evil Ahriman by thought, an idea which caused considerable difficulty because a good God was creating evil out of his own goodness and was limiting his own power. For the Median Magi or Zurvanians of the 3rd-7th centuries, the figure of Zurvan (Infinite Time) solved the problem. Zurvan (who is first mentioned on Nuzi tablets in the 13th and 12th centuries BC) now brought Ohrmazd into being after sacrificing for a thousand years. Zurvan himself had been born of light, and the Light was thus the stuff from which creation took place for Zurvanites: "From his own essence which is material light Ohrmazd fashioned forth the form of his creatures – a form of fire – bright, white, round and manifest afar" (*Greater Bundahishn*, 1.26, a 9th century Pahlavi *Book of the Primal Creation*).[4] However, this interpretation was declared heretical, and the dualism between Light and Darkness, or the Wise Lord and the Evil Spirit, God and the Devil, was left unsolved in the late *Avesta*. According to the *Gathas*, Ahura Mazda created Light and Darkness, but by the end of the tradition, Darkness had won equal status with Light.

The Manichaean Light spread to China in the 7th century and became the official religion of the Uighur state in northern Mongolia in the

8th century. It influenced the 7th century Paulicians in Armenia and Asia Minor, and was absorbed by the Bogomils in the Balkans and Bulgaria (10th-15th centuries), the Albigenses in Southern France (12th-13th centuries) and the West European Cathari (who were also in the South of France, in the 12th and 13th centuries), all of whom stressed the need to experience the Light.

6

THE TEMPLAR LIGHT

The rise of the early Templars,[1] who were only later deemed heretical, was associated with the spreading of St Bernard's Cistercian Light. The decision to found an order of monastic knights who would protect Jerusalem's Christian pilgrims was taken in 1113-5, and the foundation took place in 1118/9.

The Templars came into being at a time when the newly established Kingdom of Jerusalem was continually harrassed by Moslem armies. (The Templars' role in protecting the Kingdom of Jerusalem is preserved in the winged horse of the emblem of London's Inner Temple and in the crowned *Agnus Dei* and crusader flag, or Lamb and Flag, the emblem of the Middle Temple which now adorns the Middle Temple Hall.) St Bernard wrote the Templar Rules in 1128; it not surprisingly they contained many Cistercian features: he had renounced his career as a knight in 1112 and had entered the Cistercian monastery at Citeaux, and become the founding abbot of Clairvaux in 1115. There were just 7 Cistercian abbeys in 1118, and by 1153 there were 338 Cistercian abbeys, of which 68 were founded directly from Clairvaux, and there were 350 dependencies (54 in England).

The time of St Bernard saw a fascinating combination of events: the founding of the Templars – who may have been descendants from Valentinian Gnostics in Alexandria – and the growth of support for the dualistic Cathars in Languedoc, both of which organisations were reputed to be guardians of the Holy Grail, the chalice of the Last Supper; the setting up of numerous Black Virgins brought back from the Crusades, and the emergence of an alternative love cult of the Isis figure, the Black Virgin, who has been regarded as Mary Magdalene; the simultaneous growth of the troubadours; and the involvement in all these developments of the Secret Order of the *Prieuré Notre-Dame de Sion*, a Grand Master of which (Hugues de Payen) founded the Templars together with a co-founder who may also have been a Cathar. The *Prieuré* now aims to restore the Merovingian blood-line to the throne of France and perhaps of a united Europe. (According to one view this line began with Jesus Christ's sons by Mary Magdalene, descendants of whom apparently acceded to the throne of Jerusalem after the First Crusade.)

Both the Templars and the Cathars were put before the Inquisition and suppressed: the Cathars as a result of the Albigensian Crusade and the siege of Montségur in 1244, when the Cathar treasure (possibly including the Holy Grail) was spirited away by four parfaits or priests who were lowered by ropes down the castle walls; and the Templars in 1312, by which time their numbers included many suppressed Cathars[2] and they had come to be regarded as a heretical sect.

The Palace and Temple of Solomon

The Cistercian-Templar connection centred on Jerusalem. The first nine Templars arrived there c.1119, and Baldwin II, King of Jerusalem, gave them the site of the old Temple of Solomon. Their headquarters were in the royal palace of Solomon, in the area of the former Jewish Temple on Mount Zion (or Sion). The First Temple there had been conceived by David (2 *Samuel*, 1 *Chronicles*) and built by his son Solomon, and the Ark of the Covenant had stood in the Holy of Holies there from c.950 to c.586 BC. It contained the tablets of the Ten Commandments, and had been brought to Jerusalem by David; the Jews had carried it in the Tabernacle during their forty years of wandering in the desert under Moses. The Ark went missing c.586.BC and it was not in the Second Temple, which replaced it from c.516.BC-AD.70.

(The base of the Western wall of its courtyard still survives as the "Wailing Wall", and Jews believe the *Shekhinah*, or Divine Presence, will never leave its stones.) After 691 the site was occupied by the Moslem Dome of the Rock.

An eye-witness has left us a description of what life was like in the House of Solomon some fifty years later, in 1172. Theoderick, a German pilgrim, describes the excavations that took place during the Templar occupation[3]:

"The palace of Solomon...is oblong, and supported by columns within like a church, and at the end is round like a sanctuary and covered by a great round dome, so that...it resembles a church. This building, with all its appurtenances, has passed into the hands of the Knights Templar, who dwell in it and in the other buildings connected with it, having many magazines of arms, clothing, and food in it, and are ever on the watch to guard and protect the country. They have below them stables for horses built by King Solomon himself in the days of old, adjoining the palace, a wondrous and intricate building resting on piers and containing an endless complication of arches and vaults, which stable, we declare according to our reckoning, could take in ten thousand horses with their grooms. No man could send an arrow from one end of their building to the other, either lengthways or crossways, at one shot with a Balearic bow. Above it abounds with rooms, solar chambers, and buildings suitable for all manner of uses. Those who walk upon the roof of it find an abundance of gardens, courtyards, ante-chambers, vestibules, and rain-water cisterns; while down below it contains a wonderful number of baths, storehouses, granaries, and magazines for the storage of wood and all other needful provisions. On another side of the palace, that is to say, on the western side, the Templars have erected a new building. I could give the measurements of its height, length, and breadth of its cellars, refectories, staircases, and roof, rising with a high pitch, unlike the flat roofs of that country; but even if I did so, my hearers would hardly be able to believe me. They have built a new cloister there in addition to the old one which they had in another part of the building. Moreover, they are laying the foundations of a new church of wonderful size and workmanship in this place, by the side of the great court.

It is not easy for anyone to gain an idea of the power and wealth of the Templars – for they and the Hospitallers have taken possession of almost all the cities and villages with which Jerusalem was once enriched, which were destroyed by the Romans, and have built castles everywhere and filled them with garrisons, besides the very many and, indeed, numberless estates which they are well known to possess in other lands."

The early Templars seem to have had a mission: the involvement of St Bernard's uncle, André de Montbard, who effectively took orders from the Abbot, St Bernard; the nature of the journey of the nine; their being housed in the royal palace; and the fact that a mere nine men could not turn a war – all suggest that the first Templars were searching for something on the site of the Temple of Solomon, on St Bernard's behalf. It could have been the Ark of the Covenant, which disappeared c.586 BC, and may have been buried on the site, but their mission was secret, like the fact that their leader, Hugues de Payen was also the Grand Master of the Prieuré Notre-Dame de Sion (Zion, on whose Mount the Templars lived) which then (as now) aimed to restore the Merovingian blood-line to the throne of France. Both André de Montbard, St Bernard's uncle, and Hugues de Payen were related to Hugues, Count of Champagne, who crusaded in 1104 and joined the Templars in 1125, when he looked to St Bernard for spiritual leadership; and the role of Hugues, Count of Champagne needs to be investigated.

There is a tradition that they found the Ark of the Covenant buried in the basement of the Temple, and brought it back to Chartres, where it stood on Solomon's Table (which showed the earth, the planet and the stars in three Kabbalistic circles); and that the secret found its way into Gothic architecture in the form of buttresses shaped like the prow of a ship (punning the Ark of the Covenant with Noah's Ark, and of course the nave of a church with *navis,* the Latin for "ship" or "ark").

The early Templars became very interested in the Temple of Solomon. They took their name from it: they were known as "The Military Order of the Knights of the Temple of Solomon" and as "the Poor Knights of Christ and of the Temple of Solomon".[4] They undoubtedly absorbed some local Kabbalistic ideas about the architecture of the Temple of Solomon, and they became very interested in the Song of Solomon (10th century BC). On their return to Europe from Jerusalem in 1128 they reported to St Bernard, who increasingly based his outlook on Solomon. Between 1130 and 1145 he delivered 86 (on another count, 120, and on another, 280) Sermons on the Biblical Song of Solomon. This was possibly the Hebrew version of the Sumerian Royal Sacred Marriage in which the King "married" a fertility goddess who was represented by a temple prostitute, and St Bernard interpreted the lovers (Solomon and the Queen of Sheba) as a Bridegroom (Christ) and a Bride (the Church).

From the early Templars St Bernard absorbed the architectural plan of the Temple of Solomon, and the Kabbalistic *sefirot* (divine eminations) that were represented by pillars in the Temple, and it seems that St Bernard's Cistercians were behind the sudden and dramatic rise of the Gothic Cathedrals in the 12th century whose pillars also reflect the *sefirot*. As one observer has put it, "The spread of the Gothic style and the Temple went together.... The whole Gothic formula derives from the Cistercians."[5] The appearance of the Gothic style has been dated c.1130 (two years after the return of the nine Templars), when the earliest known pointed arches appeared in Lombardy. The pointed arch was an Islamic feature that gave churches height – and light. Gothic was first used between 1130 and 1150 at Saint-Denis, Chartres and Sens.[6] The builders of Chartres, Notre-Dame, Amiens and Reims Cathedrals seem to have been a guild called "the Children of Solomon", and the workmen were instructed in geometry by Cistercian monks and were evidently affiliated to the Order of the Knights of the Temple of Solomon.

It is possible that the Templars raised the money for the Gothic Cathedrals on behalf of St Bernard, and funded the swift rebuilding of Chartres following the fire of 1194.[7] St Bernard seems to have extended the architecture of the Cistercian Gothic Cathedrals. Although he was against the ornate style of Saint-Denis, the first Gothic Cathedral, and criticised Abbot Suger for aesthetic excesses, he was evidently in favour of the spare, unfurnished, puritanical, geometrical stone edifices that the early Gothic Cathedrals became. (There is an inherent contradiction in the Cistercian Order's ideal of self-denial, poverty, simplicity and spiritual purity on the one hand, and its reputation for aggression, military discipline, managerial efficiency and cupidity on the other hand. It is quite conceivable that the austere Cistercians who criticised Abbot Suger, the founder of Gothic, could have managed the Templar funds, which are reputed to include a treasure found in Jerusalem, and that they financed the growth of a purged Gothic style.)

THE ISLAMIC PARADISAL ROSE AND GOTHIC ROSE WINDOWS

The rose window which appeared in Gothic Cathedrals after c.1130 and embodied the Light, seems to have come from the Templars' and Crusaders' contact with the Islamic Paradise.[8]

"Paradise" is the Persian for "garden", and before 1150 the Sufi Paradise was shown as a garden and courtyard. The Mohammedan Paradise has a Cosmic Tree, the Tuba (Arabic *tuba*). A tradition of the Prophet says: "The *Tuba* is a tree in Paradise. God planted it with his own hand and breathed His Spirit into it." According to Ibn al-Arabi (died 1240) the *Tuba* manifests in the macrocosm as a Tree of Knowledge which grew from the seed of the Divine Command "Be", and in the microcosm as meditative wisdom which bears fruits in the spirit.[9] It is shown with round white flowers and appears in Persian carpets, and it may have been mistranslated by the Templars as the "tuberose". ("Tuberose" was a popular corruption from its Latin name, *polianthes tuberosa*, which was probably known in Templar times.)

The Templars seem to have absorbed the Islamic sacred architecture. The stucco inside Arab mosques (as in the Court of Lions in the Alhambra Palace, Granada) sought to transform stone into light, for "Allah is the Light of the heavens and the earth" (*Koran* 24.35) who, like an alchemist, transforms lead into gold and body into spirit (or Light);[10] and the outside of Arab mosques was frequently decorated with rose-like emblems, for sacred Islamic art was not allowed to show a human figure. The Templars seem to have interpreted the *Tuba* as a rose, and the association between

Mary and the rose reflects the Christianization of the Islamic rose after the First Crusade.

Eastern Christians revered Mary as the Mother of God, a latter-day version of the Earth Mother of Asia Minor, and Templars and Crusaders returning from the Holy Land at the end of the 11th century brought back ideas that strengthened Mariology. The French courtly love (*amour courtois*) in which a lord worshipped and served a lady like a feudal vassal, appeared in French literature at the end of the 11th century, and the new idealising of women (which women in 11th century castles welcomed) can largely be attributed to France's contact with Islamic mysticism during the First Crusade, and its ideas of love and service. The word *troubadour* seems to come from the Arabic roots *t-r-b* and *r-b* which suggest the words for God, mistress, minstrel and education, and thus derive the romantic love poetry of the troubadours from the mystical love poetry of the Sufis.[11]

Troubadours worshipped women, and this in turn strengthened Mary's position. Mary's womb was regarded as a living Grail, containing the blood and spirit of Christ, and so she was described in the medieval *Litany of Loretto* as *vas spirituale* ("spiritual vessel"): her womb was the vessel in which the divine had become manifest. The *Litany* also called her *foederis arca* or "Ark of the Covenant", and she became the Ark of a New Covenant between God and the Crusaders, whose Templars lived on the site where the Old Covenant had been housed. According to the *Litany* Mary was *domus aurea*, "house of gold" (like a Cathedral) and *Rosa Mundi*, the Rose of the World, Rose Queen of the World, Rosa Alchemica, Queen of the Most Holy Rose Garden, and Multifoliate Rose, and the rosary was told in groups of five beads to recall the five-petalled rose of Mary. The approach to Mary became the lover's approach to the Goddess of Love in the rose garden of Courtly Love, which was an allegory of Divine Love (see C. S. Lewis's *Allegory of Love*); as in the *Roman de la Rose* (c.1240) in which a dreamer fails to pick a rosebud (love) in the garden of courtly society. As Mariology grew it was inevitable that courtly and mystical love would become overtly fused, and Dante achieved this fusion by making Beatrice at once his earthly courtly lady and his guide to Paradise. Significantly Dante has St Bernard interceding with Mary.[12]

Through the Templar influence on the Cistercians, most of the French Cathedrals are dedicated to the Virgin Mary, *Notre Dame* of Divine Love, and the rose, the flower of Aphrodite, became her flower. The rose is entwined with the cult of Mary, who was often shown among roses or in a rose garden in the 15th and 16th centuries. St Bernard wrote a treatise on Mariology, the moderate cult of the Virgin, and he interpreted the Bride in the *Song of Solomon*, the Queen of Sheba, as Mary, the Queen of Heaven. The Bride/Sheba/Mary says in the *Song of Solomon* (2.1), "I am the rose of Sharon". Sharon is in Palestine, near Mount Carmel. (The rediscovery of the cult of Black Virgins which were brought back from the Crusades, often by Templars, may have been inspired by another text in the *Song* in which the Bride/Sheba/Mary says, "I am black but comely, O ye daughters of Jerusalem" (1.5).) The rose which was the symbol of earthly love for the troubadours, but which also had a Sufi meaning as we have seen, became the symbol for divine love in St Bernard's movement: Mary became the Rose without a Thorn because she was free from the "thorn" of original sin; in the Garden of Eden, or Paradise before the Fall, the rose had no thorns, which only grew as a result of original sin. St Bernard's followers, the Cistercian managers, built Mary, the Rose without Thorns who had appeared to St Bernard several times in visions, into the stones of the Gothic Cathedrals in the form of the rose window.

Again through the Templar influence on the Cistercians, rose windows suddenly appeared in France in the 12th century. The abbey church at Saint-Denis was the first in which the circular wheel of Romanesque architecture (as in Santa Maria in Pomposa) was developed into a decorated rose c.1144, after the west face had been restored under Abbot Suger (1137-40), the founder of Gothic. The designer of this rose probably also designed the rose of the north transept at Laon. (In Chartres Cathedral, the west rose is a wheel outside and a flower inside.) The experience of the towering height of early Gothic was first recorded by Abbot Suger who in 1144 felt the church transformed "that which is material into that which is immaterial" so that he was "transported from this inferior to that higher world". Saint-Denis has some verses by Suger on gilded doors: "Bright is the noble work; but, being nobly bright, the work/Should brighten the minds so that they may travel through the true lights,/To the

True Light where Christ is the true door..../The dull mind rises to truth, through that which is material/And in seeing this Light, is resurrected from its former submersion."[13] The new technique of stained glass play a part in achieving played a part in achieving this feeling of elevation.

All Gothic Cathedrals recalled the New Jerusalem of St John's *Revelation* (21.2-24): "And I John saw the holy city, new Jerusalem, coming down from God out of heaven.... And I heard a great voice out of heaven saying, Behold, the tabernacle of God is with men.... And he carried me away in the spirit to a great and high mountain, and shewed me that great city, the holy Jerusalem, descending out of heaven from God, having the glory of God: and her light was like unto a stone most precious, even like a jasper stone, clear as crystal; and had a wall great and high, and had twelve gates.... And the city lieth foursquare, and the length is as large as the breadth.... And the city was pure gold, like unto clear glass.... The glory of God did lighten it, and the Lamb is the light thereof. And the nations of them which are saved shall walk in the light of it." The architecture of the Gothic Cathedral attempted to recover this Paradisal vision, and the towering height, the elaborate gates and the effect of the glass all combined to suggest the Kingdom of God, or Paradise, which was approached through gates and which was approached through gates and which was flooded with Divine Light. The Cathedrals round Paris of c.1200 – Amiens, Reims and Notre-Dame – all developed the idea.

The Templars seem to have absorbed the stained glass technique from the 11th century Persians – Omar Khayyam himself was an Alchemist who was involved in making stained glass – and they seem to have brought the technique back to France via Venice and Bohemia, where glass was made. As soon as Saint-Denis had been built they tried the technique at Chartres where the river sand gave a very pure glass. The west facade Chartres windows were in place 1150-55, the rest by 1227. They gave a blue effect of the Divine Light throughout the Cathedral. Alchemists made the glass, and the idea passed into Alchemy: Arnold of Villanova entitled his treatise on the Great Work, *Rosarium Philosophorum*, the *Rose Garden of Philosophers*.

Besides representing the Kingdom of God, Paradise or the New Jerusalem, the Gothic Cathedral suggested the soul, the inside of which was illumined by shafts of bluish Divine Light which originated outside the stone, symbolising the work of the Light filtering into Creation from its sun-like source outside. It is in the soul that God's activity becomes perceptible to man – when the soul is dead, God is dead – and so the Cathedrals showed in their windows the living soul in the form of a Paradisal rose, a soul which would become a rose in the garden of Paradise. Part of the mystery of the rose window was that you looked at your own soul, and saw its source and destination: Paradise. In the east rose window of Laon (early 13th century) the Virgin Mary holds out a rose to mankind.

The centre of a rose window is always the *Logos*, the Word – Christ – and to anyone standing in a Gothic Cathedral it seems that Christ radiates outwards from a centre, *mandala*-like, across an immaterial and material universe, suggesting that the immaterial becomes material. The rose window is to be found at the west end of the nave and at both ends of the transept, and while different rose windows describe the past, the present and the future, they all show the origin and radiating power of Creation, and visually demonstrate the active love of God in the universe to all who gaze at them. This symbolism was extended to include the Cathedral floor. The Chartres nave rose window is above the labyrinth in the nave floor, which has a six-petalled rosette in the centre (the material manifestation), while in the western aisle of the south transept at Chartres a chink has been deliberately left in the stained glass window of Saint Apollinaire (like Pope Gregory's chink) through which a ray of sunlight strikes a particularly white stone in the floor at midday every June 21. The north rose windows glorify the Virgin Mary, who is often shown with the dove of the Holy Spirit; the south rose windows show the Resurrected Christ who at Chartres holds the Grail (c.1227); and the west rose windows show the Last Judgement. The rose windows all show many paths leading to one centre, round which there is a whirling motion. They are western *mandalas*. They show the Light *in* stones.

In the Gothic Cathedrals, Christian iconography is mixed with Neoplatonism and the metaphysics of Light that derived from St Augustine and John Scotus Erigena and suggests the order behind Creation, the *Logos* in which microcosm and macrocosm are one. Creation took place when God said "Let there be Light" (*Genesis* 1.3), and the rose windows show Creation as an explosion from a single point in the centre (a Big Bang), and to the medieval mind the Light gave order. Bishop Grosseteste (c.1175-1253), who developed a science of optics through Arab influence, thought that the heavenly spheres were filled with Light which manifested from the bodiless into bodily substance, from the eternal to the temporal world; so that Light was the creative principle in things. Rose windows act out Grosseteste's Light-filled spheres, for they suggest that just as the sun shines on a glass lens and makes fire, so an immaterial sun shining on the transparent soul makes the Light of the Spirit; and this idea is illustrated pictorially in the rose windows as the central immaterial sun radiates outwards through Light-filled spheres to bodily creation.[14]

7

The Grail Light

The reappearance of the heretical Grail legend in the West soon after 1190[1] may be associated with the rediscovery of an olive wood cup in the Celtic church of Glastonbury c.1184, but it also seems to be a reaction to the fall of Jerusalem to Saladin in 1187.

Although the legend is set in the time of King Arthur, it is imbued with a feeling for the importance of Jesus and the chalice that was brought from Jerusalem by Joseph of Arimathaea. To a contemporary reader of the crusading time the idea of a wounded Fisher King whose lands are waste could not fail to suggest Jesus's ravaged Kingdom of Jerusalem which in 1099 covered the modern Israel, south Lebanon and South West Jordan (the Holy Land). As the Grail could restore both the King and his lands to health, it would have symbolized the means of restoring the Kingdom of Jerusalem to the followers of Christ. The legend must be read against the contemporary crusading background when, as the 13th century *Mappa Mundi* shows, Jerusalem was placed at the centre of the world and under the protection of Mary (who was shown on the left panel that held the altar piece *Mappa Mundi*).

The Sufi Light of the Grail and the Cistercian Templars' Chalice

The legend of the Grail (a chalice that shone with Light) seems to have embodied and transmitted St Bernard's (and therefore the Templar) Light. The Grail emerged from the same Sufi-Islamic influence as the rose window which (as at Chartres) sometimes showed it. The Sufis, starting with Omar Khayyam, linked wine-drinking and the image of the cup with spiritual intoxication, and the Grail was at one level the Cup of Spiritual Intoxication as we have seen (pp266-274), an Islamic symbol which the returning Crusaders Christianized into the chalice of the Last Supper.

It is possible that the first Templar expedition to Jerusalem was celebrated in the Grail legends, but distanced to the time of King Arthur to preserve the secret. If so, the Templars were called the Knights of the Round Table, Hugues de Payen was Arthur, and St Bernard has been identified with Sir Galahad.[2] If the Knights of the Round Table were Templars, the Tudor rose in the centre of the 14th century Round Table at Winchester may recall the Rose of Mary, and the search for the Ark was perhaps disguised as the search for the Grail. In that case, the Kingdom laid waste was territory pillaged by the Moslems during the First and Second Crusades and the Fisher King was a composite figure of Solomon-Christ; only the restoration of the Temple through victory in the Crusades could make the lands healthy again.

Such a view explains the power of the Grail legend in the 12th century, and if it is right Wolfram von Eschenbach nearly let the cat out of the bag in 1197 by describing the Knights of the Round Table as Templars. According to one version of the Grail legend, the Grail was housed in a chapel of glass (like Paris's Sainte-Chapelle which was built between 1246 and 1248 to house relics from the Crusades), and according to another version the Temple of the Grail is in Paradise, at the centre of the world, like the Parsee sanctuary of the Holy Fire at Shiz (Gazat). The idea of a glass temple of the Grail in Paradise may be behind the Gothic Cathedrals and it is interesting that Henry Adams' magic hundred years of Gothic (1170-1270)[3] coincided with all the Grail legends.

A clue to the origin of the reappearance of the Grail legend c.1190 is to be found in the connection between Chrétien de Troyes, the first teller of the Grail story, and Philippe d'Alsace, Count of Flanders, to whom Chrétien's poem is dedicated. Chrétien lived at the court of Marie Countess of Champagne, whom Philippe tried to marry in 1182. Marie de Champagne was the daughter of Eleanor of Aquitaine, the wife of Louis VII of France and Henry II of England. She encouraged courtly romance (and the best troubadour poet Bernard de Ventadourn) at her court at Poitiers, and Marie encouraged Chrétien's courtly *Lancelot*; she was also related to Hugues de Champagne who had joined the Templars in the Holy Land shortly after his relative and feudal vassal Hugues de Payen.

The beginning of Chretien's poem says that Philippe told him the Grail story, and that his poem was composed at Philippe's request. It is possible that Philippe had access to Robert de Boron's source, "a great book on the secret of the Grail", but he may have had access to an oral tradition behind that source in Jerusalem: either something Marie had heard from Hugues de Champagne, through her mother; or something he had heard from his own father, Count Derrick of Alsace, who was in Jerusalem during the Second Crusade which collapsed when the Crusaders retreated from Damascus, strengthening the Moslems' position.

Count Derrick built a countship chapel in Brugge (the modern Bruges), the administrative centre of the countship of Alsace, in the first half of the 12th century: the chapel of St Basil. St Basil the Great, c.329-379, was a Greek church father, and four of his vertebrae were brought from Caesarea in 1100. The quasi-monastic Templars followed the two monastic Rules (the Longer and Shorter Rules) of St Basil which were used by St Benedict as well as by St Bernard, and the naming of the chapel after St Basil thus has a Templar significance. Two otherwise plain tombstones on the floor of the chapel show Grail cups and they date from the time of the rise of the Templars. Count Derrick brought back from the Second Crusade a phial of Jesus's blood which, according to tradition, he was given in 1148 by his brother-in-law Baldwin III, King of Jerusalem, and Fucher, the Patriarch of Jerusalem who led the Templar contingent against Damascus in that same year. The phial is today housed in the upstairs Chapel of the Holy Blood in Bruges.

Did Count Derrick bring the story of the Grail back from Baldwin III in Jerusalem and pass it on to his son Philippe, who told Chrétien?[4] And do the Grail cups on the two tombstones in the Chapel of St Basil link Jerusalem and France, and demonstrate the symbolic importance that was attached to the Grail during the Second Crusade a good forty years before Chrétien's poem? If so, we can understand why the Grail story has Cistercian elements that are associated with St Bernard, who planned the Second Crusade.

Alternatively, did Chrétien hear of the alleged rediscovery of the Grail cup at Glastonbury c.1184 through Marie de Champagne, the daughter of Eleanor of Aquitaine? Eleanor had accompanied her first husband, Louis VII, on the Second Crusade to defend the Kingdom of Jerusalem, and, he had stayed at the court of her uncle, Raymond of Poitiers, at Antioch. Although she was imprisoned by her second husband, Henry II of England, from 1174 to 1189, Marie was well connected and visited England, and she could well have heard of the rediscovery of the Grail cup at the court of Henry II (who would certainly have been told of the find). In which case Philippe would have told Chrétien the legendary background to the Grail which he may have heard from his father.

In the Grail legends the fall of Jerusalem in 1187 is woven with another event that was much discussed in the early 1190s: the alleged discovery of King Arthur's body at Glastonbury Abbey in 1190. Geoffrey of Monmouth had written c.1135 that "Arthur's last earthly destination was Avalon", and gravediggers came across the bones of a tall man and a stone slab seven feet below ground level, and a lead cross which said, "*Hic Jacet Sepultus Inclytus Rex Arturius in Insula Avallonia*" ("Here lies buried the renowned King Arthur in the Isle of Avalon"). The cross has since disappeared, but it was in existence in 1607 when a drawing was made of it. The remains were placed in front of the high altar in Glastonbury Abbey and became an object of pilgrimage. This event captured the public imagination and led to the mixing of Glastonbury's two main stories, of Joseph of Arimathaea and King Arthur in the Grail legends.

The Light from the Cup

The Grail was allegedly first brought to Glastonbury by Joseph of Arimathaea. We have already seen that Maelgwyn of Llandaff or Avalon, alias Melchinus (c.540), the uncle of St David, wrote that "Joseph of Arimathaea, the noble Decurion, received his everlasting rest with his eleven associates in the isle of Avalon. He lies in a bifurcated line (or linen garment) at the southern angle (or next to the southern corner) of the Oratorium over (or above) the Adorable Virgin. He has with him the two white vessels of silver" ("*habit enim secum duo vascula argentea alba*") "which were filled with the blood and the sweat of the great Prophet Jesus" (Cottonian MS). These *vascula* or cruets gave the name of the Crystal Isle to Glastonbury. The Grail itself, the cup used at the Last Supper in Joseph of Arimathaea's Jerusalem residence, may have been an ordinary cup of olive wood that was in everyday use in Joseph's house.

There are references to the Holy Grail in the 6th century. Forcatulus writes that "the Britons commemorate that Joseph brought with them the pledge and testimony of the sacred Eucharist, namely the chalice which was used by the Saviour, and placed before his most holy guests the apostles, and which is preserved by them (the Britons) as the pledge of the safety of Britain, as the palladium was that of Troy" (Fortaculus *de Gallor, Imperio et Philos, lib vii*, p989). *Greal* in British means "a collection of elements", and *Saint-Greal* means "the holy elements". Legend had it that the Grail caught some of Jesus's blood and was buried in Glastonbury, either in the earth by the Chalice Well or under the well, or under Chalice Hill – the "Chalice" in Chalice Hill of course refers to the Grail – so that the water ran round the Grail chalice. The water had miraculous healing properties for those who drank where Jesus drank or plunged into the Pilgrims' Bath, the English Lourdes, and were healed by waters that were mixed with his blood. A British hermit had a vision of St Joseph of Arimathaea and the Holy Grail c.717 (which is contained in the French monk Helinand's *Chronicles* about that time), and the closeness between Britain and Brittany in the 4th and 5th centuries during the Saxon invasions would have given impetus for the original Grail story to appeal to the French.

According to a similar tradition, Joseph or his descendants preserved the cup and later (either during the Claudian invasion of AD 42 or during the Saxon invasions) lodged it, or buried it, in the underground chapel of the Celtic church near the Chalice Well at Glastonbury, where it lay forgotten until it was found when the church was destroyed by fire in 1184 and demolished to be replaced by a building approved by Rome. In pinning down what may have happened to the Grail next, we need to summarise the sequence of events regarding the location of Joseph of Arimathaea's tomb:

AD 82 Joseph of Arimathaea buried in the wattle church of St Mary,

1184 Glastonbury (Maelgwyn of Avalon c.540); Fire destroyed wattle church of St Mary, Glastonbury, beneath which there was an underground chapel built by King Ina c.700 and laden with silver and gold (William of Malmesbury, ch XL);

1185 Norman Chapel of St Mary built on the site of the wattle church;

1367 Body of Joseph of Arimathaea discovered in a stone sarcophagus at east end of the crypt under St Mary's Chapel, whole chapel now called St Joseph's Chapel;

1662 Great Rebellion cut down Holy Thorn (June 22), Joseph of Arimathaea's stone sarcophagus and body removed and placed in the churchyard of Glastonbury church, then spent 266 years in rain and frost;

1928 Stone sarcophagus and body brought into north transept of church by L. S. Lewis, then Vicar of Glastonbury, where they now are, top of sarcophagus covered with glass; letters J.A. officially deemed to refer to John Allen, a code to conceal reference to Joseph of Arimathaea who gave up his own garden tomb to Christ.

It seems that in 1184 when the wattle church was destroyed, Joseph of Arimathaea's stone sarcophagus survived the fire in the underground chapel, and was built round in 1185, and that the Grail cup may have been uncovered (as claimed by Isabel Hill Elder in *Joseph of Arimathaea*) probably in the underground chapel. Indeed, it seems that the rediscovery of the Grail may have prompted the search for Arthur's bones, which were found in 1190. The find of the Grail would have greatly interested the Templars who were linked with the Cathars and who had been looking for it in Jerusalem and elsewhere since their foundation in 1118/9. In 1187 Jerusalem fell to Saladin.

What happened next is uncertain, and there are conflicting claims that different bowls and cups (ranging from olive wood as befits a carpenter's son to silver to magnificently jewelled) are in fact the original Grail chalice. According to one version of this tradition, the Grail passed to the Templars. It is likely that it was discovered by pro-Crusaders in 1184 when the Normans under Henry II were descending on Glastonbury to rebuild the Chapel and Romanise it, and that soon after it was passed to the Templars who may have taken it back to Jerusalem. After the fall of Jerusalem it would have been brought back to Europe, and after c.1194 it may well have been in France, lodged in Chartres Cathedral as tradition maintains. At some point it may have passed to the Cathars, and it is possible that it was smuggled out of Montségur in 1244 as tradition records; in which case the Grail may still be with descendants of the Cathars, or it may have returned to the Templars.

According to another version, the Grail remained at Montségur in 1244 and was buried in the secret underground passages. It remained hidden until the early 1930s when it was discovered by Otto Rahn, who used sacred geometry to probe Montsegur. Rahn became an SS Colonel and sent his find to Himmler in 1937. Hitler had gazed at the spear of Longinus (alias Gaius Cassius, the Roman centurion who out of compassion pierced Christ's side) in Austria in 1909; it had a nail from the cross wedged within it, and it was reputed to give a world destiny to its owner. Hitler was a will-to-power occultist under Dietrich Eckart by 1923, and one of his reasons for invading Austria was to obtain personal possession of the magical, power-giving spear, which happened in 1935. In 1945 the spear of Longinus was discovered beneath the Nuremburg Fortresss, below the Panier Platz, and is now in the

Weltliche Schatzkammer of the Hofburg, Vienna.[5] Himmler's SS had founded a new occultist organisation called the Ahnenerbe, which drew on the Manichaeans, Knights of Light and Illuminati, and sought to revive pagan beliefs about Stonehenge, the Pyramids and stone circles. Himmler took the Grail cup to the Schloss Wewelsburg and placed it on the marble pedestal in the Realm of the Dead beneath the Great Hall. In 1939 Rahn, author of *Croisade contre le Graal and La Coeur de Lucifer*, disappeared. It was alleged that he had committed suicide, but there is evidence that he was behind excavations at Montségur and other Cathar sites during the Second World War, and that he was still writing in 1945. On May 2, 1945 the Montségur Grail was put in a lead casket and buried in a glacier in Hochfeiler, Austria, 9000 feet above sea level. The casket is apparently still in the glacier, and could not be reached until it emerged between 1990 and 1995. There has been no news of its emerging.[6]

According to a third version, the Grail (if it was an olive-wood cup) remained at (or in the 13th century was returned to) Glastonbury, and it was there until c.1539 when the Abbey was dissolved. Seven of the ex-monks then fled to the Cistercian Abbey of Strata Florida, Cardiganshire, Wales, and brought with them a wooden cup. The Cistercians of course opposed the Reformation and therefore the Dissolution. The Cistercians, in fact, had always supported Welsh political and religious independence from England, and had been funded by Welsh Kings in gratitude; and it was the Welsh prince (i.e. king) Rhys ap Gruffudd (or Gruffydd) who had founded Strata Florida Abbey c.1184 (some accounts say 1164). This Abbey was also destroyed during the Reformation – all that remains now is a west doorway and some medieval tiles – and the last of the seven monks gave the cup to the Powells of Nanteos Manor, near Capel Seion, Aberystwyth. The Powells kept the cup (now a mere sliver, its edges worn away by drinkers hoping to be healed), and when Nanteos Manor was rebuilt in the 18th century the cup was displayed in the new building, where Wagner saw it, and was inspired by it to write his *Parsifal*, in 1855. Recently it was transferred to a bank (Lloyds Bank, Aberystwyth, I believe), where it now is.[7]

There are other claims for the Grail. All that can be said here is that while the Templar connection which associates the Grail with Jerusalem and

Chartres is credible, there is no evidence to support the claim; and that the Cathar connection depends on credence being given to Otto Rahn's credibility, whereas it may be that the Nazis had the wrong cup, that they found *a* cup that was associated with the *consolamentum* (see p439) but which was not the chalice of the Last Supper. It may be that the Nanteos cup is the Grail, but there is no final evidence.

The Grail legends are all Christianized accounts. Chrétien de Troyes' *Perceval* or *Le Conte du Graal* introduced the mysterious *graal* in a Christian context soon after c.1190. The *graal* was a silver cup covered with precious stones, the French *graal* coming from the late Latin *gradalis*, a dish of plenty. In Chrétien this gives off a great light when it is carried by in a procession, and Perceval later learns that the cup contained the Host, Christ's body. Robert de Boron offered a complete history of the *graal* in *Joseph d'Aramathie* or the *Roman de L'estoire dou Saint Graal* (c.1200-1210). Robert claimed to have a source, "a great book on the secret of the Grail", which (if it existed) has not come down to us, and he linked the *graal* with the cup used at the Last Supper; Robert is very interested in the cup and therefore in the blood of Christ, and behind the Old French *Saint graal* or *Saint greal* (Holy Grail) is *sang real* (Royal Blood). In Wolfram von Eschenbach's *Parzival* (1207) the Grail becomes a precious stone fallen from heaven and the idea becomes more mystical. Perceval's adventures also appear in *Didot Perceval* (1190-1215), which combines the accounts of Chrétien and Robert, and *Perlesvaus* (c.1225) which seems to have been written at Glastonbury. Malory's *Morte d'Arthur* appeared much later, in 1485.

The differing versions of the legend tell a broadly common story. The Grail is the cup used at the Last Supper in which Joseph of Arimathaea caught some of Jesus's blood either when he was on the cross, or, more probably, when he was washing Jesus's body to prepare it for burial and some blood dripped from the wounds. Later Joseph was accused of stealing Jesus's body from the tomb and was imprisoned. Jesus appears to him in light and gives him the cup and instructs him in the Mass. A dove flies into prison each day and deposits a wafer in the cup. Joseph eventually leaves Palestine with his sister and her husband Bron (sometimes Bran), and they go into exile. They make a first table of the Grail to represent the Last Supper, and lay a fish in Christ's place and leave empty the 13th seat, Judas's (the Siege Perilous). In one version, Joseph goes to Glastonbury and installs the Grail on the altar of the first Christian church, the wattle one to the Virgin Mary which was burned down in 1184, and it serves as a chalice when Mass is celebrated. In other versions Joseph remains in Europe and the cup is guarded by Bron, who is known as the Rich Fisher after he fed his followers with a single fish from the Grail, emulating Christ's feeding of the five thousand with five loaves and two fishes. All settle in Avaron (Avalon) to await King Alain, the third Grail keeper who had been converted to Christianity by Joseph; like Arviragus.

A chapel or temple is built on top of a mountain, surrounded by a river, to house the Grail, which is guarded by a priest or king. This chapel is on Muntsalvach or Monsalvat, the Mountain of Salvation or Paradise, and an order of Grail Knights comes into existence. They sit at a second table, and Mass is celebrated with the Grail keeper, who is now called the Fisher King, as priest. He is wounded in his thigh or genitals and is known as the Maimed or Wounded King. The crucified Christ is behind this Wounded King. The country round the Grail mountain becomes a barren Waste Land as a result of the Grail King's wound. The spear with which he has been struck is identified as the spear of Longinus, who pierced Christ's side when he was on the cross. The spear, the Grail and a dish-shaped platter are all in the Grail castle. By Arthur's time, a third table is set up in Avalon, the Round Table from which the Grail is absent and to which it appears at Pentecost, floating veiled in sunlight. The knights start a search for it. Perceval (or Parzival or Parsifal), the Perfect or Holy Fool; Galahad, the virgin knight and Lancelot's son; and the ordinary Bors are the only three to find it. Perceval finds his way to the castle of the Wounded King, the Fisher King, and heals his wound by asking "Whom does the Grail serve?" (Answer, the King himself.) Perceval, Galahad and Bors continue their journey and reach Sarras or Sarraz (which is near or which may be another name for Muntsalvach), where they take part in a Mass at which Christ appears, first as a child and then as the crucified, after which Galahad dies. Perceval rules in the Fisher King's place in his castle, and Bors returns to Camelot.

It is clear that there is a strong Glastonbury element in the story. The mountain could be the Tor on which St Michael's Chapel was built on the pagan top, by Lucius in AD 167 or 183, and Paradise is still a part of Glastonbury (e.g. Paradise Farm) and in names round Burnham on the approach to Glastonbury from the sea. Sarraz is close to Sarum, the old name for Salisbury. However, the Tor is too close to Camelot (Cadbury Castle) for the knights to have spent years seeking it, and Castell Dinas Brân in Wales is another possibility. (It had a cauldron that could feed five hundred.)

The story seems to have been overlaid with European and Eastern (anti-Crusader) elements, and the Grail castle could be Montségur, the stronghold of the Albigensians or Cathari ("the Pure") in Languedoc: Montsalvat is a Cathar term, and Wolfram's Lord of the Grail castle, Perilla, was also the Lord of Montségur, or Montserrat (compare Sarraz). But the Grail castle could also be the Manichaean Persian Takt-i-Taqdis (Throne of Arches), now Takt-i-Suleiman on the holy mountain at Shiz in Iran. This was a palace built by the Persian king Chosroes II in the 7th century where there was a Parsee sanctuary of the Holy Fire that is supposed to have commemorated the birthplace of Zoroaster. This sanctuary was preceded by a Manichaean circular temple called Kuh (or Mount)-i-sal-Chwadcha, the whole of which could suggest "Muntsalvach". On this spot the Sasanian kings held rituals to preserve the health of the land and when the sanctuary was destroyed, the land was laid waste as in the Grail stories. The Takt was well known as briefly possessing the True Cross, which had been found by Helena, the mother of Constantine the Great, during her pilgrimage to Jerusalem c.326. Chosroes had pillaged the True Cross from Jerusalem in 614 and this was installed at Takt-i-Taqdis until it was captured back by the Byzantine Emperor Heraclius in 629, and this link with Christianity perhaps associated the Grail legend with the Takt. There is certainly a similarity between the Takt and the description of the Grail castle in the 13th century poem *Der Jüngere Titurel* by Albrecht von Scharffenberg.[8]

Details of this castle could have reached Toledo where Sufi teachings arrived and where Wolfram's source lived, a Jewish astronomer called Flegetanis whose Arabic manuscript was reputedly given to Wolfram by a singer called Koyt. The Templars were closely connected with Cathars. (One of Hugues de Payen's co-founders may have been a Cathar, and the fourth Templar Grand Master, 1153-1170, Bertrand de Blanchefort, came from a Cathar family.) Wolfram may have been a Cathar, and the Cathars would anyway have been in touch with Toledo. The Cathars believed like the Persian Manichaean Dualists that the world was created by Lucifer; they wished to return to the world of Light from which they were separated, and the only rites permitted by their priests (*perfecti* or *parfaits*, "perfect ones", compare "Parsifal") were the mystic feast at which something like the Grail was used (the *manisola*) and the kiss which passed the Light on from one to another afterwards (the *consolamentum*).

Wolfram makes the last guardian of the Grail the Grail King's daughter's son, Prester or Presbyter (i.e. priest) John, a Christian priest-King who has not been identified with any Cathar or Templar kingdom, and who (despite being associated with Ethiopia, as we shall see on p519) ruled in the Tibetan region of Shambhala, which had a connection with the Cathars (see pp24-25).[9] He came to attention when he wrote to Pope Alexander III in 1165: "Prester John, by the grace of God king over all Christian kings, greetings to the Emperor of Rome and the King of France, our friends.... In our land there is also an abundance of wine, bread, meat, and of everything that is good for the human body...and inside our palace there is (water) and the best wine on earth, and whoever drinks of it has no desire for worldly things, and nobody knows where the (water) goes or whence it comes." (In the same year he also wrote to the Emperor of Byzantium.) Wolfram however is probably making a fictional connection; he was writing a story using historical characters, and it suited his purpose to introduce a name that had caused a public stir. We have seen (pp434-435) that the spear of Longinus is supposed to have been in the Habsburg regalia in Vienna, and to have passed to Hitler who used to gaze at it; and that it was partly to possess it, and the power over the world it was reputed to give, that the occultist Hitler went to war against Austria.

The early 13th century saw two prose versions of Robert's poem: the German romance *Diu Krone* by Heinrich von dem Turlin, in which the Grail hero is Sir Gawain and light shines from the Grail, which is covered by a cloth; and the old French *Queste del Saint Graal*, c.1220, in which the hero is Sir Galahad. This was one of the three parts of the prose *Lancelot, or Vulgate cycle*, and is to be distinguished from a later, post-Vulgate *Queste*. It is this Vulgate *Queste* that is of interest, for, besides being the link between Robert and Malory, it was written by a Cistercian who was steeped in the teachings of St Bernard, and who was writing a treatise on grace.[10]

The Grail appears at the beginning of the *Queste*. It is the evening meal in Arthur's palace, and all the knights are seated in silence. There is a peal of thunder and "at once there shone in upon them a ray of sunlight which made the palace seven-fold brighter than it was before. And straightway they were as if illumined with the grace of the Holy Spirit, and they began to look at one another.... There entered the Holy Grail covered with a white cloth; but no-one was able to see who was carrying it. It entered by the great door of the hall.... As it passed before the tables, they were straightway filled at each place with such viands as the occupant desired. When all were served, the Holy Grail departed at once so that they knew not what had become of it.... Most of them gave thanks to Our Lord for the very great honour he had done them in feeding them with the grace from the Holy Vessel."

At the outset, a "worthy old man dressed in the garb of religion" makes it clear that the Quest is for divine Truth: "This Quest is not a quest for earthly things, but is to be a search for the deep secrets and confidences of Our Lord and for the great mysteries." The knights who were imperfect fail to achieve the Quest, and those who rose highest in the world of Arthur's court sink lowest in the world of the Grail, i.e. the Light; so, Gawain, who would not accept divine help, never sees the Grail, and Lancelot, who committed adultery with Arthur's Queen, only sees it in a dream, and later his strength fails him when he is near the Grail.

Only Galahad can look at the Grail. He hears a voice say "Let those who are not entitled to sit at the table of Jesus Christ withdraw", and a man "dressed in the garb of a bishop" is carried down from heaven by four angels and seated "at the table on which was the Holy Grail". This man is Josephus, the son of Joseph of Arimathaea and he prepares "to celebrate the sacrament of the mass" and takes a wafer apparently of bread" from the Grail, from which comes forth "a man as it were quite naked, and His hands and feet and body were bleeding". This is Jesus Christ himself. Jesus hands out the "precious food" to Galahad, who fulfils the dream of every Christian Knight, to be in the position of the disciples, for as Jesus says: "Just as they ate with me at the Last Supper, so you have eaten now with me at the table of the Holy Grail", "my table where no knight has eaten since the days of Joseph of Arimathaea". This is "the bowl (or dish) from which Jesus Christ ate of the lamb on Easter Day".

The Grail, then, is a symbol of an intoxicating mystical union with God in the *Queste.* It provided an exoteric, literary version of the Light that could be readily understood by the masses in the Middle Ages, and the Celtic mysteries embody religious ecstasy. The Grail represents a grace that is withdrawn: Jesus announces that the Grail "tonight will leave the kingdom of Logres" because its people "have turned to a lower worldly life, in spite of having been nourished with grace from this Holy Vessel", and "the people of the country of Logres because of their sins lost the Holy Grail". The loss of the Grail is the cause of the collapse of Arthur's kingdom before the Saxons, and the Cistercian author of the *Queste* presumably intended this as a warning to the West, which might suffer the same fate at the hands of the Moslems unless it held on to the grace of God, i.e. the Light.

The knights of Arthur in the *Queste* at times recall Crusading knights, and in Wolfram become the Knights of the Temple (*Templeisen*); Wolfram visited Outremer to see the Templars in action, and based his Grail Knights on his visit.[11] We have seen that after the demolition of the Celtic church of Glastonbury following the fire of 1184, the Grail could have passed to the Templars at a time when they escorted Christian pilgrims in the Kingdom of Jerusalem and protected them from threatening Moslems. Descendants of the Templars (who were suppressed in 1312) may have obtained or even produced the Turin Shroud, which it is claimed carbon-dating in 1988 has now proved to have been a medieval forgery c.1350 or at any rate a brilliant painting of the face of Christ of Raphael-like quality that first surfaced in Lirey in France in the 1350s. It was first exhibited by the widow of Geoffrey de Charmy, a soldier killed at Poitiers whose namesake (probably his father) was burned as a Templar in 1314 in the same fire as the Grand Master. (There are powerful counter-claims for its authenticity.) A wooden panel painting on the wall of the double-naved Templar preceptory at Templecombe in Somerset, carbon-dated to 1280-1340, is remarkably like the face on the Turin Shroud, and it is not impossible that the Templars also had the Grail.

The Grail was a symbol of the Light before it was Christianized. It can be tracked back to the pre-Christian mysteries of Tammuz, Attis, Adonis and Mithras, where there was a Mystic Meal from a Feeding Vessel that contained the Food of Eternal Life, and we have seen that these mysteries must be interpreted in terms of the Light. These mysteries were first Christianized when Attis was identified with the Christian *Logos* (according to the Phrygian Gnostic Naassene document, 50 BC-AD 220), and when "heretical" Christian mystics adopted pagan mysteries (according to Hippolytus' *Philosophoumena*) the process of Christianization was probably completed during the Crusades when there was traffic in the relics of the Passion. If the Grail did come from these originally pagan mysteries, it is possible that the Grail legend was suppressed as a heresy in the 13th and 14th centuries, when Catharism and Templarism were suppressed. There is a suggestion that Joseph of Arimathaea had possession of certain teachings not available to the Apostles, and this would be further reason for the Grail to be suppressed.

The Grail has been tracked back to the *sacrum* of a universal pre-Christian fire-cult which later symbolized the mystery of the Trinity: a metallic mirror, or crystal or glass ball filled with water, which could produce fire from the rays of the sun like a magnifying glass.[12] If the Grail was a mirror or ball, then it had a Jewish origin – though there were Egyptian links – and was connected with the Urim and Thummim of Jewish altarware and the Ark in the Temple of Solomon (which was preserved in the Monstrance of the Christian altar). It has been claimed that such a Grail was present in all the ancient religions, and was cryptically referred to in legends; that it was known in ancient Greece. When Christianized it demonstrated that Light (the Holy Ghost or Spirit) proceeded from the Fire or sun (the Father) to the candle of the soul (the Son, the Christ) through the Grail "lens" which symbolized the Church. (Hence the importance of the "*Filioque*" clause, which originated in Toledo in the 6th century, the city where the Grail was preserved according to Wolfram von Eschenbach.) In that case this Christianized *sacrum* was at Glastonbury from the time of King Arthur until it disappeared during the Reformation, and its mysteries were the outer representation of an inner process: the outer sun represented an inner source of Light; the outer rays represented inner rays; and the outer fire represented the inner illumination.

But all the evidence points to the Grail as the chalice of Joseph of Arimathaea which symbolized the Light. It may have been taken from Glastonbury or France (where according to one medieval legend Joseph of Arimathaea's companion Mary Magdalene brought it) to Jerusalem soon after 1184. It may even have been discovered in Jerusalem soon after the Kingdom of Jerusalem was set up. It may have found its way to the Templars by Wolfram's time (1197): we have seen that Wolfram has the Templars as guardians of the Grail. During this time the Templars may have lodged the Grail (as legend asserts) for safekeeping in the Cistercian-designed Cathedral at Chartres, along with the Ark (if they found it); hence the Grail in the stained glass window at Chartres. Any Templar possession of the Grail may have been obscured by other practices of theirs, which can be seen as reactions to the Islamic threat. Some years after St Bernard's death, the Templars received a blow which marked them for the rest of their time. Shortly before his capture of Jerusalem and the True Cross in 1187 Saladin made an example of the Templars and Hospitallers he had taken prisoner. Claiming they had violated treaties with Moslem powers he beheaded 200.

It is possible that the later Templar ceremony of "Baphomet", in which Templars worshipped a bearded severed head, commemorated the beheading of the 200 whose heads were symbolized by one head; although it is also possible that the head was Christ's, the head of the Turin Shroud and of the wooden panel at Templecombe, Somerset, or of St John the Baptist; for the Templars had a Mandaean strain and Mandaeans worshipped the severed head of John the Baptist, who they regarded as the true Prophet; and the Templars' descendants, the German Johannes Brüder, also worshipped the severed head of John the Baptist. (The Baphomet is unlikely to be "Mahomet" or Mohammed, the Arabic for Baphomet meaning "Father of Wisdom" or "Father of Understanding".) The Baphomet was said by

Templars to be "the principle of beings created by God Trinity", and may have been a Primeval Man like the Kabbalistic Adam Kadmon, or a male Gnostic Sophia. The Templars had absorbed the Eastern influence, and in their later ceremonies they apparently trampled on a cross, spat at it and shouted "Yallah", which has been misunderstood as blending "Jesus" and "Allah". (This practice seems to have contributed to their being banned for Islamic heresy and magical practices, for denying Christ and sacrilege.) In fact the word probably blended "Jerusalem", "Allah" and "Salah" or Saladin (whose full name was Salah-ad-Din), and expressed disgust at the beheader Saladin's possession of Jerusalem and the True Cross. It is also possible that the trampling and spitting took place because the cross was regarded as the evil instrument of Christ's suffering.

It is certain that the Templar Order of "the poor Knights of Christ", whose Rule was written by St Bernard and who wore white mantles bearing a red eight-pointed cross, was not set up to practise denial of Christ, although it looked back to Solomon, and it is possible that the Order came to emphasise the Grail chalice for its "positive" qualities rather than the "negative" cross.

The Grail may have been passed to the Cathars by sympathetic Templars during the Albigensian Crusade against the Cathars. It may have served as a rallying point at Montségur, and been used in the Cathar *manisola* ceremony there. As the Grail was associated with Catharism, the Church attacked the Grail romances during the Albigensian Crusade, declaring them to be heretical. Significantly, Malory aside, there were no new Grail legends after c.1225, and the Grail legend may have been suppressed because of its links with the Cathars. The Grail may have been smuggled out of Montségur on the eve of its fall in 1244, either back to the Templars or to a secret hiding place that has never been found. There is a tradition that on the night before the final assault three Cathars slipped a rope over the wall and climbed down it and carried away the regalia of Dagobert II and a cup reputed to be the Holy Grail.

We can summarise the medieval history of the Grail, then, as follows:

AD 29	In Joseph of Arimathaea's Jerusalem residence for the Last Supper.
AD 36	Brought to Glastonbury via France by Joseph of Arimathaea.
Between AD 36 & 6th C AD	Deposited in the underground chapel (which was therefore the Grail chapel) of the Celtic wattle church, Glastonbury, near Chalice Well, possibly during Claudian invasion of AD 42 or during Saxon invasions.
c.1118-1149	Stories about the Grail before and during Second Crusade.
c.1184	Found in the Celtic church, Glastonbury?
c.1184-7	To Jerusalem?
c.1187	To the Templars following the fall of Jerusalem.
By c.1190	Chrétien's poem (written before 1190 when Philippe left for Crusade).
c.1197	Lodged at Chartres?
By c.1225	To the Cathars at Montségur?
1244	Smuggled out of Montségur?
By 1539	Back at Glastonbury – or had always been at Glastonbury?
16th C	If an olive-wood cup, lodged at Nanteos Manor, N. Wales.

Whatever happened to the Grail in the 13th century, Cistercian Gothic ceased to reflect it.

The main point to grasp about the Grail is that it symbolized the Light. If, as we have seen, the Grail of the *Queste* represents the Light, then it is fair to assume that it symbolises the Light in all the other treatments of the legend by Chrétien, Robert de Boron and Wolfram. Detailed analysis can make a case for this.

By the middle of the 14th century the Flamboyant style was established in the rose windows of such Cathedrals as Amiens, Sainte-Chapelle and Beauvais, and the radial style was replaced by weaving loops spreading outwards from the centre, giving the effect of tongues of flame as in the west window at Tours. The Gothic style went out in elaborate flaming fires of which the austere, simple St Bernard (judging from his criticism of Abbot Suger) would have disapproved.

8

The Kabbalist Light

The Kabbalah began as an oral tradition that, it is claimed, originated in the time of the Jewish patriarch Abraham.[1] From very early on the pure Jewish tradition became mixed with the philosophy of the Persian Magi of Babylonian Chaldea and the Neoplatonists.[2] It became corrupted by magical practices, and came to be regarded as heretical by Jews as well as by Christians.

The Kabbalist Light of the Near East, the Light of the classical Hebrew Kabbalah, made contact with the Cistercian-Gothic Light in South France after 1148 when as a result of the Second Crusade the French Jews of Languedoc, Provence and Roussillon, who had arrived as merchants from Italy, introduced the mystical Kabbalah into their Talmudic academies.[3] Their Light was reinforced by the arrival of Spanish Jews who were refugees from the Berber Moslem invasion of Spain in 1147-8. These Spanish-Arab Jews brought their Babylonian tradition to France, and with it the Persian knowledge of Manichaeism which led to the rise of Catharism after the 1140s, and the Grail legend which came to Toledo (see p438).[4] The insights of the Kabbalah greatly interested St Bernard's generation, which was fascinated by the Temple of Solomon, and the Kabbalah's vision of the New Jerusalem influenced the conception of the Gothic Cathedral. It passed into the Western tradition, mixing with the Grail legends and influencing the late medieval brightness of the 14th century Christian return to mysticism (just as it later seems to have influenced some of the plays of Shakespeare).

The Light of the Kabbalah was already very ancient. Abraham was reputed to have received it from Melchizedek, King of Salem (i.e. Jerusalem); it at least went back to the second *Torah,* which God communicated to Moses at Mount Sinai.[5] It expressed itself in early Jewish mysticism, whose Light shone in Palestine before the calamity of AD 70. Early Jewish mystics of that time saw the Scriptures as means of inner transformation, and ecstatically contemplated the *Merkava* (Hebrew for "chariot") in Ezekiel's vision (*Ezekiel* chs 1 and 10) of the divine throne.

THE LIGHT OF MERKAVA

Merkava was the earliest form of formal (as opposed to oral) Kabbalah. It grew in Palestine, but from the 7th to 11th centuries it was based in Babylonia (where angels originated), and the early *Merkava* Kabbalists were scornful of the orthodox Talmudic tradition which formed the basis of later Jewish mysticism and the later Kabbalah.

Merkava mysticism aimed to return to the original Light in the fourth and seventh heavens, and it was influenced by Gnosticism. The "explorers of the supernatural world" (*Yorde Merkava*) wrote ecstatic hymns describing the seven halls or palaces (*hekhalot*) between the visible world and the divine Light in the seven heavens. In the *Lesser Hekhalot* they described the ascent of the soul, in the *Greater Hekhalot* the descent to the throne. The descenders were the *Yorde Merkava* who see that "Lustre and brilliance are His who lives for ever" after descending into themselves.[6]

The *Merkava* mystics *viewed* God's appearance on the Celestial Throne and kept a distance between themselves and God, and in speaking of "joining" (*devekuth,* literally "adhesion") with God rather than of "union", they stopped short of union at the level of vision and did not progress to a Sufi-like surrender to the Light. The distinction between joining and union may be only a question of semantics, though, and it is significant that the prince of the divine, Metatron or the "little Adonai", underwent a fiery transformation during his ascent to the throne. Merkava mysticism was considered very dangerous unless it was properly carried out, and according to the *Talmud* could result in death. (The *Merkava* of Ezekiel's vision is the origin of Blake's line in *Jerusalem* "Bring me my Chariot of Fire" and it inspired Blake's questioning of Ezekiel in *The Marriage of Heaven and Hell*, while Blake's "fourfold vision" came from the four worlds of the Kabbalah.)[7]

The early *Merkava* Kabbalists rejected the Talmudic approach, for the Talmudic tradition stressed intellectual comprehension of revealed Scripture and rabbinical tradition rather than direct experience of God's Light. By the 4th century AD the Jewish schools taught: the Scriptures; commentaries (*Midrashim*, "expositions" or "investigations" written between the 1st and 4th centuries); translations into Aramaic (*Targumim*); and the oral tradition of rabbinic law, the *Mishna*, the core around which the Babylonian and Palestinian *Talmuds* ("teachings", "study", or "learning", written between the 3rd and 6th centuries), or commentaries on the *Mishna*, were compiled. The Hebrew *Mishna* suggests both *shanah* ("to repeat") and *sheni* ("second"), and according to Talmudic sages, a second *Torah* ("revelation") was revealed to Moses at Mount Sinai. It was "learned by repetition" or memorised and handed down as an oral tradition that ran parallel to the Scriptures. The rabbinic law or *halakhah* concerned the way things were done, from agriculture to ritual purity.

The Light only appears in the *Mishna* and *Talmuds* in so far as lights had to be symbolically blessed. There was a dispute in the *Mishna* between two Pharisaical masters and their followers as to what lights should be blessed, and when. These were commented on in the *Talmuds* that were produced in the academies of Babylonia and Palestine (chiefly at Tiberias, Caesarea and Sephoris). The two masters in the 1st century were Shammai and Hillel, and after AD 70 the Hillelites (or House of Hillel) prevailed over the Shammaites (or House of Shammai). Thus the *Mishna* (ch 8) records a dispute over the liturgies at the meal which ended the Sabbath Day; both Houses agreed that the light should be blessed first, but Shammai put Grace (the blessing of food) before spices, whereas Hillel put it the other way round. There should be no blessing of light among Gentiles, or in the presence of the dead. The *Tosefta* (or supplement) adds (ch 5) that for light to be blessed, its source (the flame) must be visible, and not just the illumination or glow. The *Gemara*, the part of the Babylonian *Talmud* which is a commentary on the *Mishna*, and which began as a commentary on the *Mishna* of Judah the Patriarch, quotes Rabbi Judah as saying that the two Houses differed over spices and light, the House of Hillel saying "The spices and afterwards the light" (ch 52), and it concludes: "Rabbi Yohanan said, 'The people were accustomed to act in accord with the House of Hillel as presented by Rabbi Judah.' " The *Gemara* debates whether the light of a furnace should or should not be blessed. The Palestinian *Talmud* (ch 8) also backs Rabbi Judah: "Spices and afterwards Light".[8]

Amid such liturgical confusion it is little wonder if the rabbis had no time to contemplate the Light of *Merkava* mysticism, and in the 7th to the 11th centuries the heads of academies under Islam (*geonim*), like the 8th century Yehudai, extended the Babylonian *Talmud* at the expense of the Palestinian one, and resisted the challenge of the antirabbinical Scripturalists (*Karaites*), while the mystics scorned the Talmudic approach.

The Light of Classical Kabbalah

The Light of the Kabbalah – the direct experience of God's Light – developed with the short, esoteric and difficult *Sefer Yetzira* (Hebrew for "Book of Creation or Formation"), which formed the basis of the classical Kabbalah. It appeared anonymously between the 3rd and 6th centuries AD, though parts may go back to Rabbi Akiba ben Joseph, a pupil of a contemporary of Rabbi Gamaliel who is mentioned in the *Acts of the Apostles*. Some parts go back to the 2nd century BC – and even, it has been claimed, back to remote Jewish antiquity, to the time of Abraham, or at least to the *Zend Avesta*, which Zoroaster is said to have taught to the exiled Hebrews in Chaldean Babylon[9] – and other parts were later additions. The *Sefer Yetzira* was influenced by Gnosticism and Neoplatonism and it claims that Creation was the work of Yahweh, the God of Israel, and that it took place on the immaterial and material levels by a process that includes 10 cosmological numbers (*sefirot*) and 22 Hebrew letters. The 10 *sefirot* are Gnostic emanations or divine powers from the One God, and with the 22 letters they form 32 paths by which God created the universe. Each number is a structure of cosmic energy in a code like the code which governs Einstein's $E=mc^2$.

All multiplicity comes from the divine unity, and the *sefirot*'s "end is fixed at the beginning, their beginning at their end, as the flames from glowing embers She-Adon Yahhid (unique) (which has) no second and in front (or to) its face One". Less literally, "the last of the *sefirot* unites itself to its first just as a flame is united with the candle, for God is one and there is no second" (1-7).

The *Sefer Yetzira* does not give the traditional names for the *sephirot*, and it does not mention the Tree of Life, which did not come into the written tradition until the 14th and 15th centuries, by which time it was fully developed, though it is reputed to be a very ancient symbol in the oral tradition, and obviously recalls the shamans' World-Tree. The idea of God as Light making creation by a downward "lightning" flash is definitely in the obscure text, however (1.6): "The *sefirot* Beli-Mah their apparition (or, aspect) as lightning (or the vision of lightning) their aim has no end.... They descend."[10] There were commentaries on the *Sefer Yetzira* by the *geonim* Sa'adia ben Joseph al Fayyumi (10th century), who pioneered a Judeo-Arabic culture which flowered in Andalusian Spain, and Hiwi al-Balkhi.

The Light of the classical Kabbalah shone in Spain and France when the rabbinic culture (950-1750) divided into two traditions: the Jews in Arab-Moslem Spain, and the Jews in Latin-Christian France and Germany. These two traditions had developed differently.

The Sefardic tradition (Hebrew *Sepharad*, "Spain"), from Babylonia brought the legend of the Grail to Andalusian Spain (Toledo) and created the Golden Age of Hebrew literature from c.1000 to 1148, writing Arabic prose and Hebrew poetry. Religious faith was redefined by a number of thinkers, and when 13th century scholars translated their Arabic and Hebrew into Latin, Jewish thought entered Western philosophy.

The Ashkenazic tradition (Hebrew *Ashkenaz*, "Germany") from Italy and Palestine entered France and Germany, and the Sefardic tradition flowed into it when the Berber Moslems attacked and wiped out the Andalusian Jewish communities in 1148 during the Second Crusade, driving refugees northwards to South France (Provence and Languedoc).

The Ashkenazic tradition brought the *Talmud and Midrash*, commentaries on the Scriptures of the *Pentateuch* (the first five books of the *Old Testament*) written between the 4th and the 11th centuries. It wrote in Hebrew, and the 12th century saw a resurgence of Jewish esotericism as the Hasidim ("pietists", German Jewish mystics) emerged c.1150. There were commentaries on the Scriptures and the *Talmud* – by Rabbi Solomon ben Isaac of Troyes, alias Rashi, for example – and in the late 12th century a new form of mystical study appeared in the Talmudic academies in Provence, Languedoc and Roussillon, the Kabbalah ("received" and therefore "tradition").

The Kabbalah, like the *Sefer Yetzira*, came from early Jewish scriptures, Neoplatonism, Zoroastrianism and Gnosticism, but it was also rooted in *Merkava* mysticism and in the *Hermetica* of Hermes Trismegistos (written 3rd century AD).[11] Hermetic sources claim that the Kabbalah is universal rather than Hebrew in origin, that it goes back to the mysteries of the Great Pyramid of Egypt, and that the Hebrew Moses was an Egyptian initiate who brought the knowledge with him to Mount Sinai as the oral tradition, or second *Torah*, which became the basis of the Mishna and the Hebrew Kabbalah. On this view, the Kabbalah leads to revelation of the invisible Light (*caballus* is Latin for "pack-horse"), its symbols are hidden in the ancient myths and legends, *Cybele*, for example, being coded Greek for "invisible Light"; and the Hebrew version is therefore a nationalistic version of a very ancient tradition.[12]

Be that as it may, the classical Hebrew Kabbalah that appeared in South France in the 12th century contained two schools. The first was a product – the chief product – of *Merkava*, a body of fragmentary texts in the form of a *Midrash* (interpretation of the Scriptures) from the Near East known as the *Midrash* of the 2nd century Rabbi Nehuny ben Haqana (to whom its oldest part was falsely attributed) or as the *Sefer ha-Bahir* ("Book of Brightness" 1150-75). The *Bahir* was a rabbinic version of Gnostic doctrines which saw the *Bible* and rabbinic law as allegories for God's manifestation in a spiritual universe, God's powers being manifested to His chosen people. The Sophia-like power in charge of the visible world was the *Shekhinah*, ("Dwelling", "Presence"), the feminine element in God who descended on the Tabernacle, according to the *Talmud*, and was the "glory of the Lord" that filled it (*Exodus* 40.34): its bright radiance, the divine Light. The *Bahir* gives the earliest known explanation of the 10 divine emanations (*sefirot*) of the *Sefer Yetzira*, and introduced the idea of a transmigration of souls (*Gilgul*) and a cosmic or spiritual Tree of Life, a mystical symbolism which traced the process of Creation from Light to matter.

The second school of classical Kabbalah arose in Languedoc between 1175 and 1200, when it moved to Spain,[13] and its main figure was Isaac ben Abraham the Blind who wrote a cosmological commentary on the *Sefer Yetzira*. He advocated a return to the Neoplatonist One, the Light, through practical contemplative mystical prayer.

The cosmological explanations of the *sefirot* in the *Bahir* and the work of Isaac together marked the foundation of the Kabbalah as it has come down to us today, and the two schools were united in the Kabbalists of Gerona, Catalonia, in the first half of the 13th century: in men such as Ezra ben Solomon, Azriel of Gerona, Jacob ben Sheshet, and Moses ben Nahman or Nahmanides.

There were two other southern European Jewish schools at this time: the anonymous school which produced the *Sefer ha-Iyyum* ("Book of Speculation"), which saw the ten *sefirot* in terms of Light, and the Spanish school around the unknown author of the *Sefer ha-Temuna* ("Book of the Image" c.1250), which gives the letters of the Hebrew alphabet a mystical significance; for, being products of God's creative power, they form the mystical image of God, and each letter represents a concentration of divine energy, and therefore "hidden lights".[14] Another Spanish movement grew up around Abraham ben Samuel Abulafia, who used the mystic Hebrew letters and aimed for prophetic inner experience of union with God similar to the experiences of the Hesychasts and Sufis, and there was also a Spanish Gnostic tradition in the 13th century.

The Primordial Point of Light, Supernal Fire or Light

The classic Kabbalah work, the *Sefer ha-Zohar* ("Book of Splendour" or literally "Radiance"), is now presumed to have been written c.1275 by Moses de Léon (1250-1305), a Spanish mystic. De Léon circulated it in Castile in the 1280s as the work of the 2nd century Palestinian rabbinic teacher, Simeon ben Yohai, and he claimed to possess the original manuscript.[15] The *Zohar* was written in the Aramaic of someone who knew Hebrew, and though it was a literary hoax it marked a turning point in Jewish mysticism, for it ranked with the *Old Testament* and the *Talmud* for several centuries afterwards. After the expulsion of the Jews from Spain in 1492, messianistic Jews used it to foretell the future of the Jews.

The *Zohar* is the most important Kabbalistic work. A *Midrash* commentary on the *Pentateuch* (the *Torah*), the *Book of Ruth* and the *Song of Solomon*, the *Zohar* describes how God manifested in ten descending divine emanations (the *sephirot*, e.g. the "Beauty" of God, the "Kingdom" of God), though the formless Infinite *Eyn Sof*, God's inner self as He was before the creation of the world, a Void, remains unknowable. (Compare Eckhart's distinction between the unknowable Godhead and the creator God). The scheme is again Neoplatonist, the incorporeal One emanating down into a material world, so that the world of nature is purely spiritual.

The *Zohar* sees the beginning in terms of the Light: "A dark flame issued from the mystery of *eyn sof*, the Infinite, like a fog forming in the unformed.... From the innermost centre of the flame sprang forth a well out of which colours issued and spread upon everything beneath, hidden in the mysterious hiddenness of *eyn sof*. The well broke through and yet did not break through the ether (of the sphere). It could not be recognized at all until a hidden, supernal point shone forth under the impact of the final breaking through. Beyond this point nothing can be known. Therefore it is called *reshit*, beginning the first word (out of the ten) by means of which the universe was created."

This primordial point is the wisdom of God (the *sefira* "*hohmah*"), the ideal thought of Creation. The idea for it (which may have influenced Dante's point some forty years later) came from de Léon's friend, Joseph Gikatilla, a Spanish Kabbalist whose *Nut Orchard* also provided the idea in the *Zohar* that mystics are people who have "penetrated to the kernel" (I.154b), the nut being the *Merkava* or Kabbalistic knowledge of the world. (Compare Julian of Norwich's "hazel nut" from the 1370s, a hundred years later, and her Infinitesimal Point.)

"The primal centre" of the "innermost light" of the divine nut, which has "shell within shell", produced the "supernal man", the Primal Man of the Kabbalah, Adam Kadmon, who comes from Zoroastrianism (one side being light, the other dark). The primal centre used the supernal man "for a chariot, and on it he descended, to be known by the appellation YHVH, so as to be apprehended by his attributes...to be named El, Elohim, Shaddai, Zevaot and YHVH, of which each was a symbol among men of his several divine attributes".

The "radiance of the glory of the Holy One" is "seen under these manifestations", and therefore "One, is the source of sea", and "in the same wise has the Cause of causes derived the ten aspects of his Being which are known as *sefirot*, and named the crown the Source, which is a never-to-be exhausted fountain of light, wherefrom he designates himself *eyn sof*, the Infinite.... Then he shaped a vessel diminutive as the letter yod, and filled it from him, and called it Wisdom-gushing Fountain, and called himself wise on its account.... Finally, 'He smites (the sea) into seven streams' (*Isaiah* 11.15), that is, he directs it into seven precious vessels, the which he calls Greatness, Strength, Glory, Victory, Majesty, Foundation, Sovereignty" (i.e. the seven lower *sefirot*). The "primal light" of Genesis 1.3 ("Let there be light") "irradiated the world from end to end...but then it was withdrawn, so as to deprive the sinners of the world of its enjoyment.... This light is put away and hidden. This light emerged from the darkness which was hewed out by the strokes of the Most Secret; and likewise from the light which was hidden away, through some secret path there was hewed out the darkness of the lower world in which inheres light."

According to Rabbi Simeon, God is a "supernal Light" or Fire which does not consume; "the white Light above neither consumes nor demolishes, nor does it ever change." "He who cares to pierce into the mystery of the holy unity of God should consider the flame as it rises from a burning coal or candle.... In the flame itself may be seen two lights: the one white and glowing, the other black or blue" which at times "turns red". "Of the two, the white light is the higher and rises unwavering" and it "remains constantly white". It is the lower light which is black, blue or red that consumes and devours and destroys, and Israel has made the mistake of clinging to this light instead of the white light, above which there "is yet another light, this one symbolising the supreme essence". "In this we see the mystery of the sacrifice. The rising smoke kindles the blue light, which then joins itself to the white light, whereupon the whole candle is wholly kindled with a single unified flame" and as with Elijah, "the fire of the Lord descends and consumes the burnt-offering" (1 *Kings* 8.38).

The same analogy explains the dependence of the soul (the black or blue light, the *nefesh*) on the body, and of the spirit (the white light, the *ruah*) on the soul, and of the super-soul (the additional light, the *neshamah*) on the spirit. Rabbi Simeon ben Yohai is therefore called "the holy lamp" throughout the *Zohar*, and the "Ancient and Inscrutable One" (God in His most hidden aspect) encircles the Israelites with his "Divine Presence" and "clouds of glory", so that they could "behold the light of the refulgent majesty of their King".

The "Radiance" of the *Zohar*, then, is the Light from which Creation came, and this is linked to the *Merkava* vision, for one part of the *Zohar* is devoted to an account of the seven Halls of God's chariot-throne. But as with *Merkava*, it is debatable whether Jewish mystics united with the divine in the same way that Christian or Sufi mystics did, and although Kabbalists despised the rational understanding of the Talmudic tradition, and sought spiritual union, it tended to be achieved with a distance between Creator and created, the perception of the divine being from a distance.

The Light, then, was in both Spanish and French Kabbalism, but in the texts it seem to have been revealed as part of a rationally grasped system rather than as a direct mystical experience. Nevertheless, the Light clearly was seen by Jewish Kabbalists throughout the Common Era, and it was only natural that after 1148 (following the Second Crusade)the Radiance of the Kabbalah should influence the construction of the French Gothic Cathedrals, whose pillars denoted *sefirot.*

The Palestinian Kabbalah

The Light of the Palestinian Kabbalah incorporated Hermetic magic. In the 14th and 15th centuries, the Ashkenazic and Sefardic streams had divided again in Provence and North Spain, and Jacob ben Ashur of Toledo had tried to unite them before the Jews were expelled from Spain in 1492. By the 16th century the centre of the Kabbalah had moved from Spain to Safed, Galilee, where Isaac ben Luria (1534-72) had enormous influence with his theosophical interpretation of the Kabbalah.

A teacher who left no writings except for three hymns and a small fragment, Luria taught that God withdrew to make room for the extra-divine, that after limiting himself He sent out the divine light into the vessels mentioned in the Zohar, which were broken. As a result the light flowed back to God or became diffused, and luminous particles – sparks of the Godhead covered in shells of evil – sank into matter and created the lower worlds. Man has a series of lives in which to help God in a "mending" (*tihkun*) operation, so that all the light flows back to God and Adam Kadmon, the highest configuration of the Light, is rebuilt when the Messiah will come. (Rabbi Shabbetai Tzevi of Smyrna proclaimed himself Messiah in answer to Luria's thought in the 17th century.)

Luria's Gnostic-Manichaean *gnosis* involved ascending up the unbroken flow of ever brighter worlds back to the Neoplatonist One, and the Lurianic *kavvanah* (the mystical intention which accompanies the ritual act of prayer) replaced the ecstatic rites whereby the Merkava mystics ascended precisely to the throne of God.

Luria's disciple in Palestine, Hayyim Vital (1543-1620), wrote *Etz Hayyim* ("Tree of Life"), the Lurianic Kabbalah, and affirmed that the radiance of the *Torah*'s divine light is reflected in the mysteries of the *Zohar*. "In every word shine many lights", the *Zohar* says (3.202a), and so the Kabbalist, meditating on the Scriptures, catches a ray "of the inexhaustible light". Luria's teacher, Moses ben Jacob Cordovero (1522-70) wrote that "the Holy One – blessed be He! – shines in the ten *sephirot*", and he regarded the *Torah* as being composed of divine letters which are configurations of the divine Light. Meanwhile Jews were coming into contact with Christians, and

Azariah dei Rossi wrote *Meor Enayim* ("Enlightenment of the Eyes"), a study of rabbinic texts which is aware of the Light.

Kabbalism led to the widespread following of the 17th century Rabbi Shabbetai Tzevi of Smyrna as Messiah. Unfortunately he was later forcibly converted to Islam, an event that was justified by one sect of disciples as liberating captive particles of divine light, and there was great disillusionment among the Jews.

In our time the main teachings of the Kabbalah have been restated for a Western New Age audience in the books of Z'ev ben Shimon Halevi (alias Warren Kenton).[16]

9

The Esoteric Light

Since the 16th century there had been an esoteric alternative to – and dissent from – Christianity in the West, a heretical non-Christian tradition of Light that had run parallel to the Christian tradition. It can be traced back to the pre-Christian Light of the ancient cultures.

By the 18th century the Industrial Revolution was under way and the West had moved to an outer, more secular vision which enfeebled the Church and impoverished Western culture. The "Age of Enlightenment" was a rational revolution that had everything to do with scientific materialism and nothing to do with the Inner Light. The new Humanism was fed by rationalism and scepticism, and by political thought which shaped the modern state system and a new governmental structure.

Since the Reformation, the Church had begun to lose its hold over Western people, and by the 18th century increasingly the inner vision was kept alive by esoteric minorities who were in reaction against – and in dissent from – the increasingly materialistic and secular Western culture. Some of these minorities belonged to esoteric cults, others (like the Romantics) shared their secret knowledge in literary groups.

Esotericists believe there is a purer, deeper, truer knowledge in their mystery cults than in the diluted, corrupt and "moribund" public religions, and this tradition has sought to preserve the Light among enclosed groups of awakened initiates, all of whom are well on along the Mystic Way, rather than pour it into a worldly Church and largely unawakened congregations. Western revivals of ancient mysteries and primitive religions have introduced initiates to the golden spiritual sun whose rays flow into the soul, and whose influxes form an important part of their theosophical systems. The danger is that these initiates may be drawn down into the occult, a hidden sub-subtradition of secret societies that follow Lucifer/Satan. (See Hagger, *The Syndicate* and *The Secret History of the West.*)

The Freemasonic Light

Freemasonry, whose heretical ceremonies channelled the Light, was the first such esoteric revival to show in the West. It began as a fraternity or guild of English stone masons and Cathedral builders in the 12th century (St Bernard's day), and when Cathedral building declined, working masons allowed honorary members to join. Freemasonry was abolished in 1547, but returned with ancient rites in the 17th and 18th centuries.

The rites go back to Egypt as the Masonic ritual itself says: "The usages and customs among Freemasons have ever borne a near affinity to those of the ancient Egyptians.... The first or Holy Lodge was opened Anno Lucis 2515, two years after the exodus of the Israelites from their Egyptian bondage by Moses...at the foot of Mount Horeb.... There were delivered...the tabernacle, the ark of the Covenant and the tables of the Sacred Law." The exodus probably took place in the reign of Ramesses II (1304-1237 BC), and it was at this time that Moses was supposed to have passed Egyptian influence to the earliest Freemasons.

"Solomon King of Israel," the ritual continues, "Hiram King of Tyre and Hiram Abiff presided over the second or Sacred Lodge, which was opened Anno Lucis 2992, in the bosom of the holy Mount Moriah.... There were revealed to (David) the plans of that magnificent Temple afterwards erected by his illustrious son."[1] The Temple of Solomon on which the masonic ritual is based, was inaugurated c.966 BC (in "the four hundred and eightieth year" after the exodus, *1 Kings* 6.1). It had been built with Egyptian assistance, for Solomon had married the Egyptian Pharaoh's daughter (*1*

Kings 3.1) and the Pharaoh, who was probably Sheshonk I of the Libyan dynasty – the "Shishak" of *1 Kings* 14.25-6 – sent 80,000 builders according to Eusebius. (Another 70,000 probably came from Tyre.) The Egyptians brought with them the craft of masonry which they had perfected on the Great Pyramid, and the stones were hewn, squared, marked and numbered in the quarries with such skill on the part of Hiram Abiff that they all fitted exactly when assembled, and it seemed that the Temple had been made by the Supreme Architect of the universe, and not by human minds.[2]

During the building of the Temple, the masons picked up the secret of the Light, and their esoteric knowledge can be revived as an initiate into Freemasonry progresses from stage to stage in a reconstructed Temple. On the altar-top of the original Holy Royal Arch were jumbled letters which arrange into JE-HO-VAH JAH-BUL-ON. This is explained in the culminating Mystical Lecture of the ritual: "It is in four languages, Chaldee, Hebrew, Syriac and Egyptian. JAH is the Chaldee name of God, signifying 'His Essence and Majesty Incomprehensible'. It is also a Hebrew word, signifying 'I am and shall be'.... BUL is a Syriac word denoting Lord or Powerful.... ON is an Egyptian word, signifying Father of All."[3] ON refers to Annu or Heliopolis, where there was a temple to Ra, and it also represents Osiris, so the "Father of All" includes the idea of Osiris-Ra, who was the Light.

Freemasonry thus preserves the mystical union with "the Eye of Ra". This mixture of Yahweh, Baal and Osiris-Ra would have been profoundly shocking to a believer in Judaism in *Old Testament* times, and the syncretism of the jumbled letters, which announce that the Light is to be found in all three cults, explains why Freemasonry has remained an esoteric cult, hiding its message in a jumble like one of the Mysteries. (There has in fact been speculation that the Hiramic drama of Freemasonry is a survival of otherwise extinct Dionysian or Osirian Mysteries.) Thus in 1614/15 the letters JHVH were carved in Hebrew – not English – within a sun (the Light) on the now disused west door of King's College Chapel, Cambridge, which was built by Freemasons in the reign of Henry VI. The proportions of the ante-chapel were based on those of the Temple of Solomon, and its vaulting resembles the Egyptian papyrus plant.[4]

The Light is central to the Freemasonic ritual. In the Ceremony of Raising to the Third Degree, the Worshipful Master says: "The light of a Master Mason is darkness visible." (This echoes a phrase in Milton's *Paradise Lost* book 1 and in Pope's "Dunciad" book 4.) "It is that mysterious veil which the eye of human reason cannot penetrate unless assisted by that light which is from above." In the Ceremony of Exaltation (from the Third Degree to the Supreme Degree), "Joshua" prays: "Grant that the Brother who now seeks to participate in the light of our mysteries may be endued with a portion of Thy divine Spirit." Later the candidate is unable to identify the contents of a scroll "for the want of light", and "Zerubbabel" says: "Let that want of light remind you that man by nature is the child of ignorance and error, and would ever have remained in a state of darkness had it not pleased the Almighty to call him to light and immortality." Later still, "Zerubbabel" asks, "Having been kept for a considerable time in a state of darkness, what, in your present condition, is the predominant wish of your heart?" to which the candidate replies, "Light." The Companions then form an arch through which the candidate will see when he is "restored to light", and "Zerubbabel" says: "We congratulate you on being admitted to the light of our Order." The candidate can now read the scroll, which ends: "And God said, let there be light, and there was light."

In the Symbolical lecture (Address of the Second Chair) "Haggai" explains the six lights Freemasons acknowledge, three lesser and three greater (which represent the Word, the creative, preservative and annihiliative powers of the Deity). These form a triangle and connect with the ceremonial ribbon, which denotes "light, being composed of two of the principal colours with which the veils of the Temple and Tabernacle were interwoven". The context of the Light has therefore been set for the Mystical Lecture on the jumbled letters, which now follows, and according to the printed ritual, the Jewel or Seal of Solomon (a double triangle) represents "that Incomprehensible Being at whose command the world burst forth from chaos into light". The Masonic hymn which is sung after the Lodge is closed invokes a "God of Light" and ends with the Masonic refrain, "So mote it be".[5]

Freemasonry was influenced by Deism in stressing the light of nature as a moral guide, and it harks back to Gnosticism. It is also linked with Templarism, which was also fascinated by the Temple of Solomon as we have seen, and which became too powerful through its links with St Bernard and the Crusades. When it was suppressed in 1312 and its grand master Jacques de Molay was burned at the stake in 1314, the Templars were driven underground, and they linked up with the Freemasons. The Masonic Sword came from the Templars, and it symbolized (according to the Symbolical Lecture) a readiness "to defend the City and holy sanctuary against the unprovoked attacks of their enemies" (i.e. Moslem infidels). It is possible that the poet Yeats was a Freemason, and that the sword he was given by the Japanese, Junzo Sato, "Sato's ancient blade" which he saw as a symbol of the soul and of "love and war" in "A Dialogue of Self and Soul", is a Masonic symbol, Freemasonry having extended to Japan. If Yeats was secretly a Freemason, then his imagery of the tower and winding stair reflect the emblem of the Second Degree Tracing Board.[6]

Freemasonry has been regarded as a descendant from Pelagianism, the 5th century heresy that salvation could be by one's own efforts and good works without proceeding through Jesus Christ (who is absent from Freemasonry); rather than by grace through faith, as St. Augustine of Hippo held. (According to Pelagius good works or evil deeds are voluntarily and freely chosen, and not a consequence of any original sin.) Hence the Church's criticism of Freemasonry, and in particular the Church's contemporary attitude, which is much more hostile than in the 1950s and firmly keeps Freemasonry outside Christianity and in the esoteric, heretical stream.[7] In fact, Freemasonry is linked with Luciferianism, a secret that is only revealed to 32nd- and 33rd-degree Masons. (See Hagger, *The Syndicate.*)

The Rosicrucian Light

Freemasonry was also linked with Rosicrucianism, which influenced it. (See Hagger, *The Secret History of the West* for a full account of the link between the two.) In the Rosicrucian ritual, the Light is represented as a golden rose.

Rosicrucianism was founded in the West in the 16th or 17th century. Paracelsus, a Swiss alchemist who died in 1541, a Neoplatonist who wrote of Nature "the light which is in her I have beheld in her", is regarded as its founder by some, but the earliest text is *Fama Fraternitatis* ("The Story of the Brotherhood of the Meritorious Order of the Rosy Cross") which was published much later in 1614. It told how Christian Rosenkreutz or Rosy Cross, a mythical hero born in 1378, travelled to Egypt and the Near East and acquired wisdom which he passed on to three others in Germany. The Brotherhood later doubled to eight, each of whom left for a different country to help and heal those in need.

There is another view that Rosicrucian doctrines flourished in ancient Egypt, and go back to the Light – the sun disc – of Akhenaton. (To this day Egyptians ask "What rose to do you wear?" on the banks of the Nile, meaning "To what esoteric sect do you belong?") According to this view, Plato, Jesus, Philo of Alexandria and Plotinus all followed Rosicrucian doctrines, though there is no direct evidence that Rosicrucianism was revived rather than founded in the 16th or 17th century.

The name of the Rosicrucians is supposed to have come from their symbol, a rose and a cross or *croix* (though there is an alternative derivation from *ros*, "dew"). The rose appeared in the shrines of Isis, and symbolized her mysteries and power, union with the Supreme. In the Middle Ages the cathedral builders put the rose into stonework as rose windows as we have seen, for the Church had taught them that Mary, the Mother of God, was the Rose Queen of the World, and the rosy cross meant that one had to love and suffer to obtain the Divine Perfection.

Perfection is obtained through thorny purgation (the Red Rose of Sorrow on a black Cross), which, when the veil is lifted, leads to illumination (the White Rose of Joy on a gleaming, shining Cross), and finally to union (the Golden Rose of Union on a red Cross). Once the initiate has achieved the goal, he must be silent about what he has learned, and so the fourth rose is the little Black Rose of Silence. Christian Rosenkreuz attends a royal wedding (compare the Royal Sacred Marriage of ancient cultures) wearing four roses and carrying a cross, and the four roses are shown round the centre of the Kabbalistic cross.

The Golden Rose of Union has an esoteric, Alchemistic meaning. "Gold contains no dross; refined in the furnace of the cleansing fires it represents the pure flame burning in the Sanctuary of the Sacred Heart, the *fire* and *light* of the Eternal Rose."[8] (Compare Eliot's "The fire and the rose are one".) The Golden Rose of Union therefore represents the Light after the Night of Spirit. Alchemy influenced Rosicrucianism: Salt, Sulphur and Mercury were in matter, and a Blazing Star or Quintessence of Fire communicated *gnosis*, i.e. the Light. The Alchemistic imagery of Rosicrucianism is deliberately obscure, and the Rosicrucian catechism asks "Why do you people speak so obscurely?" to which the answer is: "So that only the Sons of God may understand me."

The Rosicrucian ritual is entangled in Freemasonry. There are a number of higher degrees that had no part in original Masonry, and the Rose Croix appeared in France in 1754 as the 18th such degree. Like Freemasonry, it is based on the Pelagian heresy that the candidate can obtain light and perfection for himself by his own efforts without proceeding through Christ, yet in 1950 474 clergymen and 17 bishops were Perfect Princes in the Rose Croix of Heredom.

The ceremony requires the candidate to enter a Black Room which contains an altar draped in black on which hangs a black Mystic Rose. He then proceeds to the Chamber of Death, which contains a skull and crossbones, and from there he goes to a brilliantly illuminated Red Room, which is (not surprisingly) hung in red. It contains an altar that has eight steps and a Mysterious Ladder of seven steps, which the candidate symbolically ascends. It has the movable letters F,H and C (Faith Hope and Charity) on it, and I,N,R,I (*Iesus Nazarenus Rex Iudaeorum*, Jesus of Nazareth, King of the Jews; or possibly *Igne Nitrum Roris Invenitur*).

The candidate is told that the Rose is "an emblem of secrecy and silence". The Opening Ceremony has recalled the Crucifixion when "the true Light departed from us" and "the Word was lost", and from the colours of the roses we can see that the ceremony is an initiation through silence (the Black Rose) into a dying (Chamber of Death) and a rebirth through purgation (the Red Rose). The 18th degree, then, relives the esoteric meaning of the Crucifixion and stops short of the White Rose or the Golden Rose which represents the Light.[9]

Later on, Master Masons were able to take an extra nine degrees, and each degree was only conferred after studies of the Rosy Cross.

Rosicrucianism has been connected with Magic because Magic has also sought the Light. Both the magician and the mystic see the universe as a living Reality whose visible appearance veils invisible forces (the Light), but whereas the mystic opens himself selflessly to the invisible so that it works through him, the magician seeks power over the invisible to manipulate and control it and further his own ends, like Goethe's Faust.

In 1887 the Irish poet W. B. Yeats attached himself to the Theosophical Society and almost immediately witnessed a development in Rosicrucianism that involved some Theosophists. In 1887 or 1888 some more Rosicrucian manuscripts were found – these may have been fakes – and as a result of these the Hermetic Order of the Golden Dawn was established by Master Masons within the *Societas Rosicruciana in Anglia*, on the magical system of a German Rosicrucian adept, Anna Sprengel, whose name was on the manuscripts. This was a magical fraternity rather than a theosophical group, and its member adepts (like the poet Yeats and later Dion Fortune and Aleister Crowley) wore a Rose Cross on their breasts to stress its Rosicrucian origins. Many of the occult teachings of the Order of the Golden Dawn derived from MacGregor Mathers (the author of *The Kubbalah Unveiled*, 1887) from whom Yeats derived much of his imagery. The Golden Dawn itself was of course the Light, "the hidden Concealed Spiritual Sun", which the fraternity sought to approach by magical rather than mystical means. In 1890, there was a doctrinal dispute within Rosicrucianism, one set of Rosicrucianists favouring the Kabbalistic Rose, another set the Catholic Rose. The Kabbalistic Rose (which Yeats drew so elaborately in his notebooks) won the day in the end. The Order collapsed c.1940. But there are now other Rosicrucian groups.

Hermetic Magic's Light

The magic of the occultist[10] is very different from black magic and the evil actions performed by witchcraft to please devils. It goes back to the heretical

Corpus Hermeticum (see pp401-402), and especially to its treatise *Asclepius* which describes how the souls of angels and devils can enter man-made images, which become gods. (Hence the figurines left in Egyptian tombs, in which the soul of the deceased could dwell.) Nevertheless, the occult is a long, slippery slope which ends in black magic.

When the Roman Empire broke up, organised knowledge broke into fragments. Astrology, which was related to magic because it controlled the invisible forces of the planets, was attacked by Christianity and banned throughout the Dark Ages. Ptolemaic cosmology was revived in the early 13th century, and by c.1250 Western Christendom had absorbed astrology. Medieval magical text-books (*grimoires*, "black books") like the *Clavicula Salomonis* ("Key of Solomon") gave directions as to how to raise spirits. *The Sacred Magic of Abra-Melin the Mage*, another such text-book, saw the universe as being operated by angels who directed demons. It held that each man has an angel and a demon attached to his soul, and by talking to a man's Holy Guardian Angel (the unconscious layer of his self which can know the Divine) a magician could control his demon, and thus raise him if he were dead or heal him if he were sick. To be able to communicate with angels, the magician had to read holy books for six months and "inflame himself with prayer", i.e. discover the Light. The magician's Light was the same as the mystic's Light; only his interpretation and use (or abuse) of it were different.

The *Hermetica* (the source of the stream of modern magic) were rediscovered after 1450 and published – too late for this development to be included in "The Hermetic Light" (pp401-409), which deals with the ancient world – and scholars reconciled them with the *Bible* by using the Kabbalah. They played down the pagan side and emphasised the Christian side, and the Renaissance therefore saw magic as an aspect of Christianity, and the Wise Men or magicians as Christ's first disciples. Thus the magician Thomas Vaughan, the brother of Henry Vaughan the Silurist, could write: "That I should profess magic is...religion with me. Magic is nothing but the wisdom of the Creator revealed and planted in the creature. It is a name – as Agrippa saith" (the 16th century scholar magician Cornelius Agrippa) "– not distasteful to the very Gospel itself. Magicians were the first attendants our Saviour met."

Agrippa (died 1535), Charles V's court secretary, believed that everything in the universe, whether animal, vegetable or mineral, had a soul which was part of God, and that man therefore "contained within himself all things which are in God". Magic was therefore the best way to know God according to Agrippa's *De Occulta Philosophia*, which drew heavily on the contemporary Kabbalah and Hebrew letters. John Dee, a follower of Agrippa who communicated with angels through a clairvoyant and was in trouble for witchcraft, wrote that "no science gives greater proof of the divinity of Christ than magic or the Kaballah".

Later, Hermetic magicians joined Rosicrucianism, and the tomb of Christian Rosycross (i.e. Rosenkreutz) was filled with magical books, mirrors and ever-burning lamps. These took the place of the Sun in magic, and attracted forces which they then radiated, and they feature in the sexual magic of the 20th century Oriental Templars of Crowley. "Although the Sun never shined in that Vault, nevertheless it was enlightened with another Sun." The 17th century mystic Robert Fludd wrote that Rosarius's soul was "clothed with greater powers.... We see a light, as it were the Sun, but winged and exceeding the Sun of our heavens, arising from the tomb." (Compare the winged sun disc of the ancient cultures.) Thus did the magician control the invisible forces of the Light.

From then on Hermetic magic grew in influence. Even Isaac Newton was a Hermetic Alchemist, and the 18th century saw thaumaturges, and charlatans (like Cagliostro, and to some extent Saint-Germain). Astrology had declined when the Copernican revolution put the sun at the centre of creation in place of man, but the discovery of Uranus (1781) and of Neptune (1846) brought it back. The *grimoires* and works of all the scholar-magicians were codified in Francis Barrett's *The Magus* (1801).

Evangelical Dissent's Spiritual Sun: Swedenborg and Blake

By the 18th century an esoteric dissent from Evangelicalism challenged the inner vision of Christianity. Swedenborg and Blake can be seen as offshoots from the Evangelical-Nonconformist tradition – Swedenborg was a Lutheran and gave rise to the Church of the New Jerusalem – but as both men communicated with spirits and angels and practised automatic writing their Light should be treated as part of the esoteric tradition that was outside, and challenged, established Christianity. Swedenborg, in particular, had a profound influence on the later esoteric tradition. It should not however be forgotten that Swedenborg is in many ways close to Boehme.

German Pietism had influenced Sweden through the writings of Arndt and Francke, and though the Swedish religion remained Evangelical Lutheranism, the Evangelical *zeitgeist* which was opposed to the Deism of the rational Enlightenment threw up the mystic Emanuel Swedenborg (1688-1772). After an early career as a scientist and a job at the Royal Board of Mines, at the age of 55 Swedenborg began to see visions and develop clairvoyance and the power to communicate with discarnate souls. He had a vision of Christ in April 1745, and renounced worldly learning for theological writings on the *Bible* and spiritual subjects. He published over thirty books in Latin. Like Boehme, he had the gift of automatic writing – his interpretation of the *Bible, The Word Explained*, was dictated to him – and he based most of his theological writings on the Light, or, more specifically, on the correspondence between spiritual and natural light.

In *Heaven and Hell* (1758) Swedenborg distinguished the natural light of the sun from the spiritual light of "the Sun in heaven": "That which is spiritual in which heaven is, is above nature.... The Sun of heaven is the Lord, and the light there is Divine Truth, and the heat is Divine Good, and both proceed from the Lord as the Sun. From this origin are all things which exist.... The Lord is seen in heaven as the Sun, because He is Divine love from which all spiritual things exist, and by means of the sun of this world, all natural things.... That the Lord is actually seen in heaven as the Sun, has not only been told me by angels, but has also been granted to me at times to see." Swedenborg goes on to say that the loving see God as fire, while the faithful see Him as light, for "light also in the spiritual sense, is faith".

The light in heaven "exceeds by many degrees the noon-day light of the world", Swedenborg continues. "I have often seen it, even in the time of evening and night. At first I wondered when I heard angels say that the light of the world is little better than shade in comparison with the light of heaven; but now I have seen it, I can bear witness that it is so."

The angels receive light from the Divine Truth and heat from the Divine Good. Because God is Divine Truth, and Truth in heaven is light, "the Lord is called light" in the *Bible.* (Swedenborg quotes all the references to the Light and the Light of the World from the *New Testament.*) "Man's spiritual light is the light of his understanding, and the objects of the understanding are truths, which that light arranges analytically into orders, and forms into reasons." Again Swedenborg speaks from personal experience: "It has been frequently granted me to perceive, and also to see, that the light which enlightens the mind is true light (lux) quite distinct from the light (lumen) which is called natural. I have been elevated into that light interiorly by degrees, and as I was elevated, my understanding was enlightened.... This light is also Divine Wisdom and Intelligence."[11]

In *True Christian Religion* (1771), which he wrote at the end of his life when he was 83, Swedenborg restated his theology of spiritual light and heat, which pour illumination into the understanding and a Wesleyan burning into the heart. The spiritual light and heat enter everything in the universe by influx: "Life is the light which proceeds from the Sun of the spiritual world, in the midst of which is Jehovah God. Divine love forms life, as fire forms light. There are two properties in fire, burning and brilliance; its burning gives out heat, and its brilliance gives out light. Similarly there are two properties in love; one corresponds to the burning property of fire, and intimately affects the will of man, and the other corresponds to the brilliance of fire, and intimately affects his understanding. Thence a man derives love and intelligence; for...from the Sun of the spiritual world proceeds heat, which in its essence is love, and light, which in its essence is wisdom; and these two flow into the whole and every part of the universe, affecting them intimately."

Man is a receptacle for love and wisdom, and "it is therefore clear that a man's life resides in his understanding, that its character depends on his wisdom, and is modified by the love of his will." Light, life and wisdom are one and are not creatable, only the forms that are their receptacles – human and angelic minds – can be created. Man must avoid closing his mind to the spiritual light for then he is darkened by natural light, in which "he no more sees the realities of wisdom than a bat sees light at noonday."

Swedenborg asserts that "enlightenment comes from the Lord alone", and spiritual light is inwardly within natural light: "As spiritual light and heat are in natural light and heat as in their receptacle or repository, so spiritual faith and charity are in natural faith and charity. This infusion of spiritual heat and light gradually takes place as man progresses from the natural world to the spiritual world; and this he does as he comes to believe in the Lord, who...is light." The union of spiritual light and heat is therefore to be found in the union between natural faith and charity. Divine love and wisdom enter men's minds as the rays of the natural sun enter men's bodies, and "they vivify them".

Swedenborg's vision of a cosmos filled with spiritual light and heat drew on Boehme, and it had already contributed to the founding of the Martinists (who first took up the term "Astral Light" from Paracelsus) in France in 1754. (The Martinists were founded by Martinez Pasqualis and were Kabbalists who followed the Light of both Boehme and Swedenborg, and a Russian branch headed by Schwartz appeared in Moscow c.1790.) In the early 1780s, Swedenborgian societies began to appear, to interpret the Bible spiritually, and soon afterwards the first Swedenborgian congregation met for New Church worship, from whom the Church of the New Jerusalem developed. (Swedenborg himself never left the Lutheran Church.)

Swedenborg's *Heaven and Hell*, his angels, his insistence on the spiritual light and the sun, and on a New Jerusalem – all influenced a product of the Puritan tradition who was also touched by Evangelicalism, the great revolutionary English mystic, poet, painter and engraver William Blake (1757-1827). Blake always had visions of supernatural phenomena. When he was four he saw God looking through the Soho window where he lived, and when he was nine he saw in Peckham Rye "a tree filled with angels". From the Evangelical hymns of Charles Wesley and the Congregationalist Isaac Watts, Blake, a child of Nonconformist parents, obtained his stanza form of *Songs of Innocence and Experience* (1789-94). He came to Swedenborg through his artist friend John Flaxman, who had joined Swedenborg's sect by the early 1780s, and who helped pay for the printing of *Poetical Sketches* (1783).

Blake's own experience of the Light, the central experience of his life, was clearly linked to Flaxman's Swedenborgianism. In his letter to Hayley of October 23, 1804, Blake wrote that he had seen the Light after twenty years of darkness: "Suddenly, on the day after visiting the Truchsessian Gallery of pictures, I was again enlightened with the light I enjoyed in my youth, and which has for exactly twenty years been closed from me as by a door and by window-shutters.... Dear Sir, excuse my enthusiasm or rather madness, for I am really drunk with intellectual vision whenever I take a pencil or graver into my hand, even as I used to be in my youth, and as I have not been for twenty dark, but very profitable, years. I thank God that I courageously pursued my course through darkness."

Twenty years from 1804 takes us back to 1784. Blake was at the Royal Academy with Flaxman from 1779 and he may well have been illumined before the painting *Glad Day* (1780), which may therefore have both a religious and a political significance. (Blake did not distinguish religious and political Dissent, and his Swedenborgian conviction that the Light was not to be found in established churches is parallelled by a left-wing sympathy for the French and American revolutions – for example in *The French Revolution* and *America* – and by his search for a new ideal society, which he called "Jerusalem".) Blake was certainly illumined during the writing of his early *Songs of Innocence*, which go back to this time and which reflect Swedenborg.

Swedenborgianism was also present throughout Blake's long Dark Night. His patron in the late 1790s and early 1800s, Thomas Butts, was a Swedenborgian. It was the Swedenborgian Flaxman who introduced Blake to William Hayley, to work for whom Blake took the cottage at Felpham from 1800 to 1803. Blake's letters to Flaxman and Butts at this time are uninhibited about angels precisely because they all shared Swedenborg's spiritual outlook. Blake disagreed with Swedenborg's ethics – "The Marriage of Heaven and Hell" satirised and corrected Swedenborg's separation of Heaven and Hell and his condemnation of infernal energy and imagination, for Blake was on the side of the energetic-imaginative devils and against the qualities of Swedenborg's angels – but he accepted Swedenborg's view that Christ is God, that "God is very man", and that all things are One in the spiritual Light.

The Light is behind the Oneness in Blake's world. "Auguries of Innocence" (c.1803) begins with a vision of unity: "To see a World in a Grain of Sand/And a Heaven in a Wild Flower,/Hold Infinity in the palm of your hand/And Eternity in an hour." It links the Oneness with the vision of God as Light: "God Appears and God is Light/To those poor souls who dwell in Night,/But does a Human Form Display/To those who Dwell in Realms of day."

This vision of Light which can also be incarnated in a human form – the Swedenborgian idea that Jesus Christ is God – is the crowning "fourfold vision" of the verses in his letter to Butts of November 22, 1802, which, Blake writes, "were composed above a twelve month ago, while walking from Felpham to Lavant to meet my Sister". In these verses, Los (the human form of energy and imagination) appeared "in the Sun", "in fierce flames": "'twas outward a Sun, inward Los in his might." (Compare Swedenborg, who asserted that spiritual light is inwardly within natural light from the sun.) Los "flam'd in my path, and the Sun was hot" and then Blake launches into his most famous lines: "Now I a fourfold vision see,/And a fourfold vision is given to me;/'Tis fourfold in my supreme delight/And threefold in soft Beulah's night/And twofold Always. May God us keep/From Single vision and Newton's sleep!"

The single vision is the outer, sceptical, rationalistic, materialistic vision of the scientist, which is limited by the perception of the five senses. In 1810 Blake wrote in "Vision of the Last Judgment": "'What', it will be Question'd, 'When the Sun rises, do you not see a round disk of fire somewhat like a Guinea?' O no, no, I see an Innumerable company of the Heavenly host crying: 'Holy, Holy, Holy is the Lord God Almighty.' I question not my Corporeal or Vegetative (i.e. physical) Eye any more than I would Question a Window concerning a Sight. I look thro' it and not with it."

The disk like a guinea is seen with single vision. The twofold vision is the ability to see the spiritual world (or Being) behind the natural world of existence – to look *through* the windows of perception and see infinity behind a grain of sand and eternity behind a wild flower. ("If the doors of perception were cleansed, every thing would appear to man as it is, infinite.") The threefold vision is the contemplative vision in which spiritual forms – angels and the rest – present themselves. The fourfold vision is the unitive vision of the Light itself, which appears in the human form of Los ("Sol" back to front, compare the Egyptian Ra) to Blake's imaginative visualisation (the power which saw God and angels when he was a child),[12] the mystic ecstasy, "my supreme delight".

The "fourfold vision" parallels the four worlds of the Kabbalah, which Blake knew, and it dominated the years following Felpham, from 1803 on, when he wrote his long prophetic works. These are examples of automatic writing. In his letter to Butts of January 10, 1802, Blake wrote, "I am under the direction of Messengers from Heaven, Daily and Nightly," and on his deathbed he said that the credit for his works belonged to his "celestial friends". Of "Milton" (a Puritan, Nonconformist subject) he wrote to Butts on April 25, 1803: "I have written this Poem from immediate Dictation, twelve or sometimes twenty or thirty lines at a time without Premeditation and even against my Will; the Time it has taken in writing was thus render'd Non-Existent, and an immense Poem Exists, which seems to be the Labour of a long life, all produc'd without Labour or Study."

"Milton" was finished c.1808, and it incorporated parts of the abandoned "Four Zoas" (begun c.1797). The fourfold vision is pictured in an illustration to "Milton": four concentric circles surrounded by fire touch in the centre, representing through the four Kabbalistic worlds: Urthona (i.e. the eternal form of the temporal *Los,* the creative imagination), Tharmas (desire or aspiration for symbols, a figure of doubt and despair who rises when Urizen falls), Luvah (the emotions, love) and Urizen (the single vision of reason). These are the four beings (Greek *zoa,* "living creatures") or forces within the mind which end "Vala, or the Four Zoas". (Vala should be pronounced Veila to pun on Veiler, for Vala is the Veil of the natural world, which prevents people from seeing through the windows of perception to the spiritual world. Vala is thus the evil contrary of the ideally good Jerusalem.)

Jesus Christ is the bearer of the fourfold vision, and in the famous hymn "Jerusalem", which was printed at the beginning of "Milton", Blake writes of the legend that Jesus visited Glastonbury in terms of the Light of Los: "And did the Countenance Divine/Shine forth upon our clouded hills?" The prophetic poem "Jerusalem" was finished c.1820, and the "gentle souls" who guard the Fourfold Gate which opens towards Beulah (the contemplative vision) include St Teresa and Mme Guyon. At the beginning of the poem "Jerusalem" "the Divine Vision is darken'd", but the poem ends in the fiery climax of the fourfold vision of the Light. The "Heavens burnt with flaming fires,/And Urizen and Luvah and Tharmas and Urthona arose into/Albion's bosom. Then Albion stood before Jesus in the Clouds/Of Heaven, Fourfold among the Visions of God in Eternity." Then Albion, a Giant whose Gnostic or Plotinan "Emanation" the poem is about, "stretch'd his hand into Infinitude/And took his Bow. Fourfold the Vision."[13]

Romantic Neoplatonism's One Light

The *zeitgeist* of Evangelicalism led to the English Romantic movement (and, later to European Romanticism), which was also a "religion of the heart" that opposed the rational Enlightenment. (The Romantic movement was a secular echo of the religious fervour thrown up by revivalist Evangelical Protestantism in the American Great Awakening and English Methodism c.1725-1750; pantheistic Nature took the place of God and engaged the burning heart.) Blake was one of the initiators of Romanticism, and another influence on him besides Swedenborg – and on Romanticism generally – was Thomas Taylor the Platonist (1758-1835), who revived an anti-Christian Neoplatonism. Blake reconciled Taylor's pagan Neoplatonic Light with Swedenborg's spiritual Light and Swedenborgian Christianity, and there is therefore a Neoplatonist dimension to the "fourfold vision". Whereas the Metaphysical poets were very much part of the mainstream Christian tradition – many, such as Donne, Herbert and Traherne, were vicars – the Romantic poets were part of the subtradition which lay outside Christianity and the mainstream.

Taylor also influenced the second generation Romantic poet, Shelley (1792-1822). Shelley's atheism caused him to write a pamphlet, *The Necessity of Atheism*, which led to his expulsion from Oxford in 1811, and he probably came across Taylor's writings during his meetings with the philosopher William Godwin from 1812. The Neoplatonist One Light is present in Shelley's poetry from 1815 on. It is in "Alastor" for Alastor is "obedient to the light/That shone within his soul" and, on his death, a "surpassing Spirit,/Whose light adorned the world around it". It is in "Hymn to Intellectual Beauty" (1816) where an "unseen Power" visits "each human heart", the "Spirit of Beauty" whose "light alone" gives "grace and truth to life's unquiet dream". It is the "everlasting universe of things" that "flows through the mind" in "Mont Blanc" (1816). Even the famous skylark is like a glad poet "hidden/In the light of thought". "When the Lamp has Shattered" has baffled critics, but it is only saying that the heart depends on the spirit as "the light" which lies in the dust depends on the lamp, for all feelings are derived from the One Neoplatonist Spirit. Keats – "a pardlike Spirit" – passes into the One Spirit of Light on his death in "Adonais" (1821): he is "made one with Nature", with "that Power" which "has withdrawn his being to its own", which "kindles" the world. "The One remains", "the white radiance of Eternity": "The One remains, the many change and pass;/ Heaven's light forever shines, Earth's shadows fly;/Life, like a dome of many-coloured glass,/Stains the white radiance of Eternity,/Until Death tramples it to fragments" (LII). And "thou should die/If thou wouldst be with that which thou dost seek" (i.e. the white radiance of the One Light). Shelley continues: "That Light, whose smile kindles the Universe,/That Beauty in which all things work and move/...now beams on me." It is clear that the Intellectual Beauty Shelley wrote about is the Light, and Shelley is due for revival after the damaging criticism of such unillumined Professors as F. R. Leavis.[14]

The first generation Romantic poets were touched by Taylor's Neoplatonism. Coleridge (1772-1834) preached in Unitarian chapels c.1796, the development of Unitarianism in England from its 16th century roots in Hungary, Poland and Romania being another aspect of the Evangelical revival. He believed in God, but incorporated a Neoplatonism he had found in his boyhood reading. It is revealed in "Religious Musings" (1794) in which the "Passions" are "enrobed with Light" from "one Mind", "omnipresent Love,/Whose day-spring rises glorious in my soul/As the great Sun". It is in "Kubla Khan" (1798), where the "sunless sea" recalls Plotinus's sea or "lake" of material existence. It is in "Dejection: an Ode" (1802), where "would we aught behold, of higher worth", then "from the soul itself must issue forth/A light, a glory, a fair luminous cloud" of joy, from which all colours are "a suffusion".[15]

This joy is Coleridge's "shaping spirit of imagination", and as he has just said that the joy is also the "light", *ergo* the imagination comes from the Light. Coleridge knew about the Light from Plotinus. In *Biographia Literaria* (1814-17) he quotes Plotinus on the need to watch for intuitive knowledge "till it suddenly shines upon us; preparing ourselves for the blessed spectacle as the eye waits patiently for the rising sun." The imagination "shapes" in the sense that it has an "esemplastic" power, i.e. it "shapes into one" (from the Greek *eis hen plattein,* "to shape into one"). By shaping into one, the imagination as a form of the Light therefore seeks to return to the One Light from which it came, just as its operation imitates the One; for it is "the living power and prime agent of all human perception, and...a repetition in the finite mind of the eternal act of creation in the infinite I AM."[16]

Coleridge sees the creative imagination as being superior to relatively uncreative Nature – "I may not hope from outward forms to win," he wrote in "Dejection", "/The passion and the life, whose fountains are within" – and in ranking the "within" above the "outward" he is very close to Blake, who wrote, "Nature has no outline, but imagination has." The shaping light of Coleridge's imagination and Blake's sun of Los are so close, that it looks as if Blake has influenced Coleridge. Yet they met (c.1818) too late for there to be any direct influence, and must have arrived at the same concept independently. (The meeting is recorded in Crabb Robinson's diary.) There is also a strong spiritual thread in Coleridge's poems that recalls Blake. A spirit follows the Ancient Mariner's ship, and in "Christabel" Geraldine is possessed by the spirit of Christabel's mother. This goes back to Boehme (if not Swedenborg), to whom, Coleridge confesses early indebtedness in *Biographia Literaria.*

Wordsworth (1770-1850), the other first generation English Romantic poet, first met Coleridge in 1795, and later the two men were linked through the *Lyrical Ballads* and their love for the Hutchinson sisters. They went to Germany together. (It is no accident that Romanticism was born in England and Germany, the two Evangelical Protestant centres.) For

Wordsworth, however, the One was "from without in" rather than "from within out", and he is closer to Shelley in his pantheism, just as Coleridge is closer to Blake in his rejection of pantheism. Wordsworth identifies the One in the early part of *The Prelude* (1799-1805) as the "Wisdom and Spirit of the universe" (1.401), the "one great Mind" (2.257) which flows into the hearts of men and all forms of Nature (the mountains, trees, water etc). As the mind opens to the "influxes" of the One Mind – a Swedenborgian idea – an "auxiliar light" comes from the mind (2.368) and glorifies what it sees in Nature. This is Wordsworth's equivalent to Coleridge's "luminous cloud", and it results from a flowing-in of Nature. The title of the poem "Influence of Natural Objects" (1798/9), which is virtually the same as a passage in book 1 of *The Prelude*, means "The flowing-in of the Wisdom and Spirit of Nature into the heart".

"Tintern Abbey" (1798) describes an opening to the One: "Almost suspended, we are laid asleep/In body, and become a living soul..../And I have felt/...a sense sublime/Of something.../Whose dwelling is the light of setting suns,/A motion and a spirit, that impels/All thinking things, all objects of all thought." Like Shelley's Adonais, the dead pass into this One Spirit, to be "rolled round in earth's diurnal course,/With rocks and stones and trees" ("Poems on Lucy", 1799). In "Ode, Intimations of Immortality" (1803) (Wordsworth's counterpart to Coleridge's "Dejection"), Wordsworth laments his inability to see Nature "apparelled in celestial light", "the visionary gleam" which he knew as a boy. A boy who is still close to his Soul's origin in immortality "beholds the light and whence it flows", but as he grows into a man he "perceives it die away/And fade into the light of common day". These first glimpses of the light, the radiance, are "yet the fountain-light of all our day,/Are yet a master-light of all our seeing". Wordsworth writes of "the inward eye" in his famous "Daffodils" (1804), but although "influxes" of the Light flow into it, and Wordsworth hints that he himself experienced them one does not get as strong a feeling that he knew the Light as one does from the originator of "influxes", Swedenborg himself, or from mystics like Blake. Wordsworth was only part of the way down the Mystic Way; he was not towards the end as Blake was or at the end as Dante came to be, and he took his sense of the One into the Church, becoming a regular attender at Rydal church.

The other Romantic poets and thinkers were not affected by Neoplatonism. Keats wrote in his letters of "the holiness of the Heart's affections" and a "vale of soul-making", but he was supremely a poet of the senses, of what Blake called "single vision", despite his reading of Thomas Taylor the Platonist at Bailey's prompting and the hint of a spiritual Reality lurking behind the natural phenomena in his Platonic Idea of Beauty; "the mighty abstract Idea I have of Beauty in all things" as he wrote to his brother George on October 29, 1818, recalling Shelley's earlier "Spirit of Beauty" in his "Hymn to Intellectual Beauty". (Hence "Beauty is truth, truth Beauty" which is pure Platonism.) Keats' Odes are about the transience of this life, and of "one whose name was writ in water", and he found his images of timelessness, permanence and eternity in an urn and the song of the nightingale, not in the Light. Byron was almost a late Augustan.

The Light was restated as Fire in a prose work by Thomas Carlyle (born 1795), who experienced the "Fire" in Edinburgh when he was 26 (in 1821). He called it "a Spiritual New-birth, or Baphometic Fire-baptism". After a period of great wretchedness, torture, doubt and despair when he abandoned teaching in 1819 and "during three weeks of total sleeplessness", he writes, "there rushed like a stream of fire over my whole soul; and I shook base Fear away from me for ever. I was strong, of unknown strength; a spirit, almost a god" (*Sartor*, book 2, ch 7). After the experience Carlyle believed that the universe was an expression of one great indivisible Force, and his *Sartor Resartus* aimed to embody "the Divine Spirit of religion in a new Mythus...and vesture", and was influential in the 1830s. (Carlyle was interestingly a Calvinist who brought out Cromwell's letters.)

The fact that the Georgian Light was preserved in two movements that were hostile to organised religion shows how enfeebled the mystic tradition had become in the Georgian Age. Otherwise, only two followers of Boehme kept it going. There was Eckartshausen (1752-1803) in Germany who followed William Law in proclaiming the need for rebirth, and there was Saint-Martin (1743-1803) in France, an occultist who became a mystic after reading Boehme; Eckhartshausen; and the English Philadelphians Dr Pordage (died 1698) and Jane Leade (died 1704), who had also followed Boehme and claimed direct illumination from the Holy Spirit.

10

The Theosophical Light

The non-Christian esoteric tradition continued with Theosophy (Greek for "divine wisdom"), which treated the Light as a point of reference in a metaphysical system rather than as an existential experience. Theosophy can be said to have begun with the Romantic revival of interest in magic, which was continued by the French occultist Eliphas Lévi, a failed priest who was a revolutionary socialist before turning to magic in the 1850s.

Theosophy's Spiritual Sun

Lévi, like Swedenborg, regarded man as a microcosm who corresponded to the macrocosm as "a magical mirror of the universe", and he saw the human will as corresponding to the great Will of God. Lévi took the term "Astral Light" from Paracelsus and the Martinists, and maintained that the human will could mould the invisible Astral Light which permeated Nature, and shape it into visible forms. He regarded mediums as "natural magicians" who shaped Astral Light into semi-material forms at séances. The magician could control the invisible Astral Light by sending out a ray of blazing energy (requesting courage for example), which the macrocosm would beam back from the great store in the universe through the illuminating Astral Light.

Lévi wrote *Dogme et Rituel de la Haute Magie* as a devout Catholic, and he seems to have disapproved of magic, which was a "usurpation of the priesthood". He did not practise magic himself, and he received the Last Rites before he died in 1875. Nevertheless, he believed that he would be illuminated by the Astral Light through the use of the will – a form of "I want" – and his outlook is closer to magic than the selfless "*Thy* will be done" of the priest or mystic.[1]

Mme H. P. Blavatsky (1831-1891), a Russian aristocrat who claimed to have studied seven years in Tibet, started the Theosophical Movement in Russia in 1858 after being enlightened by Eastern cults, and in 1873 she came to America and founded the Theosophical Society in New York in conjunction with Col. Olcott in 1875, the year of Eliphas Lévi's death. Mme Blavatsky drew heavily on Lévi's Astral Light. She had joined the Spiritualist movement on her arrival in America – it was the time of the proliferation of Free Church sects – and Theosophy was at heart a spiritual movement. It syncretistically blended Hinduism and Buddhism, which had been rediscovered by the British Empire in India, with the Western religious and philosophical outlook; it blended the *Upanisads* and the *Bhagavad-gita* with Pythagoras, Plato, the Gnostics, and Neoplatonists, Meister Eckhart, Nicholas of Cusa, Paracelsus, Bruno (who was burned at the stake in 1600 for pantheism), Boehme and Schelling. Of all these influences, Hinduism was perhaps the strongest, for in 1879 Mme Blavatsky went to India and sat at the feet of Swami Dayananda Sarasvati, and according to Theosophy the spirit (an emanation of the Universal Spirit) passed through many incarnations on its way to perfection, when it became a Master or Mahatma.

Mme Blavatsky's *Isis Unveiled* (1877) and *The Secret Doctrine* (1888) describe an eternal universe in which God is immanent and transcendent; an oversoul in which all souls have a place (compare Richard Jefferies who wrote of the oversoul in 1883); and an evolutionary progress through seven planes to perfection, the second plane being the astral plane. Mme Blavatsky ran into considerable controversy, for she attributed *Isis Unveiled* to her Tibetan Mahatmas, but was accused of plagiarising from books in Col Olcott's library. She claimed to receive automatic writing from two dead Tibetan Mahatmas, but after an investigation in 1885, was pronounced a fraud by the London Society for Psychical Research. (This did not make much difference to the growth of the Theosophical Movement, for the ex-Fabian Annie Besant became its President in 1907.)

The Secret Doctrine includes the *Book of Dzyan*, an Oriental source which no-one has been able to identify. Concerning this Mme Blavatsky wrote to Sinnett on March 3, 1886: "Master finds it too difficult for me to be looking consciously into the astral light for my SD (Secret Doctrine), and so...I am made to see all I have to as though in my dream. I see large and long rolls of paper on which things are written and I recollect them...every section beginning with a page of translation from the Book of Dzyan."[2]

Mme Blavatsky regarded the Light as a central spiritual sun (a Platonic idea) which is both matter and force. In *Isis Unveiled*, she wrote, "It is said that 'The Sun is the soul of all things; all has proceeded out of it, and will return to it,' which shows that the sun is meant allegorically here, and refers to the central, invisible sun, GOD....Light, in short." Her view of the Light is that of the occult metaphysician fitting it into a system, rather than that of the poet or mystic who is publicly understanding a direct experience.

In *The Secret Doctrine* she writes of "the hidden Concealed Spiritual Sun" as "the Light – and Life-Giver – of the Spiritual and Psychic Realms", while in *The Key to Theosophy* (1889), a primer for initiates in the form of a Platonic dialogue, she writes: "Both the human Spirit, or the individuality, the reincarnating Spiritual Ego, and Buddhi, the Spiritual soul...were originally formed from the Eternal Ocean of Light." She refers to "the manasic mind illumined by the light of Buddhi" as a spiritual consciousness which "survives and lives for ever". Later she says: "We believe, with the Neo-Platonists and the Eastern teachings, that the Spirit (*Atma*) never descends...into the living man, but only showers...its radiance on the inner man." In this she differs from the Kabbalists who believe that the Spirit enters man's soul and is imprisoned there. Thus, "'The liberation of the mind from its finite consciousness, becoming one and identified with the infinite'...is the highest condition... but not-one of permanent duration, and it is reached only by the very *very* few. It is indeed, identical with that state which is known in India as *Samadhi*.... We (Theosophists) believe...in rare moments of ecstatic bliss, in the mingling of our higher soul with the universal essence, attracted as it is towards its origin and centre; a state called during life *Samadhi* and after death *Nirvana*." To know the Clear Light, then, is *Samadhi* in life, and *Nirvana* in death, according to Mme Blavatsky.[3]

We have seen that W. B. Yeats attached himself to the Theosophical Society in 1887. Rudolf Steiner (1861-1925), an editor of Goethe in his youth, attached himself to the Theosophical Society in 1902 but left to set up the Anthroposophical Society in 1912, anthroposophy being a theosophy that put man (*anthropos*) at the centre, and not God.

This too, was a spiritual movement, and involved a spiritual perception and knowledge from the higher self. The spiritual perception can free itself from the material world first in the etheric body and then in the astral body, and it can then take part once again in the spiritual processes of creation, Steiner writes in *A Road to Self-Knowledge* (1912). A Man then experiences Oneness and images which are memories of former incarnations, and his spiritual consciousness carries him back to a remote past, so that he experiences, "a Sun condition", which means perceiving the "ancient Sun". This is the experience of the Light, which is behind Steiner's interpretation of the experience.

In *Knowledge of the Higher Worlds* (1909-10), if a man perseveres on the astral plane, "the day will come when spiritual light will be all around him" which leads to clairvoyance through the "eyes of the spirit". This light is not the mystic Light that is seen behind closed eyes; it is rather the ability to perceive spiritually, to see the astral aura or flame round an object in the outer world. Steiner's enlightenment merely illumines the outer world and strengthens the astral body. At the end of the esoteric journey, however, "an exalted Being of Light stands before him on this path.... The soul, thus liberated from all bonds of the senses, is now confronted by the second Guardian of the Threshold.... An indescribable splendour radiates from the second Guardian; union with him lies as a far distant ideal before the eye of the soul." This is the nearest Steiner comes to describing the Light, and the fact that union with it is a "far distant" ideal shows how far from the end of the Mystic Way Steiner is, in comparison with the many unitive mystics we have been considering.[4]

George Gurdjieff (died 1949), who taught P. D. Ouspensky after their meeting in Moscow in 1915, must be regarded as part of the wider Theosophical Movement, though despite surfacing in Mme Blavatsky's Russia he was not directly a Theosophist and indeed distanced himself from aspects of the Theosophical system. A Caucasian Greek, Gurdjieff was reticent about where his system of knowledge of "work on oneself" came from. At his first meeting with Ouspensky it transpired that Gurdjieff was the anonymous "Hindu" author of a scenario for a ballet set in India, and so there may have been a *Vedanta* influence. Ouspensky himself wrote: "About schools and where he had found the knowledge he undoubtedly possessed he spoke very little and always superficially. He mentioned Tibetan monasteries, the Chitral, Mount Athos; Sufi schools in Persia, in Bokhara, and eastern Turkestan; he mentioned dervishes of various orders; but all of them in a very indefinite way."[5]

Gurdjieff regarded man as a machine who spends much of his time in a low state of consciousness. In Gurdjieff's view, man must awaken and become aware that he has four states of consciousness: sleep; waking or everyday consciousness; self-remembering or self-consciousness or consciousness of his own being; and objective consciousness, which in religions "is called 'enlightenment'". This fourth state of consciousness – compare Blake's "fourfold vision" – "is an altogether different state of being...the result of inner growth and of long and difficult work on oneself". It perceives "the unity of everything", "unity in diversity". There is much in Gurdjieff about the hydrogen of which the physical, astral, mental and fourth or divine bodies are composed, but the Absolute in Gurdjieff's system is the Light seen in terms of outer space, and its "ray of creation" is what the mystic sees: though like Mme Blavatsky – and, indeed, all the Theosophists, Gurdjieff is more interested in creating a system than in investigating direct experience of the Light.[6]

Alice Bailey (also died 1949) continued the Blavatskian tradition. Starting in 1919, she spent 30 years receiving Tibetan knowledge telepathically from a Tibetan D. K. (whom she had met in 1919) in fulfilment of Mme Blavatsky's prophecy that in the 20th century a disciple would give the psychological key to her own *Secret Doctrine*, and to the Cosmic Creation. *A Treatise on Cosmic Fire* (1925) is dedicted to Mme Blavatsky "who lighted her torch in the East and brought the Light to Europe and America in 1875", and the 1300 pages of its teachings are based on the three-page Proem to *The Secret Doctrine*. The "Fire" which is the basic element of God, the universe, the soul, the body and spirit matter in Alice Bailey can be apprehended through Illumination, and is therefore the Light: a man will "become a channel for the light of the Ego, and for the illumination of buddhi to pour through for the saving of the race.... His life must begin to radiate and have a magnetic effect upon others.... He will reach – through his own powerful vibrations – the hidden centre in each one."

Alice Bailey's next work *The Light of the Soul* (1927) is a 400-page Blavatskian commentary on the mere 16 pages of the *Yoga Sutras* of Patanjali, and besides revealing the Hindu origins of much of Theosophy, the commentary has much to say about the Light, which, it says, is thickly veiled by the three lower sheaths or bodies, which have to be thinned through purification before the Light can shine within them. After this purification the spirit is quiet and there is a pouring down of Light through the magnetic or etheric "silver cord" which links the Monad or Spirit and the physical brain, so that the soul illumines the etheric, astral and mental bodies.

The Soul or Self can then be seen as Light and the third eye develops in the region of the pineal gland. The heart centre or *chakra* opens through love, and this reveals the love of God and reveals the heart-in-head *chakra.* The emotional nature gives way to illuminated mind consciousness, and the Light can then be turned outwards and inwards to solve all problems. *Samadhi* is the "sleep of the yogi" when the real man has withdrawn from his lower threefold sheath to work on higher levels, and *Nirvana* is the condition of the adept when the three lower worlds are no longer attached to him; both are illumined states.

There are far too many references to the Light to begin to quote them in full, but the commentary includes several eye-catching headings: "*Enlightenment.* The light in the head, which is at first but a spark, is fanned to a flame which illumines all things.... *Illumination.* The gradually increasing downpour of fiery energy increases steadily the 'light in the head'.... This light becomes eventually a blaze of glory and the man becomes a 'son of light' or a 'sun of righteousness'. Such were the Buddha, the Christ, and all the great Ones who have attained.... *Illumination of perception.* The light of the soul pours forth and the man on the physical plane, in his brain consciousness, is thereby enabled to perceive that which before was dark and hidden from him.... *The shining forth of insight....* It is the capacity to pierce through all forms and arrive at that which they veil, because that reality is identical with the reality in oneself. *The illumining of the intellect....* Once the intellect is illumined, it can transmit to and impress upon the brain those hidden things which only the sons of God on their own plane know."[7]

The Light is present in Theosophy mainly as part of a system rather than as an experience; though Alice Bailey's "psychological key" goes some way towards coming to grips with the experience of the Light.

Psychology

Modern psychology has taken over the role of Theosophy – and the American New Thought – by emphasising our unconscious, irrational drives and by advancing holistic views of the universe. It has helped to attract people away from the Church and the modern psychoanalysts who first undermined reason and then overthrew it for a creative, irrational drive have probably made a contribution to the non-Christian esoteric tradition which should not be forgotten. They largely missed the Light. Freud and Adler certainly missed it. Jung and Rank came nearest to it. Jung advanced to the frontiers of religion with his theory of individuation, or attaining the Self.

Jung's knowledge of the Light is expressed in his commentary on *The Secret of the Golden Flower.* As we have seen, he quotes Hildegarde of Bingen's "I have always seen a light in my soul" and comments: "I know a few individuals who are familiar with this phenomenon from personal experience.... Its effect is astonishing in that it almost always brings about a solution of psychic complications, and thereby frees the inner personality from emotional and intellectual entanglements, creating thus a unity of being which is felt as 'liberation'." This suggests that Jung never experienced the Light himself, but that he is writing of it as a phenomenon that others have brought to his attention. His psychological commentary on *The Tibetan Book of the Dead* reinforces this view.

Nevertheless Jung's understanding was profound and in his commentary on *The Secret of the Golden Flower* he wrote, "The Golden

Flower is the light, and the light of heaven is the *Tao*...whose symbol would be the central white light (compare the... *Tibetan Book of the Dead*). This light dwells in the 'square inch', or in the face, that is, between the eyes." He quotes Edward Maitland, the collaborator of Anna Kingsford who in *Clothed With the Sun* (1888) referred to poets as "children of the sun" (the poets before c.1880, that is, not the children of darkness since the Second World War). Maitland writes: "I found myself confronted with a glory of unspeakable whiteness and brightness, and of a lustre so intense as well-nigh to beat me back." The effect of the experience was a shift in the consciousness, which was individuation: a new Self. Jung called it St Paul's feeling of "Not I (live), but Christ liveth in me."[8] Jung made his life's work the attainment of the individuation which the Light gives, and he wrote near the end of his life: "As far as we can discover the sole purpose of human existence is to kindle a light in the darkness of mere being."

Rank was not so well acquainted with the Light. He rejected Freud's view that the artist is a neurotic (which led to Trilling's reinterpretation of the classics), and in 1932 saw the artist as fulfilling the task of the hero and reaching a spiritual solution through his "will to immortality", his need "to live in the light of eternity". This meant perpetuating his will through a work of art or equivalent project; it also meant making each present moment "an Eternal Now". (Compare Eliot's placing of eternity in the here and now, where one can approach the Light by concentrating in the present.) Rank honoured the irrational and offered a new conception of personality that nourished man's creative will, and thereby opened the way for a new psychology of the Light.[9]

The Russian philosopher Ouspensky wrote, "Never in history has psychology stood at so low a level, lost all touch with its origin and meaning." The healing Inner Light puts psychology back in contact with its origin, and thus renews its meaning.

11

The New Age Light

The heretical New Age movement is an American-European spiritual awakening rather than a religious revival and though it has much in common with Transcendentalism, its roots are in the spiritual outlooks of Theosophy (including Steiner) and New Thought, whose esoteric tradition it carries forward. It reflects the multi-bodied view of Theosophy and the mental magnetism of New Thought, and stands for Holism, bringing all the spiritual movements of the past and present together and seeing them as parts of a whole. The New Age Light flows into the soul from the oceans of Light which surround us, according to the spiritual sources of the New Age.

The New Age began as a movement in the late 1960s and gathered force during the 1970s. One of the earliest communities to seek an alternative life-style to that of industrial society (a latter day variation of the Friends of God) was at Findhorn in Scotland, where the Caddys and Dorothy Maclean settled in 1962 and created a beautiful garden out of a barren waste by listening to inner voices, being in spiritual harmony with the plants and contacting their nature-spirits or *devas.* There David Spangler lived from 1970 to 1973.

The Steinerian Sir George Trevelyan provided a focus for a host of groups and organisations interested in the spirit, and the movement has spread abroad through such teachers as Paul Solomon, a Zen-influenced ex-Baptist American Minister who claims to have located a Source under hypnotism which gives readings like Edgar Cayce's Source, and who founded the Fellowship of the Inner Light which has built a modern mystery temple on a 200-acre site in the U.S.A.; Pir Vilayat Inayat Khan, the Sufi leader; the Tibetan Lama Sogyal Rinpoché; and the Hermeticist Frederic Lionel. Among those on the academic side was the Neoplatonist poet-critic (and scholar of Blake and Yeats) Kathleen Raine, the editor of *Temenos*, a journal which restated the sacred for our time. At New Age lectures and conferences throughout the world (such as the Wrekin Trust conferences in Britain) could be found a host of astrologers, healers, hypnotists who regress patients to former incarnations, dowsers, psychics, spiritualists and others, all of whom were vegetarians, and the many groups who regarded themselves as New Age took part in the annual Festival of Mind-Body-Spirit.

The Challenge of the New Age Movement/Light

The New Age has an anti-Christian outlook – its speakers sometimes describe the Church as a corpse – though Christian esotericism and mysticism are admired. If the New Age movement is the successor to Theosophy and New Thought then Spangler and Solomon are the Steiner and Trine of our time, and as one might expect from a spiritual and psychic movement, the paranormal is emphasised more than mysticism.

What makes it seem more than just another movement is its appeal to a new Age of Aquarius, which according to some has already started. At first sight this is a phenomenon of astrology, for the astrological Age of Pisces which has lasted two thousand years is either approaching an end or has already ended. However, the astrological idea has an astronomical basis in the "precession of the equinoxes"; for the vernal equinoctial point is leaving the constellation of Pisces and entering the constellation of Aquarius. The idea also echoes the Hindu *yugas* or "ages". Great natural disasters – earthquakes and tidal waves (*tsunamis*) – have been predicted by spiritual sources, including Paul Solomon's Source, as the Old Age ends, and the New Age's apocalyptic feeling is caught in Yeats' "Rough beast, its hour come round at last". (Yeats' apocalyptic view of history can be found in *A Vision.*)

The dawning of the New Age will coincide with the Second Coming of the Cosmic Christ, New Age adherents claim, and so there is a millenarian flavour to the New Age as well. They believe that the old order will be swept away by disasters that will purge and cleanse the earth, and a new spiritual order will commence in which more and more people will be illuminated and enlightened. For the New Age, for all its imprecision, is very much an Age of Light.

The New Age's Light, however, is acquired as naturally as breathing, and this is because the New Age asserts a form of Idealism. Instead of mind alone being real, Spirit or Light alone is real, and it materialises or manifests into matter as water solidifies into ice. There are oceans of Being or Light around us, which are full of thought-waves from departed spirits and hierarchies of angels or forces, and these flow into us by divine influx. (Swedenborg is behind the New Age as well as New Thought.) Man is a spiritual being who can attune to Reality, the immanent and transcendent Light. Man is a spiritually evolving being, and over the centuries he has evolved to a point where such an attunement can be more or less instant. Little is made of the sacrifices and Dark Nights of the mystics of the past; all that is needed is a more or less instant change of consciousness, a retuning, like turning the radio knob from one station to another to receive a new frequency of vibrations, and one is illumined. The New Age preaches a mysticism made easy.

David Spangler's *Revelation, the Birth of a New Age* follows the Blavatsky-Bailey pattern of transmissions from another world. Spangler (born 1945) experienced a "world of light" when he was a child in North Africa, and claims he psychically contacted a spirit or Presence, "Limitless love and truth", at Findhorn in 1970, from when he (conveniently) dates the beginning of the New Age. He did not go to sleep or lose consciousness, as Cayce did or as Solomon does, but "attuned" to the Presence via his high self, and this Presence was the Light in humanity, the spirit of the Cosmic Christ. "Because of your activity in the physical realm," the Presence told him in uncertain grammar, "your aspirations, your obedience to the Light you pour forth, it has enabled the creation of an etheric centre which is accomplishing a work not fully revealed to you.... You must become citizens, dwellers, within the New Age, fully attuned to limitlessness.... In so doing you will release an explosion of Light within your beings and from there out into this centre and the world beyond.... There is no place where Light is not.... I am the Light within all humanity."

Spangler claims that his contact with his Presence marked the Second Coming of Christ, "the educative force within creation". "The Second Coming has occurred and earth is in readiness to receive the new Christ manifestation," he writes. Man's maturity is marked by "the crown of illumination", which comes from rays from the Theosophic Solar *Logos*, which sends divine life-forces throughout the solar system and the earth's etheric body, and nourishes and educates man. (Compare Blake's Los, the sun-like source of creative energies.) The Universal Presence behind all evolution is the Cosmic Christ, which manifested in Spangler's Presence, his revelation asserts. "The Christ is the presence from which vision and revelations come." So, "the individual does not have to struggle to create a new world. He simply must learn to attune to the reality of the new world which is already here and manifesting its energies about us.... The New Age exists in the mind of the Cosmic Christ who is its overlord; from him project those energies which shall bring the characteristics of the New Age into form. These same energies exist within the individual and can be tapped by seeking consciously...to manifest those qualities and aspects of the New Age vision as we can now understand."[1]

In *Towards a Planetary Vision* Spangler explains why the New Age movement is outside Christianity: "In the New Age movement, many people have decided that Christianity has ceased to 'fill the bill'. It no longer meets the needs of modern humanity. Something else must take its place, perhaps theosophy, perhaps esotericism under many schools such as the arcane school, perhaps one of the Eastern disciplines.... There is a tendency to feel in the New Age movement that Christianity no longer is a viable proposition because it does not have the right language, it does not talk about things like reincarnation, the New Age, the Hierarchy, and so on."[2]

The New Age is compared to the Renaissance in the Introduction[3] to Spangler's *Revelation*: "David Spangler and Findhorn are, like Ficino and the Academy of Renaissance Florence, the seeds of a whole new cultural epoch." I think we are approaching a new period comparable to the Renaissance, a renaissance or rebirth of the medieval vision of the Light, but whether the New Age movement is that renaissance is another matter. In many ways Spangler is like one of the Gnostics or Manichaeans. The New Age sects rival Christianity as Gnosticism and Manichaeism rivalled the public Roman religion or early Christianity, and Spangler's Cosmic Christ recalls the Gnostic emanations, just as his revelation recalls the time of the *Apocalypse of St John* and of *The Shepherd of Hermas.* (Paul Solomon reminds me of Montanus, the 2nd century AD Phrygian pentecostalist and millenarian who went into an ecstatic state, prophesied that the Holy Spirit would descend and enlighten the faithful, and led a group of "illuminati" or "enlightened ones".)

Spangler's spiritual Presence and Solomon's spiritual Source substitute a psychic element for the mystic's direct experience of the Light, and many mystics, called upon like St Augustine to choose between the Christian Reawakening and the Manichaean-like spiritual New Age whose rise has been at the Christian expense, may prefer the Light of Eliot and Teilhard (for all his Cosmic Christ) to the possibly commercial, phoney and imprecise Presences and Sources of the New Age. I use the word "commercial" not to question the integrity of Spangler's testimony or revelation, but because there is now a Findhorn industry and the New Age groups charge for admission to lectures and conferences along the lines of private education. It must be remembered that so far as we know Christ did not charge for admission to the Sermon on the Mount, and despite its educative nature, that the Church does not charge an entrance fee.

The New Age has coincided with, or been the umbrella for, a number of revivals of primitive religion: witchcraft, black magic, Satanism, prophecy, divination, astrology, healing and drug cults. (Compare LSD and *soma,* and the doors of perception of Blake and Huxley's mescalin.) As with Freemasonry, it stands for the New Age of Lucifer. There has been a rise of differing sects and cults which parallels the proliferation of Free Churches in the 19th century. Some of these cults are harmless or even beneficial, like Pak Subuh's Subud (which passes on the illumination Pak Subuh achieved at the age of 24). The Maharishi Mahesh Yogi's Age of Enlightenment has become more controversial since it tried to teach levitation. Others are much more dubious, like Scientology, the Moon Cult, and the discredited Jones Temple Cult, which collapsed in a mass-suicide that was more like a concentration-camp mass-murder.

Such cults are dubious because they are widely believed to attempt to brainwash scepticism away. The truly illumined have an enlightened ethic – that the Light or Fire makes people naturally good – and no truly illumined person orders over-persuasive recruiting methods, detains converts against their will, bans them from seeing their families, exploits them as cheap slave labour or puts poison in their drinks. The abuse of the Light is exemplified by the Ku Klux Klan movement, the anti-Negro terrorist organisation of the American Southern whites which grew up after the Civil War and still employs fire and "sun-crowned" symbolism for racialist ends: "When the flames reached their peak, Wilkinson declared: 'Behold the fiery cross, its hallowed flame. It shall burn bright as morning for all decades to come...an inspiration, a sign of the Christian religion, a symbol of faith, hope and love.... God give us men, tall sun-crowned men who will not flinch at duty and will not lie.' "[4]

The New Age movement has absorbed many of the Middle Eastern and Far Eastern Lights. These are vigorous in their own right, and their brightness contrasts strongly with the crepuscular gloom that has spread across Christendom.

The Attraction of Cults

The Light can still be found in esoteric and religious alternatives to Christianity, then; notably in the New Age movement and in the Indian-Iranian Sufi, Hindu and Zen traditions. Many esotericists interpret it very differently from Christians however, and it is precisely their interpretation, which focuses on theosophical and spiritual systems, that has led some people to prefer the Christian Light. The rise of the esoteric groups and cults has been at Christianity's expense, just as the rise of Gnosticism challenged early Christianity before AD 150. Many people today have a choice between the sects of the main Western religions, and the esoteric cults and Eastern ways, all of which, in their different ways, offer the vision of God. So many traditions to choose from, yet there is just one experience of the Light behind closed eyes in contemplation, which all human beings can have if they set their mind to it, irrespective of outer forms. In America many more have chosen to be churchgoers than members of cults.

Despite the *coterie* nature of the various groups, the esoteric alternative to Christianity had attracted many illumined followers who before the Reformation would have gone into the Church. The Church had done little to attract them back – by offering a clear Light-based vision.

• • •

Conclusion

Western culture has spread Christendom throughout the world, and during the materialistic Industrial Revolution and the Victorian time the Light dimmed and seemed almost to have become lost. The recorded examples of the experience of the Light in the 20th century seem relatively few, although in the West both Christianity and the esoteric groups and schools hint at a continued knowledge of it. Many draw on the ideas of the heretical subtradition of Western civilization, which have contributed to the dimming of the Christian Light. Such is their following that it seems the Light is known to thousands. No religion spreads it among the masses as once happened, but it is still to be found in each higher religion. With the demise of the European empires Christendom has contracted somewhat and lost its sense of purpose, but Christianity – albeit co-existing with plural and diverse motifs from the heretical subtradition – is still the higher religion of Western civilization.

PART FOUR

THE LIGHT IN CIVILIZATIONS

And all shall be well and
All manner of thing shall be well
When the tongues of flame are in-folded
Into the crowned knot of fire
And the fire and the rose are one.

T. S. Eliot, "Little Gidding"

1

The Individual's Experience of the Light of Religion

We have reviewed the recorded visions of the Light during the last 5,000 years, and as we look back it can now be seen that the vision of the Light (or Fire) is in fact the vision of God. For this there is a wide measure of agreement over many centuries. (Dionysius the Areopagite, who insisted that God is Darkness, is in a great minority on this point.) Those who have experienced the Light are convinced they have had the vision of God, after which (for them) the word "God" becomes synonymous with the Light. By approaching God through all the recorded perceptions of the Light or Fire we have escaped easy clichés and "made the familiar strange and the strange familiar" (Coleridge); and we have taken a direct and straightforward Way that skirts round the bogs of rational proof, logical argument, and metaphysical debate whose words seem swampy beside the still clear vision that reflects the fundamental sun-like Light.

Phenomenological Method

It is now time for us to return to our phenomenological method. We have been investigating the reception of the Light in the perceiving, interpreting consciousness. We have been establishing a set of historical experiences – of perceptions and interpretations of the Light – that span 5,000 years, and we have been seeking to form a scientific picture of what the Light is in consciousness. Our objective, scientific approach to consciousness has demonstrated that consciousness includes perception of the Light. We have not gone into theories that explain the cause of the Light, for our phenomenological method has excluded all explanations of its cause.

We are now ready to complete our picture of the Light (or Fire). It was widely known in very early times, and it was desired by priest-kings. It was symbolized in sky-gods and channelled into State ceremonies through fire-sacrifices, and individuals were introduced to it through these public symbols. Religions grew round the rites of the Light, which drew peoples to it from far and wide. As time progressed numerous experiences of the Light were written down and preserved, especially in the Christian tradition. These experiences have been interpreted as (1) direct perceptions of God, or (2) revelations from God which are "beneath" God, (3) the One source of the universe which is its reflection or manifestation, (4) who is a Fire/Light or Void or spiritual sun, (5) who sends a divinising spark or influx of Light into the soul which (6) transforms or converts the ego (7) by making the heart burn and (8) by giving Eternal Life.

The Light or Fire (or God) is thus the germ or "Idea" of which the form of the universe is a reflection or manifestation. According to the Tradition, to see the Light is to see the divine unity out of which the universe came, and to experience Eternal Life. It is impossible to advance closer to God than that.

The Light as a Standard and Unifier

The sceptic may say that the mystic who sees the Light is mad – in which case the following were all mad: Patanjali, Zoroaster, the Buddha, Mahavira, Lao-Tze, Jesus, St Paul, St Clement of Alexandria, Plotinus, Mani, Cassian, St Augustine, Pope Gregory the Great, Mohammed, Bayazid, Al-Hallaj, Omar Khayyam, Suhrawardi, Hafez, Symeon the New Theologian, Hildegarde of Bingen, Mechtild of Magdeburg, Moses de Léon, Dante,

Angela of Foligno, Meister Eckhart, Tauler, Suso, Ruysbroeck, Kempis, Rolle, Hilton, Julian of Norwich, St Catherine of Siena, St Catherine of Genoa, St Gregory Palamas, Padmasambhava, Sankara, *Guru* Nanak, Hui-neng, Eisai, Dogen,Michelangelo, St Teresa of Avila, St John of the Cross, Boehme, Herbert, Vaughan, Crashaw, Traherne, Norris, Law, Cromwell, Marvell, Milton, Bunyan, Fox, Penn, Naylor, Mme Acarie, Baker, Pascal, St Francis of Sales, Mme Guyon, Wesley, Blake, Swedenborg, Shelley, Emerson, Tennyson, Browning, Arnold, Newman, Mme Blavatsky, Trine, Jung, T. S.Eliot – and a host of others who enshrine the best of Western and Eastern culture. If to see the Light is mad, then the inspiration of the greatest Western and Eastern culture has been mad – a philistine and melancholy view indeed!

No, these contemplative mystics were all sane; they were merely closer to metaphysical Reality (the Light) than sceptics are. And if I have used overkill by referring too frequently to their writings to demonstrate this, I plead that it has been necessary to present *all* the evidence to show that experiences of the Light created the religions (and heresies) of each culture and to demonstrate that the metaphysical vision which created those religions is not mad. In fact the best culture is "the greatest" precisely *because* it encapsulates (like Dante's *Paradiso*) the metaphysical vision of the Light.

The collective experience of the Light (or God) over 5,000 years lies outside the five senses and the doubting of the rational ego. The Light is a standard which resists – indeed, burns up – the secularized criteria of empiricism and rational scepticism and all world-views based solely on the senses, including the verifiability principle that has dominated modern philosophy. If the reality of the "invisible" Light (or Fire) in the foregoing experiences is acknowledged, then the materialist world of the senses (the "world of phenomena") is no longer the reality it has been for the last three hundred and fifty years.

The Light has been known in every generation of the last 5,000 years. It is a standard of truth by which to assess the philosophy of our time, and it offers an age-old metaphysical path for attaining – for directly experiencing – Reality. This metaphysical vision is so old that it is unfamiliar, and therefore "new". It is independent of all religious movements and "isms", which honour it, and it is universally available to each member of mankind. The seeker may fit it into the framework of any of the existing religions, or he may remain outside them. But whether the path he takes is the Christian, Western esoteric or Far Eastern path, or his own path, at the individual level the *Light is the Way.*

The Light illumines from the "beyond", and as such it is a standard by which man can be judged and found wanting, towards which he can progress up the Ladder of Perfection. In our time, more and more people are seeking for an answer, more and more people are potential mystics. Our examination of the Tradition has shown that answers can be found, and that there is a Mystic Way of the last 5,000 years, a metaphysical Journey to a vision of meaning and purpose which all the illumined we have been considering have known. An encounter with this transforming vision gives self-knowledge. The illumined man is the model for our time, he is the one standard by which the multiplicity of "isms" of our contemporary world can be judged.

A *guru* uses resonant words to detach the seeker from "the world of phenomena" or becoming (the physical *Maya* of the senses) so that he is ready to receive the wordless Light. The volumes of hundreds of *gurus* and saints have this same message: detachment to receive this wordless Light. We have offered the essence, the distilled wisdom, of hundreds of *gurus* and saints, for all the many experiences we have quoted carry the same message: that in the silence beyond all words can be found the wordless Light. Our accumulation of hundreds of "eye witness" accounts of the experience of the Light can only reinforce this central message: that if the seeker detaches himself from the empirical world, he can experience the wordless Light of Eternity which has profound consequences for the health of the seeker, his society, his culture and his civilization. Ultimately the vision of the Light stands against all rational and analytical philosophy, which, like the words of the *gurus*, is at best a preparation for the reception of the health-bringing Light and at worst a distraction from its Reality, an illusion.

In rediscovering the Journey to the Light, we have rediscovered an underlying metaphysical unity beneath the cultures and history of the world. The Light has been recorded for at least 5,000 years and all its cultural expressions are inter-related. All religions and heretical sects share the Light and are therefore parts of one whole, in which a multiplicity of "isms" have one unity. The Light is the common factor and underlying unity within all civilizations' metaphysical visions and all religions, and all men are therefore brothers within the Light.

The Light is therefore an ecumenical force. It is what the Christian sects have in common. In Northern Ireland, both Protestants and Catholics share the Light. It is a syncretistic force, for it is also what different religions have in common. Jews and Moslems, Hindus and Moslems and Christians and Moslems share the Light. Iranian Islam and the "decadent" Western Christianity and cultural hegemony the Ayatollahs oppose share the Light. The Light reconciles apparently opposed sects and religions, just as Clement of Alexandria reconciled apparently conflicting philosophies. The reconciling power of the Light appears at a time when Christian reunification is in the balance, and when some sort of global reunification is becoming increasingly necessary. Fundamentally, the Light is a force for peace which can unite warring Christians in Ireland and warring Jews and Moslems in the Middle East. Its power contrasts with the power of the atomic bomb. Tudor Pole (whose house at Glastonbury can be visited) marshalled the power of the Free World's Light with Churchill's blessing when he proposed the wartime minute's silence before the 9 o'clock news, during which the Free World was to beam Light at the forces of Nazi darkness.

It must never be forgotten however, that the individual's *experience* of the Light is of fundamental importance and beyond all words. We can go so far as to say that to *experience* the Light in the soul is the aim, goal, meaning and purpose of an individual's life. For the Light works in and on the soul of the individual, and his progress towards Eternity and the unfolding of his soul are of supreme importance as ends in themselves, although his progress also has an impact on the progress of his civilization. This was the knowledge traditionally guarded by the religions and made the centrepiece of the ancient civilizations.

2

Pattern and Civilizations

Universalism and the Philosophy of History

We can now return to our historical theme: the role of the Light in religion and therefore in history. History comprises the events of the past while attempts to describe and interpret the events by philosophical reflection belong to the philosophy of history.

Traditionally the philosophy of history has concentrated on explaining the direction of historical events. Its interpretations, which can vary and often have the force of theories, fall into two camps: the speculative and the analytical.

History as Linear, Cyclical and Spiral

Speculative philosophy has always assumed that history is linear (i.e. has a direction), that it has order or design and is not a random flux without pattern. Historical events are influenced by Providence according to St Augustine's theological and metaphysical approach to historical events in *City of God*; according to Bossuet's *Discours sur l'histoire universelle* ("Discourse on Universal History", 1681), which attributed the rise and fall of empires to Providence; and according to Arnold Toynbee's rejection of the pessimistic view that history is chaotic. The theological-metaphysical-Providential outlook has always regarded history as having a Providential purpose. This is not deterministic as it is advanced by the free choice of leaders, who (it is said) either further the Providential purpose or cause a reaction against their own policies which furthers the purpose.

Since the Renaissance and "Enlightenment" (in which the Light dimmed before reason) a secular speculative approach has arisen. The rationalist Enlightenment philosopher Edward Gibbon was influenced by the scepticism of Hume. In *The History of the Decline and Fall of the Roman Empire* (1766-1788) Gibbon saw Roman civilization as continuing in the East Roman and then Byzantine times until 1453, and as continuously decaying as a result of moral decadence, barbarism and religion (to which he was somewhat hostile), forces from which the enlightened European civilization would be immune. This linear view that history is a retrogression rather than progress accords with the events in the West Roman Empire until c.480, but is at variance with the facts in the East, where the Byzantine Empire grew and held the line against its opponents for a thousand years. Quite simply, Gibbon was mistaken in linking the West Roman and Byzantine Empires. Yeats attempted a wider application of Gibbon's retrogressive linear view in *A Vision* (1925, fuller version 1937). Drawing on Gibbon, whose collected works he bought with money from his 1923 Nobel Prize, and on Plato's *Laws* and the Hindu *yugas* or Ages, Yeats (or his wife's spiritual source for *A Vision* came from her automatic writing) saw history as passing through two-thousand-year-long Ages. The principle of Ages is interesting as it is distantly related to stages, but the two-thousand-year-long cycles make little contact with the precise dates of the rise and fall of the empires in each century. (It is interesting that the golden tree and bird of Yeats' 'Sailing to Byzantium', 1928, immediately came from Gibbon, who described in *Decline and Fall* vi 26 and 81 how the Byzantine Emperor Theophilus, 829-842, the last of the Iconoclasts, emulated the golden tree and "birds warbling with artificial notes" that stood in the courtyard of Haṛun ar-Rashid, the Persian Caliph of Baghdad.)

In due course, the secular speculative approach has regarded history as a science, as did Comte's optimistic positivism and Mill's view of progress.

Some speculative historians – sceptics like the more pessimistic Schopenhauer and Popper – have challenged optimistic views of history, doubting that man is perfectible or that history is leading towards a goal. To them, all historical goals are expressions of faith rather than empirical truths, and they have demanded empirical observation, testing and precision of concept. Some thinkers, like Vico, have urged historians to enter into the attitudes of the past rather than impose interpretations from their own time. Some, like von Herder, have drawn attention to the separateness of each culture in time, place and national character. (The reason perceives distinctions and differences; it is the intuition that perceives unity.) Some see history as a dynamic process, a dialectic between spirit and matter (Hegel) or an economic struggle between the ruling and working classes (Marx). In the 20th century cyclical rather than linear patterns in history have been detected by Spengler, in *Decline of the West* and Toynbee in *A Study of History*. Both were affected by the First World War, and Spengler saw civilizations as having a life cycle, whereas Toynbee's comparative study of the cycles of civilizations has been (perhaps correctly) criticised for its unscientific, inductive approach by sceptics who question all speculative systems.

We are living in a time when the speculative philosophy of history has temporarily given way to an analytical philosophy of history which directs attention not on the events of the past but on the categories and concepts of the historians who attempt to describe events; just as in philosophy itself attention has been directed not on the universe but on the concepts of philosophers who attempt to describe the universe. The first historians to examine historical categories were Dilthey and Croce, who held that history is only intelligible because historians make it so. In other words, the patterns are in the concepts of the historians rather than in the events. R. G. Collingwood investigated historical procedures and concepts in terms of past thinking (compare Vico). Some positivist philosophers of history, like Hempel, have seen history as obeying the same laws as science, while others, followers of Wittgenstein, have been sceptical about scientific models for historical concepts. Even the objectivity of history has been questioned, and some exclude value judgements from history. Such positivists, logical empiricists and analytical philosophers draw attention to what is ignored by the theorists, and reject all speculative versions of history as being over-ambitious.

Where does all this leave our Universalist approach to the history of the Tradition of the Light, and of its traditions? Clearly any Universalist view is closer to the speculative than to the analytical camp. However, our Light-based Universalist view differs from all the speculative *theories* in one important respect: it is founded on a quasi-empirical *experience* received in the intellect (the faculty of higher perception), not on speculative reason; and on the historical interpretations of that experience by the mystics and saints who have known it during the 5,000-year tradition of the Light. I therefore prefer the word "traditional" to "speculative" to describe our Universalist philosophy of history.

Nevertheless, our traditional approach extends, restores, redefines and gives new meaning to the theological-metaphysical-Providential view of St Augustine, Bossuet and Toynbee, for our phenomenological method allows us to focus on the sense of purpose in the minds of those who receive the Light rather than on the purposes of Providence; on the human response to the Providential Light rather than its guidance of the course of history. We can thus redefine the theological-metaphysical-Providential view of history in terms of an event that happens in human minds (the reception of the Light) and its effect on society (the creation of religions), and we are thus able to bring a sociological slant to the theological-metaphysical-Providential view of history. At the same time our view is scientific as it seeks to identify and describe the main Law of history as objectively as Einstein describes the Law of Relativity. Our view is not a deterministic view as the Law works through the free choice of leaders with strong personalities, whose emphasis furthers the Law or causes a reaction against their emphasis which furthers the Law.

Our view opposes the pro-secular, optimistic scientific view of Comte and Mill. As the experience of the Light is quasi-empirical our Universalist approach to the experience and tradition of the Light (as opposed to its application to history) is not subject to the criticisms of Schopenhauer and Popper that it is a matter of faith rather than empirical truth. We have been at pains to enter into the past attitudes of each of the traditions we have considered rather than to impose a 20th century idea on each one, and our view can thus withstand the objections of Vico and von Herder. (An example of a present-dominated or 20th century-dominated view of history is Francis Fukuyama's view that history has now ended as there will now be a perfect world equilibrium regardless of the stages of different traditions.) Our view accords with Hegel's conflicting dialectic between spirit and matter (the Light and Materialism), and it is directly in the tradition of Spengler and Toynbee while differing from both. Our view is both linear and cyclical: cyclical because the Light recurs in different rising and falling traditions, but linear because it spirals in a linear direction (like a spiral staircase) towards one (albeit brief and necessarily voluntary) world-wide traditions based on the Light which all traditions have in common; which I have – in contrast to *The Syndicate*'s Hellish New World Order – elsewhere called Christ's Paradisal New World Order.

History is not Random Events: The Inadequacy of Views which Deny Pattern

So, does history have a pattern, an order, a design? When we speak of a pattern in a carpet, we mean that a design has a certain regularity of recurring or similar motifs which introduce artistic order. In the same way, history has a pattern if all its traditions and religions are seen as recurring or similar motifs which give it order. A recurring connection between traditions and religions would strengthen the pattern. If we do not hold a modern version of the traditional view that history has linear order and design, then we have to adopt one or more of the following views which we have just touched on in the last few pages during our consideration of the philosophy of history:

1. History is a random flux without a pattern or direction;
2. History has a cyclical, recurrent movement;
3. History obeys the same laws as science;
4. History concerns fundamentally secular events which may

be misinterpreted by their participants in theological or metaphysical terms;

5. History has no goal, and to believe that it has is a matter of faith rather than of empirical truth;
6. History concerns the working out of economic laws and of a capitalist or Marxist dialectic;
7. History is the concepts and value judgements of the historian.

There are historical objections to each of these views that history is chaotic, and each position can be shown to be as much a matter of faith as the view that history has a goal. Each view is inadequate:

1. Leaders, creative and inventive geniuses and nations plan and behave purposively with a direction and order that contradicts notions of a patternless flux, the existence of which (in Nature as well as in history) is an unproven matter of faith;
2. Although there are cycles, or spirals, within history, and parallels between cycles (for example, between rising and falling traditions), there is no evidence that a cyclical view of history is any more reliable than a linear view, and to give cycles special importance at the expense of linear considerations without proposing spirals (which blend the cyclical and linear) is an unproven matter of faith;
3. Although historical events are governed by psychological factors and other tendencies, there is no evidence that history obeys scientific laws and such a belief is a matter of faith;
4. It has never been proved or established that secular events (or societies) have some essential superiority over events (or societies) of a theological or metaphysical nature, and while such a belief is common among those of a materialistic outlook (whose materialistic historical concepts perhaps need to be analysed) it is finally a matter of faith;
5. It has never been proved or established that history has no goal, and until there is proof any such belief is a matter of faith;

6. It has never been proved or established that history concerns the working out of economic laws, or the revolution of the working class, and followers of either theory have adopted their belief as a matter of faith;
7. Just as there is no evidence that history has no pattern, so there is no evidence that analysing historians' concepts offers a more reliable view of history than analysing historical events, and anyone who believes it does has entered the realms of faith.

These objective historical objections are supported by the inner conviction of the illumined man:

1. If history is a patternless flux, then one generation succeeds another as one wave succeeds another in the sea, and has no meaning, and there is no room for the illumined man's sense of order and purpose or his inner conviction that there is a pattern in history, notably in traditions;
2. The illumined man knows the linear inner progress of the Mystic Way, and while personal, and historical, situations may spiral and repeat themselves at different levels and times, he knows that there is a linear progression within the spiralling cycles because his own spiritual development has been linear;
3. If history is subject to the same laws as science, the illumined man knows that the laws are organic rather than materialistic and mechanistic, for his own inner life follows an organic rather than a materialistic-mechanistic model, and just as organisms are filled with the Light, so too, he has a conviction, are the organisms of history, traditions;
4. If history concerns merely secular events (and societies), then the visions of the Light that inspired the religions which have shaped history (as they did during the Crusades) are treated as secular events, whereas the illumined man is convinced that visions of the Light must be interpreted in theological or metaphysical, not secular terms;
5. The illumined man suspends rational judgement as to whether history has a goal – there is no objective evidence either way, and

to say that history has or has not a goal involves equal leaps of faith – but he knows that if history has no goal, then the aspirations and wars of individuals and nations are meaningless and senseless wastes, which, through the revealed knowledge of the Light, he has an inner conviction they are not;

6. If history is merely about economic laws or the capitalist or Marxist dialectic, then history is defined exclusively in terms of wealth and social class, a proposition which ignores the influence of the illumined man's creative depths before the Light, an influence of which the illumined man is convinced;
7. If the truth of history is in the historians' concepts and not in a set of objective events, then no event can be described objectively; the quality of the consciousness of the historian is crucial, and the illumined man knows that a sceptical historian's lack of awareness of the Light can fundamentally influence an analytical description of world traditions.

Whether viewed objectively or subjectively, then, in terms of events or concepts, the views of historians which deny pattern are no more reliable than those which locate a pattern.

Pattern through Religions: Organisms as the Unit of History

We have detailed the experiences of the Light in 25 different traditions and cultures, and have so far deliberately avoided relating them to formalised patterns. In the course of doing this we have reinterpreted history in terms of the Light. Now that we have defended the concept of pattern in history, it is time to study the pattern and draw some conclusions. First we need to investigate the unit of history. And a good place to start is cultures.

Cultures

A culture is the common way of living of a people. The classic definition was given by Edward Burnett Tylor in 1871: "Culture...is that complex whole which includes knowledge, belief, art, morals, law, custom, and any other capabilities and habits acquired by man as a member of society."[1] This complex whole grows out of primitive family groups, and it includes all a people's behaviour: their language, ideas, attitudes, values, ideals, traditions, beliefs, customs, laws, codes, institutions, tools, technology, techniques, material objects and works of art – and their rituals and religious or sacred ceremonies. When all these are regarded as historical products in their own right and in relation to each other, they cease to be aspects of behaviour and become manifestations of culture. Regarded like this, writing, tool-making, weaving, potsherds, horror of incest and belief in spirits are not so much what people do as elements in a culture.

In a growing culture religious rituals and ceremonies dominate the common social life and therefore have a great importance. They influence the common attitudes, values and ideals, and shape the common traditions, beliefs and customs. Religion is the essential element in a culture – what Toynbee in *A Study of History* called "the religious quintessence of a culture".[2] We have quoted T. S. Eliot in the epigraphs as stating that "the culture (is) essentially, the incarnation...of the religion of a people". We have seen that the Light is central to all the early religions and features strongly in their rituals and ceremonies, and that it is therefore fundamental to growing cultures.

Civilizations

A culture is an "organism" with a life of its own which it derives from its people. But a culture in turn can evolve a more sophisticated "organism" which embodies the tradition and religion of its people in a much fuller, more advanced way: a civilization. A civilization is the true unit of history. Within its "organism" a people enjoy the fullest, most sophisticated and advanced standard of living.

Several cultures evolve into a civilization when they are unified into a complex whole that can sustain different peoples and all their languages, ideas, attitudes, and values. A civilization consists of heterogeneous peoples with different cultures who have diverse roles in complex cities, and a complex economic organisation that supports the political leaders, the priests and the educated *élite*. Thus the cultures of Mesopotamian Iraq reached civilization c.3000 BC when they developed urban cities with complex food-producing and food-storage systems.

A study of a civilization would reveal that it is unified by its religion, the Light of which (the civilization's central idea) is enshrined in its rituals and ceremonies. Its religion offers a metaphysical Reality, the Light, to which diverse peoples respond, with which they identify and to which they feel they belong. As the Light is central to all religions, it is the unifying force in all growing cultures and civilizations.

As a civilization is the common way of living of all groups, classes and sensibilities of several peoples and cultures, in a traditional civilization its metaphysical vision gives meaning to the common everyday life. In early times, all the people – kings, priests, and peasants alike – shared the rituals in which everyday life met the metaphysical vision, and the religious architecture offered common analogies for sacred ideas that featured in the vision: the ziggurats provided analogies for the world mountain, and the sloping sides of the Great Pyramid offered an analogy for the rays of the sun/Light, up which the soul of the dead Pharaoh travelled back to the source. The towering spires of Cathedrals and tiers of pagodas provided similar everyday analogies for a similar vision, while in Japanese flower-arrangement three flowers symbolising heaven, earth and man make a metaphysical Taoist statement in an everyday vase.

The evidence shows that in a healthy civilization, the metaphysical vision provides analogies and echoes for all the people, and all groups and classes – artists and engineers, workers and aristocrats – share a common metaphysical ground. The artist, poet, scientist, politician and labourer all have a culture in common and a common respect for a metaphysical vision. In the case of Western civilization this vision has traditionally been Christianity. For many centuries the Christian vision inspired European artists, and the metaphysical and artistic sensibilities are obviously united in medieval paintings such as Jan Van Eyck's *Mystic Lamb* in St. Bavo's Cathedral in Ghent, and the numerous works which represent the Light as a halo round a subject's head.

A growing civilization, then, is a species of evolved culture which transmits the unifying vision of the Light and the ceremonial style that is peculiar to that civilization from one generation to another.

When the metaphysical vision fades and loses its hold, a traditional civilization's culture becomes secularized and materialistic, and begins to disintegrate. The metaphysical sensibility separates from the artistic sensibility, with the result that works of art have secular subjects. The classes separate and groups fragment, and as T. S. Eliot pointed out in *Notes towards the Definition of Culture*[3] such fragmentation means impoverishment and decay. Each class maintains its own separate culture through its elites and transmits it through the family and social institutions, while groups become divided. The arts and sciences separate.

We shall see in the companion volume to this work, *The Endless Rise and Fall of Civilizations,* that in a decaying civilization, the Light becomes lost, the civilization's unifying power is weakened, and its culture becomes excessively materialistic and diseased. The ceremonies no longer appeal. The visionary thrust that grew the civilization is absent, and economic performance becomes paramount. Unless the inner vitality is renewed there is slow decline.

But whether growing or decaying, a culture is "the common way of living of a people, that complex whole which includes knowledge, belief, art, morals, law, custom" and indeed "all a people's behaviour: their language, ideas, attitudes, values, ideals, traditions, beliefs, customs, laws, codes, institutions, tools, technology, techniques, material objects and works of art – and their rituals and religious or sacred ceremonies". We have defined a civilization as a unified complex whole of several cultures, a "whole that can sustain different peoples and all their languages, ideas, attitudes and values"; it consists of "heterogeneous peoples who have diverse roles in complex cities, and a complex economic organisation that supports the political leaders, the priests and the educated *élite*". This implies Kenneth Clark's sense of permanence (see p529). We shall see that a civilization is unified by its religion, which (Eliot believed) is incarnated in a culture.

A civilization, then, has to have (1) heterogeneous peoples, (2) a level of social organisation and stratification that creates a high cultural tradition, (3) complex "permanent" cities, (4) a complex economic organisation in which not all the citizens are producing food, (5) a mastery of technology (for example, writing, the wheel, metallurgy) and (6) last but not least, and I would argue to some extent most importantly, its own distinctive religion. A civilization is thus more than a colony, which is dependent on the mother country and lacks a distinctive religion.

25 Civilizations

Reviewing what we have already found in our broadly chronological narrative (bearing in mind that some traditions developed in parallel) of the Tradition of the Light in *Part Two* with these six elements in mind, drawing together years of research, sticking to strictly geographical groupings that do not force a pattern, retaining everyday parlance (calling it the "Egyptian" and not the "Egyptiac" civilization), and ignoring the question of distinctive religion for a moment, we can propose that our identification of 25 traditions has enabled us to identify 25 civilizations.

Using the 25 Lights we identified in *Part Two*, we can identify and list the 25 principal candidates for different civilizations. Recorded history did not begin until c.3500-3000 BC and no cultures reached the level of civilization very long before that time. These civilizations include the Indo-European Kurgans, who comprised heterogeneous peoples and despite being nomadic pastoral farmers and resembling mobile barbarians had complex cities for their time, their own distinctive tombs and religion.

Marija Gimbutas in *The Civilization of the Goddess* called their agricultural life and worship of the Earth Mother "Old European civilization", and though others have preferred to call it "Old European culture" as "civilization" implies an advanced form of social stratification, high culture and a State which the Kurgan farmers lacked in comparison with modern equivalents (see note 1 under *Part Two*, no. 1), I take the view that the social organization round the megaliths showed an advanced high culture *for their time* and spread throughout most of Western Europe, and that it can be persuasively argued that there was an Indo-European Kurgan civilizations rather than local cutlure. Their civilization absorbed a Mesopotamian influence – at first Anu and Ogma, and later, c.2400-2300 BC, Utu and Shamash – to which the building of the megaliths can perhaps be attributed.

I list the 25 now in broadly chronological or geographical order:

1. Indo-European Kurgan (perhaps builders of megaliths in Old Europe)
2. Mesopotamian (Sumerian-Akkadian and later Babylonian)
3. Egyptian
4. Aegean-Greek (including Minoan and Mycenaean)
5. Roman
6. Anatolian (including Hittite)
7. Syrian
8. Israelite (Judaistic)
9. Celtic (including Irish Celtic and Druid)
10. Iranian
11. European } together forming Western civilization
12. North American } (now centred in Europe and USA)
13. Byzantine-Russian (Christian Orthodox)
14. Germanic-Scandinavian
15. Andean (including Peruvian)
16. Meso-American (including Mexican and North American Mississippian)
17. Arab (Islamic)
18. African
19. Indian (Hindu)
20. South-East Asian (mainly *Mahayana* and later Theravada Buddhist)
21. Japanese
22. Oceanian (including Polynesian and Australian)

23. Chinese
24. Tibetan
25. Central Asian (including Mongolian) from c.500 BC

This list follows the order of the Lights set out in *Part Two*. You will see that the first ten civilizations on the list, and no. 14, are now dead; and that the remaining fourteen are still living.

All parts of the world that have an active Light are covered in this list. Countries that are not mentioned belong to one of these civilizations. (For example after 395 Greece belonged to the Byzantine civilization, then to the Ottoman/Arab civilization, and then to the European civilization.) Looking at our draft and bringing the distinctive religion of each civilization into mind, we can see that some of our civilizations have their own distinctive religion whereas others share the religion of another civilization. Numbers 1, 2, 3, 4, 5, 6, 7, 8, 10, 11, 15, 16, 17, 18, 19 and 23 all have their own distinctive religion and I should imagine there will be little disagreement about their status as civilizations as they have always traditionally been regarded as such. Let us deal with the more obvious carpings and cavils straightaway. Most of these concern the major living religions and possible alternative ways of treating geographical regions.

Maps which show Israel as having very little independent territory between 1200 and 600 BC may suggest that Israel should be regarded as a culture rather than as a civilization, but the Israelites produced their own religion and must therefore be regarded as founders of a civilization in their own right rather than as belonging to the Syrian (Phoenician-Canaanite) civilization. "Israelite" is a more accurate geographical word than "Jewish" (8) as the people of the 12 tribes were known as Israelites – the people descended from Jacob or Israel (*Gen* 32.28) – from the time of their entrance to the Holy Land, whereas "Jew" came to refer to a citizen of the Kingdom of Judah. "Arab" is now used loosely of the Arab culture throughout the Middle East, and is wider than "Arabic" which emphasises the language of the Arabs rather than the people.

It can be argued, on the grounds of their religion, that numbers 12, 13, 14, 20, 21 and 22, and parts of numbers 7 and 9, really belong to one or other of these civilizations and that 24 is related to 25. The Central Asian culture arguably began c.50,000 BC as we have seen, but recorded history did not begin until c.3500-3000 BC and the Central Asian culture did not reach the level of civilization until c.500 BC. The Irish Celtic civilization (part of 9) may be regarded as a branch of European (Christian) civilization rather than as the last stage of the Celtic (Druid-Culdee) civilization (9).

The Byzantine Empire of civilization number 13 was originally East Roman and it can be regarded as a continuation of the West Roman Empire. However, it became predominantly Greek c.626, after which it had a quite separate religion and identity from the West Roman religion and identity, and West Roman rule continued until 800. Seeing the West Roman and East Roman Empires as a continuity was Gibbon's main mistake. As a result he had to maintain that a thousand years of Byzantine growth were in fact years of decay, which puts the second part of *The Decline and Fall* at variance with the facts.

The Byzantine Empire can also be seen as a branch of the European (Christian) civilization, although it is not European and its Orthodox religion is very different from European Catholicism; and as a separate civilization from the Russian civilization, the two civilizations growing out of separate geographical regions. However it is our view that the Byzantine and Russian cultures should be seen as a continuum, as successive phases of one Orthodox tradition, with the Byzantine culture flowing into the Russian culture when the future Ivan III married the neice of Constantine Palaeologus, the last Byzantine Emperor. Both Byzantine and Russian cultures shared the same religion although they were separated both geographically (by the Mongolians and their successors, the Khanate of the Golden Horde) and linguistically. They created quite separate Empires – the Byzantine in the Mediterranean, Balkans and Anatolia, the Russian in Asia – and the Russian Emperors after 1453 wished to be regarded as Byzantine largely because they contrasted Byzantinism with Moslem Ottoman rule, equated Byzantinism with Westernisation, and preferred a Western to an Ottoman identity. The two cultures should be regarded as being linked in their Central Idea.

The Byzantine civilization could also be seen (as Toynbee saw it) as passing into the Ottoman Empire and then modern semi-European Turkey.

The latter part of the Arab civilization would then belong to a Byzantine-Ottoman civilization, with a Russian civilization unified c.1000 by Vladimir I starting out anew in its own geographical region like the American civilization rather than forming a new area of Orthodox faith. However this model is unsatisfactory. A Byzantine-Ottoman civilization would involve a major change of religion, from Orthodox Christianity to Islam, and such a fundamental change (as distinct from a shift of emphasis) does not occur in our other civilizations until they pass into their successor civilization: although the African civilization's new people were African Moslems, for example, the original African gods co-existed with Islam and were never completely eliminated as was Orthodox Christianity from Ottoman Anatolia. Moreover, the Russian civilization would on this view be younger than the European civilization (unified c.1000 as against 800) and yet be more materialistic than Europe, being under Communism, and such an atheistic outlook does not occur in other young civilizations. The collapse of Communism suggests that the Russian culture is closer to disintegration than, rather than a major threat to, Western Europe.

The Ottomans inherited Islam including Mecca. The Orthodox religion passed from the Byzantines and the Greeks to the Russians, and many of the nobility including members of the imperial family were exiled to Russia in 1453, and if we see a Byzantine-Russian continuum as one civilization based on the Greek Orthodox religion, then our view accords with our view of the other civilizations and has a consistency it would otherwise lack.

The later Syrian civilization (7) can be seen as a continuation of the Neo-Hittite branch of the Anatolian civilization which shared its gods. The Hittites, who came from Thrace, can be seen as belonging to the same race as the Greek Pelasgians and Minoans, but although they were all certainly of the same family, the Greek god Zeus was separate from the Hittite god Tarhun/Teshub and so the Hittites and Greeks came from different civilizations. The Minoan culture has been seen as a civilization in its own right, but it should be seen as part of the Mycenaean phase of the Aegean-Greek civilization, with which it shared Zeus.

But for Shinto, the Japanese civilization (21) could be seen as part of the South-East Asian (mainly *Mahayana* and later Theravada Buddhist) civilization (20), which may itself be seen as a branch of the Indian civilization. In fact S.E. Asia is a distinct geographical and cultural region, and it can be argued that there is one Austro-Asiatic civilization which includes India, China and Indo-china or S.E. Asia.

The early phases of the Oceanian civilization (22) can be regarded (without certainty) as a branch of the Indian civilization. A later phase of the Oceanian civilization can also be seen as part of the Andean civilization.

The Germanic-Scandinavian civilization (14) may be seen as a branch of a larger Indo-European "civilization" which included the Celts, although Julius Caesar regarded the Germanic tribes as being quite different and separate from the Celts.

However, although these regions were all inspired by religions from other civilizations, the use they made of their borrowed religions is their own and they produced a distinctive art; and it is more coherent to regard them as civilizations with borrowed religions than as peripheral areas to other civilizations. (The history of S.E. Asia, for example, does not gain by being studied in relation to the history of India, whose religions it borrowed; and the movements between Burma, Thailand and Khmer Indo-china have coherence if they are considered in their own right rather than as colonies of Indian and Chinese Buddhism. The North Asian Buddhist Korea should be seen as being associated with the Indianised S.E. Asian civilization rather than as a Chinese colony as its culture is a product of S.E. Asian Buddhist movements involving China, Central Asia and Japan: Korea was conquered by the Chinese, attacked by the Mongols, invaded by Japan and by the Manchus, became a Chinese tributary and was again invaded by Japan, but remained independent of both India and China.)

The Tibetan civilization (24) should be regarded as a separate civilization as it developed a distinctive religion (Tibetan Buddhism) which was adopted by the Central Asian civilization.

Africa (18) has as much right as some ancient civilizations (the Germanic-Scandinavian for example) to be regarded as a civilization in its own right rather than as a number of primitive cultures (like the pre-civilizational American Indian cultures). Although the whole of Africa has never been politically unified, the distances being too vast and the terrain too inhospitable, a coherent civilization with its own gods has spread from Egypt to Sudan to Chad and elsewhere, including Great Zimbabwe. The 25th dynasty of Pharaohs of the 7th century BC probably influenced the Bantus. The African civilization has produced its own art and an indigenous technology of considerable quality (e.g. the bronze heads of Benin which use a wax technique that is now lost, and the mortarless stone walls of Great Zimbabwe). Ever since King Solomon married the Queen of Sheba (i.e. Saba of the Sabaeans) c.930 BC?, there have been rumours of a high Sabaean African civilization with mines and riches, and the link between Prester John and Aksum[4] further attests to the relatively advanced nature of African civilization in pre-medieval and medieval times; although it must be said that legend associates Prester John with Asia, not Aksum.

The rise of Aksum may lead some to think that Ethiopia has a civilization in its own right, which began with the 6th century BC Sabaeans, expanded through the Aksumite Empire (2nd-9th century AD), and which in this century has seen the political-religious movement of Ras Tafarianism, in which "Back to Africa" Jamaicans deified Haile Selassie I (alias Ras or Prince Tafari). However, on cultural and religious grounds Ethiopia should be seen as part of the larger African civilization.

Our European civilization (11) is the civilization of the Teutonic barbarians that succeeded the Roman Empire in the West in the 5th century AD and which was converted to Christianity. Its offshoot, our North American civilization (12), can be seen as a continuation of European civilization just as the Russian civilization was a continuation of the Byzantine civilization, in which case America would now be as old as Europe. However, in our view such a perspective would be a mistake for European civilization has not come to an end, as did the Byzantine culture. America and Europe co-exist and share a common religion, as did the Roman civilization and Greece c.180 BC, and the Roman and Byzantine civilizations in the 4th century AD. If America and Europe were part of the same civilization then there would be two parts of the same civilization functioning in quite different ways – one a superpower and the other in decline – which has not happened in our other civilizations. The future prospects and interests of America and Europe are quite different. It gives greater consistency to see America as a separate civilization which is growing.

We therefore see America not as an extension of Europe but as a separate civilization in its own right. It is a geographical region with as much right to its own civilization as India, Africa or China – before Columbus it was associated with the Meso-American civilization through the Mississippi culture – and its first advanced culture was founded by a migration of religious dissidents. The settlers were inspired by religion, and they had no intention of returning to their mother country – indeed, they cut their ties with their mother country before unification – and therefore differed from other European colonialists who sought to exploit the colonial territories, make a profit and return home. America has co-existed with the European civilization and has never taken it over. America has never been invaded as has Europe, and came in on two world wars from outside; America is quite separate from the European Union, although it has taken over the leadership of the Free World.

As we have already said, our Western civilization is thus in fact an amalgam of two different civilizations. Our civilization has been called Western partly because it originated in the Western hemisphere (in Europe and then the U.S.A.) and partly because historically the Roman Empire split into the Western Roman Empire and the Eastern Roman Empire, and Charlemagne's Frankish Empire, and the later Holy Roman Empire, revived this Western Roman Empire of which our European civilization is a continuation. However Europe and North America should be regarded as belonging to separate civilizations. It may be objected that our Western (European and North American) civilization is a secular civilization and not an originally Christian civilization, but our analysis has shown that the religion of both the European and North American civilizations was always Christianity, and such an objection would indicate further evidence for maintaining that our European civilization has fallen into secular decay.

It may be thought that England, France and Germany form three separate civilizations, just as do China, Japan and S.E. Asia. However, geographical scale aside, England, France and Germany all grew through Christianity, whereas Japanese Shinto, Chinese Confucianism and S.E. Asian *Mahayana* Buddhism all grew through their own separate religions (although each influenced the other). The existence of the European Union in no way colours this conclusion. For their common Christianity would bind England, France and Germany into a European civilization even if there were no formal political link, while their separate mix of religions would separate China, Japan and S.E. Asia even if there were a formal political federation of the three. (The European Union is set to be dominated by a united Germany. It should be remembered that Germany dominated Europe throughout much of the Holy Roman Empire, 962-1806, while the European civilization grew round her, and the strength of Germany relative to the rest of Europe therefore makes no difference to our analysis.)

It could be argued that the British Isles form a separate civilization which began with the arrival of the Anglo-Saxons who drove the Celts westward; and that the British Isles are therefore not essentially part of Europe (or of the European Union). However, the 5th century Anglo-Saxon invasions should be seen as an expansion of the Germanic-Scandinavian civilization, and the Celtic retreat as a stage in the Celtic civilization. The later Christianization of the Saxons by the Celts should then be regarded as a Celtic counter-attack and the Saxons' adoption of Roman Christianity as an expansion of European influence which ended with the Norman Conquest. Thus although the British Isles missed Charlemagne's European unification and instead enjoyed Alfred's anti-Danish unification, from c.800 they took part in European civilization and in due course were as much affected by the Reformation and Counter-Reformation as was mainland Europe. The unification of England, Scotland, Wales and Ireland has parallels in the unification of France, Germany, Italy and other European countries, and the break-up of this unification as a result of a coming United States of Europe will have parallels in the break-up of other European countries. The British Empire has parallels in the Spanish, Portuguese, French, German, Habsburg/Austro-Hungarian, Italian, Belgian and Dutch Empires. In other words, the unification and imperialism of European regions were part of the process of the European civilization's development, just as the Reformation and Counter-Reformation were experienced in all the European regions. In view of their common Christianity, the British Isles and mainland Europe should be regarded as belonging to the same civilization from the 5th century despite the linguistic differences.

Australia and New Zealand differ from America. Although they belong to a geographical region, their culture was founded by convicts: deported criminals rather than religious dissidents. The lack of a religious Light during the early settlement of Australia makes it right to regard Australia (and New Zealand) as belonging to the pre-existing civilization of the geographical region of Oceania (22). Likewise, the settling of Israel after the Second World War was inspired by American-backed Zionism (which demanded Palestinian land for Nazi-persecuted Jews) and not by any religious Light, and so modern Israel should be seen as an American colony, funded by Western Jews. It is as much a colony as was the Phoenicians' Carthage, and is not the beginning of a new civilization.

The early Iranian civilization (10) can be regarded as including or excluding the Elamite culture. Elam's history runs from c.2700 BC to 639 BC and involves Old Elamite, Middle Elamite and Neo-Elamite periods. There are long dark ages during this time about which virtually nothing is known. It may be that Elam should be regarded as a separate civilization in its own right with its own Indian-sounding Indo-Iranian gods (e.g. Kiririshna). It can be regarded as an offshoot of the Indo-European Kurgan civilization. However, as it continually interacted with the Mesopotamian civilization before the Assyrians destroyed Susa and sowed Elam with salt, I have preferred to treat Elam as an early Iranian culture that mainly left its mark on the Mesopotamian civilization (e.g. destroying Ur c.2004 BC).

It is also possible to regard the Iranian civilization as now being quite separate from the Arab civilization since it was never part of the Ottoman Empire. However, in our view such a perspective would be a mistake, for its religion of Mithras and Ahura Mazda was clearly finally replaced by Islam AD c.1511, and its anti-Ottoman attitude should be attributed to the split in Arab religion between Sunnis and Shi'ites which has divided Moslems rather as the Protestant-Catholic split in Northern Ireland has divided Christians.

21 Civilizations with Distinctive Religions

We shall see that for the purposes of our argument it is right to classify civilizations with an eye to their distinctive religions. Combing more carefully through our findings in *Part Two* we can therefore regroup and renumber our draft list into 21 civilizations with distinctive religions and 4 civilizations with related religions (or early phases or later branches of the 21 distinctive civilizations) as follows:

Civilization	Distinctive God/Religion
1. Indo-European Kurgan and Megalithic in Old Europe	Dyaeus Pitar/Magna Mater (Sky Father/Earth Mother)
2. Mesopotamian	Anu/Ogma/Utu Shamash/Tammuz/Marduk Shuqamuna/Ashur
3. Egyptian	Ra/Amun/Aton Horus/Osiris/Apis
4. Aegean-Greek (Minoan/Mycenaean)	Zeus/Apollo Anat/Athene (or Athena)
5. Roman	Jupiter/Apollo Gnostic God as Light
6. Anatolian Hittite	Mistress of Animals/Storm and Weather god Tarhun or Teshub/Sharruma/Arinna
Phrygian	Cybele/Attis
7. Syrian	
Canaanite	El/Dagon/Baal/Mot/Resheph/ Molech (or Moloch) Koshar/Astarte/Anath (or Anat)
Phoenician	Baal/Astarte/Adonis
Philistine	Dagon/Ashtoreth/Baal
Aramaean	Hadad/Rammon/Atargatis

8. Israelite (Judaistic)	El Shaddai/Yahweh
9. Celtic	Du-w ("Yoo-we", cf "Yahweh")/Lug/Beli (cf Baal)/ Taran/Yesu
10. Iranian	Mithras/Zurvan (of Medes)/Ahura Mazda/Mani
Elamite	Inshushinak/Kiririshna (cf Indian Krishna)/Nahhunte/Huban
11. {European (Christian)	God as Light
{North American}	God as Light
{Byzantine-Russian (offshoots from Christian)	God as Light
12. Germanic-Scandinavian	Wodan/Odin
13. Andean	Smiling god ("El Lanzon" "the Great Image") Sun-gods: Inti/Quetzlcoatl/ Kukulcan (or Kukulan)/
14. Meso-American	Kinich Ahau/Itzamna/ Huitzilopochtli
15. Arab (Islamic)	Allah
16. African	Mwari/Nzambi/Cghene/Ngai/ Leza/Ndjambi Marunga/ Raluvhimba/Olodumare
17. {Indian	Agni/Brahman/Atman/Siva/Sakti Visnu/Rama/Krishna/Om Kar
{S.E. Asian (*Mahayana* Buddhist)	The Buddha
18. Japanese	The Buddha
Shinto	*Kami*/Amaterasu
19. Oceanian (Polynesian and Melanesian) (offshoot from Indian/ Andean)	The Buddha?/ Andean Smiling god/Inti? Io (Maoris)
20. Chinese	Shang Ti/T'ien Ti/The *Tao*

21. Tibetan — The Buddha
Central Asian (including Mongolian) — The Buddha

There may still be quibbles about points of detail: for example, the linking of the Tibetan and earlier Central Asian civilizations through Buddhism (but not the Indian civilization), the linking by juxtaposition of the Israelite (Judaistic) and Celtic civilizations (which our analysis has confirmed), our separation of the Aegean-Greek and Roman civilizations whose religions of Zeus/Jupiter are related, and our deliberate disinclination to relate the Zeus-worshipping Aegean-Greek/Roman civilizations and the Dyaeus-worshipping Indo-European civilization. (If we relate the Greeks to the Indo-European civilization, then logically we should relate the also Indo-European-inspired Iranian and Indian civilizations, which are clearly separate civilizations.) However, our broad classification is founded on a commonsense approach to history which balances the development of regional societies and peoples (for example, India) and the continuity given to their cultures over many generations by their distinctive religion (for example, by the Hindu religion). All classifications of civilizations are bound to raise questions. In view of our balanced commonsense approach, our classification should not attract undue dissent.

If we are right in our thinking, it can be seen that just as a carpet has a pattern, so this vast and elaborate Persian carpet of history has a pattern too. We have been seeking to find the pattern in the apparent tangle of design without imposing a pattern that is not there.

Toynbee's Choice of Civilizations

In his *A Study of History* the New World Order historian[5] Arnold Toynbee was confronted by the problem: what is a civilization? Over twenty-seven years he offered three conflicting lists of civilizations. In 1934 Toynbee listed 21 different civilizations, which in 1954 he changed to 23 (adding the early and little known Indus and Shang civilizations). These were:[6]

I. Full-blown Civilizations

First Generation, Unrelated to others:

Egyptiac; Andean.

First Generation, Unaffiliated to another:

Sumeric, Minoan; Indus; Shang; Mayan.

C. Second Generation, Affiliated to another:

Babylonic (to Sumeric); Hittite (to Sumeric); Hellenic (to Minoan); Syriac (to Minoan); Indic (to Indus); Sinic (to Shang); Yucatec (to Mayan); Mexic (to Mayan).

D. Third Generation, Affiliated to another:

Orthodox Christian, main body (to Hellenic); Orthodox Christian, Russian offshoot (to Hellenic); Western (to Hellenic); Arabic Muslim (to Syriac); Iranian Muslim (to Syriac); Hindu (to Indic); Far Eastern, main body (to Sinic); Far Eastern, Japanese offshoot (to Sinic).

II. Arrested Civilizations:

Eskimo; Nomadic; Osmanli; Spartan.

III. Abortive Civilizations:

First Syriac; Far Eastern Christian; Far Western Christian; Scandinavian; Medieval Western City-State Cosmos.

In 1961 in *Reconsiderations* he changed his mind and expanded the list to 30. These were:[7]

I. Full-blown Civilizations

A. Independent Civilizations:

Unrelated to Others: Middle American; Andean.

Unaffiliated to Others: Sumero-Akkadian; Egyptiac; Aegean; Indus; Sinic.

Affiliated to Others (first batch): Syriac (to Sumero-Akkadian, Egyptiac, Aegean, and Hittite); Hellenic (to Aegean); Indic (to Indus).

Affiliated to Others (second batch): Orthodox Christian, Western and Islamic (to both Syriac and Hellenic)

B. Satellite Civilizations:

Mississippian and 'South-Western' (of Middle American); North Andean and South Andean (of Andean); ? Elamite (of Sumero-Akkadian); Hittite (of Sumero-Akkadian); ?Urartian (of Sumero-Akkadian); Iranian (first of Sumero-Akkadian, then of Syriac); Korean; Japanese and Vietnamian (of Sinic);?Italic (of Hellenic); South Eastern Asian (first of Indic, then, in Indonesia and Malaya only, of Islamic); Tibetan (of Indic); Russian (first of Orthodox Christian, then of Western).

II. Abortive Civilizations

First Syriac (eclipsed by Egyptiac); Nestorian Christian (eclipsed by Islamic); Monophysite Christian (eclipsed by Islamic); Far Western Christian (eclipsed by Western); Scandinavian (eclipsed by Western); Medieval Western City-State Cosmos (eclipsed by Modern Western).

Toynbee, with different criteria, drew up lists of civilizations that are quite different from ours. He had a problem because he was not able to find what inspired civilizations. He did not see the Light as being this inspiration. He looked within history but the answer lay outside history, in the inspiration of religion which is the "incarnation" of the culture and therefore of the civilization of a people. As Toynbee himself says: "I have been searching for the positive factor which within the last five thousand years, has shaken part of Mankind...into the 'differentiation of civilization'....These manoeuvres have ended, one after another, in my drawing a blank."[8]

By not seeing the Light as inspiring a specific religion in which a civilization lives, like a caddis-fly larva in a round reed at the bottom of a pond, he offers civilizations with mixed religions. His difficulty can be seen by looking at our Egyptian civilization on the chart on pp534-535. At first he has the "Egyptiac" civilization (as he calls it) ending c.1175 BC, after the New Empire, but in *Reconsiderations* he has it ending with Islam, some 1500 years later. Similarly Toynbee lumps Iran and Islam into one civilization, whereas Islam began outside Iran and spread far wider than Iran, and seems to be a new civilization inspired by the vision of Allah.

We have seen (pp516-517) that Toynbee mistakenly saw the Byzantine civilization as including the Ottoman Empire. In other words, he maintained that the same civilization was inspired by first Orthodox Christianity, then by Islam. This breaches our "one mainstream religion per civilization" rule. (We have seen on p516 that Gibbon also got the Byzantine civilization wrong, seeing it as a continuation of the Roman civilization. As a result he saw the Byzantine thrusting growth under Justinian and his successors as deepening decline.)[9]

In *Reconsiderations* Toynbee confesses with disarming honesty to have misjudged our own Western (i.e. Christian European and North American) civilization: "I thought of the Western Civilization as being affiliated to the Hellenic Civilization exclusively.... In Christianity, which was the Western Civilization's historical link with the Hellenic, the Hellenic element was combined with, and dominated by, a Judaic one. I ought to have seen that the Western Civilization was affiliated to both civilizations."[10] Our own civilization is so often referred to as a Judeo-Christian one that we may find the Hellenist Toynbee's slip amazing. As we look at our chart on pp 534-535 we must guard against too selective an interpretation; we must seek to reflect the historical pattern that is there.

Toynbee was absolutely right to regard history as one global field rather than as a number of separate and unrelated national fields, but he attracted much needless criticism by failing to provide a clear definition of what a civilization is. He offers hints: a civilization is "a representative of a particular species of society" while civilization is "an attempt to attain the kind of culture that had been attained by citizens of a Graeco-Roman city-state". Again, civilization is "a state of society in which there is a minority that is free from the task of keeping life going from day to day, and that therefore has leisure to think and plan and direct the work of the community as a whole".[11] Toynbee quotes with approval Bagby's definition of culture as "regularities in the behaviour, internal and external, of the members of a society, excluding those regularities which are clearly hereditary in origin"[12] and Bagby's definition of civilization as "the kind of culture found in cities";

the "cities" being "agglomerations of dwellings many (or, to be more precise, a majority) of whose inhabitants are not engaged in producing food".[13]

Toynbee's definition of a civilization is incomplete for it does not take account of the centrality of religion and the Light within civilizations. In *Civilisation* Kenneth Clark contributes another layer to a definition: "Civilization means something more than energy and will and creative power: something the early Norsemen hadn't got, but which, even in their time, was beginning to reappear in Western Europe.... A sense of permanence.... Civilised man consciously looks forward and looks back."[14] In *The Law of Civilisation and Decay*, Brooks Adams does not define "civilization" but he contrasts it with barbarism and associates it with advancement in the arts and sciences, which decline when a civilization decays.[15]

Quite simply, the essence of a civilization is the mystics' reception of the Light during its genesis, which others fashion into a religion round which social cities, economic and technological organization, a high culture and the arts flourish and exude a sense of permanence. When the Light ceases to be received, the civilization atrophies and decays, its citizens having forgotten, and being alienated from, the motive force that impelled its growth and gave it impetus.

• • •

Conclusion

The theme of this book has been that civilization is based on religion, that specific civilizations are based on specific religions that all derive from their different responses to the experience of the One Light. Returning to our own list of civilizations, the chart on pp534-535 summarises the picture we have built up. It shows a number of closely related, interconnected cultures and civilizations springing from one source, each of which (as we have seen) is identified with a religion.

The chart on pp534-535 visually summarizes our view of how Lights and their religions have interconnected, as we saw in *Part Two*; and also, now we have adopted a scheme of civilizations that has arisen out of our coverage in *Part Two*, of how the *civilizations* have interconnected. Indeed, if all the Lights on the chart on pp534-535 were merged, the civilizations could all have one common Light and share one world-wide religion – an impossible, Paradisal dream. "The Light of civilization" indeed!

Having established that religions form round experiences of the Light, and having asserted that civilizations are based on religions, we are now in a position to demonstrate how civilizations rise and fall in relation to the performance (i.e. the strength or weakness) of their religions and the frequency of their experiences of the Light. We are now in a position to see how the stages civilizations go through are linked to the performance of (i.e. the brightness or dimming of the Light in) their religions and the brightness, or dimming, of the Light. That can be found in the companion volume to this work, *The Endless Rise and Fall of Civilizations.*

Appendices

Appendix 1: The Indo-European Kurgans

Extracts from a letter written by Nicholas Hagger to Dr Leon Stover, author of *Stonehenge: The Indo-European Heritage*, on September 19, 1978:

"Dear Dr Stover,

You will recall meeting me over Sunday lunch at Frank Tuohy's during your recent visit to England. (We first met in Tokyo in the 1960s.) I have been doing some research into the rise of the ancient religions, and I have just got round to the Kurgan peoples. I tried to order your book, and was told… that it is listed to appear in June 1979 – by which time I will have forgotten all the questions that burn through my mind! I would be very grateful if you could briefly answer a few of them, bearing in mind that I have read about Marija Gimbutas in books like Gerhard Herm's *The Celts*, which gives an uptodate view of the theory '*ex occidente* (as opposed to *oriente*) *lux*'.

The Kurgans were clearly the ancestors of the Greeks, Celts, Iranians and therefore of the Vedic peoples. They are traditionally regarded as having moved to the Danube between 3500 and 2300 BC. There were Indo-Europeans in Europe from at least c.4500 BC, long before Indo-Europeans moved to Iran c.2250 BC. The fault in the Libby method of dating puts Stonehenge II back from 1800 to c.2500 BC. First, a question about the megaliths. Do you believe that a number of peoples built the megaliths and that the Indo-Europeans inherited them and added to them, or do you see the Indo-Europeans as being responsible for all, or most, of the megaliths? Secondly, a question about Sumerian and Egyptian culture. Do you believe that the Sumerian and Egyptian cultures grew up independently of the Indo-Europeans, and of each other, or do you believe that the Indo-Europeans, perhaps Kurgans, exported their culture to Sumer and/or Egypt? I am particularly struck by the traces of Indo-European religion in Sumerian and Egyptian religion, and I am thinking of the fact that the Sumerians originated in the mountainous region north-east of Mesopotamia. Could they have been Kurgans? I know that the later Kurgans came into contact with Sumer and Akkad when they invaded the land of the North Pontians and Trans-Caucasians c.2300, and came into contact with a mountainous people who knew the Sumerians. I know the linguistic evidence is against it (cuneiform being so different from Indo-European languages), but could they have come into contact with descendants from their own ancestors? Who in turn had invaded Sumer? Thirdly, has your book changed any of the traditional dating of the Kurgans, including any of the rough dates above? Lastly, I would be very interested to see a photocopy of anything you found out about the change from the religion of old Europe (the matriarchal Mother Goddess) to the religion of the Indo-Europeans (the patriarchal Sky Father who fertilises the Earth Mother, the god of lightning and storm, the cult of fire etc), and the way the Indo-European religion influenced Mesopotamia and Egypt, and elsewhere.

The Kurgans are clearly at the origins of Western culture. To what extent, if any, are they at the origins of Near Eastern (Mesopotamian and Egyptian) culture? This is the overall picture I am seeking to focus through my questions.

Yours sincerely, Nicholas."

Extracts from a letter written by Leon Stover to Nicholas Hagger on October 7, 1978:

"Dear Nicholas,

It was a pleasure to receive such interesting questions from you as you asked in your letter of 19 September....

In answer to the first question, it seems on the whole that the Indo-Europeans rather added to the megalithic monuments. For example, the sun-swirls engraved on the megaliths at New Grange were made by Beaker in-migrants; rather as if Norman Mailer had came to Stratford-on-Avon and spray-painted his name on the home of William Shakespeare. Likewise, if you count the henge monument of Stonehenge I as of a piece with other megalithic monuments built by the native Neolithic population, then the bluestone pillars (Stonehenge II) erected by the Beaker migrants are an addition to that sacred circle. But perhaps what is new here is my counting the Beaker folk as Indo-Europeans, which they undoubtedly are; because I have them springing out of eastern Europe in direct response to the Kurgan migrants, who are the first Indo-Europeans.

Secondly, are the Egyptians and Sumerians Indo-Europeans, e.g., Kurgans? I would say not, although Gilgamesh may have been. On the other hand, cultural traditions never evolve in isolation. For example, the I.E. (Indo-European) cosmic tree is the polar axis of the Ural-Altaic tradition adapted to a forested environment, and assimilated to other aspects of I.E. ideology (and for the latter, see the works of Georges Dumézil). The Kurgans got their metallurgy from the Kuro-Araxes culture, located in the Caucasus region, as did the Sumerians to the south. And so I believe it is this common source that accounts for any Kurgan-Sumerian parallels – with the exception of the dynasty buried at Ur, which surely recalls that at Stepanakert. I further speculate that the Epic of Gilgamesh is a parable of good rule. At the same time it is a model for the civilizing of barbarian peoples; for its eponymous hero is a king who despoils his own city, but who learns through bitter experience to be wise and just. But these are just incidental matters in a book given to Europe, and I wouldn't want to venture more that that.

Glad to hear from you, I am yours with pleasure, Leon."

CHART OF 25 CIVILIZATIONS AND CULTURES: FROM ONE TO ONE

The Fundamental Unity of World Culture

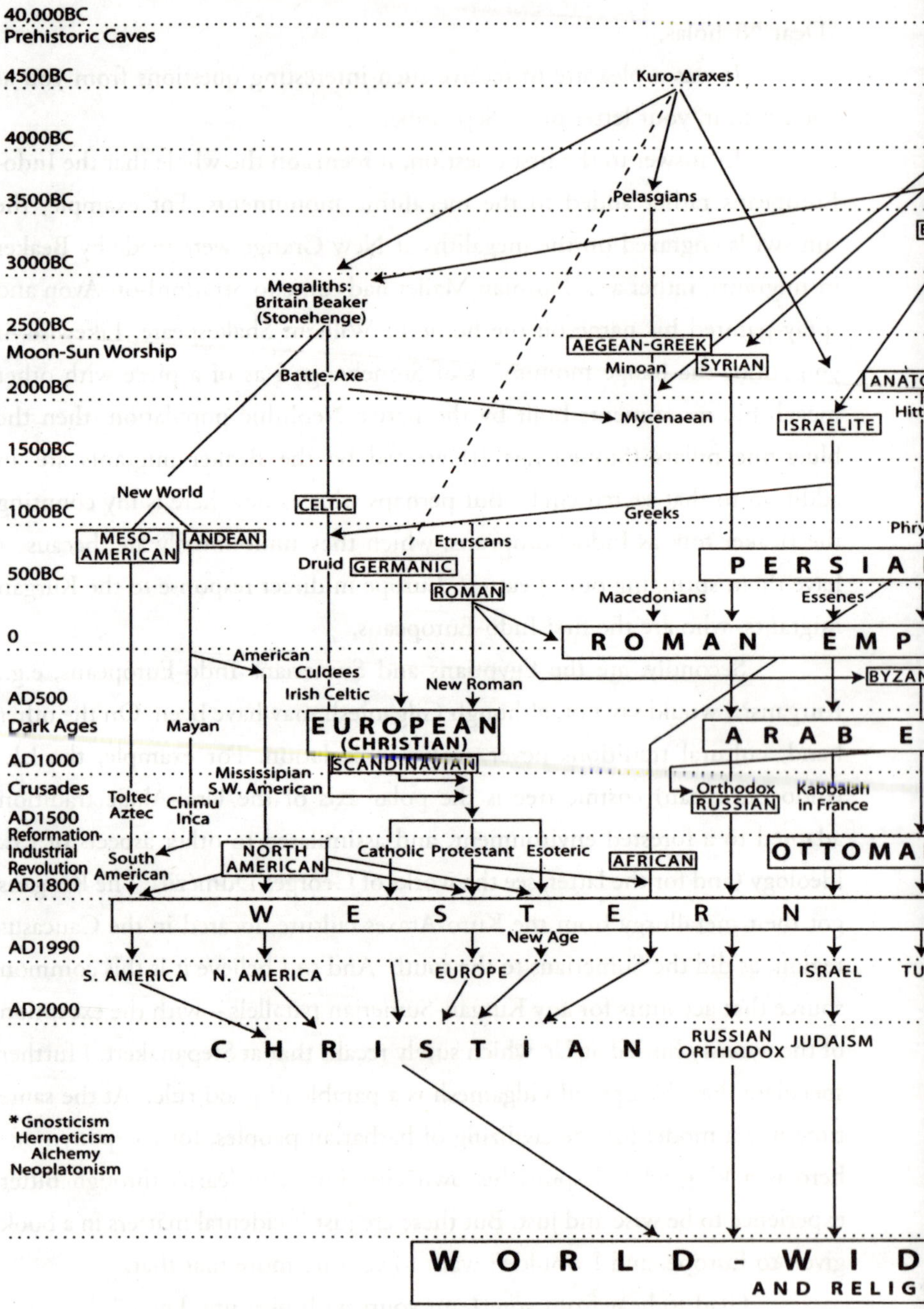

25 civilizations/major empires in boxes

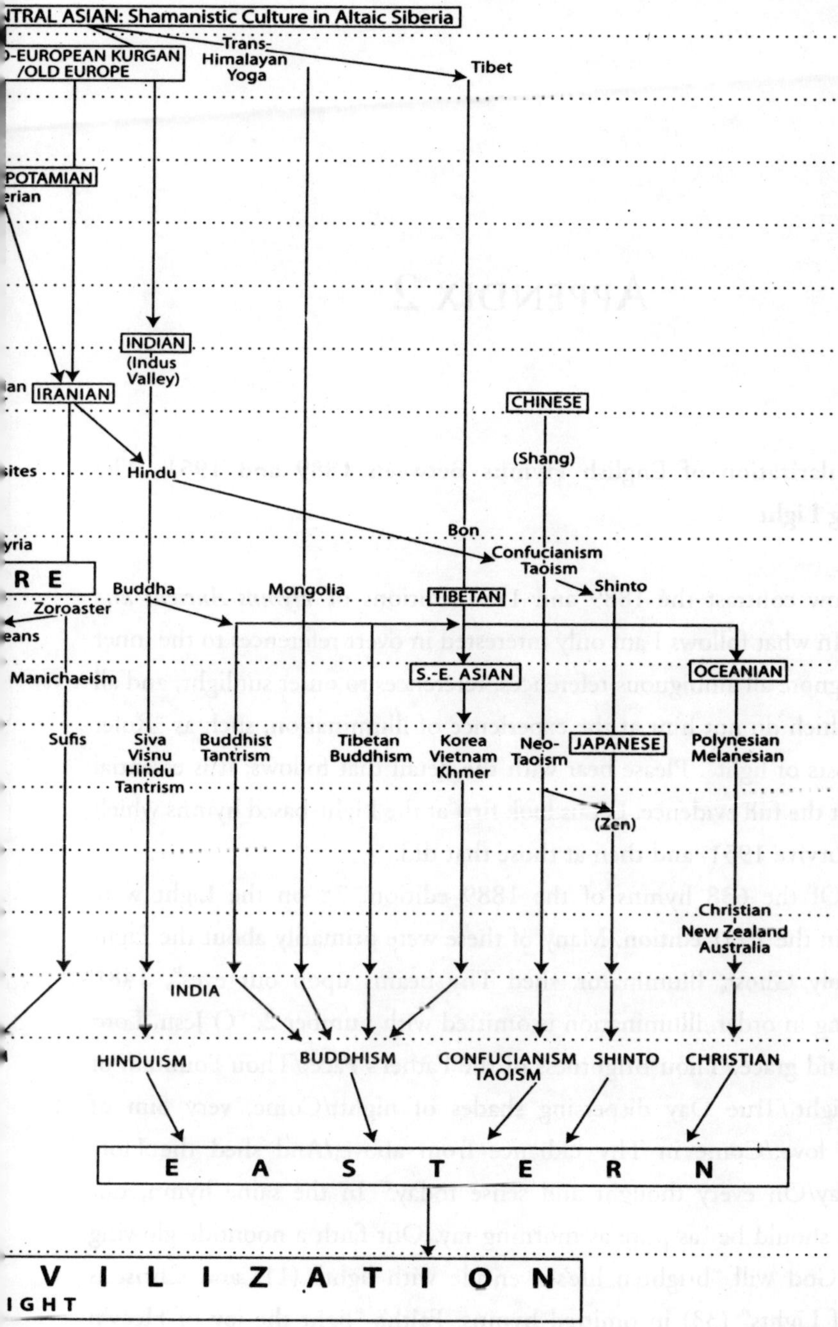

APPENDIX 2

The Secularization of English Hymns Between 1889 and 1951: The Vanishing Light

Let us now contrast the 1889 and 1951 editions of *Hymns Ancient and Modern.* In what follows I am only interested in overt references to the inner Light; I ignore all ambiguous references, references to outer sunlight, and all hymns which do not hint at the experience of illumination, such as "Ruler of the hosts of light". Please bear with the detail that follows; it is essential to present the full evidence. Let us look first at the Light-based hymns which did *not* survive 1951, and then at those that did.

Of the 638 hymns of the 1889 edition, 78 on the Light were omitted in the 1951 edition. Many of these were primarily about the Light (e.g. "Holy Ghost, Illuminator, shed Thy beams upon our eyes", 148). Proceeding in order, illumination is omitted with number 2: "O Jesu, Lord of light and grace,/Thou Brightness of the Father's Face,/Thou Fountain of eternal light,/True Day dispersing shades of night;/Come, very Sun of heavenly love,/Come in Thy radiance from above,/And shed the Holy Spirit's ray/On every thought and sense today." In the same hymn, our thoughts should be "as pure as morning ray,/Our faith a noontide glowing bright". God will "brighten life's eventide with light" (11) and Christ is "Light of Lights" (33) in omitted hymns. Faith's "light the joy of Heav'n reveals/To hearts made pure within", and we hope that "we the path may tread/Whereon its light doth shine" (42). The "Heavenly Word, Eternal Light" is asked, "Our hearts enlighten from above/And kindle with Thine own true love" (46). As "doth Thy lowly manger radiant shine.../So may our spirits glow with faith Divine" (55). Christ, "Thou Brightness of the Father's Face", is "very Light of Light" (57), and the Saviour is asked: "Thy light throughout our darkness give". St Stephen is addressed, "Like an Angel's is thy face/Beaming with celestial grace" (65), while St John's inmost spirit is filled with angelic love which was "once enkindled from above".

A brilliant image for the cauterising effect of the Light is omitted, "Lord, circumcise our hearts, we pray,/And take what is not Thine away" (71), and so is "O Jesu, while the star of grace/Allures us now to seek Thy Face,/Let not our slothful hearts refuse/The guidance of that light to use" (77). Omitted also are the mysteries of "O Christ, Who art the Light and Day,/Thy beams chase night's dark shades away;/The very Light of Light Thou art,/Who dost Thy blessed Light impart" (95).

Jesu is "Of Light invisible true Light" (141), which must seem nonsense to the unillumined, but which makes excellently succinct sense to the illuminated. I have quoted "Holy Ghost, Illuminator" (148) above. Omitted are "Each heart receives the Father's light,/The Word's enkindling glow" (152), and the hymn about the Whitsun "Day when first the light Divine/On the Church began to shine" (153). Omitted are "There is a blessed home..." where "everlasting light/Its glory throws around" (230), and the hymn about Paradise "where loyal hearts and true/Stand ever in the light" (234). Omitted are the hymns about God who "enthroned in glory, show'st/The brightness of Thy Face" (237), and the one which refers to "Thy Father's Home of light" (259). Omitted is "Clearer still and clearer/Dawns the light from Heav'n..../Pure the light within;/Thou has shed Thy radiance/On a world of sin" (305). The Baptismal hymn is omitted which includes, "This child hath scarce yet seen our earthly sun,/Yet pour him Thy light" (325).

Omitted are the hymn to the Light, "O Light, Whose beams illumine all/From twilight dawn to perfect day..../When dreams or mists beguile our sight,/Turn Thou our darkness into light" (345), and the hymn to "the Fire of Love,/The soul's Anointing from above" who should "Thy light to every sense impart,/And shed Thy love in every heart" (347). Omitted are the hymns to the Saviour which describe his Spirit as "Love's pure flame and wisdom's light" (359), and the one which draws God's attention to his lost and wandering sheep: "And kindle in their hearts the fire/Of holy love and pure desire" (363).

The hymn with the refrain "forward into light" is omitted, with its exhortation to "climb the steps of grace;/Faint not, till in glory/Gleams our Father's Face" (392). Omitted is the description of a dead bosom, "Clothed in robes of spotless white/Now it dwells with thee in light" (402). St Thomas's evidence of "Thy light" (404) and God's calling of us "out of darkness/To His own glorious light" (405) are omitted, as is the pointing of one way "to that far land where shines no sun/Because the Face of God is there" (411). The following lines about St Barnabas are omitted, "Brightly did the light Divine/From his words and actions shine" (412), as are the Lights of the Saints which are "shining full and clear" (419).

The description of Christ as "Light of Light" is omitted (422), as is the account of God calling us "to His own glorious light" (433). The brightness of the glory of the Saints is omitted – "Lord, may that grace be ours" – (446), along with the Doctors and Pastors who are true "till beside the well of life/Light in Thine own Light they see" (454).

Omitted is the plea that blessings may fill the virgin with "power to win the crown of light" so that she may "ready keep her lamp at night/To hail the Bridegroom", i.e. God. (456) (Compare St Bernard and St John of the Cross.) Omitted is the appeal to "let still Thine everlasting light/Within our souls remain;/And in the nights of our distress/Vouchsafe those rays Divine,/Which from the Sun of Righteousness/For every brightly shine" (476).

Omitted is the idea that God who "doest dwell in unapproached light" will see to it that "soon the everlasting day/Shall chase the night of gloom away" that "our brief daytime, used aright,/May issue in eternal light" (479). Omitted is the reference to the "grace of second birth" when the Redeemer will "let Thy light within us shine/That we may Thy salvation see" (486). Omitted is the appeal, "Lord, visit Thou our souls,/And teach us by Thy grace/Each dim revealing of Thyself/With loving awe to trace;/Till from our darken'd sight/The cloud shall pass away,/And on the cleansed soul shall burst/The everlasting day", i.e. "Thy Face" (488). Omitted is the plea to the Saviour to "pour down Thy radiance from above,/And make these sin-worn spirits whole" (490), as is the plea "fire our hearts with love" which should be "rekindled from above" (492). The appeal "Show Thy Face in brightness" (497) is omitted, along with the description of how Christ in the wilderness saw the Light "part reveal'd and part in cloud", "known...yet veil'd;/Else before the awful sight/Surely heart and flesh had fail'd,/Smitten with exceeding light" (503).

Omitted is the appeal to the Holy Ghost to "send down Thy Heavenly Light;/Kindle our hearts" and to grant the grace "that we of His beloved Son/May gain the blissful sight" (508). Omitted are the invocation, "One Light, one only Deity", for "One we believe Thee, Light Divine" (509), and the prayer "Lord give us light Thy truth to see" so that we shall "be perfect in the land of light" (518). Omitted are the echo of the Egyptian *Book of the Dead*, "'Tis the God Who ever liveth/'Mid the shining ones on high" (523), and the appeal "Come to our poor nature's night/With Thy blessed inward light" (524). Omitted is God's "sunshine flash'd" but "lo! His glorious face He hideth,/And men perceive it not" until, in the after-life, "all is bathed in light and glory/That once was dark or dim" (530). Omitted is the plea that the Church should "keep the old paths the father trod/In thy illumined youth" so that "seducing error shrinks and dies/At light from yonder page" (532); also the hymn about the Church which declares, "No smoother is the ancient path/That leads to light and day" (534). Omitted are the appeal to Christ to "illuminate our minds, that we may see/In all around us holy signs of Thee" (559), and the statement: "Our sins, in Thy pure light descried,/Stand out in dread array" (560). Omitted is the sign on the foreheads of the young, "that one day on each saintly brow/A glorious crown may shine" (566).

The idea that God is "far removed from mortal sight,/Dwelling in eternal light" (567) is omitted, along with "There's a bright land far away," – in fact it is as near as the soul – "/Where 'tis never-ending day", a "place,/Where men always see His face" (570). Omitted is the hymn which begins "Shine thou upon us, Lord,/True Light of men, today" that hearts may "burn/With gazing on Thy Face" and "Thy Spirit's living Flame" (580).

A hymn which speaks of God as "one Thy Light" is omitted; His "work is fire", He has "the mystic coal in hand" and came "that fire to kindle;/Fain would we Thy torches prove,/Far and wide Thy beacons lighting/With the undying spark of love:/Only feed our flame, we pray Thee,/With Thy breathings from above", and there is a reference to "His all-enlightening Spirit" (581). Omitted are the request that darkness should be "at Thy coming, light" (585), and the prayer, "Give us more light, direct our course,/Cleanse us from guile, our hearts renew;/Let not dark clouds of sin shut out/The Star of Jesus from our view" (597). The prayer "Give of Thy grace to the souls Thou hast quicken'd,/Gladness for sorrow, and brightness for gloom" (598) is omitted, together with "God through Himself we then shall know/If Thou (i.e. the Holy Ghost) within us shine" (599). The hymn for a retreat or quiet day is omitted, with its "I see from far Thy beauteous light" (600), and the hymn for the restoration of a church is omitted, its sons being seen as a "shining band", its altar as "a Throne of light" (602). The idea that God "calls to Heav'n and endless light" (614) is omitted, along with "Brightness of the Father's light" (616).

The hymn beginning "Father, before Thy throne of light", with a reference to "the brightness of Thy Face" (617) is omitted, along with the idea that God will call "us to be the portion/Which His Saints in light possess" (618). Omitted is the hymn for All Saints' Day which anticipates a time when "our knowledge/Shall be clear, unveil'd and bright;/For on God's unclouded glory/We shall gaze with cleansed sight" when we shall behold "the Unity of Substance" and see for ever "the light of light" (619). The reference to the Spirit as "fire Divine" (627) has gone, and so has "Let Thy mercy light on me..../Speak the word of power to me" (629). Finally, "There's a bright Home above, where the sun never sets", where Jesus will "show you His beautiful Face", where His "mercy grows brighter", (637) is omitted, along with "Set, Lord, in Thy most searching light/What I have done amiss" (638).

If we glance back over the above omissions, we will see that although literary criticism may identify some weak verse, much teaching has gone, and that there is much that speaks to those who have already experienced the Light. At the same time we will catch a glimpse of the religion that shaped Tennyson and Arnold, and our great-grandparents.

Of the 638 hymns in the 1889 edition, 91 which have references to the Light have been retained in the 1951 edition. However, most of these are either very well known (like "Abide with me" with its "Shine through the gloom.... Heaven's morning breaks") or else they are used on special occasions (Morning or Evening worship, Communion, Lent, the Passion, Easter, the Ascension) whose associations have priority over the idea of illumination. In many of these, the Humanistic idea of Christ's blood and love take priority over the idea of illumination.

Nevertheless, with effort the idea of Illumination can be gleaned. Again proceeding in order, Christ is "the only Light" who imparts "inward light" and must "visit then this soul of mine", piercing "the gloom of sin and grief" (number 7 in the 1889 edition). The Holy Ghost's love can "light up our mortal frame/Till others catch the living flame" (9) and bring "dawning glories of the eternal day" (12). The "*Lux Beata*" begins "O Trinity, most Blessed Light" (14) and there is the famous "Hail, gladdening Light, of His pure glory pour'd" (18). Angels are "whence Thou, Eternal Light of Light,/Art Lord of all" (19). The Holy Father is to "cheer our way,With thy love's perpetual ray" and grant us "light at evening time" (22). The Saviour is "sun of my soul" and "it is not night if Thou be near" (24). "Abide with me" (27) has been quoted above. The Saviour is asked to "make our lukewarm hearts to glow" and to "be our Light" (28).

The Light is requested: "But pass not from us with the sun,/True Light that lightenest all" (30), and when we speak the name of God, round us "there spreads a heaven of light" (32). God is "the source of life and light" (34) and "Gospel-light is glowing/With pure and radiant beams" (36). "This is the day of light:/Let there be light today" (37) is clearly about the Light, as is "Blest Creator of the light" (38), and "Creator of the starry height,/Thy people's everlasting Light" (45). Christ is the "sun" of the "soul" (47) and "as Judge, on clouds of light,/He soon will come again" (48). The Lord is asked to "shine forth, and let Thy light restore" Earth's loveliness (50), and a cloud "veils Thy glory now" (58). The famous "O come all ye Faithful" appeals to "God of God, Light of Light" (59), while "To Bethlehem straight the enlighten'd shepherds ran (61).

"The Light of Light Divine" is "true Brightness undefiled" (70), and the Eastern sages "By light their way to Light they trod" (75). The men of old "in the Heav'nly country bright/Need they no created light;/Thou its Light..." (79). The people "that in darkness sat/A glorious light have seen;/The Light has shined on them" (80). We implore "us with Saintly bands unite/In the realms of heavenly light" (121), and "in the gloomy realms of darkness/Shines a light unknown before/Lo! the heavenly light around him" (122). "All the winter of our sins/...is flying/From His Light (133) while earthly joys fade away "in that pure light of Thine" (145). "The fires, that rush'd on Sinai down" now "gently light, a glorious crown,/On every sainted head" (154). The Holy Spirit is asked to "shed a ray of light Divine": "O most Blessed Light Divine,/Shine within these hearts of Thine" (156). The Holy Ghost must "our souls inspire,/And lighten with celestial fire" and "enable with perpetual light/The dulness of our blinded sight" (157). The "Light of Lights" should "lift on us Thy Light Divine" (163). Jesus should "let Thy Light/Shine, Lord, on every heart;/Dispel the darkness of our night" (178). Lord Jesus should think of me that "I may the eternal Brightness see,/And share Thy joy at last" (185).

Jesus is "Thou Light of men" and he is asked to "shed o'er the world Thy holy light" (190), and "O quickly come, sure Light of all" (204). The gracious Spirit should come "with light and comfort from above" and "the light of truth to us display" (209). God should "show the brightness of Thy Face;/Shine upon us, Saviour, shine,/Fill Thy Church with light Divine" (218). There are "Angels of light" (223) and we are advised, "Toil, man, to gain that light" (226). True peace springs from the vision of "Light's abode, celestial Salem" where endless noon-day "from the Sun of suns is there" (232). God's courts are "in the land of light and love" and our spirit longs "for the brightness of Thy Face" (240). Whoever believeth in the truth of the Word "light and joy receiveth" (243). We should "wrestle till we see Thy Face" (248), and Jesus says " 'I am this dark world's Light' " and he is "that Light of life" (257). Jesus "turn'd thy darkness into light" (260).

Newman's famous "Lead, kindly Light, amid the encircling gloom,/Lead Thou me on" (266) speaks for itself, while "clear before us through the darkness/Gleams and burns the guiding Light", which is "the

Light of God's own Presence" (274). There are "Powers, who stand before the Eternal Light" (296), and God is "Heav'n's eternal Light" (301). "Ye Angels of light" should praise the Lord (308), and we thirst "to gaze on Thee inveil'd, and see Thy Face,/The vision of Thy glory and Thy grace" (312). God is asked, "Upon our darkness shine" (321), and He is "Thou who makest souls to shine/With light from lighter worlds above" (353). A missionary hymn asks "Can we, whose souls are lighted/With wisdom from on high,/Can we to men benighted/The lamp of life deny?" (358). "Let there be light" (360) is a refrain, and the Lord is "the Lord of light" (369).

There are "souls that wear Christ's raiment,/With crowns of golden light" (386), and of St Paul it is said "Oh, light that pierced and blinded,The zealot in his wrath" (406). Helpers "shed Thy light across our darken'd earth" (413). Faithful hearts "shall never fail/With thanks and praise his light to hail", St John is "witness to the coming Light" who will shine before Christ's "own eternal beam" (415). The Angels come "from homes of never-fading light" (424). St Simon is "one, whose zeal by Thee enlighten'd/Burn'd anew with nobler flame" (426). Heaven has "the Lamb, the Light that shineth,/And never goeth down", and hope leads to "Christ the Sun that lightens/His Church above, below" (429). The Apostles are "true lights to lighten every land" who are "in perfect glow" and in whom "the Father's glory shone" (430). The weak and poor are "full of Thy light" and the Apostles' "lights Thou has kindled/In darkness around,/O may they illumine/Our spirits within" ;God has shed round us "his own marvellous light/And call'd us from darkness" (431). The Apostles are "lights who lighten every land", who have "shed the Gospel light"; God has "call'd us to His glorious light" (432). The martyrs now "walk in golden light", "in the Beatific Vision" of God who is "Light of Light" (436).

Jesus was the "one true Light" who enabled the saints to win "the victor's crown of gold", so that "we feebly struggle, they in glory shine" (437). The martyrs are glorious spirits who shine bright, who from sufferings great "came to realms of light", for "God is their Sun" (438), and they are arrayed "in robes of light" (439). "Crowns that never fade away,/Gird and deck the Saints in light" (445), and the conqueror receives "light that ever shall endure" (447). "All light created paled" on Sinai, and those who win the fight will receive "all the glory/Of uncreated light" (460).

The "spirit of light" is to "explore,/And chase our gloom away,/With lustre shining more and more/Unto the perfect day" (525). The Word shines with "endless glory", and "still new beauties may I see,/And still increasing light" (531). The Lord is to come "when grace hath made me meet/Thy blessed Face to see" (535), and there is a land where "infinite day excludes the night" (536). This land is Zion, city of our God where "glorious things" are spoken, where "the cloud and fire appear" and "light by night", and one can be a member of Zion "through grace" (545); the "sons of light" should lift their eyes to Sion (547). Jesus is to be "light and guide" for our loved ones (595), and the Lord "glorious with His saints in light/For ever reigns", while the nations "kindle to a flame" (601). The Lord is "Light of all the earth" (611), and grace stirred within St Matthew's breast "with twofold crown of light to shine" (615). The Evangelists "flush'd the world with light" (621). Finally, there is a prayer for "a light to shine upon the road/That leads me to the Lamb", "so purer light shall mark the road" (630).

The Light is in the selection, then, even if it has to be dug out. But hymns primarily about the Light have been omitted, and by and large it is hymns which have a primary Humanistic meaning, in which the Light is secondary or even incidental, that have survived.

Note to Reader on the Sources

This book covers 5,000 years and explores civilization's roots in prehistory. Clearly all early dates are approximate. It is important that there should be a universal yardstick by which my dates and interpretations can be measured, and this is the 15th edition of the *Encyclopaedia Britannica*, which is fuller than the 16th edition and is internationally widely available in libraries. I have consulted many books, and it would be possible to give a dozen references for some notes. I have sought to simplify the process of confirming veracity by giving some primacy to the universal standard of the *Encyclopaedia Britannica.*

As I deal with 25 traditions of the Light, the sources fall into two categories: historical sources about the effect of the Light on civilizations, for example on their stone buildings (many of which are now tourist attractions); and reports on experiences of the Light. The sources are therefore a mixture of confirmations of dates and cultural statements, and pointers to where passages can most easily be found (which should be read in conjunction with the *Bibliography*).

I have taken the view that if the historical context of the Light traditions is well sourced and the experiences of the Light all have references, then the only thing to be disputed is the central concept of this work: the impact of the Light on civilizations, and history. The aim of these notes and sources is to deliver this indisputable context.

Notes And References To Sources

PART ONE

THE ORIGIN OF THE LIGHT

1. Pascal's "Fire" parchment: facsimile in Abbé Bremond's *Sentiment Religieux en France*, iv, 368; quoted in Dom Cuthbert Butler, *Western Mysticism*, p74.
2. For the four "eye-witness" accounts see St Augustine, *Confessions*, 7.10; Hildegarde von Bingen quoted in John Ferguson, *An Illustrated Encyclopaedia of Mysticism and the Mystery Religions*, p77; Finney, *Memoirs Written by Himself* 1876, p34, quoted in William James, *The Varieties of Religious Experience*, p251; and *Mother Isabel of the Sacred Heart*, pp41-3.
3. *The Secret of the Golden Flower*, trans. by Richard Wilhelm, pp106-7.
4. E. W. F. Tomlin, in *The Tall Trees of Marsland* (unpublished), swore by this view.
5. Grosseteste, *On Light* trans. by Clare Riedl, quoted in *The Age of Belief.*
6. William James, *The Varieties of Religious Experience*, p251. See Evelyn Underhill, *Mysticism* and also Michael Cox, *A Handbook of Christian Mysticism.*

7. Husserl, *Ideas* (*General Introduction to Pure Phenomenology*), e.g. pp107-9 for "bracketing".
8. Jean-Luc Aubarbier and Michel Binet, *Prehistoric Sites in Périgord*, p3. *Homo ergaster* and *homo erectus*, the first humans to walk upright, evolved in Africa 2m years ago. *Homo erectus* began to migrate from Africa 1.8m years ago and spread throughout Asia and Europe. *Homo floresiensis*, the one-metre-tall dwarf discovered in Flores, an isolated island off Indonesia, probably evolved from a *homo erectus* group cut off there 800,000 years ago. The bones of *homo floresiensis* discovered in 2004 date from around 16,000 BC. *Homo sapiens* emerged in Africa 160,000 years ago and began to migrate 70,000 years ago, replacing other *hominids*. Cro-Magnon man, who emerged c.30,000 BC, can still be identified in cranial types in France, England, Spain and North Africa; and in particular in the Dal race from Dalecarlia, Sweden and in the Guanches of the Canary Islands. These men are thought to have been absorbed into later European populations. We are descended from *homo sapiens*.
9. Quoted in James Bentley, *A Guide to the Dordogne*, pp109, 107.
10. Ferguson, *op. cit.*, p169.
11. Mircea Eliade, *Shamanism, Archaic Techniques of Ecstasy*, p503: "Animal skulls and bones found in the sites of the European Palaeolithic (before 50,000-c.30,000 BC) can be interpreted as ritual offerings."
12. Cited in Ward Rutherford, *Shamanism*, pp19, 17.
13. *EB*, 16. 638; Eliade, *Shamanism*, p4; Rutherford, *Shamanism*, p15.
14. Eliade, *Shamanism*, p86.
15. Eliade, *Shamanism*, p259.
16. Joan Halifax, *Shaman, the Wounded Healer*, p25.
17. Eliade, *Shamanism*, pp60-1 and 90-1, quoting Rasmussen, *Intellectual Culture of the Igluluk Eskimos*, pp111-113.
18. Cited in Rutherford, *Shamanism*, p19.
19. Eliade, *Shamanism*, pp155-7.
20. Eliade, *Shamanism*, p10.
21. Eliade, *Shamanism*, p205. In some shamanic traditions, e.g. among the Maori of New Zealand, there are 10 heavens; see Eliade, *Shamanism*, p492.

22. Eliade, *Shamanism*, p262.
23. Eliade, *Shamanism*, pp259-61.
24. Eliade, *Shamanism*, pp60-1.
25. Rutherford, *Shamanism*, pp113-4, 117-9.
26. Eliade, *Shamanism*, pp379-82.
27. Eliade, *Shamanism*, p156.
28. Halifax, *op. cit.*, pp19, 24-5.
29. Nigel Pennick, *The Mysteries of King's College Chapel*, pp39-41: the fan-vaulting was constructed by Freemasons, "of whom John Wastell, the Master-Mason, contracted to employ not less than sixty, for carrying on the works of this chapel" (Malden, the chapel clerk, 1759).
30. Eliade, *Shamanism*, pp60-1.
31. *EB*, II. 137; Rutherford, *Shamanism*, p140; Andrew Tomas *Shambhala: Oasis of Light*, p32.
32. Tomas, *op. cit.*, p9: "In Buddhist books of Tibet the name Shambhala is mentioned on many pages. Even before the introduction of Buddhism into Tibet in the seventh century of our era, the Land of Shambhala was shown on a geographical map in a Bon book of Tibet which is estimated to be about 2,000 years old." There is a consensus that Bon surfaced into history shortly before 1000 BC.
33. Eliade, *Shamanism*, p177: "H. Hoffmann has usefully studied the resemblances between the Bon priests' costume and drum and those of the Siberian shamans. The costume of the Tibetan oracle-priests includes, among other things, eagle feathers, a helmet with broad ribbons of silk, a shield, and a lance." The Bon priests controlled spirits by using shamanic techniques. Rutherford, *Shamanism*, p14.
34. Tomas, *op. cit.*, pp25, 33.
35. Tomas, *op. cit.*, p35, quoting a letter written by A. P. Sinnett in 1881; and p45.
36. Tomas, *op. cit.*, pp68-75.
37. Tomas, *op. cit.*, pp35-41, 53-7, 127.
38. Rutherford, *Shamanism*, p133.
39. Rutherford, *Shamanism*, pp95, 127-132, 143-5.

PART TWO

THE TRADITION OF THE LIGHT

This part of the book traces 25 traditions of the Light. The following notes include references ("*EB*", vol number, then page number) to entries in *The Encyclopaedia Britannica* (15th Edition), where many of the dates used in each tradition can be checked and verified. A list of references to *The Encyclopaedia Britannica* tradition by tradition (numbered 1 to 25) is at the end of these Notes. I have provided sources for early historical events almost lost in the mist of proto-history, which may be disputed; but have left later events, on which there is general agreement, to be confirmed from *The Encyclopaedia Britannica.* Many other sources have also been used but it is convenient to refer the general reader to one standard work, and to confine the sources to as few books as possible in the interests of manageable verification.

1. Alastair Service, *Lost Worlds*, p94; the *Collins Atlas of World History*, p8; Marija Gimbutas, *The Civilization of the Goddess, The World of Old Europe*, pp4, 7.
2. Gimbutas, *op. cit.*, p352: "The Proto- or Early Indo-Europeans, whom I have labeled 'Kurgan' people, arrived from the east, from southern Russia, on horseback. Their first contact with the borderland territories of Old Europe in the Lower Dnieper region and west of the Black Sea began around the middle of the 5th millennium BC." Also see Ward Rutherford, *Pythagoras, Lover of Wisdom*, p89.

1. The Indo-European Kurgan Light

1. Leon Stover and Bruce Kraig, *Stonehenge, The Indo-European Heritage*, pp30, 36. Also see *EB*, 2. 614. Stover and Kraig refer to Marija Gimbutas' "Old European civilization", which they call "Old European culture" as "civilization" for them implies "social

stratification, a high culture and the state". See Stover and Kraig, *op. cit.*, p24. It can be argued that works of the quality of Stonehenge were a high culture for their time when workers had little more than their bare hands. Also see Colin McEvedy, *The Penguin Atlas of Ancient History*, p20. The three periods of Kurgan expansion put forward by Gimbutas (see epigraph under "The Indo-European Kurgan Light") "seem to be confirmed by later work by Anthony and others (Anthony 1994, Anthony & Vinogradov in press)" – see L. Luca Cavalli-Sforza, "The Spread of Agriculture and Nomadic pastoralism: Insights from Genetics, Linguistics and Archaeology" in *The Origins and Spread of Agriculture and Pastoralism in Eurasia*, ed. by David R. Harris. For Anthony, see D. W. Anthony, 1994, "The Earliest Horseback Riders and Indo-European Origins: New Evidence from the Steppes", in *Die Indogermanen und das Pferd*, ed. by B. Hänsel & Zimmer, 185-95, Budapest: Archaeolingua; D. W. Anthony and D. R. Brown, 1991, "The Origins of Horseback Riding", *Antiquity* 65, 22-38; and D. W. Anthony and N. B. Vinogradov, 1995, "Birth of the Chariot", *Archaeology* 48 (2), 36-41.

2. *EB*, 2. 614.
3. Stover and Kraig, *op. cit.*, p36.
4. Stover and Kraig, *op. cit.*, p 68.
5. Stover and Kraig, *op. cit.*, p68.
6. Stover and Kraig, *op. cit.*, p68.
7. *EB*, 6. 1059; Gimbutas, *The Civilization of the Goddess*, p399; and Burkert, *Greek Religion*, p17.
8. Stover and Kraig, *op. cit.*, pp26-8.
9. Illustration in *Mysteries of the Ancient World*, p49: "Wildly gesticulating celebrants dance around a huge bull" which "decorated the wall of a shrine". The bull of the 6th millennium BC is sometimes described as an ox, as in the guidebook of the Museum of Anatolian Civilizations.
10. Burkert, *op. cit.*, p17.
11. Eliade, *Shamanism*, pp10, 206, 375-6; Rutherford, *Shamanism, The Foundations of Magic*, p63.

12. Eliade, *Shamanism*, p10.
13. Eliade, *Shamanism*, p206.
14. E. O. James, *The Ancient Gods*, pp75, 77ff.
15. O'Brien, *The Megalithic Odyssey*, pp148-9; National Trust leaflet and Rodney Legge, *Cerne's Giant and Village Guide*, pp7-12; Rodney Castleden, *The Cerne Giant*, chs 5-7, which suggest a pre-Roman origin. John North, *Stonehenge: Neolithic Man and the Cosmos*, p197, sees the Cerne Abbas Giant as a Romano-British representation of the constellation of Hercules.
16. E. O. James, *op. cit.*, p75.
17. Eliade, *Shamanism*, pp235, 269-271.
18. Gimbutas, *op. cit.*, p391.
19. Gimbutas, *op. cit.*, pp338-9: "There are more than 10,000 megalithic tombs and long barrows known in western Europe." She makes clear that these were of Indo-European origin. The megaliths seem to have spread along the coasts from the east. They are never more than a hundred miles from the sea. From the Mediterranean, the Spanish and French Atlantic coasts, they spread to Brittany and England. See Gerhard Herm, *The Celts*, pp88-90. Gimbutas, and Stover and Kraig, state that they were built at first by Neolithic farmers who had blended with Mesolithic hunters – in the case of Britain, after c.3000 BC. The idea of megalith-building seems to have been spread by a seafaring people moving northward through Spain, up the coast of western Europe and into Scandinavia – see *EB*, VI. 754. The megaliths were built after the three waves of Kurgan invasions, which suggests their Indo-European origin. The megalith-builders were superseded by the Beaker-Folk, another wave of Kurgans – see *EB*, VI. 754.
20. Gimbutas, *op. cit.*; Herm, *op. cit.*; Stover and Kraig, *op. cit.*, pp142-3.
21. Stover and Kraig, *op. cit.*, p41; Herm, *op. cit.*, p89; *EB*, VI. 754.
22. T. E. Peet, *Rough Stone Monuments and their Builders*; updated by W. B. Crow, *A History of Magic, Witchcraft and Occultism*, pp32-3. Stover and Kraig, *op. cit.*, p41; Herm, *op. cit.*, p89; *EB*, VI. 754.
23. Crow, *op. cit.*, pp32-3.
24. See "The Andean Light", note 5 for evidence that the idea for New

World temple-pyramids goes back to c.1500-1200 BC. See "The Andean Light", paragraphs 3 and 4 for 500 BC, and Crow, *op. cit.*, pp33, 53.

25. E. O. James, *op. cit.*, p121.
26. The American chemist Willard Frank Libby published *Radiocarbon Dating* (2nd edn., 1955) on a dating system based on the ratio of carbon to radioactive carbon. This became all archaeologists' measuring-scale. However, Libby's assumption that the atmosphere has always had a constant measure of radioactive carbon is wrong. In earlier years there was less radiocarbon content in the atmosphere. His dating therefore has to be adjusted by 700 years or more. See Herm, *op. cit.*, pp90-1.
27. *EB* IX. 586-7; E. O. James, *op. cit.* North, *op. cit.*, sees Stonehenge as a religious observatory designed to monitor the sun and the moon.
28. Stover and Kraig, *op. cit.*, pp65, 78, 92. *EB* IX. 587.
29. *EB* IX. 587.
30. For the axis see Hawkins and White, *Stonehenge Decoded*, and compare Thom, *Megalithic Lunar Observatories.*
31. For gematria, see John Michell, *The View over Atlantis and The Old Stones of Land's End.*
32. *EB* IX. 586-7; Stover and Kraig, *op. cit.*, ch 4.
33. See "The Egyptian Light", note 116 for Stukeley's description. The 18th-century antiquary, William Stukeley, drew attention to the serpentine avenue and associated it with Druidical serpent worship. It is more likely to be a sun symbol. See Crow, *op. cit.*, p35. Janet and Colin Bord, *Earth Rites*, p52: "The layout of the avenues and henge at Avebury was somewhat serpentine in appearance."
34. John North, *op. cit.*, pp196-204, sees the Long Man as chalked out to draw attention to the points on the ridge above where c.3500 BC the constellation Orion would cross the ridge. Other commentators have seen the Long Man in relation to the sun.
35. Mrs Maltwood's *Glastonbury's Temple of the Stars* is supplemented by Mary Caine's *The Glastonbury Giants*, which makes revisions. See Mary Caine's *The Kingston Zodiac.*

36. Maltwood, *op. cit.*; quoted in Caine, *The Glastonbury Giants*, p3.
37. Caine, *The Glastonbury Giants*, p3. Hu Gadarn has been called the founder of Stonehenge by Rev. R. W. Morgan in *St Paul and Britain*, p13, and by Isabel Hill Elder in *Celt, Druid and Culdee*, p53. Caine, *op. cit.* above, p3: "The word Somerset (says Waddell) derives from the seat of the Sumers – their capital was Somerton."
38. Flavia Anderson, *The Ancient Secret.* See http://www.celticisland.com/history%20crosses..htm: "A plain circle is often a symbol for the moon and a circle with cross within or the arms of a cross without are universal symbols for the sun. The *swastika* is a related sun symbol."
39. Gimbutas, *op. cit.*, pp361-2.
40. Stover and Kraig, *op. cit.*, pp45-51.
41. Stover and Kraig, *op. cit.*, pp105-7.
42. Stover and Kraig, *op. cit.*, pp44-8. See p46 for axes.
43. The Beaker folk are treated as Indo-Europeans by Stover and Kraig, *op. cit.*, pp62-3.
44. Stover and Kraig, *op. cit.*, pp20-1.
45. See Stover and Kraig, *op. cit.*, p55 for Stonehenge I; and pp16, 64 for Stonehenge II.
46. O'Brien, *The Megalithic Odyssey*, p131.
47. Stover and Kraig, *op. cit.*, pp28, 53-5.
48. Gimbutas, *op. cit.*; Herm, *op. cit.*, ch 5.
49. Herm, *op. cit.*, p78; O'Brien, *The Megalithic Odyssey*, p144.
50. Stover and Kraig, *op. cit.*, p142.
51. *EB*, 1. 115: "The invaders who destroyed the mainland settlements c.2200. Perhaps they came from there (i.e. Anatolia), but this remains uncertain." Also Stover and Kraig, *op. cit.*, pp142-3; E. O. James, *op. cit.*, p75: "When the Indo-Europeans migrated from their Eurasian grasslands in a westerly direction and settled on the pastures of Thessaly, they brought with them their great Sky-god…who finally was known as Zeus."
52. Burkert, *op. cit.*, p10: "Greek belongs to the group of Indo-European languages, and the scholarly reconstruction of 'Proto–Indo-European' postulates the existence of an Indo-European people in the fourth or

third millennium." However, "neither the Indo-European homeland, nor the migration of the Indo-European Greeks into Greece...can be identified conclusively on the basis of excavation finds, ceramics or burial forms." Gimbutas confirms an Indo-European invasion of the area above north Greece during the second wave of Indo-European invasions, c.3500 BC. This invasion could have brought the Pelasgians, who arrived in Greece some time before the 12th century BC, see *EB*, VII. 838. It is uncertain whether any group called themselves "Pelasgians"; the name may have been applied to all indigenous Aegean populations. Gimbutas, *op. cit.*, p344, states that the Pelasgians were matrilineal, which suggests they were not patrilineal Indo-Europeans.

53. O'Brien, *The Megalithic Odyssey*, pp144-5.
54. Stover and Kraig, *op. cit.*, pp142-3.
55. Stover and Kraig, *op. cit.*, p64; and pp194-5.
56. Stover and Kraig, *op. cit.*, p64.
57. Stover and Kraig, *op. cit.*, pp77-8.
58. O'Brien, *The Megalithic Odyssey*, pp129, 143.
59. Stover and Kraig, *op. cit.*, p142.
60. Stover and Kraig, *op. cit.*, p142.
61. Stover and Kraig, *op. cit.*, p142.
62. Stover and Kraig, *op. cit.*, pp36, 65-7; and p68.
63. *EB*, I. 900-1.
64. Stover and Kraig, *op. cit.*, p73.
65. Stover and Kraig, *op. cit.*, pp73-7.
66. Stover and Kraig, *op. cit.*, pp48-9.
67. *EB*. 2. 614-5; Herm, *op. cit.*, p81.
68. E. O. James, *op. cit.*, p75.
69. *EB*, 2. 665; *EB*, 7. 310-3.
70. O'Brien, *The Megalithic Odyssey*, pp144-5.
71. O'Brien, *The Megalithic Odyssey*, p143.
72. Booklet issued by the Avalon Research Foundation in *The Universal Voice* (1965), quoted in Percy Corbett, *Why Britain?*, p7.
73. O'Brien, *The Megalithic Odyssey*, p113 and elsewhere.

74. O'Brien, *The Megalithic Odyssey*, pp112-3.
75. O'Brien, *The Megalithic Odyssey*, pp112-3.
76. O'Brien, *The Megalithic Odyssey*, p118.
77. O'Brien, *The Megalithic Odyssey*, pp124-5.
78. O'Brien, *The Megalithic Odyssey*, pp129, 132.
79. Georges Dumézil, *Les Dieux des Indo-Européens*; referred to by implication in *EB*, X. 165: "Some scholars believe that the Tuatha De Danann were a race of pagan gods." In *Les Dieux des Indo-Européens*, Dumézil pointed to the Indo-European *Deiwos*, which described creatures in the likeness of humans but possessing superhuman powers, i.e. gods in all the European tongues – to which the Tuatha belonged, he claimed. See Rutherford, *The Druids*, p95.
80. O'Brien, *The Megalithic Odyssey*, p143, ch 9.
81. Stover and Kraig, *op. cit.*, p36.

2. The Mesopotamian Light

1. Rutherford, *Shamanism*, p11. Samuel Noah Kramer, *The Sumerians*: "It is reasonably certain that the first settlers in Sumer were not Sumerians. The pertinent evidence derives not from archaeological or anthropological sources, which are rather ambiguous and inconclusive on this matter, but from linguistics." Quoted in O'Brien, *The Megalithic Odyssey*, p134.
2. Hooke, in *Middle Eastern Mythology*, pp18-22, states that the Sumerians came into the Delta from the mountainous region to the north-east of Mesopotamia. He points out on p22 that the fir-tree is not found in the Tigris-Euphrates Delta. Rutherford, *Shamanism*, pp132-3, states that the Sumerians appeared c.3500 BC.
3. Rutherford, *Shamanism*, pp132-3.
4. Stover and Kraig, *op. cit.*, p68.
5. Rutherford, *Shamanism*, p133, who, citing Joseph Campbell, *The Masks of God* (4 vols.), states that the Sumerians appeared c.3500 BC. Hooke, *Middle Eastern Mythology*, p18, states that the Sumerians

inhabited Sumer and Akkad as early as 4,000 BC. Most prefer c.3500 BC. The *Encyclopedia of World Religions*, p64, echoes 3500 BC.

6. See Hooke, *Middle Eastern* Mythology, p70: "In Egypt Re (i.e. Ra), according to tradition, was the first king of Egypt." EB. 11. 1009; E. O. James, *op. cit.*, p79; Hooke, *Middle Eastern Mythology*, pp39-41. The Akkadian version of this poem, "The Descent of Ishtar to the Nether World", can be found in Eliade, *From Primitives to Zen*, pp321-5.
7. O'Brien, *The Megalithic Odyssey*, pp115-6.
8. E. O. James, *op. cit.*, p69; O'Brien, *The Megalithic Odyssey*, p124.
9. O'Brien, *The Megalithic Odyssey*, p117.
10. O'Brien, *The Megalithic Odyssey*, p122.
11. Kharsag Epic 1 is about the decision to settle; Epic 2 is about the arrival of the Anannage; Epic 3 is about the romance of Enlil and Ninlil; Epic 4 is about the planning of the cultivation; Epic 5 is about the building of the settlement; Epic 6 is about the Great House of Enlil; Epic 7 is about the cold winter storm; Epic 8 is about the thousand-year storm; and Epic 9 is about the destruction of Kharsag.
12. Translated by O'Brien in *The Megalithic Odyssey*, p115 and in *The Genius of the Few*, pp52-3. I have included the second version as O'Brien made revisions to his first translation.
13. O'Brien, *The Genius of the Few*, p127.
14. Stover and Kraig, *op. cit.*, p36.
15. *Myths from Mesopotamia, Creation, The Flood, Gilgamesh and Others*, p262.
16. O'Brien, *The Megalithic Odyssey*, p122.
17. O'Brien, *The Megalithic Odyssey*, p117.
18. This symbol is taken from *The Megalithic Odyssey*, p117.
19. O'Brien, *The Genius of the Few*, pp168-9.
20. O'Brien, *The Megalithic Odyssey*, p141.
21. Hooke, *Middle Eastern Mythology*, pp136-8; O'Brien, *The Megalithic Odyssey*, pp112, 139.
22. O'Brien, *The Megalithic Odyssey*, pp135-6.
23. O'Brien, *The Megalithic Odyssey*, p137.

24. O'Brien, *The Megalithic Odyssey*, pp144-5.
25. University of Philadelphia Museum Tablet No 8322, column (iii), quoted in O'Brien, *The Megalithic Odyssey*, p135. See p138 for the next few lines.
26. O'Brien, *The Megalithic Odyssey*, pp138-9.
27. O'Brien, *The Megalithic Odyssey*, p137; E. O. James, *op. cit.*, p78; Hooke, *Middle Eastern Mythology*, p20.
28. Hooke, *Middle Eastern Mythology*, pp20-21.
29. Hooke, *Middle Eastern Mythology*, pp20ff.
30. Hooke, *Middle Eastern Mythology*, p21. For Dumuzi's appeal to Utu, see J. B. Pritchard, *The Ancient Near Eastern Texts Relating to the Old Testament*, p52.
31. The Enki poem is translated by Kramer in *The Sumerians, their History, Culture and Character*, and is in Eliade's *From Primitives to Zen*, p24.
32. *EB*, 11. 974.
33. Hooke, *Middle Eastern Mythology*, p38.
34. *EB*, X. 318; *EB*, IX. 108.
35. *EB*, 11. 1010; Oates, *op. cit.*, p173, shows the sun-god Shamash being transported in his boat, rays emanating from his shoulders (Oriental Institute Museum, Chicago); British Museum picture of Shamash, the sun god, rising in the morning with flames or rays from his shoulders.
36. *EB*, 11. 1002: Louvre picture of the *stele* inscribed with Hammurabi's code, showing the king before Shamash; bas-relief from Susa, 18th century BC.
37. Michael Roaf, *Cultural Atlas of Mesopotamia and the Ancient Near East*, p163. See note 45 for winged disc.
38. Hooke, *Middle Eastern Mythology*, pp38, 21, 25.
39. For the Ziusudra quotation, see J. B. Pritchard, *op. cit.*, p44.
40. *EB*, X. 881; *EB*, 18. 1021.
41. Oates, *op. cit.*, pp172-3, allocates Nanna (Sin) to Ur, and Utu/Shamash to Sippar and Larsa. But sun-worship's replacement of moon-worship had more to do with the Kurgans' replacement of Old Neolithic Europe, and the rise of the Tammuz myth. Roaf, *op. cit.*,

p101; E. O. James, *op. cit.*, pp80, 304 (Nanna/Utu); and Hooke, *Middle Eastern Mythology*, pp39-41.

42. Roaf, *op. cit.*, p121, believes that Hammurabi may have been a vassal of Samashi-Adad I (see below/note 46). He may have identified himself with Shamash as part of his challenge to Samashi-Adad.

43. E. O. James, *op. cit.*, p119; Hooke, *Middle Eastern Mythology*, p66. Hammurabi was also Marduk's steward and was entrusted by him with supreme executive authority in Sumer and Akkad.

44. *EB*, 11. 973-4, 1005.

45. E. O. James, *op. cit.*, pp120-1; Roaf, *op. cit.*, p163, which shows Ashurnasirpal II (883-859 BC) (twice) on either side of a sacred tree with Shamash in a winged disc. See E O. James, *op. cit.*, p127: the Hittite king, Hattusilis II, ruler of Hakpis from 1275 BC, was the son of the Sun-goddess of Arinna, and as the "Great King" and "hero, beloved of the goddess", told of her power. James adds, "It was not until the death of the Hittite kings that they themselves were actually deified, like the Roman emperors." The same applied to the kings of Babylon, including Hammurabi, who were not gods during their lifetime but were sons of the goddess. For the Hittite King's being addressed as "My Sun", see *EB*, 2. 191.

46. *EB*, 11. 977; Roaf, *op. cit.*, pp112-121.

47. Oates, *op. cit.*, pp108-9, which shows an illustration captioned: "The 'sun-god tablet' from Sippar, on which Nabu-Apla-Iddina records his restoration of the ancient image of the sun-god and of his temple (c.870 BC). The king is shown being led towards an altar on which rests the sun-disk of Shamash." The tablet is in the British Museum. Most books spell the ruler Nabu-apla-iddina; *EB* spells it Nabu-apal-iddina.

48. Julian Reade, *Assyrian Sculpture*, p7, 12; a colossal human-headed winged bull stood in the inner courtyard of Ashurnasirpal II's Northwest Palace, see Roaf, *op. cit.*, p163.

49. The Hebrew word *Shemesh*, meaning "sun", is derived from its adopted root *ShMSh*. See http://www.ancient-hebrew.org/16_english.html.

50. E. O. James, *op. cit.*, pp78ff.

51. Georges Roux, *Ancient Iraq*, p82.

52. Service, *op. cit.*, p107: "The central stairway, which today ends at the gatehouse, penetrated through it and swept up to the topmost platform. There, Woolley believed, (there was) a small temple to the moon god of Ur." For the ceremony on the top of the ziggurat which represented the underworld, see E. O. James, *op. cit.*, pp140-3 ("The *Akitu* in Babylon"). For the priestess acting as Inanna, see E. O. James, *op. cit.*, pp304-5; Service, *op. cit.*, p106: "The peak of the religious calendar was the New Year festival, which occupied several days. Sacrifices and long rites, whose details are little known, were performed by priests and priestesses, musicians and sacred prostitutes. The climax of the festival came when the king celebrated the annual Sacred Marriage. He, as the god, fertilized a priestess, representing a goddess in a ritual sexual act to ensure the well-being of the people and their lands for the following year." Herodotus (*History 1*, 181-2) reported: "On the topmost tower there is a spacious temple, and inside the temple stands a couch of unusual size, richly adorned, with a golden table by its side. There is no statue of any kind set up in the place, nor is the chamber occupied of nights by any one but a single native woman, who, as the Chaldaeans, the priests of this god (Jupiter Belus), affirm, is chosen for himself by the deity out of all the women in the land. They also declare – but I for my part do not credit it – that the god comes down in person into this chamber, and sleeps upon the couch." Quoted in Stephen Bertman, *Handbook to Life in Ancient Mesopotamia*.

53. Hooke, *Middle Eastern Mythology*, p25.

54. E. O. James, *op. cit.*, pp304-5; 121: "That Babylonian kings were on occasion invited to share the couch of the Goddess as her bridegroom has been demonstrated, and it was she who was the active partner in the sacred marriage, bringing him into her bower with its couch decorated with grass and plants at the New Year Festival, to promote the growth of the fruits of the earth, to ensure prosperity in the forthcoming year, and to raise the sovereign to her divine

status....Unquestionably the king was often regarded as subservient to the Goddess, and was represented as her instrument on earth, but in his vegetation capacity his sacredness and annual renewal were dependent upon a much wider relationship with the gods, especially the local deity of the state over which he ruled, and whose favour was essential for the exercise of his royal functions in their several aspects." Service, *op. cit.*, p107.

55. E. O. James, *op. cit.*, pp78-80, 304-5; Service, *op. cit.*, p106: "The god was actually present in his temple statue....The statue in the temple had his living human counterpart, too, in the king in his palace. The god acted on earth through his king persona. The god's meals were served to the statue, then often eaten by the king."

56. See ceremonies referred to in notes 52, 54, 55 and 60.

57. Hooke, *Middle Eastern Mythology*, pp24-5. For myth and sacred marriage see Kramer, *Cuneiform Inscriptions*, pp101ff, and Chiera, *Sumerian Ritual Texts*, I. v. 14 ff. These are dealt with in E. O. James, *op. cit.*, pp78-81, 304-5. See also Hooke, *Babylonian and Assyrian Religion.*

58. *The Great Hymn to Shamash*, sections 149-50, 174-7, trans. by W. G. Lambert in *Babylonian Wisdom Literature*, p127ff, quoted in Eliade *From Primitives to Zen*, p 276. See Contenau, *Everyday Life in Babylon and Assyria*, pp116, 218, 263 and 286 for preceding points.

59. In G. Widengren, *The King and the Tree of Life*, p45.

60. E. O. James, *op. cit.*, p142: "The city was in a state of increasing commotion because Marduk was alleged to have been imprisoned in the 'mountain' of the underworld, with its reciprocal effects in the desolation of the country evidenced in the annual drought. Mock battles were fought for the purpose of securing his release and the renewal of vegetation." James makes it clear that the high mountain of the ziggurat represented the deep underworld in reverse symbolism. And so, the exoteric had become esoteric.

61. Service, *op. cit.*, pp106-7: "At Angkor in Cambodia it is clear that, to the Hindu rulers, each temple-mountain represented (and, in a sense, was) Mount Meru, the mythical mountain that was home of the gods

and stable centre of the world. It is in this light, as local world centres, that we should see the ziggurats, of which one was the Tower of Babylon or Babel." Herodotus (*History 1*, 181-2) described Nabonidus' rebuilding of Ur-Nammu's Ur ziggurat as having seven ramps in seven stages or levels spiralling round it. (He describes eight towers on seven levels.) An agate seal (9th-8th century Assyrian in style) from Babylon shows a priest before a 5-stage ziggurat or temple-tower – see Oates, *op. cit.*, p177. Oates shows an illustration of the ziggurat at Ur, *op. cit.*, p47, which is also on 5 levels. The ruined ziggurat of Ur (as opposed to Babylon) had three storeys – see *EB*, 18. 1021: "On the northeast face were three great staircases, each of 100 steps, one projecting at right angles from the centre of the building, two leaning against its wall, and all three converging in a gateway between the first and the second terrace. From this a single flight of steps led upward to the top terrace and to the door of the god's little shrine." The French archaeologist Jean-Claude Margueron saw ziggurats as "a sort of ladder inviting the deity to come down among men" – see Service, *op. cit.*, p106. This ladder united heaven and earth. See note 65.

62. Oates, *op. cit.*, pp157-60; Service, *op. cit.*, p107: "Woolley believed, a small temple to the moon god of Ur, Nanna, surmounted the whole step-pyramid composition and brought it to a height of 20 metres (65 feet). There were also signs that the terraces were planted with trees and gardens, providing an elaborately conceived temple-mountain." The Babylonian ziggurat was also known as the *Etemenaki*/Tower of Babel – on whose sides, it was thought, were the Hanging Gardens of Babylon – all three names probably describing one place. Also see O'Brien, *The Megalithic Odyssey*, p113.
63. Hooke, *Middle Eastern Mythology*, p138.
64. Hooke, *Middle Eastern Mythology*, p138.
65. Ishtar passed through seven gates of the nether world, which correspond to the seven levels of the ziggurat, each of which had a gate. The summary of "The Descent of Ishtar (i.e. Inanna) to the nether world" (Akkadian version), in Eliade, *From Primitives to Zen*,

pp321-4, reveals this symbolism: "Ishtar, goddess of life and fertility, decides to visit her sister Ereshkigal, goddess of death and sterility. As Ishtar forces her way through the gates of the nether world, her robes and garments are stripped from her. Naked and helpless, she finally reaches Ereshkigal, who instantly has her put to death. Without Ishtar there is no fertility on earth and the gods soon realise their loss. Ea creates the beautiful eunuch Asushunamir, who tricks Ereshkigal into reviving Ishtar with the water of life and releasing her. The ending of the myth is obscure; perhaps Ishtar's lover Tammuz, was released along with her." Ishtar, like Tammuz dies and is reborn, and their release from the nether world brings fertility to the earth. We are told that Ishtar

"set her mind...
to the house wherein the dwellers are bereft of light,
where dust is their fare and clay their food,
(where) they see no light, residing in darkness,
(where) they are clothed like birds, with wings for
garments...."

These lines have both an exoteric and an esoteric meaning.

66. The quotation from "The Great Hymn to Shamash", in Eliade, *From Primitives to Zen*, p276, which appears in the text before note 58 has both an exoteric and an esoteric meaning.

3. The Egyptian Light

1. See pp42-46. In their translations of the Egyptian *Book of the Dead* Sir E. A. Wallis Budge translates "*akh*" ("Shining One") as "*khu*"; R. O. Faulkner as "dweller in the sunshine"; and E. O. James as "glorified personality". When correctly translated, "Shining Ones" can be found on almost every page of *The Book of the Dead.*
2. For the Pharaoh as the physical sun of the sun-god Ra, see E. O. James, *op. cit.*, pp69, 108.
3. For the Egyptian belief in immortality in the Elysian Fields, see E. O. James, *op. cit.*, p61.

4. Toby Wilkinson, *Genesis of the Pharaohs, Dramatic New Discoveries that Rewrite the Origins of Ancient Egypt*, claims to have discovered the origin of the Egyptian civilization in the Eastern Desert, between the Nile Valley and the Red Sea, where there are rock drawings of hunters and herders and of flotillas of ships. The question is, did Wilkinson's expedition find the first Egyptians, or a desert culture (c.4000 BC) which the Egyptians absorbed? Samuel Noah Kramer wrote *History Begins at Sumer*. André Parrott in *Sumer: The Dawn of Art*: "Now that we can view the Mesopotamian Basin in all its splendour it is becoming clear that this flame which blazed up so suddenly in the Middle East, and shed so wide a light, was kindled at several points....Susa, Lagash, Ur, Uruk, Ashnunnak, Assur, Nineveh, Mari – all alike were centres whose civilization advanced from strength to strength until, at last, thanks to the genius of the few and the boldness of the many, there was wrought forth...a prodigious, many-sided art." Quoted in O'Brien, *The Megalithic Odyssey*, p112. For "Mesopotamia-first" views, see *The World's Last Mysteries*, Reader's Digest, p169 and *The Collins Atlas of World History*, pp12-15. The Mesopotamian "Shining Ones" have their counterpart in Egyptian *akhs*.

5. *EB*, V. 25. Heyerdahl's first voyage in 1947 on the *Kon-Tiki* was from the Pacific coast of South America to Polynesia to prove the possibility that the Polynesians may have originated in South America. His later voyages in 1969 from Morocco to within 600 miles of central America in a reconstructed Egyptian reed boat confirmed the possibility that pre-Columbian cultures may have originated in Egypt or been influenced by Egyptians. Budge, *The Book of the Dead (Theban Recension*, pxix: "If the known facts be examined it is difficult not to arrive at the conclusion that many of the *beliefs* found in *The Book of the Dead* were either voluntarily borrowed from some nation without, or were introduced into Egypt by some conquering immigrants who made their way into the country from Asia, either by way of the Red Sea or across the Arabian peninsula; that they were brought into Egypt by new-comers seems most probable."

6. For Ra as an African god native to On/Heliopolis/Egypt rather than an import from the east, see E. O. James, *op. cit.*, pp71, 81 and elsewhere; E. A. Wallis Budge, *The Book of the Dead (Theban Recension)*, pxxv: "It is easy to see that the debt which the indigenous peoples of Egypt owed to the new-comers from the East is very considerable, for they learned from them the art working in metals...and the art of writing. M. de Morgan...thinks that the art of brick-making was introduced into Egypt from Mesopotamia, where it was, as we learn from the ruins of early Sumerian cities, extensively practised, with many other things which he duly specifies." For Henri Frankfort's anthropological approach to archaeology and his *Kingship and the Gods*, see *EB*, IV. 281.

7. See E. O. James's notes on Frankfort in E. O. James, *op. cit.*, pp347-9, 351.

8. For Menes as Aha, see Stephan Seidlmayer, "The Rise of the State to the Second Dynasty" in *Egypt, The World of the Pharaohs*, pp25, 27, 30ff, 33; and for the last dates see p528 in the same book. See note 12 on double dating. *EB*, 6. 464 sees Aha as Menes' successor.

9. Chapter 17 of *The Book of the Dead*. The vignette illustrates both as hawks. Ra has a sun-disc on his head, Osiris has a human head and wears a crown.

10. E. O. James, *op. cit.*, pp31, 108.

11. Wallis Budge, *Egyptian Religion*, pp13-15.

12. All Archaic-period and Old Kingdom Egyptian dates are approximate. The earlier date comes from Jürgen von Beckerath, *Chronologie des pharaonischen Ägypten*, MÄS 46, Mainz, 1997. The later dating is adopted by many books on Egypt and sanctioned by Zahi Hawass, Secretary General of the Supreme Council of Antiquities and Director of the Giza Pyramids excavations. The last date is based on the chronology developed by Prof. John Baines and Dr Jaromir Malek in their *Atlas of Ancient Egypt*. Where two dates are given in this section, they refer to the first and last schemes mentioned in this note.

13. *The Book of the Dead*, ch 17, quoted by Kurt Sethe, *Urkunden des aegyptischen Altertums*, vol VI. In E. O. James, *op. cit.*, p107/327.

14. E. O. James, *op. cit.*, pp108, 174-5.
15. Mark Lehner, *The Complete Pyramids*, p34.
16. Lehner, *op. cit.*, pp23, 34.
17. Veronica Ions, *Egyptian Mythology*, p122; Flavia Anderson, *op. cit.* Also *EB*, I. 445: "As Apis-Atum he was associated with the solar cult and was often represented with the sun-disk between his horns."
18. Khufu did not take the name Ra, unlike his sons. That he regarded himself as a god is hinted at in many books and confirmed by the author's questioning of Egyptologists in Cairo. The norm may have been otherwise. E. O. James, *op. cit.*, p116, quotes Moret (*Le Rituel du Culte Divin Journalier on Egypte*, Paris, 1902, pp283ff) as contending that the Pharaoh was worshipped from the moment of his coronation, whereas Erman (*Handbook of Egyptian Religion*, London, 1907, pp37ff) held that he was only formally worshipped with temples, offerings and priests after his death.
19. E. O. James, *op. cit.*, p108.
20. For details of the coronation ceremony and toilet ceremonies, when the Pharaoh performed his renewal ritual every morning, see E. O. James, *op. cit.*, pp111-4. E. O. James, *op. cit.*, pp108ff.
21. *EB*, 18. 1021-2; *EB*, 11. 973, 1005; E. O. James, *op. cit.*, p65.
22. E. O. James, *op. cit.*, pp115-6. Also see Flavia Anderson, *op. cit.*
23. For the divine succession by hereditary sequence from father to son, see E. O. James, *op. cit.*, pp109ff.
24. Lehner, *op. cit.*, pp23-4.
25. Lehner, *op. cit.*, pp23-4.
26. Lehner, *op. cit*, p24.
27. Lehner, *op. cit*, p23.
28. James, *op. cit.*, pp169, 261.
29. Budge, *op. cit.*, plxiv.
30. I am indebted to Carol Andrews, when she was Assistant Keeper in the Department of Egyptian Antiquities in the British Museum, London for showing me pages from R. O. Faulkner's handwritten dictionary of hieroglyphs that clarify the various signs for *akh*, *akhu* and *akhty*, and for advice on a number of linguistic points in this section.

31. Budge, *op. cit.*, plxvii, lxix.
32. Budge, *op. cit.*, plxxiii. Also, Miroslav Verner, *The Pyramids*, p37: "Every Egyptian wanted to die in Egypt, to be buried there, and to be worshipped after death as an eternal memory."
33. Budge, *op. cit.*, pv.
34. Lucie Lamy, *Egyptian Mysteries*, p27. The full translation should be: "Book of the Coming Forth into Day, to Live After Death".
35. Budge, *The Book of the Dead (Theban Recension).*, plxxxviii: "The allusion being to the well-known belief of the ancient Egyptians that the journey to the Other World occupied the deceased the whole night of the day of his death, and that he did not emerge into the realms of the blessed until the following morning at sunrise."
36. But the whole burial ritual, including mummification, was generally expect to last 70 days, and sometimes took getting on for a year to complete – see Verner, *op. cit.*, p36.
37. Budge, *op. cit.*, pp3-17: hymn to Ra in papyri of Ani, Qenna, Hu-Nefer and Nekht.
38. See Budge, *Book of the Dead (Papyrus of Ani)*, pp xci-xciii, on monotheism behind polytheism.
39. Lamy, *op. cit.*, pp23-4, on initiation.
40. Lehner, *op. cit*, pp23-4. *EB*, X. 881.
41. Lehner, *op. cit*, p24.
42. Lamy, *op. cit.*, pp24-5: "It is impossible not to relate this inner light to the Pharaonic word for light, *akh.* This word, often translated as 'transfigured', designates transcendental light as well as all aspects of physical light....*Akh* indeed expresses all notions of light, both literally and figuratively, from the Light which comes forth from Darkness to the transcendental light of transfiguration."
43. Lamy, *op. cit.*, p25.
44. The white ibis can still be seen round Luxor; drive by convoy – because of the military situation – from Luxor to Abydos and you will pass hundreds of ibises standing by the water of the roadside canals.
45. Lamy, *op. cit.*, pp24-6.
46. Lamy, *op. cit.*, p25.

47. Edith Schnapper, *The Inward Odyssey*, p129.
48. Sir F. Petrie, *Personal Religion in Egypt Before Christianity*, p49.
49. The first translation of 81A, is, like the translations so far, from Sir E. A. Wallis Budge's *The Book of the Dead*. These translations are not always accurate. R. O. Faulkner's *The Ancient Egyptian Book of the Dead* is more accurate. It is from this book that the third translation of 81A is taken. The second translation of 81A is quoted in A. Bothwell Gosse's *The Lily of Light*.
50. Lamy, *op. cit.*, p25, which speaks of the "pre-existent *Akhw*" i.e. *Akhu* (as *w* is sounded *u*). Also see page reproduced in Hagger, *The Fire and the Stones* from R. O. Faulkner, *Concise Dictionary of Middle Egyptian*, which shows the hieroglyph for *Akhu*, which is defined as "sunlight, sunshine". As the *Akh* is "pre-existent", the sunshine is "pre-existent", i.e. underworldly.
51. Lehner, *op. cit*, pp14-16.
52. *The World's Last Mysteries*, Reader's Digest, p190.
53. See I. S. Edwards, *The Pyramids of Egypt*, pp290-1: Spell 508; and pp139-40 for the Sphinx.
54. Ian Shaw and Paul Nicholson, *The British Museum Dictionary of Ancient Egypt*, p152. Lehner, *op. cit.*, p108. For the *cartouche* of Khufu's name (*hwfw*), see Alberto Siliotti, *Guide to the Pyramids of Egypt*, p50, which shows a *cartouche* in red ink of Khufu, bearing his name and the year of his reign – "the seventeenth year of the (cattle) census". This was discovered on the walls of the highest weight relief chamber by Wvyse and Perring in 1837.
55. Lehner, *op. cit.*, p108. Also Lehner, *op. cit.*, p29: "In the Pyramid Texts, *Akhet* is written with the crested ibis and elliptical land-sign, not with the hieroglyph of the sun disk between two mountains that was used later to write 'horizon'." This also applies to note 56.
56. Lehner, *op. cit*, pp33, 108; Verner, *op. cit.*, p189.
57. R. O. Faulkner, *Concise Dictionary of Middle Egyptian*, *Akhty* described as "horizon-dweller, especially of god" or "horizon-dwelling" – see note 50 for page reproduced in Hagger, *The Fire and the Stones*, showing *Akhty*.

58. Verner, *op. cit.*, p236: "Recently Vasil Dobruv has suggested that Djedefra built the Sphinx as a gesture of filial piety connected with the establishment of the local divine cult of Khufu." Djedefra, Khufu's son and successor, was the first Pharaoh we know to take the title "Son of Ra". Khufu did not take the name "Son of Ra", and it is known that he persecuted temple priests. The indications are that he wanted himself to be worshipped as a god. The Sphinx may bear his face staring serenely at the sun, and the secret of the Sphinx may be: Khufu's divinity. If one of his sons was responsible for the Sphinx, the statue could be intended to placate Khufu's people by reassuring them that his successor had subordinated himself to Ra.

59. Lehner, *op. cit*, p108, 29.

60. Lehner, *op. cit*, pp108, 29, 6; Lamy, *op. cit.*, p25.

61. For the derivation from *pur*, "fire", see Verner, *op. cit.*, 460. "Pyramid" is also derived from the Greek for "wheaten cake"; see Lehner, *op. cit*, p460.

62. Lehner, *op. cit*, p23.

63. Lehner, *op. cit*, pp112-3; Verner, *op. cit.*, pp202 and 41, 45: "After his death the ruler became one of the eternal stars near the North Star....The dead pharaoh went north to become one of the eternal stars around the North Star that never set.". Lamy, *op. cit.*, p28: "In 2700 BC, the Pole was occupied by Alpha Draconis, the star around which turned the Circumpolars – called the 'indestructibles' since they never disappear below the horizon. Thus they were the symbol of immortality."

64. Lehner, *op. cit*, p112; Verner, *op. cit.*, p202.

65. Lehner, *op. cit*, pp28-9; Lamy, *op. cit.*, p25. Verner, *op. cit.*, p44: "The pharoah's ultimate goal was to rise as high as the sun that 'shone over the horizon.'"

66. See quotation in note 65.

67. Lamy, *op. cit.*, pp25,28.

68. Lehner, *op. cit.*, p114.

69. Verner, *op. cit.*, p203: "According to a legend recounted by Diodorus Siculus, Khufu ultimately was not buried in his pyramid. Medieval

Arab historians mention the existence of a mummy-shaped coffin and the ruler's bodily remains but do not say where they lay."

70. Lehner, *op. cit.*, pp99-100, 103.

71. Lehner, *op. cit.*, p114. It was Rainer Stadelmann who suggested that the unfinished state of the subterranean chamber meant that it was intended to resemble the Underworld cavern.

72. For the *cartouche* of Khufu, see Siliotti, *op. cit.*, p50. "Wonderful is the White Crown of Khufu" – reported to the author by an Egyptologist accompanying him inside the Great Pyramid.

73. Verner, *op. cit.*, p203. See note 69.

74. Verner, *op. cit.*, pp202-3. That the cracking in the ceiling of the King's Chamber made the Great Pyramid unsafe was first claimed by the Polish architect Koziński.

75. Knowing what we do about the respect and reverence for the Pharaoh, we can safely conclude that no Pharaoh could be submitted to the indignity of being buried in an unfinished tomb.

76. Lehner, *op. cit.*, pp38, 108.

77. By Rainer Stadelmann, *Pyramiden*, L.A.IV, 1982, pp1205-63; and *Die ägyptischen Pyramiden: vom Ziegelbau zum Weltwunder*, Mainz, 1985.

78. See R. G. Torrens, *The Golden Dawn and the Inner Teachings*, pp150-1 for treatment of the Great Pyramid as "Light" and an initiation into the mysteries of the *akh*.

79. Marsham Adams, *The House of the Hidden Places* and *The Book of the Master*, both published in 1895, suggested that the Great Pyramid was used for ceremonies of initiation; that the postulant goes through the symbolic ritual of *The Book of the Dead*, which is full of doors opening and closing, and finally lies in the tomb of Osiris, the Hidden Light. See Torrens, *op. cit.*, pp11, 65, 150-2. Also see Verner, *op. cit.*, p450.

80. There is no evidence that the ramp was originally called the Path of the Just; this may be a relatively modern label giving it a ceremonial purpose. Compare "King's Chamber", "Queen's Chamber" – which are relatively modern labels.

81. See note 79.

82. Manfred Lurker, *The Gods and Symbols of Ancient Egypt*, p114: "The Egyptian sphinx was, with only a few exceptions in representations of some queens of the Middle Kingdom, shown as male, unlike the Greek sphinx which was female. Also, the Egyptian sphinx was viewed as benevolent, a guardian, whereas the Greek sphinx was invariably malevolent towards people. The sphinx was the embodiment of royal power."

83. For example, Alberto Siliotti, *Guide to the Pyramids of Egypt*, preface by Zahi Hawass; Farid Atiya, *The Giza Pyramids*; Verner, *op. cit.*

84. This view is reflected by Rainer Stadelmann in "Royal Tombs from the Age of the Pyramids", in *Egypt, The World of the Pharaohs*, p75.

85. Reported to me by an Egyptologist who accompanied me to the Giza Pyramids in 2005; hinted at in several books.

86. See note 58.

87. See note 58.

88. Semti-Hesep-ti is referred to in Budge's 1899 edition of *The Book of the Dead*, p210, as reigning "c.4266 BC". This 1st-dynasty dating is clearly very wrong. Semti is missing from many lists of 1st-dynasty Pharaohs.

89. Lehner, "The Sphinx", in Zahi Hawass and others, *The Treasures of the Pyramids*, pp179, 184; Lehner, *op. cit.*, p132; Verner, *op. cit.*, p237.

90. Lehner in Hawass, *op. cit.*, p180: "The Sphinx must have been a repellent to dangerous forces."

91. Erik Iverson, *Obelisks in Exile*, vol 1, quoting Pliny's *Natural History*, 36. 14. 64.

92. For *sekhem*, see Budge, *The Book of the Dead (Theban Recension)*, plxii.

93. Besides having *akh* in his own name Akhenaton called his new city Akhetaton (now Tell el-Amarna). *EB*, I. 629.

94. *EB*, I. 321.

95. *EB*, I. 629.

96. The Aton's rays end in healing hands which hold the *ankh* (life) to Akhenaton and Nefertiti in a tablet in the Staatliche Museum, Berlin.

97. E. O. James, *op. cit.*, pp206 and 302: "This ephemeral Aton cult was the first and only attempt to reduce a pantheon of polytheistic deities

to a single all-embracing heavenly Creator. Thus, Yahweh among the Hebrews was the only god of Israel."

98. To be exact, Copernicus proposed the heliocentric system in which the sun is at rest near the centre of the universe and that the earth, spinning on its axis once every day, revolves annually around the sun. Akhenaton gave priority to the sun, but there is no evidence that he approached the precision of Copernicus.

99. "Hymn to Aton", line 53, in Eliade, *From Primitives to Zen,* pp28-33.

100. R. J. Williams' introduction and translation in D. Winton Thomas (ed. by), *Documents from Old Testament Times,* in Eliade, *From Primitives to Zen,* p27. "Hymn to Aton", lines 94-8, in Eliade, *From Primitives to Zen,* pp28-33.

101. As only Akhenaton knew the Aton, he was between the Aton and the people and was worshipped as the incarnation of the Aton.

102. Eliade, *From Primitives to Zen,* p27.

103. "Hymn to Aton", line 54: "You created the earth according to your will, being alone."

104. The hieroglyphic sign denoting "life" was the *ankh.* Temple reliefs show the king being offered the *ankh* sign by the gods, suggesting that the *ankh* also represented eternal life as well as good health in this life. Shaw and Nicholson, *op. cit.,* p34.

105. See note 101.

106. See note 95.

107. *EB,* 1. 402: "The funerary religion dropped Osiris, and Akhenaton became the source of blessings for the people after death. The figure of Nefertiti replaced the figures of protecting goddesses at the corners of a stone sarcophagus."

108. The link between the Aton and Rosicrucianism is less than evidential, and must inevitably be somewhat conjectural.

109. Author's research in Egypt; conversations with Egyptologists.

110. See list compiled by Jürgen von Beckerath, *Chronologie des pharaonischen Ägypten,* MÄS 46, Mainz, 1997, in *Egypt, the World of the Pharaohs,* ed. by Schulz and Seidel.

111. See *EB,* VI. 754: "The idea of megalith building appears to have been

spread during the Late Neolithic Period by a seafaring people moving northward through Spain, up the coast of western Europe, and into Scandinavia." Were these seafarers Egyptian? There is evidence of Egyptian trade reaching round the Mediterranean – there is evidence of trading expeditions to Syria and Nubia in the Early Dynastic Period (c.3100-c.2686 BC), see *EB*, 6. 464. There is evidence that the Egyptians colonized the East Coast of Australia, where writing in Egyptian hieroglyphic script is prolific; this colonization began c.2000 BC–seehttp://www.geocities.om/australiandesertcats/hypothesis/hypothesis.html. If the Egyptians could reach Australia c.2000 BC, why not Britain? Also see Flavia Anderson, *op. cit.*

112. Flavia Anderson, *op. cit.*; Stover and Kraig, *op. cit.*, p38: "Today we know…that Egypt is not the oldest (Mesopotamia is)."
113. Flavia Anderson, *op. cit.*
114. Booklet on Chalice Well, Glastonbury; Flavia Anderson, *op. cit.*
115. For *Neter*, the oldest ancient Egyptian word for God, see http://www.hwt-hrw.com/page6.php. "*It-Neter*" means "father of the god"; "*Hem Neter*" means "Servant of the god"; "*Jemjra Hem-Neter*" means "high priest"; "*Jemjra Hemet-Neter*" means "high priestess". "*Whmw*" means "a class of priesthood that acts as an oracle and intermediary between *Neter* and the people". It is just as likely that the axes on Stonehenge were carved by the Battle-Axe culture. For a discussion on the double-bitted *labrys* of Minoan Crete in relation to Stonehenge, see Stover and Kraig, *op. cit.*, p112.
116. Flavia Anderson, *op. cit.*; Service, *op. cit.*, p187: "The people of Avebury started to build around this mound in about 2600 BC, forming a stepped cone that rose…to a flat top. The resemblance to the step pyramids of Egypt at this stage is obvious." See Lurker, *op. cit.*, p108: "The Apophis serpent was the most pre-eminent of evil powers as the opponent of Re (i.e. Ra)." The Avebury serpent went through the sun's disk, according to Dr William Stukeley (1687-1765): "An illustration drawn by Stukeley for his book on Avebury shows a great stone serpent whose head rested at the now-destroyed

Sanctuary on Overton Hill and whose body was formed by West Kennet Avenue and Beckhampton Avenue. The 'bulge' of Avebury in the body of the serpent Stukeley explained as a circle through which the serpent is passing." See http://www.britannia.com/wonder/stukeley.html.

117. Flavia Anderson, *op. cit.*

118. Crow, *op. cit.*, pp36-7.

119. Dr. W. J. Perry, quoted in Flavia Anderson, *op. cit.*

120. Stover and Kraig, *op. cit.*, p106: "What megalithic tombs seem to have in common, apart from stone construction, is some astronomical bearing specifically with the sun. The entranceways of British and Breton passage graves most often face eastward, as do the higher ends of the long barrows where the burials are deposited."

121. However, see *EB*, VI. 754: "All of the monuments share certain architectural and technical features, demonstrating that the disseminators of the megalith idea came to dominate the local populations of many areas. The carving of similar magical symbols on many of the monuments also shows an underlying unity of beliefs."

122. Stover and Kraig, *op. cit.*, pp73-7, on dagger and axe carvings on stone no. 53.

123. Stover and Kraig, *op. cit.*, p75; Stover and Kraig, *op. cit.*, p107, give the analogy of graffiti by artists spraying the name of Norman Mailer on the home of William Shakespeare.

124. Crow, *op. cit.*, pp35-7.

4. The Aegean-Greek Light

1. Gimbutas, *op. cit.*, pp368 (account of expansion of Kurgans towards N, Greece c.3500), pp372-3 (Kurgan apsidal houses in Macedonia, N.E. Greece, Central and Southern Greece); and p385 (map of Kurgan expansion from c.3500 BC), pp387-9 (the Vučedol shift south).

2. E. O. James, *op. cit.*, p41. O'Brien, *The Megalithic Odyssey*, p144. For Pelasgians, see *EB*, 8. 407: "As waves of Greek-speaking peoples

moved south into the peninsula during the 2nd millennium BC, they absorbed Pelasgian (pre-Greek) cults such as those of the primitive oracle at Dodona."

3. E. O. James, *op. cit.*, p42; Stover and Kraig, *op. cit.*, pp65-70 (Battle-Axe) and 71, 74-6 (Mycenaeans).
4. E. O. James, *op. cit.*, pp70, 75.
5. Eliade, *Shamanism*, p10: "The only great god after the God of the Sky or the Atmosphere is, among the Altaians, the Lord of the Underworld, Erlik (=Ärlik) Khan." Burkert, *op. cit.*, p287: "A grotto (i.e. in Eleusis)...was dedicated to Pluto, Lord of the Underworld."
6. Burkert, *op. cit.*, pp46 (*wanax*), 50 on divine kingship.
7. The Delphic oracle probably came from Anatolia; E. O. James, *op. cit.*, p243. For the Delphic oracle's originating in the Mycenaean period, see E. O. James, *op. cit.*, p242. The origin of the Delphic oracle is conventionally dated to the very end of the 9th century BC; see *The Classical Oxford Dictionary*, p445, and Burkert, *op. cit.*, p114.
8. Apollo may have come from Anatolia; his cult on Delos can be dated to the 8th century BC. The Homeric "Hymn to Apollo" (see Eliade, *From Primitives to Zen*, pp52-4) can be dated to the 7th century BC for the Delian part and perhaps the 5th century BC for the Delphic part. He was very early identified with the sun, and so with the sun-god Hyperion who is invoked by the 7th-century BC Hesiod (*Theogony. 371ff, cf134ff*). In the Homeric Hymn he is referred to as Phoebus (*phoibos*) Apollo some half-a-dozen times, and is addressed as Lord Phoebus, suggesting that his role was from the outset similar to that of Shamash.
9. See notes 2 and 8.
10. E. O. James, *op. cit.*, pp41-2.
11. E. O. James, *op. cit.*, pp67-8.
12. Burkert, *op. cit.*, p37: "The horns and the double axe..., after a long pre-history which begins in Anatolia,...finally reached the shores of Crete."
13. See "The Indo-European Kurgan Light", note 9.
14. Burkert, *op. cit.*, p37-8.

15. Burkert, *op. cit.*, p64; also E. O. James, *op. cit.*, p131.
16. Burkert, *op. cit.*, p64; *EB*, VI. 922. For Minos as a dynastic title rather than an individual, see Diodorus Siculus, 4.60.2-5, who distinguishes between two Minoses over three generations; quoted in *The Oxford Classical Dictionary.*
17. E. O. James, *op. cit.*, p133 (Mount Ida); *The Oxford Classical Dictionary*, p408, quoting Strabo 10.4.8; Plato, *Leg.* 624a, *Minos* 319b; Homer, *Odyssey*, 19.179. The normally excellent Burkert, quoting the same sources, *op. cit.*, p25 states *eight* years instead of nine.
18. Burkert, *op. cit.*, p29; *The Oxford Classical Dictionary*, p987 (*labrys*).
19. E. O. James, *op. cit.*, p130.
20. E. O. James, *op. cit.*, pp131-2.
21. E. O. James, *op. cit.*, pp41-2; *EB*, 1. 115-6.
22. In the National Museum, Athens; see illustration in Sinclair Hood, *The Arts in Pre-historic Greece*, p163.
23. Rosettes "picture-frame" a draughtboard from the palace at Knossos c.1600 – Hood, *op. cit.*, p118. As the influence of the neolithic Great Mother (*Magna Mater*) declined so the influence of the Egyptian sun-cult increased.
24. E. O. James, *op. cit.*, p43.
25. See "The Syrian Light", note 4, which shows that the cult of Baal was known from c.1500 BC. Anat was Baal's sister. See *EB*, 1. 115-7 for migrations to Greece and Crete from Anatolia. E. O. James, *op. cit.*, p226. Also *EB*, 8. 407: "(The Mycenaeans) came into contact with the Minoan nature religion. As a result, Zeus himself acquired a Cretan origin as well as a consort in…Hera. Athena, the palace guardian, became Zeus's daughter." Athena was adopted by the Mycenaeans from Anatolia via Crete, where she was Anat. But see Burkert, *op. cit.*, p139: "Whether the goddess is named after the city or the city after the goddess is an ancient dispute….The goddess most probably takes her name from the city; she is the Pallas of Athens." (Pallas is obscure; it was interpreted sometimes as "Maiden", and sometimes as "weapon-brandishing". However, see *EB*, I. 617: "She is

associated primarily with Athens, to which she gave her name." Compare Burkert, *op. cit.*, p138: "...the introduction of the horse and war-chariot from Anatolia to Greece about 1600...." Burkert, *op. cit.*, p37: "After a long pre-history which begins in Anatolia, (horns and the double axe) finally reached the shores of Crete."

26. Athena Parthenos.
27. *EB*, I. 343; *EB*, I. 617.
28. *EB*, I. 617.
29. Booklets about the Greek island of Aegina, from where the spear tip could be seen glinting in the sun.
30. The Parthenon was built between 447 and 438 BC, and external decorations and carvings continued until 432 BC. Its frieze and sculptures embodied the central idea between the withdrawal of the Persians and the war with Sparta. See *EB*, VII. 774. The gold and ivory statue of Athena guarded the Athenian Light.
31. E. O. James, *op. cit.*, p45.
32. "Bull's flesh", see the Dionysiac section, (p72); "Ear of corn", see the Eleusinian section (p73); and fire, see the Orphic section (p75).
33. Ferguson, *op. cit.*, p125: "Mystery. From the Greek word *myein* 'to keep one's mouth shut', hence a secret revealed to initiates and generally not to be disclosed to others." Also, "Mystery, from root of *muein* to close (the lips or eyes)" – *Shorter Oxford English Dictionary.* Also "Mystic, from *mustes* one intiated into mysteries" – *Shorter Oxford English Dictionary.* For *mustes* in mysteries, see Burkert, *op. cit.*, pp286-7.
34. E. O. James, *op. cit.*, p226.
35. E. O. James, *op. cit.*, p226.
36. Burkert, *op. cit.*, pp290-2.
37. Ferguson, *op. cit.*, p48.
38. Ferguson, *op. cit.*, p49.
39. *EB*, III. 561 ('Dionysus').
40. See E. O. James, *op. cit.*, p226 for Dionysiac bull-eating and Zeus; *The Oxford Classical Dictionary*, pp480-1.
41. Burkert, *op. cit.*, pp223-5.

42. Burkert, *op. cit.*, p116; E. O. James, *op. cit.*, pp242-4.
43. Goblet D'Alviella, *The Mysteries of Eleusis*, page before title page.
44. D'Alviella, *op. cit.*, pp19-23; James, *op. cit.*, pp164-5.
45. Ferguson, *op. cit.*, p53.
46. For the Eleusinian *Philosophoumena*, Ferguson, *op. cit.*, p53. For the "wonderful light", see Plutarch, *De Anima*, fragm VI, 2, quoted on D'Alviella, *op. cit.*, p21. Also, E. O. James, *op. cit.*, pp163-5.
47. D'Alviella, *op. cit.*, p25.
48. For the analogy between grain and the spirit, see D'Alviella, *op. cit.*, p39: "Just as our farmers are mindful of preventing spoilage of the grain, which carries the future harvest in its bud, so our distant forefathers endeavoured to prevent the spirit, which had to give life to the following harvest, from disappearing or degenerating while awaiting the sowing season. Now the spirit as well as the body is exposed to old age and decay. It was thus prudent to allow it to undergo a rejuvenation, to bring it to a rebirth." Compare A. Bothwell-Gosse, *The Lily of Light*, p3: "Man was taught…to subject his soul to be cultivated…, by sharing figuratively in the various agricultural operations, thereby inducing spiritual growth."
49. For the first two quotations, see Scholiast on Aristophanes, *The Frogs*, 158; and *Ephemeris Archaiologike*, journal of the Archaeological Society at Athens, 1883, p82. For the last quotation see *Homeri Carmina, In Cererem*, line 480ff. A different translation is in Ferguson, *op. cit.*, p54 and D'Alviella, *op. cit.*, p23.
50. Hippolytus, *Philosophoumena*, v.8; Plutarch, *On the Soul*, quoted in Stobaues IV, trans. by George Mylonas in D'Alviella, *Eleusis and the Eleusinian Mysteries*.
51. D'Alviella, *op. cit.*, p84.
52. Ferguson, *op. cit.*, p136.
53. Ferguson, *op. cit.*, p137.
54. Ferguson, *op. cit.*, p137.
55. Ferguson, *op. cit.*, p137.
56. E. O. James, *op. cit.*, p285; see *The Classical Oxford Dictionary*, p1079, for Orphic abstention.

57. See Ferguson, *op. cit.*, p137; and E. O. James, *op. cit.*, pp225-6 for Phanes as Light.
58. E. O. James, *op. cit.*, pp284-5 (Pythagoreans) and 289-90 (Plato). Around 530 BC Pythagoras emigrated to Croton in southern Italy, where Orphism was established. Burkert, *op. cit.*, pp296-301 ("Orpheus and Pythagoras").
59. Ward Rutherford, *Pythagoras, Lover of Wisdom*, p11. The northern Hyperboreans were also thought by some to be the British.
60. Burkert, *op. cit.*, p300.
61. Rutherford, *Pythagoras, op. cit.*, p11.
62. Rutherford, *Pythagoras, op. cit.*, pp80-2.
63. *EB*, 14. 539; Rutherford, *Pythagoras, op. cit.*, p59.
64. Burkert, *op. cit.*, pp325-6 (Orphism). Plato, *Phaedrus* 250, c: "pure was the light that shone around us, and pure were we, without taint of that prison house which now we are encompassed withal, and call a body, fast bound therein as an oyster in its shell."
65. Plato, *Republic*, VII, 514-5. "Subterranean cavern" is mentioned in the first three lines of Book VII.
66. James, *op. cit.*, pp289-90.
67. Plato, *Republic* VII, 540, translated in Hamilton and Cairns as: "We shall require them to turn upward the vision of their souls and fix their gaze on that which sheds light on all, and when they have thus beheld the good itself they shall use it as a pattern for the right ordering of the state."
68. Plato, *Cratylus* 439c and *Phaedo*, 65d, 75d, 78d, 100b. See *EB*, 14. 536: "The Good is the supreme beauty that dawns suddenly upon the pilgrim of love as he draws near to his goal....The Good holds the place taken in later philosophers by the God who is thought of as the 'Light of the world'."
69. Plato is held to have believed that Greek philosophy came from the "fountains (or springs?) of the West" – for example Italy and Sicily; i.e. from the Orphic and Eleusinian mysteries, and not from the east. There is no reference to Plato's belief in *The Collected Dialogues*, ed. by Hamilton and Cairns. Arguably the inspiration for the western

"origin" came from the east. See "The Meso-American Light", note 22.

70. *EB*, 14. 532: "On the execution of Socrates in 399 BC, Plato and other Socratic men took temporary refuge at Megara with Euclid....The next few years are said to have been spent in extensive travels in Greece, in Egypt, and in Italy." If Plato did become an initiate at the Temple of Isis at On, Heliopolis, it would have been between the execution of Socrates in 399 BC and his founding of the Academy about 387 BC.

71. Plato's Light passed through Julius Caesar and Mark Antony to Egypt. See "The Roman Light", note 17.

5. The Roman Light

1. For the c.1200 BC date, see *EB*, 15. 1085: the legendary founding of Rome by the Trojan Aeneas in the 12th century BC may have been an early Etruscan contact. The legend was familiar to Etruscans from the 6th century BC. For c.800 BC onwards, see *EB*, III. 984. Rome was founded by Romulus in c.754 BC.

2. E. O. James, *op. cit.*, p75; Burkert, *op. cit.*, p17; *EB*, 15. 1060.

3. *EB*, 15. 1061: having expelled the Etruscan kings, Rome, faced with a shortage of grain, arranged for grain to be imported from Cumae. Greek religion was imported with it, including the Olympian gods, the Sibyl of Cumae and Cumaean notions of the Underworld. (A temple is said to have been dedicated to a Sibyl in 493 BC – E. O. James, *op. cit.*, p248.)

4. *The Oxford Classical Dictionary*, p123: "Apollo's arrival in Rome during a plague in 433 BC was due to a recommendation of the Sibylline Books (Livy 4.25.3): to avert the plague, a Temple of Apollo Medicus was vowed and built...where there had already been an Apollinar, presumably an open cult-place of the god (Livy 3.63.7, for the year 449)." The temple was built in 432 BC – *The Oxford Companion to Classical Literature*, p34 – and completed in 431 BC.

5. For *rex sacrorum*, see *EB*, 15. 1065, 1086. *The Oxford Classical Dictionary*, p1311.
6. *EB*, 15. 1061; Joscelyn Godwin, *Mystery Religions in the Ancient World*, p38.
7. *EB*, 15. 1121. The cult of Isis was first introduced at the time when Julius Caesar, Mark Antony and Octavian all had contact with Cleopatra. For the 3rd-century pagan Alexandrian Lights, see pp401-9.
8. *EB*, 15. 1063: "*Garhapatya*, 'house-father's fire.'"
9. *The Oxford Companion to Classical Literature*, p178.
10. For Sol, see *The Oxford Classical Dictionary*, pp1420-1. For Sol in alchemy, see, for example, Salomen Trismosin, *Splendor solis* ("Splendour of the Sun"), 1598 – *EB*, 1. 435. Many texts show a sun in an alchemist's cauldron.
11. *EB*, 15. 1064-5.
12. *The Oxford Classical Dictionary*, p917: "The Elect, to whom all worldly occupations and possessions were forbidden,…." Ferguson, *op. cit.*, p115: "Escape from mortifying the body, through an extreme asceticism, including vegetarianism and abstenance from sex."
13. H. R. Ellis Davidson, *Gods and Myths of Northern Europe*, pp55, 56, 70, 140-1 (Mercury); 82, 86 (Hercules); 57 (Mars).
14. *The Oxford Companion to Classical Literature*, p205.
15. *The Oxford Classical Dictionary*, pp1420-1 (Sol/Jupiter, *Sol Invictus*); 992 (Sol/Mithras).
16. *The Oxford Classical Dictionary*, p213. Also see note 15 for Jupiter/Sol.
17. The Egyptian Royal Mysteries worshipped the Pharaoh and his parents. Mark Antony adopted Dionysus in Athens by 39 BC, and he and Cleopatra could now be presented as Osiris (identified with Dionysus) and Isis, linked in a sacred marriage for Asia's prosperity – *The Oxford Classical Dictionary*, p115. Octavian/Augustus made Apollo his special god as a reaction to this – *The Oxford Classical Dictionary*, p123. As a result of Cleopatra's relationships with Julius Caesar, by whom she had a son, Caesarion/Horus, and Mark Antony, the Greek Mysteries passed into the Egyptian Royal Mysteries: Demeter

(Eleusis) into Isis/Cleopatra; Dionysus into Osiris/Mark Antony; with Orpheus also identified with Osiris as both were torn to pieces.

18. This pattern (Pharaoh as Horus etc.) applied until Cleopatra, who became Isis, her son becoming Horus. Isis was identified with Cybele via Demeter – see note 21.
19. Horus became identified with Apollo under Augustus, who took Apollo as his main god – see note 17. Augustus was Pharaoh/Horus/Apollo.
20. *The Oxford Classical Dictionary*, p676-7.
21. Herodotus, 2. 59, 156.5; quoted in *The Oxford Classical Dictionary*, p768. Also Godwin, *op. cit.*, pp120-1.
22. *The Oxford Companion to Classical Literature*, pp299, 391.
23. Aristides, *Orat Sac*, III, p500 ("from Isis a Light"); Porphyry, *De Mysteriis*, II. 8 ("the eye of the body"); Apuleius, *Golden Ass*, p286.
24. Ellis Davidson, *op. cit.*, pp140-1, 219-221.
25. Jessie Weston, *From Ritual to Romance*, pp157 (Vegetation Deity as Attis-Adonis) and 204 (Christian God).
26. Weston, *op. cit.*, pp8, 90, 150 (Attis-Adonis), and 204 (Christ).
27. Weston, *op. cit.*, pp165 (quoting Cumont), 204.
28. Weston, *op. cit.*, pp146 (Attis-Adonis) and 148 (Eucharist).
29. D'Alviella, *op. cit.*, pp116-8.
30. Quoted in D'Alviella, *op. cit.*, p107.
31. D'Alviella, *op. cit.*, pp107-8.
32. Godwin, *op. cit.*, p121.
33. Ean Begg, *The Cult of the Black Virgin*, p14.
34. Begg, *op. cit.*, pp14 and 133-5 (Rocamadour).
35. *EB*, 15. 1065: "Constantine the Great declared the sun his Comrade on Empire-wide coinages and devoted himself to the cult until he adopted Christianity in its stead." Also *The Oxford Classical Dictionary*, p1421. Constantine was converted to Christianity in 312 and became Emperor of both East and West in 323. The chief imperial worship of Jupiter-Sol then ended.
36. George Jowett, *The Drama of the Lost Disciples*, ch XVIII; Corbett, *op. cit.*, pp33-5.

6. The Anatolian Light

1. *EB*, V. 67: "Probably originating from the area beyond the Black Sea."
2. *EB*, V. 67: "Hittites, ancient Indo-European people who appeared in Anatolia at the beginning of the 2nd millennium BC." Also see, *EB*, 1. 815: "The third phase of the Early Bronze Age (the final centuries of the 3rd millennium BC) appears to have been a time of major migrations. About 2300 BC a great wave of Indo-European invaders, speaking a Luwian dialect, seems to have swept over Anatolia from the west, occupying practically the whole southwestern part of the peninsula." For Hittites taking over the land of the Hatti, see E. O. James, *op. cit.*, p32 and the Hattic (or Hattian) language see *EB*, IV. 948.
3. *EB*, 1. 817.
4. *EB*, 1. 818.
5. *EB*, 1. 819. See*EB*, IX. 8 for Achaeans/Ahhiyawa as Sea Peoples, and *EB*, I. 56 for identification of the Achaeans with the Mycenaeans.
6. *EB*, 1. 821.
7. *EB*, 10. 307; and *EB*, V. 463 ("Israelite").
8. *EB*. 1. 821.
9. *EB*, 2. 191. For the relationship between the Hittite king and the Storm and Weather god, see E. O. James, *op. cit.*, pp93,127-130.
10. *EB*, 2. 191: "The king and queen were her (Arinna's) high priest and priestess."
11. *EB*, 2. 191: "She (Arinna) is always called a sun goddess, and sun disks appear as emblems in her cult, but there are indications that she may originally have had chthonic, or underworld, characteristics." Hence her similarity to Apollo.
12. *EB*, 2. 191 (Istanu); and *EB*. 1. 1058 (Shams).
13. *EB*. 1. 821.
14. *EB*, 2. 192: soon after Hattusas fell c.1180 BC, the Luwians moved eastward. The East Luwians' chief goddess was Kubaba, who later became Cybele. Attis was part of the Cybele cult myth. Cybele was known in Greek and Roman literature from 5th century BC onward – see *EB*, IV. 700.

15. For Attis, see Ferguson, *op. cit.*, pp42-3 and *EB*, 2. 193. Also E. O. James, *op. cit.*, pp97-8. For Corybantes and dervishes, see Jessie Weston, *op. cit.*, p90.
16. Ferguson, *op. cit.*, pp42-3; the Christian Prudentius, *Peristephanon*, X. 1011-50, in Eliade, *From Primitives to Zen*, *op. cit.*, pp302-3.
17. Ferguson, *op. cit.*, p43; Godwin, *op. cit.*, p111; *The Oxford Classical Dictionary*, p416; E. O. James, *op. cit.*, pp97-8.
18. S. Angus, *The Mystery Religions and Christianity*, pp135-6; in Eliade, *From Primitives to Zen*, *op. cit.*, p304.
19. Weston, *op. cit.*, p146.
20. *The Oxford Classical Dictionary*, p416: "By the 5th century BC Cybele was known in Greece." For the Phrygian cap, see *EB*, VII. 973.

7. The Syrian Light

1. The cult of Dumuzi-Tammuz was found in most of the major cities of Sumer in the 3rd and 2nd millennia BC and was known before c.2600 BC – see *EB*, IX. 796. Adonis was identified with Tammuz – see *EB*, I. 97. The Adonis cult gradually emerged alongside the Tammuz cult. Also see *EB*, 1. 97; *The Oxford Classical Dictionary*, p12.
2. Hippolytus, *Philosophoumena*, or *The Refutation of all Heresies*, pp185-6:

   "Hail Attis, thou mournful song of Rhea!
   Assyrians call thee thrice-longed-for Adonis;
   All Egypt calls thee Osiris…"

   Weston, quoting this passage, comments on "this practical identification of all the Mystery-gods with the Vegetation Deity Adonis-Attis." See Weston, *op. cit.*, pp156-7.
3. E. O. James, *op. cit.*, p297.
4. Hooke, *op. cit.*, p81; E. O. James, *op. cit.*, pp91, 122-3. For 1500 BC, see *EB*, I. 703: "Knowledge of Baal's personality and functions derives chiefly from a number of tablets uncovered from 1929 onward at Ugarit (modern Ras Shamra), in northern Syria, and dating to the middle of the 2nd millennium BC.…The worship of Baal was

popular from the 14th century BC onward in Egypt."

5. *EB*, I. 703.
6. Weston, *op. cit.*, pp35, 37-8, 99, 157. Compare D'Alviella, *op. cit.*, p39, quoted in "The Aegean-Greek Light", note 48; and Bothwell Gosse, *The Lily of Light*, pp2-3.

8. The Israelite Light

1. Hooke, *op. cit.*, pp103-4 for "first Hebrew" and "middle of 18th century BC". The temple to Nanna on the Ur Ziggurat (22nd-21st centuries BC) predates Abraham. Also, *EB*, 17. 939-40, 1.12.
2. *EB*, 1.11-12.
3. On the *stele* of Hammurabi, the king is represented as receiving the collection of laws known as the Code of Hammurabi from Shamash. See "The Mesopotamian Light", note 36. Also, Hooke, *op. cit.*, p147.
4. *EB*, 1. 12.
5. *EB*, X. 786: Vowels were added to the consonants of YHWH, making YeHoWaH, i.e. Jehovah. Christian scholars after the Renaissance and Reformation used Jehovah in place of YHWH. 19th and 20th century scholars restored Yahweh.
6. *EB*, X. 786: "The meaning of the personal name of the Israelite God has been variously interpreted. Many scholars believe the most proper meaning maybe He Brings Into Existence Whatever Exists (*Yahweh-Asher-Yahweh*)" – i.e., Creator, First Cause. See also E. O. James, *op. cit.*, p217.
7. For the two locations, see Laurence Gardner, *Lost Secrets of the Sacred Ark*, p4.
8. Nigel Pennick, *The Mysteries of King's College Chapel*, pp86-8.
9. See Leo Schaya, *The Meaning of the Temple*, pp362-4, which confirms from the oral tradition of Talmudic and rabbinical writings that the Tabernacle contained the Divine Light. For the *Shekinah*, see Hooke, *op. cit.*, pp146, 151-2, referring to *Exodus* 33.7: "When he (Moses) entered into the Tent the pillar of cloud, the *Shekinah*, descended and

stood at the door of the Tent and Yahweh talked with Moses out of the cloud, while all the people watched from their tent-doors."

10. Corbett, *op. cit.*, pp48-9.
11. Corbett, *op. cit.*, pp48-9.
12. For Judah/Israel, see Jowett, *op. cit.*, p223.
13. *EB*, X. 258 (Assyrian reliefs). Also Corbett, *op. cit.*, pp48-9.

9. The Celtic Light

1. *EB*, 3. 194, 1071.
2. *EB*, 3. 1073-4.
3. *EB*, 3. 194.
4. *EB*, 3. 1074; for Nemi, see note 16.
5. *EB*, 3. 1074. For Gauls, see *EB*, 7. 960. For lack of temples, see *EB*, 3. 1071. For Stonehenge III, see Stover and Kraig, *op. cit.*, pp80-1.
6. *EB*, III. 674: "The earliest known records of the Druids come from the 3rd century BC."
7. Morgan, *op. cit.*, p14. See Rev C. C. Dobson, *Did our Lord Visit Britain as they Say in Cornwall and Somerset?*, for a note on Morgan's great scholarship and reliability.
8. Morgan, *op. cit.*, p14.
9. Morgan, *op. cit.*, p14.
10. Morgan, *op. cit.*, p14; *EB*, 3. 1069. For Beli/Apollo, see *EB*, 3. 1070; and Rutherford, *The Druids*, p131.
11. Morgan, *op. cit.*, p15; Elder, *Celt, Druid and Culdee*, p65.
12. Elder, *Celt, Druid and Culdee*, pp89-90.
13. See note 14.
14. *EB*, 3. 1071 (*dru-vid*) and Rutherford, *The Druids*, p67 (*dru-vid*); Elder, *Celt, Druid and Culdee*, p52 (*dru-thin*).
15. *EB*, 3. 1069.
16. See Elder Pliny, *Natural History*, for the cutting of the mistletoe. Quoted in Herm, *op. cit.*, p143; see Frazer, *The Golden Bough*, p930 for God's incarnation in mistletoe.

17. Rutherford, *The Druids*, pp24-5; *EB*, 3. 1071.
18. Rutherford, *The Druids*, pp24-6.
19. *EB*, 3. 1069 (pantheon);
20. For Awen, see http://www.druidorder.demon.co.uk/awen.htm. The first recorded reference to the Druid pagan Awen was in Nennius' *Historia Brittonum* (c.796), which was based on earlier writings by the Welsh monk Gildas. He refers to Talhearn "Tad Awen" ("the Father of Awen") during the reign of King Ida of Northumbria (547-559). Awen means flowing (*aw*) spirit (*en*), and is found in Welsh poems from the 6th to 13th centuries, particularly in the *Book of Taliesin* where the poem "The Chair of the Sovereign" refers to "the three Awens", chants "similar to the Hindu Om or Aum". The medieval poem "The Hostile Confederacy" says: "The Awen I sing,/From the deep I bring it,/A river while it flows." There are references to obtaining Awen by drinking from the cauldron of the goddess Ceridwen. The Awen also descends in the form of a hawk according to the poet Henry Vaughan, in a letter to John Aubrey. Awen is paralleled by the Hindu goddess-spirit Shakti – and Kundalini – and by Ceridwen, the giver of Awen; also by Dan or Dana, or Danu or Anu, the goddess of the Tuatha de Danaan (or tribe of Danu). Awen is like the Melanesian Mana. For the "ineffable name of the Deity", see Morgan, *op. cit.*, p15, who also states: "The Druids, contrary to the Mosaic account, made the creation of man simultaneous with that of solar light."
21. Morgan, *op. cit.*, p15: "The symbol of the ineffable name of the Deity (was) three rays or glories of light."
22. Rutherford, *Shamanism*, p37: "Caesar mentions the Druidic custom of measuring time by nights rather than days, a relic of which survives in our own 'fortnight' or 'fourteen nights'."
23. It is likely that the acorn, the fruit of the oak, was the staple food of the Celts.
24. The common source would be the Indo-Europeans, whose culture emerged in Mesopotamia and thence Egypt, and in the Celts.
25. Morgan, *op. cit.*, pp14-15. Jowett, *op. cit.*, p78.

26. Jowett, *op. cit.*, pp200-5, 73, 116. For Lug, see *EB*, 3. 1069 and Herm, *op. cit.*, p155-6.
27. Flavia Anderson, *op. cit.* (Trinity); and Elder, *Celt, Druid and Culdee*, p66 (tree). Schedius, *Treatise de Mor. Germ*, xxiv and Thomas Maurice, *Indian Antiquities*, vol VI, p49; cited in Elder, *op. cit.* above, pp 66,70.
28. Elder, *Celt, Druid and Culdee*, p66.
29. Elder, *Celt, Druid and Culdee*, pp67-8.
30. Elder, *Celt, Druid and Culdee*, pp85-6 (festivals); Morgan, *op. cit.*, p15 (germs/Creation) and Ferguson, *op. cit.*, p107 (Logos): around Plato's time, "the Jewish thinkers began to fill the gap between God and man with…the *Memra* or Word of god: in *Genesis* God speaks and it is done; His Word is His self-expression and it is with power. Jews in Alexandria, of whom Philo is the best known, desirous of bringing together Greek and Jewish insights, equated this with the Logos." There may be Jewish influence on the Druid Creator's speaking his name.
31. Jowett, *op. cit.*, pp204-6.
32. *EB*, III. 380.
33. Rev. L. S. Lewis, *St Joseph of Arimathaea at Glastonbury*, pp191-4.
34. *EB*, I. 554: "Assumptions that a historical Arthur led Welsh resistance to the West Saxon Advance from the middle Thames are based on a conflation of two early chroniclers, Gildas and Nennius, and on the *Annales Cambriae* (c.950-1000)."
35. Details of Arthur's legendary and allegedly historical life can be found in many books, for example Richard Barber, *King Arthur in Legend and History* and Geoffrey Ashe, *King Arthur's Avalon.*
36. *EB*, 3. 200. See Elder, *Celt, Druid and Culdee*, pp120-4 for British suspicion and scorn at Rome's attempt to convert the English. Also see note 39.
37. Quoted in Morgan, *op. cit.*, p 125. See Bede, *Ecclesiastical History of the English People*, bk 3, ch 29.
38. In Bede, *Ecclesiastical History of the English People* (Penguin), 60 BC ends on p48 and AD 156 begins on p49. For the marginalizing of the Celtic Church, see Harry Rosenberg, "The West in Crisis", in *The History of Christianity* (Lion Handbook), p222.

39. See *EB*, 3. 284-5; Elder, *Celt, Druid and Culdee*, pp134-5 for Irish Celtic decline. See *EB*, 3. 202 for invasions of Norsemen. Also see Harry Rosenberg "The West in Crisis", in *The History of Christianity* (Lion Handbook), pp221-4: "Celtic Christians object".

10. The Iranian Light

1. Herm, *op. cit.*, p78.
2. For 2250 BC see McEvedy, *op. cit.*, pp24-5, which shows a map of Iranians moving to what is now Iran in c.2250 BC. For 1700 BC, see *EB*, 9. 867. For 1500 BC, see *EB*, 12. 288: "In a cuneiform tablet of the 15th century BC…Mithra (i.e. Mithras) is invoked as the god of oath."
3. *EB*, 9. 868.
4. See *EB*, 9. 872. Also *EB*, 19. 1174 (Gushnasp). The sacred fire at Gushnasp is referred to in the Zoroastrian "general confession" – see R. C. Zaehner, *The Teachings of the Magi*, p121.
5. *EB*, 19. 1171.
6. *EB*, 19. 1169-70; Raymond Van Over, *Eastern Mysticism*, p289.
7. *EB*, 19. 1169-71.
8. *EB*, 19. 1169-70.
9. *EB*, 12. 288-90.
10. *EB*, 9. 870.
11. *EB*, 19. 1173.
12. Van Over, *op. cit.*, pp295-9, and Champion and Short, *Readings from World Religions*, pp92-5 (Yashts/Gathas). E. W. F. Tomlin, *Philosophers of East and West*, p106 (*Dadistan-i-Dinik).*
13. E. O. James, *op. cit.*, pp279-80.
14. *EB*, VI. 482-3: "It is disputed whether the Magi were from the beginning followers of Zoroaster….Rather it appears that they constituted a priesthood serving several religions. The Magi were a priestly caste….From the 1st century AD onward the word in its Syriac form (Magusai) was applied to magicians and soothsayers, chiefly from Babylonia." In other words, before the 1st century AD the Magi taught the idea behind several religions, i.e. the Light.

15. *EB*, VI. 483: "As long as the Persian Empire lasted there was always a distinction between the Persian Magi, who were credited with profound religious knowledge, and the Babylonian Magi, who were often considered to be imposters." After Cyrus, the Persian Magi taught in Chaldean Babylon, and "as early as the 3rd century, the Magi were thought of as kings". The Magi were dualists; Aristotle said in *Peri philosophias* ("On Philosophy") "that the Magi preached the existence of two principles, Oromasdes and Areimanios" – see *EB*, 19. 1173.
16. *EB*, VI. 483 ("magician"): "The name derives from the Persian Magi." And *EB*, VI. 482 ("Magi"): "From it the word magic is derived."
17. Champion and Short, *op. cit.*, p85; and *EB*, 19. 1176. For a picture of the Fire-temple at Naqsh-e-Rostam (also known as Naqsh-i-Rustam), see *Encyclopedia of World Religions*, Octopus, pp134-5.
18. *EB*, 9. 870.
19. Ferguson, *op. cit.*, pp120-2; *EB*, 12. 289; E. O. James, *op. cit.*, pp317-8. Also see Zaehner, *The Teachings of the Magi*, p128 (Primal Bull).
20. See Godwin, *op. cit.*, p56: "The king may even be a god himself, descended to earth in a temporary physical body for the benefit of mortals....The situation is closely paralleled in Tibet, whose Dalai Lamas are regarded as *Tulkus* (incarnations) of Avalokiteshvara (i.e. Avalokitesvara)."
21. Godwin, *op. cit.*, pp56-7.
22. Godwin, *op. cit.*, p98, which states that the cult of Mithras was officially recognised in Rome in the later 2nd century AD.
23. E. O. James, *op. cit.*, p318
24. *EB*, 12. 290; Franz Cumont, *Mysteries of Mithra*, pp2, 89, 97, 162-4, 180.
25. *EB*, 12. 290; Flavia Anderson, *op. cit.*, pp251-2.
26. E. O. James, *op. cit.*, p317; *EB*, 12. 289-90; Cumont, *op. cit.*
27. By Godwin, *op. cit.*, p98.
28. Ferguson, *op. cit.*, p121; Cumont, *op. cit.*, pp2, 89, 97, 162-4, 180.
29. Ahura Mazda and Mithra represented the Lord of Truth, which would burn The Lie – Champion and Short, *op. cit.*, p85.

30. Champion and Short, *op. cit.*, p85.
31. In Zaehner, *The Teachings of the Magi*, p26; quoting *Pahlavi Texts*, pp41-50.
32. Menok i Khrat, 1.94; in Eliade, *From Primitives to Zen*, *op. cit.*, p361.
33. *EB*, 16. 438.
34. *EB*, 16. 440; *EB*, 9. 868-9.
35. Tamara Talbot Rice, *The Scythians*, pp85-6.
36. *EB*, VIII. 904.
37. *EB*, 19. 1172.
38. *EB*, 9. 870: "The Sasanian period is noted for the rise of a Zoroastrian state church." *EB*, 19. 1172.
39. *EB*, 19. 1174 (Farnbag). Also *EB*, 19. 1172.

11. The European Light

1. There are other claims. Ken Clayton's *Jesus Identified* adduces evidence to claim that Jesus was an Essene, Onias the Just, who was killed c.63 BC.
2. I have seen Gururaj, the founder of the British Meditation Society, go into divine union with the Light. Half a dozen of those present (I was not one of them) reported that they saw his aura turn lilac and shine.
3. For "*Gestapo*", see Jowett, *op. cit.*, ch 4, title: "The Saulian *Gestapo* and the Exodus AD 36." For a vivid description of the Reign of Terror against Christians in which Paul enthusiastically participated, see Ernle Bradford, *Paul the Traveller*, pp54, 66-8.
4. *EB*, 13. 1090.
5. Hans Jonas, *The Gnostic Religion*, p40: "A sensational find at Nag-Hammadi (Chenoboskion) in Upper Egypt has brought to light a whole library of a gnostic community, containing in Coptic translation from the Greek hitherto unknown writings of what may be termed the 'classical' phase of gnostic literature: among them one of the major books of the Valentinians, the *Gospel of Truth*." "Naj-Hammadi" is a better spelling for the Egyptian town.

6. Jonas, *op. cit.*, pp37-8.
7. Jonas, *op. cit.*, pp42-3, 40.
8. Jonas, *op. cit.*, p37; *EB*, I. 228 (Alexandria, School of); and *EB*, 13. 734-6.
9. *EB*, I. 422 (Antioch, School of).
10. Quoted in Ferguson, *op. cit.*, p40.
11. *EB*, 4. 710, 711.
12. *EB*, VI. 302.
13. See Ferguson, *op. cit.*, p144 for Philo and the *memra.*
14. *EB*, VI. 302.
15. *EB*, 4. 711.
16. *EB*, 4. 711.
17. *EB*, 13. 735-6.
18. G. R. S. Mead's translation, pp320, 322-3, and ch 32. Quoted in Head and Cranston, *Reincarnation: The Phoenix Fire Mystery.*
19. *EB*, VI. 869.
20. See *EB*, 15. 1131-2 for anti-barbarian reaction and the Germanic hegemony (in this and next two paragraphs).
21. *EB*, 2. 364-8; and Dom Cuthbert Butler, *op. cit.*, pp96-101 (epistemological doctrine).
22. After the first literal translation, I have quoted the Penguin translation by R. S. Pine-Coffin, pp146-7, which is marginally more accurate than other versions.
23. For "*augoeides*" see G. R. S. Mead, *The Doctrine of the Subtle Body in the Western Tradition,* p59; quoted in Metzner, *Opening to Inner Light,* p86.
24. For the Western tradition of the Light via St Augustine, Pope Gregory the Great and St Bernard, and numerous references to the Light which I have not quoted, see Dom Cuthbert Butler, *op. cit.* For most of the quotations for St Augustine, see pp79-123.
25. For Dionysius, see Stace, *The Teachings of the Mystics*, pp137-8; F. C. Happold, *Mysticism,* pp36 and 63; Dom Cuthbert Butler, *op. cit.*, p68; Ferguson, *op. cit.*, pp47-8; references in Underhill, *op. cit.*; *EB*, VIII. 266; and Capps and Wright, *Silent Fire,* pp36-40.

26. *EB*, VIII. 266.
27. For most of the quotations for Pope Gregory the Great, see Dom Cuthbert Butler, *op. cit.*, pp 124-53.
28. For the West Roman Empire, see *EB*, 4. 542-5. For the quotations from St Bernard, see Dom Cuthbert Butler, *op. cit.*, pp154-180, and Capps and Wright, *op. cit.*, pp48-52.
29. *EB*, VI. 38: "Lanterns of the dead, small stone structures with windows in the upper part, in which lamps were placed to mark the position of a cemetery at night. Their use, which seems limited to western and central France, is probably due to a traditional survival of primitive Celtic rather than Christian ideas." For the Lantern of the Dead at Sarlat, see James Bentley, *A Guide to the Dordogne*, p208.
30. Ferguson, *op. cit.*, p77. Also see Capps and Wright, *op. cit.*, pp52-9; Underhill, *op. cit.*, pp115, 276. Also see, Matthew Fox, *Illuminations of Hildegard of Bingen.*
31. For Mechthild, see Ferguson, *op. cit.*, pp116-7. Also see Capps and Wright, *op. cit.*, pp78-82. For Joachim, see Ferguson, *op. cit.*, p93.
32. Capps and Wright, *op. cit.*, p63 (Father of lights); Happold, *op. cit.*, pp210-217 (*The Four Degrees of Passionate Love*).
33. For the background of the Crusades, see *EB*, 5. 304-10. For St Francis, see Ferguson, *op. cit.*, p62 (crucifix at S. Damiano) and p63 (*Canticle of the Sun*), and Ferguson, *op. cit.*, p25 (*The Little Flowers of St Francis*). Also, *EB*, 7. 682-3. Underhill, *op. cit.* and Capps and Wright, *op. cit.* For the Franciscans John of Parma, see Underhill, *op. cit*, p237; and Jacopone see Ferguson, *op. cit.*, p90.
34. For the quotations in the first two paragraphs see Ferguson, *op. cit.*, p13. Also see Capps and Wright, *op. cit.*, pp82-8. For the remaining quotations, see Angela de Foligno's *Le Livre de L'Experience des Vrais Fideles*, ed. by M. J. Ferré, English translation, pp24, 189, 186, 181. (In Underhill, *op. cit.*, pp342, 282, 331-2, 293, 350-1 and elsewhere).
35. For Bonaventura, see Underhill, *op. cit.*, pp124 (fire most truly God) and 106 (Energizing Fire).
36. The quotations are from Dante, *Paradiso*, trans. by Dorothy Sayers and Barbara Reynolds, Cantos 28-33, pp301, 319, 321, 328, 330, 343-7. For the letter to Can Grande, see William Anderson, *Dante the*

Maker, p321, which claims that the letter was written to justify Dante's claim to divine illumination. For background to Dante, see *EB*, 5. 481-5. For Dante and the Beatific Vision, see William Anderson, *Dante the Maker*, pp72-3, 153, 165, 274-5, 282-3, 296-7.

37. See Ferguson, *op. cit.*, p196.
38. For Eckhart, see Capps and Wright, *op. cit.*, p111 (spark of the soul); Underhill, *op. cit.*, p305 (God is at home); Capps and Wright, *op. cit.*, p116 (Father of lights); and Capps and Wright, *op. cit.*, p112 (ravished into the light). For the other quotations see Stace, *op. cit.*, pp157 (sermon 23) and 154 (sermon 21). Also see *EB*, 6. 187-8. Also see Happold, *op. cit.*, pp238-248.
39. For the quotations from Tauler, see Ferguson, *op. cit.*, pp190-1 (Friends) and Capps and Wright, *op. cit.*, pp129-131 (Divine illumination).
40. For the Friends of God, see Ferguson, *op. cit.*, p64. For Suso, see Ferguson, *op. cit.*, pp180-1 (Heaven/inaccessible light). See Underhill, *op. cit.*, pp186-8 for Shining Brightness, hidden light, *Servitor.*
41. For Merswin see Ferguson, *op. cit.*, p118. See Underhill, *op. cit.*, p370 for von Crevelsheim (enveloped in light).
42. For the first quotation, see Underhill, *op. cit.*, p56, and Ferguson, *op. cit.*, p194.
43. For *The Mirror of Simple Souls*, see Underhill, *op. cit.*, p219 and Ferguson, *op. cit.*, p120. For the first quotation from Ruysbroeck, see Stace, *op. cit.*, p172 (Eternal Brightness). The quotations from *The Adornment of the Spiritual Marriage*, chs 1-3, quoted in Stace, *op. cit.*, pp163-4 (para 1); 165 (para 2); and 167 (para 3). The quotation from the *Book of Supreme Truth*, ch 8, is on p170.
44. For Groote and the first quotation, see Ferguson, *op. cit.*, pp71-2. For Kempis quotations, see Kempis, *The Imitation of Christ*, pp1, 5, 62, 82-83, 117, 134, 170, 173, 182, 224-5.
45. For the quotation from Nicholas of Cusa, see Happold, *op. cit.*, p308. For background to Rolle, see Ferguson, *op. cit.*, p158 and *EB*. VIII. 641. Quotations from Rolle, *The Fire of Love*, trans. by Clifton Wolters are on pp92-3, 45, 88-9, 46, 106, 114.

46. *The Cloud of Unknowing*, ed. by Evelyn Underhill, pp58, 50, 107-8.
47. The quotations from *The Ladder of Perfection* (2.24-6) can be found in Happold, *op. cit.*, pp284-90. See p283 for Hilton and Dionysius.
48. Julian of Norwich, *Revelations of Divine Love*, trans. by Clifton Wolters, pp80, 121, 201, l80, 209, l03. For background on Julian of Norwich, see Ferguson, *op. cit.*, p96 and *EB*, V. 632.
49. For Kempe's "boisterous", see Ferguson, *op. cit.*, p100. See Langland, *Piers the Ploughman*, trans. by J. F. Goodridge, pp162-4.
50. See Ferguson, *op. cit.*, p37 for background and first paragraph on Catherine of Siena. Also *EB*, II. 642. For the quotations in paragraph 2, see Underhill, *op. cit.*, pp398, 221-2; and in paragraph 3, see Capps and Wright, *op. cit.*, pp145-8.
51. For the first paragraph (end of Renaissance), see Underhill, *op. cit.*, p467. For background to St Catherine of Genoa, see Ferguson, *op. cit.*, pp36-7. For the quotations in the second, third and fourth paragraphs, see Underhill, *op. cit.*, pp181-2, 247, 221, 202. St Catherine of Genoa's conversion can be found in Capps and Wright, *op. cit.*, pp151-5.
52. For this last point see Baron Von Hugel, *The Mystical Element of Religion as studied in St Catherine of Genoa and her Friends*, vol 2, p34. Von Hugel shows that, contrary to some comment, Catherine did not bypass the Illuminative way and pass straight from Purgation to Union, and his remarks on light and fire are worth reading: vol, 1 pp270-1, 277-8, 290-2.
53. In Villari, *Life and Times of Savonarola*, p744.
54. For the quotation from Luther, see *EB*, 11. 189.
55. In *Calvin Commentaries*, ed. by Joseph Haroutunian and Louise Pettibone Smith, p52.
56. The first four poems, *Non So Se S'è; Vorrei, Voler, Signore; E Son Giganti*; and *Un Gigante v'è Ancor*, are in *Michelangelo, a Self-Portrait*, ed. by Clements pp93, 69, 167, 76-7. The last poem is in *The Age of Adventure*, ed. by de Santillana, p155, and the phrase "metaphysics of light" is on p151.
57. The quotations from Blosius are in Dom Cuthbert Butler, *op. cit.*, pp71 and 197.

58. For the quotations from Ignatius, see Underhill, *op. cit.*, pp58 and 272.

59. The quotations from St Teresa, in order, can be found in: Capps and Wright, *op. cit.*, p179; St Teresa's autobiography, *The Life of St Teresa,* which is in Stace, *op. cit.*, pp182, 179; Underhill, *op. cit.*, p371; the *Interior Castle*, extracts of which are in Happold, *op. cit.*, pp317-8 and Stace, *op. cit.*, pp184-5; and finally in Underhill, *op. cit.*, p393.

60. The quotations from St John of the Cross, in order, can be found in: Dom Cuthbert Butler, *op. cit.*, pp206-7; Stace, *op. cit.*, p194; and *The Dark Night of the Soul*, revised Zimmerman, pp1-2, 57, 84-6, 88, 103-4, 110, 119, 175-6.

61. The poems can be found in *St John of the Cross, Poems*, trans. by Roy Campbell (who himself lived in Toledo where St John was imprisoned in 1577, and knew the Carmelite martyr Eusebio), pp45, 61, 71, 85 and 99.

62. The quotations in paragraphs 1-3 on Boehme can be found in Underhill, *op. cit.*, pp255-8 and 227; those in paragraphs 4-8 come from Boehme's *Aurora*, pp82-4, 1, 31, 34-6, 718-9, 40-3, 239-43, 706-7, 714-5 and 721. Those in paragraphs 9 and 10 can be found in Underhill, *op. cit.*, pp229-30, 119, 421, 313-4, 357, and in Capps and Wright, *op. cit.*, p 163.

63. See *John Donne, Poems*, ed. by Hayward, and *Donne's Sermons, Selected Passages with an Essay*, ed. by L. P. Smith, numbers 58, 63, 71, 81, 111, 124, 140, 146, 148.

64. See *The Metaphysical Poets*, ed. by Gardner, p137 for the first quotation from Herbert; p95 for the quotation from his brother; pp321, 267-8, 269-70, 271-2, 275-6, 277-8, and 280-1 for the quotations from Vaughan the Silurist; pp212-3 for the quotation from Crashaw; pp117-8 for the quotation from Quarles; and pp290-1 for the poetic quotation from Traherne. The quotations from *Centuries of Meditation* are in Happold, *op. cit.*, pp340-1.

65. For the Cambridge Platonists, see *EB*, II. 477. The quotations from Norris are in *The Metaphysical Poets, op. cit.*, pp303-4.

66. The quotations from Law are in Happold, *op. cit.*, pp347-352.

67. For Niclaes, see *EB*, IV. 44 (Familists). For Edward VI as Josiah, who became king of Judah c.640 BC at the age of eight, and Elizabeth I as Deborah, who inspired the Israelites to victory over their Canaanite oppressors (*Judges* 4 and 5), see Diarmaid MacCulloch, *Tudor Church Militant, Edward VI and the Protestant Reformation*, pp14-15, 18, 199.
68. For Anabaptists, see *EB*, I. 333-4. For Denck, see Ferguson, *op. cit.*, p12 (Anabaptists). For "Spark of Truth", see *EB*, III. 464.
69. *EB*, VII. 105.
70. *EB*, 2. 713.
71. *EB*, I. 421.
72. See Firth, *Oliver Cromwell and the Rule of the Puritans in England*, pp39 (Cromwell's conversion) and 470-2.
73. The quotations from Marvell are in *The Metaphysical Poets, op. cit.*, pp241 and 257.
74. The quotations from Milton's "Paradise Lost" (ed. by Darbishire) are from 1.73, 85, 245; 10.65; 3.375-380; and 3.1-52.
75. The quotations from Bunyan are in the Collins *Pilgrim's Progress*, pp15, 189, 190, 193, 195, 196, 197, 282, 273, 381.
76. The quotations in the first three paragraphs on Fox are from ch 1 of the *Journal*. They can be found in Capps and Wright, *op. cit.*, pp165-70, and the one in the fourth paragraph is in Underhill, *op. cit.*, p 178. Also see *EB*, 7. 743-6 (Friends).
77. William Penn, *No Cross, No Crown*, "The Lord's Candle"; in *The Quaker Bedside Book*, compiled by Bernard Canter, p40.
78. The quotations from *Fox's Epistles* are from pp299-300 and p14. The remaining quotations are in A. Neave Brayshaw's *The Quakers, their Story and Message*, pp 45-7, 50-1. See *The Quaker Bedside Book, op. cit.*, p39 for "the Light of Christ" and "that of God". For "that of God in every man", see *EB*, 7. 743.
79. For Nayler, see *EB*, VII. 231-2.
80. *Fox's Epistles*, see note 78.
81. In *The Quaker Bedside Book, op. cit.*, p34.
82. In *The Quaker Bedside Book, op. cit.*, p35.

83. *The Quaker Bedside Book*, *op. cit.*, p39.
84. For the quotations from Winstanley, see Ferguson, *op. cit.*, p210; and *EB*, X. 709.
85. For the quotation from St Francis of Sales, see Dom Cuthbert Butler, *op. cit.*, p73.
86. For the quotations from Father Baker, see Dom Cuthbert Butler, *op. cit.*, pp74, 204.
87. The quotation from Marie of the Incarnation is from her Autobiography, in Capps and Wright, *op. cit.*, p206.
88. The "Fire" parchment is quoted in Dom Cuthbert Butler, *op. cit.*, p74.
89. The quotations from Pascal's *Pensées* can be found, in order, in the Everyman edition, pp58, 78, 118, 156, 64, 161, 162, 71-2.
90. Ferguson, *op. cit.*, p153 (Quietism).
91. See *EB*, I. 281 (Alumbrados), which states that "exterior forms of religious life were unnecessary for those who had received the 'light.'" Compare Ferguson, *op. cit.*, p11 (Alumbrados), which does not bring out this point.
92. For the *Illuminés*, see Ferguson, *op. cit.*, p85. For the Weishauptian Illuminati, see Hagger, *The Secret History of the West* and *The Syndicate*. For Quietism, see Ferguson, *op. cit.*, p153. For background to Molinos and the first quotation from Molinos, see Ferguson, *op. cit.*, p122; and for the second quotation, see Underhill, *op. cit.*, p324.
93. The quotations from Madame Guyon can be found in Underhill, *op. cit.*, pp184, 322, 246-7, 265 and 431.
94. For Pietism, see Ferguson, *op. cit.*, p145, and *EB*, 14. 455-61 (Spener and von Zinzendorf).
95. See *EB*, 9. 64 for Hus/Scriptures.
96. For Moravians, see Ferguson, *op. cit.*, p123. For what Bohler taught Wesley, see Lecky, quoted in Arnold Lunn, *John Wesley*, p112.
97. See *EB*, 19. 760 for heart-warming.
98. See *EB*, 19. 759 for brand.
99. All the quotations from the English poets can be found in standard Oxford, Everyman, Penguin or Faber editions of Dryden, Pope,

Tennyson, Browning, Matthew Arnold. Sir Edwin Arnold's "The Light of Asia" (1879) can be found in *The Wisdom of China and India*, ed. by Lin Yutang, pp 380-490.

100. E. I. Watkin, *Philosophy of Mysticism*, p388, quoted in Dom Cuthbert Butler, *op. cit.*, pp275-8.

101. Yeats's poems can be found in his *Collected Poems* and Lionel Johnson's in anthologies. For Hegel's Idealism, see *EB*, 8. 728, and for Kierkegaard's attack on Hegel's philosophy see *EB*, 10. 466. For the quotation from Berdyayev, see *EB*, I. 993.

102. For the poems by MacNeice and Auden, see *The Penguin Book of Contemporary Verse* ed. Kenneth Allott. The quotations from Gascoyne's *Journal* are from pp140-1. Thomas's poems can be found in his *Collected Poems*, and the poem by Raine is in Ferguson, *op. cit.*, p155.

103. The quotations from Hölderlin can be found in his *Selected Verse*, and the quotation from Goethe comes from Part One of the two-part Penguin *Faust* (pp45-6).

104. See *Bibliography* for two volumes containing Rilke's poems. In 1912 Rilke experienced vibrations passing into him from the interior of a tree in the garden of Schloss Duino. In a letter of November 13, 1925 Rilke wrote to von Hulewicz: "We are the bees of the Invisible.... The Angel of the Elegies has nothing to do with the angel of the Christian heaven.... The Angel of the Elegies is the creature in whom that transformation of the visible into the invisible we are performing already appears completed." The mystic certainly collects the honey of the Invisible to accumulate it in the hive of the visible, and seeks to transform himself into an Angel of the Invisible, but he does it through the Light, which Rilke does not appear to have known. Rilke's "mysticism" was a sensitivity to the vibrations of Nature.

105. The quotations from Mallarmé and Valery can be found in a number of anthologies. See the *Bibliothèque de la Pléiade* (Gallimard) for most of the greater French writers; Stéphane Mallarmé, *Poems*, trans. by C. F. MacIntyre; and Geoffrey Brereton, *A Short History of French Literature* on Mallarmé and Valery.

106. See Sebastian Bullough, *Roman Catholicism*, pp67-8, and Arseniev,

Mysticism and the Eastern Church, pp120-4. The quotations from the *Liturgy of St James* in the next paragraph but one can be found in Arseniev, pp129, 132, 138 and 135. See p124 for the main point, that the liturgies represent the descent of the *Logos*. For lighted candles, see *New Catholic Encyclopaedia*, entry for Light.

107. The quotations from the *Liturgy of St James* can be found in Arseniev, *op. cit.*, pp129, 132, 138 and 135. See *New Catholic Encyclopaedia*, entry for Light.

108. St Thérèse is known as the dove of Lisieux in contrast to St Teresa, who is known as the eagle of Avila. She was an extremist, who once said: "I do not believe I have ever been more than three minutes at a time without thinking of (God)." See Michael Cox, *A Handbook of Christian Mysticism*, p236.

109. See Ferguson, *op. cit.*, p208 for the first and last quotations; and Capps and Wright, *op. cit.*, p225 for the middle quotation (Plato/*Iliad*).

110. The quotation can be found in Capps and Wright, *op. cit.*, pp237-9.

111. The quotation can be found in Capps and Wright, *op. cit.*, pp243-4.

112. All the quotations from Eliot are in his *Collected Poems*.

113. The quotation can be found in Capps and Wright, *op. cit.*, pp230-3.

12. The North American Light

1. See Yukio Irie, *Emerson and Quakerism*, for Emerson's knowledge of the Light.

2. Trine, *In Tune with the Infinite*, pp115, 197, xi-xii, 35, 31, 4, 49, 32, 112, 61.

3. See *EB*, 15. 118-9 for Protestant evangelism and ecumenism.

13. The Byzantine-Russian Light

1. See *EB*, 15. 1127 for the founding of Constantinople: "This 'New Rome,' established in 324 on the site of Byzantium and dedicated in

330, rapidly increased in population as a result of favours granted to immigrants."

2. See *EB*, 15. 1126-7 for Constantine's Christianization of Sol.
3. See Ferguson, *op. cit.*, p10 for Christianized alchemy.
4. *The Sayings of the Desert Fathers*, trans. by Sister Benedicta Ward, pp1-7. See also Arseniev's classic, *Mysticism and the Eastern Church.*
5. In W. N. Perry, *A Treasury of Traditional Wisdom*, p318; from Gregory of Nyssa, *Works*, 1893, p379.
6. The quotations can be found in Ferguson, *op. cit.*, p93 (John of Lycopolis) and p112 (Macarius).
7. See *The Sayings of the Desert Fathers, op. cit.*, pp75, 186, 11 for the stories concerning John, Silvanus and Arsenius.
8. The unattributed quotations from St Symeon are in *EB*, IX. 733 (vision of light); and Ferguson, *op. cit.*, p184 (Fire uncreated). Also see Ferguson, *op. cit.*, p106: "Symeon the New Theologian saw a light like dawn shining from above, growing brighter and brighter, and himself at the centre of the light; he saw the light permeating his physical being and turning him completely to fire and light."
9. For Hesychasm, see Ferguson, *op. cit.*, p77. The quotations from St Gregory Palamas come from Ferguson, *op. cit.*, p138 (uncreated light); and *EB*, 13. 905 (quotations in next paragraph).
10. See *EB*, 9. 1178 and *EB*, 6. 157 for Ivan III/Sofia.
11. Dostoevsky, *The Idiot* (Penguin), p258.
12. Tolstoy, *Anna Karenin*, p768.

14. The Germanic-Scandinavian Light

1. *EB*, 8. 40.
2. *EB*, 8. 40.
3. *EB*, 8. 40.
4. *EB*, 8. 40.
5. *EB*, 8. 40-1.
6. *EB*, 8. 43-4.

7. *EB*, 8. 36-7. For Asgard, see H. R. Ellis Davidson, *Gods and Myths of Northern Europe*, pp28, 31.
8. *EB*, 8. 36. For Odin as shaman, see Davidson, *Gods and Myths of Northern Europe*, pp147-9, e.g.: "The shamanistic element in the worship of Odin can hardly be doubted."
9. *EB*, 8. 36.
10. For Sleipnir, see Davidson, *Gods and Myths of Northern Europe*, p26 and elsewhere. For Odin as Great Shaman, see Rutherford, *Shamanism*, p93. Also Eliade, *Shamanism*, pp380-1.
11. For Tiwaz/Tyr, see Davidson, *Gods and Myths of Northern Europe*, pp57-60. For Tyr/Tuesday, see *EB*, 8. 38.
12. See *EB*, IX. 712 for the *swastika* as an Indo-European symbol found on ancient Mesopotamian coins and in early Christian and Byzantine art; and among Hindus, Jainas, Buddhists and Mayas. H. R. Ellis Davidson associates it with Thor in *Gods and Myths of Northern Europe*, p83, but twenty years later with Odin in *Scandinavian Mythology*, p55. She says, on p54 of *Scandinavian Mythology*, that both Thor and Odin replaced Tiwaz. The *swastika* was originally associated with Tiwaz, which is how it is treated here.
13. For Frigg/Friday, see *EB*, 8. 38.
14. *EB*, 8. 37 for Thor and Davidson, *Gods and Myths of Northern Europe*, pp86-7 and 191, for Thor's association with the sacred oak.
15. For the identification of Thor and Jupiter, see Davidson, *Gods and Myths of Northern Europe*, pp81, 86-7.
16. See Davidson, *Gods and Myths of Northern Europe*, p79.
17. Davidson, *Scandinavian Mythology*, pp72-3.
18. Davidson, *Scandinavian Mythology*, pp33-4 (grove sacrifices) and 46-8 (Odin hanging on tree). Also see *EB*, 8. 36.
19. Davidson, *Scandinavian Mythology*, p124.
20. Davidson, *Gods and Myths of Northern Europe*, pp173, 179; and Davidson, *Scandinavian Mythology*, pp121, 124, 104. Calvary, i.e. the Christian cross of Calvary.
21. The quotations from "The Dream of the Rood" and "Christ II (The Ascension)" are in *Anglo-Saxon Poetry*.

22. For the Christianization of Anglo-Saxon England, see *EB*, 3. 199-204; and of the Germanic peoples, see *EB*, 8. 39-40 and Johannes Brøndsted, *The Vikings*, pp285-291 (Denmark, Norway, Sweden). For the inscription at Jelling, see Gwyn Jones, *A History of the Vikings*, p117.
23. Jones, *op. cit.*, pp360-4 (Aggersborg, Fyrkat and Trelleborg) and 20-1 (Pytheas).

15. The Andean Light

1. See Friedrich Katz, *The Ancient American Civilizations*, pp11-12: "The primitive races of America originated in Asia....The peoples of ancient America bear striking physical resemblances to the Mongolian peoples of Asia....The Behring (i.e. Bering) Strait between Alaska and Siberia is the most favourable crossing place from the old to the new world." On July 5, 2005 it was reported in the *Times* that almost 270 human footprints about 40,000 years old have been discovered in volcanic ash at the edge of a lake in Mexico. They show that a community of *homo sapiens* lived in the Valsequillo Basin, near Puebla in central Mexico, suggesting that the first settlers reached the West Coast from Japan or other Pacific Ocean Communities rather than over the Bering Sea. This will be questioned and the discovery does not immediately overthrow the theory that the original migration took place over the Bering Strait. The discovery does not alter the fact that the Mongoloid features of American Indians originated in shamanistic Asia.
2. Katz, *op. cit.*, p12: "Remains of blunt stone implements... have...led some scholars to the conclusion that man has existed in America for thirty-five to fifty thousand years." Katz cites Alex D. Krieger in *Prehistoric Man in the New World.*
3. *EB*, 1. 843-4.
4. For example the Huaca del Sol and Huaca de la Luna in the Moche valley. Compare Teotihuacan. Pre-Toltec pyramids in Mexico within the Meso-American tradition of the Sun and Moon are linked by a "Avenue of the Dead". See Katz: "The greatest construction of the first

two centuries in Teotihuacan was the Sun Pyramid which was designed for religious purposes." In both instances we are reminded of the overlapping moon-cult and sun-cult in Ur and on other ziggurats.

5. Robert McC. Adams, in *The Evolution of Urban Society*, pointed to similarities between Mesopotamia c.3900-2300 BC and Mexico from AD 1-1519, which he maintained had no direct connection. However diffusionists can demonstrate a connection through the arrows on chart on pp534-535. See Katz, *op. cit.*, pp9, 10, 13 for the case against Egyptian influence and p44 for Egyptian pyramids being exclusively places of burial, unlike South American pyramids. See Katz, pp18, 54, 77 for similarities between Mesopotamian and South American pyramids. For tombs hidden in South American pyramids, see *EB*, 11. 946. See H. de Terra, *Man and Mammoth in Mexico*, quoted in Crow, *op. cit.*, p53, for New World pyramids dating from 500 BC.
6. *EB*, 9. 259.
7. *EB*, 9. 259-60.
8. *EB*, 9. 259.
9. *EB*, 9. 259.
10. *EB*, 1. 849 (conquest of Chan Chan); *EB*. II. 728 (10 temple-pyramids); *EB*, 9. 261 (dwelt with the sun).
11. *EB*, 9. 260.
12. *EB*, 9. 260.
13. *EB*, 9. 261.
14. *EB*, 9. 261.

16. The Meso-American Light

1. *EB*, 11. 934, 938-9.
2. *EB*, 11. 946 (Itzamna); *EB*, V. 824 (Kinich Ahau). Also *EB*, 11. 721: "Itzamna, Lord of the Heavens, who ruled over the pantheon, was closely associated with Kinich Ahau, the sun." Also *EB*, 11. 944 (Tikal).
3. *EB*, 11.721-2.

4. *EB*, 11.721.
5. See *EB*, 11.720-1 for details of the maize god, Yum Kaax, and the cloud and rain god Metsabok.
6. *EB*, I. 152; *EB*, 11.722.
7. *EB*, 11.721.
8. *EB*, 11.720. For the jaguar's being associated with the night, see *EB*, 11.946 and *EB*, 2. 550.
9. See John S. Henderson, *The World of the Ancient Maya*, pp84, 181, 205.
10. *EB*, 11.721.
11. *EB*, 2. 549.
12. *EB*, 11.948.
13. *EB*, IX. 892.
14. *EB*, 2. 550.
15. *EB*, 2. 550-1.
16. *EB*, VI. 938.
17. *EB*, VI. 938: "The magnitude of such public works and the distribution of temples suggest a dominant religious cult and a cadre of priest-rulers."
18. *EB*, VI. 938.
19. See Eliade, *From Primitives to Zen*, pp11-13.
20. *EB*, 17. 305, 308: "Without the active participation of every individual in the group, it was believed that the life-giving sun would not return from his 'winter house' after the solstice; the rain would not fall nor could the crops grow."
21. *EB*, 17. 308: "Without human help in an annual cycle of ceremonies, the cosmic order would be in danger of breaking down."
22. *Ex oriente lux* is a much-quoted Latin proverb. Civilization is traditionally supposed to have spread from the east, although Plato is held to have claimed that it spread from the west, i.e. via the Orphic and Eleusinian mysteries. Arguably, the western mysteries had been earlier inspired from the east. See "The Aegean-Greek Light", note 69.

17. The Arab Light

1. *EB*, 1. 1057.
2. *EB*, 1. 1057.
3. See *EB*, V. 461: Israel was a united kingdom under Saul, David and Solomon (c.1020-922 BC) and later merely "the northern Kingdom of Israel, including the territories of the 10 northern tribes (i.e. all except Judah and part of Benjamin), that resulted from a revolt led by Jeroboam I and lasted from 922-721 BC". Assyria dispersed these 10 northern tribes in 721 BC.
4. *EB*, 1. 1058 (El/Ilah); *EB*, 1. 1045 (Dhu-Samawi).
5. *EB*, 1. 1045.
6. *EB*, 1. 1045.
7. *EB*, 1. 1058.
8. *EB*, 9. 927: "Some (Arabs) were identifying the God of the Jews and Christians with Allah, the Lord of the Ka'bah."
9. *EB*, 12. 606.
10. *EB*, 12. 607 (Medina); and *EB*, V. 649 (Black Stone).
11. See *EB*, 12. 606-9 (Mohammed); *EB*, 1. 1047 and 9. 929 (Ummayads); *EB*, V. 308 (Imam).
12. *The Koran,* trans. by N. J. Dawood, pp211-2.
13. For Sufism see Van Over, *op. cit.*, pp341-351; R. A. Nicholson, *The Mystics of Islam,* ch 2 (*Illumination and Ecstasy*) and ch 3 (*The Gnosis*); and Laleh Bakhtiar, *Sufi, Expression of the Mystic Quest.* Also, *EB*, 9. 943-4 (Sufism).
14. For the quotation from Rabi'a, see Van Over, *op. cit.*, p343. For Dhu an-Nun's *ma'rifah* and Bayazid's *fana*, see *EB*, 9. 943. See Nicholson, *op. cit.*, ch 2, "Illumination and Ecstasy", for the concepts in the 2nd-5th paragraphs; and also Van Over, *op. cit.*, pp348-51. The quotation from Ziyad al-Arabi can be found in Stace, *op. cit.*, pp204-5. The quotation from Junayd is in Eliade, *From Primitives to Zen*, p523, and the last quotation from Dhu an-Nun (Beacon) can be found in Eliade, *From Primitives to Zen*, p522.
15. For the quotations from Bayazid, see (in order) Van Over, *op. cit.*,

p346 (and also Stace, *op. cit.*, pp201); Ferguson, *op. cit.*, pp6-7; Nicholson, *The Mystics of Islam*, pp57, 51; and Ferguson, *op. cit.*, pp6-7.

16. See Nicholson, *The Legacy of Islam*, p218 for the account of the crucifixion of al-Hallaj, which is in Eliade, *From Primitives to Zen*, p524.
17. For the first quotation from al-Hallaj, see Ferguson, *op. cit.*, p73. The first quotation from Nuri is in Nicholson, *The Mystics of Islam*, p94.
18. The quotation from al-Niffari is in Eliade, *From Primitives to Zen*, p525.
19. The quotation from Abu Said is in Nicholson, *The Mystics of Islam*, p118.
20. The quotation from Hujwiri is in Nicholson, *The Mystics of Islam*, p159.
21. See Stace, *op. cit.*, pp206-7 for Avicenna's *Stages of the Mystical Life*; and Ann Fremantle, *The Age of Belief*, p117.
22. For the quotation from Baba Kuhi, see Nicholson, *The Mystics of Islam*, p59. For Mohammed mysticism, see *EB*, 9. 943, 945. See Eliade, *From Primitives to Zen*, p526 for al-Ghazali's autobiography/conversion; Van Over, *op. cit.*, pp358-9 for the last quotation (walks in his light).
23. See *Mishkat Al-Anwar*, trans. by W. H. T. Gairdner for the niche of lights.
24. For Omar Khayyam see *EB*, VII. 530. For Omar, Nizam and the last quotation (roses), see the introduction by Ernest Rhys to the Everyman's edition of the *Rubaiyat*, pp3-6.
25. The two Fitzgerald versions are in one edition in Heron Books and in the Everyman's edition, the introduction to which contains a full record of Omar's relationship with Nizam. I have avoided Fitzgerald's translations here. The first quotation is translated by Swami Gavinda Tirtha in *The Nectar of Grace* (1941) and the rest are by E. H. Whinfield (in Van Over, *op. cit.*, pp400-2, which gives the evidence for Omar's Sufism), except for "the Flask of Wine" which is in Fitzgerald's first version, quatrain 11.

26. The quotation from Sana'i of Ghazna is in Van Over, *op. cit.*, p389.
27. For the quotations from al-Arabi (in order) see Nicholson, *The Mystics of Islam*, p155, 87; Stace, *op. cit.*, pp212-3; Nicholson, *The Mystics of Islam*, pp, 102-3 and 155.
28. See Stace, *op. cit.*, pp207-210 for the Simurgh, and compare Edward Fitzgerald's translation in Happold, *op. cit.*, pp229-32; also Van Over, *op. cit.*, p418.
29. The quotations from Rumi (in order) appear in: *Rumi, Poet and Mystic*, trans. by R. A. Nicholson, pp42 (stars), 166 (lamps), 189 (veils), i.e. Masnavi 1.754, 3.1259, 3.1286; Nicholson, *The Mystics of Islam, op. cit.*, p106; Van Over, *op. cit.*, p409; Happold, *op. cit.*, p227 (also in Ferguson, *op. cit.*, p160); and Underhill, *op. cit.*, pp87, 134, 389. See also A. J. Arberry's translation, *Mystical Poems of Rumi.*
30. The quotation from Iraqui is in Happold, *op. cit.*, p224.
31. The quotation from Sa'di is in Ferguson, *op. cit.*, p162.
32. The quotations from Hafez (in order) appear in: Nicholson, *The Mystics of Islam, op. cit.*, p88; Jacob Needleman (ed. by), *The Sword of Gnosis*; Van Over, *op. cit.*, pp419-20.
33. The quotations for Jami (in order) appear in: Nicholson, *The Mystics of Islam, op. cit.*, pp80-1 (also in Happold, *op. cit.*, p222); Happold, *op. cit.*, p221; Van Over, *op. cit.*, pp421-4; and Underhill, *op. cit.*, p127.
34. For Kabir, see Bankey Behari, *Sufis, Mystics and Yogis of India*, p242, and for the quotations from Sarmad see, pp112-3, 115, 118.
35. For the rise of the Ottomans, see *EB*, 9. 934-6 and *EB*, 1. 1048-9. The quotations in the last paragraph (in order) are in Behari, *op. cit.*, pp125, 181, 184; Van Over, *op. cit.*, pp396-7; and in Happold, *op. cit.*, pp223 and 224.
36. See A. Faber-Kaiser, *op. cit.*, for a full account of the Ahmadi claim.

18. The African Light

1. *EB*, VI. 809.
2. See *EB*, 1. 282: "By 2000 BC (the Egyptians) were sending

expeditions to the far south (Nubia and Ethiopia)....By 1000 BC (Egypt's) power was in decline, and the centre of royal authority moved southward into Nubia. The main successor state was that of Kush....In the 8th century BC the Kushites invaded Egypt and established a dynasty in Upper Egypt for about a century."

3. *EB*, VI. 809; *EB*, 1. 282.
4. *EB*, VI. 809; *EB*, 1. 282.
5. *The World's Last Mysteries*, Reader's Digest, pp234-5.
6. See Rutherford, *Shamanism*, for African religion (e.g. pp15-16) and early Egyptian religion (e.g. pp21-2) being shamanistic. For Olorun, see Service, *op. cit.*, pp134-5.

19. The Indian Light

1. See *EB*, V. 349 for Indus Valley dates; and *EB*, 9. 339: these dates were proposed by Sir Mortimer Wheeler.
2. *EB*, 9. 346.
3. *EB*, 9. 346. Also see *EB*, 8. 908.
4. Van Over, *op. cit.*, p41: "Some time around 2000 to 1500 BC the Aryan tribes began invading India from the north." *EB*, 9. 346.
5. *EB*, 9. 346.
6. See *EB*, 9. 339 and 343-4 for the horned cross-legged god from whom Siva evolved; also see *EB*, IX. 244-5. For Siva evolving from the Vedic god Rudra, see *EB*, VIII. 710-1. Also see *EB*, 8. 910: "Rudra developed into the Hindu god Siva." Van Over, *op. cit.*, p40: "Non-Aryan gods, such as Siva, became identified with Aryan gods, such as Rudra."
7. *EB*, 8. 909.
8. *EB*, 8. 909.
9. For the concepts in this paragraph (*tapas*, *yajna* etc.) see Jeanine Miller, *The Vision of Cosmic Order in the Vedas*, pp12-28, 231, 241 – and p210 which states that "the secret creative Fire 'whom men find in their heart'...was sorely misunderstood until only recently"; and

Professor Jan Gonda, *The Vision of the Vedic Poets*, which states (p272) that "belief in a light which, being suprahuman in origin and penetrating into the heart of the inspired poets, illumined their mind, was the complement of the conviction that these poets owe their praeternormal knowledge and their religious and political inspiration to 'visions', that they 'saw' the truth about the deeds and power of the gods which they formulated in their hymns. These authors, indeed not rarely, alluded to an internal light which is in the heart of the poet or to which he gains access in his heart.... This light is brought into connection with the sacral world of the inspired poet. The expression 'bearing light in the mouth'... is in 10.67.10 applied to the poets who magnify Brhaspati (the Lord of prayer)."

10. Quoted in Champion and Short, *op. cit.*, p27.
11. Mandala II Hymn 4 of *Rig Veda*; and see R. C. Zaehner, *Hinduism*, pp19-20.
12. Van Over, *op. cit.*, vol 1, p66.
13. Quoted in Van Over, *op. cit.*, p42. The translations from the *Upanisads* and *Bhagavad-gita* which follow are taken from the Mentor editions (translator Swami Prabhavananda).
14. For the Gandharvas/Pururavas, see Eliade, *From Primitives to Zen*, pp248-51. For the dates (c.1000 to 500 BC, and 600 BC) see *EB*, 8. 910 and 911. Quotations from the *Upanisads* can be found in a number of editions. See the *Bibliography* for one of these.
15. Quotations from the *Bhagavad-gita* can be found in a number of editions. See the *Bibliography* for one of these.
16. See Alice Bailey's Theosophical commentary, *The Light of the Soul*, for this last date, which is discredited.
17. Quotations from Patanjali's *The Yoga Sutras* can be found in *The Wisdom of China and India*, ed. by Lin Yutang, pp120-132.
18. For the founding of Buddhism, see *EB*, 3. 404-5. For Nirvana, see Champion and Short, *op. cit.*, p161, and Stace, *op. cit.*, pp70-1. For the Buddha's Fire Sermon, see Champion and Short, *op. cit.*, p183 (also in Van Over, *op. cit.*, pp245-6).
19. See the *Buddhacarita* ("Acts of the Buddha") by the 1st century AD

Indian poet Asvaghosa; from a Tibetan MS translated in *The Buddhist Scriptures*, ed. by Conze, p50.

20. Champion and Short, *op. cit.*, pp156-7.
21. *The Buddhist Scriptures, op. cit.*, p63. The second account comes from the *Maha-Parinibbana-Sutta* of the Digha-Nikaya; see Stace, *op. cit.*, p75.
22. For the Buddha's last sermon, see Van Over, *op. cit.*, pp220-2.
23. *Majjhima-Nikaya*, 1.485; in Eliade, *From Primitives to Zen*, *op. cit.*, p576.
24. Van Over, *op. cit.*, p300.
25. For the *Sacred Book of the Jainas and the three Jewels*, see Champion and Short, *op. cit.*, pp149-52.
26. *Akaranga Sutra*, 5th lecture, 6th lesson; in Van Over, *op. cit.*, pp308-9.
27. Van Over, *op. cit.*, p309.
28. *Buddhacarita*, or "*The Acts of the Buddha*"; quoted in *Buddhist Scriptures*, trans. by Conze, pp50-1.
29. The quotations in the *Dhammapada* can be found in *The Wisdom of China and India*, ed. by Yutang, pp335, 337, 353
30. The quotation from the *Surangama Sutra* can be found in *The Wisdom of China and India*, ed. by Yutang, pp525-8.
31. For 1st century AD, see *EB*, VI. 500.
32. Zaehner, *Hinduism*, p86.
33. Zaehner, *Hinduism*, pp84-89.
34. Zaehner, *Hinduism*, pp84-89.
35. Most of the quotations from the Saivite saints can be found in Van Over, *op. cit.*, pp188-9, 191, 180, 183 and 193.
36. For 5th century AD, see *EB*, 8. 896. Also Ferguson, *op. cit.*, p185.
37. See Evans-Wentz, *Tibetan Yoga and Secret Doctrines*, pp32, and elsewhere for *Kundalini* Yoga; and Fokke Sierksma, *Tibet's Terrifying Deities*, for the sexual symbolism in Tibetan religion. See Philip Rawson, *Tantra, the Indian Cult of Ecstasy*, generally.
38. Rawson, *The Art of Tantra*, p164, for *rasa*-juice.
39. For an autobiographical account of a contemporary experience of

Kundalini see *Gopi* Krishna's *Kundalini, The Evolutionary Energy in Man.*

40. See Evans-Wentz, *Tibetan Yoga and Secret Doctrines*, pp156-61, for *Tummo.*
41. The quotations are from Evans-Wentz, *Tibetan Yoga and Secret Doctrines, op. cit.*, pp183, 195, 206-7.
42. From *Mila Khabum*, the *Biography of Milarepa* by "the mad yogi from g Tsan" (12th-13th centuries). In Evans-Wentz, *Tibet's Great Yogi Milarepa*, pp199-202.
43. For Sankara or *maya* see Zaehner, *Hinduism, op. cit.*, pp75-7.
44. The quotations for Sankara come from Van Over, *op. cit.*, pp159-62, 166-8.
45. In T. M. P. Mahadevan, *Ten Saints of India.*
46. For the Kali *yuga* see Zaehner, *Hinduism, op. cit.*, pp62, 104-6, though the length of the Kali *yuga* is incorrectly stated as 1800 years. It should be 1200 years, a multiple of 12.
47. Quoted in Zaehner, *Hinduism, op. cit.*, p99.
48. See *EB*, II. 442-3 (Caitanya and Caitanya movement) for Caitanya's *bhakti.*
49. See Max-Pol Fouchet, *The Erotic Sculpture of India.*
50. The first quotation from Nanak is in Ferguson, *op. cit.*, p129; the last two are in M.A. Macauliffe *The Sikh Religion* (6 vols), quoted in Champion and Short, *op. cit.*, pp286 and 303.
51. The quotation from Ram Das is in Van Over, *op. cit.*, p333.
52. For the Moghul rule and Shah Jehan (or Jahan), see *EB*, VII. 84. For the inscription about Paradise, see Daniel Wolfstone, *Golden Guide to South and East Asia*, pp225-6: "In the Dewan-i-Khas, the Hall of Private Audience, Shah Jehan left this inscription: 'If there be paradise on earth, it is here, it is here.'" I found this inscription in 1967.
53. For Indian reform movements including *Brahmo Samaj*, see *EB*, 8. 918. Ramakrishna's vision is quoted in Mahadevan, *op. cit.*, p110, and Zaehner, *Hinduism, op. cit.*, p162.
54. Both stories are from *The Gospel of Sri Ramakrishna*, trans. by Swami Nikhilananda, pp356 and 388.

55. From notes taken from a talk by Vivekananda in the house of an American disciple, Mrs Sara Bull, and printed for private circulation in 1913.
56. Aurobindo, *The Life Divine*, p64 and ch 1. Quoted in Stace, *op. cit.*, pp50, 52.
57. The temple experience of Ramana Maharishi is quoted in Mahadevan, *op. cit.* The other quotations from Ramana come from *Erase the Ego*, pp30-6.
58. See A. Osborne, *Ramana Maharishi*, pp34, 77 and 90.
59. Ananda Coomaraswamy, *The Vedas*, pp108-110, 112, 115-6.
60. For a poem about the message of the Ryoanji stone garden, see Hagger, "The Silence", in *Collected Poems.*
61. Jean Klein, *Neither This Nor That I Am*, pp vii, 135, 137.
62. Gopi Krishna, *op. cit.*, pp13, 243.

20. The South-East Asian Light

1. For the *Mahayana* schools in this section see *EB*, 3. 406-8 and Ernest Wood, *Zen Dictionary*. See Stace, *op. cit.*, p84 (*Maha-* etc.), and p85 (*Diamond Sutra*).
2. For *Lankavatara Sutra* see the translation from Sanskrit by D. T. Suzuki (1932), p196.
3. See Stace, *op. cit.*, pp79-82 for *Awakening of Faith.*
4. For the *Mahayana* schools see Ernest Wood, *Zen Dictionary.*
5. See note 60 in "The Indian Light".
6. *Japan the Official Guide* (Japanese Ministry of Transportation 1963), p247.
7. In Eliade, *From Primitives to Zen, op. cit.*, p509.
8. For Tantric Buddhism or Vajrayana, see *EB*, X. 329. The quotation from the *Bhagavata-Purana* is in Eliade, *From Primitives to Zen, op. cit.*, pp253-4.
9. See Kukai's account of his initiation into Shingon in *Memorial Presenting a List of Important Sutras*, which he addressed to the

Emperor on his return from China; in Eliade, *From Primitives to Zen, op. cit.*, pp314-7.

10. See George Coedès, *Angkor, an Introduction*, pp29-30, 32 for the cult of the Angkor god-king.

11. For Buddhist architecture, see *EB*, 3. 396 (*caityas/stupa*). For the spreading of Buddhism, see *EB*, 3. 407-13. For the final quotation, see Marco Pallis, *Is There Room for "Grace" in Buddhism?* In *The Sword of Gnosis*, ed. by Needleman, p275.

21. The Japanese Light

1. For Bon in Japan, author's personal experience and research. For the Mahayana influence on Taoism, see *EB*, 3. 408; and for the origin of Shinto in Taoism, see *EB*, 16. 672.
2. *EB*, 16. 671-2.
3. *EB*, 16. 672.
4. The "nesting boxes" I observed in the palace of my pupil, the Emperor Showa's second son.
5. For future shamans as birds, see Rutherford, *Shamanism*, p53: "According to both the Tungus of eastern and the Yakuts of north-eastern Siberia, the souls of future shamans repose in nests among the high trees of the Upper World." Also see Eliade, *Shamanism*, pp40, 70-1, 205, 272-3, 480-1. See the Shinto writer Izawa Nagahide on the 800 "myriads" of Shinto myths, quoted in Champion and Short, *op. cit.*, p43. For Shinto and Zen see Wood, *op. cit.*, p96.
6. *EB*, 16. 673.
7. *EB*, 16. 673.
8. Author's research. I confirmed that the imperial chrysanthemum represents the Golden Flower by questioning a member of the Imperial family. See Richard Wilhelm "A Discussion of the Text", in his translation of *The Secret of the Golden Flower*, p9: "'Golden Flower' (*Chin Hua*), in an esoteric connection, includes the word 'light'. If one writes the two characters one above the other, so that they touch,

the lower part of the upper character and the upper part of the lower character make the character for 'light' (*kuang*)." See pp323, 338.

9. For Zen, see *EB*, X. 872, and Stace, *op. cit.*, pp88-101. Also see Fung Yu-lan, *The Spirit of Chinese Philosophy*, chapter 8, "The Inner-Light School of Buddhism", for *Tao*-sheng and the pre-*Ch'an* Light.
10. In Ferguson, *op. cit.*, p35.
11. When in 661 Shen-hsiu wrote, "The mind is the stand of a bright mirror.../do not allow it to become dusty," Hui-neng wrote, "Buddha-nature is forever clear and pure, where is there any dust?" This showed a more profound grasp and Hui-neng became the Zen Master. Quoted in *EB*, V. 192 and (in a different translation) Ferguson, *op. cit.*, p80.
12. For *zazen*, see *EB*, 3. 386; and *EB*, X. 868.
13. For Seami and the *yugen* see *EB*, X. 868 (Zeami, i.e. Seami). Also Arthur Waley, Introduction to *The Nō Plays of Japan*, pp21-2.
14. Waley, Introduction to *The Nō Plays of Japan*, p21.
15. From Hashida, *Shobo genzo shakui*, 1.142-64, selections trans. in De Bary (ed. by), *Sources of Japanese Tradition*, pp251-2; in Eliade, *From Primitives to Zen*, *op. cit.*, p511.
16. D. T. Suzuki, *Essays in Zen Buddhism*; in Stace, *op. cit.*, pp90-2, 95.

22. The Oceanian Light

1. See *EB*, 13. 444 for S.E. Asian migration to Oceania c.20,000 BC and into the Christian era. For the Huns as descendants of the Mongolian Hsiung-nu and their appearance on the South Russian steppe AD c.370, see *EB*, 9. 597.
2. *EB*. VIII. 99-100. See *The World's Last Mysteries*, Reader's Digest, p98 for the arrival of S.E. Asians in Polynesia c.500.
3. See *Encyclopedia of World Religions*, p41.
4. For *mana*, see *EB*, 14. 782-3 and *Encyclopedia of World Religions*, p41.
5. For the invasion of c.800 see *The World's Last Mysteries*, Reader's Digest, pp98-9, and for the invasion of c.1100 see *EB*, 6. 131-2: the

fact that the middle period of long-eared statues began in about 1100. Dr Brigham and his pupil Max Freedom Long, an American who studied Hawaiian and wrote *Growing into Light* and *The Huna Code in Religions*, championed the view that Huna is a lost ancient teaching.

6. Long, *The Huna Code in Religions*, p28. See Long's two books for the next two paragraphs.
7. For *moai*, *ahu* and long ears, see *EB*, 6. 131-2 and *The World's Last Mysteries*, Reader's Digest, pp95-8.
8. *EB*, 6. 132. Also *The World's Last Mysteries*, Reader's Digest, pp100-1.

23. The Chinese Light

1. *EB*, 4. 300-2.
2. See *EB*, 4. 422 for Shang Ti; and *EB*, 4. 302 for the move to *Yin*.
3. See *EB*, 4. 303-5 for Chou. For Zoroastrian dualistic influence on Taoism see, J. C. Cooper, *Yin & Yang, The Taoist Harmony of Opposites*, ch 13, pp104-9 ("Taoism and Zoroastrianism"): "Zoroastrianism...has points in common with both Taoism and Confucianism....Zoroastrianism goes further than either Taoism or Confucianism in its dualist aspect; instead of the *yin-yang* interplay, each being interdependent and containing the germ of the other within itself and all being in a state of flux, Zoroastrianism offers a sharp division between the opposites of good and evil since 'each exists in and by its own essence in endless antagonism'." For the history of Taoism, see *EB*, 17. 1044-50. For the quotation from Chuang Tzu see W. T. de Bary, *Sources of Chinese Tradition*, pp70-5; in Eliade, *From Primitives to Zen*, *op. cit.*, p604.
4. All the preceding quotations from the *Tao Te Ching* are taken from Wing-Tsit Chan's translation, *The Way of Lao Tzu*, and variant readings in brackets are from R. B. Blakney's translation. Arthur Waley's translation is in *The Way and its Power*; in Eliade, *From Primitives to Zen*, *op. cit.*, p599.

5. For the *I Ching* and the tortoise, see *EB*, V. 281. Also, James Legge, the *I Ching*, p14. For Wen Wang, see *EB*, 4. 303.
6. For Wen Wang, see *EB*, V. 281. James Legge, in his introduction to the *I Ching*, p6, calls Wen Wang "Wan": "The Yi (i.e. *I*), so far as we owe it to king Wan, was made in the year BC 1143 or 1142, or perhaps that it was begun in the former year and finished in the latter."
7. Legge edition of *I Ching*, *op. cit.*, pp357-9.
8. For Shang Ti dwelling in *T'ien* (Heaven), and for *Yin* and *Yang*, see *EB*, 4. 424. For *T'ien* (Heaven) and Earth (*Ti*), see *EB*, 4. 426. For the Temple of Heaven and Heaven round/Earth square, see *EB*, 14. 7.
9. *EB*, 4. 346.
10. For Neo-Taoism, Ko Hsuan/Ko Hung and the effects of Tantrism, see *EB*, 17. 1048-50. For the alchemical techniques in the last three paragraphs see Philip Rawson and Laszlo Legeza, *Tao, The Chinese Philosophy of Time and Change*, pp27-9.
11. *The Secret of the Golden Flower*, trans. by Richard Wilhelm, p6.
12. *The Secret of the Golden Flower*, trans. by Richard Wilhelm, a text which Richard Wilhelm obtained in Peking in 1920. For the quotations which follow (in order) see pp21-3, 30-1, 33, 49-51, 53, 55-6, 58.
13. The quotation from Su Tung-p'o is in Yutang, *op. cit.*, p1067.
14. "The Book of Consciousness and Life", in *The Secret of the Golden Flower*, pp69, 74, 76, 77-8.

24. The Tibetan Light

1. Tantrism appeared c.400 – see Ferguson, *op. cit.*, p185. For Bon, see *EB*, X. 995: Tibetan Buddhism incorporated "shamanistic features of the indigenous Tibetan religion, Bon." For Bon passing into Tantrism, see *EB*, IX. 995 (Tibetan Buddhism), and *EB*, 3. 387: "Tibetan Buddhism has adopted also in modified form many practices from the pre-existing Bon cult, such as oracular priests, some local divinities,

and a notion of divine kingship." See *Encyclopedia of World Religions*, pp179-80: Tibetans believe that the Bodhisattva Avalokitesvara became incarnate as their spiritual head, the Dalai (meaning "oceanwide") Lama, and that each Dalai Lama reincarnates in the body of a child. See *EB*, I. 676 for Avalokitesvara, who dwells on the mountain Potala and whose images are placed on hilltops. He is the creator of the fourth world, which is the actual universe in which we live, and inherited the characteristics of the Bon Sky Father. He successively reincarnates in each Dalai Lama.

2. For Tantrism entering Hinduism in the 5th century, see *EB*, 8. 896. For Tantrism entering Buddhism in the 8th century, see *EB*, II. 137. For Tantrism entering Buddhism in S.E. Asia, see **pp315-316**: it spread to China in the 8th century but had begun to spread by the 6th century.
3. *EB*, X. 329: Vajrayána (Tibetan Buddhism) flourished from 6th to 11th centuries. Also *EB*, 3. 387: the period of transimission from India to Tibet was 7th to 11th centuries. Transmission was a slow process, and centuries are necessarily approximate.
4. See *EB*, II. 137: "The original features of Bon seem to have included a cult of divine kingship, the kings being regarded as manifestations of the sky divinity (reformulated in Buddhism as the reincarnation of lamas); an order of oracular priests."
5. For King Khri-srong-Ide-brtsan's active encouragement of Buddhism, see *EB*, 3. 388. *The Yoga of Knowing the Mind* is in *The Tibetan Book of Great Liberation*, ed. by W. Y. Evans-Wentz; the following quotations coming from pp203, 205, 212, 215, 218-9, 221-2, 227, 229-30, 238-9.
6. One of the seven treatises in *Tibetan Yoga and Secret Doctrines*, ed. by W. Y. Evans-Wentz; with a translation and commentary by his Tibetan *guru*, Lama Kazi Dawa-Samdup. For the line of transmission see pp58, 101-2, 155-6, 241-2. The quotations are from pp225, 229 (*Yoga of the Clear Light*) and (*Yoga of the After-Death State*) 234, 236-9.
7. See *Tibetan Yoga and Secret Doctrines*, *op. cit.*, p234 note 2, where

Evans-Wentz writes on the fifth of the Six Teachings (*Yoga of the After-Death State*): "The serious reader should not fail to refer to the *Tibetan Book of the Dead* which contains a comprehensive and authoritative commentary on our present text."

8. See *The Tibetan Book of the Dead*, ed. by W. Y. Evans-Wentz. The quotations are from pp91, 90, 95-6.
9. *Idem*, pp90 note 3, 102 note 3.
10. *Idem*, p213.
11. *Idem*, pp2, 35.
12. Suggestions by Jung in *The Tibetan Book of the Dead*, *op. cit.*, ppxlviii-xlix, where the quotations can be found. Jung of course understood the Secret of the Golden Flower.
13. *Idem*, pxlix.
14. For the Tibetan Buddhist sects, see *EB*, 3. 388-9.
15. For *mandalas*, see *EB*, VI. 555-6. For *mandalas* originating in Bon-po, see Giuseppe Tucci, *The Theory and Practice of the Mandala*, p24: "This construction of the world, this magical reflection of the universe, is also to be found in the...Bon po, that is to say of the indigenous Tibetan religion. The Bon po Masters construct *mdos* or symbolical representations of the world." For the last quotation (Enlightened One), see Lama Govinda, *Creative Meditation and Multi-Dimensional Consciousness*, pp60-2.
16. Tucci, *op. cit.*, p78.

25. The Central Asian Light

1. *EB*, 3. 1119-20.
2. See *EB*, 12. 370: the *Hsiung-nu* created a great tribal empire in Mongolia in the 3rd century BC, and were succeeded by Turks and Mongols who were probably their subjects. There is a lack of convincing archaeological or historical evidence, but there is a broad consensus that the *Hsiung-nu* ruled the Mongolians, who therefore migrated with the *Hsiung-nu*.
3. For the rise of the Mongols, see *EB*, 12. 370-4 and *EB*, 4. 341.

PART THREE:

SUBTRADITION: THE HERETICAL LIGHT IN WESTERN CIVILIZATION

1. The Essene Light

1. *EB*, III. 965. The Essenes observed the Law of Moses, the Sabbath and ritual purity, and professed belief in immortality and divine punishment for sin. But they denied the resurrection of the body and shunned Temple worship, living in monastic communities such as Qumran. They were persecuted, see next paragraph.
2. *EB*, III. 965. Also, Ferguson, *op. cit.*, pp55-6 (Jewish sect).
3. Quoted in Edmond Bordeaux Szekely, *The Teachings of the Essenes from Enoch to the Dead Sea Scrolls*, p14. See pp11-13 for *Therapeutae*, Mareotis and agriculture. The Essenes seem to have identified Yahweh with the sun and to have renounced sex and money – see Ferguson, *op. cit.*, pp55-6. Pliny the Elder's account is in *Historica Naturalis* concerning Judea AD c.70.
4. Quoted in Szekely, *The Teachings of the Essenes from Enoch to the Dead Sea Scrolls*, p14.
5. Quoted in Tomas, *op. cit.*, p89: "The secret teaching of the East affirms that the Brotherhood of Essenes was responsible for the origination of Christianity and that Jesus himself was an Essene like John the Baptist....Bishop Eusebius...declared that 'the ancient Therapeutae were Christians and their ancient writings were our gospels and epistles.'"
6. Tomas, *op. cit.*, p88: "In 1967 Tibetan *émigrés* published a *Tibeto-Shanshun Dictionary* in India which included texts from ancient Bon books. One paragraph is extremely interesting: 'The wonder-worker Esses then came to the land of Shanshun-Mar (north Tibet).' Another passage describes how this Teacher Esses (or Eshe) preached in Persia in the first century of our era. Esses is shown among the supreme gods of the Bon cult." Also see note 19.

7. See note 6. For the Essene Heavenly Father (of the evening communions)/Earthly Mother (of the morning communions), see Szekely, *The Teachings of the Essenes from Enoch to the Dead Sea Scrolls*, pp31, 34.
8. Szekely, *The Teachings of the Essenes from Enoch to the Dead Sea Scrolls*, p12 (Esnoch) and 29 (Esrael).
9. For the Essene *Book of Moses*, see Szekely, *The Gospel of the Essenes*, pp25-8. Also see Szekely, *The Teachings of the Essenes from Enoch to the Dead Sea Scrolls*, ch 2 on Moses' Law. See *EB*, 19. 1176 for Iranian influence during the exile at Babylon.
10. See *EB*, 19. 1176 for the impact of Iranian light/dark dualism, which influenced scroll texts such as *The War of the Sons of Light Against the Sons of Darkness*. Also see Szekely, *The Teachings of the Essenes from Enoch to the Dead Sea Scrolls*, ch 3 for Zoroastrian influence on the Essenes and the Essene Tree of Life.
11. *The Book of Enoch*, trans. by R. H. Charles. The quotations (in order) are from pp92-4, 41-2, 44, 57 (last two in the last line).
12. *EB*, III. 905: "This portrait of Enoch as visionary was influenced by the Babylonian tradition of the 7th antediluvian king, Enmenduranna, who was linked to the sun god and received divine revelations. The story of Enoch reflects many such features of the Babylonian myth."
13. *The Gospel of Peace of Jesus Christ by the disciple John*, ed. by Szekely, first published 1937; and *The Gospel of The Essenes*, trans. by Szekely, in which the *Unknown Books of the Essenes* and *The Lost Scrolls of the Essene Brotherhood* can be found. These include the Essene *Book of Moses, The Communions*, the Essene *Book of Jesus*, the Essene *Gospel of John* and the Essene *Book of Revelations*. I have preserved the "thou" and "thy" of the translations to capture the atmosphere of the Bible, through which Jesus is traditionally approached.
14. See Szekely, *The Teachings of the Essenes from Enoch to the Dead Sea Scrolls*, p34 for the Light and Ahura Mazda ("This Communion with the Heavenly Father, the Creator, the Light the Ahura Mazda of Zoroaster, was the Essenes' central communion"), and pp18 and 44 for the Essene "ocean of life and thought".

15. *The Gospel of Peace, of Jesus Christ by the disciple John*, ed. by Szekely, p60.
16. *EB*, 11. 1018: "The Qumran sect, a Jewish monastic group known in modern times for its preservation of the Dead Sea Scrolls held a doctrine – found also in later Jewish sects – of a messianic pair: a priestly messiah of the house of Aaron (the brother of Moses) and a royal messiah of the house of David." See *EB*, 10. 154 for spiritual Son of Man/earthly Son of God.
17. *EB*, 11. 1018; *EB*, 10. 154. And see Hagger, *The Secret History of the West*, Appendix 3, p507.
18. See D. E. Nineham, *Saint Mark*, p408.
19. A. Faber-Kaiser, *Jesus Died in Kashmir*, which seems to hinge on the testimony of two German missionary doctors Marx and Prancke, whose 40-volume diary, dated 1894, was photographed by a Professor Hassnain in a lamasery (monastery) at Leh, the capital of Ladakh, a mountainous region between Kashmir and Tibet. The doctors referred to some manuscripts discovered by Nicolai Notovich, a Russian traveller at the end of the 19th century, at the lamasery of Hemis. Notovich claimed that Jesus (Isa) had been in India, Tibet and Ladakh during the 18 missing years. The German missionaries did not believe Notovich's information, and nor do those in charge of the Ahmadiyya movement. It must be remembered that ever since Madame Blavatsky returned from Tibet, Tibet was a place from which travellers could bring back such stories and be believed. The letter from Pilate is quoted on pp23-4.
20. For the view that the marks on the Turin Shroud are not bloodstains but radiation burns, see Brent and Rolfe, *The Silent Witness.*

2. The British Druid Light

1. See Morgan, *op. cit.*, p12 for 3903 and Seth.
2. See the immensely knowledgeable Jowett, *op. cit.*, chs 5 & 6 for the connection between the Druidic Celts and Samaria and the Hebrew influence on Druidism.

3. Jowett , *op. cit.*, pp49-53 for Ephraim, K'Omri, I-Saccasuns etc. and the white bull of Israel/lost 10 tribes under Ephraim – also see p223. See Morgan, *op. cit.*, pp12-13 for white bull.
4. See Morgan, *op. cit.*, p13 (Hu) and 11 ("The Truth against the World"). Also Jowett, *op. cit.*, pp48-9. Also see Elder, *Celt, Druid and Culdee*, p53.
5. For *si'uns*, see Elder, *Celt, Druid and Culdee*, p84. The claims are mostly made by several authors, including Morgan, *op. cit.*, pp12-13 and Jowett, *op. cit.*, chs 5 and 6.
6. This tradition was first put forward in 1860 by Morgan in *St Paul in Britain*. Evidence from Roman writers contained in this scholarly book has since been restated and amplified in Jowett, *op. cit.*; Rev C. C. Dobson, *Did our Lord Visit Britain as they say in Cornwall and Somerset?*; Rev L. S. Lewis, *St Joseph of Arimathaea at Glastonbury, or the Apostolic Church of Britain*; and J. W. Taylor, *The Coming of the Saints*. It has been restated in Corbett, *op. cit.*
7. Rev. Dr Margoliouth, *Jews in Britain*, vol I, p23; vol III, p198 – quoted in Elder, *Celt, Druid and Culdee*, p68.
8. Morgan's translation from the original manuscript, quoted in *St Paul in Britain*, p73.
9. See L. S. Lewis, *op. cit.*, ch.4; and also Victor Dunstan, *Did the Virgin Mary Live and Die in England?*
10. L. S. Lewis, *op. cit.*, *Appendix* 3, "Kinships of the Holy Family".
11. Baronius add ann 306, Vatican MSS, *Nova Legenda*, cited in Elder, *Celt, Druid and Culdee*, p102.
12. Lewis Spencer, *The Mysteries of Britain*, pp62-5.
13. See L. S. Lewis, *op. cit.*, Appendix 1, pp151-4, for the full story. The tomb is today covered with a glass top.
14. For how Caractacus/the British Royal Family took the British Light to Rome, see Morgan, *op. cit.*, chs 3 and 4; Jowett, *op. cit.*, ch 12, "The Royal British Founders of the First Christian Church at Rome, AD 48," and ch 18 on Constantine; Elder, *Celt, Druid and Culdee*, chs 4 and 10; and other works mentioned in note 6.
15. For the tradition that St Paul was in Britain, see Morgan, *op. cit.*, ch

4; Jowett, *op. cit.*, ch 16; and Elder, *Celt, Druid and Culdee*, p144, who notes that the tradition has been accepted by numerous writers including Theodoret (4th century), Venantius (6th century), the Patriarch of Jerusalem (7th century), Ussher and Stillingfleet.

3. The Gnostic Light

1. See the classic on Gnosticism, Hans Jonas, *The Gnostic Religion.*
2. Jonas, *op. cit.*, pp34-5 and 42-7 where the *gnosis* is seen as illumination throughout.
3. The pseudo-Clementine "*Clement of Rome*", *Homilies and Recognitions*, ed. T. de Lagarde, *Clementina*, Leipzig, 1865, (Rec. II. 49) quoted in Jonas, *op. cit.*, pp109, 346. The information and quotations which follow come from Jonas.
4. All quotations from Mandaean texts are taken from Jonas, *op. cit.*, pp49-91, where each is attributed.
5. Jonas, *op. cit.*, p284 under the heading "ecstatic illumination".

4. The Hermetic Light

1. All quotations in this and the next paragraph are taken from Jonas, *op. cit.*, pp148-153, and the version in brackets is from the Far West translation of *Hermetica.*
2. See Jonas, *op. cit.*, pp158-9.
3. *Hermetica, Libellus* 6, 7, 10, 11, 13; the *Hymn* in *Libellus* 13.
4. See Torrens, *op. cit.*, p87 for this and the next paragraph.
5. For an introduction to Alchemy, see Stanislas Klossowski de Rola, *Alchemy, The Secret Art* and Jacques Sadoul, *Alchemists & Gold.*
6. *Rosarium Philosophorum* (16th century), Stadt-bibliothek Vadiana, St Gallen MS, quoted in de Rola, *op. cit., pp19-20.*
7. For Plotinus, see Elmer O'Brien, *The Essential Plotinus*, and R. T. Wallis, *Neoplatonism.* Also see *EB*, 14. 573-4 and Ferguson, *op. cit.*, pp146-7.

8. See Macrobius' commentary on Cicero's Dream of Scipio , and Keith Critchlow's pamphlet, *Chartres Maze, a Model of the Universe?*
9. All quotations from Plotinus are from *Enneads*, 6.9; most are quoted in Stace, *op. cit.*, pp114-121. Also see Happold, *op. cit.*, pp182-9. The Light is seen in terms of the sun in a quotation from *Enneads* (in Happold, *op. cit.*, p188): "And what are we to think of as surrounding the One in Its repose? It must be a radiation from It while It remains unchanged, just like the bright light which surrounds the sun, which remains unchanged though the light springs from it continually."
10. Porphyry, *Life of Plotinus*, quoted in Collins, *Christian Mysticism in the Elizabethan Age*, p10. The first quotation in this paragraph (light of *Nous*) is in Happold, *op. cit.*, p188.
11. The first quotation in this paragraph is in Ferguson, *op. cit.*, p147; the second in Underhill, *op. cit.*, p207.

5. The Manichaeist Light

1. For Mani, see Jonas, *op. cit.*, ch 9, pp206-237. Also *EB*, 11. 442-7 and Ferguson, *op. cit.*, pp114-5.
2. See M. R. James, *The Apocryphal New Testament*, pp364 (Bardesanes) and 411 ("The Hymn of the Pearl").
3. From Nani's *Shahpurakan*, quoted in Al-Biruni's *Chronology of Ancient Nations* – cited in Jonas, *op. cit.*, p230.
4. For Zurvan (time), see *EB*, X. 903 and *EB*, 19. 1173.

6. The Templar Light

1. For a full account of the historical background of the Templars, see Edward Burman, *The Templars, Knights of God*; Ean Begg, *The Cult of the Black Virgin*; and Baigent, Leigh and Lincoln, *The Holy Blood and The Holy Grail.* Also *EB*, IX. 879.
2. For the suppressal of the Cathars, see Arthur Gurdham, *The Great Heresy, the History and Beliefs of the Cathars.* The Cathars really merit

their own section, "The Cathar Light". Readers will find the equivalent of this in Hagger, *The Secret History of the West*, ch 1, "The Cathar Revolution".

3. Theoderick, *Description of the Holy Places*, pp30-2, quoted in Burman, *op. cit.*, pp64-5.
4. Burman, *op. cit.*, pp13, 20.
5. Louis Charpentier, *The Mysteries of Chartres Cathedral*, pp71-2.
6. William Anderson, *The Rise of the Gothic*, pp13, 11-12 for the dating to 1130 and Islamic origin of Gothic.
7. Charpentier, *op. cit.*, ch 18.
8. See Cowen, *Rose Windows*, p41: "Much of the inspiration of this new art came from crusaders and pilgrims returning from the Holy Land. One of the routes passed through Venice and Bohemia, whence came new techniques and materials." Also William Anderson, *The Rise of the Gothic*, pp11-12 for the Islamic influence on the origin of the Gothic style, including "the pointed arch from North Africa through Sicily, and events such as the capture of many Moslem craftsmen among the thousands of prisoners taken in 1064 at the siege of Barbastro (some 200 miles inland from Gerona), added greatly to the range of possibilities in Western Christian architecture." For the four gardens of the Islamic Paradise, see Bakhtiar, *op. cit.*, pp28-30.
9. See Bakhtiar, *op. cit.*, p 57.
10. See Titus Burckhardt, *Art of Islam*, pp77-80 on the Alchemy of Light.
11. Ferguson, *op. cit.*, p199.
12. See John Matthews, *The Grail, Quest for the Eternal*, pp14-15.
13. For the Gothic, stained glass and rose windows, see Henry Adams, *Mont Saint-Michel and Chartres*, p100, quoted by E. Panofsky in *Meaning in the Visual Arts*, p162; and in Painton Cowen, *Rose Windows*, p7. The poem is in Panofsky, *Abbot Suger on the Abbey Church of St Denis and its Art Treasures*, pp47, 49.
14. For Grosseteste and rose windows as demonstrating Light-filled spheres, see Cowen, *op. cit.*, p96.

7. The Grail Light

1. For an introduction to the Grail, see *EB*, IV. 665-6. Also see Richard Barber, *The Holy Grail*; Geoffrey Ashe, *King Arthur's Avalon, The Story of Glastonbury*; and for a popular retelling of the main Arthur stories, Roger Lancelyn Green, *King Arthur and his Knights of the Round Table*. For Joseph of Arimathaea bringing the Grail to Glastonbury and the discovery of King Arthur's skeleton at Glastonbury, see the books mentioned in note 6 of "The British Druid Light" (Part 3, no. 2). For the Fisher King and Muntsalvach, see John Matthews, *The Grail, Quest for the Eternal*, pp6,76.
2. Burman, *op. cit.*, p29, quoting Daniel-Rops, *Cathedral and Crusade*, pp111-3.
3. Cowen, *op. cit.*, p99.
4. Evidence that Derrick was the father of Philippe was supplied to me by the British Library, who found details of the relationship in *Dictionnaire de la Noblesse*, 3rd edn. Paris 1866 (1969 reprint), Kraus, Liechtenstein vol 8 (BL shelfmark 2101.66); I had intuitively stumbled on the relationship when visiting Bruges. Also see Matthews, *op. cit.*, p22: "Provence, like Languedoc, was the centre of Catharism and Manichaean beliefs and even of Sufi teachings brought from the east via Spain and the Pyrenees."
5. Trevor Ravenscroft, *The Spear of Destiny*, p353.
6. For the occult and Hitler, Himmler, Rahn and the Grail, see Ravenscroft, *op. cit.* throughout, and Nigel Pennick, *Hitler's Secret Sciences*, pp164 (Rahn) and 176-7 (Hochfeiler).
7. For the Grail and the Cistercian Strata Florida Abbey and Nanteos Manor, see Reader's Digest *Folklore, Myths and Legends of Britain*, p383, and Geoffrey Ashe, *King Arthur's Avalon*, p279, which I have followed up with my own research.
8. For the Iranian theme in this paragraph, see Matthews, *op. cit.*, pp23, (Chosroes II), and 24-5 (Takt, Heraclius, Shiz, Kuh-i-sal-Chwadcha).
9. See Tomas, *op. cit.*, ch 9, p101, for Wolfram von Eschenbach's possible reference to the Grail as a stone, perhaps the Chintamani Stone of Shambhala. See Rutherford, *Shamanism*, p144 for the possibility that

some Cathars found sanctuary in Tibet.

10. For Cistercian influence, see William Wistar Comfort's introduction to his translation of the *Queste del Saint Graal,* from which the quotations in the next four paragraphs are taken, pp10, 12, 15, 215-221. (See also *The Quest of the Holy Grail,* trans. by P. M. Matarasso, and John Matthews, *The Grail, the Quest for the Eternal.*)

11. For the "puzzling" link between the Knights of the Grail and Templarism see Jessie Weston, *From Ritual to Romance,* pp100, 187; a book that inspired a modern treatment of the disastrous loss of the Grail by a modern mystic: T. S. Eliot's "The Waste Land". For points in the next paragraph, see Weston, *op. cit.*, pp146, 149, 163, 166 and 170, though Weston does not make the crucial connection between the Grail and the Light.

12. See Flavia Anderson's *The Ancient Secret,* which is out of print but which can be obtained in the reserve stock of the Kensington Library, Phillimore Street, London. See this for the full argument, which is very detailed.

8. The Kabbalist Light

1. That the oral tradition of the Kabbalah began with Abraham is claimed by the most prominent modern interpreter of the Kabbalah, Warren Kenton (alias Z'ev ben Shimon Halevi) in *Tree of Life,* pp17-18: "It is said that Abraham the father of the Hebrew nation received the original Teaching from Melchizedek, King of Salem, who was also a priest of the most High God." See *EB*, V. 650-1 for the Kabbalah from 1st century AD. For the nationalistic corruption of a once pure universal Kabbalah, see Hagger, *The Secret History of the West,* Appendix 2, "The Two Kabbalahs" and Nesta Webster, *Secret Societies and Subversive Movements,* p11; and *EB*, 10. 185-8 (Jewish Mysticism).

2. See note 1. Also see Jonas, *op. cit.*, pp33, 39-41 for a pre-Christian Jewish tradition mixing with Hellenistic pagan, Babylonian and Egyptian traditions.

3. See *EB*, 10. 320 (Second Crusade/Provence); and Baigent, Leigh and Lincoln, *The Holy Blood and the Holy Grail*, p44: "Languedoc had much in common with Byzantium. Learning, for example, was highly esteemed....At Lunel and Narbonne, schools devoted to the Cabala (i.e. Kabbalah) – the ancient esoteric tradition of Judaism – were thriving."
4. For the Almohad Berber invasion of Spain, see *EB*, I. 266. For Sefardic Jews preserving Babylonian rather than Palestinian Jewish traditions, see *EB*, IX. 28.
5. See *EB*, VI. 769 for Melchizedek's meeting with Abraham on his return from battle. He gave Abraham bread and wine – and perhaps the first oral Kabbalah. Abraham gave him a tithe (one-tenth) of the booty.
6. For *Merkava*, see *EB*, VI. 807. See Leo Schaya's *The Universal Meaning of the Kabbalah*, pp75, 92 for the Light in the fourth and seventh heavens.
7. See Professor Gershom Scholem, *Major Trends in Jewish Mysticism*, pp5, 122-3 for the distinction between ecstasy and union, and Stace, *op. cit.*, pp221-2 for a comment critical of Scholem which I have followed.
8. For the blessing of light in the *Mishna, Tosefta* and Babylonian and Palestinian *Talmuds*, see Jacob Neusner, *Invitation to the Talmud*, pp56, 77, 153-4, 204-5. See also *The Talmud*, selections trans. by H. Polano.
9. According to Adolphe Franck, *The Kabbalah* (1843), last chapter.
10. See Carlo Suarès, *The Sefer Yetzira*, pp72, 71 for the literal quotations, and Ferguson, *op. cit.*, p166 for the more modern version.
11. *EB*, 10. 186: "Jewish thinkers who attempted to harmonize the biblical-rabbinical tradition with Greco-Arab philosophy, whether of Neoplatonic or Aristotelian inspiration."
12. The French Hermeticist Frederic Lionel is one such Hermetic source. But Emile Grillot de Givry in a chapter on Jewish, Christian Kabbalists in *Illustrated Anthology of Sorcery, Magic and Alchemy* points out that "during the last part of the 18th century there was a new race of mere superficial Kabbalists, such as the Comte de Saint Germain

and Cagliostro who spread a kind of dechristianized Kabbalism mixed with oriental elements of debatable value" and that the Tarot "was seized upon", and the Book of Thoth; and this was not the most reliable of traditions.

13. For the two schools of classical Kabbalah, see *EB*, 10. 185-6.
14. See Scholem, *On the Kabbalah and Its Symbolism*, trans. by R. Manheim, p 80.
15. See Scholem's introduction to *Zohar, the Book of Splendour*, for an account of the authorship. The quotations from the *Zohar* that follow are taken from pp27, 28, 78-80, 29-30, 38-40, 44, 47, 55, 82.
16. For the Lurianic and Shabbetaian Kabbalah, see *EB*, 10. 188-9. For the Light in the Kabbalah, as a modern living system rather than a historical one, see William Gray, *The Ladder of Lights*; W. E. Butler, *Magic and the Qabalah*; and the books of Warren Kenton (alias Z'ev ben Shimon Halevi).

9. The Esoteric Light

1. For an overview of post-1717 Freemasonry, see *EB*, IV. 302. In fact, Freemasonry is much older than that. For the two quotations see Walter Hannah, *Darkness Visible*, pp109 (*Explanation of the First Degree Tracing-Board*) and 173 (*Address of the Third Chair; the Historical Lecture*).
2. See Alex Horne, *King Solomon's Temple in the Masonic Tradition* for full details of the building of the temple. The identification of Sheshonk I is in Abraham Malamat, *The Kingdom of David and Solomon.*
3. Hannah, *op. cit.*, p182 (*Address of the First Chair; Mystical Lecture*).
4. See Nigel Pennick, *The Mysteries of King's College Chapel*, pp86, 67.
5. For the quotations in the previous two paragraphs, see Hannah, *op. cit.*, pp140, 160, 162, 165, 175-6.
6. That Yeats was a Freemason was first suggested to me in conversation by Frank Tuohy, author of *Yeats.* For full details of Sato's one-foot-three-inch, 600-year-old, short samurai sword, see Shotaro Oshima,

W. B. Yeats and Japan. See also Kathleen Raine, *Yeats the Initiate*, for Yeats' Rosicrucianism and membership of the Order of the Golden Dawn.

7. See Rev. John Lawrence, *Freemasonry – a Religion*? for a hostile judgement on Freemasonry by the Church.
8. For an introduction to Rosicrucianism, see Christopher McIntosh, *The Rosy Cross Unveiled*. Also *EB*, VIII. 677. See A. Bothwell Gosse, *The Rose Immortal*, p44 for the White, Red, Golden and Black Roses.
9. See Hannah, *op. cit.*, pp202-7 for the ritual of the 18th degree.
10. For an introduction to the magic of the occultist and for many of the points in this section (*Corpus Hermeticum*, *grimoires*, *Vaughan*), see Francis King, *Magic, The Western Tradition*, especially pp7-16.
11. For an overview of post-1846 Evangelicalism, see *EB*, III. 1009 (Evangelical Alliance). The quotations from Swedenborg are from *Heaven and Hell*, pp72-4, 79-83; and (in the next three paragraphs) *The True Christian Religion*, pp58-60, 302, 416.
12. Underhill, *op. cit.*, points out (p280) that Blake regarded his visions as "corporeal" rather than "imaginary": they were actual perceptions of the "real and eternal world". "I know," Blake wrote in a letter, on August 23, 1799, "that This World Is a World of Imagination and Vision. I see Everything I paint In This World, but Every body does not see alike. To the Eyes of a Miser a Guinea is far more beautiful than the Sun.... As a man is, so he sees" (Nonesuch edition, p835).
13. The quotations from Blake, in order, come from the Nonesuch edition, pp900 (his illumination), 118,121 ("Auguries of Innocence"), 859-62 (fourfold vision), 652 (guinea), 855 and 866-7 (letters to Butts), 375 (the hymn "Jerusalem"), and 434 and 564 ("Jerusalem").
14. For an overview of Romanticism, see *EB*, VIII. 653-4. The quotations from Shelley, in order, are in the Penguin edition, sel. by Isabel Quigley, pp63, 69, 71-2, 74, 182, 283, 265 and 269.
15. The quotations from Coleridge, in order, are in the Penguin edition, sel. by Kathleen Raine, pp88 ("Kubla Khan"), and 95-6.
16. The first quotation from *Biographia Literaria* is from ch 12 and refers to *Enneads* 5.5. The definition of imagination is from ch 13. Both are on pp190-1 of the Penguin edition, sel. by Kathleen Raine.

10. The Theosophical Light

1. For an overview of Theosophy, see *EB*, 18. 276-8 and Ferguson, *op. cit.*, p195. See Ferguson, *op. cit.*, p104 for Lévi, "Closer to magic than to mystical religion". See Francis King, *Magic, the Western Tradition*, for a fuller account of magic.
2. In H. P. Blavatsky, *The Secret Doctrine*, vol 1 pp27-34.
3. The quotations from Mme Blavatsky, in order, come from *Isis Unveiled*, p270; *The Secret Doctrine*, vol 1, p481; *The Key to Theosophy*, pp105, 175, 101, 11-12.
4. The quotations from Steiner, in order, come from *A Road to Self-Knowledge*, pp118-9, 153-4, and from *Knowledge of the Higher Worlds* pp35-6, 208-9, 211.
5. P. D. Ouspensky, *In Search of the Miraculous*, pp6, 36, 278, 87.
6. Ouspensky, *op. cit.*, pp141-2, 278, 87.
7. Alice Bailey, *A Treatise on Cosmic Fire*, p863; *The Light of the Soul*, pp180, 253-4.
8. *The Secret of the Golden Flower*, *op. cit.*, pp106-7, 101, 103-4.
9. See Ira Progoff, *The Death and Rebirth of Psychology*, for a full account of the rebellion of Jung and Rank, although there is no mention of the Light. See p262 for the "will to immortality".

11. The New Age Light

1. David Spangler, *Revelation, the Birth of a New Age*, pp47-50, 159, 161, 173, 175.
2. Spangler, *Towards a Planetary Vision*, p122.
3. Introduction by William Irwin Thompson to Spangler, *Revelation, the Birth of a New Age*.
4. Reported by no less an authority than *The News of the World*, London, March 19, 1978.

PART FOUR

THE LIGHT IN CIVILIZATIONS

1. Edward Burnett Tylor, *Primitive Culture* (1871).
2. Arnold Toynbee, *A Study of History*, vol 8, p499.
3. T. S. Eliot, *Notes towards the Definition of Culture*, p26.
4. João de Barros, Book on Portuguese explorations, 1552: "These structures" (i.e. Great Zimbabwe) "are very similar to some found in the land of Prester John, at a place called Acaxumo, which was a municipal city of the Queen of Sheba, which Ptolemy calls Axuma."
5. For Toynbee's record as a servant of the New World Order, see Hagger, *The Syndicate*, pp31-2 and elsewhere. Throughout his long service at the Royal Institute of International Affairs he worked tirelessly for a world government. In a speech made in Copenhagen in 1931 he declared: "We are at present working with all our might to wrest this mysterious force called sovereignty out of the clutches of the local national states of our world. And all the time we are denying with our lips what we are doing with our hands." (Lindsay Jenkins, *Britain Held Hostage*, p51.)
6. Toynbee, *op. cit.*, vol 12, *Reconsiderations*, pp546-7.
7. Toynbee, *op. cit.*, vol 12, *Reconsiderations*, pp558, 560-1 (*A Re-survey of Civilisations*).
8. Toynbee, *A Study of History*, one-volume edition, p97.
9. Toynbee regarded the Ottoman Empire as the Orthodox Christian universal state, see Toynbee, *op. cit.*, pp353-4 for numerous references. Gibbon's *Decline and Fall of the Roman Empire* continues the story of the Roman civilization deep into the Byzantine period.
10. Toynbee, *op. cit.*, vol 12, *Reconsiderations*, p549.
11. Toynbee, *op. cit.*, vol 12, *Reconsiderations*, pp284, 273, 335.
12. Toynbee, *op. cit.*, vol 12, *Reconsiderations*, p272.
13. Bagby, *Culture and History*, pp84, 95, 162-3, quoted in *A Study of History*, one-volume edition, p43.
14. Kenneth Clark, *Civilisation*, pp15, 17.
15. Charles A. Beard's Introduction, p xxxvii, to Brooks Adams, *The Law of Civilisation and Decay*.

CHECK LIST OF REFERENCES IN *THE ENCYCLOPAEDIA BRITANNICA'S MACROPAEDIA*

Tradition/ Civilization	Volume of Encyclopaedia Britannica	Pages	Heading
1. Indo-European	6	1059-1063	*Europe, Ancient*
Kurgan and			
Megalithic/Old	2	611-616	*Balkans, History of the*
European	3	193-197	*Britain, Ancient*
	3	1071-5	*Celts, Ancient*
2. Mesopotamian	11	967-993	*Mesopotamia and Iraq, History of*
	11	1001-1006	*Mesopotamian Religions*
3. Egyptian	6	464-488	*Egypt, History of*
	6	503-509	*Egyptian Religion*
4. Aegean-Greek	1	112-122	*Aegean Civilizations*
	8	324-390	*Greek Civilization, Ancient*
5. Roman	15	1085-1133	*Rome, Ancient*
	15	1059-1064	*Roman Religion*
	9	1076-1084	*Italic Peoples, Ancient*
	9	1114-1126	*Italy and Sicily*
	3	547-557	*Byzantine Empire*

See also Joscelyn Godwin, *Mystery Religions in the Ancient World*, The Imperial Cult, pp56-58

6.	Anatolian	1	813-825	*Anatolia, Ancient*
		2	189-193	*Asia Minor, Religions of*
7.	Syrian	17	931-953	*Syria and Palestine, History of*
		2	189-193	*Asia Minor, Religions of*
8.	Israelite	17	939-951	*Syria and Palestine, History of*
		10	302-328	*Judaism, History of*
9.	Celtic	3	1071-1075	*Celts, Ancient*
		3	1068-1071	*Celtic Religion*
		3	198	*Britain, Ancient*
		3	199-208	*Britain & Ireland, History of*
		3	284-286	"
		7	960-962	*Gaul*
10.	Iranian	9	829-860	*Iran, History of*
		9	867-872	*Iranian Religions*
		19	1171-2	*Zoroastrianism and Parsiism*
		11	442-447	*Manichaeism*
11.	European	4	540-545	*Christianity before the Schism of 1054*
		12	139-142	*Middle Ages*
		9	1119-1112	*Italy and Sicily*
		5	298-310	*Crusades*
		15	108-120	*Protestantism, History of*
		15	1002-1019	*Roman Catholicism, History of*
12.	North American	18	946-999	*United States, History of*
		15	108-120	*Protestantism, History of*

13. Byzantine-Russian	3	548-571	*Byzantine Empire*
	16	39-88	*Russia and the Soviet Union, History of*
	6	152-162	*Eastern Orthodoxy, History of*
	5	298-310	*Crusades*
14. Germanic-Scandinavian	8	40-4	*Germans, Ancient*
	8	33-40	*Germanic Religion and Mythology*
	15	1127-1132	*Rome, Ancient*
	11	926-934	*Merovingian and Carolingian Age*
	16	304-312	*Scandinavia, History of*
15. Andean	1	839-854	*Andean Civilization, History of*
	9	259-261	*Inca Religion*
16. Meso-American	11	935-954	*Meso-American Civilization, History of*
		719-22	*Mayan Religion*
	2	548-552	*Aztec Religion*
17. Arab	1	1043-1051	*Arabia, History of*
	3	623-645	*Caliphate, Empire of the*
	9	926-937	*Islam, History of*
	1	1057-1059	*Arabian Religions*
18. African	1	206-209	*Africa*
	17	274-298	*Southern Africa, History of*
	1	285	*African Peoples and Cultures; Religions*

19. Indian	9	336-428	*Indian Subcontinent, History of the*
	8	908-920	*Hinduism, History of*
	3	403-414	*Buddhism, History of*
20. S.E. Asian	17	231-3,	*Southeast Asian Peoples, Arts of*
		250-271	
	3	510-515	*Burma, History of*
	16	718-723	*Siam and Thailand, History of*
	3	681-689	*Cambodia, History of*
	19	120-131	*Vietnam, History of*
	3	412-413	*Buddhism, History of*
21. Japanese	10	57-91	*Japan, History of*
	10	109-115	*Japanese Religion*
	16	671-676	*Shinto*
	3	409-410	*Buddhism, History of*
	4	1101-1102	*Confucianism, History of*
22. Oceanian	13	443-448	*Oceanian, History of*
	6	130-132	*Easter Island*
	14	777-784	*Polynesian Cultures*
	11	864-870	*Melanesian Cultures*
	2	412-421	*Australia, History of*
	13	50-55	*New Zealand, History of*
23. Chinese	4	297-402	*China, History of*
	4	422-428	*Chinese Religion*
	4	1099-1103	*Confucianism, History of*
	3	403-413	*Buddhism, History of*
	17	1044-1050	*Taoism, History of*

24. Tibetan	18	378-382	*Tibet, History of*
	3	386-388, 397, 401	*Buddhism*
	3	1141	*Central Asian Peoples, Arts of*
25. Central Asian	3	1118-1122	*Central Asian Cultures*
	12	370-376	*Mongols*
	3	1122-1143	*Central Asian Peoples, Arts of*
	3	407-408	*Buddhism, History of*
(For Visual Arts of each civilization:	19	174-487	*Visual Arts East Asian/ Western*)

The main reference appears first and the remaining references are in descending order of priority.

BIBLIOGRAPHY

Adams, Henry, *Mont Saint-Michel and Chartres*, New York, 1959.

Adams, Marsham, *The Book of the Master*, Murray, 1895.

Adams, Marsham, *The House of the Hidden Places*, Murray, 1895.

Adams, Robert McC., *The Evolution of Urban Society*, Chicago, 1965.

Al-Ghazali, *Mishkat Al-Anwar*, trans. by W. H. T. Gairdner, Ashrat, 1952.

Anderson, Flavia, *The Ancient Secret*, Gollancz, London.

Anderson, William, *Dante the Maker*, Hutchinson, 1980.

Anderson, William, *The Rise of the Gothic*, Hutchinson, London, 1985.

Angela De Foligno, *Le Livre de L'Experience des Vrais Fideles*, ed. by M. J. Ferré, Paris, 1927.

Anglo-Saxon Poetry sel and trans. by R. K. Gordon, J. M. Dent, London, 1957, which includes *The Dream of the Rood*, *Christ II* (*The Ascension*), and Wulfstan's *Address to the English.* (Original versions for the first and third poems can be found in *Sweet's Anglo-Saxon Reader*, revised by C. T. Onions, OUP, London, 1954.)

Angus, S., *The Mystery Religions and Christianity*, London, 1925.

Apocryphal New Testament, trans. by M. R. James, OUP, London, 1975.

Apuleius, *The Golden Ass*, trans. by Robert Graves, Penguin, London, 1950.

Arber, Agnes, *The Manifold and the One*, John Murray, London, 1957.

Aristophanes, *The Frogs.*

Aristotle, *Metaphysica.*

Arnold, Sir Edwin, *The Light of Asia*, 1879.

Arnold, Matthew, *A Selection* by Kenneth Allott, Penguin, London, 1954.

Arnold, Matthew, *Culture and Anarchy*, ed. by J. Dover Wilson, Cambridge, London, 1979.
Arnold of Villanova, *Rosarium Philosophorum.*
Arseniev, Nicholas, *Mysticism and the Eastern Church*, Mowbrays, London, 1979.
Ashe, Geoffrey, *King Arthur's Avalon, the Story of Glastonbury*, Collins, London, 1957.
Asvaghosa, *Buddhacarita.*
Atiya, Farid, *The Giza Pyramids*, Cairo, 2004.
Aubarbier, Jean-Luc and Binet, Michel, *Prehistoric Sites in Périgord*, Ouest France, 1985.
Augustine, St, *City of God.*
Augustine, St, *Confessions*, trans. by R. S. Pine-Coffin, Penguin, London, 1961.
Aurobindo, Sri, *The Life Divine*, Arya, Calcutta, 1949.
Bachelard, Gaston, *The Psychoanalysis of Fire*, Beacon, U.S.A. 1964.
Baigent, Michael; Leigh, Richard and Lincoln, Henry, *The Holy Blood and the Holy Grail*, Corgi, London, 1983.
Bailey, Alice, *A Treatise on Cosmic Fire*, Lucis, London, 1977.
Bailey, Alice, *The Light of the Soul*, Lucis, New York, 1927, 1972.
Bakhtiar, Laleh, *Sufi, Expression of the Mystic Quest*, Thames and Hudson, London, 1976.
Barber, Richard, *King Arthur in Legend and History*, Boydell Press, 1973.
Barber, Richard, *The Holy Grail, Imagination and Belief*, Allen Lane, 2004.
Bauval, Robert and Gilbert, Adrian, *The Orion Mystery, Unlocking the Secrets of the Pyramids*, William Heinemann, 1994.
Bede, *Eclesiastical History of the English People*, Penguin, 1955
Begg, Ean, *The Cult of the Black Virgin*, Arkana, London, 1985.
Behari, Bankey, *Sufis, Mystics and Yogis of India*, Bombay.
Bentley, James, *A Guide to the Dordogne*, Viking, London, 1985.
Bertman, Stephen, *Handbook to Life in Ancient Mesopotamia*, Facts on File, Inc, 2003.
Bhagavad-gita, The, The Song of God, trans. by Swami Prabhavananda and Frederick Manchester, Mentor, U.S.A., 1957.

Blake, William, *Complete Poetry and Prose*, ed. by Geoffrey Keynes, Nonesuch, 1927 and 1956.

Blavatsky, H. P., *Isis Unveiled*, Rider, London, 1877.

Blavatsky, H. P., *The Key to Theosophy*, Aryan Theosophical Press, London, 1923.

Blavatsky, H. P., *The Secret Doctrine*, Theosophical University Press, 2 vols, U.S.A., 1970.

Boehme, Jakob, *Aurora*, trans. by John Sparrow, ed. by C. J. Barker and D. H. Hehner, Watkins, London, 1914.

Book of Enoch, *The*, trans. by R. H. Charles, SPCK, London, 1917 and 1976.

Bord, Janet and Colin, *Earth Rites*, Granada, 1982.

Bothwell-Gosse, A., *The Lily of Light*, Watkins, 1935.

Bradford, Ernle, *Paul the Traveller*, Allen Lane, 1974.

Brayshaw, A Neave, *The Quakers, their Story and Message*, Friends Home Service Committee, London, 1921.

Brent, Peter and Rolfe, David, *The Silent Witness*, Futura, London, 1978.

Brereton, Geoffrey, *A Short History of French Literature*, Pelican, 1956.

Brøndsted, Johannes, *The Vikings*, Penguine, 1960.

Browning, Robert, Sel. by W. E. Williams, Penguin, London, 1954.

Buddhist Scriptures, The, trans. by Edward Conze, Penguin, London, 1959.

Budge, Sir E. A. Wallis, *Egyptian Religion*, Routledge, U.K., 1899.

Budge, Sir E. A. Wallis, *The Book of the Dead (Papyrus of Ani)*, Routledge, London, 1899 and 1974.

Budge, Sir E. A. Wallis, *The Book of the Dead (Theban Recension)*, Routledge, London, 1899 and 1974.

Bullough, Sebastian, *Roman Catholicism*, Pelican, London, 1963.

Bunyan, John, *The Pilgrim's Progress*, Collins, London.

Burckhardt, Titus, *Art of Islam*, World of Islam Festival Publishing Co., 1976.

Burkert, Walter, *Greek Religion*, Basil Blackwell, UK, 1987

Burman, Edward, *The Templars, Knights of God*, Crucible, London, 1986.

Butler, Dom Cuthbert, *Western Mysticism*, Arrow Books, London, 1922 and 1960.

Butler, W. E., *Magic and the Qabalah*, Aquarian, London, 1964.

Caine, Mary, *The Glastonbury Giants* (pamphlet).

Caine, Mary, *The Kingston Zodiac* (pamphlet).

Campbell, Roy, trans. by *St John of the Cross, Poems*, Penguin, London, 1960.

Capps, W. H., and Wright, Wendy M., Silent Fire, *An Invitation to Western Mysticism*, Harper & Row, U.S.A., 1978.

Cassian, John, *Conferences.*

Champion, S. G., and Short, G., *Readings from World Religions*, Premier Fawcett, U.S.A, 1959.

Charpentier, Louis, *The Mysteries of Chartres Cathedral*, Research into Lost Knowledge Organisation, London, 1972.

Chaucer, Geoffrey, *Prologue to the Canterbury Tales*, trans. by Nevill Coghill, Penguin, London, 1982.

Chiera, *Sumerian Ritual Texts*, London, 1924.

Clark, Kenneth, *Civilisation*, BBC/John Murray, 1973.

Clayton, Ken, *Jesus Identified*, Belvedere, London, 1978.

Clements, Robert J., *Michelangelo, a Self-Portrait*, Prentice Hall, U.S.A., 1963.

Cloud of Unknowing, anon, ed. by Evelyn Underhill, Watkins, London, 1946.

Cœdes, George, *Angkor, an Introduction*, OUP, London, 1963.

Coleridge, Samuel Taylor, *Poems and Prose*, selected by Kathleen Raine, Penguin, London, 1957.

Collins, J. B., *Christian Mysticism in the Elizabethan Age*, 1940.

Compton, Piers, *The Broken Cross*, Veritas, Australia, 1984.

Contenau, G., *Everyday Life in Babylon and Assyria*, Arnold, U.K.

Coomaraswamy, Ananda, *A New Approach to The Vedas*, Luzac, London, 1933 and Prologos Books, U.S.A., 1976.

Coomaraswamy, Ananda, *Hinduism and Buddhism*, Philosophical Library, New York, 1943.

Cooper, J. C., *Yin & Yang, The Taoist Harmony of Opposites*, Aquarian, 1981.

Corbett, Percy E., *Why Britain?*, R. J. Press, Newbury, Berks, U.K., 1984.

Cowen, Painton, *Rose Windows*, Thames and Hudson, London, 1979.

Cox, Michael, *A Handbook of Christian Mysticism*, Crucible, London, 1986.

Critchlow, Keith, *Chartres Maze, a Model of the Universe?*, Research into Lost Knowledge Organisation, London, 1975.

Crow, W. B., *A History of Magic, Witchcraft and Occultism*, Aquarian, London, 1968.

Cumont, Franz, *Mysteries of Mithra*.

Dally, Stephanie, trans. by, *Myths from Mesopotamia, Creation, The Flood, Gilgamesh and Others*, Oxford University Press, 2000.

D'Alviella, Goblet, *The Mysteries of Eleusis*, Aquarian, London, 1981.

Daniel-Rops, H., *Cathedral and Crusade: Studies of the Medieval Church 1050-1350*, Dent, London, 1957.

Dante, *Paradiso*, trans. by Dorothy Sayers and Barbara Reynolds, Penguin, London, 1962.

Davidson, H. R. Ellis, *Gods and Myths of Northern Europe*, Pelican, London, 1964.

Davidson, H. R. Ellis, *Scandinavian Mythology*, Hamlyn, London, 1984.

De Bary, W. T., *Sources of Chinese Tradition*, Columbia, U.S.A., 1960.

De Givry, Emile Grillot, *Illustrated Anthology of Sorcery, Magic and Alchemy*, Causeway Books, U.S.A., 1973.

De Rola, Stanislas Klossowski, *The Secret Art of Alchemy*, Thames and Hudson, London, 1973.

De Santillana, Giorgio, ed. by *The Age of Adventure*, Mentor, U.S.A., 1956.

Dobson, Rev. C. C., *Did Our Lord Visit Britain as they say in Cornwall and Somerset?* Covenant, London, 1936.

Dodds, F. R., *The Greeks and the Irrational*.

Dostoevsky, Fyodor, *The Brothers Karamazov*, Penguin, London, 1960.

Dostoevsky, Fyodor, *The Idiot*, trans. by Magarshack, Penguin, London, 1958.

Dryden, John, *Poems*, introd. by Bonamy Dobrée, J. M. Dent, London, 1954.

Dumézil, Georges, *Les Dieux des Indo-Européens*, Paris, 1952.

Dunstan, Victor, *Did the Virgin Mary Live and Die in England?*, Megiddo Press, U.K., 1985.

Edwards, I. S., *The Pyramids of Egypt*, Pelican, London, 1947, 1961.

Elder, Isabel Hill, *Celt, Druid and Culdee*, Covenant, London, 1973.

Elder, Isabel Hill, *Joseph of Arimathaea*, Real Israel Press, Glastonbury, 1979.

Eliade, Mircea, *From Primitives to Zen*, Collins, London, 1967.

Eliade, Mircea, *Shamanism, Archaic Techniques of Ecstasy*, Princeton University Press, U.S.A., 1964.

Eliot, T. S., *Collected Poems*, Faber, London, 1963.

Eliot, T. S., *Family Reunion*, Faber, London, 1958.

Eliot, T. S., *Idea of a Christian Society*, Faber, London, 1939.

Eliot, T. S., *Little Gidding in Four Quartets*, Faber, London, 1958.

Eliot, T. S., *Notes towards the Definition of Culture*, Faber, London, 1957.

Eliot, T. S., *Tradition and the Individual Talent*, in *Selected Prose* ed. by John Hayward, Penguin, London, 1958.

Encyclopedia of World Religions, Octopus, London, 1975.

Evans-Wentz, W. Y., ed. by, *Tibetan Yoga and Secret Doctrines*, OUP, London, 1958 and 1977.

Evans-Wentz, W. Y., *Tibet's Great Yogi Milarepa*, OUP, London.

Evans-Wentz, W. Y., *The Tibetan Book of the Dead*, OUP, London, 1927 and 1976.

Evans-Wentz, W. Y., ed. by, *The Tibetan Book of the Great Liberation*, OUP, London, 1954 and 1977.

Faber-Kaiser, A., *Jesus Died in Kashmir*, Sphere, London, 1977.

Faulkner, R. O., *A Concise Dictionary of Middle Egyptian*, Griffith Institute.

Faulkner, R. O., *The Ancient Egyptian Book of the Dead*, Guild, London, 1985.

Ferguson, *An Illustrated Encyclopaedia of Mysticism and the Mystery Religions*, Thames and Hudson, London, 1976.

Finnery, *Memoirs by Himself*, U.S.A., 1876.

Firth, Sir Charles, *Oliver Cromwell and the Rule of the Puritans in Englands*, OUP, U.K., 1900 and 1961.

Fitzgerald, Edward, *Rubaiyat of Omar Khayyam*, Dent, Everyman's, London, 1928 and 1935.

Fouchet, Max-Pol, *The Erotic Sculpture of India*, Allen and Unwin, London, 1960.

Fox, George, *Journal*, ed. by N. Penney, Cambridge, 1911.

Fox, Matthew, *Illuminations of Hildegard of Bingen*, Bear, New Mexico.

Franck, Adolphe, *The Kabbalah*, University Books, U.S.A., 1843 and 1967.
Frankfort, Henri, *Ancient Egyptian Religion*, Colombia, 1948.
Frankfort, Henri, *Kingship and the Gods,* Chicago, 1948.
Frazer, Sir James G., *The Golden Bough*, Macmillan abridged edition, London, 1963.
Freeman, Laurence, *Light Within*, Darton, Longman and Todd, London, 1986.
Fremantle, Ann, *The Age of Belief, the Medieval Philosophers*, Mentor Books, U.S.A., 1954.
Fung Yu-Lan, *The Spirit of Chinese Philosophy*, Routledge, London, 1947.
Gardner, Laurence, *Lost Secrets of the Sacred Ark*, Element/Harper Collins, 2003.
Gascoyne, David, *Paris Journal, 1937-1939*, Enitharmon, 1978.
Gibbon, Edward, *The Decline and Fall of the Roman Empire*, Penguin, 1960.
Gimbutas, Marija, *The Civilization of the Goddess, The World of Old Europe*, HarperSanFrancisco, 1991.
Godwin, Joscelyn, *Mystery Religions in the Ancient World*, Thames and Hudson, London, 1981.
Gonda, Jan, *The Vision of the Vedic Poets*, Mouton, The Hague, 1963
Goethe, Johann Wolfgang von, *Faust*, parts 1 and 2, trans. by Philip Wayne, Penguin, London, 1959/1961.
Gosse, A. Bothwell, *The Lily of Light*, Watkins, London, 1935.
Gosse, A. Bothwell, *The Rose Immortal*, Watkins, London, 1958.
Govinda, Lama, *Creative Meditation* and *Multi-Dimensional Consciousness*, Theosophical Publishing House, London, 1966.
Graves, Robert, *The White Goddess*, Faber, 1948/1997.
Gray, William, *The Ladder of Lights*, Helios, U.K., 1975.
Green, Roger Lancelyn, *King Arthur and his Knights of the Round Table*, Puffin, 1953.
Grosseteste, Bishop, *On Light*, trans. by Clare Riedl, Marquette University Press, U.S.A., 1942.
Guénon, René, *East and West*, Luzac, London, 1941.
Guénon, René, *The Lord of the World*, Coombe Springs, U.K., 1983.
Guénon, René, *The Multiple States of Being*, Larson, U.S.A., 1984.

Gurdham, Arthur, *The Great Heresy, The History and Beliefs of the Cathars*, Neville Spearman, U.K., 1977.

Hagger, Nicholas, *The Secret History of the West*, John Hunt, 2005.

Hagger, Nicholas, *The Syndicate*, John Hunt, 2004.

Halevi, Z'ev ben Shimon *(alias* Warren Kenton), *Adam and the Kabbalistic Tree*, Rider, London, 1974.

Halevi, Z'ev ben Shimon *(alias* Warren Kenton), *A Kabbalistic Universe*, Rider, London, 1977.

Halevi, Z'ev ben Shimon *(alias* Warren Kenton), *School of Kabbalah*, Gateway, London, 1985.

Halevi, Z'ev ben Shimon *(alias* Warren Kenton), *The Tree of Life*, Rider, London, 1972.

Halevi, Z'ev ben Shimon (alias Warren Kenton), *The Way of Kabbalah*, Rider, London, 1976.

Halifax, Joan, *Shaman, the Wounded Healer*, Thames and Hudson, London, 1982.

Hannah, Walter, *Darkness Visible*, Augustine, London, 1952.

Happold, F. C., *Mysticism, A Study and an Anthology*, Pelican, London, 1963.

Haroutunian, Joseph and Smith, Louise Pettibone, *Calvin Commentaries*, Westminster Press, Philadelphia, U.S.A., 1958.

Harris, David R., *The Origins and Spread of Agriculture and Pastoralism in Eurasia*, UCL Press, 1996.

Hawass, Zahi and others, *The Treasures of the Pyramids*, The American University in Cairo Press, 2003.

Hawkins, Gerald, and White, John B., *Stonehenge Decoded*, Fontana/Collins, London, 1966.

Head, Joseph and Cranston, S. L., Reincarnation: *The Phoenix Fire Mystery*, Indian Press/Crown, New York, 1977.

Heidegger, Martin, *Being and Time*, 1927.

Heidegger, Martin, *Introduction to Metaphysics* , Doubleday, U.S.A., 1961.

Henderson, John S., *The World of the Ancient Maya*, Cornell, U.S.A., 1981.

Herm, Gerhard, *The Celts*, Weidenfeld and Nicolson, London, 1976.

Hermetica, Far West Press, U.S.A., 1977.

Hilton, Walter, *The Ladder of Perfection*, London.
Hippolytus, *Philosophoumena.*
Hölderlin, *Selected Verse*, ed. by Michael Hamburger, Penguin, 1961.
Hood, Sinclair, *The Arts in Prehistoric Greece*, Penguin, UK, 1978
Hooke, S. H., *Babylonian and Assyrian Religion*, London, 1953.
Hooke, S. H., *Middle Eastern Mythology*, Pelican, London, 1963.
Hopkins, Gerard Manley, *A Selection of His Poems and Prose*, Penguin, London, 1958.
Horne, Alex, *King Solomon's Temple in the Masonic Tradition*, Aquarian, London, 1972.
Hua-Yang, Liu, *The Book of Consciousness and Life in The Secret of the Golden Flower* (q.v.).
Husserl, Edmund, *Ideas, General Introduction to Pure Phenomenology*, Allen and Unwin, London, 1969.
Huxley, Aldous, *The Perennial Philosophy*, London, 1946.
Hymns Ancient and Modern, old edition 1889, William Clowes, London, 1904.
I Ching, trans. by James Legge, Dover Publications, New York, 1963.
Ions, Veronica, *Egyptian Mythology*, Newnes Books, 1968, 1982, 1986.
Irie, Yukio, *Emerson and Quakerism*, Kenkyusha, Japan, 1967.
Isabel, Mother, *Mother Isabel of the Sacred Heart*, Kingscote Press, London, 1916.
Iverson, Erik, *Obelisks in Exile*, Copenhagen, 1968.
James, E. O., *The Ancient Gods*, Weidenfeld and Nicolson, London, 1962.
James, M. R., *The Apocryphal New Testament*, OUP, U.K., 1924 and 1975.
James, William, *The Varieties of Religious Experience*, Collins, Fontana, London, 1960.
Jefferies, Richard, *The Story of My Heart*, London, 1873.
Jonas, Hans, *The Gnostic Religion*, Beacon, U.S.A., 1963.
Jones, Gwyn, *A History of the Vikings*, OUP, London, 1984.
Jowett, George, *The Drama of the Lost Disciples*, Covenant, London, 1961, 1975.
Julian of Norwich, *Revelations of Divine Love*, trans. by Clifton Wolters, Penguin, London, 1966.

Kafka, Franz, *The Castle*, Penguin, London.
Katz, Friedrich, *The Ancient American Civilizations*, Phoenix, 1972.
Kempis, Thomas à, *Of the Imitation of Christ*, OUP, World's Classics, U.K., 1906.
King, Francis, *Magic, the Western Tradition*, Thames and Hudson, London, 1975.
Kingsford, Anna, and Maitland, Edward, *Clothed with the Sun*, London, 1888.
Kirk, Bishop Kenneth, *The Vision of God*, James Clarke, U.K., 1977.
Klein, Jean, *Neither This Nor That I Am*, Watkins, London, 1981.
Knox, Ronald, *Captive Flames*, London, 1940.
Koran, The, trans. by N. J. Dawood, Penguin, London, 1956.
Kramer, Samuel Noah, *Cuneiform Inscriptions*, Oxford, U.K., 1923.
Kramer, Samuel Noah, *Sumerian Mythology*, New York, 1961.
Kramer, Samuel Noah, *The Sumerians, their History, Culture and Character*, Chicago, U.S.A., 1963.
Krishna, Gopi, *Kundalini, the Evolutionary Energy in Man*, Shambhala, U.S.A., 1971.
Lambert, W. G., *Babylonian Wisdom Literature*, Oxford, U.K., 1960.
Lamy, Lucie, *Egyptian Mysteries*, Thames and Hudson, London, 1981.
Langland, *Piers the Ploughman*, trans. by J. F. Goodridge, Penguin, London, 1959.
Lawrence, D. H., *The Plumed Serpent*, Penguin, London, 1961.
Lawrence, Rev. John, *Freemasonry – a Religion?*, Kingsway, London, 1987
Lehner, Mark, *The Complete Pyramids*, the American University in Cairo Press/Thames & Hudson, 1997.
Lewis, Rev. L. S., *St Joseph of Arimathaea at Glastonbury, or The Apostolic Church of Britain*, James Clarke, U.K., 1922 and 1976
Long, Max Freedom, *Growing into Light*, DeVorss, U.S.A., 1955
Long, Max Freedom, *The Huna Code in Religions*, DeVorss, U.S.A., 1965
Lunn, Arnold, *John Wesley*, Cassell, London, 1929.
Lurker, Manfred, *The Gods and Symbols of Ancient Egypt*, Thames and Hudson, 1974.
Macauliffe, M. A., *The Sikh Religion.*

Macrobius, *Commentary on Cicero's Dream of Scipio*, trans. by W. H. Stahl, Columbian University Press, New York.

Mahadevan, T. M. P., *Ten Saints of India*, Bharan's Book University, Bombay.

Malamat, Abraham, *The Kingdom of David and Solomon*, Biblical Archaeological Reader, vol 2, New York, 1964.

Mallarmé, Stéphane, *Poems*, trans. by C. F. MacIntyre, University of California Press, 1957.

Maltwood, Katharine, *Glastonbury's Temple of the Stars*, Watkins, London, 1935.

Marcel, Gabriel, *Metaphysical Journal (1913-23)*, Paris, 1927.

Matthews, John, *The Grail, Quest for the Eternal*, Thames and Hudson, London, 1981.

McEvedy, Colin, *The Penguin Atlas of Ancient History*, Penguin, 1967/1978.

McIntosh, Christopher, *The Rosy Cross Unveiled*, Aquarian, 1980.

Mead, G. R. S., *The Doctrine of the Subtle Body in the Western Tradition*, Stuart and Watkins, London, 1967.

Merton, Thomas, *Contemplation in a World of Action*, London.

Merton, Thomas, *The Silent Life*, London, 1957.

Metaphysical Poets, The, ed. by Helen Gardner, Penguin, London, 1957.

Mietzner, Ralph, *Opening to Inner Light*, Century, London, 1987.

Michell, John, *The Old Stones of Land's End*, Garstone, U.K., 1974.

Michell, John, *The View over Atlantis*, Garstone, U.K., 1972.

Miller, Jeanine, *The Vision of Cosmic Order in the Vedas*, Routledge and Kegan Paul, London, 1985.

Milton, John, *The Poetical Works*, ed. by Helen Darbishire, OUP, London, 1958.

Morgan, Rev. R. W., *St Paul in Britain*, Covenant, London, 1860, reprinted.

Mylonas, George, *Eleusis and the Eleusinian Mysteries*, Princeton, U.S.A., 1961.

Mysteries of the Ancient World, National Geographic Society, 1979. 1985.

Mystical Poems of Rumi, trans. by A. J. Arberry, University of Chicago Press, U.S.A., 1968.

Myths from Mesopotamia, Creation, The Flood, Gilgamesh and Others, trans. by Stephanie Dalley, Oxford University Press, 1989.

Needleman, Jacob, ed. by *The Sword of Gnosis*, Arkana, London, 1986.

Neusner, Jacob, *Invitation to the Talmud*, Harper and Row, New York, 1973.

Newman, John Henry Cardinal, *Apologia Pro Vita Sua*, ed. by A. Dwight Culler, Houghton Mifflin, U.S.A., 1956.

Nicholson, R. A., *Rumi, Poet and Mystic*

Nicholson, R. A., *The Legacy of Islam*, London, 1939.

Nicholson, R. A., *The Mystics of Islam*, Routledge and Kegan Paul, London, 1914 and 1975.

Nijinsky, Vaslav, *The Diary of Vaslav Nijinsky*, London, 1936.

Nineham, D. E., *Saint Mark*, Pelican, London, 1963.

North, John, *Stonehenge: Neolithic Man and the Cosmos*, HarperCollins, 1996.

Oates, Joan, *Babylon*, Thames and Hudson, 1979, 1986.

O'Brien, Christian, *The Genius of the Few, The Story of Those Who Founded the Garden in Eden*, Dianthus Publishing Ltd., 1985.

O'Brien, Christian, *The Megalithic Odyssey*, Turnstone, U.K., 1983.

O'Brien, Elmer, S. J., *The Essential Plotinus*, Hackett, U.S.A., 1964.

Osborne, A., *Ramana Maharishi.*

Oshima, Shotaro, *W .B. Yeats and Japan*, Hokuseido Press, Japan, 1965.

Ouspensky, P. D., *In Search of the Miraculous*, Routledge, London, 1964.

Panofsky, Erwin, trans. by and ed. by, *Abbot Suger on the Abbey Church of St Denis and its Art Treasures*, Princeton, U.S.A., 1979.

Panofsky, Erwin, *Meaning in the Visual Arts*, London, 1970.

Pascal, Blaise, *Pensées*, trans. by W. F. Trotter, Dent, London, 1931.

Peet, T. E., *Rough Stone Monuments and their Builders*, London and New York, 1912.

Pennick, Nigel, *Hitler's Secret Sciences*, Neville Spearman, London, 1981.

Pennick, Nigel, *The Mysteries of King's College Chapel*, Thorsons, London, 1974.

Perry, Whitall N., *A Treasury of Traditional Wisdom*, Allen and Unwin, London, 1971.

Petrie, Sir Flinders, *Personal Religion in Egypt before Christianity.*

Pistis Sophia

Plato, *The Collected Dialogues including the Letters*, ed. by Edith Hamilton

and Huntington Cairns, Princeton University Press, 1982.
Pliny, The Elder, *Natural History.*
Plutarch, *De Anima* (*On the Soul*).
Poland, H., ed. by and trans. by, *The Talmud,* Warne, 1969.
Pope, Alexander, *Collected Poems,* ed. by Bonamy Dobrée, J. M. Dent, London, 1959.
Porphyry, *Life of Plotinus.*
Prehistoric Man in the New World, ed. by Jesse D. Jennings, Edward Norbeck, Chicago, 1964.
Pritchard, J. B., ed. by *The Ancient Near Eastern Texts Relating to the Old Testament,* 2nd edition, Princeton, U.S.A., 1955.
Pritchard, J. B., *The Times Atlas of the Bible,* Times Books Ltd., London, 1987.
Progoff, Ira, *The Death and Rebirth of Psychology,* Delta, U.S.A., 1964.
Prudentius, *Peristephanon.*
Quaker Bedside Book, The, compiled by Bernard Canter, Hulton, London, 1952.
Queste Del Saint Graal, trans. by William Winston Comfort, London; also trans. by P. M. Matarasso as *The Quest for the Holy Grail,* Penguin, London, 1982.
Raine, Kathleen, *Defending Ancient Springs,* Golgonooza, U.K., 1985.
Raine, Kathleen, *Yeats the Initiate,* Dolmen and Allen and Unwin, London, 1986.
Ramakrishna, *The Gospel of Sri Ramakrishna,* trans. by Swami Nikhilananda, Ramakrishna-Vivekananda Centre, New York, 1942.
Ramana, Maharishi, *Erase the Ego,* 1974.
Rasmussen, Knud, *Intellectual Culture of the Igluluk Eskimos,* trans. by William Worster, Copenhagen, 1930.
Ravenscroft, Trevor, *The Spear of Destiny,* Samuel Weiser, New York, 1982.
Rawson, Philip, *Tantra, the Indian Cult of Ecstasy,* Thames and Hudson, London, 1973.
Rawson, Philip, *The Art of Tantra,* Thames and Hudson, London.
Rawson, Philip, and Legeza, Laszlo, *Tao, The Chinese Philosophy of Time and Change,* Thames and Hudson, London, 1973.

Reade, Julian, *Assyrian Sculpture*, British Museum, 1983.
Reader's Digest, *Folklore, Myths and Legends of Britain*, London, 1977.
Rice, Tamara Talbot, *The Scythians*, Thames and Hudson, London.
Rig Veda Samhita, ed. by Max Muller, 4 vols, 2nd edn., London, 1890-2; trans. by R. T. H. Griffith, Varanasi, 1963 (reprint of 1899).
Rilke, Rainer Maria, *Duino Elegies*, Hogarth Press, London, 1959.
Rilke, Rainer Maria, *The Book of Hours*, trans. by A. L. Peck, Hogarth Press, London, 1961.
Roaf, Michael, *Cultural Atlas of Mesopotamia and the Ancient Near East*, Time-Life books, Amsterdam, 1991.
Rolle, Richard, *The Fire of Love*, trans. by Clifton Wolters, Penguin, London, 1972.
Roux, Georges, *Ancient Iraq*, The World Publishing Co., 1964.
Rubaiyat of Omar Khayyam, trans. by Edward Fitzgerald, Everyman, 1928.
Rumi, Poet and Mystic, trans. by R. A. Nicholson, Unwin, 1968.
Rutherford, Ward, *Pythagoras, Lover of Wisdom*, Aquarian, London, 1984.
Rutherford, Ward, *Shamanism*, Aquarian, London, 1986.
Rutherford, Ward, *The Druids*, Aquarian, London, 1978.
Sadoul, Jacques, *Alchemists& Gold*, Neville Spearman, 1972.
St John of the Cross, *The Dark Night of the Soul*, revised by Rev. Benedict Zimmerman, James Clarke, U.K., 1973.
Schaya, Leo, *The Universal Meaning of the Kabbalah*, Allen and Unwin, London, 1971.
Schnapper, Edith, *The Inward Odyssey*, Allen and Unwin, London, 1965.
Scholem, Prof. Gershom, *Major Trends in Jewish Mysticism*, Schocken.
Scholem, Prof. Gershom, *On the Kabbala and Its Symbolism*, trans. by R. Manheim, Schocken.
Schulz, Regine and Seidel, Matthias ed. by, *Egypt, The World of the Pharaohs*, Könemann Verlagsgesellschaft mbH, 1998.
Schuon, Frithjof, *From the Divine to the Human*, World Wisdom, U.S.A., 1981.
Schuon, Frithjof, *Gnosis, Divine Knowledge*, John Murray, London, 1959.
Schuon, Frithjof, *Light in the Ancient Worlds*, World Wisdom, U.S.A., 1965.
Schuon, Frithjof, *Logic and Transcendence*, Perennial, U.K., 1984.

Schuon, Frithjof, *Survey of Metaphysics and Esoterism*, World Wisdom, U.S.A., 1986.

Schuon, Frithjof, *The Essential Writings of Frithjof Schuon*, ed. by Seyyed Hossain Nasr, Amity House, New York, 1986.

Schuon, Frithjof, *Transcendent Unity of Religions*, Faber and Faber, London, 1953.

Secret of the Golden Flower, The, trans. by Richard Wilhelm, Harcourt, Brace and World, New York, 1962.

Service, Alastair, *Lost Worlds*, Collins, 1981.

Sethe, Kurt, *Urkunden des degyptischen Altertums*, Leipzig, 1903.

Shaw, Ian and Nicholson, Paul, *The British Museum Dictionary of Ancient Egypt*, The British Museum Press, 1995.

Shelley, sel. by Isabel Quigley, Penguin, London, 1956.

Sierksma, Fokke, *Tibet's Terrifying Deities*, Tuttle, U.S.A., 1966.

Siliotti, Alberto, *Guide to the Pyramids of Egypt*, The American University in Cairo Press, 1997.

Sir Gawain and the Green Knight, trans. by B. Stone, Penguin, 1959; original ed. by Sir Israel Gollancz, OUP, London, 1940.

Smith, Logan Pearsall, *Donne's Sermons, Selected Passages with an Essay*, Oxford, U.K., 1919 and 1932.

Snow, C. P., *The Two Cultures: and a Second Look*, Cambridge, U.K., 1964.

Spangler, David, *Revelation, the Birth of a New Age*, Findhorn, U.K., 1977.

Spangler, David, *Towards a Planetary Vision*, Findhorn, U.K., 1977.

Spink, Canon Peter, *Spiritual Man in a New Age*, Darton, Longman and Todd, London, 1981.

Spink, Canon Peter, *The Path of the Mystic*, Darton, Longman and Todd, London, 1983.

Spence, Lewis, *The Mysteries of Britain*, London.

Stace, Walter T., *The Teachings of the Mystics*, Mentor, U.S.A., 1960.

Stadelmann, Rainer, *Pyramiden*, L.A.IV, 1982

Stadelmann, Rainer, 'Royal Tombs from the Age of the Pyramids', in *Egypt, The World of the Pharaohs*

Steiner, Rudolf, *A Road to Self-Knowledge*, Steiner Press, London, 1975.

Steiner, Rudolf, *Knowledge of the Higher Worlds*, Steiner Press, London,

1969.
Stover, Leon and Kraig, Bruce, *Stonehenge, the Indo-European Heritage*, Nelson-Hall, Chicago, 1978.
Strachan, Francoise, ed. by *The Aquarian Guide to Occult*, Mystical, Religious, Magical London and Around, Aquarian, London, 1970.
Suares, Carlo, trans. by, *The Sepher Yetsira*, Shambhala, U.S.A., 1976.
Suzuki, D. T., *Essays in Zen Buddhism*, Rider, London.
Swedenborg, Emanuel, *Heaven and its Wonders and Hell*, Swedenborg Society, London, 1937.
Swedenborg, Emanuel, *The True Christian Religion containing the Universal Theology of the New Church*, Dent, London, 1933.
Szekely, E. B., *The Gospel of the Essenes*, C. W. Daniel, London, 1974.
Szekely, E. B., trans. by, *The Gospel of Peace of Jesus Christ by the disciple John*, C. W. Daniel, London, 1937, and 1973.
Szekely, E. B., *The Teachings of the Essenes from Enoch to the Dead Sea Scrolls*, C. W. Daniel, London, 1978.
Tacitus, *Annals*, Penguin, London.
Taylfor, J. W., *The Coming of the Saints*, London, 1906; Covenant, 1969; Artisan, U.S.A., 1986.
Tennyson, Alfred Lord, *Collected Poems*.
The Cloud of Unknowing, ed. by Evelyn Underhill, Watkins, London, 1946.
The History of Christianity, a Lion Handbook, 1977.
Theologia Germanica, ed. by Susanna Winkworth, *Golden Treasury Series*, 1907.
The Oxford Classical Dictionary, 3rd edition, ed. by Simon Hornblower and Antony Spawforth, Oxford University Press, 1996.
The Oxford Companion to Classical Literature, compiled and ed. by Sir Paul Harvey, Oxford University Press, 1937.
The Penguin Book of Contemporary Verse, ed. by Kenneth Allott, 2nd edition, 1962.
Thérèse de Lisieux, St, *Histoire d'une Ame*, Paris, 1898.
The Sayings of the Desert Fathers, trans. by Sister Benedicta Ward, Mowbrays, London, 1975.
The Secret of the Golden Flower, trans. by Richard Wilhelm, Harcourt, Brace

& World, 1931.
The World's Last Mysteries, Reader's Digest, 1977.
Thom, *Megalithic Lunar Observations*, OUP, U.K., 1971.
Thomas, D. Winton, ed. by *Documents from Old Testament Times*, Nelson, London, 1958.
Thomas, Dylan, *Collected Poems*, J. M. Dent, London, 1959.
Tomas, Andrew, *Shambhala: Oasis of Light*, Sphere, London, 1977.
Tomlin, E. W. F., *The Approach to Metaphysics*, London, 1947.
Tomlin, E. W. F., *Philosophers of East and West*, Oak-Tree Books, London, 1986.
Tolstoy, *Anna Karenin*, trans. by Edmonds, Penguin, London.
Torrens, R. G., *The Golden Dawn and the Inner Teachings*, Samuel Weiser, New York, 1977.
Toynbee, Arnold, *A Study of History*, Oxford University Press 12 vols, U.K., 1934, 1939, 1954, 1961.
Toynbee, Arnold, *A Study of History*, revised one-volume edition , OUP/Thames and Hudson, London, 1972.
Traherne, Thomas, *Centuries of Meditation*, Mowbray, U.K., 1975.
Trine, Ralph Waldo, *In Tune with the Infinite*, Bell, London, 1923.
Tucci, Giuseppe, *The Theory and Practice of the Mandala*, Rider, London, 1961.
Tuohy, Frank, *Yeats*, Thames and Hudson, London.
Tylor, Edward Burnett, *Primitive Culture*, 1871.
Underhill, Evelyn, *Mysticism*, Methuen, London, 1911 and 1960.
Upanisads, The, Breath of the Eternal, trans. by Swami Prabhavananda and Frederick Manchester, Mentor, U.S.A., 1957.
Van Over, Raymond, *Eastern Mysticism*, Mentor, U.S.A., 1977.
Verner, Miroslav, *The Pyramids, The Mystery, Culture and Science of Egypt's Great Monuments*, The American University in Cairo Press, 2002.
Villari, Professor Pasquale, *Life and Times of Girolamo Savonarola*, trans. by Linda Villari, T. Fisher Unwin, London, 1888, reprinted.
Von Hugel, Baron, *The Mystical Element of Religion as studied in St Catherine of Genoa and her Friends*, 1908.
Waley, Arthur, *The No Plays of Japan*, Allen and Unwin, 1921/1954.

Waley, Arthur, *The Way and its Power*, Grove Press, New York.

Wallis, R. T., *Neoplatonism*, Duckworth, London, 1972.

Waterfield, Robin, *René Guénon and the Future of the West*, Crucible, London, 1987.

Watkin, E. I., *Philosophy of Mysticism*, London.

Way of Lao-Tzu, The, trans. by Wing Tsit Chan, Bobbs-Merrill, U.S.A., 1963.

Way of Life, Lao-Tzu, The, trans. by R. B. Blakney, Mentor, U.S.A., 1955.

Webster, Nesta H., *Secret Societies and Subversive Movements*, Christian Book Club of America, 1925.

Wesley, John, *Selections from the Journal*, ed. by Hugh Martin, London, 1955.

Weston, Jessie, *From Ritual to Romance*, Doubleday Anchor, U.S.A.

Whitehead, Alfred North, *Process and Reality*, in Whitehead, An Anthology, sel. by Northrop and Gross, Cambridge University Press, London, 1953.

Widengren, G., *The King and the Tree of Life*, Universitets Arsekrift No 14, Uppsala, 1951.

Wilkinson, Toby, *Genesis of the Pharaohs, Dramatic New Discoveries that Rewrite the Origins of Ancient Egypt*, Thames and Hudson, 2003.

Wolfstone, Daniel, *Golden Guide to South and East Asia*, Far Eastern Economic Review, 1963.

Wood, Ernest, Zen *Dictionary*, Pelican, London, 1977.

Wordsworth, William, Collected Poems.

Yeats, W. B., *Collected Poems*, Macmillan, London, 1958.

Yoga Sutras of Patanjali, The, trans. by Alistair Shearer, Bell Tower, 2002.

Yutang, Lin, *The Wisdom of India and China*, Random House, New York, 1942.

Zaehner, R. C., *Hinduism*, OUP, London, 1966.

Zaehner, R. C., *The Teachings of the Magi*, Sheldon Press, 1975.

Zohar, The Book of Splendour, sel. and ed. by Prof. Gershom Scholem, Rider, London, 1979.

